ANCIENT TURKEY

Students of antiquity often see ancient Turkey as a bewildering array of cultural complexes. *Ancient Turkey* brings together in a coherent account the diverse and often fragmented evidence, both archaeological and textual, that forms the basis of our knowledge of the development of Anatolia from the earliest arrivals to the end of the Iron Age.

Much new material has recently been excavated and unlike Greece, Mesopotamia, and its other neighbors, Turkey has been poorly served in terms of comprehensive, contemporary and accessible discussions of its ancient past. *Ancient Turkey* is a much needed resource for students and scholars, providing an up-to-date account of the widespread and extensive archaeological activity in Turkey.

Covering the entire span before the Classical period, fully illustrated with over 160 images and written in lively prose, this text will be enjoyed by anyone interested in the archaeology and early history of Turkey and the ancient Near East.

Antonio Sagona is Professor of Archaeology at the University of Melbourne. He is an elected Fellow of the Society of Antiquaries (London) and the Australian Academy of Humanities, and has carried out fieldwork in Turkey, the Caucasus, Syria, and Australia.

Paul Zimansky is Professor of Archaeology and Ancient History at the State University of New York, Stony Brook. He has excavated in Iraq, Iran, Syria, and Turkey. His academic specialties are Hittite and Urartian cultures, early cities, and the archaeology of writing.

Routledge World Archaeology

Forthcoming:

Prehistoric Britain, 2nd edition, Timothy C. Darvill

ANCIENT TURKEY

Antonio Sagona and Paul Zimansky

LONDON AND NEW YORK

First published 2009
by Routledge
2 Park Square, Milton Park, Abingdon, Oxon OX14 4RN

Simultaneously published in the USA and Canada
by Routledge
270 Madison Ave, New York, NY 10016

Routledge is an imprint of the Taylor & Francis Group, an informa business

© 2009 Antonio Sagona and Paul Zimansky

Reprinted 2009

Typeset in Sabon by
RefineCatch Limited, Bungay, Suffolk
Printed and bound in Great Britain by the
MPG Books Group

British Library Cataloguing in Publication Data
A catalogue record for this book is available from the British Library

Library of Congress Cataloging in Publication Data
A catalog record for this book has been requested

ISBN: 978–0–415–48123–6 (pbk)
ISBN: 978–0–415–28916–0 (hbk)
ISBN: 978–0–203–88046–0 (ebk)

CONTENTS

PREFACE

This book was written because of the continuing dearth of general, accessible, and up-to-date surveys on ancient Turkey before the Classical period. While there are a number of excellent period- and site-specific works, students and teachers have faced the persistent difficulty of reading and synthesizing an enormous and often bewildering amount of literature before they can formulate a general narrative on the principal periods and areas of innovation and culture. The task of covering in one volume so vast a topic—from the earliest arrivals to the end of the Iron Age—is daunting to say the least, but we have decided to take the plunge and divided the task between us: AS is responsible for the periods up to the end of the third millennium BC (Chapters 1–5), whereas PZ continues the story to the arrival of Persian influence at the end of the Iron Age (Chapters 6–10). This exposition makes no claim to be comprehensive, neither is it a detailed narrative. Rather, we hope that it provides a readable and well-balanced book for those who wish to understand the main cultural expressions of Turkey's ancient past. Hence, it would be pedantic and uncalled for to load the text with the heavy apparatus of scholarship. Nonetheless, we hope that the references provided will enable the curious to make their own way into the various topics.

Anyone who writes a book as wide ranging as this, ventures, often with trepidation, into areas outside their comfort zone. We have been fortunate and grateful that many friends and colleagues have helped us during the writing and preparation of this book, and, although we cannot mention them all, we are sincerely grateful to them. The debts we have incurred are many and range from permission to reproduce photographs and drawings (even though not all were used owing to limitations of space), through providing information on topics less familiar to us, to sustained conversations over many years. All these played an important part in shaping this book and accordingly we would like to express our sincere gratitude to the following: Mikheil Abramishvili, Guillermo Algaze, Ruben Badalyan, Nur Balkan-Altı, Scott Branting, Charles Burney, Stuart Campbell, Elizabeth Carter, Özlem Çevik, Altan Çilingiroğlu, Simon Connor, Ben Claasz Coockson, Şevket Dönmez, Bleda Düring, Refik Duru, Turan Efe, Aslı Erim-Özdoğan, Marcella Frangipane, David French, Christoph Gerber, Savaş Harmankaya, Ömür Harmanşah, Harald Hauptmann, Ian Hodder, Mehmet İşıklı, Peter Jablonka, John Kappelman, Kakha Kakhiani, Steve Kuhn, Clemens Lichter, Catherine Marro, Timothy Matney, Roger Matthews, Marcel Otte, Mihriban Özbaşaran, Mehmet Özdoğan, Aynur Özfırat, Vecihi Özkaya, Aliye Öztan, Giulio Palumbi, Anneliese Peschlow-Bindokat, Jacob Roodenberg, Christopher Roosevelt, Michael Rosenberg, Mitchell Rothman, Curtis

Runnels, Claudia Sagona, Oya Sarı, Klaus Schmidt, Ulf-Dietrich Schoop, Veli Sevin, Ludovic Slimak, Sharon Steadman, Gil Stein, Françoise and Geoffrey Summers, Mary Voigt, and Aslıhan Yener. We are very appreciative to the staff of various museums in Turkey, too many to list here, for their support over the years in allowing us to study material held in their collections.

Special thanks are owed to Sharon Steadman, Mary Voigt and Aslıhan Yener, who generously made available to AS papers in advance of their publication, a gesture for which he is most grateful. Among those who read and commented on various parts in draft, providing excellent advice and counsel, we thank Claudia Sagona, Caroline Spry, and Elizabeth Stone. We would also like to thank the cohorts of students, who, over the years, have acted as sounding boards for our formative ideas. Their questions and insightful comments have helped to sharpen our focus.

In a book of this type, images are immensely important. Three individuals have played a key role in standardizing, adapting, and redrawing the illustrations:

- Claudia Sagona spent many hours preparing the drawings and photographs for Chapters 1–5, and many more again reformatting them as AS changed his mind, often on a regular basis
- Chandra Jayasuriya drew the illuminating maps, and we are grateful for her care and professionalism
- Elizabeth Stone created almost all of the plans in Chapters 6–10 and several of the line drawings, taking time off from her own work on Iraq and remote sensing to apply her considerable graphic skills to the illustrations.

To the staff at Routledge, we extend our thanks for their patience and understanding in the long gestation of this book. AS would like to thank the University of Melbourne for financial support and research leave, especially in 2007, which enabled him to undertake the writing of his chapters. We also acknowledge with gratitude that the publication of this work was assisted by a publication grant from the University of Melbourne.

Finally, we must express the huge debt of appreciation we owe to our wives, Claudia Sagona and Elizabeth Stone, for their constant support.

Antonio Sagona
University of Melbourne

Paul Zimansky
Stony Brook University, NY

ACKNOWLEDGMENTS

We are grateful to the following individuals, publishers, journals and institutions that have given permission for their illustrations to be used here in exactly the same form as the original; other persons and publications are acknowledged separately in the captions.

Front cover: Hirmer Verlag (Munich)

Figs 2.3 and 5: Otte, M., Yalçınkaya, I., Taşkıran, H., Kozlowski, J. K., Bar-Yosef, O., and Noiret, P. (1995c) The Anatolian Middle Paleolithic: new research at Karain Cave, *Journal of Anthropological Research* 51: 287–299, figs 3–5

Fig. 2.6: Reprinted with permission of Wiley-Liss, Inc., a subsidiary of John Wiley & Sons, Inc., from Kuhn, S. L. (2002) Paleolithic archaeology in Turkey, *Evolutionary Anthropology* 11: figs 5–6

Fig. 2.9: Reproduced courtesy of Nederlands Instituut voor het Nabije Oosten from Rosenberg, M. (1994) Hallan Çemi Tepesi: Some further observations concerning stratigraphy and material culture, *Anatolica* 20, fig. 13; Rosenberg, M. and Peasnell, B. (1998) A report on soundings at Demirköy, an aceramic Neolithic site in eastern Anatolia, *Anatolica* 24: figs 4–5

Fig. 2.11: 1–2: Otte, M., Yalçınkaya, I., Leotard, J.-M., Kartal, M., Bar-Yosef, O., Kozlowski, J., Bayon, I. L., and Marshack, A. (1995a) The epi-Palaeolithic of Öküzini cave (SW Anatolia) and its mobiliary art, *Antiquity* 69: 931–944

Fig. 3.8: 3: Deutsches Archäologisches Institut, Orientabteilung, Urfa-Projekt

Figs 4.6; 4.7: 1, 4; 4.8: 3–4; 4.16: 1: Reproduced courtesy of the British Institute at Ankara from Mellaart, J. (1963) Excavations at Çatal Hüyük: Second preliminary report, 1962, *Anatolian Studies* 13: pl. VI: b; Mellaart, J. (1964) Excavations at Çatal Hüyük: Third preliminary report, 1963, *Anatolian Studies* 14: pls II: c, IV: a, XIII: b, XIX: a, XXIV: a; XXIV: b

Fig. 4.8: 1: Reproduced courtesy of Badisches Landesmuseum Karlsruhe and Niğde Museum from Badischen Landesmuseum Karlsruhe (ed.) 2007 *Vor 12.00 Jahren in Anatolien: Die ältesten Monumente der Menschheit*, p. 253. Konrad Theiss Verlag GmbH: Stuttgart. Fig. 4.8: 2: Reproduced courtesy of the Çatalhöyük Research Project from Hodder, I. (2006) *The Leopard's Tale: Revealing the Mysteries of Çatalhöyük*. London: Thames & Hudson, fig. 99.

Fig. 5.27: Reproduced courtesy of Hermann Müller-Karpe (1974) from his *Handbuch der Vorgeschichte*. Bd. 3, *Kupferzeit*. Munich: Beck.

1

INTRODUCTION

Nature has been generous with Turkey, endowing it with gifts of land, minerals, plants, and animals. Geographically, Turkey straddles two continents, linking mainland Europe with Asia across the narrow straits of the Bosphorus and the Dardanelles. These, along with the Sea of Marmara in between, form the only sea passage from the Black Sea to the Aegean. European Turkey (Thrace), to the north of the Sea of Marmara, shares borders with Bulgaria and Greece. Asian Turkey, much of which is known locally as Anatolia (or Anadolu), is very much bigger in area and borders Syria and Iraq to the south and southeast, Iran and Armenia to the east, and Georgia to the northeast. The Black Sea, the Aegean, and the Mediterranean all wash the long coastlines. The name Anatolia is a relatively modern term first used in the 10th century AD. Before then the country had been loosely referred to by classical writers as "Asia," or as "Asia Minor" to distinguish it from the continent of that name.[1] In pre-classical times it had no name at all, since it had never been sufficiently united politically for its frontiers to be defined.

The landscape of Turkey is extraordinarily complex and dominated by mountains, part of a broad belt of ranges extending westward from Iran into the heart of Europe. An east–west peninsula, stretching from Trans-Caucasus to the southeast extremity of Europe, Turkey's shape and alignment has promoted the notion of a bridge-land, an overused metaphor that probably goes back to time when Asia Minor was perceived as the land between Classical Greece and Achaemenid Persia.[2] While it is true that this geographical circumstance allowed Turkey to function as a land link between two continents, we should not categorize Turkey simply as a corridor. Indeed, even a casual glance at Turkey's cultural achievements will reveal that it was also responsible for nurturing a kaleidoscope of innovative ancient societies. In studying the human occupation of this formidable mountainous terrain, we have constantly to be aware of its intricate and broken nature that separates into seven broad geographical regions (Figure 1.1).

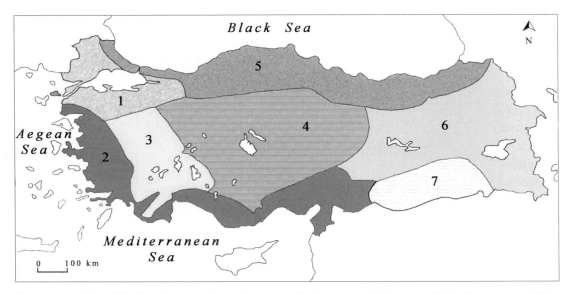

Figure 1.1   Map of Turkey showing the main geographical regions: 1 Marmara. 2 Mediterranean. 3 West central. 4 Central. 5 Black Sea; 6 Eastern. 7 Southeastern

For ancient Turkey cultural patterns are better understood if they are seen as mutually interacting with physical features and related bioclimatic elements.

THE LAND AND ITS WATER

Turkey's structural evolution has been shaped by tectonic plate shifts, significant seismic activity and the effect of volcanism since the mid-Tertiary. Frequent and major earthquakes, together with volcanic phenomena, are signs that these powerful earth forces are still active today.[3] Anatolia and Iran are the two halves of the Mobile Belt Province that has been literally squeezed by the African and Eurasian tectonic plates (Figure 1.2). This massive tectonism created the Pontic Mountains, a virtually continuous belt of folded ranges across northern Anatolia, and the Taurus and Anti-Taurus Mountains, a similar belt across the south, rimming either side of an ancient platform. In the west, rift valleys (grabens) and raised blocks (horsts) create the irregular coastline of the Aegean. On the other side of the peninsula, the tangled highland topography of eastern Anatolia merges into the Caucasus and into the Zagros, creating some of the most rugged topography in the Middle East. In easternmost Turkey, this complex culminates in the massive cone of Mount Ararat (Ağrı Dağı), towering 5145 m above the Armenian borderlands. To its southwest is Lake Van, which fills a great basin 128 km long.

A basic understanding of plate movements and faulting proves useful in appreciating some of the background elements of the Anatolian landscape that we will visit throughout this book.

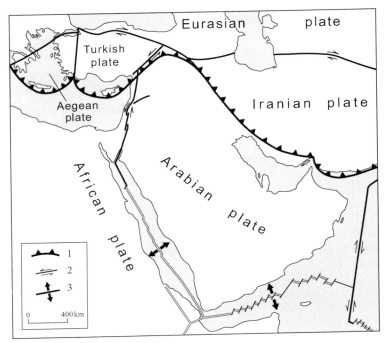

Figure 1.2 The complex system of tectonic plates in the Middle East. Note the convergence of tectonic zones in eastern Turkey (adapted from Held 1994: map 3–2)

Volcanism, for instance, brings with it mineralization along the various plate contacts, which has furnished Turkey with more nonfuel mineral wealth than any other region in the Middle East. Most (although not all) metallic ores occur in mineralized rocks, and Turkey has extensive deposits of copper, iron, lead, silver, and gold among others. Obsidian (volcanic glass), so prized in early prehistory, and amply attested in the eastern and central regions of Turkey, was also formed as part of this process. Emphasizing Anatolia's mountainous character should also remind us that it is a well-watered land. Long winters cover these mountains with heavy snowfalls that turn the ranges into a source of water, with melting snows and spring rains supplying the headwaters of the major rivers of the Middle East—the Euphrates (Turkish, *Fırat*) and Tigris (Turkish, *Dilce*), and the Kura and the Araxes (Turkish, *Aras*), to mention but a few. Finally, we should note that the east–west fracture lines have determined the main avenues of communication, such as the Kelkit–Çoruh trough and the longitudinal Erzurum plain, which track the path of the notorious North Anatolian Fault that runs south of the Pontic. There is, of course, extensive crossfaulting that has created important north–south passes, but on the whole the topography of Turkey is conducive to an east–west flow. With this we should delve a little further into the physical structure of the various regions (Figure 1.3).[4]

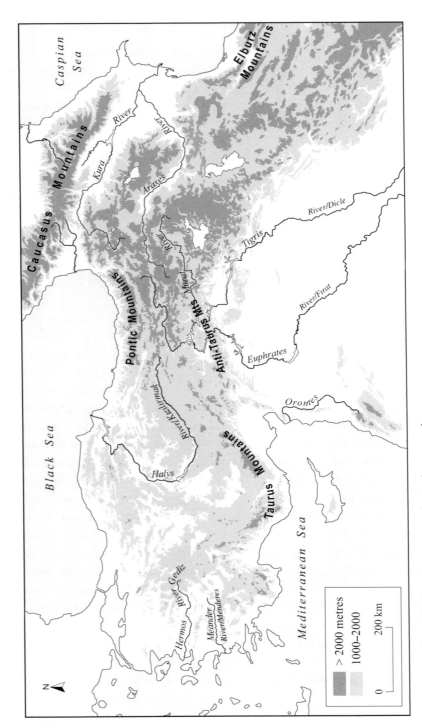

Figure 1.3 Map of Turkey showing its physical topography

CLIMATE AND VEGETATION

Putting aside the vagaries of contemporary global warming, the climate of Turkey is one of extremes. Coastal Turkey is mostly humid, with parts of the western shores never experiencing frost, yet the eastern highlands can be covered with snow for several months of the year. Shielded from rain-bearing winds by mountains, the central plateau of the interior is semiarid, yet the Black Sea coast has an abundance of precipitation, with annual rainfall reaching about 2500 mm. In outlining the modern vegetational zones of Turkey, or indeed of the Near East, it is the *potential* natural plant cover that is reconstructed by palynologists and ecologists rather than the actual present day cover. This should be evident by looking across Turkey's landscape today. Deforested for the most part, it is a stark testimony of millennia of human interference on a grand scale. Ecologists have calculated that about 70% of Turkey has the potential to maintain a forest cover, and yet today only 14% can be considered arboreal vegetation of which more than half is coppiced woodland.[5] Over 30 years ago, Zohary sketched the modern vegetation of the Near East,[6] and since his monumental work others have refined the vegetation patterns. Here we follow the reconstruction proposed by van Zeist and Bottema, who identify nine broad vegetational zones (Figure 1.4).[7]

From these broad potential vegetation patterns, we need to move back in time and observe the history of climate change and plant cover. Given that plants in the eastern Mediterranean area are closely tied to a cycle of winter rain and summer drought, the patterns of ancient vegetation can be reconstructed from palynological evidence, which is sometimes integrated with lake-level readings for more accurate determinations. In interpreting the pollen diagrams, we should bear in mind the differences in rainfall needs, with trees requiring more rainfall than shrubs and herbs.

Turkey has 10 pollen diagrams that are relevant to Late Quaternary and Holocene vegetation history, with most cores taken in regions west of the Euphrates (Figure 1.5: 1). This constitutes the largest body of data from western Asia, but should nonetheless be studied against the information from neighboring regions, including Iran (the fundamental core from Lake Zeribar), Syria, and the Caucasus, which has many pollen diagrams, the most recent from southern Georgia.[8]

The pollen diagram from Lake Van (Figure 1.6: 1) broadly matches that from Lake Zeribar in general character, namely a treeless steppe vegetation gradually giving way to oak woodland. But unlike the radiocarbon-dated Zeribar core, the chronology of the Van diagram has been problematic, owing to the use of varve counting.[9] Even so, it remains a key source on ancient highland vegetation, and its dating has been rectified somewhat through new data from a nearby peat bog. The pollen curves we now have from Van and Zeribar both show the gradual replacement of herbs such as *Artemisia* and chenopods, typical of cold steppe landscapes, by an oak and pistachio woodland around 10,500 years ago that reaches its full extent some 4000 years later.

This transition from steppe to woodland is also apparent in the pollen diagrams from west Anatolian sites, with the spread of trees occurring between 11,000 and 9000 years ago.[10] While

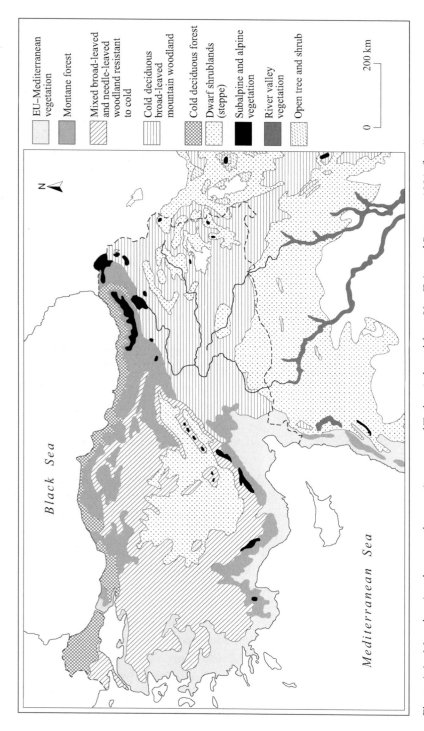

Figure 1.4 Map showing the natural vegetation zones of Turkey (adapted from Van Zeist and Bottema 1991: fig. 4)

Legend:

- EU–Mediterranean vegetation
- Montane forest
- Mixed broad-leaved and needle-leaved woodland resistant to cold
- Cold deciduous broad-leaved mountain woodland
- Cold deciduous forest
- Dwarf shrublands (steppe)
- Subalpine and alpine vegetation
- River valley vegetation
- Open tree and shrub

0   200 km

Black Sea

Mediterranean Sea

N

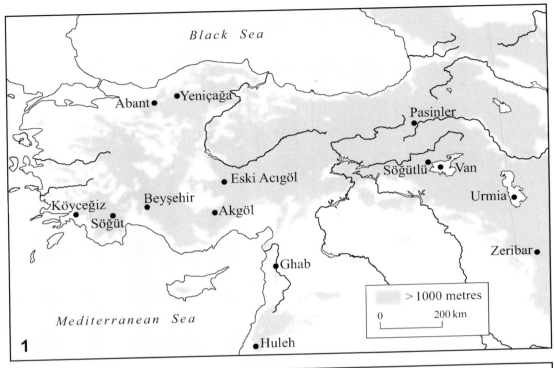

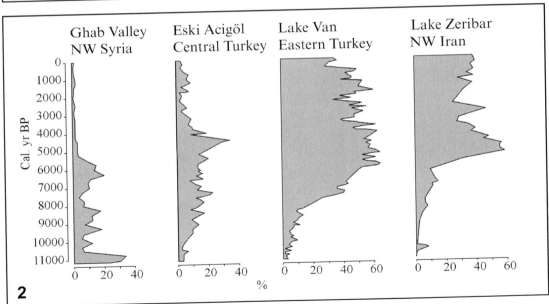

Figure 1.5 **1** Location of pollen core sites in Turkey. **2** Pollen curves of *Quercus* (oak) from four key sites plotted on similar timescales. The diagrams show a clear trend, with established early Holocene oak woodland in Syria gradually spreading to the highlands of Anatolia and Iran during the mid-Holocene (adapted from Connor 2006; Roberts 2002; Yasuda et al. 2000)

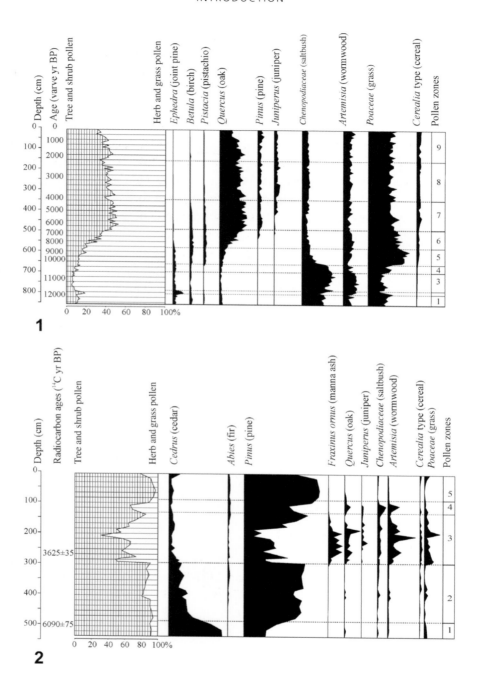

Figure 1.6 **1** Pollen diagram from Lake Van, eastern Turkey (adapted from Van Zeist and Woldring 1978; Wick et al. 2003). **2** Pollen diagram from Beyşehir Gölü, southwestern Turkey, showing the dramatic change in the curve as a result of forest clearance (adapted from Roberts 1990, 2000)

oak dominated the eastern highlands in the early Holocene, here in the western Taurus, it shared the forest cover with pine, cedar and juniper, with pine eventually becoming the most common tree (Figure 1.5: 2). A similar trend is reflected in the pollen count taken from the northwestern cores.[11] This decline in oak is of particular interest because it coincides with a rise in plants such as olives, walnuts, vines, and hemp between 3500 and 2000 years ago, which corresponds roughly to the Late Bronze through Iron Age in the archaeological record. Climate and volcanic activity are unlikely causes for this shift. Rather, this interlude in the pollen records from western Anatolia, the so-called Beyşehir Occupation Phase (Figure 1.6: 2), is a stark testimony to human agency.[12] It reflects the influence that farmers, who cleared the forests to make way for crops and their herds had on the landscape. The most likely forest clearance procedure was slash and burn (or swidden) cultivation—burning down woodland and cultivating with hoes in the ash-enriched soil. Plough agriculture, suited to the grass cover of the plains, would not have been used among the charred stumps and tangled roots. This deforestation was largely responsible for the disappearance of oak woodlands in southern and western Anatolia, which enabled the hardier pine to take hold wherever it could in an already eroded terrain. At the moment, however, Neolithic landuse is not detectable in the pollen records of Anatolia, a situation that will no doubt change with an increase in the precision and number of pollen diagrams.[13]

NOTES

1 See Georgacas 1969 for a detailed discussion of the etymology of the name Asia.
2 Greaves 2007.
3 The most detailed account of tectonics is found in Dixon and Robertson 1984; see also Fisher 1978.
4 A general introductory geography is Dewdney 1971. Accounts of Turkey in relation to the Middle East can be found in Held 1995 and Anderson 2000.
5 Van Zeist and Bottema 1991: 23.
6 Zohary 1973.
7 Van Zeist and Bottema 1991.
8 Connor 2006 thoroughly reviews these pollen data as a background to his own palynological field work in Georgia, southern Caucasus.
9 Van Zeist and Bottema 1977 (Zeribar); van Zeist and Woldring 1978 (Van); for more recent palynological studies around Lake Van, see Bottema 1995; Wick, Lemke, and Sturm 2003.
10 Bottema and Woldring 1984; Bottema and Woldring 1990; Vermoere et al. 2002.
11 Beug 1967; Bottema and Woldring 1990.
12 Roberts et al. 1997; Roberts 2002.
13 For an interpretation of the Zeribar diagram involving anthropogenic factors, see Pullar 1977.

2

EARLIEST ARRIVALS

The Palaeolithic and Epipalaeolithic
(1,000,000–9600 BC)

In Europe, the Palaeolithic, covering the period from the first appearance of tool-using humans in Africa to the retreat of the Ice Age at ca. 11,000 BC, has attracted attention for well over a century.[1] The study of this vast stretch of prehistory in Anatolia, by comparison, is a fledgling field, which is represented by only a handful of systematically excavated sites and a comparatively small number of dedicated researchers (Figure 2.1).[2] One reason for this situation is the difficulty of finding early Palaeolithic sites, which are often covered by later sediments and represented by ephemeral traces of human activity. Even so, the *Türkiye Arkeolojik Yerleşmeleri* (TAY—Turkish Archaeological Settlements) project has listed over 200 localities bearing Palaeolithic artefacts.[3] The other, more pertinent, reason for this sparsity of knowledge is neglect. Until very recently the Palaeolithic has simply been overshadowed by the intensity of research devoted to the later historic cultures. Yet it offers enormous potential to world prehistory, especially given the penchant for travel of *Homo erectus* and his relatives. As the most likely path anatomically modern humans took as they migrated from Africa through the Near East to Europe and central Asia, Anatolia no doubt played a crucial role in the peopling of the Old World. It is most likely, for instance, that Dmanisi, in southern Georgia, currently the earliest known hominid site outside Africa, where rich hominid (*Homo ergaster*) and artefactual finds have confirmed settlement between 1.7 and 1.8 million years ago, was reached by crossing Anatolia.[4]

During this time, which defines the boundary of the Plio-Pleistocene, the Anatolian peninsula was generally quite warm and humid.[5] With the onset of the glacial ages, climates changed significantly to colder and drier conditions.[6] Glaciers covered the highest peaks in the Taurus and Pontic mountains where they extended to as low as 1700 m. Elsewhere peri-glacial conditions (thawing during the day, freezing at night) were widespread, creating colluvial soils. Among the most conspicuous footprints of the Quaternary (Pleistocene) era are the numerous lakes that were formed, some as early as the Pliocene, through progressive uplifts and

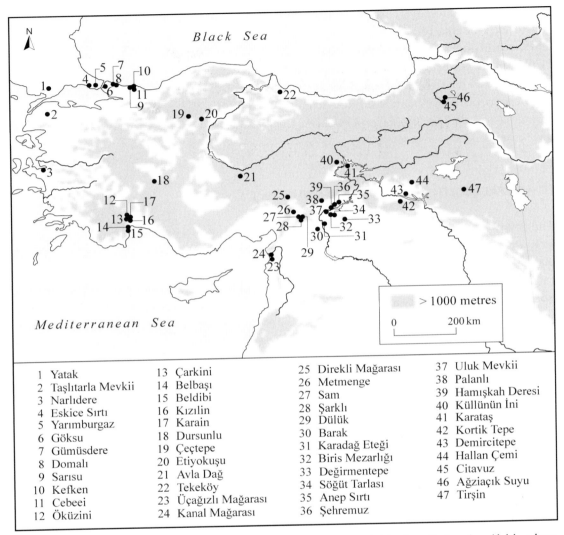

Figure 2.1 Map of Turkey showing the Palaeolithic and Epipalaeolithic sites. Only a handful has been excavated

1 Yatak	13 Çarkini	25 Direkli Mağarası	37 Uluk Mevkii
2 Taşlıtarla Mevkii	14 Belbaşı	26 Metmenge	38 Palanlı
3 Narlıdere	15 Beldibi	27 Sam	39 Hamışkah Deresi
4 Eskice Sırtı	16 Kızılin	28 Şarklı	40 Küllünün İni
5 Yarımburgaz	17 Karain	29 Dülük	41 Karataş
6 Göksu	18 Dursunlu	30 Barak	42 Kortik Tepe
7 Gümüsdere	19 Çeçtepe	31 Karadağ Eteği	43 Demircitepe
8 Domalı	20 Etiyokuşu	32 Biris Mezarlığı	44 Hallan Çemi
9 Sarısu	21 Avla Dağ	33 Değirmentepe	45 Citavuz
10 Kefken	22 Tekeköy	34 Söğüt Tarlası	46 Ağziaçık Suyu
11 Cebeei	23 Üçağızlı Mağarası	35 Anep Sırtı	47 Tirşin
12 Öküzini	24 Kanal Mağarası	36 Şehremuz	

downdrops. The most notable are Tuz Gölü (Salt Lake) in the heart of Turkey, Lake Burdur and a handful of others in the southwest, and Lake Van in the east.[7] In addition to these, a series of shallow lakes once dotted the central Anatolia plateau around Konya. Together, these bodies of water created a unique climatological background, which must be appreciated when studying cultural developments in Anatolia. Multiple shore terraces indicate that the size of these lakes changed, expanding or contracting with respect to rainy conditions (pluvials) or arid periods.[8] At times, the lakes contained fresh, or mildly brackish, water, enough to support populations of the clam *Dreissencia*. Even though these bodies of water would have attracted the early hominids, the Anatolian interior must have been a bleak and wind blown landscape in the early Pleistocene, judging from the sediments of storm waves at the base of the now dried-up lakes, and the sand dunes that developed once the lake waters receded.[9] When sea levels dropped in the Pleistocene at the peak of the glaciations, the Anatolian coastal lines changed accordingly, and became deeply incised. These coastlines are now submerged, but during the glacial stages would have experienced extremely cold and semiarid conditions. The configuration of the Aegean would have looked the most different during the Pleistocene, because its low broad shelf would have extended further west.

LOWER PALAEOLITHIC (ca. 1,000,000–250,000 BC)

The prospects the Palaeolithic holds have been vividly demonstrated with the recent discoveries at Kaletepe Deresi 3 (KD3), in central Anatolia, which have pushed the boundaries of human occupation back to 1 million years ago.[10] Just as exciting are the fragments of a *Homo erectus* calvaria (frontal bones and parietals) discovered accidentally in a block of travertine stone quarried at Kocabaş, near Denizli.[11] These fossils are of profound significance for Turkey. Dated to about 500,000–490,000 years ago, not only do they represent the first Middle Pleistocene hominid remains from the peninsula, but they also provide insights on the health of these early immigrants. The lesions identified at the base of the cranium are pathological evidence that the individual suffered from tuberculosis (*Leptomeningitis tuberculosa*), which inflames the meninges, the membrane that surrounds the brain. This significant discovery is poignant testimony that tuberculosis, once thought to be a fairly recent disease of only a few thousand years, was among the perils the first hominids faced as they left Africa. The earliest human ancestors to migrate out of Africa were protected against the ultraviolet rays of the intense sun of their homeland by their presumably dark skin. But as they moved from tropical lands north into temperate Eurasia, this protection became a problem, preventing the absorption of a requisite amount of vitamin D from sunlight, which, in turn, adversely affected their immune system.

The earliest human attempts in culture are best traced through stone artefacts. Effective and abundant, these tools provide the only continuous series of cultural markers. A particularly important series is emerging at Kaletepe Deresi 3, situated amidst the volcanic landscape of the plateau where the soft volcanic tuffs have eroded, exposing older, artefact-bearing layers that under normal circumstances would not be visible.[12] The rock formations of Cappadocia are a striking example of this process. Near Kaletepe Deresi 3 is the extensive Kömürcü obsidian source. Other volcanic rocks in this area such as basalt were also utilized for tool making. Six layers of tephra (R1–R6) in the upper levels of the 7 m deposit are particularly valuable for dating the recent volcanic activity; geochemical characterization of the R1–R5 tephras have linked them to the Acıgöl tuffs assigned to a minimum eruption date of 160,000 years ago. The Kaletepe Deresi 3 sequence comprises two major and interlocking cycles: The sedimentary deposition and the archaeological levels, which, in turn, are ascribed to cultural phases.

The long and uninterrupted sequence at Kaletepe Deresi 3 shows clear changes in the production of stone tools from volcanic rocks such as obsidian, rhyolite, andesite, and basalt. By the end of the 2005 season, some 4000 lithic artefacts were recovered; animal bones, by the same token, are scarce, perhaps owing to the acidic nature of the soil. The earliest cultural phase, I, is of singular significance. Acheulian handaxes—the first such artefacts recovered in situ in Anatolia—were found in levels V and VI–XII, presently confined to a small area. Only obsidian was used for these handaxes which have been worked on both surfaces (bifaces); andesite and other rocks were utilized for polyhedrons, cleavers, and choppers. Overall, this assemblage is clearly at home with the Acheulian tradition of southwest Asia. Level IV has a different character—choppers, chopping tools, and large flakes struck from andesite and rhyolite cores; obsidian was rarely exploited in this level. Phase II has a flake-dominated stone industry manufactured from obsidian. Thick flakes with unprepared striking platforms were also modified into denticulates and notched tools. The best parallels from Anatolia are found at Yarımburgaz and Karain E (assemblage A). Further work needs to address the apparent restricted utilization of obsidian in the Lower and Middle Palaeolithic which is confined to the volcanic provinces, a situation that is at odds with the widespread trade in the Neolithic.

Quite different in character is the slightly younger (900,000–780,000 years) site of Dursunlu where a deeply buried layer, exposed in an open cut lignite mine northwest of Konya, has yielded a rich deposit of remarkably preserved plant and animal remains, interspersed with a sample of stone artefacts.[13] Giant deer (*Megalaceros*) were a common sight in the Pleistocene, roaming the cool steppe landscape around Dursunlu, with horses, cattle, mammoth (*probiscideans*), and other wildlife. Birds, including herons, egrets, geese, ducks, and waders, attracted to the food afforded by the shallow lakes, were also abundant. Some 175 stone tools, mainly knapped from quartz, show no evidence of bifacial flaking. Rather they comprise simple flakes with few signs of further modification.

Two other Lower Palaeolithic sites stand out for their fine sequences: Yarımburgaz Cave, in the vicinity of Istanbul, and Karain Cave, near Antalya. They belong to clusters of sites located along the coasts of the Mediterranean and the Sea of Marmara.[14] Despite its unfortunate destruction, Yarımburgaz Cave remains the key site for the Lower Palaeolithic. The cave had two entrances, an upper and lower. Palaeolithic cultural material was found in the lower chamber, which also contained a substantial amount of fossil bear bones (*Ursus deningeri*).[15] None of the bear bones shows any cut marks or modification by humans, suggesting that the 40 or so individual animals died during hibernation. This curious association of stone tools and bear bones indicates that the cave was home to both humans and beasts, albeit not concurrently. It seems that in winter bears hibernated (and sometimes died) in the cave, and when they left in the spring, humans moved in, using Yarımburgaz Cave as a seasonal shelter. This "dual occupancy" also accounts for the apparent mixing of sediments and the relative homogeneity of the assemblage. Nonetheless, this arrangement appears to have suited all parties. Various archaeometric techniques, including electron spin resonance (ESR), indicate this arrangement lasted a long time (ca. 330,000–130,000 years ago).

Stone tools at Yarımburgaz were manufactured from flint (the principle raw material), quartz, and quartzite (Figure 2.2).[16] Excavations yielded 1674 lithic artefacts that show a close link between function/technique and choice of stone. Tools knapped from quartzite, the hardest of the three main materials, amount to no more than 237 artefacts, but comprised the bulk of chopping tools. Flint and quartz, by way of contrast, were preferred for the production of flake tools, the majority of which (about a third of the total assemblage) were retouched. Flint flakes are mostly rectangular or oval in shape, contrasting with the usual triangular forms of the Middle Palaeolithic (Mousterian). The total absence of prepared striking platforms—the Levallois technique—that so characterizes the Mousterian assemblages of Western Europe is another prominent difference. The Yarımburgaz repertoire, then, is predominantly a flake industry with flake tools outnumbering core tools eight to one.

Karain Cave forms part of an extensive karstic system, situated in an area with plenty of raw material for the manufacture of stone tools, mostly cobbles and pebbles of radiolarites. First explored in the 1960s by Kökten, renewed investigations since 1985 have provided a very important sequence of settlement.[17] Lower and Middle Palaeolithic deposits were found in the main chamber, Karain E, where the sequence reaches a depth of 10 m. Five geological units (I–V, in descending order) each with a number of sedimentary deposits were equated with archaeological layers (A–I). Whereas averages determined from ESR and TL (thermoluminescene) readings from the upper deposits confirm occupation around 250,000 years ago, estimations based on the correlation with oxygen isotope stages push the earliest peopling of the cave to about 500,000 years ago.[18]

The importance of the long Karain sequence is its capacity to show the technical and typological evolution of the lithic industry, from simple to refined, with associated shifts in raw material procurement and discard patterns. During the Lower Palaeolithic stone tools were produced outside the cave using local material. Within the cave five levels of occupation (Layers A–E) have been distinguished that can be divided into two technological groups (Figure 2.3). The earliest, Layer A, has an assemblage that broadly resembles the one at Yarımburgaz in its simple toolkit, comprising mostly small notched and denticulate flakes that have been expediently struck off cores with no signs of core preparation. No heavy-duty tools, in the form of choppers or bifaces, were found. According to the excavators this assemblage recalls the Clactonian industry of Europe, defined in part as a thick flake industry knapped without hard percussion, possessing smooth striking platforms, and displaying heavily retouched edges. As time progressed, production technology at Karain became more sophisticated. The general trend was from thick, well-retouched scrapers and a limited array of tools through essentially the same repertoire, but with a higher number of denticulates in Layer B (proto-Charentian) towards thinner tools, displaying controlled retouch, and a more specialized and varied toolkit in the uppermost layer.

In Layer C, the presence of a sidescraper with a partial retouch on both surfaces has been compared with the Acheulio-Yabrudian or Mugharian facies of the Levant, but otherwise the Acheulian traditions in the Levant are absent at Karain.[19] Nonetheless, the Charentian

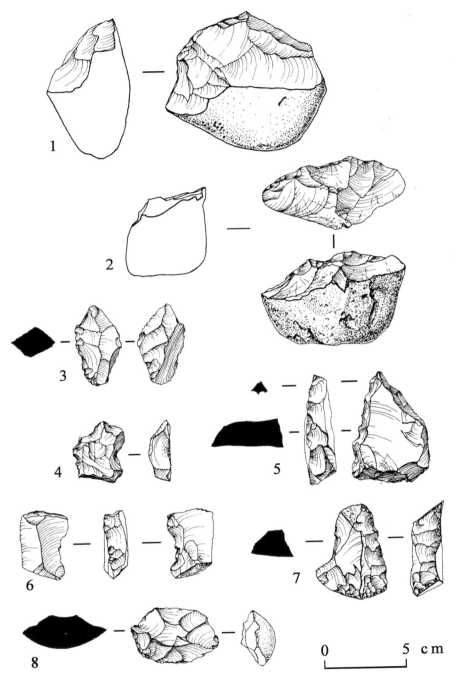

Figure 2.2 Lower Palaeolithic stone tools from Yarımburgaz Cave: **1, 2** Choppers. **3–7** Flake tools. **8** Flint core (adapted from Kuhn 2003)

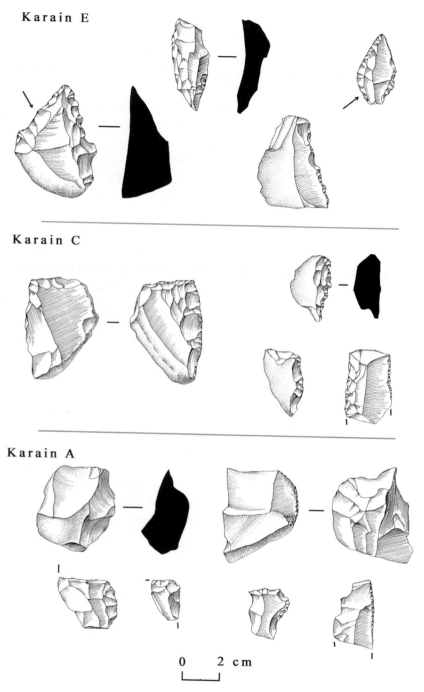

Figure 2.3   Lower Palaeolithic stone tools from Karain Cave, Levels A, C, and E (adapted from Otte et al. 1995c)

character of the industry continues through to Layer E, when sidescrapers, some displaying fine marginal retouch, increase in number. The inhabitants at Karain Cave hunted wild sheep and goat, whose bones prevailed among the faunal remains, although deer were represented too. Bear bones were also collected at Karain Cave, but there were not as many as at Yarımburgaz.[20]

These sequences—Karatepe Deresi 3, Yarımburgaz, and Karain—highlight a conspicuous feature of Lower Palaeolithic Anatolia, one that it shares with Greece, namely the presence of two different assemblages or stone tool industries.[21] One industry, found concentrated in the northwest corner, is characterized by core choppers and flake tools, and a conspicuous absence of bifacial handaxes. This chopper- and flake-dominated industry is found across the Balkans, Greece, and central Europe where they are sometimes referred to as "small tool industries." By contradistinction, central and eastern Turkey are largely defined by an assemblage based on handaxes that resemble the well-known Acheulian types found in western Europe, Caucasus, the Levant, and Africa.[22] Bifacial tools are particularly prevalent at open-air sites strung along the ancient terraces of the Euphrates and Orontes rivers. But, apart from the Kaletepe Deresi 3 examples, the finds from Turkey have been collected from the surface, offering little chronological control.[23] Even so, there is enough evidence to show that Anatolia is where two worlds met in the Lower and Middle Palaeolithic. This geographic division in Anatolia is defined by what Curtis Runnels recently termed the "Arsebük Line," essentially a continuation of a modified "Movius Line" that divides the Acheulian tool users of Europe, Africa and western Asia from the chopping tool industries of East Asia (Figure 2.4).[24]

This geographical division is not easy to explain, and many views have been put forward, succinctly summarized by Runnels.[25] What has become abundantly clear is that the Lower Palaeolithic stone tool traditions of Europe and the Near East are distinguished by diversity. Bifacial handaxes and cleavers, choppers and small tool industries, as well as simple and sophisticated technologies are all features that form part of two varied and widespread industries that were contemporary for good stretches of time, if not the entire Lower Palaeolithic. According to some, this coexistence has rendered the linear evolutionary model that argued for a chronological progression from Oldowan through Acheulian to Mousterian as untenable.[26] Others, however, maintain that flake-dominated assemblages are an archaic industry (the so-called Clactonian/Tayacian) that represents groups of earlier immigrants into Eurasia than those who brought the bifacial handaxes.[27]

Of all the explanations, the most persuasive are those that posit the two assemblages may be the product of either different environmental zones, or representative of functional distinctions. Sites with handaxes are scattered across terrain in Turkey that is generally 600 m above sea level, whereas core choppers assemblages are found at lower elevations that would have been associated with warmer and wetter climatic conditions. Moreover, the rather amorphous toolkit of core chopper industry suggests there was no need for specialized tools, possibly reflecting ample supplies of wood. This pattern is also broadly consistent with evidence from Europe. Contrariwise, the occurrence of handaxe assemblages at open-air sites and the association of nonbiface

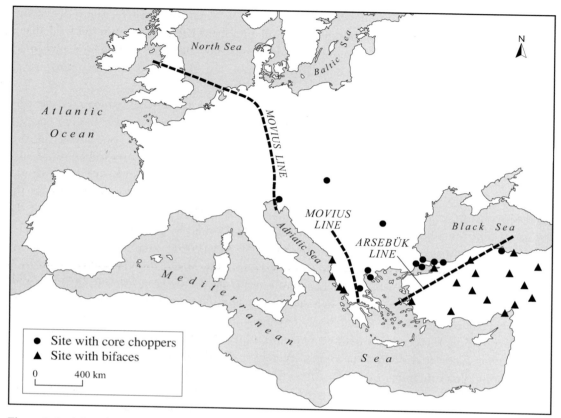

Figure 2.4 Map showing the re-alignment of the Movius Line and its continuation in Anatolia where it has been termed the Arsebük Line (adapted from Runnels 2003)

industries with cave sites suggest separate functions.[28] This view would gain strength if it could be shown through detailed comparative analyses that the flake tools associated with the handaxe assemblages are technically similar to those of the core chopper repertoire.

This brings us to the important issue of presence and absence of elements in assemblages, which has also called into question the mode of stone tool classification. There is now a shift away from clustering lithic artefacts into groups of retouched tools (typologies) to studying reduction processes, and the use and discard of tools (*chaînes opératoires*). According to this approach, the final forms of the tools are not as fundamental as the technology and processes used to *produce* them. Using this methodology, it has been argued that the Lower Palaeolithic had very linear production patterns, which were directly linked with the raw material. This resulted in parallel technological trajectories—specific reduction techniques applied to particular stones producing a limited range of tools that nevertheless displayed diversity over a time and space. This contrasts with the more flexible Middle Palaeolithic production processes, discussed later, that produced a standard array of flakes and blades through one or two reduction methods. The tools were then modified even further into a range of shapes and edge type by retouch. So while the assemblages from both periods show diversity, this feature was determined at the commencement of the reduction process in the Lower Palaeolithic and at the end in the Middle Palaeolithic.

MIDDLE PALAEOLITHIC (ca. 250,000–45,000 BC)

The most important Middle Palaeolithic sequence in Anatolia is Karain Cave. In Layer F, significant technological changes and procurement patterns appear that clearly link the upper deposits (F–I) with the Mousterian industry (Figure 2.5). Among the new traits are the use of the Levallois technique that replaces abrupt retouch, the appearance of Mousterian points, and the preference for sidescrapers over denticulates and notched tools. Tools were modified and used in a more intense fashion, with evidence for the complete reduction of cores. There is also a greater variety of raw materials. Although the stone used was still local, the occupants of the cave went further afield for raw material to produce large flakes. Towards the end of this Middle Palaeolithic deposit, in Layer I, tools were quite small and the assemblage as a whole was not so Levallois in character; in addition to radiolarites, sandstone and quartzite were utilized for the first time. Overall, the technique employed by the knappers of Karain and the shapes of the tools they produced are redolent of the Zagros cave sites rather than the Levantine Mousterian. The small leaf-shaped points from layers H–I also resemble the bifacially worked tools from the Balkans and central Europe.[29] Moreover, the amount of debitage in the sequence suggests that stone tool production in the Middle Palaeolithic was now an indoor activity. Kocapınar, Beldibi-Kumbucağı and Kaletepe Deresi 3 have comparable Mousterian assemblages, although not as extensive, or as well studied, as yet.[30]

A group of fossil hominids was discovered in Karain Layer F (geological unit III.2). Several distinguishing traits, such as a pronouncedly receding chin and the frontal disposition of the incisors, suggest they belong to Neanderthals. This identification is potentially very significant for just like the Denizli *Homo erectus* remains it sheds light on early migrations. The Karain fossils not only attest the presence of Neanderthals in Anatolia around 250,000–200,000 years ago, well before they reached the Levant (123,000–120,000 years ago), but also suggest that they migrated from Europe when the glaciers had reached their maximum extent during the Oder stage (oxygen isotope stage 8).

Nearly 20,000 mammalian bone fragments were recovered, but only about 15% could be identified. Even so, the Karain faunal record is noteworthy. Four taphonomic groups could be distinguished: (a) consumption refuse—animals that were hunted and transported back to the cave by humans, including goats and sheep (dominant throughout the sequence), various deer (fallow, roes and red), and wild boar, aurochs, and equids; (b) workshop debris—animals (hippopotami and elephants, ovicaprine horns, and deer antlers) prized for their bones, which were carved into objects, rather than for nutritional value; (c) competitors—carnivores such as bears,

Karain I

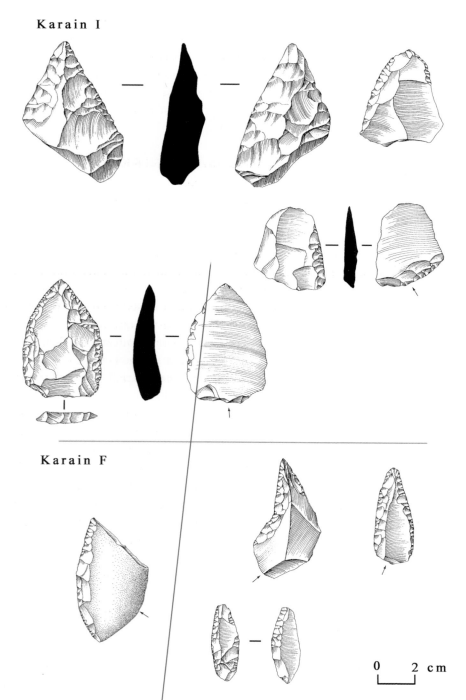

Karain F

0   2 cm

Figure 2.5 Middle Palaeolithic stone tools from Karain Cave, Levels F and I (adapted from Otte et al. 1995c)

wolves, foxes, and hyenas, which also used the cave for shelter; (d) intrusions—animals (small birds, hares, hedgehogs among others) that could have been transported to the cave by predators and raptors. While a few animals have an ambiguous position, whether as prey of human or animal predators, this analysis does show some clear patterns. One thing that is clear is that like at Yarımburgaz before it, the occupants at Karain shared their abode with wild animals. At Kaletepe Deresi 3, a mandible and two molars of a primitive form of equid are worth noting.

UPPER PALAEOLITHIC AND EPIPALAEOLITHIC (ca. 45,000–9600 BC)

At the beginning of the Upper Palaeolithic (ca. 45,000–40,000 BC), stone tool industries in Near East display an important element. They retain archaic Levallois features, but also embrace the production of blades that were struck off prismatic cores. In Anatolia, representation of the initial Upper Palaeolithic is scant. There are fewer sites ascribed to this period than the better known Lower and Middle Palaeolithic, and the subsequent Epipalaeolithic (or late Upper Palaeolithic) when these blade technologies were replaced by microliths. While this situation may reflect a general research bias in the field, this cannot explain the lack of evidence in the intensely surveyed regions around Marmara and in the southeastern region. More likely is that Anatolia, like Greece, was sparsely settled in the initial Upper Palaeolithic. This circumstance stands in sharp contrast to developments in the northern Balkans, the Caucasus, the Zagros region, and the southern Levant where occupation between the Upper Palaeolithic and Neolithic reveals no major gaps.

Presently, Uçağılı and Kanal caves both located near the Mediterranean shore of the Hatay province, and close to the mouth of the Orontes River, offer the best evidence for the early Upper Palaeolithic. Uçağılı is a collapsed cave investigated some 15 years ago. Three main cavities were opened, with Locus 2 yielding the most detailed deposit (1.5 m) which comprised four layers. There is general agreement that the lithic industry resembles those in the Levant, especially Lebanon (Figure 2.6). Two different assemblages are represented at Uçağılı: The earliest deposit has endscrapers, burins and retouched blades like those found at Ksar ʿAkil (Lebanon), whereas in the higher levels pointed blades produced through the bipolar technique are conspicuous and are again redolent of tools from Ksar ʿAkil and also the Antelias shelter near Beirut. Accelerator mass spectrometer (AMS) places the earliest levels between 41,000 and 43,000 years ago, and the latest range from 28,000 to 33,000 years BC. The Kanal assemblage also has strong southern connections. Both the Uçağılı and Kanal assemblages were produced from high-grade flint in the form of pebbles; the white cortex suggests they were procured from a source as nodules rather than from the sea shore. Blades predominate and can be retouched and unretouched, although flakes were still produced; the ratio is about 2:1. Generally broad, most blades were turned into endscrapers with a facetted platform and a pronounced bulb of percussion indicative of a hard hammer. This variety of lithics has generated discussion on nomenclature. The excavators refer to the Uçağılı tools as Aurignacian, using the number of flat endscrapers as a guide, though

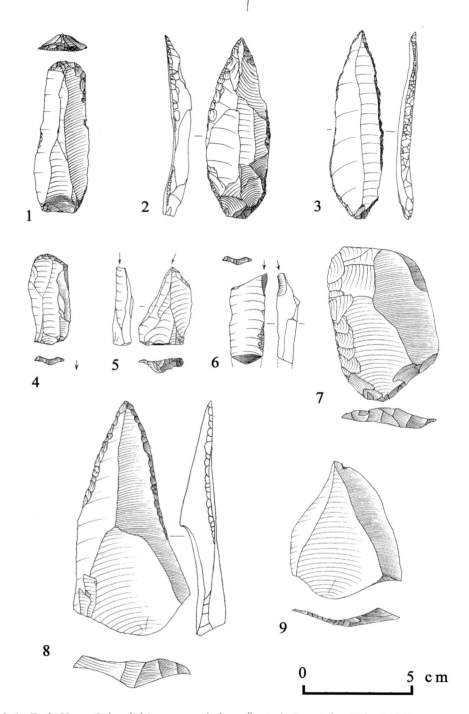

Figure 2.6 Early Upper Palaeolithic stone tools from Üçağızlı Cave (after Kuhn 2002)

others prefer Ahmarian because of the high proportion of retouched and pointed blades termed el-Wad points.[31] But there were differences between the Hatay sites and other initial Upper Palaeolithic sites around the east Mediterranean, namely the absence of certain key types, including Emireh and Umm et-Tlel points.[32]

In addition to stone, tools were manufactured from bone, including square-sectioned points found in the earliest levels. Judging from the quantity of modified shell remains, it is clear that the inhabitants at Uçağılı were fond of personal ornaments.[33] Together with those from Ksar ʿAkil, the Uçağılı beads and pendants made from various marine gastropods comprise the earliest evidence for jewellery in the Near East, and are comparable in date to similar objects from Africa and eastern Europe. This widespread used of personal ornaments in the Upper Palaeolithic points to the emergence of external symbolic human behavior. Whereas wearing jewellery may not represent a fundamental leap in human cognition, it nonetheless represents another stage of communication expressed through body decoration. Uçağılı has also yielded a rich sample of animal bones, mostly herbivores (wild goats, and fallow and roe deer), with some game birds and tortoises.[34]

Evidence for the end of the Palaeolithic, or Epipalaeolithic, is found across much of Anatolia, but the best evidence for the early stages again comes from the warm Mediterranean coast and the southeastern region. Near Antalya we have a cluster of caves—Beldibi, Belbaşı, Karain B, and especially Öküzini—that offer a picture of life towards the end of the Ice Age.[35] At the commencement of the earliest phase at Öküzini (ca. 17,800 BC), we witness further changes in lithic industries. Initially, the blank blades were modified into endscrapers, burins, and perforators that bear some resemblances to elements from the Kebaran tradition. In Layer 3, the narrow blades are snapped into microlithic tools (triangles, trapezes, lunates, and microburins), and later still (10,500 BC) the tools became even smaller, with cores now quite irregular. The tool kit at the very end of the Pleistocene also had a considerable number of awls, needles, and spatulas carved from bone, making it quite diversified. Moreover, the presence of grinding stones in the earliest levels points to emergence of intensive exploitation of plant foods. Faunal remains at Öküzini also show shifts in hunting patterns. Ovicaprines (mostly goats and some sheep) predominate throughout the sequence, but fallow deer and other forest animals increase to 40% of the sample in the uppermost deposits of the Pleistocene.

While the Epipalaeolithic along the Mediterranean littoral has affinities with the traditions in the southern Levant, some have argued that elsewhere in Anatolia it appears to be home grown.[36] Likewise this coastal region lies outside the "nuclear zone" of wild cereals where the first experiments with agriculture occurred in the eighth millennium BC. These observations are rather significant in terms of their developments that marked the Neolithic. As the focus of settlement shifted towards the foothills of the Taurus Mountains, the Mediterranean coast of Anatolia, like those of Syria and Lebanon, was abandoned and resettled only much later at Mersin and other sites.

In the southeast, a number of groups began to change their behavior in a remarkable way. For the first time in Anatolia, they built houses and lived in them year round. We will deal with this fundamental shift in settlement organization more fully in the next chapter. Whether one ascribes these settlements to the Epipalaeolithic or the early Pre-Pottery Neolithic A is a moot point, given that the boundary between the two periods is still quite blurred. Nevertheless, the earliest sedentary communities have been identified at Hallan Çemi, Demirköy, Körtik Tepe and the earliest level at Çayönü.[37] In central Anatolia, we have the mound at Pınarbaşı, which although dated around 8500–8000 BC, has a microlithic assemblage of stone tools that is typical of the very end of the Epipalaeolithic.[38]

At Hallan Çemi calibrated radiocarbon readings stretch back to the end of the 11th millennium BC, making it roughly comparable in date to Jerf el Ahmar and the earliest occupation at Abu Hureyra 1 in Syria. The earliest dwellings at Hallan Çemi (Level 3) were stone built, C shaped and no more than 2 m in diameter.[39] Of the four structures completely exposed in Level 2, three were well paved with sandstone slabs, and of these, one was large (about 4 m in diameter) and centered by a small, plastered basin (Figure 2.7). Judging by their sturdy construction (sandstone slabs), size (up to ca. 5–6 m in diameter), and installation (semicircular stone bench), the four buildings in the uppermost level appear to have served a public function rather than a domestic role. Similar round huts have been found at Çayönü (subphase 1), where they were partly sunken into the ground.[40] Built with walls of reed or wattle and mud plaster, over time these small huts gradually assumed an oval shape. In these earliest levels at Çayönü, the deceased were buried in pits dug in open spaces or under the floor of the huts, in a tightly flexed position, accompanied only by a few pieces of ochre.

Both settlements reflect the emergence of community planning and a new sense of social awareness expressed through the public domain. At Hallan Çemi houses and other features, including low, round, plastered platforms, define a large central open area about 15 m across. The large amount of animal bone and fire-cracked stones found within them have been interpreted as the remains of communal feasting. At Çayönü open spaces were used for storage, stone knapping and dumping rubbish, possibly the remnants of feasting, too.[41] Chlorite and limestone bowls finely ornamented with geometric and naturalistic designs from Hallan Çemi and Körtik Tepe, and a range of pestles with sculpted handles (Figures 2.7 and 2.8), comparable to those further south at Nemrik 9 and Tell Magzalia, were part of the paraphernalia used to prepare food for public consumption.[42]

As the focus of daily activities, these houses of the late Epipalaeolithic were also imbued with symbolic connotations that reflected the new circumstances of their builders. Whether it is the sense of settlement planning, suggesting some sort of social control, or the internal organization of space that becomes more apparent a little later, the emphasis placed on the house and settlement is clear. Communities were not only on the cusp of domesticating food resources, but they also experimented with new modes of social arrangement. This change in the social cohesion of sedentary groups was reflected later in the Pre-Pottery Neolithic by exuberant symbolism, but its roots are to be found in these earliest formative villages. These groups of circular hut-like structures, then, had an impact on the development of communal life that went far beyond their simple constructional technique.

F. ~~xxxxx~~
Bin
Hair
Shawl

T.

Legs
Washing
Sorting papers
Bin.

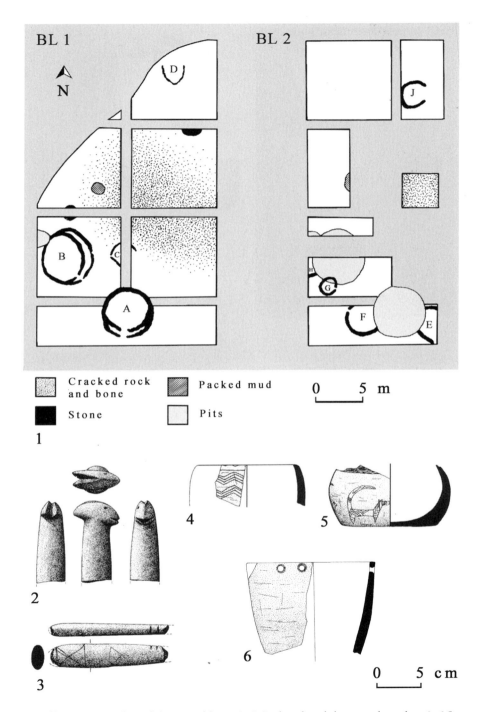

Figure 2.7 Hallan Çemi: **1** Plan of the round huts. **2, 3** Sculpted and decorated pestles. **4–6** Stone vessels (adapted from Rosenberg 2007)

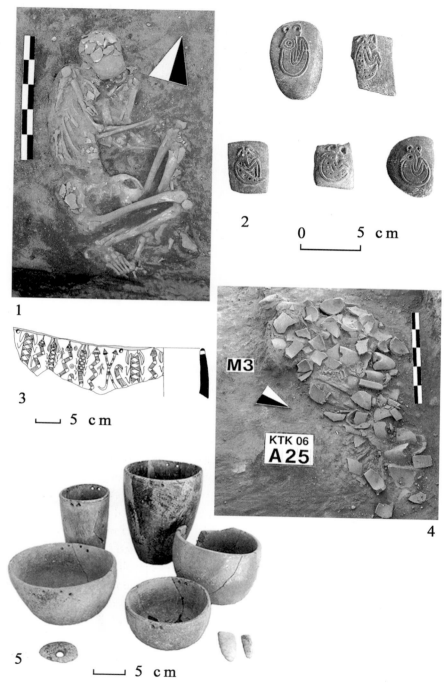

Figure 2.8 Körtik Tepe: **1** Burial in flexed position. **2** Decorated stone objects. **3** Drawing of chlorite vessel richly decorated with incised representations of snakes and other reptiles. **4** Deposit of fragmented stone vessels. **5** Group shot, showing stone vessels with perforated rim, pendant, and polished tool artefacts (adapted from Özkaya and Sarı 2007; Schmidt 2006)

The chipped stone industry from Hallan Çemi and Çayönü shows clear links with the northern Zagros culture province. The Hallan Çemi repertoire includes scalene geometric tools and some rare but distinctive examples of Nemrik-type projectile points (Figure 2.9).[43] These are also found at Demirköy, whose artefacts are generally placed between the end of Hallan Çemi and the beginning of Çayönü.[44] Missing from Hallan Çemi is any trace of Levantine influence such as the side-notched el-Khiam point.[45] These notched points are present, however, in small numbers in the Pre-Pottery Neolithic industry at Çayönü, which has many burins, notched tools, and endscrapers (but few retouched tools, including hollow-based points) that begin to increase by the end of the period. Some of these tools, as well as shaft straighteners, are found at Demirköy.[46] Flint was the main medium, with obsidian utilized only rarely at Çayönü. Analysis of the sheen that many stone tools bear along their edge indicates that a wide variety of tasks were performed from food processing to building—the cutting of silicious plants, whether for constructing of superstructures (reeds) or for food, must have been a constant preoccupation.

ROCK ART AND RITUAL

The appearance of art and its implications for cognitive processes has captured interest in Palaeolithic studies generally, yet it is a curiously neglected field in Turkey. Rock art is found in three mountainous regions of Anatolia: (a) the Taurus Mountains starting in the Hakkâri region (Tirşin, Şat and Çatak), westwards to Palanlı, in Adıyaman, and beyond to Antalya where Beldibi and Özükini are decorated; (b) the easternmost highlands running north from Van (Put Köyü and Başet Dağı), not far from the Hakkâri group, through Pasinler (Yarnak or Yazılı Cave) and Kars (Kağızman, Azat and Katran Kazanı); (c) Tekerlek Dağı, ancient Mount Latmos, in western Anatolia. Collectively, these sites encompass the principal categories of rock art: Pictographs (painted images), petroglyphs (carved, or more precisely, pecked, motifs), and engravings (incisions). Recent advances in dating rock art, whereby minute organic samples are analyzed using accelerator mass spectrometry, have not been applied to any Anatolian rock art site as yet. Samples tested include pigments such as ochres that are mixed with fat, organic particles trapped below the layers of chemical coating (rock varnish) that build up on the rock surface over time, and even the chemical constituents of rock varnish itself (although this technique has its critics). Consequently, the chronology of rock art in Anatolia is still based on the rather subjective approach of placing different styles in a temporal sequence without any firm evidence, stratigraphic or other, to support it. Some of the sites mentioned earlier are ascribed to the Neolithic, but given the vagaries of dating and the relatively small number of studies, they are dealt with here together.

One of the largest concentrations of rock art in the Near East is located about 2850 m above sea level on the Tirşin Plateau, in the Hakkâri region.[47] Images are either carved or incised on blocks of andesite that are scattered over a vast area, but clustered into two groups within close proximity to each other: Kahn-ı Melkan and Taht-ı Melkan. The majority of representations are

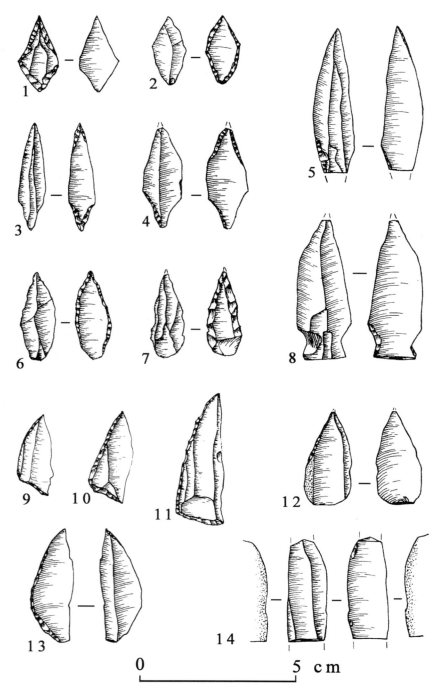

0 5 cm

Figure 2.9 Epipalaeolithic stone tools from Demirköy (1–8, 12–14) and Hallan Çemi (9–11): **1, 2** Nemrik points. **3, 4** Tanged points. **5** Triangular point. **6, 7** Foliate points. **8** Güzir type point. **9–11** Scalene triangles. **12** Obliquely backed point. **13** Lunate. **14** Sickle blade (adapted from Rosenberg 1994; Rosenberg and Peasnall 1998)

of animals, including wild cattle, bison, ibexes, deer, and wild goats, which are depicted in a realistic or stylized fashion (Figure 2.10). Realistic figures are generally larger in scale, with lines running from back to belly often compartmentalizing the body of the beast, such as in the image of an antelope (Figure 2.10: 4). Bulls are often portrayed with a lowered or turned head and massive shoulders, such as the one depicted on a block over 2 m high (Figure 2.10: 6). We even have a hybrid creature, a two-headed beast, combining features of deer with a bull. Humans are rarely shown, and invariably in a schematic manner, such as the curious and well-endowed male figure with pronounced genitalia, ribs, fingers, and toes (Figure 2.10: 3). A recent redating of the Tirşin rock art places it within the Pre-Pottery Neolithic, based largely on stylistic similarities it shares with Göbekli Tepe, especially in the rendering of the bull.[48] A nearby site, apparently aceramic Neolithic, and the altitude of the Tirşin Plateau that would have precluded occupation before the postglacial optimum are also used to argue for a later date. Another reckoning suggests stylistic comparisons between the animal figures depicted at Palanlı and the Hakkâri Mountains with those painted on Halaf pottery of the sixth millennium BC.[49] Even so, firmer evidence would be useful.

In Antalya, Beldibi C has a number of artworks, including a carved fish, an incised image of a bull with its head turned back, and a running stag.[50] At Öküzini, a large bull is rendered in a realistic fashion in red paint on the wall, and nearby is a cluster of apparently human stick figures and a schematic ibex. The general similarity this art shares with sites scattered across the Mediterranean, especially Italy, with the relatively rare representations at some Natufian sites has suggested an Epipalaeolithic date. In the first report, Bostancı also published a small pebble (5 cm) from Öküzini that was incised with a crude image of a bovid.[51] On closer examination under a microscope, the pebble revealed a more delicate overengraving of the bovid, which was surrounded by schematic "weapons" used in a symbolic hunt (Figure 2.11: 1).[52] This seemingly diminutive artefact assumes some significance. In the first instance, despite the absence of bovid bones from Öküzini, artists were clearly familiar with aurochs and had an aptitude in depicting them. It is also important for the similarity it shares with the imagery found on mobiliary and cave art from the late Upper Palaeolithic of western Europe. The representation of the "killing" on the Öküzini pebble is particularly important because microscopic study has shown that not only do the symbolic weapons and wounds reveal different hands at work, they were apparently also incised at different times. This renewal of a ritual killing, or the general practice of renewing prehistoric art, is an activity we will encounter later in the Neolithic, especially at Çatalhöyük.

In the Van region, the canyon that separates the village of Yedisalkım and Başet Mountain is peppered with up to 60 caves, yet only four are decorated with paintings.[53] They are all located on the south slope and were deliberately chosen for their difficult access—the lowest is 20 m above ground level, the highest nearly 80 m. The richest gallery is the so-called Cave of Maidens that has over 90 figures executed in red or dark brown paint (Figure 2.12: 1). Whereas the red images are realistically depicted, the dark brown ones are stylized and apparently are the most recent given that they sometimes superimpose the red figures. The cave comprises two

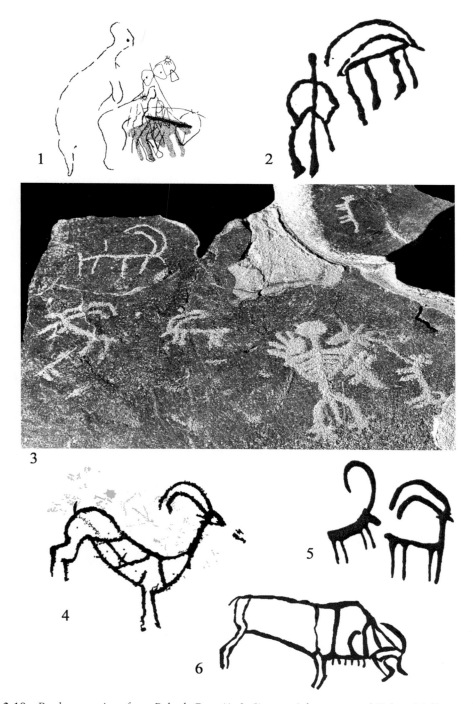

Figure 2.10   Rock engravings from Palanlı Cave (1, 2, 5), near Adıyaman, and Kahn-ı Melkan and That-ı Melkan on the Tirşin Plateau (3, 4, 6), in the Hakkâri region (adapted from Anati 1968; Özdoğan 2004)

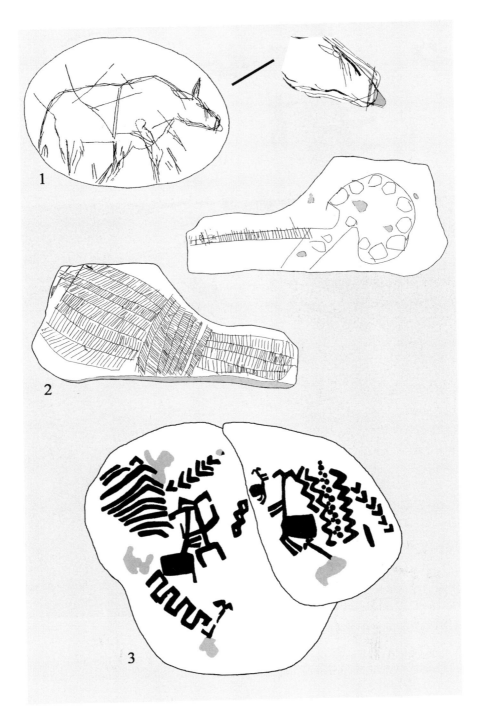

Figure 2.11 **1** Incised pebble from Öküzini, depicting a bovid and hunter. The details are recognizable under a microscope. **2** Two faces of another pebble—one has a circular motif with a ladder-like attachment, whereas the other has a clustered of "ladders" (adapted from Otte et al. 1995a). **3** Rock painting from Latmos showing geometric motifs and figures (adapted from Peschlow-Bindokat 2007)

Figure 2.12 **1** Rock painting from the Cave of Maidens, near Van. **2** Rock face with engravings from Çamılı, in the Kars province (adapted from Belli 2003b; Photo: Antonio Sagona)

chambers, both are decorated, Chamber 2 more so, with ceilings heavily blackened from soot. Wild goats and deer are the most commonly depicted animals across sweeping panels; they are well executed, often with a narrow midriff. Humans, both male and female, are generally smaller in size, schematically rendered and usually with their arms outstretched above their heads as if dancing. Sometimes, they are depicted with exaggerated features—thighs and legs (females), and the phallus. Absent are the accoutrements of hunting—bows and arrows, and other hunting gear. Importantly, the overall arrangement of the galleries is not orderly, suggesting the art was rendered at different times and wherever space permitted. The figurative art at Put Köyü (also known as Yeşilalıç) is also located in the Van province. They comprise engravings and paintings of humans and animals, mostly goats, and the occasional cross motif.

Further north, in the Kars province, we find rock art in several districts. One is located in the Kağızman district, in the environs of village of Karaboncuk, also referred to as Çamışlı and Yazılı Kaya.[54] Again the remoteness of the site, at an altitude of 3134 m, is conspicuous. Here we find large, smooth-faced panels engraved with many images of animals depicted with precision, especially stags with massive antlers (Figure 2.12: 2). Nearby is another cluster at Çallı, where the sites of Büyük Pano and Küçük Pano show skilfully engraved ibexes with sweeping horns; a lattice motif may represent a hunting net. At Azat, the animals are mostly painted, but they do not appear to be as gracefully executed even if they have suffered from weathering. In Pasinler, we have Yarnak (or Yazılı) Cave, again remote, which has been decorated with red stylized animal and human figures, with the occasional abstract motif.[55]

The art from Latmos clearly belongs to a different tradition. Here there are no engravings or carvings. Stylized human figures are interspersed with what appear to be reptiles and geometric motifs (dots, vertical zigzags, herringbone, battlements), all executed in red paint (Figure 2.11: 3). The anthropomorphic figures have T-shaped or M-shaped heads, and their arms are often raised. Like other rock art, chronology is problematic. Using the rendering of the female figures, Anneliese Peschlow-Bindokat is inclined to link them to the art of the Hacılar culture of the Late Neolithic.[56]

So what are we to make of this rich imagery? Any attempt to answer this question requires us to enter the complex and untidy world of human visual perception. Art is a notoriously difficult phenomenon to define, not least because it involves a range of media and activities. It is further complicated by the western notion of aesthetics, an 18th-century construct designed as a set of limited responses to fine arts (painting, sculpture, architecture, poetry, and music) as distinct from technical or decorative arts. Western appreciation of art requires "beauty" to be judged and emotions to be affected without any reference to context or utility, a state that has been referred to as "disinterested contemplation."[57] These criteria are not generally applicable to nonwestern art, in our case prehistoric art, where the boundaries between the aesthetic and utilitarian, and social and religious activities are blurred. Taking this line of thought, it seems that the production of prehistoric art was probably part of social and ritual events that might have included dancing and miming.

The importance lay not in the production of art—a transient event—but its role in reaffirming social cohesion. Indications are not lacking that much of nonwestern art strives not for the *effect* (the finished product), but for the *affect*, namely capturing the qualities brought about magically and, perhaps, momentarily by whatever activity is being performed. In the art of the Australian Aborigines, to use a distant example, the act of delineation whether drawing or painting was (and still is) in itself efficacious in some way of solidarity. This best explains why paintings are sometimes executed on top of existing pictures, so as to bring about a chaotic palimpsest of superimposed images. One way of explaining the difference between nonwestern and western art, then, is that in the former the reality and efficacy is in the *act performed* and the *reality captured* there and then, rather than in the *act communicated* and *reality repeated*. In other words, it could be argued that certain nonwestern art involves a magical process.

This leads us to phosphenes and shamanism, topics that curiously have not been discussed much in Anatolian circles, despite many studies focused on their relevance to Eurasia and prehistoric Europe.[58] Briefly, phosphenes are the kaleidoscopic range of images that the human visual system can generate under a range of conditions, including pressure, darkness, sound, and so on. Some have argued that, broadly speaking, these phosphenes bear a striking similarity to the abstract geometric patterns depicted in prehistoric art. Taking it one step further, other researchers believe that these patterns were induced by shamanic practices. Shamanism is an ecstatic religious phenomenon characterized by an ideology of cosmic flight, undertaken for enlightenment or healing and achieved through a trance state. Many religions have mystical exaltations when people speak with the spirit world and become the vehicle for communication with the divine.[59] Even though shamanism is most often associated with hunter-gatherer cultures, especially those of Siberia (whence we get the term "shaman," connoting one who is excited, moved, or raised) it is now recognized that shamanic behavior is ubiquitous. Indeed, in a discussion on the sociology of ecstasy, Lewis cogently argues that "possession" phenomena are universal in character and feature in many religions and societies at various times to the present.[60]

Just as some art should not be viewed through modern western eyes, so too the defining features of shamanism should not be seen as "irrational" behavior. One such behavior is the altered states of consciousness most shamans experience. These trances are marked by vivid hallucinations, which can be achieved through the ingestion of a hallucinogenic substance, sensory deprivation (absence of light and sound), vigorous dancing, and rhythmic sound (such as drumming and chanting) to mention a few modes. Shamans, who can be either men or women, are possessed by spirits, which they incarnate. Importantly, shamans never lose control over the spirits and it is this command that empowers them reputedly to cure the afflictions of the believer.[61] But their other supposed abilities include changing and controlling natural elements such as weather and animal behavior, and predicting the future.

Although one should be careful to avoid making a simple analogy between shamanic practices that have been recorded in the recent past and the material remains in archaeology, there are nonetheless some commonalities that are strikingly similar irrespective of time, place, or society. According to some researchers, these similarities are universal because they are responses of the human nervous system while in a state of altered consciousness. These similarities need not detain us here. Suffice to say that three stages of neuropsychological experiences have been identified.[62] Briefly, when under a trance a shaman generally first sees moving luminous geometric forms, then attempts to interpret them as more tangible objects, and, finally, in the third stage of trance, the subject can have the sense of traveling through a latticed vortex, which terminates in a bright light, to emerge in a frightening world of intensely real hallucinations, comprising demons, animals, and bizarre settings. In this final state, surroundings become animated and shamans can feel that they change into the animals they see. By becoming their hallucinations, they experience a sense of flight, or to "blend" into the features around them. In line with this argument, then, prehistoric art in Anatolia becomes a more fruitful and engaging field of study if it is divorced from the western notion of aesthetics and viewed within a framework of neuropsychological experiences.

NOTES

1 The Palaeolithic is an archaeological stage that is coterminous with the geological epochs from the Plio-Pleistocene transition to the beginning of the Holocene. More specifically, the Lower Palaeolithic covers the period from the late Pliocene to about the end of the Middle Pleistocene, whereas the Middle and Upper Palaeolithic equate with the Upper Pleistocene.
2 Kuhn 2002.
3 Harmankaya and Tanındı 1996.
4 Gabunia et al. 2000; Lordkipanidze et al. 2008; Vekua et al. 2002.
5 Roberts and Wright 1993. The Pliocene is the last geological epoch of the Tertiary geological period. It ended about 1.8 million years ago, when the Pleistocene epoch of the Quaternary period began. The geochronological division of the Pleistocene is as follows: Lower (or Early) began ca. 1.8 million years ago, the Middle about 780,000 years ago, and the Upper (or Late) around 127,000 years ago. It ended around 10,000 years ago, when the Holocene (or postglacial) epoch began. Both the Pleistocene and the Holocene form part of the Quaternary geological period.
6 Bottema and van Zeist 1981.
7 Erol 1978.
8 Karabıyıkoğlu et al. 1999; Kuzcuoğlu et al. 1999.
9 Fairbridge et al. 1997.
10 Slimak et al. 2006; Slimak et al. 2008.
11 Kappelman et al. 2008.
12 Slimak et al. 2006; Slimak et al. 2008.
13 Güleç et al. 1999.
14 Runnels and Özdoğan 2001.
15 Arsebük et al. 1992; Stiner et al. 1996.
16 Kuhn 2003; Kuhn et al. 1996.
17 Kökten 1955; Otte et al. 1995a; Otte et al. 1995c.
18 Otte et al. 1998: table 1.
19 Otte et al. 1995c.
20 López Bayón 1988.
21 Runnels 2003.

22 Bar-Yosef 1994; Ljubin and Bosinski 1995.

23 Kuhn 2002: 202; Taşkıran 1998; Yalçınkaya 1981.

24 Runnels 2003. Güven Arsebük (Istanbul University) led investigations at Yarımburgaz Cave, whereas Hallam Movius, an American archaeologist based at the Peabody Museum of Archaeology at Ethnology, was a specialist on Palaeolithic Europe. See also Kuhn 2003: 153–155.

25 Runnels 2003: 199–200.

26 Kuhn 2003: 153.

27 Otte et al. 1995c: 297.

28 Kuhn 2002: 207.

29 Kuhn 2002: 202.

30 Bostancı 1966; Minzoni-Dèroche 1987.

31 Kuhn et al. 1999.

32 Kuhn et al. 1999.

33 Kuhn et al. 2001.

34 Kuhn 2002: 205.

35 Albrecht et al. 1992; Bostancı 1959, 1962; Esin and Benedict 1963.

36 Balkan-Altı 1994a: 143–144.

37 Badischen Landesmuseum Karlsruhe 2007. For a Near Eastern perspective, see Aurenche and Kozlowski 1999.

38 Watkins 1996.

39 Rosenberg 1994, 1999. Baird in Badischen Landesmuseum Karlsruhe (ed.) 2007.

40 Bıçakçı 1998; Özdoğan 1999: 42–44.

41 Özdoğan 1999.

42 Rosenberg 1994; Rosenberg and Davis 1992; Özkaya and San 2004.

43 Rosenberg 1999.

44 Rosenberg and Peasnell 1998.

45 Caneva et al. 1998; Rosenberg 1999.

46 Rosenberg and Peasnell 1998.

47 Uyanık 1974.

48 Özdoğan 2004.

49 Mellaart 1975: 162–164.

50 Anati 196; Bostancı 1959.

51 Bostancı 1959.

52 Otte et al. 1995b.

53 Belli 2001, 2003b.

54 Belli 2006.

55 Başgelen 1988.

56 Peschlow-Bindokat 2003.

57 Winter 2002.

58 Bednarik 1990; Clottes and Lewis-Williams 1998; Lewis-Williams 2002; Lewis-Williams and Pearce 2005. For Anatolia, see Sagona and Sagona (forthcoming).

59 See, for example, Furst 1972.

60 Lewis 2003: 15–31.

61 For opposing views on shamanism and spirit possession, see Eliade 1964: 437–440; Lewis 2003: 43–45.

62 Helvenson and Bahn 2003.

3

A NEW SOCIAL ORDER

Pre-Pottery Neolithic (9600–7000 BC)

By the closing phase of the Glacial Period, from about 11,000 BC, the world was fundamentally transformed in two ways. First, global warming led to profound environmental changes, including the rise in sea level caused by the melting of glaciers and the geographical spread of vegetation and animals into temperate areas that were warmer and wetter than before. In the Near East, these ameliorating changes were interrupted by a cold and arid spell called the Younger Dryas (ca. 10,800–9600 BC), which was followed by so-called climatic optimum (ca. 9600–5000 BC), when winter days were mild and the summer nights humid.[1]

The second transformation was caused by the human response to these ecological adjustments, accelerating social and economic pursuits in new directions. In the Near East, an area that exercised a critical influence on neighboring lands, among the most significant was the shift from mobility to a settled life in villages, which brought with it new social structures. Whereas earlier undertakings very much depended on group cooperation, the acumen of individuals and the nuclear family gradually determined survival and success, with the home (or *domus*) becoming the focus of activities.

Yet another change was the gradual adoption of farming and with it new technologies, which steadily spread through most of Europe, bringing a more abundant and dependable source of food through cultivation of crops and the domestication of animals. But the most fascinating change related to the human experience itself. Increased complexity of social dynamics heralded novel ways of thinking that were at times expressed in a vivid symbolism through art. Initially, public cult buildings with monumental stone sculptures and later decorated houses equipped with installations gradually transformed the cultural landscape.

So profound and widespread were these changes in human history that their impact has been compared to the Industrial Revolution, which, ironically, ended the pre-eminence of agriculture as the economic propellant. The magnitude of these early postglacial (or Holocene) episodes did not escape Vere Gordon Childe, who, some 70 years ago, summed them up in the enduring metaphor—the Neolithic Revolution.[2] While today few would disagree that these events were indeed momentous, providing as they did the circumstances in which civilizations could appear a few millennia later, there is far less talk of a "revolution." There are, in fact, no clear-cut divisions between gathering food and complete dependence on cultivated plants. Radical though the innovations were, the change was not abrupt. Nonetheless, a mosaic of regional events presents us with a clear and convincing overall pattern—farming totally transformed the conditions of human existence.

THE NEOLITHIC: A SYNERGY OF PLANTS, ANIMALS, AND PEOPLE

Archaeological terminology can potentially mislead, so we will attempt to review, however summarily, certain key definitions and concepts. When it was first coined, in the 19th century, Neolithic emphasized technological change. It was part of a model based on northern European archaeological remains that distinguished cultural transformations solely on the basis of development of tool technology, first of stone, and, subsequently, of bronze and iron. Although Neolithic assemblages do indeed indicate changes in stone industry, some of the implements such as mortars and pestles, and other polished stone tools, once thought to be Neolithic in origin can now be attributed to the older Epipalaeolithic period. Equally, the criterion of permanent settlement need not be exclusive to agricultural societies. In the Near East, the notion of "sedentary hunter-gatherers," first attributed to the Epipalaeolithic Natufian communities of the Levant, who exercised considerable control over the rich and varied resources for subsistence around their settlements, has been well accepted.[3] The term Neolithic, then, is one of convenience, more than it is of precision.

The long period of the Neolithic in Anatolia (and the Near East) is divided into two broad phases on the basis of ceramic technology. The Anatolian pre-pottery (or aceramic) phase extends from about 9600 to 7000 BC and is further subdivided, largely on the basis of stratigraphy and the evolution of artefacts, into a Pre-Pottery Neolithic A (PPNA), Pre-Pottery Neolithic B (PPNB), and Pre-Pottery Neolithic C (PPNC). This is followed by the Pottery Neolithic (PN), which is also refined down into an early and late phase.[4] In recent years, the distinguishing traits of the "Neolithic package" have had to be redefined too, from one that focused almost exclusively on crops and food processing tools to clusters that include domestic space (or mode of living), sacred space (or cult), symbolism, farming, human genetics and the spread of language, which varied according to region and period.

Early agriculture is a daunting subject.[5] Even a sketch of the story can easily burst its banks, but Anatolia's crucial role in this process demands some comment. The predisposing conditions of the Fertile Crescent towards agriculture have been known for some time. An impressive arc of land, broadly defined, it stretches from the southern Levant through the plains of Syria and across the foothills of southern Anatolia to the mountains of Iran and all the way down to the tip of the Persian Gulf. Embracing a diversity of ecosystems that enclose the river valleys of Meso-potamia, the Fertile Crescent was a cornucopia in the climatic optimum. The significance of these "hilly flanks," as opposed to the lowland plains, was recognized early on by Robert Braidwood, who maintained that farming originated in those regions where the progenitor of the principal domesticates grow naturally.[6] In the 1940s, he led a team from the Oriental Institute in Chicago to investigate the site of Jarmo in northern Iraq, and, in the 1960s, he initiated a collaborative project with Halet Çambel of Istanbul University extending across the southeastern provinces of Siirt, Diyarbakır and Urfa, focusing on the site at Çayönü.

Regardless of this abundance of plants and animals suitable for domestication, the crucial role that wheat and barley played in the development of the human circumstance in the Near East cannot be overemphasized. Just as civilization in East Asia was based on the cultivation of millet and rice, and the New World was dependent on maize and potatoes, so too wheat and barley fuelled the engines of Near East. Domesticated animals—mostly sheep, goats, and cattle—did, to be sure, supplement the kitchen, but wheat and barley remained the staples. As we shall see later, however, the very beginnings of sedentary life were not based on the intensive exploitation of cereals, but on a subsistence strategy that drew on a range of food resources. Even so, the significance of wheat and barley in shaping the trajectory and character of Near Eastern society will become very apparent when we examine the emergence of complex societies. In essence, the ability to produce food surpluses from the fertile lands of Greater Mesopotamia and its neighbors provided elite groups with both wealth and power.

Within the Fertile Crescent, three zones have attracted particular attention: Southeastern Anatolia, the Levantine Corridor (extending north from the Dead Sea along the Jordan Rift to Damascus, and then following the Middle Euphrates in the Syrian desert), and the Zagros Mountains. The essentials of agriculture are the cultivation of crops and the raising of animals. How these practices came about and at what places and times is not a simple task to explain, but most opinions advance three basic factors: Climatic change, an increase in population densities, and improving technologies. The view that farming was adopted because hunting-gathering pushed communities into a marginal existence, threatened with starvation and little leisure time, a perspective that has its roots in 19th-century thinking, has long been abandoned. Indeed, it is well known that farming requires a large investment of energy and resources. The more inten-sive the farming practice—ploughing, weeding, irrigating—the greater the productivity, but greater too is the labor input per person.[7] A combination of environmental changes, sedentism, and population pressure might well have stimulated attempts to increase food resources as hunting-gathering areas became overcrowded.[8]

While the abundance of seasonal resources would have allowed communities to abandon their mobile existence, it would also have enabled them to relax their birth control mechanisms, a necessary constraint on nomadic groups.[9] So the transition from gathering wild cereals to planting and harvesting them might have been prompted by the greater number of mouths to feed. But for others the need to cultivate plants arose as a means of coping with the stresses of the Younger Dryas, a period of climatic instability, which would have reduced the wild food sources and prompted the storage of grain for lean times.[10] The need to store food would have encouraged sedentism, which in time led to the depletion of wild food resources around settlements. According to this reckoning, then, the genesis of plant domestication could be viewed as a type of risk management brought on by Younger Dryas.

Whatever prompted change, the process was gradual, as Eric Higgs and Michael Jarman noted many years ago.[11] According to them the apparent binary opposites of "wild" and "domestic" and "hunter-gatherer" and "farmer" obscure the continuum between ranges of related subsistence patterns. The difference between a "crop" and a "weed," for instance, is largely a cultural construct that reflects the economic value a plant may have to humans. Likewise, selective hunting patterns could be interpreted as a form of animal management, although less focused and intensive than herding. What interested Higgs and Jarman was the changing relationship between human communities and the plants and animals they exploited.[12] Thus, they preferred to speak of the relationship between humans and their environment as one of mutual dependence, in which the change from Mesolithic to Neolithic was essentially one of degree rather than one of kind.

Following this line of thought, the notion of agriculture, broadly defined, involves human efforts to modify the environments of plants and animals to increase their productivity and usefulness. What distinguished early farmers was their systematic and purposeful alteration of the environment, which resulted in fundamental genetic changes. We shall look at the archaeological record of the earliest stages of domestication in Anatolia a little later.

This focus on subsistence strategies has been a consuming passion for many archaeologists and scientists involved in the Neolithic. The discourse of animal and plant husbandry, and the logic of formalist economics, have given way to a range of other interpretations. The notion that material culture must be understood as sets of symbols embedded with meaning now looms large in Neolithic studies. In this new mode of thinking, social factors have garnered the most exciting new insights. Barbara Bender and Brian Hayden, for example, have emphasized that feasting and the consumption of food may underlie the adoption of farming.[13] The argument is straightforward, namely that members of a community in which the practice of reciprocity was esteemed achieved status and dominance by throwing feasts. The larger the banquet, the more likely guests could not respond on equal terms, leading to indebtedness. The limited wild resources available to hunter-gatherers would have precluded such occasions, but agriculture enabled determined individuals to till the fields and amass food surpluses that could be used in social competition, which, in turn, may have led to an increase in interpersonal conflict.

Jacques Cauvin, however, would have us believe otherwise. He proposes that a fundamental change in belief systems and ritual propelled communities towards agriculture and a sedentary way of life.[14] The exuberant symbolism of the Pre-Pottery Neolithic is seen as the positive human response to explaining how the world is structured and their relationship with the numinous. For Cauvin, then, the Neolithic revolution was a symbolic one that involved a profound leap in human cognition. This view is not one that is shared by Jean Perrot, who would prefer us to believe in long-term processes that draw on memory and the capacity human ingenuity, as much as the circumstances of the time.[15] This long-term perspective (*longue durée*) that views Neolithic achievements as part of broader structural history not only follows others who have applied the approach of the Annales School to the study of ancient societies, but more specifically it also echoes the sentiments expressed by Higgs and Jarman.[16] Some of the latest ideas on the Neolithic have responded to the question of whether language moved with the first farmers.[17] This is an issue that has engaged not just archaeologists, but linguists and geneticists too. With regard to Anatolia and Europe it specifically concerns the matter of whether the Indo-European family of languages spread with the first farmers.[18] Despite some earlier strident views, there appears to be no consensus.

What is clear from this necessarily brief review is that the transition from hunting and food-gathering ways of life to agricultural communities and systems of food production was not a straightforward process. It was both a long-term occurrence and an involved one. Like the Neolithic period itself, it is best understood as the synergy of a number of causes and consequences: Climate change compounded by alterations of the environment by humans, food resource stress, population growth, technological developments, human ingenuity and adaptability, and a new social organization that prompted innovation.

NEW PERSPECTIVES ON THE NEOLITHIC FROM TURKEY

Despite the intense interest that post-Pleistocene adaptations have generated over the last few decades, Anatolia was seen until recently as the "Cinderella" region of the Neolithic Near East, suffering from undeserved neglect at the expense of the Levantine corridor, which is deemed by some to be the core area of development and innovation. Without denying the significance of Levantine developments, Mehmet Özdoğan quite correctly argues that this imbalance is reflective of research trajectories that have accorded the Levant, implicitly at the very least, with primacy in economic innovation.[19] Even when the irrefutable and indeed dazzling evidence of an Anatolian Neolithic began to appear in the 1960s at Çayönü, Çatalhöyük, and Hacılar, researchers were reluctant to promote these sites to the front line in the "Neolithization" process, attempting instead to explain their existence as outliers involved in the highland trade of obsidian. In many ways, the Taurus Mountains were seen as a cultural frontier as much as geographical limit. As sites emerged in southeastern Turkey, they were described as secondary or marginal to the Levant, whereas those located further north, in the highlands, were simply too far removed from the action to be considered seriously.

Not only has the Neolithic been associated above all with the study of economic subsistence strategies, its way of life has been essentially perceived as a struggle—farmers scratching a living in semiarid environments—that was often contrasted with the idyllic existence of hunters and gatherers. According to the views of the day, the stimulus behind development in the Neolithic was environmental stress, a concept that could be comfortably accommodated in the Levant, but not in resource rich Anatolia. These two issues—economics and ecology—dictated the nature of research design. Consequently, animal bones and carbonized seeds were seen as more relevant subjects of study than cult centers and crafts, just as catchment analyses overshadowed religious ideology and social organization. This focus on economics was linked to another influential assumption, namely that the earliest sedentary peoples must have been cultivators. With the notion of "sedentary hunter-gatherers" still a distant concept, artefacts were ascribed functions within a farmer's toolkit, rather than part of forager's equipment.[20] Mortars and pestles were used, it was said, to process domesticate grains rather than wild nuts and seeds.

Current attitudes towards the Anatolian Neolithic have changed quite dramatically. Since the early 1980s, investigations at sites south of the Taurus Mountains like Nevalı Çori and Göbekli Tepe, continuing the narrative from Epipalaeolithic Hallan Çemi and Körtik Tepe, have opened a new chapter in the history of humanity. Indeed, for some, the remarkable cult buildings in this region form the very roots from which the later practices of Mesopotamian temple societies emerged.[21] Discoveries further north are no less significant. Pre-pottery sites like Cafer Höyük, in the Euphrates Valley, Aşıklı Höyük, in central Anatolia, and many ceramic Neolithic sites leave no doubt about the achievements of early agrarian communities in Anatolia. Just how far Neolithic studies in Anatolia have advanced is amply demonstrated with the recent publication of *Türkiye'de Neolitik Dönem (Neolithic Settlements in Turkey)*, a handsome production that surveys some 30 key sites and regions.[22] This is a far cry from the mid-1950s when no archaeologist was prepared even to contemplate a Neolithic period for the peninsula.

The rethinking of Neolithic has spilled over into other issues. One of these concerns the notions of core and periphery. Whereas some still reckon that the Neolithic did have a core area, a good number are persuaded by the arguments that the earliest Neolithic communities of the Near East belonged to a cultural formation zone.[23] This notion of a "supra region" maintains that communities within it shared ideas and technologies irrespective of social organization and variations in subsistence patterns. These zones do not imply homogeneity, neither do they raise the scepter of diffusionism. Rather, they refer to cognate geographical areas that develop along a similar and broadly defined cultural trajectory, although at the same time displaying internal diversity in material culture. Most importantly, the dynamics within these formation zones were defined by cultural contact—through emulation, exchange, or migration—which Renfrew has called "peer polity interaction."[24] Some have qualified this notion and pointed out that there is no evidence to indicate that development in this formative period was triggered by stress or competition, but instead that prosperity was gained by a sharing of knowledge, others see a direct link to warfare.[25] Although the exact boundaries of the earliest formative zone are still vague, broadly speaking, it covered a vast area that stretched from the Zagros Mountains across the Taurus range to the Turkish Upper Euphrates, and down to the southern Levant. Equally important is the environmental diversity of this zone. From high plains and thickly forested mountains, it descends in altitude through riverine locations to alluvial plains and semiarid lands. Interestingly, the boundaries of this zone lasted for some 4000 years from the 11th millennium BC to the early centuries of the sixth, during which time no communities appear to have made any attempt to colonize other regions.

In Anatolia, Neolithic settlement has been identified in three broad regions (Figure 3.1):[26]

1 Southeastern Anatolia. The regions south of the Taurus Mountains, especially Urfa and Diyarbakır, but including the Upper Euphrates, have evidence for the earliest developments. These run parallel with those in the Zagros Mountains and the Levantine corridor with which they share considerable similarities.
2 Another locality is north of the Taurus, on the plateau, encompassing Aksaray, Konya, and the Lake District. It is distinctly different in character and more deeply rooted in "Anatolian" tradition. Cultural connections extended beyond these areas to Greece, where aspects of Thessalian material culture, ceramics in particular, links it to southwestern Anatolia.
3 Western Anatolia. Most information on this area is less than two decades old and derives from the Marmara region, but includes the newly emerging evidence around Izmir. Situated at the gateway to Europe, northwestern Anatolia felt the greatest influence from the Balkans, and it is no surprise that the coastal regions of the west have connections with the Aegean.

North-central and northeastern Anatolia, by contradistinction, remained curiously devoid of Neolithic settlement.[27] Whether these regions were subjected to geomorphological processes

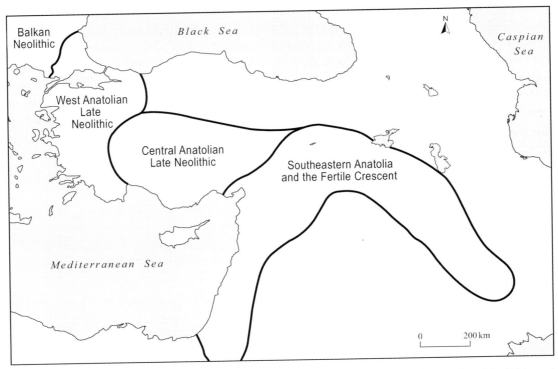

Figure 3.1 Map of Anatolia showing the three cultural formation zones of the Anatolian Neolithic and neighbouring Balkan Neolithic (adapted from Özdoğan 1999a)

that have buried Neolithic sites, or experienced adverse climates, or whether they were sparsely populated, perhaps by communities of hunters and gatherers, is far from clear. Presently, evidence from the northeastern highlands indicates that village societies moved into this rugged terrain as late as the fifth millennium BC, which seems a curious paradox given the established Neolithic sequences in Trans-Caucasia.[28]

The three concentrations of Neolithic occupation noted earlier can be reduced even further to two, using the Taurus Mountains as the boundary, which effectively separate different economic subsistence strategies and environmental conditions. From the beginning of the Neolithic through to the Bronze Age, western and central Anatolia together with the Balkans, an area extending from the shores of the Mediterranean to the Danube River, formed one large zone. This region should be distinguished from the zone of Greater Mesopotamia and the Levant, including the southeastern Anatolia (or the Near Eastern zone), which developed along its own path.

In the Near East, despite its ecological diversity, arid and semiarid conditions necessitated a number of risk management strategies. One was a heavy reliance on cereal agriculture that was developed through irrigation farming, which, in turn, required a large labour force. The rich alluvium of Mesopotamia soon responded favorably to this type of management and agricultural surpluses provided wealth that saw the emergence of elite groups in later centuries. In the Anatolian–Balkan zone, however, the ecological zones were more varied and allowed for a range of economic options. The productivity of the land was relatively uniform throughout the zone, so we do not witness the early emergence of social groups whose power was based on agricultural surpluses. These fundamental differences also led to the development of two early settlement types. One, south of the Taurus, soon developed into towns, and later evolved into urban centres, states and empires. The other did not expand its complexity, but instead metamorphosed into variations of itself. We will trace these changes in subsequent chapters.

BEGINNINGS OF SEDENTARY LIFE

Several features distinguish the formative stage of the Neolithic in the Near East:

1 its origins in the Epipalaeolithic
2 its longevity—an episode stretching some 4000 years
3 the large size of many sites (so-called "mega-sites")
4 a high level of sociopolitical complexity manifested by monumental public buildings, striking art, a stratified society, and elaborate cultic practices
5 vibrant internal dynamics that sustained such large enterprises.

Whereas not so long ago such attributes were viewed as individualistic or unique, we now realize that they are widespread, having been identified from the southern Levant to the Taurus

Mountains. Similar sites are probably also located further east along the mountainous arc in the foothills of the Zagros, but we must await the resumption of systematic fieldwork in those regions to verify this.

For the moment, it appears that the Pre-Pottery Neolithic cultures in Anatolia were introduced. This judgment is not at odds with the rather abrupt appearance of villages in the 10th millennium BC in the southeast. Neither does it contradict the evidence on the other side of the Taurus. The concepts of settlement layout and sophisticated craft items from the plateau have no precursors in the Mediterranean late Upper Palaeolithic-Epipalaeolithic sequences, which in any case represent a totally different lithic tradition.

Views are divided on the pedigree of the Anatolian Pre-Pottery Neolithic. Michael Rosenberg prefers the Zagros region, drawing attention to similarities in lithic technology between Hallan Çemi and late Zarzian sites such as Zawi Chemi Shanidar.[29] At both, blades were produced from single platform cores and modified into geometric shapes, such as scalene triangles. Equally noteworthy, according to Rosenberg, is the absence of certain chipped stones, including backed and truncated blades, which characterize the Natufian assemblage of the Levant. For Mehmet Özdoğan, by way of contrast, none of the Epipalaeolithic or Palaeolithic substrata in the Levant or northern Iraq has the cultural complexity in terms of art, architecture, and social life that could be compared to the Pre-Pottery Neolithic. For him, the north Pontic region, embracing the Balkans, offers a more plausible connection.[30] This area is well known for its developed Upper Palaeolithic, which is characterized by notable achievements in mobiliary art, social organization, and a sophisticated lithic assemblage (Epi-Gravettian) based on bullet core technology. Moreover, and in contradistinction to Anatolia, the Neolithic cultures of the north Pontic are late, dispelling any notion of continuity. But exactly how two geographically distant regions— the north Pontic and the Taurus—connected remains to be seen.

Pre-Pottery Neolithic occupation has been identified in a range of environments (Figure 3.2).[31] In the southeast, there is a concentration that stretches from the Tigris alluvial plains (if we include the Epipalaeolithic sites of Hallan Çemi, Demirköy and Körtik), across the foothills (Çayönü), and plateaux (Nevalı Çori, Göbekli Tepe and Gürcütepe) south of the Taurus Mountains, to the Upper Euphrates (Cafer Höyük, Boytepe, and Çınaz). On the plateau, in central Anatolia, Pınarbaşı and Aşıklı Höyük afford the earliest dates.[32] In redefining the Neolithic, it has become apparent that apart from Çayönü, which is located on arable land, most Anatolian Pre-Pottery Neolithic sites are not situated in a terrain conducive for farming. Göbekli, for instance, is perched on top of a mountain, Nevalı Çori is located at an altitude of 490 m, and Suberde is situated in the northeastern foothills of the western Taurus range, on the edge of the Anatolian plateau. It is also important to note that most Pre-Pottery Neolithic communities preferred to settle in proximity to mountains rather than on the plains, as was once thought. Whether the mountains themselves will yield substantial evidence of Neolithic occupation, has yet to be determined.

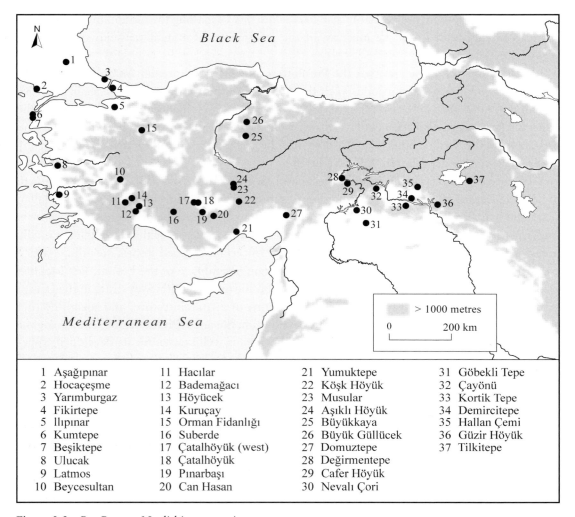

Figure 3.2 Pre-Pottery Neolithic occupation

1 Aşağıpınar
2 Hocaçeşme
3 Yarımburgaz
4 Fikirtepe
5 Ilıpınar
6 Kumtepe
7 Beşiktepe
8 Ulucak
9 Latmos
10 Beycesultan
11 Hacılar
12 Bademağacı
13 Höyücek
14 Kuruçay
15 Orman Fidanlığı
16 Suberde
17 Çatalhöyük (west)
18 Çatalhöyük
19 Pınarbaşı
20 Can Hasan
21 Yumuktepe
22 Köşk Höyük
23 Musular
24 Aşıklı Höyük
25 Büyükkaya
26 Büyük Güllücek
27 Domuztepe
28 Değirmentepe
29 Cafer Höyük
30 Nevalı Çori
31 Göbekli Tepe
32 Çayönü
33 Kortik Tepe
34 Demircitepe
35 Hallan Çemi
36 Güzir Höyük
37 Tilkitepe

Origin of the village

In a classic study published in 1972, Kent Flannery explored the problem of the origin of the village as a settlement type, a subject he revisited 30 years later.[33] Flannery identified two types of village that, in his view, reflected two socioeconomic structures. The first type comprises compounds of round huts often arranged in a circle or oval, with storage facilities in a central communal area. Following analogous settlements plans from modern communities, Flannery persuasively argued that these prehistoric compounds accommodated an extended family, with the cell-like huts most likely used as the residence for individuals rather than an entire family. The second type of settlement was closer to a true village plan and comprised multiroom rectilinear houses that had domestic quarters and storage facilities under the one roof. These houses were generally better built and were large enough for a nuclear family. The key issue here is not simply one of shape, but the social and economic structures underlying the designs. To quote Flannery, the distinction is between: "(1) societies where small huts are occupied by individuals and storage is shared and (2) societies where large houses are occupied by whole nuclear families and storage is private."[34] At the core of this distinction is the nature of risk management. On the one hand, in the first type of society, the group shares food, as well as the risk and rewards. The closed plan of the nuclear family houses, on the other hand, with its private storage areas, is an incentive to increase production without the need to share resources. This move from open plan communal storage to private facilities, from an extended family compound to nuclear family houses, is a fundamental shift that can be observed in Anatolia and throughout the Near East.[35] The reason behind this change is aptly put by Flannery: "I suspect that Prepottery Neolithic societies grew so fast, and settlements became so large, that not every family considered itself closely related to its neighbors to be willing to share the risks and rewards of production."[36]

Architecture forms an important part of the archaeological record, so it is worthwhile briefly reviewing the basic building techniques that we will encounter.[37] Anatolia has an abundance of raw materials for building. It has no end of stone, plenty of earth, and, in antiquity, vast tracts of timber. These together with small plants constitute the most basic building materials. Rock structures are common in Anatolia. Rock is the longest lasting building material. But it has drawbacks, too. It is a weighty material and awkward to manage, and its energy density means a large amount of heat is required to keep a building warm. Wood, like rock, is a generic building material that can be used to build in most climates. Cut into lumber such as planks, wood is a very strong and flexible material.

Mixing earth, sand and chaff, or other fibrous material, such as dung, easily produces mud bricks.[38] Shaped using frames and dried in the sun, they offer significant advantages in hot dry climates, and have a long history in Anatolia. Mud brick houses remain cooler because they store and release heat very slowly. Also known as adobe, from the Spanish word for mud, a pithy description of this technique is provided by *The Farmers' Handbook*, published by the Department of Agriculture, New South Wales, Australia, about a century ago:

As their name (Adobe) implies, these buildings are constructed of sun-dried, but unburnt bricks. For buildings of this character, material like clay, which is unsuitable for Pisé-work, can be used. The bricks are made in a wooden mould, and are 16 in long, 8 in wide, and 6 in thick. A man can mould about 100 per day. They are laid in a similar manner to other bricks, the mortar used being wet loam, or even the material of which the bricks are made . . . Buildings constructed of these bricks are substantial and cool, and very similar in character to Pisé buildings.[39]

Looking at modern vernacular mudbrick architecture in Anatolia and neighboring regions, there appears to be a cultural divide between (a) the flat plate tradition of southeast Turkey that extends to Mesopotamia, and is the modern Arab type; (b) the adobe block tradition, which is found north of the Taurus, extending across to Europe, and now the norm in Turkey; (c) and a modern compromise tradition found in villages in the southeast.[40] The approximate extent of the first two of these traditions is also reflected in antiquity.

Rammed earth construction, also known as *pisé de terre* or simply *pisé* was not as popular as mud bricks in Anatolia, but its simplicity of construction, cheapness, and durability account for its long history of use.[41] On the technique of building in *pisé*, we can turn to Pliny, whose account is as succinct as it is informative:

> Have we not in Africa and in Spain walls of earth, known as "formocean" walls? From the fact that they are moulded, rather than built, by enclosing earth within a frame of boards, constructed on either side. These walls will last for centuries, are proof against rain, wind, and fire, and are superior in solidity to any cement. Even at this day Spain still holds watch-towers that were erected by Hannibal. (Pliny *Natural History* 25: 48)

Elaborating a little further, to construct a rammed earth wall, a mixture of damp earth, sand, clay, and a stabilizer such as lime is compressed into a wooden frame (shutters) with the use of a rammer, creating a solid wall of earth. The wall frames are removed once the earth is compressed, and the wall is allowed to dry and cure. Soils used for *pisé* building should not be light or as stiff as clay, but should have a gravelly consistency that enables cohesion. Floors made of *pisé* were quite common in antiquity.

Architecture involving a light framing of poles and twigs (wattles) was utilized in regions north of the Taurus Mountains. A woven latticework of wattles that is daubed with a mixture of clay and sand and sometimes animal dung can create an effective structure often in the form of small, detached one-roomed structures, or as component parts of a mud brick or timbered building. We also know from numerous house models from Europe where wattle and daub buildings were common that roofs were gabled or pitched and not flat.

The interior of walls and floors were often plastered with lime, as were storage pits to keep them clean. Lime plaster can be readily produced by heating limestone (calcium carbonate) to a temperature of about 900°C to create quicklime, or burnt lime (calcium oxide). Water is then added to produce slaked lime (calcium hydroxide). The production of gypsum (calcium sulfate dihydrate), a very soft mineral, required even less effort—the heating to a temperature of 100–200°C.

Southeastern Anatolia

With its large exposures and numerous building levels Çayönü continues the story from Hallan
Çemi, providing the most comprehensive picture of a Pre-Pottery Neolithic village in Anatolia
(Figure 3.3). Around 9400 BC, the settlement changed markedly with the construction of buildings based on a grill plan (subphase 2).[42] House floors were no longer semi-subterranean, but
elevated on unusual pebble foundations, which reveal a tripartite plan (Figure 3.4): A northern
half with parallel rows of supporting stones ("grills"), a rectangular central room furnished with
fireplace and lime-plastered floor, and, at the southern end, stone-paved cells flanking an
entrance. The need for elevation may have arisen because of tendency to flooding and dampness,
for unlike today's harsh dry conditions, the Ergani Plain then experienced wetter conditions
with a landscape that harbored marshes, swamps, and rivers.

Despite the shift from round to rectilinear houses, conceptually an architectural revolution,
builders at Çayönü continued to use wattle and daub for the superstructure, which was probably vaulted.[43] Moreover, the popularity of grill structures, together with the uniformity they
display in size and plan, and their arrangement around open spaces point to a community with a
clear sense of settlement layout. Inside their houses, inhabitants organized their space more
effectively than before. A scatter of bone and stone tools and debris over the parallel foundations, for instance, suggests they carried out craft activities at the back of the building, whereas
tasks requiring heavy ground stone objects (pestles and grinding stones) were found in the
central room. The cells near the entrance, too small for habitation, may have provided storage.
Equally important is the observation that some of the centrally located buildings also have a
concentration of exotic artefacts and raw materials, with minimal evidence of manufacture,
suggesting a socioeconomic differentiation among households.[44] In terms of mortuary practice,
the deceased continued to be buried either as individuals or with their kinsmen beneath
courtyards or the floors of buildings.

By the beginning of the early Pre-Pottery Neolithic B, around 8700 BC, grill buildings were
being modified and improved as they were slowly transformed into channelled buildings (Figure
3.4).[45] During this change, builders experimented with foundation types, eventually preferring
parallel rows of stone that were gradually placed closer together (resembling drainage channels)
to form a "platform." Whatever the plan of the supporting stones, the floors of these houses
were now lime plastered and sometimes painted red, and separated from the foundations by a
layer of organic material, possibly branches. But the most dramatic change that occurred during
the channelled building subphase was the switch from a post framework to the use of chaff-
tempered mud (a forerunner to mud bricks) for the construction of walls. Accordingly, roofs
changed in design from vaulted, wattle and daub arrangement to flat and earthen. At about this
time, the dead were disposed of in a new manner. Secondary burials, including the collection of
skulls, were now the norm, and foreshadow a custom that took on massive proportions in the
following subphase, with the Skull Building (Figure 3.5: 1).[46]

Channel buildings are also found at Nevalı Çori, in Urfa, where five building levels display

Figure 3.3   Aerial view of Çayönü showing the stone foundations of various building types (Photo: courtesy Mehmet Özdoğan)

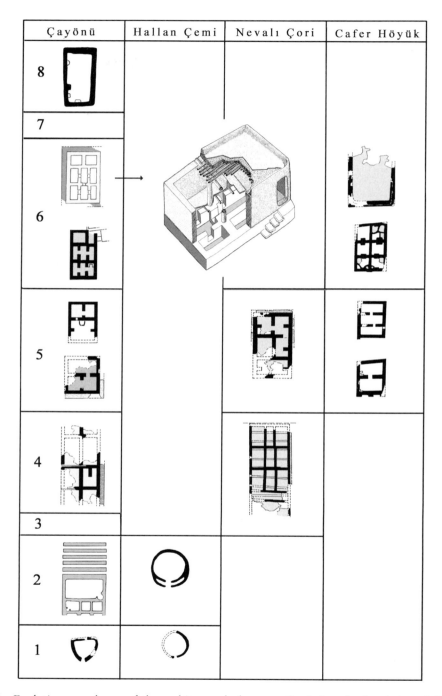

Figure 3.4 Evolutionary scheme of the architectural phases at Çayönü and related sites: **1** Wattle and daub huts. **2** Grill plan buildings. **3** Channelled houses. **4** Cobble-paved houses. **5** Cell plan buildings. **6** Cell plan to large room transition. **7** Large roomed buildings (adapted from Bıçakçı 1998)

Figure 3.5 Çayönü: **1** Aerial view of the Skull Building (BM2). **2** Flagstone Building. **3** *Terrazzo* Building (Photos: courtesy Mehmet Özdoğan)

variations on the theme.[47] Depending on the number of lateral and longitudinal supports, a house should have more than nine compartmentalized foundation units, and channels that connected to gutters which ran along the outside. Measuring 18.20 × 6.20 m, House 26 in Level II was the largest structure and probably accommodated an extended family. Like most channelled buildings, it comprised two parts—a long main room and a smaller annex at the front.

Towards the end of the early Pre-Pottery Neolithic B, the use of space and planning began to change. Houses and workshops at Çayönü, now oriented along a different axis, were localized in the western part of the settlement. The most important development, however, was the significance assigned to a communal open space. Not only was this space large at both Çayönü and Nevalı Çori, but two features defined the area clearly from the residential sector: Numerous roasting pits and public structures, which were isolated and conspicuous. At Çayönü we have the "Flagstone" and "Skull" buildings (Figure 3.5: 1, 2), whereas Nevalı Çori boasts an impressive cult building, which are dealt with later.[48]

Around 8000 BC the inhabitants of Çayönü again introduced new concepts in architecture and settlement plan, which point to an ever developing labour force. Named after the type of flooring, the cobble-paved building subphase is sometimes considered transitional (Figure 3.4). Its most impressive structure is buttressed and called the *Terrazzo* Floor building, distinguished by a base layer of limestone riverine cobbles and rocks set in a concrete-like reddish matrix (Figure 3.5: 3).[49] Its surface has an eye-catching layer of finer pinkish pebbles that were smoothed and polished to a hard finish; two pairs of white-pebbled, parallel lines at both ends of the room add further definition. By this time the popularity of the open courtyard began to decline. Although still enclosed by houses, its purpose shifted to butchering and bone tool production.

The use of cobbled floors also occurs at Cafer Höyük, near Malatya, where in the early phase a large structure with a tripartite plan (Level X) replaced a two-roomed house (Level XII).[50] But the Cafer residents did not lavishly copy the building practices at Çayönü, as is evident by their preference for large (90 × 25 × 8–9 cm) mud bricks similar in size to those used later in Syria and elsewhere, including Gritille further down the Euphrates River.[51] According to Cauvin, the uniformity of these bricks over a wide area is suggestive of a standardized unit that originated in Syria.[52]

The mode of social interaction seems to have changed by the end of the Pre-Pottery Neolithic B, when these closed courtyards all but disappeared. We may speculate that activities were now carried out mostly in houses or on rooftops. Houses were large and had high stone foundations that resembled units of cells (hence "cell buildings") that supported thick mud brick walls.[53] Their proportions and internal plans were different too, and became more diverse as time progressed. Rooms were internally divided to provide discrete spaces for specific functions, indicated by the different types of artefact found within them. Basements were also utilized, for storage and burials, and access between the various cells was provided by openings in the foundations. But open spaces seem to have persisted at Cafer Höyük (Levels VIII–V), where buttressed, mud brick cell houses with hearths and storage bins most likely had an upper story.[54]

The last Pre-Pottery building phase at Çayönü (subphase 8) is poorly documented, but the settlement, now much smaller, was different enough to warrant the term "Large Room."[55] New planning concepts were clearly in force, which disregarded most of the earlier sense of uniformity in regard to planning, orientation, and construction techniques. Buildings consisted of one or two large rooms with clay floors and generally were not as well constructed. Only stones were used if the house walls were thin, but for the wider foundations that were now set in trenches, mud bricks were deemed more suitable.

North of the Taurus Mountains

The picture from central Anatolia is vastly different. We have no sense of an extended or evolving Pre-Pottery Neolithic sequence as exists in the southeast, rather we are confronted at the outset with a handful of sites of Pre-Pottery Neolithic B date, chief among them Pınarbaşı A, Aşıklı Höyük, Kaletepe, and Musular. Of these, Aşıklı Höyük is a fully fledged settlement and best demonstrates the indigenous character of the Early Neolithic of central Anatolia, from which Çatalhöyük, Hacılar, and Can Hasan descended.[56]

Aşıklı's settlement plan, architectural concepts and material assemblage do not resemble any known cultural horizon from either southeastern Anatolia or the Levant. Three principal levels (designated 1–3 from top to bottom) and numerous superimposed building phases with minimal variation in conceptual planning were defined at Aşıklı. Level 2 affords a clear plan of a village—tightly packed houses conforming to the so-called agglutinative plan—with an enclosure wall surviving along the eastern edge of the settlement (Figure 3.6). The village is divided in two by a cobble-paved road that runs from the banks of the Melendiz River through the southwestern corner of the settlement. South of the road is a complex of structures (HV) and a large, red painted room (designated T), most likely public monuments. To the north is the residential quarter, with a few neighborhoods defined by narrow alleyways 0.5–1.0 m wide, but on the whole there is very little space between the structures. Remains from the few courtyards around the settlement suggest that they served as work spaces and dumps, as the accumulation of debris from Trench 4 G–H reveals. Here, it seems, the residents knapped obsidian, worked antler and bone into tools, and also processed their food.

Domestic structures at Aşıklı were built of long and wide mud bricks—up to 100 cm in length and 30 cm wide—set directly onto the ground; one cluster of buildings, constructed late in Level 2, was founded on stone blocks. Each house had independent walls, and comprised a single room, mostly likely a workshop, or a group of two to three rooms joined by doorways. Access into the house, however, was through the roof and down a portable ladder. None of the houses had a front door, so communication between houses was across the roofs, which were probably at different heights. Postholes were discerned as shallow discoloration surrounded by stones. Houses are rectangular or subrectangular in plan and have very few storage facilities.[57] The exception is House TM that had a couple of storage bins, one circular and sunken into the floor,

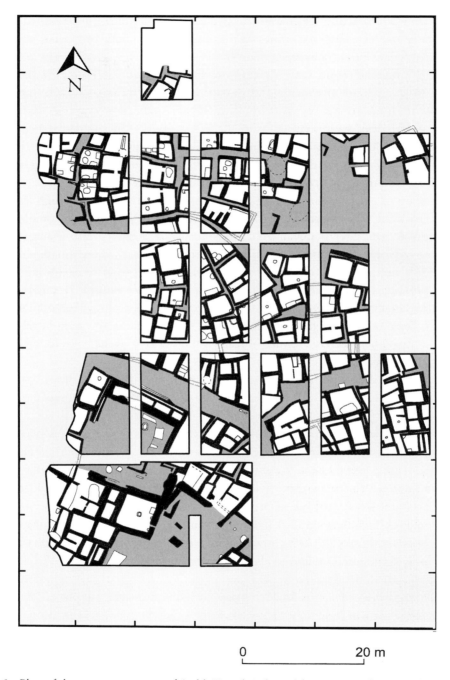

Figure 3.6 Plan of the western segment of Aşıklı Höyük (adapted from Esin and Harmankaya 1999)

along the north wall. Hearths are generally nestled into a corner of the one-roomed houses and paved with large pebbles; large flat stones set vertically into the floor or a canal to capture the ash defined their edge. Floors consisted of two layers—a basal layer of small pebbles and a thick topcoat of clay; in some rooms woven mats were spread across the floors.[58] Walls, too, were coated with mud, on both the inside and outside, and sometimes at regular intervals. The interior walls of some rooms revealed traces of fugitive colors—red, pink, and yellow. At Aşıklı some of the dead were kept close to the living—buried in simple earthen pits under floors. Despite the 400 rooms or so that have been exposed, only 70 burials have been found, suggesting there may be a nearby cemetery. The deceased were laid to rest in a variety of positions—foetal, on their back, or on their side bent at the knees.[59]

A combination of excavation and surface stripping exposed a similar though less extensive plan at Can Hasan III, in the southern plateau.[60] The tops of walls revealed a complex of tightly packed rectilinear structures many of which did not share a party wall. Houses have walls constructed mostly of beaten earth (*pisé*), although some mud bricks were found; wood, by way of contrast, does not appear to have been used for reinforcement. Houses did not have door-ways, again pointing to a roof entrance. The practice of building houses directly on top of the wall lines of earlier structures also foreshadows the practice at Çatalhöyük. Room interiors are mud plastered and occasionally painted red. Some floor surfaces are particularly hard and compact, and strengthened by a mixture of small pebbles. Two ovens were found. They were built of clay and embedded into the wall.

Suberde Level III shows poorly preserved remains of mud brick buildings with plastered floors, and burnt fragments of wattle and daub, probably from roof or partitions.[61] Suberde is of much later date (7650–6750 BC) and, according to Duru, the lack of pottery (except for a few sherds in the uppermost prehistoric deposits, some large clay bins and fragments of clay figurines) may be an intentional cultural practice rather than chronological indicator.[62] The wild boar paraphernalia—tusks, figurines and bones—is suggestive of cultic practice.

In western Anatolia, the occurrence of a pre-pottery phase is rather vague. Evidence is emerging from Çalca and Keçiçayırı, but at present mostly in the form of a typology from surface finds and soundings, including pressure flaking technology, projectile points, edge ground axes, and bone spoons and hooks.[63] A clear stratigraphy would certainly help to resolve the issue of the earliest levels at the small mound of Hacılar, termed "Aceramic Hacılar I–VII" by Mellaart, but reclassified to the Early Pottery Neolithic by Duru.[64] The basis of this rethinking is a small number of plain, dark-faced sherds found in situ on a red floor reached in one of 28 exploratory trenches dug in the plain around the small mound. Tempting though this suggestion is, without a stratigraphic link between Mellaart's aceramic floor and that found by Duru it must remain a possibility only. We do not have a coherent plan of the settlement of Aceramic Hacılar I–VII available, owing to the restricted size of the sounding in the lowest deposits, but features such as the use of large mud bricks link it to Aşıklı.[65] It is not clear whether houses shared a wall, or where doorways are evident. Floors had a base of small pebbles, coated with a layer lime plastered, stained red and burnished, which continued up the wall forming a dado; replastering occurred frequently. A few fragments of wall plaster suggest that above the dado, walls were covered with a cream colored plaster and painted with red designs. House furnishings were few, including a low raised platform probably used to elevate grindstones and a cupboard—one in Level VI was fully enclosed and items were retrieved through a couple of small holes. Hearths and ovens were situated in the courtyard and like floors also had a base of pebbles; a mud brick kerb defined their edge.

Ritual, art, and temples

Southeastern Anatolia

In recent years, the spectacular discoveries at Göbekli Tepe (9600–8000 BC) and Nevalı Çori (8600–7900 BC), perched in the lower rocky slopes of the Taurus Mountains, overlooking the lowlands of Urfa, have prompted a major upheaval in our understanding of ritual practice in the Pre-Pottery Neolithic. In the first instance, they have articulated in a superb manner the emergence and gradual elaboration of special (nondomestic) buildings built by communities of sedentary hunter-gatherers. We knew about the existence of public buildings from the earlier excavations at Çayönü, to be sure, but the date, preservation and monumentality of buildings uncovered at these Urfa sites have ushered in another level of complexity, not least of which is the notion, in the case of Göbekli, of a special ritual site serving a region. Whereas at Nevalı Çori both houses and temples are located within proximity of each other, Göbekli has only temples. Its lowest sequence, Level III, is represented by a series of stone-built circular structures up to 20 m in diameter (Figures 3.7 and 3.8) that are presently the earliest temples on earth.[66] Monumental size, T-shaped pillars (some reaching a height of 5 m), benches running along the wall, and the use of sculpture, as integral architectural traits, are their distinguishing features. The pillars vary in size: the two largest are positioned in the centre, whereas a series of smaller ones are embedded into a bench. Their date in the second half of the 10th millennium BC makes them roughly contemporary with Qermez Dere (north Iraq) and Jerf el Ahmar (Syria), which are seen as the antecedents. In Level II, the Göbekli temples are rectilinear, although they still retain the other attributes.

The cult buildings at Nevalı Çori are no less fascinating. There, excavations revealed a squarish building in Level II that clearly had a special purpose (Figure 3.9).[67] Built of stone and whitewashed, it measured 13.90 by 13.50 m. Thirteen monolithic pillars with T-shaped capitals were set into a wide bench that ran along the interior wall. Two similar pillars had been presumably set at the centre of the paved flooring. Other features include a podium, which the excavators believe contained a cult statue, and a niche. Discarded fragments of sculpture from the earliest cult building that did not survive were found embedded within the structure. Its successor, Temple III, was smaller in size, having been built directly within the walls of its predecessor. Its plan and features remained basically the same with the exception of the two central pillars that

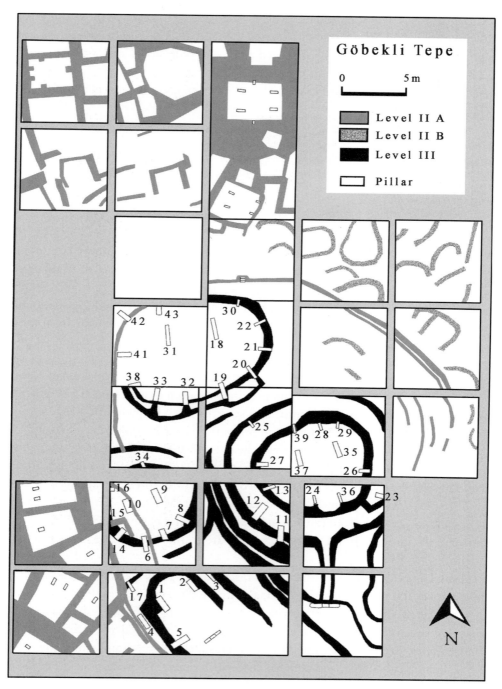

Figure 3.7 Plan of Göbekli Tepe showing the plans of the circular (Level III) and rectilinear (Level II) temples (adapted from Schmidt 2007)

Figure 3.8 Decorated T-shaped pillars from Göbekli Tepe: **1** Pillar 43 showing a richly decorated surface.
2 Aurochs, quadruped, and bird. **3** Rampant lion. **4** Aerial view of Enclosure D, Göbekli Tepe
(Photos: courtesy Deutsches Archäologisches Institut (1, 4) and Harald Hauptmann (2, 3))

1

2

Figure 3.9 Aerial views of the Nevalı Çori temples: **1** Level II. **2** Level III (Photos: courtesy Harald Hauptmann)

are now decorated with two arms holding hands. At this time a larger than life-size limestone head, bald with snake attached to its back, was reused as building material (Figure 3.10: 2). Indeed, with one exception, all 11 pieces of sculpture, largely human-animal compositions, were found in secondary positions. Whether the intention was apotropaic, or whether the sculpture was ritually broken, or simply had a utilitarian function as another building block is difficult to say.

Another distinguishing feature of these Pre-Pottery Neolithic cult buildings is their powerful imagery. At Göbekli, the T-shaped pillars are richly decorated with low relief art that is predominantly animalistic, featuring rampant lions, wild cattle (aurochs), foxes standing on their hind legs, wild donkeys and pigs, birds of prey, cranes, scorpions and snakes among other creatures (Figure 3.8). These figures are portrayed individually, or grouped; sometimes they are empanelled between linear geometric patterns. On one pillar, a net pattern forms the background of a bird scene, as if to show capture. There is no reference here to domestic animals and remnants of domesticated plants and animals have not been recovered from Göbekli. Here a community still very firmly ensconced in the hunt created the striking imagery and monumentality. Perhaps the most spectacular composition is found on pillar no. 43 with its diverse repertoire of motifs and animals figures (Figure 3.8: 1). Dominating the central area is a bird, its curved beak and folds around the neck indicative of a vulture. Above its left wing is a circle and further to the right is another smaller bird curiously depicted as if to fit the space. Above this bird is yet another, possibly an ibis, to judge by its long legs. Three rather strange box-like objects with semi-circular handles each associated with a small depiction of a creature—its "animal determinative"—are juxtaposed along the top of the pillar. In the lower scene is a clearly depicted scorpion positioned above a bird and beside a fox. Finally, in the bottom right-hand corner, is a most interesting depiction—a headless male clearly identifiable by his erect penis. Although this figure is diminutive compared to the animals, it carries a strong stylistic resonance of the floating, headless humans depicted on the so-called vulture painting at Çatalhöyük, which we will deal with in the next chapter. Ithyphallic human statues and the depiction of male genitalia on all animal mammals further emphasize the male sex. An exception to this is the sexually explicit figure of a woman with legs akimbo carved on the floor of one of the temples. The depiction of cranes at Göbekli is particularly interesting. Whereas their torso is easily identifiable, they appear to have thick, clumsy legs with knees bent forward rather than back. It has been suggested that these are meant to show human legs, implying that they represent either a hybrid creature, or a human dressed as a crane. The extent of this monumental Pre-Pottery Neolithic culture is only just becoming apparent, now that we know what to look for. A carved pillar found on Nemrut Dağ, in the Adıyaman province, suggests that it could be fairly extensive south of the Taurus.[68]

Sculpture from Nevalı Çori is invariably worked in soft limestone and shaped with flint implements.[69] Meaning was often conveyed through hybrid creatures combining animal and human features—snake-men and bird-women. Moreover, arrangements are reminiscent of totem poles, with figures superimposed and melded into each other. One fragment of bird sculpture is such piece. Most likely belonging to a much taller original, it shows the bird (possibly a raptor) on top of two human heads, facing outwards and wearing netted headgear (Figure 3.10: 1). The profile of the opposing human heads, a theme that appears to run through this monumental art, has suggested to the excavators that the T-shaped pillars within the buildings are in fact schematic side-on renderings of the human form, much like a Janus figure. Another fragment, also part of a composite arrangement, and the only piece not found in a cult building, simply shows a human head, possibly female. Different is an ithyphallic statue in the form of a stela found in Urfa that stands nearly 2 m high. The figure, wearing a necklace, is bald with deeply set eyes, originally plugged, and hands placed above the penis, now broken. Fragments of stelae and stone phalluses found at Göbekli and among surface finds probably belonged to similar statues. Another intriguing sculpture depicts two human figures, with arms outstretched and possibly dancing, flanking a turtle.

So how should we interpret these remarkable sites, with their monumental architecture and vivid iconography replete with animal symbolism? First, is the megalithic architecture itself that created the context. As discrete, thick walled structures, the temples would have focused attention on the imagery and ritual activities. It is also likely that the buildings would have been quite

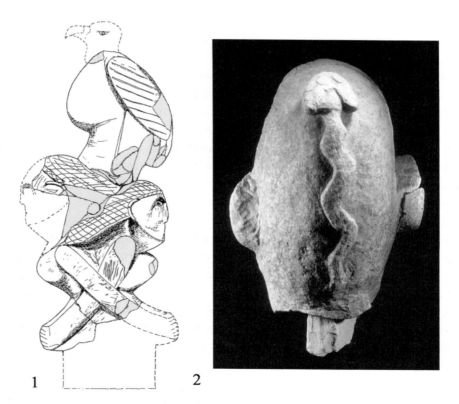

1 **2**

Figure 3.10 Limestone sculptures from Nevalı Çori: **1** Limestone sculpture showing a bird on top of a pair of human heads (adapted from Hauptmann 1999). **2** Back of a larger than life-size human head with an applied snake (Photo: courtesy Harald Hauptmann)

dark inside. So the surrounding physical conditions, as with any sacred space, no doubt heightened the emotional experiences of participants. More importantly, the temples themselves were clearly public buildings and their public display no doubt promoted communality.[70] Group cohesion of this type may well have served to bond communities like Göbekli and Nevalı Çori—neither nomadic hunters nor sedentary farmers—and assisted them in adjusting to their new circumstances. Then we have the explosion of highly visual symbolism. This overt imagery is no doubt linked to the importance placed on ritual in social life. These communities needed to explain their new world order and they did so through symbolism. In fact, as the wild, natural world was being controlled, so too was society. That is, vibrant symbolism was, as Marc Verhoeven has aptly suggested, "an expression of the desire to control ritual behavior and the supernatural world, in order to control the human world."[71]

But how can we explain the preponderance of animal imagery, explicitly wild animals and, in particular, birds? Here we need to recall what we said about ritual and rock art. One of the similarities between the late Palaeolithic rock art sites and the Pre-Pottery Neolithic sites is the prevalence of an animalistic iconography. The main difference is the type of settlements—one group comprises natural open-air sites or caves, whereas at Göbekli and Nevalı Çori we have built environments. I would propose that another similarity between the two periods is the prominent role played by shamanism in ritual. As we have seen, the last stage of a trance is often connected to a hallucinogenic transformation into an animal, especially birds, because experiencing a "cosmic flight" is one of the most common elements of shaman's altered state of consciousness. This association between humans and birds, and the concept of "taking flight," is well illustrated in a documentary film of the Kwakiutl Indians, who live along the British Columbia coast, made in 1914 by Edward Curtis, an American frontier photographer.[72] In one scene Thunderbird, a human dressed as a bird, is seen standing at the prow of the war canoe flapping his wings. Although one should not imply that Curtis' documentary portrays shamanic behavior, it nonetheless vividly captures the human-bird linkage in animation. It is not unreasonable, then, to suggest that the purpose of the reliefs depicted at Nevalı Çori and Göbekli was to capture the presence of this or that animal.

Another Pre-Pottery Neolithic practice should be mentioned here, namely the seemingly unusual custom of "burying" a building at the end of its lifespan. This practice of deliberately filling a room with soil or mud bricks, as if to accord a structure humanizing qualities, was first identified by David French at the Chalcolithic site of Can Hasan, and has since been detected elsewhere.[73] At Çayönü two special buildings of the Pre-Pottery Neolithic B period are noteworthy: The Flagstone (FA) Building and the Skull (BM1) Building, which in part retained the traditional oval plan (Figure 3.5: 1–2). Both were buttressed, but only partially preserved.[74] The Flagstone structure had a floor of large limestone slabs and three undecorated stele that were broken before it was "buried." Monumental standing stones were probably also used in the Skull Building whose association with death is found in two shallow pits that contained multiple burials sealed by its earthen floor.

It was in the cobble-paved subphase (the third evolutionary stage) that the Skull Building

(BM2) developed to its full capacity as a house of the dead. The remains of some 600 individuals, most represented by partial skeletons, were found in the building. Now rectangular in plan, it was renewed three times and comprised rooms, a courtyard, standing stones, and "altar." The quantity of skeletal material and the diversity of mortuary practices left no question with regard to purpose. Separate crypts contained numerous skulls and long bones carefully arranged, and the remains of decapitated primary burials. Primary and secondary burials of headless individuals were also found under the pavement, and in many of these cases, as those burials in crypts, they were accompanied by gifts—beads and pendants made from boar's tusk, shell, and so on.[75] In its last phase, the excavators found a cache of 49 burnt and crushed skulls on the floor, as if they had been stored on a shelf prior to the building's destruction. The end of its existence was intentional as it was dramatic—it was burned and buried under a thick layer of pebbles that formed the floor of the subsequent Terrazzo Floor building mentioned earlier.

The practice of terminating a building continued into the earlier Cell subphase, when houses were emptied of personal ornaments (but not utilitarian objects), sealed at the doors, and buried. Open areas were ritually buried too. The founding of the Pebbled Plaza (of the Cobble-paved subphase) provides a good example. It featured two rows of undecorated stelae and two grooved slabs that were deliberately broken and buried under the Earth Plaza (of the Cell subphase) that superimposed it.

Central Anatolia

As in general settlement planning, cultic symbolism in central Anatolia differs from that in the southeast. The situation at Aşıklı is curious. It has a probable complex of public monuments south of the paved road, but there is a conspicuous scarcity of figurative art (only one small, clay animal figurine).[76] The sturdy architecture consists of a casemate construction adjacent to the road, and a large structure (Building HV) that is separated from nearby Building T by a narrow courtyard (HJ). The interior walls of Building T were painted red, as was the polished floor, which was laid thickly (up to 8 cm) from a mixture of ground tuff and water. A low bench ran along the north, west, and south walls, whereas the east wall was fitted with a large hearth and canal that connected with the exterior. Another hearth, domed and made of mud brick, was situated in the adjacent courtyard (HG), which was paved with blocks of basalt and later plastered with clay. In another room (AB), two double graves were found underneath the floor: One containing the remains of a young woman and an elderly man, the other a woman and an infant. This room was painted a purplish-red. Given the careful finish of Building T, its well-proportioned fitments, and position within the complex overlooking the Melendiz River, the excavators suggested that it functioned as a shrine; at the very least it was a building of some importance. As a public structure, it has been compared to Building A at contemporary Musular, located less than half a kilometre away, which is distinguished by fine, lime plastered floors that were painted red and burnished (Figure 3.11).[77] Raised benches—one ran along three walls

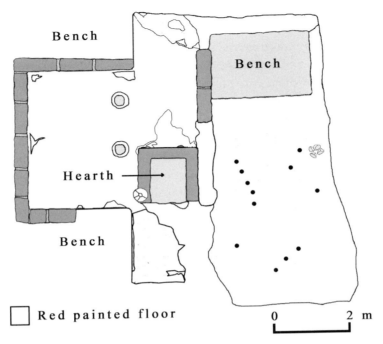

Figure 3.11 Plan of a Musular building with red painted floor (adapted from Özbaşaran et al. 2007)

creating a cul de sac—a central hearth, and a pair of flat stones that probably supported wooden roof posts were the interior elements. Missing from Aşıklı and Musular, however, is any sense of highly charged symbolism that emerged later at Çatalhöyük, in the Konya Plain. Perhaps symbolic connotations at Aşıklı were attributed to well-crafted bone belt fasteners and polished stone beads, or items made material long since perished.

Economy

It could be argued that the most significant resources possessed by Anatolia were the seven primary domesticates (emmer wheat, einkorn wheat, barley, sheep, goats, cattle, and pigs) that ranged across the Fertile Crescent.[78] Other foods, including nuts and legumes, provided variety. The change in economic subsistence mentioned earlier is difficult to document in its initial stages because the differences in hard anatomy between wild and domestic animals are often not distinct. Other indicators are needed. In animals, it involves understanding population structures that are reflected in age/sex ratios of bone remains. Keeping and managing animals within settlements (herding and husbandry), for instance, are behavioral patterns of control that eventually led to morphological change. At the centre of this long process is the question of what actually constitutes a domestic animal. Current debate suggests there were two stages.[79] First, came the control of wild herds through selective hunting patterns, which would not have resulted in the biological changes of animals. Then, in the second stage, animals were herded into settlements. This separation from the wild herds required new management practices that eventually brought about a morphological change, including a reduction in the size of the animal, and, in the case of domesticated sheep and goats, a change in the structure of their horns, from roughly four-sided cross-section to a triangular one.

Wild sheep and goats had a more defined geographical distribution than the wild ancestors of cattle and pigs, which are found beyond western Asia. Red sheep (*Ovis orientalis*), or moufflon, was very much at home in the rugged landscape of the Taurus-Zagros arc. Although it reached as far south as the Negev, it was not a popular food source there. The bones of sheep and goat are often indistinguishable, hence the group term "ovicaprine." Judging by the quantity of sheep bones at sites such as Abu Hureyra and Çayönü, it appears that the first steps towards the sheep domestication were taken in northern Syria and southeastern Anatolia (Figure 3.12). Even so, the distribution of the bezoar (*Capra aegagrus*), the wild ancestor of domestic goats, can be

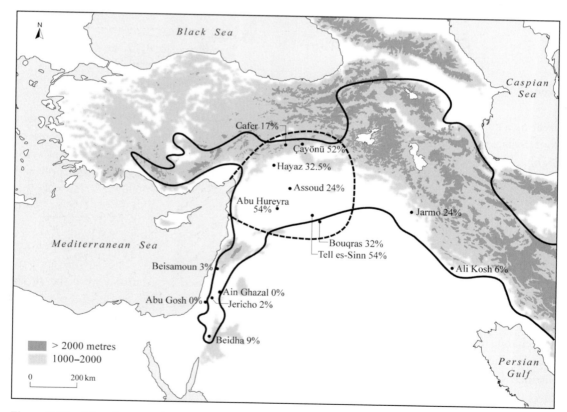

Figure 3.12   Map showing the area in which sheep were first domesticated set against the vast homeland of their wild ancestors. Percentages refer to the amount of sheep bones found in assemblages dated between 7000 and 6200 BC (after Smith 1995)

66

roughly defined and it is more expansive than the moufflon, extending into the southern Caucasus and the Elburz Mountains. More sites hunted the bezoar, or Persian wild goat, including Cafer Höyük, but it was probably first domesticated around Ganj Dareh, in the Zagros.

Emmer wheat (*Triticum turgidum dicoccoides*) and barley (*Hordeum vulgare spontaneum*) carpeted the full length of Fertile Crescent, whereas wild einkorn wheat (*Triticum monococcum boeoticum*) is absent in the Levant, but covers much of Anatolia (Figure 3.13). Plants, unlike animals, can have their genetic composition changed far more rapidly, between 20 and 200 years, although radiocarbon dating lacks the precision to establish whether wild einkorn, emmer wheat, or barley was the first cereal to be domesticated. Genetic studies of einkorn wheat have suggested that the Karacadağ Mountains, in the Diyarbakır region of southeastern Turkey, may have been where it was first domesticated.[80] By comparing the DNA makeup of a range of wild einkorn wheat with cultivated einkorn lines (*Triticum m. monococcum*), scientists have been able to identify a cluster of 11 lines whose wild and cultivated varieties match very closely. These phylogenetic analyses also compare well with the archaeological record. Not far from Karacadağ, on the upper and lower fringes of the Fertile Crescent, are a number of Early

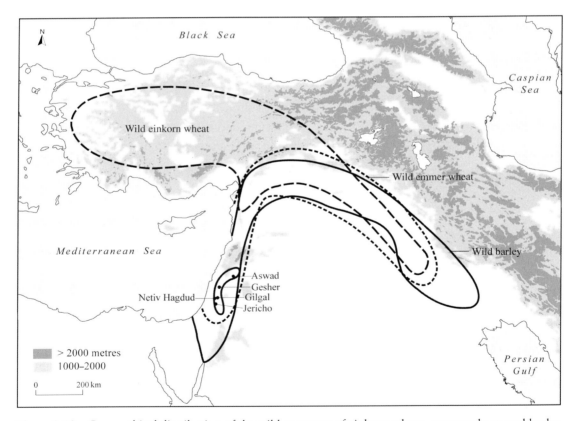

Figure 3.13 Geographical distribution of the wild ancestors of einkorn wheat, emmer wheat, and barley (adapted from Smith 1995)

Neolithic sites—Cafer Höyük, Çayönü, and Nevalı Çori—that have yielded samples of both wild and cultivated einkorn.[81] The change from wild to domestic cereals required the modification of only a few genes, which was caused unintentionally by foragers when they cut the plants. In the wild, cereals have a brittle stem (rachis) that enable the loosely attached seeds to self-disperse and reseed the fields. Domestic cereals are distinguished from their wild progenitors by the presence of a sturdier spike, requiring people to discard the husk from around the seed. By harvesting the cereals before they dispersed, and then planting some of them in the subsequent year, early farmers would have promoted the tougher variety, which in natural circumstances would have clung to the stem and not necessarily scattered.

Despite the prevalence of sedentary lifestyles, hunting and gathering was still a basic component of daily life. Moreover, the shift towards husbandry and cultivation was gradual, but by no means uniform. Not surprisingly, the archaeological record reveals site-specific exploitation of the natural resources. At Hallan Çemi, for instance, the community managed to lead a fully sedentary lifestyle while procuring the bulk of their food through hunting and gathering. They collected high protein foods such as wild almonds and pistachio, and also exploited lentils and vetches, which were favored at Çayönü in the Pre-Pottery Neolithic A.[82] But unlike their Natufian neighbors further south, they did not gather cereals, which explains the negligible quantity of sickle blades among their stone tools. The significance of this subsistence model—a reliance on plant resources other than cereals—is that it runs counter to the generally perceived notion that cereal exploitation played a central role in the transition from mobile to sedentary economies.

The patterns of animal exploitation at Hallan Çemi are no less surprising. Whereas most animal bones—including sheep/goats, pigs, deer, bears, and various birds and fish—belong to wild individuals that were hunted, a small but significant percentage point to fledgling attempts at animal husbandry.[83] But sheep and goats, commonly assumed to be the most amenable and earliest domesticates, were not the subjects. Rather, Hallan Çemi's inhabitants preferred to experiment with pigs. Both the age and sex ratios point to pigs being maintained and butchered at the site. This happened much earlier than at Çayönü, where pigs may have been kept towards the end of the early Pre-Pottery Neolithic B (Channel Building subphase). Prior to that the community depended entirely on wild game.[84]

Just before the first pigs were raised at Çayönü, people began to collect wild emmer and einkorn, though pulses still formed the bulk of their nonmeat diet.[85] In time, however, as cereals were cultivated, they became the main staples in the subsistence diet, certainly by the end of the Pre-Pottery Neolithic B period (Cell houses). By then sheep and goats were fully domesticated and they too began to replace their wild counterparts in the kitchen.[86] A similar sort of picture is attested at Nevalı Çori, though Göbekli has yielded no evidence to suggest that its inhabitants either cultivated cereals or practiced animal husbandry. Yet another picture has emerged at Cafer. There the community was fully agricultural (cereals and pulses) from the start, but did not keep animals in the settlement. Indeed, their hunting patterns are distinct and indicate a shift towards larger animals that provided more meat.[87]

Apart from showing us that the trajectory of Early Neolithic societies in southeast Anatolia was different to that pursued in the Levant, these economic data also support the view that, in the shift to food production, domesticated resources were supplements to the diet rather than staples.[88] In the case of Hallan Çemi, for instance, the young pigs consumed by its inhabitants would have been seen as a type of dietary insurance, that is, an early form of risk management geared towards the possible depletion of wild local resources. Nonetheless, in time communities began to rely less on wild foods, preferring instead to grow plants and herd animals, thereby ensuring a steady supply.

Pınarbaşı A, in central Anatolia, offers some interesting zooarchaeological patterning.[89] Most of the animal remains show no trace of morphological change, but doubt still surrounds sheep and goats, the largest category (less than 50%), which may have been herded. Other animals include wild pig (20%) and cattle (about 12%). Clearer evidence of human control has come from Aşıklı Höyük where over 70% of the animal bones that display all the morphological characteristics of wild fauna are caprine. Yet the proportionally large quantity of bones belonging to sheep and goat, and the fact that most were juvenile (under 4 years of age) suggest that these animals were herded and the young consumed for food.[90] A similar picture is reflected at Suberde, where sheep were the main source of meat for the villagers, who also consumed goat, cattle (*Bos*), pig, and red deer.[91] Other species, including dog, are represented in smaller quantities. According to Perkins and Daly this was a hunters' settlement—all animals were wild apart from the dog. However, their comment that none of the sheep was older than 3 years argues against this. Without detailed data, the situation is difficult to assess, but indications are that the inhabitants at Suberde herded sheep and managed them by culling. Whether this practice was applied to other species is difficult to say. At Can Hasan III *Bos* was the main source of meat, although sheep/goat, pig, and an equid (probably onager) were also on the menu. But the village had an agricultural economy, and the predominant cereals were bread wheat and club wheat, emmer, wild and domestic einkorn and two-row hulled barley.[92]

Contact and exchange: The obsidian trade

Obsidian (volcanic glass) had a special role in the ancient Near East, engendering a most enduring trade network, which lasted several millennia. It occurs naturally when acidic volcanic lavas cool rapidly and transform into a vitreous material that was highly prized in antiquity for the making of tools. Its hardness and predictable conchoidal fracture made obsidian as desirable as flint, if not more so, whereas its brittleness also ensured the sharpest of edges with even the most expedient technology.[93] Such are the qualities of obsidian that it was also used to manufacture luxury items, including polished mirrors.[94] Usually black, obsidian can also come in a range of colors from gray and brown, through dark green and red, to translucent. Sometimes it is mottled or banded, combining two different colors. But it is obsidian's geochemical qualities that make it particularly useful for archaeology, enabling its distribution across much of the Near East to be tracked over time.

Several geochemical qualities of obsidian should be noted. First, obsidian is an unstable product that recrystallizes over geological time. Generally, deposits younger than 10 million years old offer the best quality obsidian; older deposits are mostly unsuitable for tool working. This characteristic has a significant implication for archaeology because only some of the recorded sources were exploited. Impurities and recrystallization rendered the others of no use to the ancients. So a distinction ought to be made between "archaeological" and "geological" obsidian. Second, individual obsidian sources have diagnostic trace elements. Although the composition within a single flow may vary, it is far less than the difference between flows, permitting each source to be attributed with its own geochemical fingerprint. Finally, unlike metals whose makeup is altered through recycling practices, manufacture and usage do not change the physical and chemical properties of obsidian, making it an extremely sensitive indicator in provenance studies such as trade. Several methods are available to detect the trace elements with varying degrees of accuracy.[95]

In the Near East, obsidian occurs naturally in distinct regions in Anatolia and Trans-Caucasus, areas that have witnessed complex geological activity since the Miocene.[96] Obsidian outcrops in three regions in Anatolia—the west, the centre (Cappadocia), and the eastern highlands (Figure 3.14: 1). Of these, the central Anatolian sources—Acıgöl, Göllü Dağı, Nenezi Dağı, Hasan Dağı, Erciyes Dağı, and Karakören—which fall within the Aksaray–Nevşehir–Niğde triangle have been studied the most.[97] Two tuffs distinguish the Acıgöl source, but only the Upper Acıgöl Tuff, at the peak of Koca Dağı, has an abundance of black obsidian. Even so, within this tuff only the East Acıgöl ante-caldera, the richest obsidian area of the Acıgöl complex, was exploited in prehistory.[98] Göllü Dağı (Çiftlik), with six separate deposits and two geochemical groups (west and east), was also extensively utilized. Substantial workshops, notably those at Kömürcü and Kaltepe, are carpeted with stone-working debris—cores, blades, and flakes—much of it highly standardized that suggests some form of organized production.[99] A complimentary source to Göllü Dağı is Nenezi Dağı, which has an obsidian workshop on its western plateau. Hasan Dağı is conspicuous—a large stratovolcano, near Aksaray. So, too, is its obsidian, which is the only source in central Anatolia to contain quartz. But there is no convincing evidence that Hasan Dağı was ever used. The same can be said of Erciyes Dağı, whereas the deposits near Karakören village have only a couple of tools ascribed to them.

Two distinct obsidian sources are known in western Anatolia, and a third is inferred from geochemical analyses. The two known deposits, located relatively recently, are Yağlar and Sakaeli-Orta. Artefacts from Güdül have shown a different range of trace elements, which has fuelled the view of another as yet undiscovered source located somewhere nearby in the Galatian Massif.

The eastern Anatolian obsidian sources are less well known, although recent sampling and analyses are making headway in better understanding these extensive flows.[100] Two broad regions in the east contain obsidian—the northeastern highlands and the basin of Lake Van.

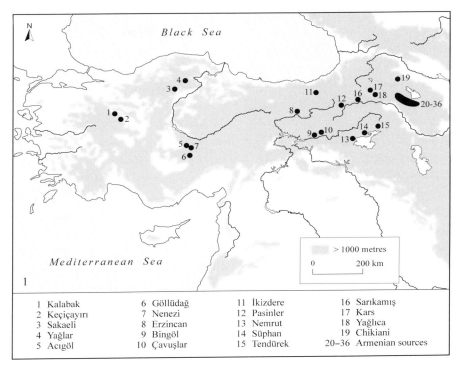

1 Kalabak	6 Göllüdağ	11 İkizdere	16 Sarıkamış
2 Keçiçayırı	7 Nenezi	12 Pasinler	17 Kars
3 Sakaeli	8 Erzincan	13 Nemrut	18 Yağlıca
4 Yağlar	9 Bingöl	14 Süphan	19 Chikiani
5 Acıgöl	10 Çavuşlar	15 Tendürek	20–36 Armenian sources

Figure 3.14 **1** Main obsidian outcrops in Turkey. **2** Blocks of obsidian embedded in a soft tuff at Büyükdere, near Pasinler, eastern Turkey (Photo: Antonio Sagona). **3, 4** Obsidian tools found strewn across the ground at the Büyükdere source (Photos: courtesy Lee McRae)

Those in the northeast include Pasinler, Güzelyurt, Ömertepe, İkizdere, Erzincan, and Sarıkamış. The Pasinler source is the most extensive, stretching from its northernmost point near Calyazı village, located at an altitude of 2356 m, down through two plateaux—one a vast area north of Büyükdere village—to the bed of the Büyükdere River, a tributary of Aras River, which cuts through the Malikom Gorge. The obsidian at Büyükdere is black and gray in color, and embedded in a soft gray or pale brown tuff (Figure 3.14: 2). Strewn across the ground is clear evidence of expedient tool manufacture (Figure 3.14: 2–3). Meanwhile, waterworn cobbles that were certainly utilized in antiquity can be found beyond the Büyükdere River to the town of Pasinler, where they settle along the rocky banks. Two relatively nearby sources are located at Güzelyurt (Tambura) and west of Ömertepe (Pulur), whose mound was investigated by Hamit Z. Koşay. Güzelyurt obsidian was of no practical use to the ancients, being poor in quality, and the Ömertepe sources are thinly scattered on the eastern slope of Güney Dağı. Further west another source is located at Boztepe, near Erzincan, but like Güzelyurt it is not suitable for stone tool production, showing no regular conchoidal fracture and a considerable amount of crystals. The Sarıkamış source is extensive and outcrops in a couple of locations, but the best known is the cutting along the Erzurum to Kars road. Obsidian from Sarıkamış varies in color, but black and mottled red-black are the most common. Finally, we also have a source in the Pontic Mountains at İkizdere positioned between the villages of Büyük Yayla and Çağırankaya Yayla. Not well studied, and perhaps not exploited in antiquity, this formation appears to have different flows, some of which is eye-catching red and red-black banded obsidian.

Obsidian of the southeastern region, which stretches from Bingöl to the Iranian border, is part of a complex geological area precisely where the various plates collide. Two phases of volcanism are evident, the second of which created the stratovolcanoes of Süphan Dağı and Ağrı Dağı (Mt. Ararat). Further tectonic activity also created the peralkaline obsidian flows at Nemrut Dağı and Bingöl. Analyses of the Bingöl source have revealed two distinct groups. A peralkaline type[101] (Bingöl A), gray or green in color, is found at the small flow of Orta Düz, which has been redistributed through river action to Çavuşlar, where rounded cobbles can be found. The second group, a cal-alkaline variety (Bingöl B) gray or black in color, is located at the flow dome Alatepe and redistributed to Çatak. Nemrut Dağı is a stratovolcano (2935 m high) with a vast caldera now containing Lake Nemrut. Obsidian from this source can be divided into two types based on location—from outside and from inside the caldera. Black to semitransparent obsidian can be found on the slope of the mountain and along the edge of the caldera, but it is not homogenous and contains a lot of crystals, making it unsuitable for knapping. Another variety, however, is like the Bingöl B variety distinctly green in color, owing to their peralkaline state, and easily distinguishable from other obsidian groups in Anatolia. Obsidian also occurs in the Muş basin, near the village of Mercimekkale, but no analyses are available as yet. Süphan Dağı, rising to 4434 m, is the second highest peak in Anatolia. Analyses of its obsidian reveal two groups (Suphan I and II), which have impurities very similar to those of Göllü Dağı, Acıgöl, and Erzincan. Near Süphan is Meydan Dağı, with flows of gray and black obsidian around its large caldera. Finally, there is the high shield volcano at Tendürek, south of Doğubayazıt, where obsidian has been observed near its crater summit. But as yet no analyses have been performed on these outcrops.

Communities in southeast Anatolia were already engaged in sustained cultural interaction with their neighbors from the time the first round huts were founded at Hallan Çemi. This degree of community organization is seen in the procurement of copper ore and obsidian, both imported from sources as far away as 150 km, which suggest that the inhabitants were also involved in a long distance network of exchange. Making use of the major natural thoroughfares across the rim of the Fertile Crescent and down the Levant Corridor, obsidian from sources north of the Taurus was traded, initially in small quantities and probably as part of a gift exchange system, to communities as far as 1000 km from the sources.[102] Equally remarkable is the longevity of this trade. Beginning in the Epipalaeolithic, it peaked in the seventh and sixth millennia BC, but continued in a piecemeal fashion well into the historic period. In its heyday it was the most enduring exchange network of the ancient Near East. No doubt other valued commodities such as plant products were also trafficked along the same axes of communication, but these have not survived in the archaeological record.

Some insight into the nature of this pre-urban trade is afforded by the ethnographically well-documented exchange systems of Melanesia, where shell bracelets (*Spondylus*) are exchanged between trading partners together with a host of more mundane items such as food and pottery.[103] These modes of Melanesian trade survive up to the present because the items exchanged were not precious and were of no interest to the outside world. Similarly, we may assume that the trade and demand of high value materials such as metals and lapis lazuli prompted the eventual fragmentation of the obsidian network in western Asia.

The late Pleistocene hunter-gatherers were the first to exchange obsidian. From about 14,000 to 12,000 BC, a small quantity of obsidian from central Anatolia crossed the Taurus Mountains and reached the northern Levant where it was fashioned into geometric Kebaran tools. At the other end of the Fertile Crescent, Bingöl obsidian made its way to the Zarzian communities of the northern Zagros Mountains. The subsequent cold snap of the Younger Dryas did not impact on the trade. Indeed between 12,000–9500 BC the Middle Euphrates appears to have become an intermediary region between the central Anatolian sources and the Natufian communities of the Levant, while the Bingöl source continued to supply the Zagros region, as tools from Zawi Chemi indicate. Then, with the amelioration of the climate, larger quantities of obsidian were circulated during the Pre-Pottery Neolithic A period. The two regions of central Anatolia and Bingöl remained relatively discrete exchange zones, although we now find eastern obsidian finding its way to the Levant through the Middle Euphrates. When Pre-Pottery Neolithic B was fully established, obsidian criss-crossed the Near East, even reaching Cyprus and the Middle Zagros. Towards the end of that period the trafficking of obsidian was increasingly being controlled by a number of large nodal settlements, such as Bouqras and Tell Abu Hureyra, in Syria, Ain Ghazal, in Jordan, and Çatalhöyük. During the Pottery Neolithic, the obsidian exchange system develops into a highly reticulated one. The most significant change to the previous network is the diversification of routes and sites that handled obsidian, effectively breaking the monopoly of the nodal Pre-Pottery Neolithic sites and the Middle Euphrates route. Obsidian now reached the northern Levant, which hitherto appears to have been settled by Mesolithic forest foragers, through the plain of Cilicia and the coast.

Stoneworking technologies and crafts

Although technology in the Pre-Pottery Neolithic is first and foremost lithic, we should flag the extraordinary finds of native copper from Çayönü, 200 artefacts and fragments in all, which are the earliest known metal objects in the Near East.[104] Quantity aside, it is the sustained nature of the metallurgical activity, showing the development from cold hammering to the earliest stages of pyrotechnology, that is so important. Copper tools in the form of solid needles and reamers, hooks as well as beads and rings, begin to appear at the end of the early Grill building subphase. Most objects were hammered from nodules of copper that occurred naturally. Some were annealed and hardened. Even before this we find malachite pieces worked into small beads among the deposits of the Round hut subphase. Several thousand of these malachite beads were found throughout the pre-pottery deposits. This precocious metal working no doubt had much to do with the settlement's location only 20 km from the rich copper mines at Ergani Maden. Even so, the use of copper during the Pre-Pottery Neolithic A implies a detailed understanding of the region and its resources. While obsidian sources are for the most part conspicuous, copper ores are less accessible and embedded in the mountainous terrain. Native copper was also worked at Aşıklı Höyük for grave goods, although not with such precociousness.[105]

By the early Pre-Pottery Neolithic B, pressure flaking techniques are introduced at Çayönü such as those used on Byblos points, and there is a greater exploitation of obsidian especially for the production of "Çayönü" double-backed blades. Broadly similar techniques and procurement patterns in earliest levels at Cafer, where microliths are particularly popular and the Çayönü blades are absent, confirm architectural parallels (Figure 3.15). Connections still largely point to the Zagros sites (Jarmo, M'Lefaat, and Magzalia), but we see attempts to communicate with villages in the Middle Euphrates region of Syria (Mureybit IV and Abu Hureyra). The initial preference for flint over obsidian (from Bingöl), the technique of bipolar knapping on naviform cores, and the popularity of certain stone tools (Byblos point) are seen as evidence for extensive networking.[106] Naviform core technology used to produce long, straight blades from opposed platform-prepared cores is particularly noteworthy. These blades were used to manufacture large projectile points, which, as we shall see, have implications for increased conflict in the Pre-Pottery Neolithic B. Further insight into the nature of these technologies is gained by a flint workshop at Hayaz located downstream of Gritille, where flint is also favored.[107]

In central Anatolia, obsidian was favored for stone tool production. It was procured from the Kayırlı and Nenenzi sources, near Göllüdağ, and brought to Aşıklı as nodules for fashioning, although workshops are also found near the sources themselves.[108] Among the variety of tools,

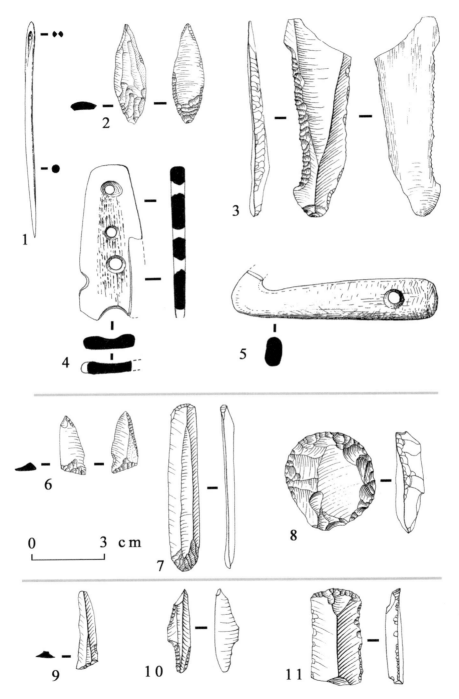

Figure 3.15   Stone and bone tools from Cafer Höyük. *Late phase*: **1** Bone needle. **2** Flint projectile point. **3** Obsidian "Çayönü tool." **4, 5** Perforated bone tools. *Middle phase*: **6–8** Obsidian tools. *Early phase*: **9, 10** Obsidian tools. **11** Flint tool (adapted from Cauvin et al. 1999)

scrapers and retouched blades are the most common. At Suberde, the small size of the tools and the use made of waste flakes indicate that obsidian was not readily accessible. Many flint sickle blades have a sheen that comes from cutting cereal stems or reeds. Can Hasan III tools, again predominately obsidian, are finely retouched and included end- and flakescrapers, awls, *lames écailles*, heavy backed blades and smaller versions, some obliquely truncated.[109] Flint was mainly used for sickle blades that are sometimes denticulated. Waste from the manufacture of obsidian tools is clearly evident, contrasting with the more prudent use of flint. Ground stone artefacts are abundant too, especially at Çayönü, where hand stones come in a wide variety of shapes.[110] Grinding slabs, axes, spheres (or round sling stones), grooved stones for straightening arrow shafts, and pestles also show the predilection of subsistence activities.

While bone equipment in the southeast is extensive and displays the ebb and flow of fashion, overall morphological types are quite standard and long lived at Çayönü.[111] These types include needles, spatulae, and chisels. Bone and antler handles and sickles are not very common. Bone was also worked at Can Hasan III and the range of tools—points, scoops, pins, spatulae (that could also be netting spacers), and beads—attest to a flourishing industry. Among the Çayönü ornaments, beads are by far the most common.[112] Starting with shell beads in the Round building subphase, polished, stone beads of many different shapes and sizes soon proliferate, as well as spacer beads with multiple perforations (Figure 3.16). Bone and malachite beads were also produced. Fancier still are the marble and basalt bracelets, plain and grooved, found at Cafer.[113]

COLLAPSE OF THE PRE-POTTERY NEOLITHIC

Many have pondered on why such vibrant Pre-Pottery Neolithic B cultures, distinguished by large sites, monumental architecture and captivating art, eventually fizzled out across the Near

Figure 3.16 Shell and stone ornaments from various subphases at Çayönü (adapted from photos: courtesy Mehmet Özdoğan)

East.[114] Their finale, termed the Final Pre-Pottery Neolithic B or Pre-Pottery Neolithic C, witnessed a marked decline in every category of material culture, ending with either the abandonment of sites or their reduction in size.

To understand this episode we need to be reminded of the trajectory of the aceramic Neolithic, which, put simply, is as follows:

1 Early Pre-Pottery Neolithic (and/or late Epipalaeolithic): Small settlements, occupied year round by complex hunters and gatherers, with modest communal spaces and public structures used for feasting and related activities that bonded the community.
2 Late Pre-Pottery Neolithic (the *dénouement*): Large settlements with monumental temples and art, reflecting an elaborate cult, which was sustained by an organized economy, requiring a significant investment of energy by a hierarchically structured society.
3 Final Pre-Pottery Neolithic: A deterioration of cultural activities that lead to sites being abandoned or shrinking in size. Either way it reflects a flow of population away from large sites and the establishment of a network of small sites across the landscape.

While this trajectory fits the rise-and-fall paradigm, Michael Rosenberg appropriately reminds us that bigger is not necessarily better.[115] That is, the benefits reaped by individuals living in a large community can be offset by the effort they invest in maintaining the infrastructure, surpluses, and networks. Conversely, smaller groups experienced less stress, yet maintained a manageable and flexible lifestyle.

Two mechanisms appear to have enabled the shift to a reduction of site size. First came the full domestication of sheep and goats that provided farmers with more flexible subsistence strategies, which permitted them to exploit new ecological niches.[116] This flexibility, in turn, coincides with the peopling of areas beyond the boundaries of the original formation zone, including the plateau and the west Anatolian region.[117] Some have argued that, in the Levant at least, deteriorating climatic conditions such as aridity may have triggered this movement into new lands.[118] However, this seems unlikely for Anatolia, where the extensive suite of pollen diagrams (see Chapter 1) show forests reached their peak about 7000 BC. If anything, the full expansion of the forest cover, limiting as it would suitable grazing areas, might have prompted groups to seek areas more conducive to farming.

How, then, can we explain the Anatolian scene? Rosenberg has put forward a persuasive idea, based on observed changes in stone technology, that merits serious consideration.[119] Towards the end of the Pre-Pottery Neolithic the lithic repertoire is distinguished by the utilization of naviform cores from which long, straight-sided blades were struck. Whereas smaller blades produced from earlier techniques could have been shaped into a variety of forms, only blades knapped from naviform cores were big enough to manufacture large projectile points that were attached to the shafts of spears or javelins. Given issues of balance and aerodynamics, these large points were not suited as arrowheads, but designed for accurate and forceful penetration at close range. Some points were also designed to snap once they had hit their target, so that even if they did not kill on impact they would certainly have inflicted pain and infection. With no evidence for changes in hunting patterns, Rosenberg argues that large projectile points are indicative of warfare. While he is not the first to suggest that the rise of the Neolithic ran parallel to an increase of group conflict, the changes in lithic technology he observes point to "a change in the conduct or intensity of such conflict."[120] The implications for this are significant. It appears that the development of large Pre-Pottery Neolithic B sites brought with it a rise in social conflict, which eventually lead to the disaggregation and dispersal of communities, which were not inclined to live in an atmosphere of tension. In the next chapter, we will follow the development of the clustered village lay out, already observed at Aşıklı Höyük, which, according to Rosenberg, is overtly defensive, a view expressed many years ago by Mellaart, but which had hitherto lost appeal.

CONCLUDING REMARKS

We have seen that many features distinguish the Pre-Pottery Neolithic period in Anatolia. One is the gradual evolution of sedentary life from the modest huts and permanent camps of the Epipalaeolithic to the fully fledged villages with substantial public buildings (temples in some cases) of the Pre-Pottery Neolithic B. Another is the overt emphasis on ritual expressed through striking iconography. A third feature is the clear time lag between the earliest village communities, which subsisted through hunting and gathering, and the gradual adoption of a farming economy. Finally, and perhaps most intriguing of all, is the emergence of cultural regionalism and divergent ways of thinking, which is evident when settlements north and south of the Taurus Mountains are compared. Briefly, settlements in the southeast comprise free-standing structures that conform to a rigid plan and orientation, and form part of a domain that embraced open spaces. By contradistinction, settlements north of the Taurus are far more organic in nature even though they too adhered to strict building codes. Their closely packed neighborhoods, minimal open spaces, and rooftop access into buildings provide a starkly different communal organization. But differences are not limited to buildings. Mortuary practices are at variance too: In the southeast the secondary treatment of skeletal remains and the use of communal burial sites were the norm, whereas in central Anatolia families preferred to bury their dead beneath the floors of their houses. And despite obvious interaction between the two regions—central Anatolian obsidian was used in the southeast—their stone tool working techniques developed along different trajectories.

NOTES

1 Bottema 1991; Bottema and Van Zeist 1981; Bottema and Woldring 1984; Perrot 2002: Figure 1; Van Zeist et al. 1975; Van Zeist and Bottema 1982.

2 Childe 1936.
3 Bar-Yosef and Belfer-Cohen 1992.
4 There have been several attempts to change these admittedly universal and arbitrary terms into more regionally specific nomenclature (e.g., Özbaşaran and Buitenhuis 2002), but given the patchiness of our archaeological record for Neolithic Anatolia it is best for the time being to adhere to conventional terminology.
5 The following provide useful lead-in studies: Bellwood 2005; Clutton-Brock 1989; Smith 1995; Zohary and Hopf 2000.
6 Braidwood 1960: 134. Less well known is the earlier work of Russian botanist, Nikolai Vavliov (1952), who attempted to define the centers of origins of cultivated plants, in which he included the southern Caucasus.
7 See the first explanation of this view in Boserup 1965.
8 Binford 1968.
9 Hassan 1973.
10 Bar-Yosef and Belfer-Cohen 1991; McCorriston and Hole 1991.
11 Higgs and Jarman 1969.
12 For a development of the view on the relationship between humans and plants, see Rindos 1984, who believed that agriculture was the unintentional outcome of this association.
13 Bender 1978; Hayden 1995. For the view that dance was fundamental to social cohesion in the Neolithic, see Garfinkel 2003.
14 Cauvin 2001.
15 Perrot 2000.
16 Bintliff 1991; Knapp 1992. For a critique of the *longue durée*, see Kristiansen and Larsson 2005: 32ff.
17 Bellwood and Renfrew 2002.
18 For a recent and thorough review on the question of the spread of Indo-European languages, see Anthony 2007.
19 Özdoğan, M. 1995, 2002.
20 Bar-Yosef and Belfer-Cohen 1991 on the first definition of this term.
21 Özdoğan 2002, 2005; see also Verhoeven 2002a.
22 Özdoğan and Başgelen 2007. This is the second edition of Özdoğan and Başgelen 1999.
23 For emphasis on the Levant, see, among several, McCorriston and Hole 1991. On "formation zones," see Özdoğan 1993, 1996a, 2005.
24 Renfrew 1986.
25 Cf. Özdoğan 2005: 18–23, with Watkins 1992 and Rosenberg 2003, who see an increase in social conflict.
26 Özdoğan 1999a: 11.
27 Sagona and Sagona 2004 (northeast region), and Matthews 2007 (north-central region).
28 On Trans-Caucasia, see Chataigner 1995; Kiguradze 2001; the earliest radiocarbon dates from northeastern Anatolia come from exploratory soundings at Pulur, near Erzurum, Işıklı 2007.
29 Rosenberg 1999.
30 Özdoğan 1999c.
31 Badischen Landesmuseum Karlsruhe 2007; Gérard and Thissen 2002; Özdoğan and Başgelen 2007.
32 For a list of all the central Anatolian Neolithic sites, see Gérard 2002.
33 Flannery 1972, 2002.
34 Flannery 2002: 421.
35 Byrd 1994; Sagona 1993; Schachner 1999; Watkins 1990.
36 Flannery 2002: 421.
37 Individual entries in Oliver 1997 provide useful lead-in articles on a range of topics pertaining to

vernacular architecture. I would like to thank Miles Lewis for pointing me in the right direction on matters architectural by providing me with some useful references.

38 Dethier 1982; Williams-Ellis et al. 1947: 59–65.
39 Synnot 1911.
40 I would like to thank Miles Lewis (University of Melbourne) for this insightful observation.
41 Williams-Ellis et al. 1947: 22–58.
42 Özdoğan 1999: 44–47.
43 Schrimer 1988, 1990.
44 Davis 1998.
45 Özdoğan 1999.
46 Özdoğan 1999.
47 Hauptmann 1988, 1999: 70–74.
48 Hauptmann 1993; Özdoğan and Özdoğan 1998.
49 Özdoğan 1999.
50 Cauvin 1985; Cauvin et al. 1999.
51 Ellis and Voigt 1982.
52 Cauvin 1989; Cauvin et al. 1999: 90.
53 Bıçakçı 1995.
54 Cauvin et al. 1999: 91–93.
55 Özgoğan 1999: 53–54.
56 Esin et al. 1991; Esin and Harmankaya 1999.
57 Esin and Harmankaya 1999; Özbaşaran 1998.
58 Esin 1998a: 91.
59 Esin and Harmankaya 1999: 126.
60 French et al. 1972.
61 Bordaz 1968.
62 Duru 1999: 187; Thissen 2002: 324.
63 Efe 2005; Özdoğan and Gastov 1998.
64 Duru 1989.
65 Mellaart 1970a: 3–5.
66 Hauptmann 1999; Schmidt 2004, 2006, 2007.
67 Hauptmann 1993.
68 Hauptmann 2000a.
69 Hauptmann and Schmidt in Badischen Landesmuseum Karlsruhe (ed.) 2007.
70 Verhoeven 2002b.
71 Verhoeven 2002a: 248–249; cf. Hansen 2006.
72 Curtis 1914.
73 French 1963: 35.
74 Özdoğan and Özdoğan 1998.
75 Özdoğan 1995, 1999.
76 Esin and Harmankaya 1999: 130.
77 Özbaşaran 2000: fig. 3; Özbaşaran et al. 2007: figures 3–4.
78 Smith 1995.
79 Smith 1995.
80 Heun et al. 1997.
81 For another view that places the centre of plant domestication in the Near East in the Levantine corridor, see McCorrsiton and Hole 1991.
82 Rosenberg et al. 1995.

83 Rosenberg et al. 1995.

84 Özdoğan 1999: 44.

85 Van Zeist and Roller 1994.

86 Lawrence 1982.

87 Cauvin et al. 1999: 100.

88 Rosenberg 1999.

89 Martin et al. 2002: figure 1; Watkins 1996.

90 Buitenhuis 1997.

91 Perkins and Daly 1968.

92 French et al. 1972.

93 See Disa et al. 1993 for the effectiveness of obsidian when compared to modern metal surgical steel blades.

94 Conolly 1999a.

95 X-ray fluorescence (XRF), instrumental neutron activation (INAA), proton induced x-ray emission and proton induced gamma ray emission (PIXE/PIGME), and, the most sensitive method, measuring parts per billion, laser ablation inductively coupled plasma mass spectrometry (LA-ICPMS).

96 Badalyan et al. 2004; Cauvin et al. 1998; Jackson and McKenzie 1984; Oddone et al. 2003; Yılmaz et al. 1987.

97 Poidevin 1998.

98 Chataigner 1998.

99 Balkan-Altı et al. 1999.

100 Kobayashi and Sagona 2008.

101 Peralkaline obsidian has a relatively high iron and zirconium content and the amount of alumina is less than that of sodium and potassium oxides combined; cal-alkaline obsidian comprises more than about 60% silica and an equal proportion of calcium oxide, potassium oxide, and sodium oxide; alkaline obsidian which contains a higher than average amount of sodium than potassium. For a technical discussion, see Shackley 2005.

102 Mauss 1990.

103 Leach and Leach 1983; Malinowski 1920.

104 Maddin et al. 1991; Yener 2000.

105 Esin 1995; Yener 2000.

106 See, for example, Caneva et al. 1998.

107 Ellis and Voigt 1982; Roodenberg 1979–80; Voigt and Ellis 1981.

108 Balkan-Altı 1994b; Balkan-Altı et al. 1999.

109 French et al. 1972.

110 Davis 1982.

111 Özdoğan 1995.

112 Özdoğan 1995.

113 Maréchal 1985.

114 See, for example, Rollefson and Köhler-Rollefson 1989.

115 Rosenberg 2003.

116 Bar-Yosef and Meadows 1995.

117 Badischen Landesmuseum Karlsruhe 2007; Özdoğan and Başgelen 2007.

118 Rollefson and Köhler-Rollefson 1989.

119 Rosenberg 2003: 94–99.

120 Rosenberg 2003: 95. Cf. Watkins 1990.

4

ANATOLIA TRANSFORMED

From Pottery Neolithic through Middle Chalcolithic (7000–4000 BC)

The transition between Pre-Pottery Neolithic and Pottery Neolithic in Anatolia, a span of time straddling the turn of the eighth and seventh millennia BC, is curiously indistinct. Yet the subsequent changes transformed the long-established traditions of the pioneer sedentary groups. The production of ceramic vessels is one such break with the past. Even though clay was used sparingly well before now, this technological innovation of transforming clay by heat marks a convenient reference point with which to divide the Neolithic into two broad periods.[1] As with all technological achievements, the invention of pottery was accompanied by changes in social behavior that now very much revolved around the home and the hearth, which became the fixed points of human existence.

Pottery Neolithic is also distinguished by the expansion into new areas and the development of regional traits. The Lake District and the Marmara region emerged as well-defined and distinct groups, and recent investigations at Ulucak show that the western coastal region is shaping up to be yet another discrete Neolithic zone, with strong Aegean connections. This adoption of a Neolithic lifestyle in disparate areas was gradual, and we must always be aware of the timelag between, say, the establishment of Pre-Pottery settlements in central Anatolia about 8500 BC and the onset of early Pottery communities in western Anatolia around 6500 BC.[2]

Finally, in the seventh millennium we also witness a shift in the character of cult ritual. The drama of religious activity was no longer performed in and around large temples, but instead was centered within the domestic domain. Buildings where cult activities were carried out are for the most part similar in plan to houses. It seems that the home became the liminal space where residents and their ancestors, often buried beneath the floor, interacted and mediated with the numinous. Religious imagery also changed. Sometimes vivid, at other times muted, we can nonetheless detect new iconographic elements at sites north of the Taurus. Highly evocative wall paintings and well-articulated female figurines are the most eye catching. In other instances, the iconography is subtle and embodied in utilitarian objects. Whatever the imagery, the encounter with the divine and the language of sacred space appears to have changed.

POTTERY NEOLITHIC (ca. 7000–6000 BC)

Houses and ritual

Southeastern Anatolia and Cilicia

Mezraa-Teleilat, a mound positioned near the banks of the Euphrates (Figure 4.1: 1), is of paramount importance. Its uninterrupted sequence, with well-preserved architectural layers bridges the critical timespan between Pre-Pottery and Pottery Neolithic. The crucial horizon in the Mezraa-Teleilat sequence is the third, which is sandwiched between the late Pre-Pottery Neolithic B (Phase IV) with its cell-plan buildings and the early Pottery Neolithic (Phase II) distinguished by its so-called corridor-houses.[3] Calibrated radiocarbon readings place Phase III at the very end of the eighth millennium BC.[4] Its village was composed of wooden or wattle and daub huts with rounded corners. Burnt areas with sunken floors are suggestive of hearths, whereas a cluster of pits filled with river pebbles and ash appears to have been fire pits constructed to maintain heat. Amidst these freestanding structures, pottery makes its appearance, tentatively at first, but increasing in quantity towards the end of the settlement. Strewn on the floor were fragments of ceramics—well finished with a crisp fabric—and a series of limestone figurines.

Many recent studies have been devoted to figurines, mostly seeking to determine their function and purpose. Approaches vary greatly and range from sound analysis through speculation to assertions based on modern ideologies. For Anatolia, the most persuasive views have been those of Mary Voigt who has emphasized the archaeological context, mode of disposal of figurines, and the signs of wear and breakage they bear.[5] She significantly modified the criteria for figurine classification Peter Ukco proposed some 40 years ago, but retained his broad functional groupings, which were based on ethnographic observation: Cult figures, vehicles of magic, initiation figures, and toys.[6] Each of these categories has its own specific attributes of wear and damage. Cult figures, for instance, are unlikely to be associated with ordinary refuse and would show little sign of wear, whereas toys are often randomly distributed in domestic debris and display considerable damage and wear, as one would expect. Following this line of thought, Voigt draws attention to established patterns of human behavior as the basis for any interpretation.

Although none of the Mezraa-Teleilat III figurines could be definitively associated with a structure, none was recovered from a refuse pit.[7] On the whole, the figurines are crudely worked with little attempt to smooth over tool marks. The fugitive traces of red paint some bear, suggests that they may have been painted. Three types of figurine exist. Seated figures—these

Figure 4.1 Mezraa-Teleilat: **1** Aerial view showing the excavations in the foreground and the Euphrates River in the background. **2** Cell buildings, Level IIB2 (Photos: courtesy Mehmet Özdoğan)

vary in size from 2.7 to 11.5 cm in height. They are inclined backwards, as if seated on an armchair. The angle at the back and the flatness of the surfaces suggests that the figurines were embedded into a wooden frame. The face is the most delineated component of the body; legs are simple and pointed, and the torso is shaped by straight surfaces, suggestive of a robe. Arms are generally stubby and protrude in front; in a couple of figurines they are placed on the sides. Even though phalluses are obvious on only some figurines, the homogeneity of these schematized figurines suggests, according to the excavators, the same male deity or person is represented. Only two fragments of standing figures have been found and these, too, are roughly shaped. Finally, the most numerous group are phallic symbols. Most are schematized, though some are incised with detail, leaving no doubt what they represent. The human figures belong to a type with southern connections termed Assouad. Examples been found at a number of sites strung along the Euphrates, including Gritille and Tell Sabi Abyad (in Syria), pointing to an indigenous tradition of the southern Taurus. This overt symbolism of maleness continues the earlier Pre-Pottery Neolithic notion of male fecundity without the monumentality.

The Mezraa-Teleilat III culture is considered intrusive, but it is followed, in Phase II, by a significant change that revived the local elements of the Pre-Pottery Neolithic B. Massive structures (the corridor houses) built from light colored mud bricks characterize Phase II and define an architectural tradition that continued to develop until the Halaf period of the Early Chalcolithic (Figure 4.1: 2).

Across the Amanus Mountains, the long sequence at Yümük Tepe, near Mersin, in the broad fertile plain of Cilicia, is the chronological cornerstone for the Anatolian Pottery Neolithic and Chalcolithic periods of Anatolia.[8] Although the Second World War severely interrupted John Garstang's work—an air-raid on Liverpool destroyed much information held in his office— renewed excavations by Isabella Caneva and Veli Sevin have refined the sequence.[9] Exactly how the 33 building levels discerned by Garstang should be divided is still a matter of debate, and one that largely concerns ceramics.[10] But the division of the Neolithic is as follows: Early Neolithic (XXXIII–XXVI) and Late Neolithic (XXV–XX).[11] The small exposure in the lower levels precluded a settlement plan, but there was a gradual shift from small, rectangular rooms to large enclosures.[12] Notable are a series of stone-based circular "silos" placed between two large structures in Level XXIV. Later still, in Level XXIII, structures are built with slabs of mud (oblong bricks) that were placed on top of stone foundations.

Central Anatolia

The Early Pottery Neolithic in central Anatolia is rich and well developed. We have an ever increasing amount of evidence from Çatalhöyük, the largest known Neolithic site in Anatolia. Measuring about 500 × 300 m and rising 17.5 m above the surrounding Konya Plain, the east mound has revealed a deep and extremely well-preserved Neolithic deposit that stretches from about 7400 BC to the end of the seventh millennium BC. Çatalhöyük West was established later, in the Early Chalcolithic period. Despite intensive excavations between 1961 and 1963 by James Mellaart, who opened broad areas, providing some of the clearest settlements plans for pre-historic Anatolia, only a fraction of the settlement was exposed, and its full occupational sequence has not been determined as yet.[13] His spectacular finds dazzled an unsuspecting discipline and they remain the focal point of any discussion on the site. Mellaart's results have prompted the current renewed excavations that began in 1993 under the direction of Ian Hodder, whose onsite and post-excavation strategies embrace all that contemporary archae-ology has to offer.[14] Understandably, the two approaches vary considerably and have supplied images of life in the Neolithic that differ in their degrees of resolution. Whereas Mellaart worked on a grand scale, opening up large areas that provided the big picture, Hodder and his team have focus on the micro scale, supplying very detailed information on the history of small areas such as single rooms.

Mellaart differentiated 15 building levels (0–XIII from top to bottom), but did not reach virgin soil, which he claimed was probably several meters below the present ground level of the plain. Ever since the publication of his preliminary findings, Mellaart and others have argued that the settlement showed remarkable continuity in plan throughout its many rebuildings with Levels VIII–II affording us the best information on architecture.[15] Of these, Level VI (divided into subphases A and B, top to bottom respectively) was destroyed by a catastrophic fire, but is the best preserved.[16] Whether the entire settlement or only part of it was burnt is difficult to say given the large areas that are not excavated, but the fire appears to have been quite devastating. Although details of Mellaart's stratigraphy have been questioned, the new investigations have essentially supported the idea of continuity, viewing the entire sequence as a gradual process of minor changes.[17] Recently, however, the degree of architectural continuity has been disputed. Bleda Düring has shown that the use of space and building patterns did change at Çatalhöyük, especially between Levels VI and V, reflecting transformation in social behavior and attitudes.[18]

A glance at Figure 4.2 reveals that in the early period (Levels VIII to VIB) Çatalhöyük was a village of roughly rectangular houses that were tightly packed into blocks.[19] Houses did not share party walls and as such comprised separate structural entities. The lack of alleyways and doors, other than between the main room and its adjacent storeroom, suggests that communica-tion between buildings was through the roof, following the earlier practice at Aşıklı. Ladders must have been common sights at Çatalhöyük. They were attached to all buildings, usually against the south wall where their imprints and remains have been found. Roof openings also acted as chimneys. Even so, the rooms must have been smoke filled, judging by the high number of incidences of black lung among the skeletal material. Daylight entered the rooms from small apertures set high on the walls, which suggests that houses were of varying heights or some how split level. Thick beams of juniper and an infill of mud, twigs and reeds supported by two wooden posts ensured that the roof was sturdy and, no doubt, flat. Buildings had no founda-tions and were constructed of mud bricks and wood. Rooms were of a standard size with little variation in furnishings. Main rooms were often roughly square in plan and occasionally had a

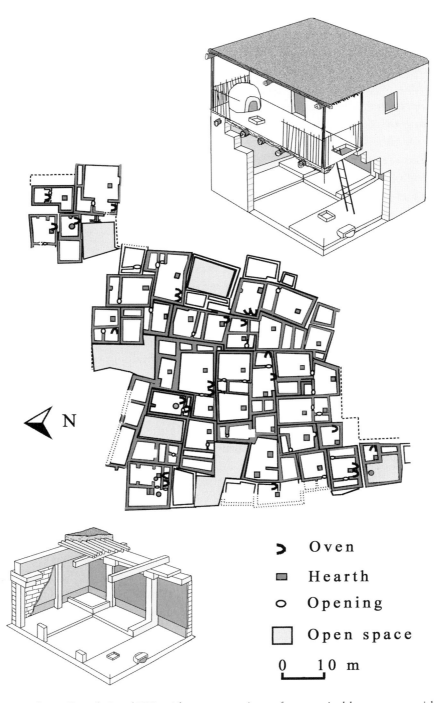

> Oven

▪ Hearth

○ Opening

☐ Open space

0   10 m

Figure 4.2 Plan of Çatalhöyük Level VIB with reconstructions of two typical houses, one with an upper story (adapted from Cutting 2005 and Mellaart 1967)

storeroom. These units were generally modest in this earlier period, covering and area about 40 m^2 (Figure 4.2). On the inside, walls were well plastered, as were floors, which were kept remarkably clean. It seems that most of the manufacturing activities were conducted outdoors, with the space inside buildings used for domestic activities such as food preparation. The thick deposit of superimposed layers of plaster (up to 40, in one case) suggests that residents spruced up the interiors regularly. Around each room were standard fitments: Low platforms, presumably for sitting and sleeping, benches, cupboards, and hearths.

Perhaps the most remarkable aspect of this early settlement plan is the extent to which residents ensured that new buildings were constructed on the same ground, in the same manner and according to the same plan as those of their ancestors. A code of building clearly existed at Çatalhöyük and it was adhered to in the strictest terms. From Level VIII onwards, the settlement became more crowded. As families grew larger, the predilection of continuing the architectural traditions of their forebears on the same land meant that virtually every available space was built on. The settlement became more agglomerated as time went on, so that by Level VII–VIA Çatalhöyük was a densely clustered settlement of essentially similar buildings. While this mode of construction may have served a practical purpose, namely to utilize the walls of older houses as foundations, it seems that it had more to do with social identity.[20] What we see is a phenomenon that inextricably bound households with their ancestors and associated belief systems. This explanation does have appeal, although we should not discount the functionalist view altogether. While it is unlikely that the clustered mode of building served as a measure against floods, it may well have had a defensive purpose if, as mentioned in the previous chapter, one maintains that social conflict increased at the end of the Pre-Pottery Neolithic. Many of the Level VIA structures were burned, deliberately so it seems, and, according to Mellaart, one room (no. 44), the "Leopard Shrine," filled with rubbish after the fire, recalling the burying of the Çayönü buildings.[21] This apparent ritual burning of structures became a widespread Neolithic practice that extended across into Europe.[22]

In Level V around 6500 BC, or just later, the ancestral settlement plan was modified. Change was already in the air, with many buildings of VIB not rebuilt in VIA. Those that were kept became noticeably larger, and open spaces represent a radical shift in planning (Figure 4.3). Alleyways and open courtyards, which were used by residents to dump their rubbish, now separated clusters of buildings. Doorways linked certain buildings in Level IV when large communal ovens were preferred over individual ones in each building. This new schema also changed the accessibility of building units.[23] In the early settlement, certain buildings, especially those decorated with elaborate symbolism, were difficult to reach, perhaps intentionally so. Often located in the heart of a cluster of buildings, they could only be accessed by walking across the rooftops of several houses. Whether there were boundaries and zones where only certain folk could cross is difficult to say, but by Level V open spaces and doorways made most buildings easy to reach.[24] What caused this change is uncertain. Perhaps the devastation of the fire itself prompted the residents at Çatalhöyük to reassess their situation and implement changes.

Many rooms were richly decorated with eye-catching wall paintings, fixtures, plastered clay

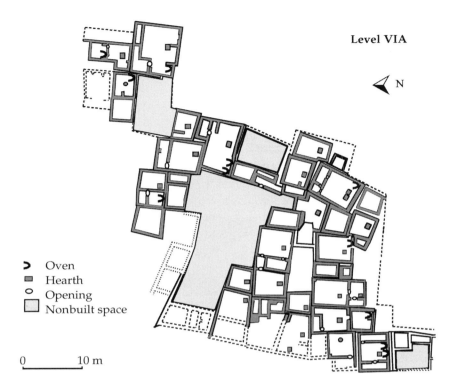

Figure 4.3 Plan of Çatalhöyük Level VIA (adapted from Cutting 2005 and Mellaart 1967)

reliefs, and cut-out silhouettes each replete with symbolism, leading Mellaart to designate them shrines.[25] The term has lost favor recently in some circles primarily because to some the word "shrine" has connotations of religious exclusivity, in societies where religious worship and daily activities are conducted in separate buildings or locations.[26] At Çatalhöyük, however, shrines are the same size and have similar features (bins, platforms, ovens, and so on) as domestic houses. Why certain buildings have elaborate ornamentation, but others only some embellishments, and yet others still have none is not altogether clear. Does this differentiation mean that certain buildings were more important centers of ritual, or do we have a process whereby all or most buildings were gradually decorated? That is, do we have preserved in the archaeological record a snapshot of a cyclic phenomenon of household ornamentation?

Painted walls depicted a range of compositions from simple red panels to large and intricate polychrome scenes that covered the room. Geometric and linear patterns that may have imitated textile designs adorned many walls (Figure 4.4: 2). Figurative representations are found too. Scenes showing humans surrounding or in association with various animals, such as stags and bulls, may represent hunting, or they may depict a public spectacle of taunting animals in which only certain members of society were allowed to partake (Figures 4.4: 3 and 4.5).[27] That some of these animals are shown with their tongues hanging out may also suggest that these creatures

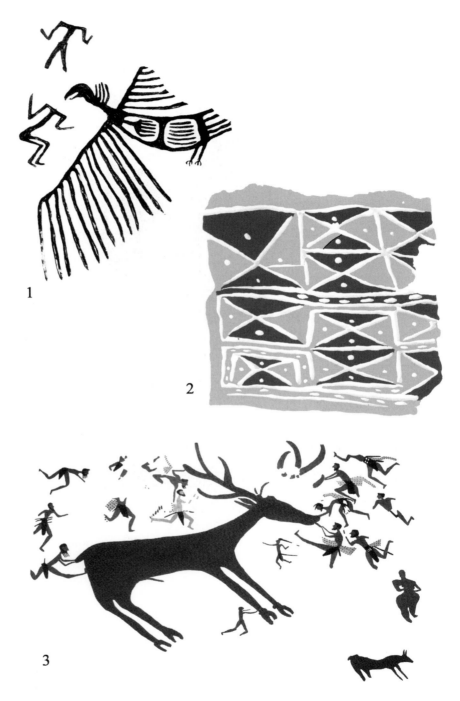

Figure 4.4 Çatalhöyük wall paintings excavated in the 1960s: **1** A vulture or raptor attacking a pair of small, headless human figures (Level VII). **2** A grooved, painted geometric pattern, executed in three colours—white (grooves), black, and red (Level VII). **3** Bearded men, some wearing leopard skin garments, taunting a stag rendered in a larger size. A female figure is positioned on the right of the scene (adapted from Haydaroğlu 2006)

Figure 4.5 Çatalhöyük wall painting excavated in Level V, in the 1960s, showing a large red bull taunted by men, some dressed in leopard skin garments. A female figure can be seen under the bull (adapted from Haydaroğlu 2006)

were dead. Aspects of mortuary rites, namely the defleshing of the dead, may be alluded to in a dramatic painting with red birds of prey circling over lifeless human figures (Figure 4.4: 1), some headless, which recalls the diminutive figure of a headless male on Pillar 43 at Göbekli. Roger Matthews made the insightful connection between Mellaart's suggestion that the birds may, in fact, represent humans dressed as birds and a deposit of wings of birds of prey found at Zawi Chemi Shanidar, in northern Iraq, dated to the ninth millennium.[28] Indeed, as suggested in the previous chapter, the practice of dressing as a bird is well recorded in modern shamanistic rituals. There are also scenes that appear to show humans dancing, an activity which probably promoted social cohesion.[29] Stencilled handprints offer even more realistic human impressions, whereas a possible landscape scene, showing a settlement (depicted as a series of squares) below a mountain, has generated considerable interest since it was found.

The reliefs are no less fascinating. Among the more easily recognizable images are complete spotted leopard-like animals and various animal heads (Figure 4.6). Bizarre features include wild boar jaw bones, animal skulls, and, in one case, vulture beaks, that are encased in a clay features. A type of relief figure thought to represent a deity is shown with arms and feet outstretched in a spreadeagle position (Figure 4.7: 1), and most often interpreted as a goddess giving birth. In one case, the figure is painted with a net pattern (Figure 4.7: 4), in another it is situated above a pair of bull's horns set into the wall; bull's horns were also set into small pillars and benches. A close examination of the original excavation photographs, however, indicate that the subsequent reconstruction of these splayed images has been liberal, making them more human like than they probably were. Indeed, a comparison of the original Çatalhöyük excavation photograph with the more recent finds from Göbekli and Nevalı Çori suggests that these figures are most likely animals (reptiles?) and not humans or goddesses (Figure 4.7: 2).[30] A Çatalhöyük stamp seal in the form of a bear also resembles the splayed relief figures (Figure 4.7: 3).[31]

The way ritual space was constructed at Çatalhöyük varied. Düring has shown, for instance, that buildings richest in ritual paraphernalia are not always the largest, a point that did not escape Mellaart.[32] Moreover, while burials are often associated with reliefs in a small number of buildings, paintings are rarely associated with either mouldings or the dead. Finally, and most important in terms of discontinuity, all the figurative mouldings belong to the early settlement (Level VI and earlier), whereas the "hunting" scenes were all found in later shrines.

The spirits of the dead are pervasive in the domestic arena at Çatalhöyük. The remains of ancestors are numerous and some display symbolic elaborations. Mellaart found some 480 burials and a further 250 were exposed by the new excavations.[33] Building 1 alone had 62 burials. Three burial types have been recognized: Primary, secondary, and disturbed, with the first being the most common. Funerary rites appear fairly standard: Usually wrapped in skins, basketry, or textiles (Figure 4.8: 3–4), the deceased were placed in a pit, in a flexed position, under the platforms within houses. Certain individuals were sprinkled with red ochre, but most were accompanied by gifts, including wooden vessels that were carbonized when fire swept through the compound (see later). Partial burials suggest a more protracted ritual that may have involved the removal of flesh from bodies.

1

2

Figure 4.6 Çatalhöyük relief decorations excavated in the 1960s: **1** Reconstruction of plastered and painted relief of a pair of leopards, Level VIA (adapted from Mellaart 1964). **2** Seven bull horn cores embedded into a bench, Level VI (Photo: courtesy the British Institute at Ankara)

93

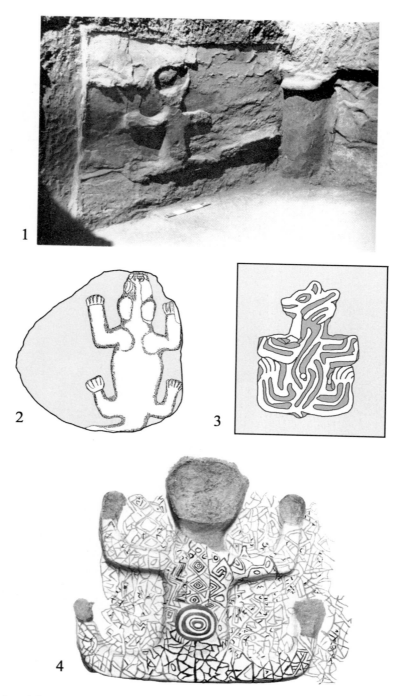

Figure 4.7 **1** Splayed figure in relief from Çatalhöyük "Shrine E", Level VI B (Photo: courtesy the British Institute at Ankara). **2** Reptile carved in relief from Göbekli (adapted from Hauptmann 1999). **3** Stamp seal in the form of a bear from Çatalhöyük (adapted from Hodder 2006), **4** Splayed figure decorated with a net pattern executed in red, orange, and black paint on a white background, at Çatalhöyük "Shrine" VII.23 (adapted from Mellaart 1964)

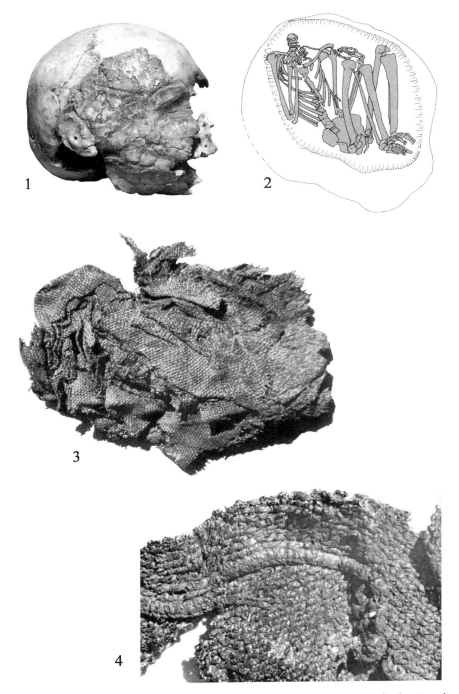

Figure 4.8 **1** Plastered skull from Köşk Höyük (Photo: D. Johannes, courtesy Badisches Landesmuseum Karlsruhe). **2** Articulated burial without skull (adapted from Hodder 2006). **3** Woven cloth from House E VI, 1, at Çatalhöyük. **4** Detail of 3, showing weave and seam (Photos: courtesy the British Institute at Ankara)

In some instances, the skull was removed without disturbing the rest of the skeleton (decapitation burials; Figure 4.8: 2). What happened to the head after its selection was dramatically attested in 2004 with the discovery of a plastered skull.[34] This is a rare find for Anatolia, constituting one of only two examples, the other found at Köşk Höyük (Figure 4.8: 1).[35] The caching of skulls extends back to the Anatolian Pre-Pottery Neolithic (Çayönu and Nevalı Çori), of course, but the concept of plastering, painting, and modelling skulls is best illustrated in the Levant, where the Jericho Pre-Pottery Neolithic B examples still resonate with vitality.[36] But why were skulls removed and cached? The usual explanation is ancestor worship, and, judging by ethnographic comparisons, there is some truth in this view. That some skulls were plastered also suggests they were displayed. Yet the fact that some skulls of children were treated in this fashion sits uneasily with the notion of an ancestor. What is more, most plastered skulls are abnormally wide and some were probably deliberately deformed when the children were alive. So there seems to be some association between purposeful deformation at birth and the removal of skulls for ritual treatment after death.[37] Taking this one step further, the human skulls may have been honored in this fashion because they were understood as the seat of "life force" whence stemmed fecundity, well-being and vitality.

No discrimination in terms of age or sex has been recognized, with about half of the skeletons uncovered in the current investigations at Çatalhöyük being those of children. Moreover, there appears to have been a reason, as yet unknown, for the burial of infants and neonates near hearths and ovens, normally situated at the southern end of the house. The people of Çatalhöyük were not healthy by modern standards. Analyses of human bones indicate that domesticated plants formed the core of their diet, which was not well balanced. Stunted growth, tooth decay, black lungs, and anaemia were among the maladies suffered. And the frequency of osteoarthritis points to strenuous physical activity.

Figurines form an important component of the ritually constructed spaces at Çatalhöyük. Over 250 figurines and fragments have been documented from Mellaart's excavations, and they can be grouped into three distinct categories:[38]

1 Small clay figures of animals and humans—these are generally expediently produced with pinched features and lightly baked, possibly "passively" fired by their placement near a hearth. They were found in levels IX to IV embedded between bricks and bunched in rubbish pits. Voigt quite correctly puts forward the view that, whatever their symbolic meaning, both human and animal representations must be studied as a group given their uniform treatment and context. Moreover, the similarities they share with distant sites such as Gritille, in southeastern Turkey, lend themselves to the idea of a widespread set of beliefs and practices.

2 Large clay figures—14 of these finely modelled statuettes were found with over half recovered from one building (AII.1) in Level II. The largest and best known figurine from Çatalhöyük is that of an ample woman seated in a chair flanked by two standing cats that form the arms of the chair (Figure 4.9: 3). Their tails extend across the woman's back and over her shoulders. Between the woman's feet is a head with facial features, suggestive of a newborn child.

Originally about 20 cm in height, this figure was found deposited at the bottom of a bin, possibly associated with grain and thus the notion of fecundity. Quite likely it was placed there carefully and deliberately, just as were eight other large figures that found clustered around a hearth in the same structure. Judging by the fine artistry they display (Figure 4.9: 1), their specific context, iconic elements, and, in some case, signs of intentional breakage,[39] we can assume these were cult figures.

3 Stone figures—these can be both realistic and highly schematic, the latter usually a modified pebble or rock (Figure 4.9: 2). They are clustered in Levels VI (especially VIA) and VII, with only four recovered from the later Levels V–II. Some of these stone figures, like their clay counterparts, appear to have been deliberately broken before disposal, perhaps when Level VI was intentionally burned.

The attribution of sex to figurines is usually quite difficult, but it seems that all the clay figures from the earlier excavations at Çatalhöyük represent females, whereas more of the stone figures could be firmly identified as male than females. This observation together with the chronological spread of the figurines suggests that a significant paradigm shift occurred between levels VI and V, corresponding to the change in settlement plan noted earlier. Religious practice in the early settlement at Çatalhöyük involved stone figures, a good number male, which have stylistic connections with art produced at the pre-pottery sites of the southeast. During later periods at Çatalhöyük, the female representations, often steatopygous, emphasizing buttocks, pregnancy, and ample bodies became more prominent. Whereas these female figures may have been deities, although there is less talk of "mother and fertility goddesses" in recent years, one could equally argue that their purpose was to emphasize femaleness and sexuality. If this were the case, the change in imagery may point to a change in gender relations.

The sophistication of Çatalhöyük can easily overshadow the existence of contemporary mobile communities that were still part of the landscape. A seventh millennium BC rock shelter at Pınarbaşı is one such site. A series of ovens and irregular fire pits, later filled with bones and stone, provide a glimpse of food preparation and consumption.[40] Erbaba, by the same token, was fully agrarian.[41] Although the stratigraphic sequence, I–III in descending order, is problematic and difficult to verify without further investigations, wide exposures confirm the central Anatolian type of a cluster of tightly packed rectangular buildings. The main difference is the use of stone for building walls, preserved up to 1.57 m at one point. Slabs of limestone were superimposed and stabilized with mud mortar. The floors of the rooms were substantially sunken—in some cases 40 cm below the surface of the mound. Many rooms were not fully excavated, making a contextual analysis quite difficult. But ovens, clay benches, and painted features were noted. One building, in Area D, had 10 layers of occupation and only in the latest deposit was a doorway constructed; prior to that it seems entry was through the roof.[42]

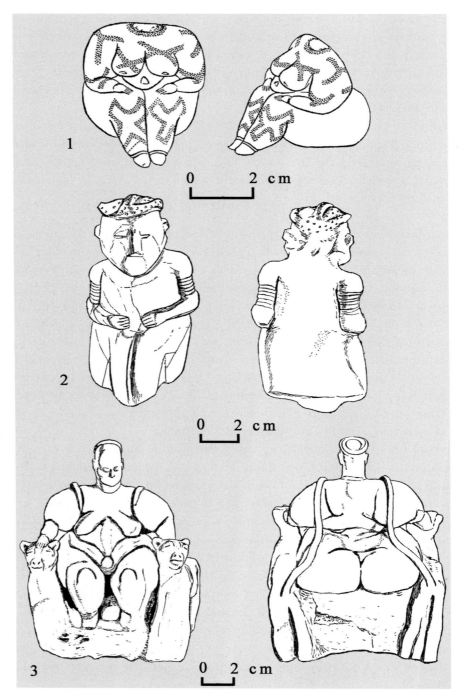

Figure 4.9 Two types of Çatalhöyük figurine: **1, 3** Large clay figurines. **2** Stone figure (adapted from Mellaart 1963)

Western Anatolia and the Aegean coast

While farmers were establishing themselves in the Konya Plain, other groups had reached the Lake District where they founded settlements like Hacılar, Kuruçay, Höyücek, and Bademağacı.[43] Here the display of symbolism is much more subdued than in the Konya Plain. There are no wall paintings or relief sculpture, and cult activities may well have focused on well-crafted objects and figurines.

An impressive fortification wall with a pair of semi-circular towers, exposed along a 26 m segment, surrounded the Neolithic village at Kuruçay.[44] More coherent plans, however, are found at Höyücek where two large rectangular rooms were built with a combination of rectangular (lower wall) and plano-convex (upper wall) mud bricks. The rooms were separated by a pair of smaller storage areas, well furnished with cupboards, bins, and clay benches, and together formed a religious complex and designated the "Shrine Phase" (Figure 4.10).[45] Particularly suggestive of a cult function is a large marble basin, filled with pottery vessels, and associated smaller marble containers placed near a staircase of solid clay that no doubt led to an upper story. A pit with thousands of flint blades and a scatter of deer antlers and jaw bones add to the symbolic connotations of the room. After a gap in occupation, Höyücek was reoccupied in the Late Neolithic (ca. 6450–6100 BC), when the inhabitants built five unconnected and parallel stretches of wall. Their purpose is unclear, but concentrations of ample-bodied female figurines, one on a plaster bench, schematized figurines, stone tools, and various ceramic containers, according to the excavators, warrant the term "Sanctuaries Phase."

Female figurines have been found in considerable numbers at Kuruçay and Höyücek (Figure 4.11: 8–9).[46] The Kuruçay examples are generally upright, with arms hanging at their sides or folded across their breasts. Their heads are long and thin with hair shown either braided down the back of the neck or pulled back in a bun. In some cases, the feet are incised to portray toes. Figurines from the Sanctuaries Phase at Höyücek show a greater variety of positions, including seated and cross-legged. Heads are pegged, sometimes with a piece of bone. One figurine bears traces of white paint, whereas others are decorated with impressed dots or incised with lines to indicate clothing and jewellery, or the pubic region. While some figurines are fulsome, others are rather schematic and "sack shaped"—rectangular bodied with stubby arms.

Bademağacı presents something quite different—freestanding mud brick houses supported by wooden beams and posts were separated by alleyways and courtyards (Figure 4.12).[47] Each unit was equipped with a round oven, storage facilities, a portable hearth, and grinding stones. This settlement concept did not come from the Konya Plain, with painted red floors comprising the only connection.

The Late Neolithic settlement at Hacılar is roughly contemporary with the end of the Çatalhöyük sequence. Houses had mud walls built of plano-convex bricks, 50 cm², set on stone foundations, and were arranged neatly in blocks.[48] Timber was also liberally used. Twelve houses were uncovered, each with a main room and a kitchen area to the side constructed of wattle and daub, some measuring as much as 10 × 4 m. Residents no longer entered their

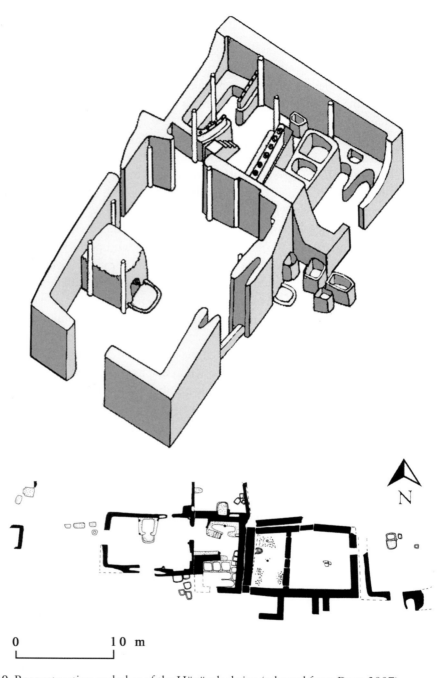

0   10 m

Figure 4.10 Reconstruction and plan of the Höyücek shrine (adapted from Duru 2007)

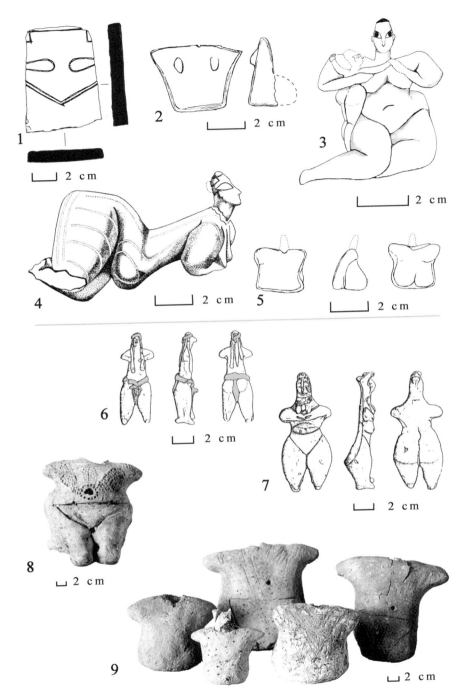

Figure 4.11 Figurines from western Anatolia: Hacılar: **1** Stone plaque. **2** Figurine. **3, 4** Statuettes. **5** Schematic figurine (adapted from Mellaart 1970a). **6, 7** Ulucak (adapted from Çilingiroğlu et al. 2004). **8, 9** Höyücek (Photos: courtesy Refik Duru)

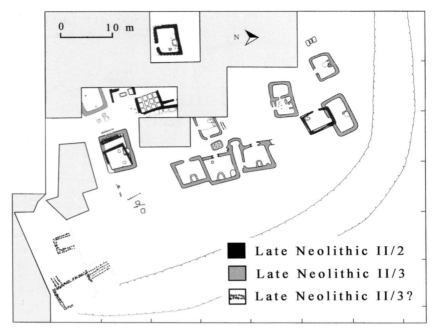

Figure 4.12 Plan of Late Neolithic Bademağcı, Level II (adapted from Duru 2007)

homes through the roof. Instead, they used a double door of wood located on the long wall facing the courtyard and laneways. Kitchens were sometimes located on either side of the entrance, on the exterior, and screened by partitions of brushwood and plaster. Opposite the entrance was a square oven with a hearth defined by a kerb and fixed against the back wall. Other fixtures included cupboards and rectangular clay boxes to collect embers. But the Hacılar houses had no benches along the base of the walls such as those at Çatalhöyük and Can Hasan. Residents at Hacılar also had little taste for red painted floors, and they preferred to bury their dead outside the settlement in a cemetery. Superimposed levels of debris and two stout postholes suggest that the main rooms probably supported an upper story built of a light material, which was accessed from the courtyard and up a flight of mud brick steps. Judging by the size of the main rooms, their uniformity, and the domestic nature of the equipment, including grindstones, it is clear that these buildings were houses for a nuclear family of about five people.[49] The walls of a Hacılar house were well plastered, but plain, suggesting that textiles perhaps provided both color and texture. A discrete cemetery, regrettably never systematically excavated, also distinguished Late Neolithic Hacılar.[50] Gifts included pottery vessels, initially, and possibly statuettes and anthropomorphic containers later on.

The tradition of female figurines with exaggerated features continues at Late Neolithic Hacılar, where no male or animal figurines are represented. They were found mostly in the upper story of the three houses in Trench Q, where grain was dried. Level VI yielded most of the 76 figurines, which Mellaart classified into four types: Statuettes, figurines, schematic figurines, and stone slabs with incised features (Figure 4.11: 1–5).[51] Of these the statuettes were finely crafted (hence the distinction from "figurines") from red or buff clay; black paint is often used to depict details. The statuettes varied in size from 24 cm to 7 cm, and displayed considerable diversity in posture and detail. Women are shown in a variety of poses—reclining, seated, enthroned (with animals), and standing—and are represented nude or wearing a skirt. Heads were made separately and attached to the body; cruder figurines probably had a wooden peg head. Attention is paid to hairstyles on the statuettes: Hair is shown either pulled up in a bun on top of their head, or hanging down the back as a pigtail.

In a reinterpretation of their context and function, Voigt suggests that these statuettes served as teaching devices or initiation figures.[52] Her view is based on their diversity of shapes that lend themselves to be handled rather than displayed, as they would have been if cult objects. Indeed, it appears that the Hacılar statuettes reflect the different stages of a woman's life and their sexuality, sometimes quite explicitly.[53] Here at Hacılar, as at Çatalhöyük the emphasis is on femaleness that may suggest a change in gender roles, or at least recognition of the crucial role played by women in an agricultural village.

A site with considerable potential is Ulucak Höyük, close to Izmir and the Aegean coast, where excavations are uncovering a substantial Late Neolithic village with connection to both the Lake District and Thrace (Figure 4.13).[54] Radiocarbon determinations suggest that the earliest occupation so far reached (Levels Va and IV) stretched from the very end of the seventh millennium BC to the first half of the sixth. The excavators prefer to call these levels Late Neolithic, as opposed to Early Chalcolithic, because they cannot detect any major stratigraphic change. Not even painted wares, generally held as the hallmark of the Early Chalcolithic, can be used to differentiate. A rambling wattle and daub building of at least five rooms, with one room approximating a rough square (ca. 4.7 × 4.5 m), distinguishes the earliest level. This plan is rather unusual for post framework constructions, which are usually freestanding and single. Pottery vessels, stone tools, and loom weights, and the large number of sling missiles, in excess of 200, are suggestive of a workshop. Lying above this deposit is a mud brick village with a plan—an agglomeration of closely packed houses—that shows clear connections with the plateau. When areas needed to be expanded the *pisé* technique was also used, although the level of workmanship is generally inferior. Nonetheless, three modes of building—wattle and daub, mud brick, and *pisé*—were used to build the Neolithic settlement at Ulucak. Figurines with generous thighs—one is a male with loincloth, long hair, and a headband (Figure 4.11: 6–7)—and associated hearths provide a glimpse of domestic ritual.

Northwest Anatolia

Towards the mid-seventh millennium BC, farming communities settled in the northwest of Anatolia around the Marmara Sea, the last destination before agriculture spread to southeast

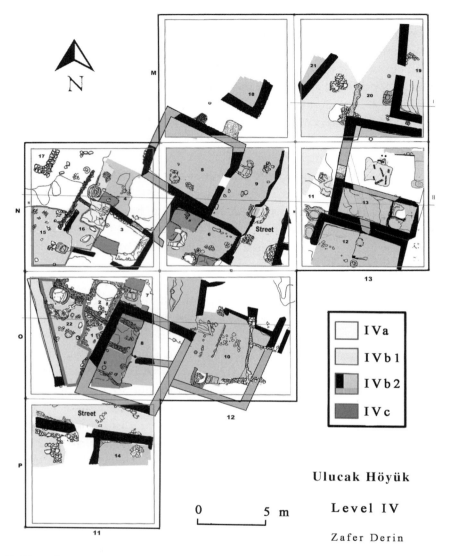

☐		I V a
▨		I V b 1
◼		I V b 2
▦		I V c

Ulucak Höyük

0   5 m

Level IV

Zafer Derin

Figure 4.13 Plan of Late Neolithic Ulucak Höyük, Level IV (adapted from Çilingiroğlu et al. 2004)

Europe. It did not take long and the region soon became a frontier zone, funneling influences from the Balkans and the Anatolian plateau.[55] In the Early Pottery Neolithic this intermingling is more pronounced in architecture and lithic industries than in pottery. At Pendik and nearby Fikirtepe, the settlement consisted of small, circular or oval huts built of wattle and mud plaster.[56] Their floors were sunken below the level of the ground.

The Late Neolithic is better known, largely through excavations at Hoca Çeşme (Phases IV and III), Yarımburgaz (a cave 30 km northwest of Istanbul), Aşağı Pınar, and the inland site of

Ilıpınar. Strong connections with the heartland of the Balkans can been seen in the design and construction of the earliest village at Hoca Çeşme.[57] Substantial circular houses were built from thick posts driven into bedrock, and surrounded by a stone wall over a metre thick. A series of regularly placed postholes suggest that a wooden palisade defined its inner face. This mode of planning continued until Phase II, when residents changed the plan and built rectangular houses similar to those at Karanovo I in Bulgaria. The walls are thin and constructed of mud slabs reinforced by a framework of posts. Inside, they were furnished with domed ovens, bins, and clay platforms.

Methodical excavations at Ilıpınar and Aşağı Pınar are providing a wealth of information. Three construction methods are represented at Ilıpınar.[58] Two types occur simultaneously in phases X–VII (6000–5700 BC) and are especially apparent in a large exposure—the "Big Square" (W 12/13 and X12/13). One made extensive use of timber and is distinguished by a series of aligned postholes that supported earthen walls, whereas the other structures had walls built of mud slab, actually slabs cut from natural clay deposits. The third mode of construction, using mud bricks, comes into vogue in Ilıpınar VI (5700–5500 BC), the Early Chalcolithic.

The original Ilıpınar village, perhaps no more than 10 to 15 freestanding, post wall houses (Figure 4.14), was arranged in a radial fashion around a spring. By the end of its lifespan 300 years later, the settlement comprised about 30 dwellings each with its own exterior space, such as shared courts and pathways. Later houses were rebuilt in line with the floor plans of earlier ones, suggesting the existence of family plots of land. Carefully aligned rows of posts were driven up to 50 cm into the earth and, in some cases, latched together using rope. The gaps between the posts were then filled with beaten earth (pisé); no evidence of a wattle and daub technique was recovered. Central posts supported ridge beams of the roof that was most likely gabled and reed covered, as they were in parts of the Balkans and beyond. Covering an area about 30 m², these houses probably constituted space for a nuclear family. Internal features were rarely preserved. The exception is the burnt house from phase X.[59] On entering the house, the visitor would have noticed a central hearth (but no oven as such), and in the corner opposite the entrance were storage bins and food-processing tools such as grindstones and obsidian blades. Along a side wall was a platform that presumably elevated a grinding slab, making the task of preparing food less back breaking. The floor was beaten mud, although neighboring houses had wooden floor boards. Lying on the floor was a large horned animal figurine, and stone and bone beads. What makes this post house settlement so interesting is that despite its overtly Balkan character, its material culture, especially its ceramic assemblage, reflects an Anatolian lineage. Similar houses are emerging from Aşağı Pınar (Figure 4.15).[60] Mortuary rites associated with this post house settlement at Ilıpınar are quite different to those on the plateau. The dead, mostly children, were laid to rest in the foetal position in simple earthen pits behind the house, in a roughly circumscribed area that can be called a burial ground; the skeleton of an adult found on a wooden board is an exception.[61] Osteoarthritis and anaemia were among the maladies, while grooves detected on the front teeth of females were probably formed through weaving and basket making.

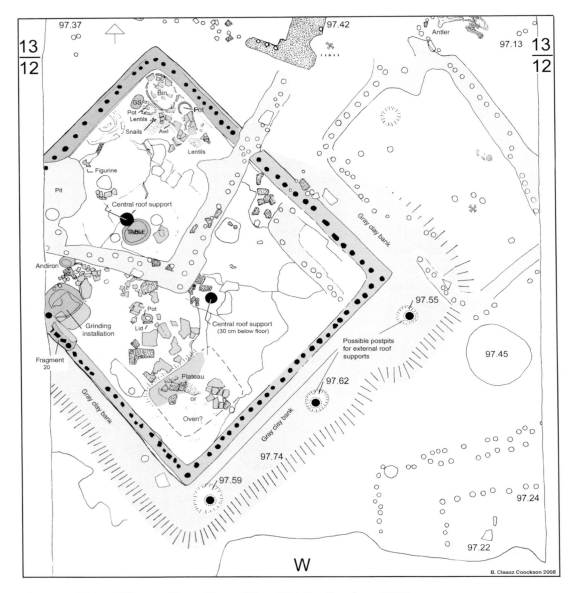

Figure 4.14 Plan of Ilıpınar "Burnt House," Level X (after Coockson 2008)

Judging by the size and layout of the mud slab structures at Ilıpınar, they too appear to have been freestanding houses. Rectangular in shape, their walls constructed of large mud slabs (clay) were founded on wooden boards that extended across the entire floor area of the dwellings. Similar mud slab structures were recovered at Menteşe, in the Yenişehir basin, where evidence of genuine wattle and daub structures is also attested.[62]

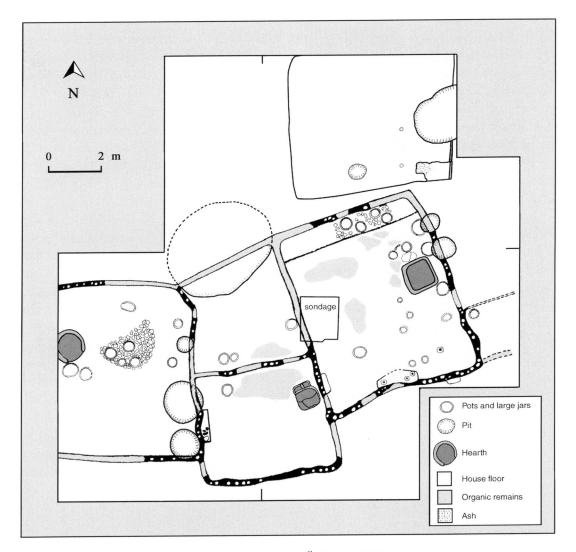

Figure 4.15 Plan of Aşağı Pınar Level VI (adapted from Özdoğan 2007)

Seeing red

Even though meanings escape us, we have seen that through the use of imagery and material culture Neolithic societies constructed and used complex symbolic systems. This unique ability to link a concept with a symbol, whether material or abstract such as language, is, par excellence, the hallmark of *Homo sapiens*. One of the most potent carriers of symbolic meaning is color. Yet despite the extensive ethnographic evidence for color symbolism among contemporary societies, this topic has received relatively little exposure in archaeology, and even less in

Anatolia.[63] Following Victor Turner's commentary of the ritual ceremonies of the Ndembu of Zambia, many researchers support the idea that white, black, and red form a basic color triad, which carried similar meanings across many societies.[64] This view is strengthened by linguistic and perception studies, which have revealed a series of complex biological, social, neurophysiological, and psychological factors involved in both the naming of color and its perception.[65] It is now generally maintained that in most languages, color terminology is based on a seven-stage evolutionary sequence.[66] The basic color terms are "white" and "black," the monochromatic colors, which are followed by red. This process of naming is, in turn, connected with the complex physics and physiology of human vision, which is trichromatic like that of certain primates.[67] Of all colors, red is the most salient primary color the visual system can perceive, subjectively advancing closer to the observer than any other equidistantly placed color.

Given the prominence of red in the Neolithic, it is the social context of *redness* that is so intriguing. Here we will restrict ourselves to the cultural significance of the color red, and ochre, its most common material referent, and briefly survey the available evidence for prehistoric Anatolia. Ochre is an earthy iron ore whose color is determined by the quantity of iron oxide. The higher the amount, the redder the ochre, like haematite; by heating yellow ochre (limonite, goethite), its color can be changed to red. Impurities such as cinnabar and clay can also affect the color and texture of ochre. These elements need to be considered because, judging by recorded instances of ochre procurement in the recent past, expeditions sometimes travelled through hostile territories and endured many privations to mine "proper" ochre, even though other sources were readily available.[68] The archaeological record is replete with examples of ochre usage. They are found across five continents and extend back to the Middle Palaeolithic, with the evidence from Qafzeh Cave, in Israel, being the most thoroughly examined.[69] To judge by ochre's multifarious uses in contemporary cultures such as body adornment, ritual cleansing, and medicinal purposes, we only have a portion of the prehistoric picture. Even so, what has survived provides ample testimony on two primary uses of ochre. It was (and still is) the dominant pigment used to decorate caves and rock shelters, and, since the time of Neanderthals, who signalled a new awareness of self-existence by burying their dead, there is persistent and extensive evidence for red ochre's symbolic role in mortuary practice. This took the form of sprinkling ochre, occasionally profusely, over the deceased, or placing pieces of ochre around the body.[70] Ochre was used well before rock art and burials. At the lower Palaeolithic site of Terra Amata, in France, 60 pieces of ochre, some with abraded edges ("crayons"), were scattered among the debris of a camp, and probably used to color objects, skins, or the inhabitants themselves.

The desire of humans to decorate their bodies in any number of ways, from body art through hairstyles to clothes, enables messages to be transmitted that are understood by members within that society. Ethnography enlightens us on the magical properties of red, and its role and primacy in body art.[71] When people decorate their bodies they do so for one or more purposes— social, ritual, physical/sexual, practical, and pleasure.[72] In ritual contexts such as rites of passage and ceremonies, red is often accorded profound significance. It is, above all, symbolic of blood and signifies life, but its association with hunting and war also means it can stand for aggression or good fortune. Red is also seen as being endowed with beneficent properties and accordingly is rubbed on the ill to promote health and vigor, or on those who have overcome an ordeal. At special ceremonies such as the birth of a child or marriage, red is used liberally, and is seen as the color of celebration and goodwill. Daubing specific body parts (such as ears and eyes) in red can also enhance the functionality of those parts. Finally, in ritual circumstances red is also linked with cosmology and often used in shamanistic rituals as a means of protection. In social contexts, a well-decorated body that is both colorful and shiny is often seen as a prerequisite of high status. In highland New Guinea, for instance, an individual's chances of becoming the "big man" are determined by the elaborateness and variety of his body decoration, the size of his gifts, and the nature of the entertainment. Coloring hair red and decorating erogenous parts of the body are two of many methods of sexual allurements, especially among young men and women who flaunt sexuality, prowess, strength, and beauty.

In Neolithic Anatolia, we have seen that ochre was primarily used in mortuary rites and to paint walls and floors of houses. Taking a cue from the above review, it would seem that sprinkling a corpse with ochre overcame the pallor of death and "infused" the deceased with life and blood. Likewise, we should not assume that walls were painted primarily in red simply because ochre was ubiquitous. Instead, the color red should be also appreciated for its symbolic and social significance. As a color that expresses vigor, vitality, and fecundity, and heightens sensory perception, red should be seen as part of the package of paraphernalia that was embodied within the ritually constructed spaces of many Neolithic buildings.

Invention of pottery

Across the Near East, clay was utilized for a number of purposes in the Pre-Pottery Neolithic—to coat floors, to construct house fixtures such as hearths, ovens and storage facilities, and to craft a variety of objects like figurines and geometric shapes (spheres, cones, and discs among them).[73] Even so, it is the invention of portable pottery containers that defines the exploitation of clay as a resource. In Anatolia, this happened around 7000 BC and its occurrence has been conventionally used in archaeology to separate pottery-using communities from their forebears who did not create clay vessels.[74] People have used receptacles for storing and carrying food and water since earliest prehistoric times. Ethnographic observations and scraps of evidence from archaeological contexts suggest that reeds, twine, gourds, wood, animal skins, and other organic substances were used (Figure 4.16: 1).[75] These materials had the advantage of being light in weight and economical. But with permanent settlements came the gradually increasing need for durable storage facilities. Pits dug into the ground and occasionally plaster lined for cleanliness were suitable, but, of course, not portable. This necessity for sturdy everyday containers combined with the characteristics of clay—its plasticity that allowed the artisan to produce myriad shapes and its durability when baked—prompted the creation of terracotta vessels.

Ceramic artefacts hardened from fired clay together with stone tools and ornaments are the

Figure 4.16 1 This carbonized oval wooden container and lid from Çatalhöyük burial in E VI, 10 reminds us that containers manufactured from perishable materials were also used in addition to pottery (Photo: courtesy the British Institute at Ankara). **2** A Dölek potter burnishes leather hard vessels before firing them (Photo: Antonio Sagona). **3** Building vessels by hand. At Dölek, pottery manufacture is a household activity and skills are passed from mother to daughter (Photo: Antonio Sagona)

most durable objects manufactured in prehistory (Figure 4.16: 2–3). Yet despite their toughness ceramic vessels generally have a short lifespan because they are prone to breakage and wear. These characteristics plus clay's ubiquity have made pottery a primary source in archaeology. Stylistic analysis, by far the most common form of investigation in Anatolian archaeology, looms large in chronological studies. In addition, pottery can provide useful information on formal and functional aspects of ancient societies, such as manufacturing technology and firing techniques. It can convey meaningful information about social behavior such as cooking habits, commensality, and also the scheduling of activities—potting was most likely a seasonal pursuit.[76] Yet others have argued that the shape, surface treatment and ornamentations of pottery containers have symbolic connotations that can be decoded.[77] These aspects are mentioned in passing because they have been hardly pursued in Anatolia and offer enormous scope for future research.

The earliest stage of pottery manufacture in Anatolia was not uniform, a pattern not inconsistent with the rest of the Near East. Evidence from Çatalhöyük, Mezraa-Teleilat, and Yümüktepe (Mersin) shows that it took a while for the usefulness of this fledgling technology to be embraced fully. Pottery from Neolithic Anatolia can be grouped into two broad categories that, bearing in mind time lags, roughly define the Early and Late ceramic Neolithic: (a) Dark coloured wares stretch from the southeastern regions, where they are known as Dark-Faced Burnished Ware (DFBW), to the shores of the Marmara Sea and beyond, into Bulgaria, where the monochrome repertoire may be considered distinct echoes. These wares are quite coarse and are often associated with the first wave of settlers, with the more distinct assemblages in the north representing the final stages of the movement; (b) red-slipped wares with a highly burnished surface and a finer paste are found concentrated in western Anatolia. Sometimes decorated with white painted designs, which increase in the Early Chalcolithic period, these red wares are generally ascribed to a later part of the ceramic Neolithic.

The fabrics of these two broad groups (dark and red wares) probably point to different cooking practices between the initial wave of settlers and those who followed.[78] There are many regional variations on these two themes, especially with regard to decoration, and what follows is a brief overview of main types drawn from a number of key sites.

Cilicia and the southeast

The Syro-Cilician region is dominated by Dark-Faced Burnished Ware, which characterizes the deposit at Tell el-Judeideh (Amuq A and B), the lower Neolithic levels at Mersin (XXXII–XXVII) and Mezraa-Teleilat IIIA, extending down the Syrian coast to Ras Shamra VB–VA and beyond to Byblos.[79] Shapes are simple and open—round and shallow bowls, hole-mouth pots and wide-bellied jars, sometimes with ledge handles, are the most common (Figure 4.17). Their well-burnished surface usually extended partly inside the vessel, and is sometimes impressed or incised with rows of neat dots, short curved lines (executed with the thumbnail or the edge of a

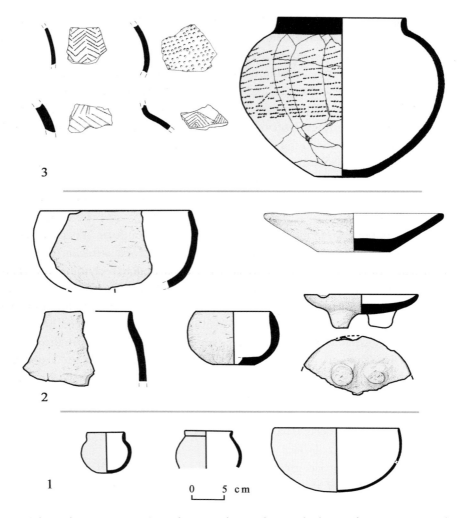

Figure 4.17 The earliest pottery in Anatolia: **1** Dark-Faced Burnished Ware from Amuq A and B. **2** Coarse Mezraa-Teleilat IIC ware. **3** Impressed pottery from Mezraa-Teleilat IIB (adapted from Braidwood and Braidwood 1960; Özdoğan 2007)

shell), and bolder notches produced with the end of stick or bone. At Mezraa-Teleilat, a substantially different local product that is coarse in fabric follows this style. Later still, in Level IIB, vessels are ornamented with distinctive impressed patterns.

Central Anatolia

Although Mellaart suggested that pottery was found throughout Çatalhöyük, beginning in Level XII, current investigations appear to show that it started a little later, in Level XI, and continued to be fairly rare up through to Level VIII.[80] The significant quantity of baskets and wooden containers found in association with the ceramics suggest that foodstuffs were most likely carried and stored in organic containers, which may even have been used to "cook" food. Heated clay balls, found in large numbers in these earliest levels, could have effectively roasted grain held in organic containers. The earliest pottery from Çatalhöyük is handmade with thick walls built with coils or slabs of clay. Many vessels are mottled with dark patches from being fired at low temperatures in an uncontrolled open kiln. Hole-mouth jars, sometimes bearing knob handles, and oval bowls are common. After Level VI, vessels were fired to a range of dark colors and potters switched from chaff to grit inclusions, which have thermal qualities more suitable for cooking and may point to changes in kitchen practices. Although the same basic forms continued, vessels are now better manufactured with thinner walls and a higher polished surface. Later, mottled wares again become more common and new shapes emerged. Despite the exuberance of the painted rooms at Çatalhöyük, and the high level of skill displayed by other crafts, Neolithic pottery was not seen as medium that required much attention.

Dark burnished vessels from Kösk Höyük III are particularly striking for their relief decoration.[81] One jar is anthropoid—facial features, including coffee bean-shaped eyes, are applied to the narrow neck, and a pair of arms and female breast that are placed on the upper body. Another portrays three figures, apparently dancing, whereas yet another jar is decorated with a stag's head, with its impressive 12 point antlers painted white to contrast with the dark surface. Late Neolithic red-slipped jars, cups, and bowls with flaring sides are well represented at Musular, Kösk Höyük and from material collected from the surface at a number of sites.[82]

Western Anatolia

The change in ceramic traditions from dark colored wares to red-slipped ones is well represented in the Lake District. It is apparent at Bademağacı and Höyücek, which also foreshadows the white-on-red painted horizon in its uppermost levels (Figure 4.18).[83] Whereas Refik Duru prefers to place this shift at about 7000 BC or earlier, Schoop has argued for a later date around 6500 BC.[84] Open, simple shapes are the norm among the red-slipped horizon, with some bearing vertically pierced cylindrical lugs and basket handles. Although there are a few links between the Early Settlements Phase at Höyücek and Çatalhöyük VI–V, on the whole, connections between the Lake District and the Konya Plain are not strong.

From the beginning of Hacılar's ceramic phase, its potters produced fine wares. Initially pale coloured, they changed to red and brown slipped by levels VII and VI, which were distinguished by a high burnish.[85] Decoration was not so common. Some pieces had applied ornamentation in the form of animal shapes and human heads, others, more rare still, were painted with red on cream linear or curvilinear patterns (Figure 4.18: 9). More characteristic was applied ornamentation. In the Elmalı Plain further south, the Late Neolithic period is represented only by surface

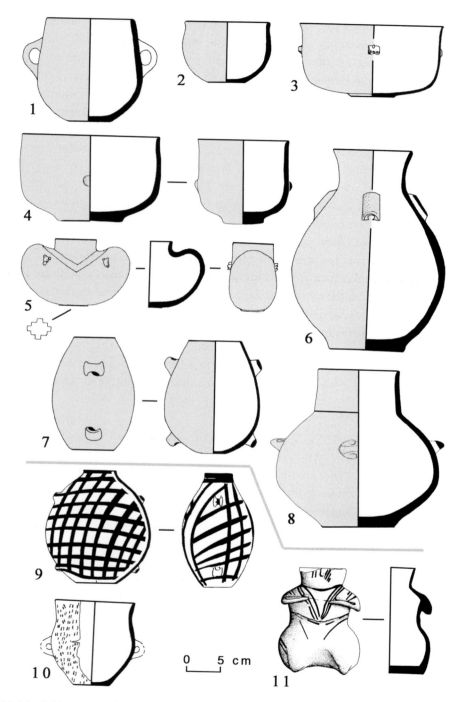

Figure 4.18 Neolithic pottery from western Anatolia: **1** Dark-faced ware, Höyücek. **2** Pale-faced ware, Höyücek. **3–8** Red slipped ware from Hacılar VI (3, 7), Höyücek (5, 6) and Ulucak IV (4, 8). **9, 11** Red-on-white painted ware from Hacılar VI (9) and Ulucak IV (11). **10** Impressed ware, Höyücek (adapted from Çilingiroğlu et al. 2004; Duru and Umurtak 2005; Mellaart 1970a)

survey sherds collected at a few sites, notably Akçay Höyük, Gökpinar and Tekke where fabric, shape and features such as tubular lugs connect them with Hacılar IX–VII.[86]

A parallel sequence is emerging at Ulucak, where brown wares are gradually superseded in quantity by red-slipped pottery.[87] A small number of cream-coloured sherds in the lowest levels also demonstrate links with the Konya Plain, but the absence of painted pottery at Ulucak and the occurrence of impressed wares, an Aegean feature, highlight regional differences with Lake District sites (Figure 4.18: 10).

Northwest Anatolia

In the northwest, pottery assumes primacy in defining cultural sequences. Özdoğan attributes the earliest group of ceramics to Fikirtepe, a site near Istanbul, which has an inventory distinguished by its dark burnished and incised ceramics (Figure 4.19).[88] The stratigraphical position of this assemblage below Yarımburgaz Layer 4 type pottery at both Ilıpınar and Demircihöyük, both well dated by radiocarbon analysis, indicates that the Fikirtepe culture, as it has come to be known, spanned some six centuries from 6200 to 6700 BC. At Fikirtepe itself Early (Archaic) and Late (Classical) phases of pottery have been discerned.

The early assemblage, found also at the nearby site of Pendik, comprises vessels with a gritty paste and a dark well-burnished surface, occasionally tending towards pale reddish-brown; at Ilıpınar X they tend to be chaff tempered. Shapes are redolent of other areas—mostly hole-mouth jars, straight-sided bowls and pots with ledge handles or lugs that are sometimes perforated. Ornamentation is rare and generally incised, and patterns are geometric such as rows of hatched triangles. It seems that the nature of decoration was village specific.

In the Late Phase, pottery is fired red, and a new ware distinguished by a lustrous black burnished surface makes its appearance. Grit is the preferred temper and added in reasonable quantity. Hole-mouth jars lose favor to bowls and pots with an S-profile. Incised decoration and rectangular vessels gain in popularity. Finger and nail impressions begin to appear especially on Ilıpınar IX and Menteşe vessels; grooves also make a fleeting appearance. The material from Yarımburgaz Layer 5, the earliest level at that site, and Hoca Çeşme IV are sometimes seen as transitional between Archaic and Classic Fıkırtepe.[89]

Fıkırtepe pottery has been found throughout the areas fringing the southern shore of the Sea of Marmara down to the Eskişehir-Kütahya region.[90] Aşağı Pınar, in Thrace, is one of the northernmost sites, but evidence in the surrounding region is more sporadic, owing to a scarcity of investigation. Over the modern political border, in Bulgaria, it is well represented by what is called the "monochrome phase" at such sites as Koprivets and Krainitsi.[91] The earliest levels at Hoca Çeşme, IV and III are coterminus with the Fikirtepe material (Figure 4.20).[92] Tubular lugs and applied ornaments, including animal and human motifs, show strong connections with the Lake District in the southwest and attest to Anatolian roots of the early Hoca Çeşme tradition; they are also at home in Thessaly but do not belong to the Aegean or to the

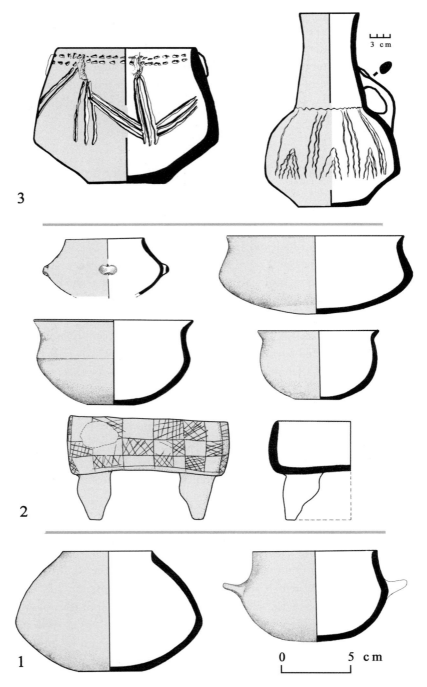

Figure 4.19 Neolithic pottery from northwest Anatolia: **1** Early Fikirtepe phase. **2** Late Fikirtepe phase. **3** Developed Fikirtepe (or Yarımburgaz 4) phase (adapted from Özdoğan 1999b; Özdoğan et al. 1991)

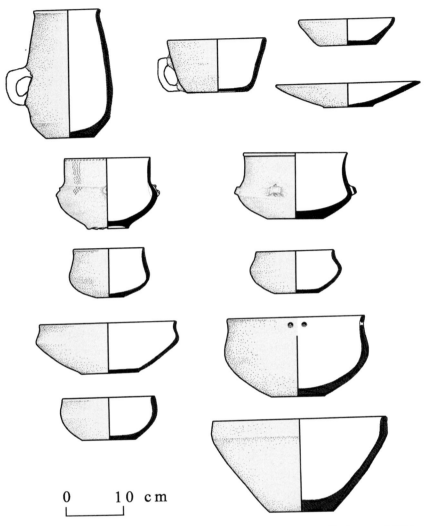

Figure 4.20 Pottery from Hoca Çeşme, northwest Anatolia (adapted from Özdoğan 1999b)

Balkans. Pottery remains basically the same in Hoca Çeşme III, with some fine vessels displaying geometric motifs, although we now see the appearance of coarse wares that are found at proto-Sesklo assemblages in Greece, but not at Karanovo. Therefore, Hoca Çeşme III is earlier than the Karanovo sequence.

Other crafts and technology

The large amount of sophisticated artefacts manufactured from a range of exotic raw materials is testimony to both to the skills of the craftspeople and to the extent of their procurement networks.[93] While the nature of the exchange system remains uncertain—we do not know, for instance, whether the export of manufactured goods supplemented the subsistence economy—it is clear is that it involved long distances and was effective. At Çatalhöyük, for instance, the furthest point of contact, the Red Sea, some 1000 km to the south, provided cowrie shells that were set into the eye sockets of the dead before burial, recalling the plastered skulls from Jericho. Dentalium and cockle shells were closer at hand—they were gathered from the Mediterranean along the south coast of Anatolia. And date palm phytoliths may suggest the use of carrying baskets manufactured in Syria, Mesopotamia, or the Levant. Raw copper ore was most likely mined from the Ergani mine in southeastern Anatolia, about 500 km away, whereas the lead was mined at the Cilician Gates to the east. Copper was fashioned into various items, including beads, pendants, tubes, and rings. The production of copper beads was simple. Native copper was hammered into sheets, cut into strips, and rolled into beads. Galena and cerussite, lead minerals, were also used to make beads.[94] A comparable level of copper production, albeit on a smaller scale, is evident at Mersin, Hacılar, and in the Amuq Plain.[95] Pale coloured tabular flint, rare though it was, came from further east still, in Syria. Obsidian, as we have seen, is a central Anatolian commodity in plentiful supply, and the Çatalhöyük samples derive from Cappadocian sources of Göllüdağ and Nenezi Dağ some 250 km to the north, not Hasan Dağ as was originally thought. Local materials included ochre, azurite, and white marble and basalt, which were worked into mortars and pestles. Even the transport of timber from the surrounding mountains would have required considerable organization given the quantity used in building construction.

On the whole, Late Neolithic sites of Anatolia did not produce sophisticated stone tools. This stands in sharp contrast to Pre-Pottery Neolithic cultures.[96] In the seventh millennium BC, stone tools are limited typologically and reflect a more restricted technology of production. Bullet cores and microlithic features are absent. Instead, the basic tool type is the large blade. Projectile points are also distinct types, but only during the first half of the early Pottery Neolithic, up to the appearance of red-slipped ceramics of the Late Neolithic, when they disappear from the greater part of Anatolia to replace sling stones as the weapon of choice. Çatalhöyük, however, is somewhat of an exception. Up to seven stone industries have been identified at Çatalhöyük, ranging from expedient flakes to superbly crafted blades. As for figurines and pottery, the obsidian artefacts show changes in typology and production before and after Çatalhöyük VI. From Level V onwards the industry is characterized by pressure flaking, prismatic cores, and blades that may indicate a more intensive exploitation of domestic foods.[97] Concentration of tools in certain rooms, and caches of quarry blanks that were buried near the hearth and accessed when tools needed to be knapped, reflect a specialized industry. Among the most famous obsidian objects from Çatalhöyük were polished mirrors that were valued enough to be placed in burials as a gift. It is entirely possible that like red ochre, black obsidian was considered a highly symbolic material imbued with magical properties. The Hacılar chipped stone industry is poor and characterized by flint (never obsidian) blades and sickle blades, although some microliths were found clustered in Level VI.[98] There is ample evidence of ground stone objects—querns and mortars, pounders, and highly polished greenstone axes. In the Marmara region, stone tool industries, like architecture, show that the coastal and inland sites represent contrasting traditions. The microliths, bullet cores and scrapers at Fikirtepe and Pendik reflect the continuation of the rich Epipalaeolithic technology known as the Ağaclı tradition. Ilıpınar, by way of contrast, shares with central Anatolia the lack of any formal tool types.[99]

Nearly 50 clay stamp seals were found at Çatalhöyük, complementing a few more from other sites in the southwest; smaller and less detailed versions are found in the northwest (Figure 4.21: 1–10). These Neolithic stamp seals from Anatolia are generally large compared to Late Chalcolithic examples that were used to impress lumps of clay as a means of maintaining control over the storage and distribution of commodities. No clay sealings (discarded impressed lumps of clay) have been found at Çatalhöyük, suggesting that these stamps seals had other functions such as body or textile decoration. But like later seals, these early versions appear to have had an emblematic status and often accompanied their owners to their graves. Most seals have a geometric pattern, but two recent examples are noteworthy:[100] A fragment portraying the spotted body of leopard, and a bear shown spreadeagle (Figure 4.7: 4), both recalling wall decorations.

Rich and varied assemblages of bone artefacts have been unearthed at a number of sites (Figure 4.21: 11–18). Sharp and round points, burnishers, gouges, hook and eye fasteners, pendants, and beads are among the many forms manufactured, primarily indoors, from a wide range of animal taxa. Spindle whorls point to clothes that were manufactured from woven textiles rather than animal skins and held together with bone toggles and belt hooks. Spatulae with decorated handles were also finely produced from bone and are sometimes ornamented with animal heads. Among the distinctive equipment of the Fikirtepe culture are bone spoons with grooved or twisted handles that come in a variety of shapes and sizes, and bone polishers. Bone spoons are rare in the rest of Anatolia, where they may have been carved from wood, but are a common feature in the southeastern European Neolithic and its white-on-red painted wares, after which they peter out. They are also noteworthy at Ilıpınar where there is evidence of a thriving bone and antler industry among the post structures, but not the mud brick village. Given their elaborateness, spoons might have been a type of status symbol in Thrace and southeastern Europe.

Economy

Çatalhöyük had a fully fledged agricultural economy. Among the crops, domestic wheat (emmer and bread wheat) that is not native to the region was important.[101] In addition, farmers cultivated einkorn wheat and barley, bitter vetch and peas, and most likely irrigated their fields using

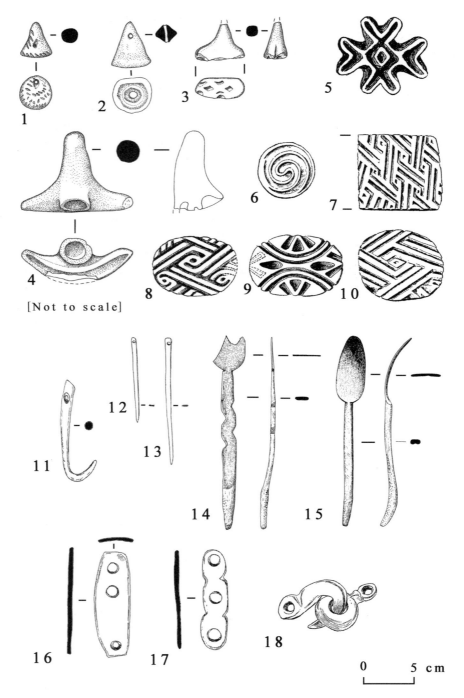

[Not to scale]

Figure 4.21 Stamp seals and bone work: **1–4** Hoca Çeşme. **5–13, 16–18** Çatalhöyük. **14, 15** Ilıpınar (adapted from Mellaart 1964; Özdoğan 1999b; Roodenberg 1999)

simple methods. Animals were also reared, but only the bones of sheep and goats indicate they were fully domesticated. They comprise about 70% of the animal bones found at Çatalhöyük. This is contrary to earlier views that suggested cattle were domesticated.[102] Although wild cattle are considerably larger than their domesticated counterparts, new data indicate that their horn cores are, in fact, indistinguishable.[103] Even though cattle contributed to a small proportion of food consumption, it is interesting that they are amply reflected in much of the symbolism, which was associated with wild and not domesticated animals. Significantly, there appear to be no changes through time in the number or types of animal that were kept and in the range of plants that were cultivated. But only future work will determine whether the way food was processed, stored and discarded was modified, possibly in line with new codes of social behavior. Although their farming practices were advanced, the residents of Çatalhöyük still engaged in hunting and foraging to balance their diet. They had a taste for pistachio nuts, almonds, and juniper berries, to name some of the plant foods, as well as wild boar, ass, horse, and various birds, mostly waterbirds such as geese and ducks. Interestingly, in view of the prominence of the leopard in wall art, only a single bone (a pierced claw) has been found. This has lead to the view that some sort of taboo or perhaps reverence surrounded the leopard.[104]

Hacılar was an agricultural settlement. Cultivated einkorn, emmer, bread wheat, barley, lentil, purple pea, and bitter vetch were recovered from Level VI. Only the dog appears to have been domesticated. The northwest region displays two modes of subsistence that reflect its varied environment. One (at Ilıpınar) is typically agropastoral, depending on domestic animals and cultivated plants with supplements provided by foraging and collecting wild resources; the other, represented at coastal sites, shows a heavy, but not exclusive dependence on fish, shellfish, and wild animals.

Concluding remarks on the Ceramic Neolithic

Looking at the Neolithic as a whole, villages north of the Taurus during the Pre-Pottery and Early Pottery Neolithic conform to the clustered plan. These are represented at Aşıklı, Çatalhöyük XIII–VI, Can Hasan III, and Erbaba. By contrast, during the Late Pottery Neolithic and Early Chalcolithic, only one site (Can Hasan I) continues this tradition, the rest adopted the open settlement plan. The Early and Late Pottery Neolithic periods can also be broadly distinguished through imagery. The vivid symbolism of decorated walls and interiors so apparent at Çatalhöyük, gave way to ritual practices that focused on statuettes, pottery, and, presumably, textiles. It seems that the need for artistic expression found an outlet in pottery manufacture and other crafts rather than wall painting.

The period after 6500 BC represents a period of expansion and transformation. The impetus behind the establishment in the Lake District of a large number of small villages, such as Erbaba, which resembles Çatalhöyük in plan and ceramics, is seen as deriving from the Konya Plain.[105] Yet the connections between these two regions diluted considerably as time progressed.

Likewise, the spread of the Neolithic package to the northwestern region a little later (at Demircihöyük, Fikirtepe, Ilıpınar, and Menteşe) might be linked to the momentum generated in the Konya area.[106] The contrasting evidence from the coastal and inland sites located in the northwestern region suggests a mingling of traditions—one was brought to the area by farming communities from west of the Central Anatolian plateau, the other essentially belonged to the greater Balkan region and developed from indigenous Epipalaeolithic traditions.

SPREAD OF FARMING INTO EUROPE

The knowledge of cereal cultivation and animal domestication was transmitted, imperceptibly to any single generation, from the Fertile Crescent across the Anatolian plateau to southeastern Europe, and eventually to its central and western regions in the fourth millennium BC. It would be prudent, then, to say a few words about the establishment of farming communities in southeastern Europe up to the Hungarian Plain, which represents the first stage of a complicated transformation of the European landscape, the so-called "Neolithization of Europe." that stretched from about 7000 to 4000 BC.[107] When the Near Eastern dates are set against those from Neolithic settlements in Europe, a progressive spread westward of the knowledge of agriculture, if not the farmers themselves, is the likely sequence. There is no archaeological evidence to support the independent development of farming in southeastern Europe, but much that points to a clear cultural break between the mobile Mesolithic communities and the intrusive Neolithic village-based societies.[108]

With new elements not native to Europe—wheats, barley, sheep, and goats—came a new lifestyle that changed the face of Europe forever. Cattle and pigs were also kept, but there is some argument that these were native to temperate Europe. This new way of life also brought with it timber-framed buildings arranged in clusters, and, less frequently, mud brick structures, distinctive burial types, clay figurines with coffee bean-shaped eyes, bone spoons and hooks, stamp seals, slings, polished stone axes, and a variety of pottery, including the distinctive prismatic polypod vessels otherwise known as "cult tables."[109] This Neolithic package also promoted a new set of values and opportunities, but the exact nature of this transformation is still not altogether apparent.[110] Clearly, there was considerable contact between communities from the Near East and Europe, but what is not altogether obvious is whether this took the form of colonization—immigrant farmers seeking new land—or native groups adopting foreign staples and ideas.[111]

We know very little about native communities in the Balkans between 10,000 and 7000 BC, with most of our evidence coming from the Danube gorges south of Belgrade and Franchthi Cave, in the northeast Peloponnese. These local foragers had varying subsistence strategies ranging from fishing for tunny in Greece through exploitation of game and plants at home in river and forest settings. Some mitochondrial DNA (mtDNA) studies of extant European populations certainly suggest that indigenous populations of southeastern Europe, already predisposed to new technologies and in contact with neighboring communities, played a role in the transition from foraging to farming.[112] But this argument cannot be applied to the whole of the Balkans, which would have been sparsely populated before the influx of farmers. Even so, taking a cue from the debate surrounding the "Uruk expansion" discussed in the next chapter, it would be wise to leave both options open.

There are a number of considerations that one should be aware of when delving into the archaeology of the Balkans. First, information is disseminated in a number of languages (at least eight), and inevitably similar geographical features and archaeological cultures have different terms. The Hungarian "Körös" culture, for instance, equates with the Romanian "Criş." This has led to temporal equations, involving a number of terms such as the Kremokovci–Karanovo I Complex and the Starčevo–Körös–Criş Complex. Second is the patchiness of the evidence, which is certainly not unique to the Balkans. Radiocarbon determinations, when they are available, must be assessed with respect to the variability between different laboratories and the reliability of sampling techniques. Finally, one should be aware that pottery styles loom large in the definition of cultural horizons in the Balkans (and Europe)—*Bandkeramik* or linear pottery, corded ware, bell beaker and so on—but these in themselves do not comprise separate cultures.

Communities practicing a Neolithic lifestyle appeared suddenly in the Balkans.[113] Broadly speaking, cultural divisions are noticeable between the southern Balkans and its neighbor in Greece, and the central and northern Balkans, which looked north towards temperate Europe. Communication between the regions meant that very similar pottery is found across the Balkans, but linking it to Anatolian sequences is not straightforward. The abrupt appearance of dark coloured ceramics in Crete (Knossos IX), for instance, is difficult to explain. But the detection of key Y-chromosome haplogroups that occur in Crete and Anatolia and not elsewhere in the Aegean, together with the occurrence of bread wheat from Knossos, point to direct connections between the Aegean island and sites from southwest and central Anatolia.[114]

We are on firmer ground when dealing with decorated pottery with painted designs executed in red, black, or white paint. Across southeastern Europe different styles begin to appear with red-on-white wares favored in northern Greece, whereas white-on-red ceramics distinguish the early levels at Karanovo in Bulgaria. Whatever the color combination, the similarity of decorative designs and concepts between painted assemblages from the Balkans and the Hacılar and Can Hasan sequences, clearly point to inter-regional dynamics, if not migrations. Shapes for the most part are simple—deep open bowls and globular jars—and occasionally feature tubular and ledge handles. Unusual shapes include square or rectangular jars, and bowls with oval mouths.

Towards the end of the Early Neolithic in the Balkans, which equates with the end of the Early Chalcolithic in central and western Anatolia, painted wares start to wane in both areas. What emerge in the Balkans are the formative elements the Vinča culture, distinguished by an assemblage of black burnished ceramics decorated with grooves and incisions. On the broader scale, we need to remember that the Vinča culture is contemporary with the Ubaid of the Near East, which we encounter later.

EARLY AND MIDDLE CHALCOLITHIC (ca. 6000–4000 BC)

With the commencement of the Early Chalcolithic period we enter a somewhat obscure period, but no less significant. Indeed, falling between the two "revolutions"—agricultural and urban— it is important as the seedbed for aspects of complexity that led to major sociopolitical changes in the late fourth millennium BC. At the same time it is an elusive interlude to define. For the greater part of Anatolia the transition from the Late Neolithic to the Early Chalcolithic (ca. 6000 BC) does show change but not enough to suggest a major break of tradition.[115] If factors other than adoption of copper metallurgy conventionally used to define the Chalcolithic are taken into account, the significance of the transition from the Neolithic is reduced. Indeed, in many respects the character of Early Chalcolithic cultures was essentially Neolithic.[116] Stone continued to be the preferred medium for tool technology with copper artefacts, few in number and range, largely produced for prestige purposes. The economic basis of village life remained largely unchanged, too.

Even so, in Cappadocia the slump in the number of permanently occupied settlements experienced at the end of the Neolithic was reversed with the establishment of new villages that nonetheless avoided old sites. While settlement patterns around the Konya region remained basically the same, even though there was shift from Çatalhöyük East to Çatalhöyük West, portable hearths and a new type of pottery point to different modes of cooking.[117] Obsidian tools also changed, no longer displaying the sophistication of prismatic blades.

Then, around 5500 BC, the beginning of what we conventionally term the Middle Chalcolithic, many sequences north of the Taurus Mountains ceased, leading Ulf-Dietrich Schoop to reckon that "the greater part of the second half of the sixth millennium may still be considered a 'dark age' in respect to our knowledge of cultural development."[118] Shortly after this curious stretch, in the Late Chalcolithic period (which we shall discuss in the next chapter) there was a change of tempo in social organization and innovation that led to an upsurge in technological advancements. Across Anatolia centres of populations had also established networks of communications with distant lands.

Like so many periods, the Chalcolithic is bedevilled by considerable confusion over chronology and nomenclature. A bewildering set of inconsistencies has made it difficult to understand the unfolding of cultural developments after the Neolithic. At the base of this confusion are the seemingly incompatible Near Eastern and Aegean chronologies, which have sandwiched Anatolia in a collision of terms and dates. In eastern Turkey, for instance, indigenous Anatolian sequences need to be keyed into the broader and established framework of Greater Mesopotamia and the perplexing chronology of Trans-Caucasia, which has its own peculiar problems.[119] Meanwhile, the central and western areas of Turkey rub uneasily with the Aegean sequence, whereas sites along Black Sea littoral jockey within the framework of Greater Eurasia, or the so-called Circumpontic zone.[120] Schoop has discussed these problems and those associated with early methods of excavations in a thorough and persuasive study.[121]

Regional variations

Eastern Anatolia

In the Early Chalcolithic period much of the territory south of the Taurus was associated with the Halaf tradition that stemmed from Upper Mesopotamia. In the Near East this was a period of cultural integration, despite regional variations, that stretched over eight centuries (ca. 6000–5200 BC). Defined by a sophisticated assemblage of painted pottery, occasionally executed in polychrome and ornamented with geometric and naturalistic motifs, this complex had a far-flung distribution, extending from the Upper Euphrates region around Malatya-Elazığ to the middle of Mesopotamia in Syria and Iraq, and incorporating the plains of Cilicia and Amuq, the southern part of the Lake Van region, and the western borders of Iran fringing the Zagros mountains. Other cultural indicators are distinctive circular architecture, an organizational system that used seals, and an elaborate craft production especially well reflected in worked obsidian that was in great demand, and part of a long-distance trading network. Although these southern interconnections were pervasive throughout southeast Anatolia, they appear for the most part to have been more directional than uniform.

Of paramount significance is the new evidence from the site of Domuztepe, in Kahraman Maraş, a huge settlement of 20 hectares, making it one of the largest prehistoric sites of the Near East.[122] Since 1995 three main cultural phases have been discerned in several operations: Phase A-1 (Late Halaf, ca. 4750–4500 BC), and Phases A-2 (formerly, Post-Halaf A) and A-3 (formerly, Post-Halaf B), covering about 4500–4300 BC. Several examples of round structures with a rectilinear entrance passage were exposed—the classic and somewhat inaptly termed *tholoi* houses—that were built with either rammed earth or mud bricks. Rectangular mud brick buildings continue throughout this phase into the Ubaid. This combination of "keyhole" and rectilinear architecture is also attested at Çavı Tarlası, near Hassek Höyük, and Kurban Höyük.[123]

It is the so-called Death Pit of Phase A-2, however, that warrants special attention. This seemingly simple arrangement, an earthen grave approximately 3 m in diameter and 1.5m deep, belies a complex funerary deposit and associated ritual feasting.[124] Essentially, the Death Pit is the site of a mass burial, containing layers the disarticulated bones of at least 40 individuals and a large number of animals, mixed with ash, broken pottery, and other artefacts. The sequence of deposition is rather important. First, a subrectangular pit was dug and the soil dumped along the southern edge, creating a bank. Then came two deposits of animal bones (Fill A and B), found interleaved with layers of silt. The nature of the silting, caused by rain or possibly the deliberate pouring of a liquid, suggests a relatively short interval. The third and final stage of the process saw two other fills deposited on either side of the bank of earth. Fill C, laid on top of the first animal remains, consisted largely of a hard-packed matrix of earth, ash, human, and animal bones that rose above the original level of the pit, forming what the excavators describe as a raised hollow. This might suggest that the original dimensions of the pit were too small and that the fill had been literally packed in (by stomping?). The adjacent Fill D contained few or no human bones, and apparently comprised mostly domestic refuse, including animal bones that were more fragmented that those recovered from Fill C.

The patterns of animal bones as determined by age, sex and species are also telling.[125] Domestic animals—cattle, sheep, goats, pigs, and some dogs—are in the majority, with only a very small quantity of wild taxa cuts of meat thrown in the pit, among them those of gazelle, equid, deer, and bear. Whereas the range of animals from the Death Pit tallies with that recovered from the settlement, the relative proportions are markedly different. Most notable are cattle bones, which are overrepresented in the pit compared to the domestic quarters, and pig that are significantly fewer. This emphasis on valuable animals for ritual consumption is also reflected in the high percentage of adult female cattle and sheep/goat. While there is no evidence that the animals were sacrificed in any special manner, in so far as the method of butchery did not differ greatly between the two areas, the animal bones recovered from the Death Pit were more complete and articulated. This might reflect not only different taphonomic processes through better preservation conditions, but also different cooking techniques and modes of eating. It seems that participants of the feast may not have been as fussy about consuming all the meat and marrow, as they were accustomed to do.

Mersin certainly fell under the influence of the Halaf in Levels XIX–XVII, which enriched the local painted pottery, but Western Cilicia was on the fringe of this tradition. The settlement plan is still rather vague, though a large rectangular structure and a circular outdoor oven, both stone based, can be discerned. It is not until we reach Mersin XVI that we have a coherent settlement plan. Garstang exposed part of a carefully planned fortified village surrounded by a thick fortification wall, with two projecting towers flanking the gateway, which led down to the river, or to the central courtyard. Abutting the interior of the circuit wall is a row of tightly packed squarish rooms, each with its own enclosed courtyard. Slit windows allowed light into the rooms, which were otherwise furnished with standard domestic equipment—benches, hearths, grinding stones, and so on.

Along the Turkish Euphrates and its tributaries Halaf ceramics have been found at Tülintepe, Korucutepe, and Çayboyu in the Keban region, and further down at Samsat and nearby sites.[126] In the Diyarbakır region it occurs at Gerikihacıyan, and beyond at Tilkitepe and Yılantaş near Van.[127] Painted and plain Halaf pottery are represented in Amuq C and D, whereas further north we have Domuztepe, and west there is Mersin, which despite local painted wares has strong links with Amuq D. Halaf vessels have an orange to buff biscuit, and, when painted, designs are executed in red, orange, dark brown, or black. In the late period, bichromy was achieved by varying thicknesses of paint. A single thin layer of paint produced an orange effect, for instance, and a thicker layer produced dark brown. Rare are the splendid polychromatic designs, where white is used as a highlight. The artistry and technical competence of Halaf pottery improved through time, reaching the highest level of sophistication in the late period. Potters were fond of rich designs that were repetitive and minute. Bands or panels filled with an bewildering array of motifs—including pendant triangles, circles, stipples, fish scales, net patterns, wavy lines, and zigzags, to mention a few—are rendered with precision and neatness, features that stand in sharp contrast to the bold and large patterns western Anatolian ceramics. The bull's head, or *bucranium*, motif is the most representational design of the Halaf period. There is evidence to support the view that the naturalistic *bucranium* designs were earlier, and that they later became increasingly stylized until they were reduced to an abstract, geometric shape.

Some of the most intriguing painted sherds belong to a jar from Domuztepe that is decorated with a scene showing two-storied, gable-roofed buildings, separated by trees and pots. In the foreground, a chequered pattern, possibly matting, appears to support the field evidence that architecture at the site was constructed of various materials. On top of the structures are rows of long-necked birds. Apart from providing us with a vivid impression of buildings, these sherds are important from a technical perspective, attempting to show as they do several sides of a building on a flat two-dimensional surface. The fringe elements of the Halaf horizon are well attested at Mersin where black burnished wares ornamented with white-filled pointillé designs occasionally boast horned handles that are redolent of ceramics from the Konya Plain. These were associated with the local painted ware that extended south to Ras Shamra.

The Ubaid, a complex that originated in the plains of southern Mesopotamia, follows the Halaf. A northern variant of the Ubaid culture appears around 4500 BC in the area of Anatolia earlier occupied by Halaf communities. These northern traits that developed in the Tigris piedmont and eastern Jezirah are well documented at Tepe Gawra, and belong to the latest development of the Ubaid, which can be loosely ascribed to the Middle Chalcolithic.[128] Trade was no doubt part of the continued contact with the south, and along the Turkish Euphrates we note a concerted effort to exploit natural resources in the Late Ubaid period. At Değirmentepe, the presence of foreign traditions is most apparent in the use of stamp seals that were used to mark merchandise in an evolving system of administration and accounting. The impressions of these stamp seals, the clay sealings (also known as *bullae* and *cretulae*), show a distinctive regional style with geometric motifs, horned animals, vultures, and human figures, possibly shamans.[129] Nearby, Ubaid traits appear at Norşuntepe, Korucutepe, and Tepecik. One of the distinctions of the Ubaid is pottery, both painted and monochrome, among which so-called Coba bowls, vessels with a scraped surface named after Sakçegözü (Coba Höyük), are the most common. Ubaid pottery is far more haphazardly painted than Halaf. Loose patterns of festoons, zigzags, and other linear designs are executed in a purplish-brown paint on clay often baked to greenish buff. Ubaid traits are found at Amuq E (Tell esh-Sheikh ware), Gedikli (near Sakçegözü), Mersin XV–XIIB and around Maraş. At the other end of the Taurus, Ubaid traits occur at Tilkitepe and among the surface material from the Ağrı region.

The central plateau

After Çatalhöyük East, material recovered from exploratory trenches and collected from the surface at Çatalhöyük West and the excavations at Can Hasan, near Karaman, provide the best evidence for settlement in the central region. For the most part, Chalcolithic buildings at Can Hasan never used stone as a foundation course. According to David French, Can Hasan 3 represents a turning point in architecture at the site shown by the use of standardized mud bricks and the size and symmetry of the excavated building. Interestingly, however, he also notes "that the walls of Layer 3 had been deliberately constructed on the top of Layer 4 walls."[130] French surmises that this may have been for stability, but we have come across this tradition at Çatalhöyük, and it is tempting to consider this a carry over of a Neolithic practice that firmly connected people with place.

Level 2B has been ascribed as transitional between the Early and Middle Chalcolithic, whereas Level 2A is seen as fully developed Middle Chalcolithic, although its structures are fewer in number and poor in preservation compared with those in Level 2B. Again, we notice the enduring central Anatolian Neolithic tradition of tightly grouped independent structures without any intervening courts or alleyways (Figure 4.22). The avoidance to share a party wall is clear and deliberate. The best preserved building, Structure 3, whose walls stand over 3 m high, has an intact doorway linking the main room with the anteroom. Most rooms have a squarish plan, and each is well built, using mud bricks of uniform size ($80 \times 40 \times 10$ cm). Several internal buttresses strengthened the walls and created a series of niches, many of which were fitted with a bench. There is some evidence that walls were coated with white plaster, and fragments of red-on-white painted plaster suggest some rooms were ornamented with geometric patterns. All Level 2B structures appear to have had an upper story of sorts that would have created a staggered roofline, whereby the floor of the roof of the lower story was the floor of the upper. Entry to all the lower rooms was through the roof, which comprised closely set beams superimposed by a layer of branches and reeds laid perpendicular to the beams, and sealed, in turn, by clay and white plaster.[131] Level 2A largely constitutes the rebuilding of a few 2B structures, but the standard of building techniques appears to have dropped.

The Late Chalcolithic settlement at Can Hasan Level 1 is poorly preserved, but it is clear that it had a completely different layout to the previous period. Open spaces ("courtyards"), not apparent in the Middle Chalcolithic, are now incorporated into the plan and fitted with ovens, bins, and partitions. Buildings appear to have been modified fairly frequently, perhaps because this part of the settlement was built on a slope at that time. Nonetheless, on the inside, houses were well maintained—walls were thickly coated with white plaster and the floors covered with hard white clay.

The ceramics of Can Hasan 2B began largely as a mixture of painted (red-on-cream wash) and burnished wares; vertical and horizontal rows of zigzag lines are the basic painted patterns.[132] Gradually, the quality of both types improve, and the burnished fabrics (gray, red-brown and buff) have their surfaces both well polished and incised; in the last building level a new pottery type appears—white-slipped red ware with painted designs of simple horizontal lines and cross-hatched triangles executed in brown or black. Although the incised wares do not occur in Can Hasan 2A, the various painted and plain wares provide a link. But what distinguishes Can Hasan 2A are large jars elaborately decorated with polychrome designs of

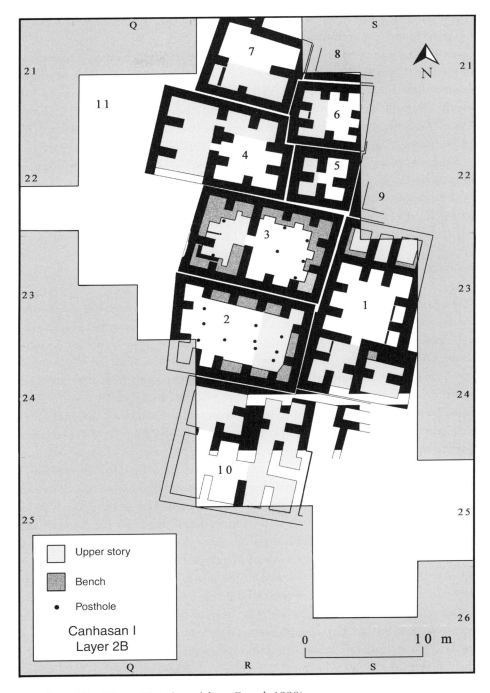

Figure 4.22 Plan of Can Hasan 2B (adapted from French 1998)

chevrons and hatched patterns fired to distinct shades or buff and orange. Similarly striking pottery has been found at Çatalhöyük West.

Influences from southeastern European were now penetrating further into Anatolia than before. In the central plateau and especially at Alişar Höyük black burnished carinated vessels with decorated fluted patterns recall the Vinča horizon.[133] Dishes with thickened rims ornamented in this fashion have been compared to those found at Anza IVA, Vinča-Belo Brdo, Vesselinovo in the Balkans, and with examples at Can Hasan 2b and Yarımburgaz 0. Influences associated with post-Vinča horizons (i.e., Maritsa, Pre-Cucteni and Gumelnitsa) are also apparent at a number of central Anatolian sites such as Büyük Güllücek, Dundartepe, İkiztepe, Yazır Höyük, Boğazköy-Yarıkkaya, Gelveri-Güzelyurt, and Bucak Hüyücek (Figure 4.23).[134] Whether evidence comes through excavations or field surveys, the chronology of central Anatolia remains a major obstacle.

Western Anatolia

Within this broad region three Chalcolithic clusters can be identified: The southwestern, the Aegean coast, and the area in between. The Early Chalcolithic settlement at Hacılar (V–III) has left traces. Those inhabitants who continued to live at the site appear to have reorganized its plan—the area occupied by the previous Late Neolithic settlement (Hacılar VI) was turned into courtyards.[135] Hacılar II provides good evidence of a southwestern Anatolian village from the first half of the sixth millennium BC. The settlement assigned to Level IIA was oblong in shape and enclosed by a thick mud brick wall equipped with small buttresses.[136] Several activity areas could be discerned around a main central courtyard—a residential quarter in the west, potters' workshop within the courtyard, a cluster of cooking areas, and two possible shrines (Figure 4.24). An average house had a doorway, facing the courtyard, which led directly into an anteroom that was attached to the main room. Most houses were fitted with a square or rectangular oven set into the floor of the main room, storage bins, and benches; some houses also supported an upper story. The number of querns and mortars found lying on the floor of the central courtyard associated with lumps of red and yellow ochre, painting utensils, clay modeling tools, and stacks of unused pottery are suggestive of a craft area reasonably identified as a potters' workshop. Another specialist area is located in the northwest corner where large amounts of grain strewn across the floor, equipped with storage bins and two large, oval ovens, point to a granary. The architectural complex at the other end of the settlement, the eastern side, was partitioned with brushwood barriers, partly roofed, and fitted with the usual features of a domestic area. A stone-lined well was also found nearby.

Whether the large building to the northeast corner is a shrine, as Mellaart proposes, is a moot point. Open plan in layout, the building has thin walls like those of the potters' quarters, suggesting that it did not have an upper story. His judgement is largely based on size of the building, fragments of painted plaster associated with a niche, remains of standing stones, a

130

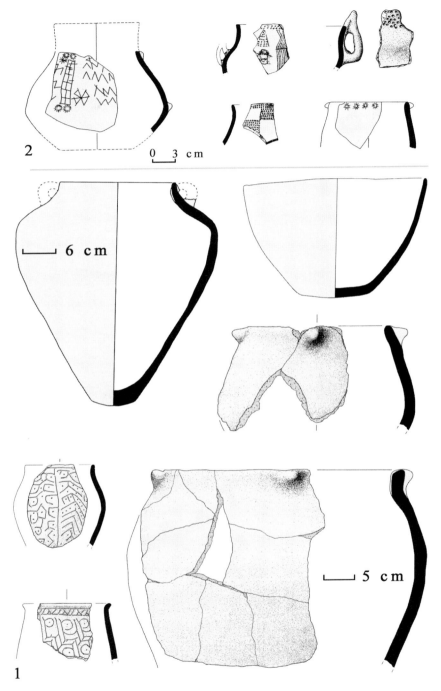

Figure 4.23 Early to Middle Chalcolithic pottery from central Anatolia: **1** Yarıkkaya. **2** Büyük Güllücek (adapted from Orthmann 1963; Schoop 2005)

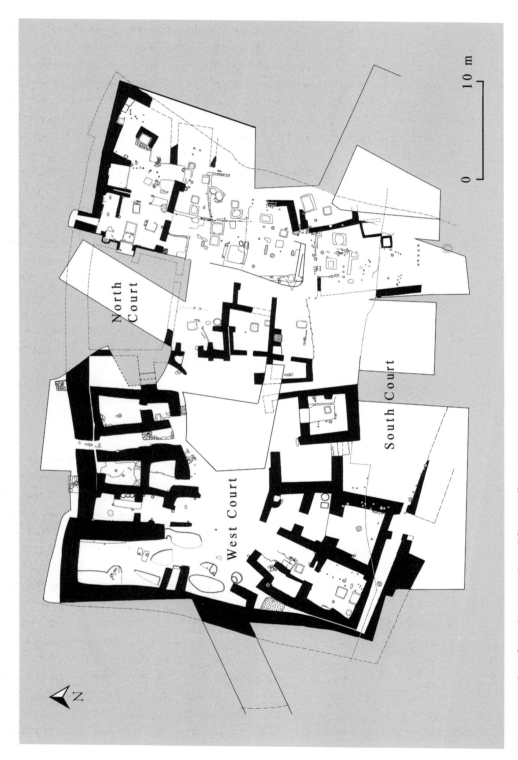

Figure 4.24 Plan of Hacılar II A (adapted from Mellaart 1970)

stone slab, two clay-lined holes, and five burials, one a double grave (mother and child). But in every other respect this room appears to be similar to those designated as domestic. Another room, in the southwest corner, which contained "ritual" pots—a stylized human head and a figurative representation of a human and animals—is also ascribed a shrine status. While all these features may have had a ritual purpose, their setting is clearly domestic. Hacılar IIA was partly burnt and rebuilt (IIB) along the western half. The smaller settlement with substantially fewer hearths suggests that some of the inhabitants left.

After the destruction of Hacılar IIB, the settlement was rebuilt, possibly by newcomers. Although only part of the Hacılar I settlement was excavated, the plan is noticeably different (Figure 4.25). Two blocks of houses were uncovered, radially arranged around a central courtyard. Approximately a fifth of the settlement was excavated, and there was no differentiation in activity areas—the rooms were clearly residential. No doorways were found, pointing to an upper story that was presumably entered in the normal manner from a courtyard on top of the

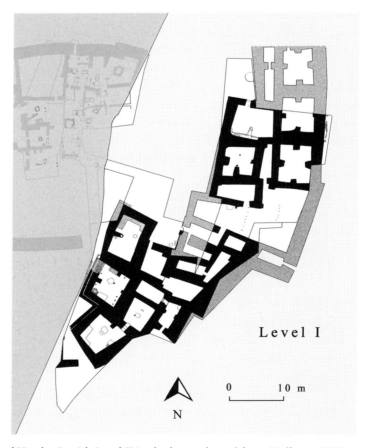

Figure 4.25 Plan of Hacılar I, with Level II in shadow (adapted from Mellaart 1970)

mound, although little evidence survives apart from a few postholes. Rooms were mostly square and internally buttressed. They were generally fitted with benches and hearths that were raised on a platform, whereas domed ovens were found in the courtyards. Floors were coated with mud plaster, as were the walls, and covered with woven mats. But these basement rooms appear to have been empty apart from the material that collapsed from the upper story. Mellaart suggested that the plan of this settlement—with the back walls of the houses forming an unbroken façade—is defensive. But there is no evidence to support this idea. Roughly contemporary with Hacılar I is Kuruçay Level 7, a settlement of the clustered houses.[137]

Striking red-on-cream painted pottery is generally seen as the hallmark of the Early Chalcolithic period in southwestern Anatolia (Figure 4.26), which nonetheless develops from the end of Late Neolithic. Moreover, the Hacılar painted style of linear decoration appears to be quite localized, extending as far south as Karain. Painted patterns on the Hacılar repertoire vary—one portrayed stylized versions of Late Neolithic applied motifs, another depicted textile designs, using positive and negative techniques. The range of forms increased—there are now oval cups, and, in Level II, the appearance of anthropomorphic vessels and spouted jars. Monochrome ceramics continued to be manufactured, but were fewer in number than in the previous phase. Statuettes also showed changes. They are larger, more standarized, often painted to display garments, and devoid of animals and children. Potters continued to experiment with new forms—oval and subrectangular shapes, square cups, and ovoid butter churns. But, on the whole, vessels became more open, and the most popular shapes were carinated bowls and jars with wide necks. Among the most notable vessels are the painted anthropomorphic seated figure with prominent eyebrows and noses, and eyes that are either painted defined by chips of inlaid obsidian. Corpulent statuettes were still made, but now alongside a new type—stylized figurines with narrow waists. In the Elmalı Plain only a few sherds have been found of the Hacılar painted variety. Most of the Early Chalcolithic pottery from Elmalı simply shows a continuation of the Late Neolithic tradition—coil-built monochrome vessels of rounded forms.

While the period between the end of the Hacılar culture and the beginning of the Beycesultan Late Chalcolithic has been described as "the greatest possible break imaginable,"[138] traditional chronology has also assumed that there was little if any gap. We now realize that a hiatus of considerable length of time separates the two periods into which we can now place the Elmalı Plain (Kızılbel and Lower Bağbaşı), Kuruçay, Ilıpınar, basal Demircihöyük, and Orman Fidanlığı.[139] The Elmalı sites are also significant because of the evidence they provide for relations with the east Aegean. Ceramic features such as strap handles decorated with knobs, pans with high walls and pierced rims, and the occasional incised design have parallels in the earliest deposits at Emporio on Chios (Levels X–IX), at Tigani on Samos, and the cave sites on Kalymnos.[140] Geographically, this communication between the Elmalı Plain and the eastern Aegean could have been effected using a maritime route—along the western and southern coastline and then up to the plain—or an overland one—following the Büyük Menderes to the Burdur area and then to Elmalı.

Figure 4.26 Early Chalcolithic red-on-white painted pottery from Hacılar II–I (adapted from Mellaart 1970)

Northwest Anatolia

About 5700 BC, the inhabitants at Ilıpınar erected a mud brick building directly over debris of the post houses belonging to phase VII (Figure 4.27).[141] As the settlement grew, it shifted to the west so that the mud brick village juxtaposed rather than superimposed the post house settlement. Houses were no longer single-roomed freestanding units, but multiroomed and closely grouped together. This change no doubt transformed behavior. Within the house separate activity areas are discernable—cooking and food processing, for instance—each compartimentalized by a thin partition (Figure 4.28). In phase VA, one house had an upper story where food was processed evidenced by grinding stones; the ground floor, contrariwise, was used for storage. This shift in mode of construction and organization is abrupt, as it is puzzling. At a time when connections with the Balkans were increasing and those with the central Anatolian plateau were waning, the change in building techniques does not appear to lie in cultural ties, but was possibly prompted by a drier climate spell, even though no conclusive evidence has been found. This view that communities in northwest Turkey were experimenting with architecture as a response to climatic changes is supported by the sudden appearance of post houses during the third millennium BC at the nearby site of Hacılartepe.[142] The end of the settlement at Ilıpınar is defined by a crudely constructed, oval pit (3 × 5 m) that was dug about 50 cm into the earth. This semi-subterranean structure had an earthen bench and was equipped with an oven, hearths, grinding slabs, and jars full of grain. It seems that when the mud brick settlement was eventually abandoned, people continued to till the fields and occupy the area in a semi-permanent fashion.

Potters from the mud brick village at Ilıpınar produced distinctive squat pots ornamented with excised patterns, carinated open bowls with wavy line designs, and square vessels. This is attributed to the Developed Phase of the Neolithic Fikirtepe sequence, even though it is absent at Fikirtepe. Similar types have been found at Yarımburgaz Layer 4, and Toptepe; and some of the Demircihöyük Ware E material could be considered transitional between Fikirtepe and Yarımburgaz 4.[143] While the overall impression is one of general continuity from the Late (Neolithic) Fikirtepe, the details of the connection are not altogether clear. At Yarımburgaz 4, for instance, pottery is elaborately decorated, sometimes all over, with excised and impressed patterns. And forms now include tall-necked jars with a low belly. Ceramics from Hoca Çeşme II show new influences, namely the introduction of barbotine pottery also known as "surface roughened" in southeastern Europe (Figure 4.19: 3). Their surface treatment is unmistakable: The exterior, except for the rim which was burnished, was deliberately roughened by gouging and scratching, to contrast with the inner face that was given a smoothing or burnishing. This ware type proved popular and, shortly after its introduction towards the end of Phase II, quickly dominated the assemblage of the following period. Connections are clearly Balkanic where this barbotine pottery is found in earlier contexts associated with red-painted wares at Karanova I, Starčevo, Körös and Criş. The latest phase at Hoca Çeşme, I, reveal three horizons on the basis of floors and pits: Level Ic is distinguished by the predominance of barbotine ceramics ornamented with nail impressions and "organized barbotine" decoration. These elements belong to the western

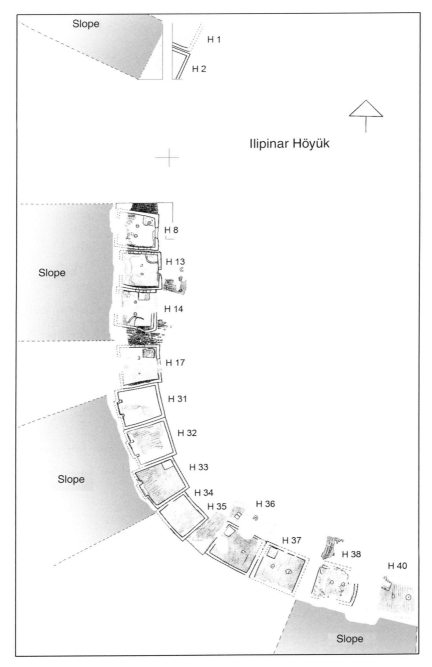

Figure 4.27 Plan of Ilıpınar Level VI (after Roodenberg and Alpaslan Roodenberg 2008)

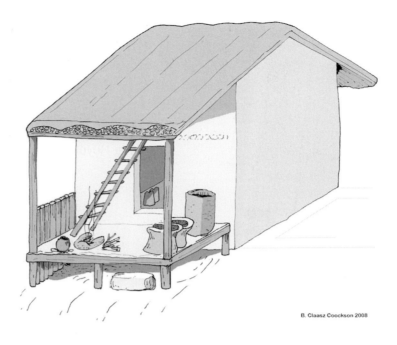

B. Claasz Coockson 2008

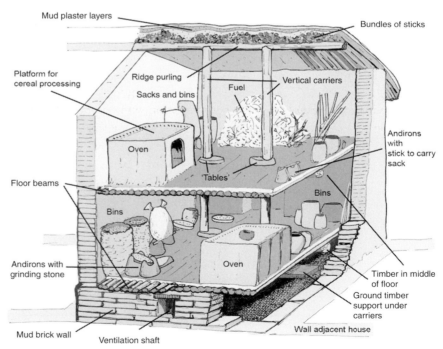

Figure 4.28 Exterior and interior view of a mud brick house of Ilıpınar VI (after Coockson 2008)

Balkans. In eastern Thrace this pottery is intrusive at Yarımburgaz 0 and Toptepe II–IV, and more recently at Orman Fidanliği (Levels I–V), where painted ceramics also reflect connections to the southwest regions; Level Ib includes rectangular and triangular vessels with excised or incised designs, carinated profiles, open bowls with thickened rims and high feet, punctate and fluted ornamentation, and horned handles; Hoca Çeşme Ia is typically defined by dark coloured open bowls burnished patterns on both surfaces. Stylistically, this assemblage has connections with Toptepe I, and Ilıpınar V, and further afield, with late Karanovo III and early Karanovo IV, Vinča A or A/B, and Tsangli/Larissa.

Metallurgy

Technically, Early Chalcolithic metalwork is virtually indistinguishable from that of the Neolithic, except for the copper pins and small ornaments at Mersin XXII–XXI and Hacılar, which suggest an interest in small luxury items. Proficiency becomes more evident in the Middle Chalcolithic. The copper mace head and bracelet from the burial of an adult male at Can Hasan is testimony of this. Originally thought to be cast from pure copper, the shaft-holed solid mace head (5.3 by 4.32 cm) appears to have been hammered into shape from a mass of native copper. But the most significant metallurgical development in the early fifth millennium BC comes from Mersin, where Garstang recovered axes, chisels, and other tools cast in simple open moulds.[144] Moreover, some of the tools revealed traces of tin, arsenic, and even lead, effectively making them low-level bronze objects. While arsenic may have been a naturally occurring, hence arsenical copper, tin, and lead certainly do point to a rudimentary understanding of smelting mineral ores. Thus the transition from cold hammering through melting and casting to the threshold of smelting was realized. That threshold in the experimentation with polymetallic ores was crossed in the subsequent levels (XVI–XIV) at Mersin, when a large repertoire of tools—axes, adzes, chisels, and pins—were produced containing good quantities of tin (1.3–2.1%) and arsenic (1.15–4.25%). The significance of these Mersin tools cannot be overstated. Presently, as the earliest smelted and cast metal items in Anatolia, they represent a technological breakthrough that enabled later metalsmiths to produce items that were significantly larger and more complicated than was possible by simple cold hammering.[145]

NOTES

1 Schmandt-Besserat 1974, 1977.
2 Düring 2006: 13, figure 1.2.
3 Karul et al. 2001; Karul et al. 2004.
4 Özdoğan 2007: 199.
5 Voigt 2000, 2007a. I would like to thank Mary Voigt for giving me a copy of her 2007 paper before it went to press.

6 See Voigt 2000: table 2 for attributes of these functional classes based on ethnographic and ethno-historical sources.

7 Özdoğan 2003a.

8 Garstang 1953.

9 Caneva and Sevin 2004.

10 Garstang's periodisation for the earliest levels is as follows (1953: 2): Early Neolithic (XXXIII–XXVII), Late Neolithic (XXVI–XXV), Early Chalcolithic (XXIV–XX), Middle Chalcolithic (XIX–XVII and XVI), and Late Chalcolithic (XVB–XIIA).

11 Schoop 2005: 96–99. Cf. the slightly different attributions by Caneva and Sevin 2004.

12 Garstang 1953: figures 12, 24 and 38.

13 Düring 2006: 130–247; Mellaart 1967; Todd 1976.

14 Hodder 1996, 2000, 2005a, 2005b, 2005c, 2007.

15 No final report is available on the Mellaart excavation. Mellaart 1967, an overview, has a listing of the detailed preliminary reports.

16 It may seem incongruous to say that a fire "preserves," but structures built of mud brick or organic material like those at Çatalhöyük burn quickly and collapse equally as fast, a process that smothers the fire and seals their content.

17 Cessford reply in Düring 2002: 230.

18 Düring 2001, 2006.

19 Cutting 2005.

20 Düring 2001; Hodder 2006; Matthews 2002.

21 Hodder 1996: 365; Mellaart 1964: 78.

22 Stevanovic 1997.

23 Düring 2001.

24 Although it has been argued that these courtyards were mostly rubbish dumps and therefore did not aid accessibility, it remains to be seen whether this was the case throughout the site, and whether courtyards were used this way throughout their lifespan. That is, were the courtyards only dumps when they entered the archaeological record?

25 Mellaart 1967.

26 While "ritually elaborate buildings" has been suggested (Düring 2001) as a more suitable concept, the reaction against "shrine" seems perhaps a little overzealous given that it can mean "a place hallowed by some memory" (*Oxford English Dictionary*).

27 Matthews 2002: 93.

28 Matthews 2002: 94.

29 Garfinkel 2003.

30 Voigt 2000.

31 Hayadaroğlu 2006: 62.

32 Düring 2001; Mellaart 1975: 101.

33 Haydaroğlu 2006; Hodder 2005a; Mellaart 1967.

34 Hodder 2006: figure 7.

35 Badischen Landesmuseum Karlsruhe 2007: 251–253.

36 Kuijt 2000 on skull caching in the Levantine Neolithic.

37 Verhoeven 2002a: 249.

38 Hamilton 1996: 215–217; Voigt 2000. For comments on figurines from the renewed excavations, see Meskell and Nakamura 2006, who group them into three types—anthropomorphic, zoomorphic, and miscellaneous—with the first group subdivided into human, humanoid, and schematic.

39 See Grinsell 1961, 1973 on the notion of "killing" objects, even though his study examines breakage in funerary contexts.

40 Watkins 1996.

41 Bordaz and Bordaz 1982. For full listing of reports, see Düring 2006: 248–259.
42 Bordaz 1969: 60.
43 Duru 1999.
44 Duru 1994b.
45 Duru and Umurtak 2005.
46 Duru 1994a: pls 185–193; Duru and Umurtak 2005: pls 111–170.
47 Duru 1996b, 1997a, 1997b, 1998, 2000a, 2000b, 2002.
48 Mellaart 1970.
49 Eslick 1988.
50 Mellaart 1970a.
51 Mellaart 1970a: 166–176.
52 Voigt 2007a.
53 For instance, following Mellaart's original interpretation published in his preliminary reports that were later sanitized for the final publication (1970), Voigt 2007a argues that Mellaart 1970: figure 227 is not "a young woman dressed in a leopard skin, playing with her son," but a two people copulating. Likewise Mellaart 1970: 201 does not depict "a young girl in position of childbirth," but rather a young woman's sexual readiness.
54 Çilingiroğlu and Abay 2005; Çilingiroğlu et al. 2004.
55 Efe 2000; Özdoğan 2006; Steadman 1995.
56 Bittel 1969/1970; Harmankaya 1983; Özdoğan 1983; Pasınlı et al. 1994 (Pendik).
57 Özdoğan 1998.
58 Gérard 1997; Roodenberg 1995, 1999a; Roodenberg and Alpaslan Roodenberg 2008; Roodenberg and Gérard 1996; Roodenberg and Thissen 2001.
59 Roodenberg 1993.
60 Karul et al. 2003.
61 Roodenberg and Alpaslan-Roodenberg 2008.
62 Roodenberg 1999b; Roodenberg et al. 2003.
63 Sagona 1994b; Jones and MacGregor 2002.
64 Turner 1966.
65 Hovers et al. 2003; Sagona 1994b and references therein.
66 Kay and McDaniel 1997.
67 Hovers et al. 2003.
68 See Sagona 1994b for examples pertaining to the Australian Aborigines.
69 Hovers et al. 2003.
70 For a review, see Sagona 1994b. So prolific was the use of ochre in Bronze Age east-central Europe that both pit graves and catacomb graves are sometimes referred to collectively as the "ochre grave culture."
71 Sagona 1994b.
72 Brain 1979.
73 The sherds from Beldibi (Bostancı 1959: 51–57) represent a Neolithic intrusion into a late Mesolithic assemblage. Other Mesolithic sites, Karain (Kökten 1955), Belbaşı (Bostancı 1962), Carkini and Öküzini (Esin and Benedict 1963) did not yield any ceramic artefacts.
74 Schmandt-Besserat 1977.
75 Arnold 1985; Rice 1987.
76 Arnold 1985.
77 Hodder 1982.
78 Özdoğan 2005.
79 Braidwood and Braidwood 1960; Caneva and Sevin 2004; Garstang 1953; Karul et al. 2004.

80 Atalay 2005; Last 2005; Mellaart 1967.
81 Öztan 2007: figures 13–18.
82 Özbaşaran 2000; Öztan and Özkan 2003; Öztan 2007; Todd 1980.
83 Duru and Umurtak 2005: 181–194.
84 Schoop 2002.
85 Mellaart 1970.
86 Eslick 1992.
87 Çilingiroğlu and Abay 2005; Çilingiroğlu et al. 2004.
88 Özdoğan 1983, 1999b.
89 Özdoğan 1999b.
90 Efe 1993.
91 Özdoğan 1999: 214.
92 Özdoğan 1998.
93 Mellaart 1967.
94 Yener 2000: 24.
95 Yener 2000: 25.
96 Balkan-Atlı 1994a; Özdoğan 1999b: 211–212.
97 Carter et al. 2005; Conolly 1999.
98 Mellaart 1970.
99 Özdoğan 1999b.
100 Haydaroğlu 2006: 62–67; Türkcan 2005.
101 Asouti and Fairbairn 2002; Fairbairn et al. 2005.
102 Perkins 1969.
103 Martin et al. 2002.
104 Hodder 2006.
105 Thissen 2002: 18.
106 Thissen 2002: 19.
107 Efstratiou 2005.
108 Colledge et al. 2004; Rowly-Conwy 2003; Zohary and Hopf 2000.
109 Perlès 2001: 52–63; Schwarzberg 2006.
110 Hodder 1990; Whittle 1985.
111 Pinhasi et al. 2005; Tringham 2000.
112 Renfrew and Boyle 2000; Semino et al. 2000.
113 Bailey 2000; Tringham 1971, 2000.
114 Broodbank and Strasser 1991: 236–237; King et al. 2008: 210–11. Cf. the earlier study that sparked off the discussion on genetics and the Neolithic, Ammerman and Cavalli-Sforza 1984.
115 Schoop 2005; Yakar 1991, 1994a, 1994b.
116 On the degree of continuity in central Anatolia, see Gérard and Thissen 2002.
117 Baird 2002.
118 Schoop 2005: 358.
119 Such is the need for a stocktake that no fewer than three conferences have been convened in recent years to address these issues. See Marro and Hauptmann 2000; Postgate 2002; Rothman 2001.
120 Chernykh 1992; Kohl 2007.
121 Schoop 2005.
122 Campbell et al. 1999.
123 Algaze 1990; Von Wickede 1984.
124 Campbell et al. 1999; Carter et al. 2003. See also short annual reports in *Anatolian Archaeology*.
125 Kansa and Campbell 2004.

126 Algaze et al. 1994.
127 Korfmann 1982; LeBlanc and Watson 1973; Marro 2007.
128 Rothman 2002.
129 Esin 1994.
130 French 1998: 25.
131 French 1998: figure 22.
132 French 2005.
133 Efe 1990: 102–113; Özdoğan 1993; von der Osten 1937: figure 67.
134 Hauptmann 1969; Özdoğan 1993; Parzinger 1993a.
135 Mellaart 1970a: 23–25.
136 Mellaart 1970a.
137 Duru 1994a, 1996a.
138 Mellaart 1970b: 326.
139 Eslick 1980; Özdoğan 1999b.
140 Eslick 1980.
141 Gérard 1997; Roodenberg 1995; Roodenberg and Gérard 1996; Roodenberg and Thissen 2001.
142 Roodenberg 1999a.
143 Özdoğan et al. 1991 (Yarımburgaz and Toptepe); Thissen 1995 (Ilıpınar); Seeher 1987a (Demircihöyük).
144 Caneva 2000; Garstang 1953. Originally found in Level XVII, the copper objects have been reassigned to Level XVI by Caneva.
145 Efe 2002.

5

METALSMITHS AND MIGRANTS

Late Chalcolithic and the Early Bronze Age
(ca. 4000–2000 BC)

In Anatolia, the Late Chalcolithic roughly equates with the fourth millennium BC (4000–3100 BC), although as with most matters on chronology, there are several variations on the timespan and nomenclature.[1] There is general agreement, however, that the period is a turning point in cultural developments, foreshadowing achievements and connections in the Early Bronze Age. For this reason it is best to treat the two periods together. A distinguishing feature of the Late Chalcolithic is the emergence of new socioeconomic systems controlled by those in power whose voracious appetite to display their status and wealth fuelled a quest for resources. This need for items of luxury and new technologies—the main manifestations of their authority—ensured the geographical expansion of cultural boundaries, particularly evident in the Euphrates Valley where the Near Eastern and Anatolian worlds collided. During the Chalcolithic period, Near Eastern communities pushed into the central Taurus region, to the very threshold of central Anatolia. This level of cultural interaction, spurred on by trade, increased in the subsequent centuries so that at the end of the Early Bronze Age much of the Anatolian peninsula was involved in an extensive network, stretching from the shores of the Aegean to the northern territories of Syro-Mesopotamia.

Owing to the intensity of investigations along Euphrates Valley in recent years, it makes sense to start the survey of regional developments there, moving eastwards to its borders with the Caucasus and Iran, and then to examine the evidence in the central and western regions.

LATE CHALCOLITHIC (ca. 4000–3100 BC)

Euphrates area and southeastern Anatolia

The change of tempo in the Late Chalcolithic was most marked along the Euphrates Valley. Significant organizational changes emerged in eastern Anatolia, matched by an upsurge in technological innovations and cultural interaction. But the nature and force of these changes varied throughout the east. From the cultural milieu of the Ubaid horizon, a series of local complex polities emerged that can best described as chiefdoms, while understanding that the development and nature of these societies were by no means uniform, neither did they necessarily lead to the formation of states.[2] One was localized in the Upper Euphrates, north of the Taurus Mountains, and bore clear affinities with the Amuq Plain, whereas the other occupied the lowlands south of the mountains (the Jezirah and Karababa regions) and was distinguished by its local Late Chalcolithic that spread across much of north Mesopotamia and Syria (Figure 5.1). Overlapping with both of these is what has been labelled Gawran, a horizon emanating from northern Iraq, and best expressed in Gawra XI-A, with its round house and sequence of temples.[3]

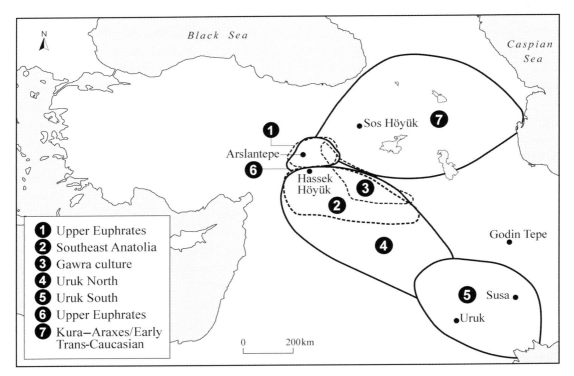

Figure 5.1 Map showing the main Late Chalcolithic cultural zones in eastern Anatolia and adjacent regions: **1–3** (4000–3500 BC). **4–7** (3500–3000 BC)

During the second half of the fourth millennium, the area below the Taurus Mountains, the northern reaches of Mesopotamia, experienced intensive contact with southern merchant venturers. Contact between indigenous communities and Uruk Mesopotamia is seen at several places, but is especially well documented at Hacınebi. At Hassek Höyük we have an actual colony of Late Uruk type, which raises a concept of colonization that will concern us shortly. Repercussions of this mercantile activity were felt north of the mountain range too, especially in the Malatya and Elazığ regions, where local cultures adopted Mesopotamian forms of administration. At Arslantepe (Level VIA), centralized economic activity is reflected in a well-preserved complex that contained many seal impressions (known as *cretulae* or *bullae*)[4] and wheelmade pottery. Emerging connections with different cultural environments farther east, most notably with Trans-Caucasus, are also clearly evident by the presence of handmade, red-and-black burnished pottery. The rugged highlands northeast of the Taurus, contrariwise, developed its own character, one that drew on the Trans-Caucasian experience.

The Late Chalcolithic period in Anatolia has been dominated by studies on the phenomenon referred to as the Uruk expansion. This occurrence is defined by the dispersal of a distinctive inventory of material culture, including ceramics, iconographic motifs, architecture, and terracotta wall cones, and administrative procedures (attested by seals and sealings, and proto-cuneiform tablets). These are linked with southern Mesopotamia, especially at the site of Uruk-Warka, to distant lands such as the Upper Euphrates and Upper Tigris regions in Turkey, northern Syria, western Iran, and Egypt. Over the last decade or so, this episode of history has once again gripped archaeologists with a fervor that is no less a phenomenon than the period itself. A generation of new fieldwork has seen an outpouring of literature that has not only harnessed the evidence, but also grappled with various conceptual frameworks.[5] Key among these is the view, eloquently espoused by Guillermo Algaze in 1993,[6] that the Mesopotamian heartland, the southern alluvium investigated by Robert Adams in his pioneering surveys, deeply affected others regions around its periphery. Algaze argues that regions such as the Middle Euphrates in Syria and the Taurus intermontane zone beyond, which formed part of Greater Mesopotamia, started to experience dramatic shifts in social, political, and economic organization that were prompted by developments on the alluvium.

These ideas drew on the results of a host of new investigations. Even though located it was on the very limits of the Uruk world, near Malatya in the Upper Euphrates drainage basin, Arslantepe stands pre-eminent for two reasons. First, the exemplary work carried out by the Italians since 1961 has shed enormous light on an important complex settlement. The methodical excavations that emphasiz broad horizontal exposures have taken full advantage of this well-preserved site. Second, this project constitutes without a doubt some of the best work currently being carried out on an early state administrative center in southwest Asia. It has shown that the formation of early state systems was not limited to Upper and Lower Mesopotamia, but included parts of highland eastern Anatolia along the Euphrates, which developed along its own trajectory.

In the same year that Algaze published his seminal work, which explained the dynamics of an expanding Uruk world as viewed from the alluvium, Frangipane offered a perspective from the highlands and reminded us that the pulse of complexity did not beat only in the plains.[7] She indicated that complex social structures emerged in the Syro-Anatolian region well before contact with the Mesopotamian Uruk culture. Indeed, the picture now emerging is one of a mosaic of interacting polities (rather than a single centre) that sprang up in Greater Mesopotamia from the late fifth millennium BC, each of which reacted differently to the Uruk impact—some embraced it, others had no choice but to accept it, whereas others again filtered those elements which they saw as useful. As we shall see, Arslantepe's distinctiveness lies in its highland location ("peripheral" to the Uruk heartlands) and the nature of its administrative complex, which is based around contiguous temples.

Although the chronology of the fourth millennium BC in southwest Asia remains loose in parts, comprehensive analyses of radiocarbon determinations from across Greater Mesopotamia support the view that the Uruk expansion was not short lived (3300–3100 BC), as was once thought.[8] In fact, it appears to have extended over the Middle and Late Uruk periods in the south, and lasted from about 3800 to 3100 BC.[9] The appearance of typical south Mesopotamian Middle Uruk ceramic forms such as the ubiquitous bevelled-rim bowls at Hacınebi B2 suggest that this influence was felt in southeastern Turkey just before 3600 BC.

Clearly, the term Uruk is not always apt when referring to indigenous communities that occupied lands surrounding the southern alluvium of Mesopotamia. A more overarching terminology is required. Frangipane proposed three Late Chalcolithic phases plus a Late Uruk period for the Syro-Anatolian and Upper Mesopotamian regions, a proposal largely followed by Helwing.[10] The latest pronouncement stems from the Sante Fe conference on the Uruk world, which appears to have a broad consensus and is used here. Five stages of the Late Chalcolithic (LC 1–5) are identified, stretching from 4200 BC to 3100 BC.[11] These are roughly equivalent to the Early, Early Middle, Late Middle, and Late Uruk sequences of southern Mesopotamia.

Before we turn to the evidence, let us continue with a few more conceptual issues. While the sway southern Mesopotamia had on surrounding regions well outside its immediate boundaries has been well known for some time, it is the nature of this expansion as well as the relationship between the Uruk intruders and the local populations that have prompted the greatest discussions. Were these intrusive settlements true colonies, or were they enclaves attached to host communities? Is the material assemblage implanted and pure, or does it simply display influences from the south ("Uruk like")? Did the southern settlers mix with the indigenous community, or did they keep to themselves, resolutely pursuing their business? These and other questions have focused attention on the social transformations and dynamics that occurred when Uruk settlers met indigenous societies. More importantly, they highlight the difficulties of identifying this cultural contact, because unlike the recognition of the Old Assyrian commercial enclaves of second millennium BC Anatolia, our understanding of the Uruk expansion relies on archaeology alone.

Several factors need to be considered in any attempt to discern the degree of Uruk influence in the Taurus region:

- distance between the Mesopotamian heartland and the eastern Anatolian sites they affected;
- the level of social and political complexity of the Anatolian communities in whose regions the Mesopotamians settled;
- relative organizational structures—the intrusive colonial network versus the established indigenous systems;
- the nature and intensity of trade between settlers and host communities—balanced or one sided;
- power interchanges between southern cities and their colonies, and, in turn, between the colonies and host societies;
- intermarriage between the immigrant groups and local populations.[12]

Three types of Uruk settlement have been detected outside the homeland by applying these criteria to archaeological evidence.[13] First is the *colony*, which Stein aptly defines as:

[A]n implanted settlement established by one society in either uninhabited territory or the territory of another society. The implanted settlement is established for long-term residence and both spatially and socially distinguishable from the communities of the host society. The settlement at least starts off with a distinct formal corporate identity as a community with cultural/ritual, economic, military, or political ties to its homeland, but the homeland need not politically dominate the implanted settlement.[14]

Implicit in this overarching definition is the view that only state-level societies establish colonies, which, in terms of Uruk settlements, were small in size compared to their parent cities on the alluvium. While acknowledging that a formal relationship exists between colonies and their homeland states, it also allows for a certain degree of flexibility—colonies need not be totally prevailed on by their parent states, neither do colonies themselves necessarily dictate the organizational activities of their host societies. These stand alone Uruk sites have been interpreted as "stations" that acted as intermediaries (the main nodes of communication) between sites in the Mesopotamian periphery and city-states of the alluvium. They are distinguished from contemporary local settlements by their niched façade temples, walls embedded with ceramic cones forming colorful geometric patterns, tripartite houses with a middle hall, and a complete repertoire of Uruk pottery. Hassek Höyük, near Samsat in southeastern Turkey, is generally seen as an example of a small Uruk station, although Helwing would prefer to describe it as a Syro-Anatolian site that gradually acquired Uruk traits.[15]

The second type of Uruk settlement is an *enclave*—a foreign quarter of traders established within a pre-existing local site, or at its edge, and with the agreement of the host community. The nature of these settlements has been compared to the later and better known Old Assyrian *karum*, situated in central Anatolia, where foreigners and locals coexisted to engage in trade. Once thought to have been founded only in the highlands, deep within the mountains of the Taurus and Zagros, Uruk enclaves have now been discovered on the plain, most notably at

Hacınebi Tepe, a small site (3.3 hectare) located just north of the Birecki ford in southeastern Turkey.

Population replacement and presumably some use of force distinguish the third type of Uruk settlement—a *large enclave*. This situation envisages foreign settlers taking over pre-exisiting centres with a thriving economic network. Of the three types of Uruk settlement, these are the most difficult to discern. Evidence from Kuyunjik, the high mound at Nineveh, and at Tell Brak, points to a discontinuity in local Late Chalcolithic traditions. Whether this was linked with an increased presence of Uruk settlers is difficult to say at the moment.[16] In Turkey, no settlements of this type have so far been discovered. The large site of Samsat, once thought to belong to this category, was probably at the centre of a cluster of indigenous settlements, where a limited range of Uruk items gained favor among the local elites.[17]

Scholars generally agree on one issue, namely that this expansion was fuelled by the desire of the growing powerful elite of southern Mesopotamia to obtain natural resources in order to construct buildings and manufacture goods that would legitimize their claim to authority. Herein lies a curious paradox. Whereas the extraordinary fertility of alluvium of lower Mesopotamian generated the agricultural surpluses that became the foundations for the earliest known urbanized state societies, the plains were not endowed with many of the raw materials requisite for the development of ancient complex societies. These commodities and luxury items, including timber, metals (especially copper, tin, gold, and silver), semiprecious stones (lapis lazuli and carnelian), chlorite, and obsidian, had to be obtained from distant lands.[18]

In their quest for resources, the main centers of lower Mesopotamian took advantage of the long-established routes of exchange and communication, such as the Euphrates River, and in the process instigated changes to existing social, economic, and political structures in the areas they settled. The extent of Uruk influence was so successful and vast, covering several thousand square kilometers, that good reason beyond the desires of vainglorious rulers would have been required. The construction of typically Uruk temples far from the homeland and the link between administration and temples (although these traits were by no means universal, especially in Anatolia) seem to suggest that political and religious ideology acted as a mitigating double helix for expansionism.

Late Chalcolithic 1 and 2 (LC 1–2): 4300–3650 BC

The lowest levels at Norşuntepe were reached on the West Terrace (Levels 40–38) and on the south slope (JK 17, strata 28–12), which revealed part of a large building, although no coherent plan was recovered. A few Ubaid-like painted sherds enable it to be assigned to the latest phase of the Ubaid (or Terminal Ubaid).[19] The predominant fabric, however, is Dark-Faced Burnished Ware. Both form and ornamentation—small knobs, incised geometric designs and impressed grain motif—link these vessels with Amuq D/E.[20] The subsequent horizon at Norşuntepe (West Terrace 37–35) is characterized by Coba bowls.[21] Built by hand or on a *tournette* with plenty of chaff temper, Coba bowls have been found at many sites south of the Taurus Mountains, ranging from Mersin in the west through the Amuq and Maraş Plains to the Jerzirah, incorporating the Urfa and Adıyaman regions. They occur at sites in the Anti-Taurus, but further east around Malatya, and the Altınova Plain they tend to evolve into a different profile. Their easternmost occurrence appears to be the Muş Plain.[22]

Late Chalcolithic 3 (LC 3): 3650–3450 BC

The Late Chalcolithic period is defined by two periods at Arslantepe that show a continuity of development. In the earlier period, VII, attributed to the early fourth millennium BC to about 3300 BC, a fledgling central authority was established and its presence is seen in monumental architecture. In the early and middle levels of this period, the settlement was already quite extensive and covered much of the mound. Evidence of town planning is seen in the segregation of residential and ceremonial buildings.[23] Domestic houses, mostly rectangular in plan, were located in the northeast sector. Inside they were furnished with ovens and basins, and their floors sealed the graves of kin.

The western sector had a different character that is registered by imposing buildings positioned at what was then the highest vantage point on the site. The structures had thick walls that were built using a distinctive mud brick technique—edged with one or two rows of bricks—and the central wall cavity was then packed with mud and mud brick fragments. On the interior surface, the walls were plastered and painted with geometrical designs executed in red and black, foreshadowing similar depictions in the next period. Wall paintings in the first half of the fourth millennium BC, however, are fairly rare. At Norşuntepe a house wall is decorated with a sketch in black and red of an animal with an elongated body and a mane of frizzy "hair," whereas downstream at Tell Halawa, in Syria, we have a more complicated scene, also painted in red and black, apparently showing human figures encircling a large face.[24] Although their meaning is unclear, these curious images point to an Upper Euphrates tradition in the Late Chalcolithic period.[25] Arslantepe VII buildings are also distinguished by the use of mud brick columns that were thickly coated in plaster, a feature that links it to Tell Brak.[26] That some of the rooms within the complex were used for storage is evident by the large number of pottery containers, grinding stones and pestles that were found on the floor. Although no clay sealings (cretulae) were recovered, the concentration of clay lumps in room A582 suggests that some form of administrative record keeping was practiced. Overall, then, the impression is one of importance that points to an emerging social and political complexity.

The upper level of Period VII at Arslantepe, located immediately below the structures of Period VIA, marks an important development and is represented by another series of imposing structures. One group consisted of juxtaposed oblong rooms (A850–842), originally thought to be storerooms, but now judged to be craft areas by the presence of ochre and the debitage of stone tool production.[27] Nearby is a building (A900) of different character; it is monumental with a tripartite plan and has all the hallmarks of a ceremonial building redolent of structures erected in the southern alluvium of Iraq. Inside, the walls bore traces of paintings, but better preserved were two pairs of niches that were set one into each of the short walls of the *cella*, on either side of the entrance. A large podium and an accompanying fireplace set into the center of the floor would have enhanced the notion of ceremony. But this complex served another purpose, namely as a place to store and distribute commodities. This is vividly attested by hundreds of mass-produced bowls found strewn across the floor; others were stacked high upside down. Grouped neatly in one corner of the room, clay sealings were a reminder of past dealings. These buildings and the operations that they sheltered argue for a growing and powerful administrative elite that had clear political affiliations with the Syro-Mesopotamian region.

The beginning of Period VII at Arslantepe not only heralded changes in political and administrative structures; it also witnessed the emergence of new modes of pottery production that lasted for almost a millennium. Like architecture and settlement patterns, these novel traits, apparent in a range of different pottery shapes and fabrics, reflect basic changes in social organization and economic activities that spread across Greater Mesopotamia, including the Upper Euphrates region of Turkey.[28] Over this vast area pottery is ascribed to the broad horizon termed Chaff-Faced, which emphasizes the large quantity of straw inclusions that was added to the paste and clearly visible on the surface of vessels. The typology of these wares was first defined in the Amuq where they characterize periods E (at Tell Kurdu) and F (at Çatal Höyük) of the sequence, though their chronology still lacks precision.[29] No longer interested in decorative pottery of high quality, such as that which characterized the earlier centuries, households now demanded wares that best served their new needs. Aesthetics gave way to mass production, and variety was replaced by standardization in a move that saw pottery production move out of the household to a centralized workshop. With the gradual specialization of crafts that mirrored the emergence of a stratified society, the emphasis was now on speed and quantity.[30] The use of the potter's mark during this period may have been how wares of individual workshops within a centralized manufacturing process were distinguished.[31]

Arslantepe VII pottery is largely coarse. Only a few fine examples were found that date to the very end of the period, and they do not belong to the chaff-tempered tradition. Coarseness of paste among chaff-faced vessels varies according to the size of each vessel, but in all cases containers were dipped into a thin slip, often red-orange, and some (Chaff-Faced Ware) were then given a perfunctory burnish when dry. In general, while the Arslantepe repertoire reflects the general trend that occurred in northern Syria and Mesopotamia, technical and typological differences are noticeable. Shapes are limited, and open forms were the most popular (Figure 5.2). Noteworthy are the mass-produced bowls that come in two broad types in the earlier levels: (a) Rounded bowls, which are flint scraped around the bottom, often bearing a potter's mark at the base on the exterior, a type that grew out of the so-called Coba bowl; (b) conical bowls with a wide, flat base, not string cut, and a potter's mark on the lower internal wall.[32]

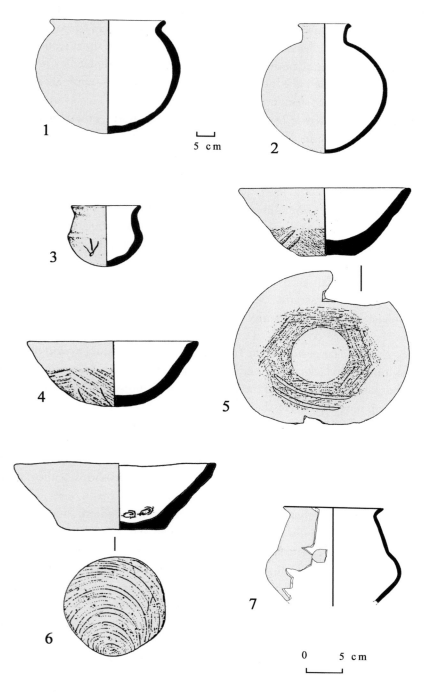

Figure 5.2 Pottery from Arslantepe VII (Late Chalcolithic 2): **1–6** Coarse Chaff-Faced Ware, some of which bear the potter's marks. The bowls are mass produced and have a flint-scraped surface. **7** Red-black burnished jar (adapted from Frangipane 2000)

Changes appear in the pottery repertoire of the late levels of Arslantepe VII, which, although registered by only a handful of fragments of new wares, are very significant in foreshadowing later developments, in Period VIA. They are represented by burnished ware and a fine, wheel-made grit-tempered fabric found scattered among the predominantly Chaff-Faced Ware of the temple and multiroomed complex.[33] Burnished pottery amounts to less than 2% of the total ceramic assemblage, and can be best distinguished on the basis of color into three group: Red-black, monochrome (red through gray to brown), and black. Red-black ware also points to a controlled firing technique that allowed potters to achieve a scheme of contrasting colors—black on the outside and red on the inside for closed forms such as jars, and the reverse for open forms like bowls. Significantly, these burnished wares were found in the very latest stages of this phase, constructed immediately before the temple complex of VIA, and were not recovered from the columned building. They point to new cultural influences emanating from eastern Anatolia and Trans-Caucasus, where communities of farmers and pastoralists, bearing none of the social or political complexity found along the Euphrates corridor, began to make their presence felt in the Malatya region around 3500 BC. We will discuss these societies later on.

Late Chalcolithic 4 (LC 4): 3450–3250 BC

Following the local Late Chacolithic Hacınebi A settlement, the community began to gravitate towards southern influences. This new settlement, Hacınebi B, shows a mixture of local traits and elements associated with the initial spread of Uruk tradition from the south. At Hacınebi colonists formed a minority and were located in the northeast corner of the B2 settlement, which regrettably was badly disturbed by modern pits. The absence of fortifications, weapons, or violent destructions suggests that Mesopotamians and Anatolians lived in relative harmony for several centuries, estimated to be between 300 and 500 years.[34] Moreover, there is no indication that the Uruk settlers controlled the Hacınebi community either economically or politically.

Only context and a holistic interpretation of the artefactual evidence can distinguish between a foreign enclave and a site that displays exotic influence through the importation or emulation of foreign goods. In the case of Hacınebi, two different patterns of behavior are apparent when the overall assemblage is compared and contrasted. The division in ceramics and their localization in different parts of the site catch the eye first. The mercantile quarter has yielded a full assemblage of mostly "Middle Uruk" ceramics, including the predominant grit-tempered, bevelled-rim bowl (Figure 5.3). This differs from the largely chaff-tempered Amuq F repertoire found across the rest of the site.[35] Also, many Uruk ceramics—but none of the local Amuq F vessels—bear dribbles of bitumen, reflecting the distinctly Mesopotamian practice of coating certain containers. Significantly, the bitumen from Hacınebi matches the chemical composition of sources in southern Mesopotamia and in the Deh Luran plain, suggesting bitumen was imported to southeast Anatolia. Not only were the ceramic forms between the two areas different, but functional variations are apparent—the Anatolian vessels are typically domestic and

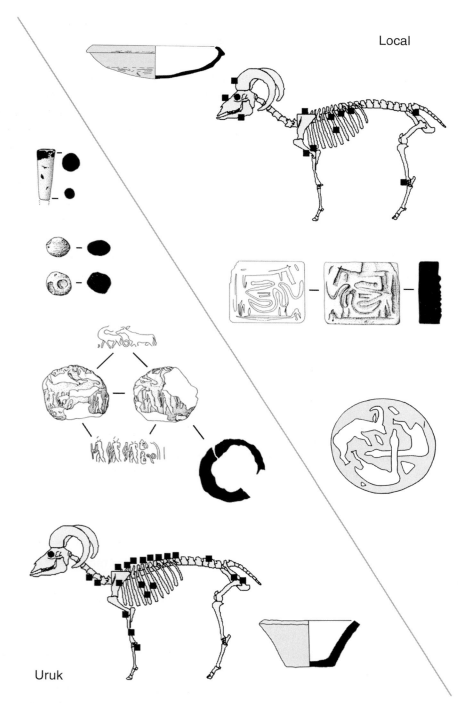

Figure 5.3 The contrasting assemblages of the Hacınebi B settlement (Late Chalcolithic 4), showing the different patterns of behavior between the local population and the Uruk settlers (adapted from Stein 1999a)

were used for food storage, preparation, and serving, whereas the overwhelming amount of bevelled-rim bowls (90%) in the Mesopotamian quarter suggest the importance of specialized activities.

These two groups also differed in their culinary practices. The Mesopotamians preferred sheep and goat, and only occasionally ate beef and pork, whereas the Anatolians relished all four types of meat equally. Moreover, the way meat was butchered and the modes of food preparation differed between those living in the enclave and the rest of the inhabitants (Figure 5.3).[36] The chipped stone industry is less differentiated, although Canaanean blades and simple blades associated with the Uruk assemblage are smaller. In this context, the discovery of two well-baked clay sickles, though curious, is nonetheless telling of a practice that is characteristic of alluvial plains of southern Mesopotamian where stone is sparse.[37] Finally, the administrative technology of business was different. The Anatolians at Hacınebi authenticated accounting transactions with north Mesopotamian square or round stamp seals that feature lions and caprids. They used these seals to impress clay sealings attached to cloth sacks, wooden boxes, bundles of matting, and leather bags. Uruk merchants, by way of contrast, employed a south Mesopotamian system of recordkeeping, involving cylinder seals and other devices. The repetitive impressions of processions of animals or human figures left by these seals were found on a different range of items, including a sealed clay ball containing tokens, a clay tablet, and jar sealings and stoppers.

Late Chalcolithic 5 (LC 5): 3250–3000/2950 BC

The last phase of the Late Chalcolithic is well represented both north (Arslantepe) and south (Hassek Höyük) of the Taurus Mountains. Hassek Höyük measures about 1.5 hectares in area and is one of several sites along the Euphrates that exhibit Uruk material. Excavations revealed a fortified settlement (Level 5), roughly oval in shape, dominated by a pair of compartmentalized buildings of the "Mittelsaal" type similar to those found further south at Habuba Kabira-süd (Figure 5.4: 1). The compound also included grain storage facilities and work areas. Although the ceramic assemblage at Hassek reveals a strong presence of types of Uruk origin such as bevelled-rim bowls, spouted jars, and four-lugged jars, the local chaff-tempered ceramics are equally well represented (Figure 5.5).

During the last third of the fourth millennium BC, Arslantepe (Period VIA) was drawn inexorably into the Late Uruk Mesopotamian exchange network. Excavations have uncovered a complex of public buildings (I–IV), termed a "palace," clearly evident in the largest exposure on the southwestern slope (Figure 5.6). Not necessarily the residence for royalty, the complex was rather a centre for various public functions carried out under the auspices of those in power. Two monumental temples, A and B, which share virtually similar ground plans and internal fitments, dominate the complex. Temple A was added after the establishment of the palace, as is seen by its bent axis, attached to a hewn-out section of the earlier structure. Access to Temple

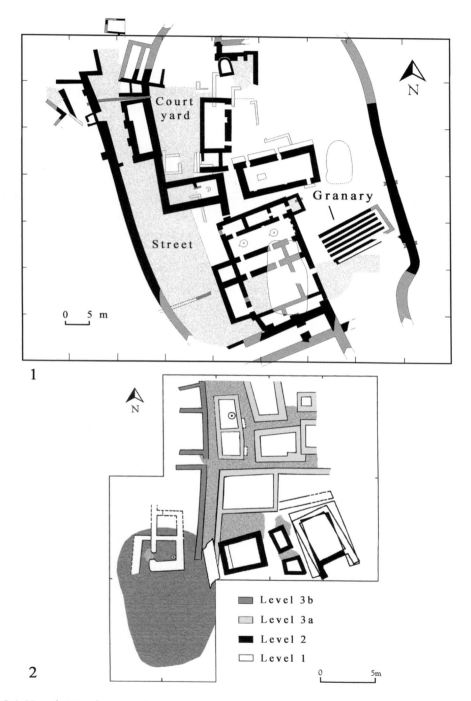

Figure 5.4 Hassek Höyük: **1** Level 5, the Late Chalcolithic settlement. **2** Level 3, the Early Bronze Age settlement (adapted from Behm-Blancke 1992)

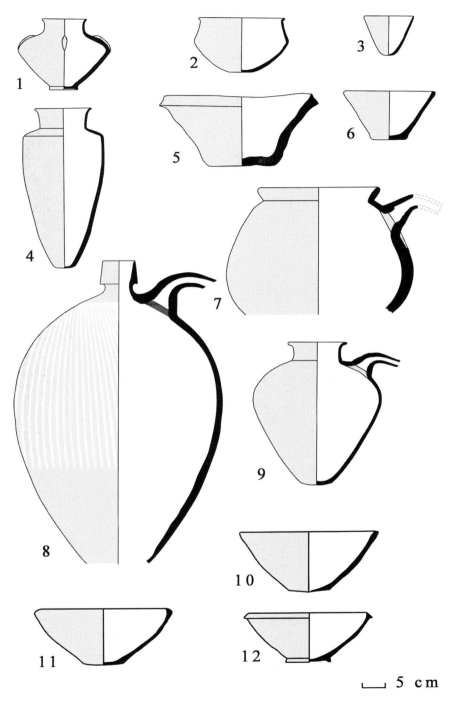

Figure 5.5 Characteristic types of Uruk and local pottery (Late Chalcolithic 5) from Hassek Höyük (adapted from Helwing 2002)

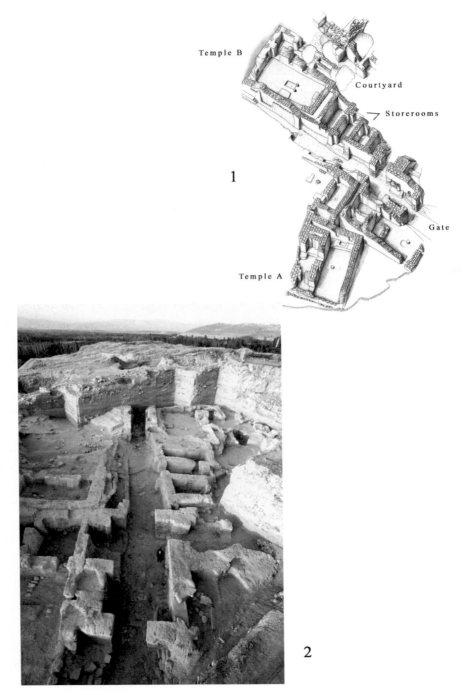

Figure 5.6 Arslantepe: **1** An isometric view of the Period VIA (Late Chalcolithic 5) complex (adapted from Frangipane 2007). **2** An aerial view of the same complex (Photo: Robert Ceccacci, courtesy Marcella Frangipane)

B in Building IV, the earliest building, was indirect, via a monumental gate, an oblong room paved with irregular stones, and a long corridor, flanked by storerooms. Platforms located on either side of the gate appear to have served as guard posts. On the west side of the storerooms is a large courtyard surrounded by further rooms that have been only excavated in part. Sections of other features and buildings, such as a monumental building near Temple B, await full exposure.

Temple B has a bipartite plan, comprising a broad room (the *cella*) and a narrower, compartmentalized attachment, through whose long eastern wall one entered. At the entrance, a series of red and black paintings that decorated the walls of the vestibule area would have demanded attention. Of these, the liveliest is the stylized image of a male figure with raised arms, standing in front of an altar or table, which is under a canopy (Figure 5.7: 1). Along the corridor and in rooms surrounding the *cella* itself, the sense of aesthetics was different. Here the walls were textured with concentric lozenge motifs set in relief and applied with a stamp, a mode of decoration that is similar in conception to that found in the Level III temples at Uruk.

The other temple, A, is part of Building I, which together with Building II was constructed on terraced areas and oriented differently to the earlier buildings.[38] But in floor plan Temple A mirrors its predecessor. The eastern wall of the *cella* featured two elevated niches set above a basin and bench that was lime plastered like the other walls. Traces of a red and black painting were found on the east wall, and at its base, on the bench, were the bones of goat, cattle, and a boar, possibly the remains of an offering. A white plastered podium centred the floor of the *cella*. In an adjoining room, at the entrance to the temple, parts of a wall were decorated with a stamp in a similar manner to Temple B, except, in this case, concentric oval motifs were set in relief and painted in red to contrast with the white background. Sealings do attest to some economic activity in this latest area, but the smaller quantity reflects a declining market. It seems that the writing was on the wall, so to speak, and not long after this public precinct, that so well reflected an early state system, it was abandoned and subsequently burnt.

Evidence of economic activities carefully controlled by an administrative system is found throughout the complex, but the most compelling are the 2000 plus *cretulae* found in concentrations. Importantly, these impressed lumps of clay were not found strewn haphazardly across the site, instead most were carefully discarded once they had served their purpose, whereas others were found in situ near the objects and commodities they sealed.[39] These contextual patterns reflect a clear chain of administrative operations, involving three stages—those that were in use when the building was destroyed, those that had been recently used and placed in the corner of the storeroom, and those that were discarded (neatly in dumps) once they had served their purpose. Careful examination of the back of the *cretulae* enabled the identification of the objects that were sealed: Sacks, some tied with a wooden peg; pots, with a cloth covering the opening, were plugged at the mouth, or had a *cretula* attached to the neck or shoulder; baskets and wicker lids; and, perhaps most fascinating of all, a system of door closures, including pin tumbler locks (Figure 5.8). The quantity and sophistication of designs point to a rich tradition of local glyptics.

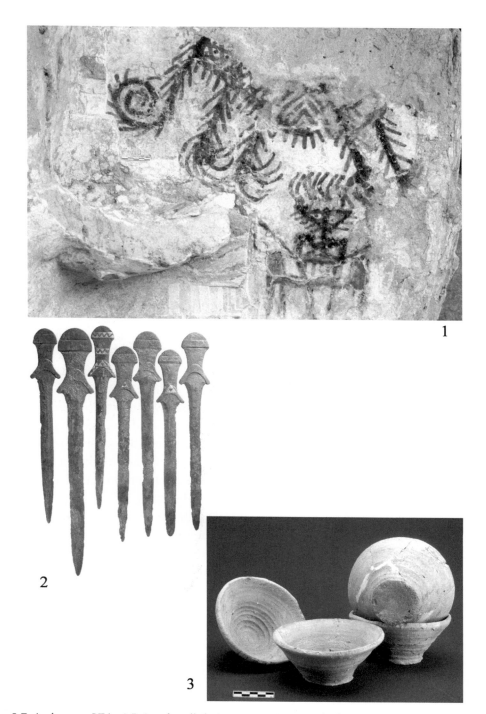

Figure 5.7 Arslantepe VIA: **1** Painted wall design portraying a male figure beneath tendrils and volutes. **2** Daggers fashioned from arsenical copper—one is decorated with a fine silver pattern. **3** Mass-produced conical bowls (Photos: Robert Ceccacci, courtesy Marcella Frangipane)

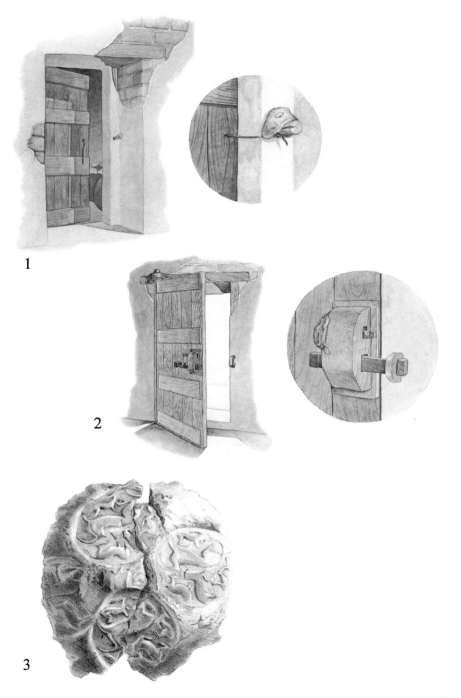

Figure 5.8 Arslantepe VIA locking systems as determined by the type and discard patterns of impressed lumps of clay (*cretulae*): **1** Rope and peg. **2** Wooden toothed lock that foreshadowed the Yale lock by some five millennia. **3** A lump of clay with seal impressions that depict arrangements of animals (Drawn by T. D'Este and Mario Cabua, courtesy Marcella Frangipane)

Both cylinder and stamp seals were used to impress the lumps of clay. In both cases, stylized animal motifs (goats, lions, and deer), often rampant or interlaced, predominate, with humans making only a rare appearance. Interestingly, very few actual seals have been found. If the variety of seal designs is any indication of the level of sophistication of administration, then it must have been fairly elaborate at Arslantepe, and probably involved a bureaucracy of officials whose duties no doubt included the accountability of transactions.

Precious items were clearly stored in this complex, evidenced by the 21 arsenical copper items, mostly swords (Figure 5.7: 2) and spearheads discussed later, which were found in Room A 113, in Building III. So not only did this palace serve as a place of worship, but the physical linkage of the temples to a series of storerooms demonstrates that the area also functioned as an economic and administrative centre, as in previous centuries.

Despite the remarkable continuity in architecture and administrative aspects between Periods VII and VI, the pottery inventory shows an abrupt change. Four different ware types replace the chaff-faced horizon that dominated the greater part of the fourth millennium BC:

1 wheelmade fine or semi-fine buff pottery that is similar to, but not an exact copy of, "Plain Simple Ware" of the Syro-Mesopotamian plain, including Reserved Slip Ware;
2 coarse mass-produced bowls, redolent of Period VII, except for a paste that now has grit inclusions;
3 Red-Black Burnished Ware that made an appearance in the last centuries of Period VII
4 kitchen ware.

This break with tradition should not be viewed as an instance where foreign peoples substituted the local population, but rather as the adoption of new fashions and techniques of manufacture that new lines of communication promoted.

Although the four different ceramics represent new connections with markedly different cultural spheres, including an increase in the interplay with Trans-Caucasus, it is with the highly centralized and developed Late Uruk culture of Mesopotamia that Arslantepe VIA dealt with most. The inventory of shapes found at Arslantepe is now quite standardized, suggesting an even greater degree of administrative control than in the previous period (Figure 5.7: 3). The potter's mark, once an identifying symbol of individual artisanship, disappears. Even so, potters at Arslantepe catered for local needs, which did not slavishly mimic customs elsewhere. Although we have an abundance of necked jars decorated in reserved slip (south of Taurus) and high-stemmed bowls (central Anatolia), the repertoire at Arslantepe is far more restricted when compared with adjoining regions. The end of this administrative complex was swift and violent. Around 3000 BC, Arslantepe VIA burnt completely, leaving behind a thick deposit of charred and mud brick debris that sealed its former splendour.

Eastern Highlands

The rugged terrain east of the Euphrates River did not engender a centralized authority. Instead, the greater part of the population still lived in villages, with a rural lifestyle that involved tilling the land and raising stock. Around 3500 BC, or slightly earlier, the character of the eastern Anatolian highlands began to change, reflected primarily by the appearance of visually striking pottery fired to a red and black color scheme. Handmade, well burnished, and often decorated, these ceramics form one of the most distinctive archaeological horizons of the ancient Near East, referred to in literature as Kura-Araxes, Early Trans-Caucasian, or Karaz.[40] The suite of material culture stretched across a remarkably wide area, encompassing eastern Anatolia and the Turkish Upper Euphrates, southern Caucasus (except the westernmost part of Georgia), and northwestern Iran. It has also been found in considerable quantity in later Early Bronze Age contexts in the Amuq (H–I) where Robert and Linda Braidwood designated it Red-Black Burnished Ware, a term that emphasizes the distinctive color scheme.[41] Further south still, a related artefact assemblage occurs in the Levant, where its conspicuous presence comes in a derivative form named after the site of Khirbet Kerak (modern Beth Yerah), in northern Israel.[42] Longevity also distinguishes the Kura-Araxes horizon. In some regions like the northeastern Anatolian highlands, where we have a suite of reliable radiocarbon readings from Sos Höyük, it endured for more than 1500 years.

Even though the Kura-Araxes horizon spanned across the entire Early Bronze Age of eastern Anatolia—indeed most discussions of this horizon concern the third millennium—in recent years attention has focused on its crucial formative stage that is deeply embedded in the Late Chalcolithic period. Whereas the Kura-Araxes horizon does, at first glance, give the distinct impression of widespread homogeneity, leading some to suggest it represents the material culture of a discrete ethnic group,[43] the high degree of regionalism should not be underestimated. Even so, unmistakably similar modes of architecture and artefact types are recurrent over an astonishingly wide geographical zone. These traits include: Rectilinear, subrectangular, and circular houses built of mud brick, wattle and daub, and stone; portable and fixed hearths that are often anthropomorphic or zoomorphic in style; a wide range of hand-built burnished pottery often displaying a contrasting color scheme of black, gray, brown, and red, and sometimes bearing elaborate ornamentation; a simple range of bronze objects often with a high content of arsenic; well-crafted bone implements; standardized horned animal figurines; and a standardized stone tool repertoire that is manufactured primarily from obsidian in the eastern areas and characterized by the tanged projectile point.

The Late Chalcolithic is of singular importance in addressing the perplexing question of the Kura-Araxes' genesis. Did this ubiquitous phenomenon emanate from a single point of origin and thence spread rapidly throughout the highlands, or did the "package" of traits come together through active communication between neighboring communities? Was there a stimulus that prompted its rapid spread? Chronological issues aside, what were the internal developments of this horizon? At the moment, the starting point for a discussion of the late prehistory of Anatolia east of the Euphrates is the mound of Sos Höyük, near the town of Pasinler, in the province of Erzurum, which has yielded an important Late Chalcolithic deposit (Period VA).[44] To this can be added the surface finds collected from surveys conducted in a number of regions—Erzurum, Bayburt, Van, and Iğdır among others[45]—that assist in constructing the development of the highland communities east of the Euphrates.

The most conspicuous architectural feature of Sos Period VA, dated between 3500/3300 and 3000 BC, is a large, curved wall (Figure 5.9: 2–3).[46] Measuring 2.5 m wide, the foundation of the wall is constructed with a packing of small stones and hard clay. Although only part of the wall has been exposed, it appears to have encircled the core of the settlement. With such a broad base, the superstructure, presumably built of mud brick and wood, must have had a commanding view of the surrounding plain. In terms of its construction, we are certain about three things. First, the earliest settlers at Sos Höyük did not build the wall—their material remains are found on floor levels that predate its construction. Second, the wall was destroyed at least twice. And, finally, after the initial collapse, possibly caused by an earthquake, the wall was not rebuilt immediately, which is attested by the remains of dwellings that are sandwiched between the two building phases of the wall.[47] One other characteristic of Sos Höyük should be noted, namely the central role of the hearth in the domestic domain. This is evident not only by the quantity of hearths, portable and fixed, but also by the practice of building hearths directly above the earlier ones, highlighting the importance of place.

After the first collapse of the wall residents built a circular freestanding house that was constructed entirely of mud bricks (Figure 5.9: 1). An almost complete refit of an obsidian pebble reconstituted from the flakes collected on the floor (Locus 4244) demonstrates that stone working activities were clearly carried out in the house.[48] In the center of the house and built into the floor was a circular hearth that would have caught the eye as one entered the doorway on the western side. Portable hearths, ceramic vessels, and other items were on the floor. Radiocarbon analyses of charcoal place this round house within the period 3350 to 3000/2900 BC.

Although Kura-Araxes ceramics have been much discussed, they do not constitute the only repertoire of pottery during the Late Chalcolithic. Indeed, the relationship between the earliest Kura-Araxes pottery and contemporary pottery horizons provides the clearest indicator of change in this formative period. Several distinct ware types have been identified (Figure 5.10):

1 Sioni ware, named after the eponymous site in Georgia, has distinctive features that include very decorative rims—incised, impressed, serrated, or wavy—and broad bands of combed decoration.[49] Ornamentation on uncombed vessels is incised *after* firing. The small sample of body sherds at Sos VA probably marks the approximate western border and very tail end of this tradition.[50] Further east, however, it has been found in the province of Ağrı, generally in small amounts, except at Sarıgül and Çetenli.[51] More recently it has appeared in excavations at Kohne Pasgah Tepesi in the Koda Afarin Valley, northwestern Iran.[52]

2 "Drab" ware is the term assigned to a local pottery tradition found throughout northeastern Anatolia, but it does not occur in the Lake Van basin.[53] Some vessels from Sos Höyük have

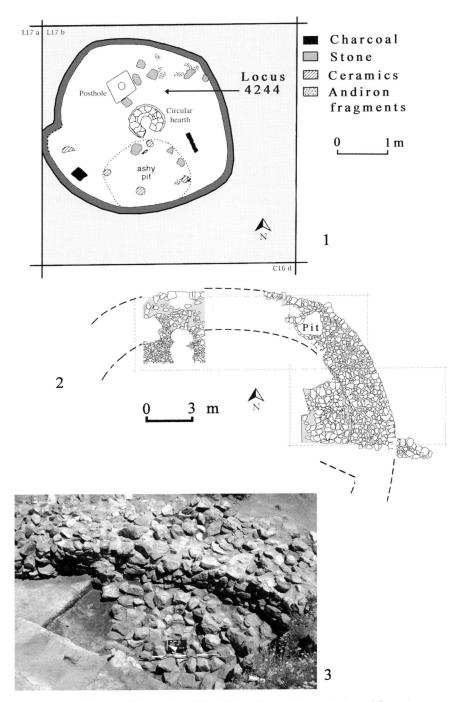

Figure 5.9 Late Chalcolithic Sos Höyük, Level V: **1** Plan of round house (adapted from Sagona and Sagona 2000). **2, 3** Segment of the circular stone wall that surrounded the centre of the village (Photo: Bronwyn Douglas)

textile impressions either on the interior surface, or sandwiched between two layers of clay, a method that continued into the third millennium.[54]

3   Chaff-Faced Ware, the hallmark of Amuq E/F and widespread through northern Mesopotamia and northern Syria, has turned up in considerable quantities around Doğubayazit and Lake Van.[55] These discoveries fill a crucial gap and make sense of the long known Amuq parallels in Caucasus, including those at Maikop, in the northwestern corner.

4   Another ware is named after Tilki Tepe, near Van, where it was first identified; it also occurs in considerable quantities at nearby Yılantaş.[56] Vessels are built from a chaff-tempered buff clay, and have a well-polished outer surface. Some pieces also bear painted decoration, often in fugitive red or black. Presently, Tilki Tepe ware is restricted to sites located east of Lake Van, and at Tekhut in Armenia, suggesting a small distribution zone, extending to the middle Araxes Valley.

5   Black burnished ware has a well-levigated paste and a polished surface. The radiocarbon analysis of a charcoal sample from an exploratory trench at Pulur (Erzurum) produced a reading of 4242–4075 BC (OZG 367) at one sigma confidence, suggesting that this ware could be pushed back to the fifth millennium BC.[57]

6   The final group represents the formative stages of the Kura-Araxes tradition and has been provisionally termed "proto-Kura-Araxes."[58] Its contrasting scheme of black and red surfaces is easily recognizable as a Kura-Araxes attribute, and points to experimentation with a controlled firing atmosphere. Its exterior surface is generally black and well burnished. Yet it differs from "classic" Kura-Araxes pottery of the Early Bronze Age in two ways: First, certain pieces display incised ornamentation that is a more typical attribute of Sioni pottery, and, second, the vessel walls tend to be thinner than those produced in the third millennium BC. Noteworthy is the jar type with a globular body and comparatively tall neck that can be either convex or slightly swollen, which foreshadows its popularity in the third millennium. Hemispherical bowls and flat lids with a loop handle at the centre are also part of the repertoire.

From this mix, we can detect a number of dynamics at play. Radiocarbon dates place the earliest Late Chalcolithic levels at Sos Höyük (VA) on a par with the columned building at Arslantepe VII at around 3550 BC.[59] Importantly, whereas proto-Kura-Araxes and black burnished wares were recovered in the earliest Sos VA deposits, they are not present in the Arslantepe columned building. At Arslantepe, red-black ware appears in the very latest phase of Period VII sandwiched between the columned building and the VIA complex. Equally significant is the appearance of red-black and black burnished pottery in Trans-Caucasus around 3350–3000 BC. This suggests that eastern Anatolia currently has earlier contexts for red-black and black burnished wares than does Trans-Caucasus. However, this evidence does *not* imply that the Kura-Araxes horizon originated in eastern Anatolia. The picture is far more complicated than that. New information is accelerating a shift from the single homeland hypothesis to one that views cultural interaction across the highland, stretching from the Euphrates to the southern Caucasus, as

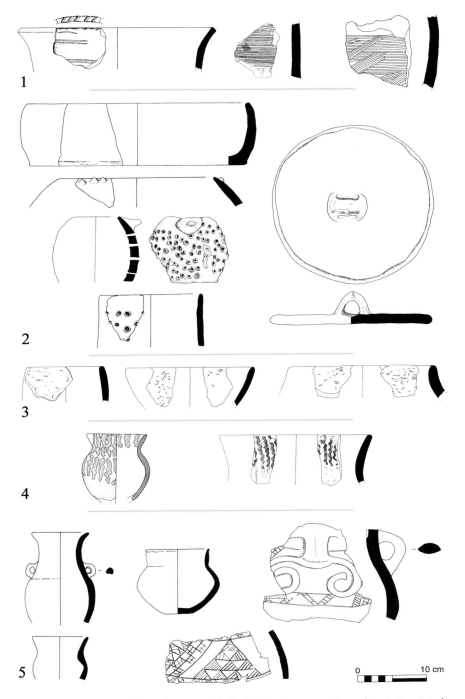

Figure 5.10 Main pottery types from the Late Chalcolithic of eastern Anatolia: **1** Sioni (adapted from Marro 2007a). **2** Drab ware (adapted from Sagona and Sagona 2000). **3** Chaff-Faced Ware (adapted from Marro 2007a). **4** Tilkitepe ware (adapted from Korfmann 1982; Marro 2007a). **5** Proto Kura-Araxes (adapted from Sagona and Sagona 2000)

the driver in the formation of the Kura-Araxes package. The red and black color scheme may well have been an Anatolian contribution, but attributes such as small handles set at the juncture of the neck and shoulders and tall (slightly swollen) necked jars are firmly embedded in the Trans-Caucasian Chalcolithic. Rothman aptly described the nature of these highland dynamics as "ripples in a stream of movement of pastoral nomads, traders and small farmers back and forth in the larger region."[60] Moreover, according to him, this movement was prompted by the search for specific natural resources, especially metal ores, population densities, and the adaptation to a range of environmental zones. Recent pollen data from Georgia, pointing to an increase in rainfall and temperature (a "climatic optimum") beginning after 4000 BC, also suggest that environmental change may have been a factor in economic strategies and expansion.[61]

Western Anatolia

Compared with the eastern regions, the fourth millennium in western Anatolia, which here includes the central plateau and northern coastal regions, remains rather obscure with the southwest providing the most reasonable picture. Beycesultan, in the upper reaches of the Menderes (Maeander) Valley, offers a deep sequence of immense value for tracing the continuity of occupation. The earliest arrivals at the site established their village on virgin soil in Late Chalcolithic. Once thought to precede immediately the local Early Bronze Age, it now seems better to place this first settlement earlier at 3800–3400 BC, with Kuruçay (Levels 6A–4) following, as the lead up to the third millennium.[62] Late Chalcolithic pottery from Beycesultan (Levels XL–XX) can be grouped into four phases dominated by a dark ware with a burnished surface that is sometimes decorated with a matt white paint. Shapes are simple and serviceable, consisting of flat dishes with outcurving sides, open bowls with thick everted rims, and large and small jugs with one handle linking rim to shoulder. Architecture is poorly understood for these lowest levels, but mud brick buildings with a main rectangular room and attached anteroom are clearly discernable.

Meanwhile at Kuruçay alleyways and paths separated freestanding, single structures (Figure 5.11: 1).[63] Despite these spaces between the buildings—cross walls blocked circulation at certain points—there does not appear to have been a predetermined plan for the settlement. One building (XXII) was considered a sacred space because of the concentration of ceramics of uncommon forms. Otherwise buildings appear to have been domestic—large enough to accommodate three to five members of a family and sometimes equipped with an oven in the corner. In Level 4 multiroomed units—one main room with storage rooms attached—suggest some social or economic differentiation. At Bağbaşı, in the Elmalı Plain, the Late Chalcolithic is poorly preserved, but enough survives there and at other sites in the region to indicate the spread of this southwest tradition to northern Lycia.[64]

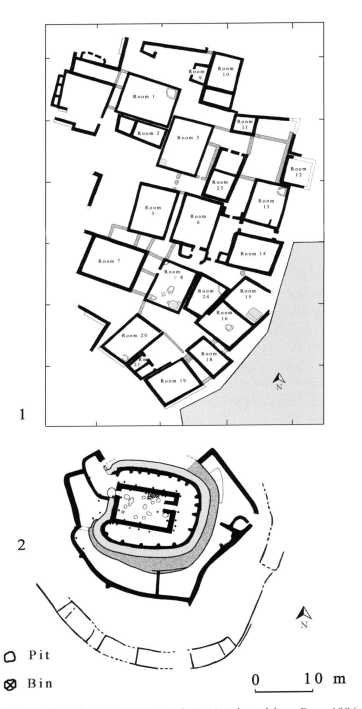

Figure 5.11 **1** Plan of Late Chalcolithic Kuruçay, Levels 4–6A (adapted from Duru 1996a). **2** Plan of Late Chacolithic Karataş (adapted from Eslick 1988)

Northwestern Anatolia and the Pontic Zone

The evidence for the northwest and Pontic regions is patchy. Pattern-burnished ware characterizes Kumtepe B, in the Troad, and has been found at other sites on the Gelibolu Peninsula and around the Sea of Marmara.[65] Late Chalcolithic marble figurines of the so-called Kilia type with a flat, "cut-out" body and ovoid head were found at Tigani IV, Pekmez and several sites in the northwest and the Aegean.[66] Black burnished wares with white painted ornaments occur at Yazır Höyük, Orman Fidanlığı VII, and the Konya Plain.[67] Bowls at Orman Fidanlığı were also decorated with oblique bands of lines pendant from the rim, which can be notched and rippled.[68] Forms include bowls with sharply everted rims and rounded pots with spurred handles. The Late Chalcolithic burials at Ilıpınar, which are not associated with a known settlement, have nonetheless offered evidence on mortuary rites (Figure 5.12).[69] Unlike the Neolithic burials, these fourth millennium graves sometimes had two individuals, mostly adults, who were placed in a contracted position together with pottery and metal objects.

İkiztepe, the key site in the Black Sea region, incorporates four small mounds, two of which have been investigated extensively. Even so, its stratigraphy is difficult to interpret, with nomenclature complicating matters further; much material attributed originally to the Early Bronze Age has been reassigned to the Late Chalcolithic.[70] Discoloration of soil and rows of post holes point to the use of timber and wattle and daub in the construction of freestanding houses, conforming to a rough square or rectangular plan usually with an anteroom. Fixed clay hearths were set into the floors. Potters produced a restricted range of simple shapes that are also attested at Dündartepe—hole-mouth jars sometimes with triangular ledge handles and deep bowls with inverted rim, often producing a sharp profile, are the most common.

Central Anatolia

Of all the Anatolian regions in the Late Chalcolithic period, developments in central Anatolia, in particular the north central region, are the most difficult to comprehend, a situation that no doubt owes much to its geographical circumstance—a cusp region open to influences from neighbors. The Alişar Regional Project, incorporating renewed investigations at Alişar Höyük and new excavations at nearby Çadır Höyük, has done much in recent years to clarify the situation.[71] It appears that after the relative obscurity of the Middle Chalcolithic, clusters of sites emerged centred around larger settlements such as Alişar and Çadır.

Alişar Höyük, in the bend of the Kızılırmak, is a key site with a 12 m deep deposit, but has a rather confusing stratigraphy and nomenclature. For a long time it was thought that the many levels before the Early Bronze Age II should be compressed into 500 years with a baseline about 3000 BC. It is more reasonable, however, to extend the beginning of the sequence well into the middle of the fourth millennium.[72] The American excavators labelled eight Chalcolithic levels in Early (Levels 19–15) and Late Chalcolithic (Levels 14–12). A distinctive type found both at

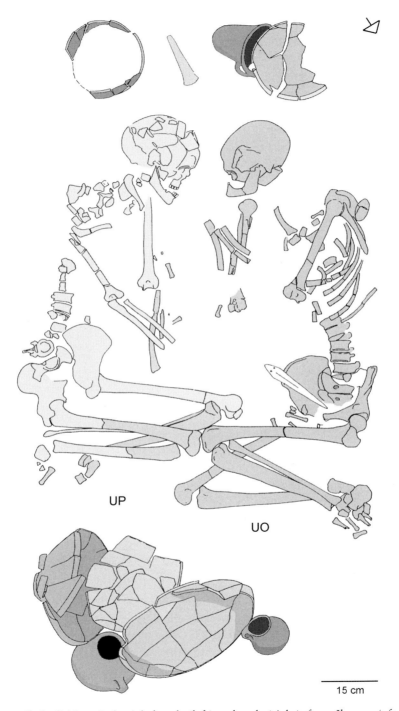

UP

UO

15 cm

Figure 5.12 Late Chalcolithic twin burial, female (left) and male (right), from Ilıpınar (after Roodenberg and Alpaslan Roodenberg 2008)

Alişar and Alaca Höyük is the tall and slender stemmed bowl, or "fruitstand," which is well burnished and sometimes fluted horizontally (Figure 5.13). Pedestalled jars, and cups with one handle and a low carinated belly were also part of the repertoire.

Çadır Höyük, by way of contrast, provides a clearer picture. Several features of the settlement, including a large stone gateway and accompanying enclosure wall, sizeable courtyards and nondomestic buildings (the so-called Burnt House), suggest the community had an administrative system responsible for public works. Concentration of spindle whorls, stone debitage, hearths, and quantities of grain scattered across the courtyards show that these public areas probably served a number of purposes. Ceramics from central Anatolia point to considerable interaction with surrounding regions. Contact with southeastern Europe, for instance, is reflected in dark vessels often black burnished, bearing punctate ornamentation, incised geometric patterns filled with a white paste, and white painted designs. This range is particularly well attested at Büyük Güllücek.[73] Then there are influences that may stem from the east. A predilection for black burnished surfaces and the use of small, decorative knobs are known from the Kura-Araxes culture province. Indeed, the interface between central and eastern Anatolia, mentioned some 30 years ago by Ufuk Esin and Güven Arsebük, is a topic that has found favor once again.[74] But what distinguishes the Çadır assemblage is the number of highly burnished bowls with an *omphalos* (concave) base and other vessels decorated with a red painted band, applied after firing.

EARLY BRONZE AGE (ca. 3100–2000 BC)

By the Late Chalcolithic, sites in the Taurus region were part of a more widespread tradition that extended across the northern Syro-Mesopotamian plain to the southern alluvium of Iraq and southwestern Iran. This vast and variegated region was the seedbed for civilization—a new order of life made possible by mixes of human skills, needs, and natural resources. We have seen these factors at play already, as in the case of the spectacular flowerings of the Neolithic period. Yet for all the spectacular achievements of these earliest village communities, they foreshadowed rather than reflected civilization.

It is worth considering for a moment just what it is we are looking for. Although the emergence of civilization represents one of the crucially important episodes in human history, the concept itself is not an easy one to define adequately. Most general definitions of civilization stress that it represents "an advanced stage in human social development" (*Oxford English Dictionary*). That is without doubt, but we still have to determine how advanced or developed and along what lines. Some have sought to identify the features that distinguish "civilized" societies—monumental buildings, cities, and irrigation have all been suggested, and, as we approach the threshold of literacy, writing has been suggested as a credential too. Although we may think that these attributes are typical of a civilization, those early civilizations that developed outside the Greater Mesopotamian region have shown us that they need not be found together. But what

Figure 5.13 Main pottery types from the Late Chalcolithic of central Anatolia (adapted from Schoop 2002)

these features and others besides have in common is social, political, and economic *complexity*. They all point to a level of human interaction that offered more diversity and elaboration of experiences than ever before, crystallizing in the third millennium BC.[75]

Cities, centers, and villages

We should move now to more concrete matters and delineate, however summarily, some of the markers that registered this new order. The concept of civilization is inextricably linked with another phenomenon that emerged in this period—that of the city. Today our image of a city is one of a huge metropolis teeming with millions of residents, mostly strangers to each other, who are engaged in myriad activities a city has to offer. Although an ancient city would be hardly recognizable to us, we are nevertheless talking about the same phenomenon. There are many definitions of a city, ranging from those that give primacy to population size through the complexity of its administrative system, to the specific skills of its residents. Essentially, at its most basic level, an urban center within the context of early civilizations is an entity that provided a number of specialized functions when compared to the greater hinterland. This often meant that the greater proportion of the population of a centre was engaged in activities other than food production. For this reason cities and towns are sometimes viewed as structurally similar and specialized settlements, which are distinguishable largely, and often arbitrarily, on the basis of size.

Certainly, the relative size of an ancient city or town when compared with the overall population of the surrounding area is a characteristic that needs to be considered. In the ancient Near East, a city that served as a provincial centre would normally have had a few thousand inhabitants, although calculating ancient populations sizes is always a notoriously difficult task. Another feature of a city is the number of activities that it can support when compared to a village, for instance. The burgeoning consumer market of an ancient city promoted a focused division of labor, enabling some to free themselves from farming and seek gainful employment in specialized roles such as craftsmen, bureaucrats, and merchants.

Finally, while geographers naturally stress the emergence of new settlement patterns and the centrality of urban centers ("the central place"), one needs to remember that a city is part of a network and therefore very much dependent on neighboring satellite settlements. Whereas the underlying determining force that brought together these dense populations to form cities in southern Mesopotamia appears to have been large-scale irrigation agriculture, in the northern regions rain-fed farming was also practiced. In both regions, communal effort was needed to expand and maintain the fields. Hence determining the function of a city is important. The earliest Near Eastern cities were, above all, the center of a region, and often had administrative, economic, and political roles, providing services such as central storage and manufactured products, as well as law and order. They were also actively engaged in an increasingly organized network of long-distance trade. As such, some cities formed the core of small polities called city-states, which comprised stretches of farmland and interdependent settlements.

Although changes apparent in settlement patterns and economy are defining criteria, they offer only part of the picture. Another crucial aspect is the nature of central governmental authority, which anthropologists refer as a state level of sociopolitical organization. It is clear that within an urban setting people began to grow apart in terms of power and wealth. Populations gradually became divided into social and economic classes in a stratified society. Status was based less on kinship and social prestige, which was largely ascribed, as in the ranked societies of earlier periods, and more on designated roles in highly specialized bureaucracies in which some groups of people had more access to political office, authority, and wealth than others. These new and powerful bureaucratic institutions controlled much of the decision making and were responsible for the centralization of certain activities such as religious ritual, legalized use of force and the economy. These new leaders were the elites of society and they legitimized their positions and conferred value on institutions they controlled. The construction of monumental temples and palaces was one way they consolidated their standing.

Although civilization can be defined conceptually, its manifestations are by no means uniform. So far we have discussed the social and political organisation of Greater Mesopotamia to which southeastern Anatolia belongs.[76] What type of social systems did the rest of Anatolia, north of the Taurus, harbor? The cultural landscape in this region was far more variegated (Figures 5.14 and 5.15), and the transformation processes in the two regions—Mesopotamia and Anatolia—are quite distinct.[77] Whereas the various terms and nomenclature for this transitional period confuse matters—"towns," "town-like settlements," "city-state," and "proto-city-state"—Özlem Çevik quite correctly points out that the difference is much more fundamental.

In southeastern Anatolia, we can trace the transformation from villages through towns to the large centers of the first half of the third millennium (Samsat, in the Karababa Basin, ca. 10 ha), and finally cities in the mid-third millennium BC (Titriş Höyük, in the Bozova region, ca. 43 ha, and the exceptionally large Kazane Höyük, in the Urfa province, ca. 100 ha). When cities emerged, the regions south of the Taurus established polities based on a four-tiered hierarchy of settlements, whereby the largest (20–43 ha) formed the core in a mutually beneficial network of exchange and support, involving towns (5–15 ha), tertiary centers (2–5 ha), and hamlets (0.1–1.0 ha). The function of each component of these urban conglomerates is not easy to disentangle, such as those of towns like Kurban Höyük and Lidar Höyük, although an extensive potters' workshop at the latter is suggestive of its primary function.

North of the Taurus Mountains, two broad settlement patterns are apparent, roughly dividing at the Euphrates River. Eastwards, the highlands lacked any form of centralized authority until the first millennium BC, and in the Early Bronze Age their character was entirely rural.[78] Small farmsteads, averaging 1–2 ha, are scattered across the rugged terrain to the highest altitudes. In the Upper Euphrates Valley, in the Malatya-Elazığ region, the situation differed. There Norşuntepe dominated the Altınova Plain in the Early Bronze Age I when it grew to 3.2 ha, only to decrease substantially a few centuries later.[79] The Malatya Plain reflects similar circumstances, where Arslantepe expanded to about 4 ha. In central Anatolia, the largest centers

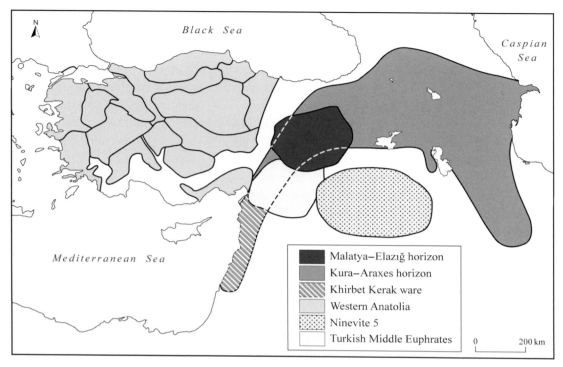

Figure 5.14 Map of Early Bronze Anatolia showing the main cultural zones

on the plateau were about 10 ha in size. Even though Alişar (28 ha), Acemhöyük (56 ha) and Karahöyük and Kültepe (50 ha) are larger, Çevik quite rightly suggests that their maximum expansion can be reasonably attributed to later developments. The western regions conform to an approximately similar pattern—the largest Early Bronze Age sites such as Troy and Karataş averaged between 5 and 13 hectares, with Beycesultan (30–40 ha) being the exception.

On size and site distribution alone, then, Anatolia appears to have had three types of socio-political transformation in the Early Bronze Age: *urbanization* in the southeastern region whereby large cities controlled their hinterland through a highly organized administrative system; *centralization* in western and central Anatolia, where the largest sites enjoyed only a loose control of the surrounding area; and a *rural landscape* in the eastern highlands that harbored villages with no indication of any hierarchy.[80]

Before we turn to specific regional issues we need to mention one other important development that incorporated much of Anatolia and peaked in the Early Bronze Age III period, namely trade. Across much of southeastern, central, western Anatolia and beyond into the Aegean, we witness the emergence of innovations that are suggestive of an extensive network of interaction.[81] We have already made reference to growing central authorities and the changing nature of settlements that now included upper and lower towns, fortification systems, and monumental public buildings. Wheelmade pottery, although manufactured in the southeast for over a

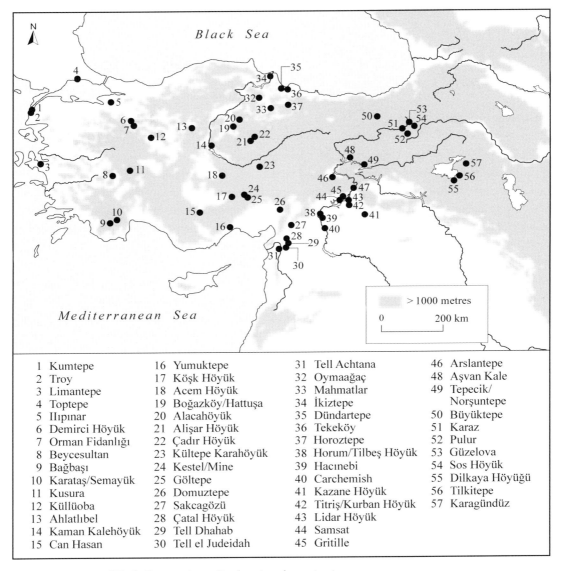

Figure 5.15 Map of Early Bronze Anatolia showing the main sites

1 Kumtepe	16 Yumuktepe	31 Tell Achtana	46 Arslantepe
2 Troy	17 Köşk Höyük	32 Oymaağaç	48 Aşvan Kale
3 Limantepe	18 Acem Höyük	33 Mahmatlar	49 Tepecik/
4 Toptepe	19 Boğazköy/Hattuşa	34 İkiztepe	Norşuntepe
5 Ilıpınar	20 Alacahöyük	35 Dündartepe	50 Büyüktepe
6 Demirci Höyük	21 Alişar Höyük	36 Tekeköy	51 Karaz
7 Orman Fidanlığı	22 Çadır Höyük	37 Horoztepe	52 Pulur
8 Beycesultan	23 Kültepe Karahöyük	38 Horum/Tilbeş Höyük	53 Güzelova
9 Bağbaşı	24 Kestel/Mine	39 Hacınebi	54 Sos Höyük
10 Karataş/Semayük	25 Göltepe	40 Carchemish	55 Dilkaya Höyüğü
11 Kusura	26 Domuztepe	41 Kazane Höyük	56 Tilkitepe
12 Küllüoba	27 Sakcagözü	42 Titriş/Kurban Höyük	57 Karagündüz
13 Ahlatlıbel	28 Çatal Höyük	43 Lidar Höyük	
14 Kaman Kalehöyük	29 Tell Dhahab	44 Samsat	
15 Can Hasan	30 Tell el Judeidah	45 Gritille	

millennium, appears in western Anatolian contexts around the mid-third millennium BC, and thence found its way to the western Aegean. Likewise, distinctive ceramic forms began to circulate across the peninsula: west Anatolian depata, tankards, and cutaway-spouted jugs, for instance, were transported eastwards, whereas "Syrian bottles" and wheelmade plates were exotic tableware items north of the Taurus. Many have argued that the quest for metals drove this new economic system. The acquisition and control of precious metals—gold, silver and tin—fuelled a shift in social structures in which items of precious metals acted as indicators of status and power.

Regional survey

Southeast Anatolia

After the collapse of the Uruk colonial network, interregional exchange patterns continued within substantially different organizational structures. The centralization of authority and its various manifestations virtually disappeared, and did not re-emerge until about 2600–2500 BC, when large urban centers and their polities began to dominate the landscape in response to a resurgence of Mesopotamian influences. Sandwiched between these two periods, the Early Bronze Age I–II developed a sociopolitical system that was essentially rural, attested by the small towns and villages scattered across the Anatolian foothills and plains.

In the Turkish Lower Euphrates Valley, our picture is determined largely by field surveys in those riverine areas that have now been flooded by the Atatürk, Birecik, and Carchemish dams.[82] Our understanding of settlements in the plains, however, is poor, with the recently published results of the survey of the Harran Plain providing reasonable data.[83] Stratified sequences, too, are relatively few and architectural exposures are restricted, a situation exacerbated by the drowning of a number of key centers, most notably Samsat. Even so, we can point to a number of changes in the early centuries of the third millennium.

In the first place, we can note a marked reduction in the size of sites. Kurban Höyük, for instance, a bustling village of four hectares in the Late Chalcolithic (Period VI) contracted to one hectare in the subsequent period. This pattern of a decrease in site size from the late fourth to the early third millennium BC is also reflected in the surrounding region where a number of settlements of similar dimensions are situated.[84] A comparable shift in settlement pattern occurred at Hassek Höyük. There, walled enclosure gave way to groups of small houses (Figure 5.4: 2). Survey results, on the other hand, show that the *number* of sites actually increased in the post-Uruk period. These two features—a reduction in the size of settlements and an increase in their number—suggest a demographic shift to the countryside. Whereas this change from townsfolk to villagers may have accounted for a good portion of the population, others may well have adopted a more nomadic existence, making their presence in the archaeological record less visible.[85]

At first glance, the regional system linking these hamlets appears largely nonhierarchical. Yet some maintain that the three-tiered settlement structure of the preceding centuries basically continued in albeit substantially modified form, with fewer large sites.[86] Samsat and Carchemish were now the dominant sites along the Turkish Lower Euphrates and therefore probably became nodes for communication. A landscape dotted with many small sites would not have encouraged a closed system rather than regional integration, with production based largely around households. This change in settlement pattern may also reflect the shifting routes of trade that appear to have favored the Khabur and Tigris basin rather than the Euphrates in the early third millennium BC.[87] Even so, while trade may have been scaled down along the Turkish Euphrates corridor, it certainly did not collapse.[88] Grave goods in the form of metal artefacts and jewellery items from the Birecik and Hassek Höyük cemeteries leave no doubt that many families were still prosperous.

Two broad culture provinces can be discerned, even though nomenclature and chronology remain matters of considerable debate:[89] A western zone, stretching from the Amuq Plain (Hatay) to the Euphrates River, which is distinguished by a ceramic horizon that includes Late Reserved Slip, Plain Simple Ware, and Red-Black Burnished Ware;[90] and an eastern region-based zone in the Tigris drainage system where the Ninevite 5 assemblage is common. The main trend at the beginning of the third millennium is the disappearance of chaff-tempered wares and their replacement with grit-tempered Plain Simple Ware, which was already present in smaller quantities in the Late Chalcolithic period.[91] Core types like hemispherical bowls with thickened or folded rims are now associated with a range of new shapes: Cups with a sinuous profile (the so-called *cyma recta* curve) and delicate ring base, and bowls with a pedestal or stemmed base (Figures 5.16 and 5.17). Late Reserved Slip Ware, a development of the earlier Late Chalcolithic version, and its eye-catching ornamentation, is not as common, but present in all sequences. The third fabric group is cooking pot ware, represented by handmade simple bowls and round-bodied pots with a hole mouth.

Radical shifts in social and political structures and innovations in metal technology characterize the Early Bronze Age III ca. 2500–2000 BC. Large cities and centers developed at Tirtiş, Samsat, Lidar, and Kazane south of the Taurus, as southeastern Anatolia became absorbed into the far-flung territorial network of the Akkadian Empire. As with the Uruk phenomenon, what is not altogether clear is the degree of influence external dynamics had in the emergence of urbanism in southeastern Turkey. Tirtiş Höyük, the capital of a small city-state that lasted about 300 years (2500–2200 BC), is a crucial site. The growth of the city has been elucidated through a skillful combination of detailed geophysical prospection and select excavation.[92] Covering an area of 43 ha, the site comprises a high mound, where presumably the ruler lived amidst the central administrative quarters, and suburbs that stretched across the lower and outer town sectors. A massive fortification wall surrounded the entire city; at some distance was the cemetery. The overall plan is suggestive of a highly organized, central authority with a clear predetermined idea of design. Large public buildings, constructed both on the high mound and in the lower areas, were the focal points of a comfortable and bustling city. Substantial terraces point to the levelling of areas before the construction of the domestic quarters, which were provided with wide streets, well-built houses of standard plan that were fitted with sewerage facilities. That the houses closest to the high mound were larger, may point to the status of its occupants. Yet despite the urban character of Titriş, the frequent occurrence of sickle blades in houses indicates that its residents were still closely tied to the land and the agricultural cycle. Other specialized activities include textile manufacture, wine production, and the knapping of

Figure 5.16 Main pottery types from the Early Bronze Age I–II southeastern Anatolia. All are from Hassek Höyük (adapted from Gerber 2005)

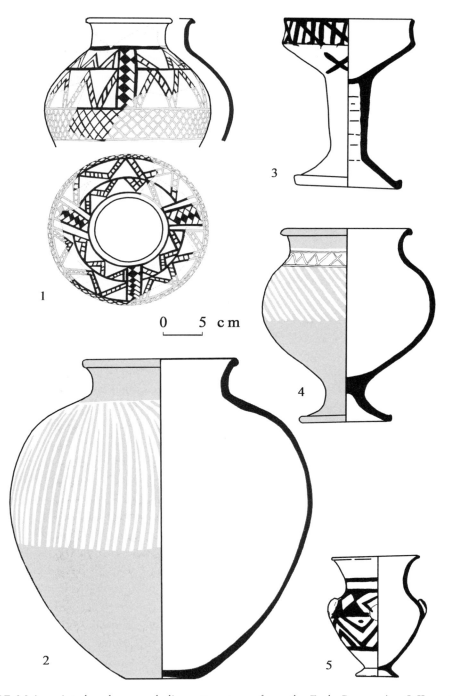

Figure 5.17 Main painted and reserved slip pottery types from the Early Bronze Age I–II southeastern Anatolia: **1, 2** Hassek Höyük. **3–5** Birecik cemetery (adapted from Gerber 2005; Sertok and Ergeç 1999)

Canaanean blades. Kurban Höyük and Lidar Höyük were secondary centres, both with scaled-down features that are redolent of Titriş.[93]

The ceramic repertoire expands significantly during the mid-third millennium (Figure 5.18). New shapes such as cups with a corrugated surface augment the Plain Simple Ware assemblage, and vessels that belong to cooking pot ware have triangular handles attached to the rim to aid portability. Among the new wares are: Horizontal reserved slip ware, now decorated with different patterns; Karababa painted ware, with geometric designs executed in a dark red paint; comb wash ware, distinguished by the combing of a painted surface; and metallic ware, a highly fired, crisp fabric with a consistent fine gray biscuit that was used to manufacture, among other shapes, the Syrian bottles (Figure 5.22: 7, 10).

East-central Anatolia (Turkish Upper Euphrates)

Around 3000 BC the impressive Uruk-influenced palace and temple complex at Arslantepe collapsed, and with it centralized organization. What followed was striking change in the nature of the settlement and sociocultural dynamics at Arslantepe and in the greater Malatya-Elazığ region, highlighted by the comingling of several cultural traditions.[94] Syro-Mesopotamian influence is still clearly discernable in ceramics—a Plain Simple Ware and Late Reserved Slip horizon with provincial Ninevite 5—but this is embedded in a strong east Anatolian and Trans-Caucasian context. These relations were not, to be sure, uniform. For instance, although one can now correlate the sequences at the Arslantepe and Norşuntepe, their developmental phases were certainly not mirror images. Two primary factors are behind this somewhat heterogenous picture. One is geographical location, which exposed sites in the Malatya Plain, for instance, to different foreign trends to those in the Altınova, which had a more direct access to the Upper Tigris route; and the relative isolation of Murat Valley ensured that foreign influences were well diluted before they reached sites like Taşkun Mevkii. The second reason has to do with the nature of the contact itself, which continued to be directional rather than uniform.

At Arslantepe, pastoral groups introduced a lifestyle and cultural heritage that had deep roots in Trans-Caucasus. These folk, bearers of the red-black ware that was already in circulation within Period VIA complex, took advantage of the vacuum to establish a settlement that is distinguished by two subphases: Period VIB1 (Early Bronze Age IA) followed in quick succession by VIB2. The earliest was a village of freestanding huts, mostly irregular in plan, but conforming generally to a rectangular shape with rounded corners. These dwellings had wattle and daub walls supported on a framework of wooden posts—mud brick was used sparingly—and a sunken floor. Excavations reveal small clusters of huts sometimes joined by rows of postholes, which probably delineate partitions that penned in livestock. The village was short lived, but its material was remarkably homogenous, comprising handmade red-black pottery of the Trans-Caucasian type. The subsequent and more substantial settlement (Period VIB2) has a similar organization of space and house design, but is constructed with mud bricks. For

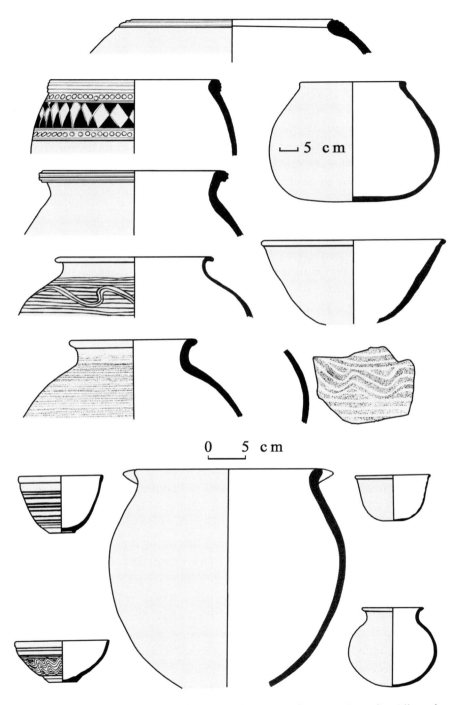

Figure 5.18 Main pottery types from the Early Bronze Age III southeastern Anatolia. All are from Kurban Höyük (adapted from Algaze 1990a)

example, one house has a main room furnished with a circular hearth set into the center of the floor, and an anteroom used for storage. Intriguing is the combination of a conceptually Trans-Caucasian settlement with a ceramic assemblage that has a considerable amount of pale colored, wheelmade vessels, recalling the earlier Syro-Mesopotamian traditions of the VIA complex.

There is no settlement at Norşuntepe that is contemporary with Arslantepe VIB1. The hiatus in occupation that began around 3300 BC continued until 2900 BC, when, like Arslantepe VIB2, it came under the pervasive influence of Syro-Mesopotamia in the Early Bronze Age IB, which at Norşuntepe corresponds to Levels 30–25.[95] In the earliest layers (30–28), a substantial perimeter wall built of mud bricks on stone foundations surrounded Norşuntepe, like the ones at its neighbors Tepecik and Tülintepe. A limestone cylinder seal with a herringbone pattern of the Jemdet Nasr style, typical of Amuq G, and a bronze pin with a twisted head common at Carchemish, and among the grave goods in the Birecik cemetery, confirm this southern influence.[96] For the most part, houses were freestanding, rectilinear structures constructed of mud bricks, though in Level 26 two multiroomed buildings were partly exposed. Mostly pits follow in Level 25.

Meanwhile, in the Murat Valley, which was isolated from the main traffic with northern Syria, we find an intriguing connection with western regions. At Pulur (Sakyol) the settlement of Level X was laid out in a radial fashion, the *Anatolisches Siedlungsschema*, with adjoining houses and a communal central court (Figure 5.19: 1).[97] Yet the household fittings and contents—mud brick benches, horseshoe-shaped hearths with anthropomorphic decoration, ash pit and elaborately ornamented red-black pottery—are redolent of the Kura-Araxes (Early Trans-Caucasian) tradition. So here we see another tantalizing aspect of cultural interplay at work, this time combining a western concept of village layout, with an eastern sense of domestic space. We should place Taşkun Mevkii, with its juxtaposition of freestanding wattle and daub and mud brick buildings, and few examples of metalwork and Jemdat Nasr seals, within this context too.[98]

During the Early Bronze Age II A (2700–2600 BC), the Syro-Mesopotamian influence at Norşuntepe (Levels 24–21) started to wane, with a noticeable rise in Trans-Caucasian black burnished (Kura-Araxes) ceramics that are now associated with red-on-cream Malatya-Elazığ painted vessels, whose ladder motifs mimic the relief designs on the burnished ceramics.[99] Architectural designs changed rapidly from a round house (Level 24), through a wattle and daub structure (Level 23) to multiroomed, mud brick buildings (Level 21).[100] Arslantepe, by way of contrast, has no corresponding settlement during this interval. Following this, standardization set in and profound changes were experienced at Norşuntepe. Wattle and daub houses (*Pfosten-häuser*) are the norm from Level 20 through 14 at Norşuntepe (Early Bronze Age IIB). They have typical features—rounded corners, benches along the walls, and an eye-catching, horned hearth in the centre—well known from inner Georgia, in Trans-Caucasus.[101] The Norşuntepe dwellings also yielded considerable evidence of metallurgical activity, including crucibles and a bivalve mould for a shaft hole axe. As elsewhere in the region, ceramics show various influences, although Kura-Araxes predominates. Similar structures are also found at Değirmentepe III,

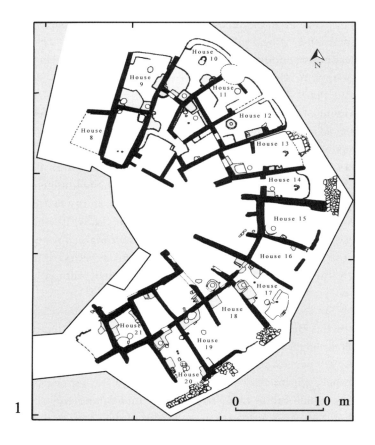

Figure 5.19 Early Bronze Age architecture from the Euphrates region of east-central Anatolia: **1** Pulur (Sakyol) Level X (adapted from Koşay 1976). **2** Norşuntepe (Early Bronze Age III) jars in Storeroom 7, Horizon VII (adapted from Koşay 1976; Photo: courtesy Harald Hauptmann)

north of Norşuntepe,[102] but at Arslantepe pits and lack of architecture in Period VIC indicate that it was still not permanently occupied.

In terms of socioeconomic complexity, Noşuntepe reached its apogee in the Early Bronze Age III period (Levels 13–6), which lasted some 500 years (2500 to 2000 BC), as indeed did a number of sites in the Altınova Plain. Three superimposed building levels of a palatial complex are well preserved on the summit of the mound and are designated Levels 8–6. Distinguished by blocks of storage rooms and workshops, the settlement was most expansive in Level 6, with a store-room complex that extended across the summit of the site, measuring over 70 m along its length. The many in situ jars leave no doubt that this was an economic center of considerable importance (Figure 5.19: 2). Interestingly, compared to the Late Chalcolithic complex at Arslantepe VIA, the Norşuntepe "palace" is conspicuous by the absence of any features that can be interpreted as cultic. Prosperity is also recognizable at Korucutepe (Phase E) where a large and sturdy building (6 by 9 m), termed "the hall" by the excavators, contained a nest of three horseshoe andirons placed on top of a circular raised hearth.[103] Despite its period of instability, Arslantepe emerged in the Early Bronze Age III as a permanent settlement, though nowhere as grand as Norşuntepe.

In addition to the Syro-Mesopotamian ceramic wares that have already been dealt with, in the third millennium the Upper Euphrates is distinguished by two handmade horizons—the Kura-Araxes red-black burnished pottery and the Malatya-Elazığ painted vessels. Kura-Araxes pottery shows some very general trends from Early Bronze Age I to Early Bronze Age III. Relief decoration, for instance, appears to be more popular in the earlier centuries than incised and fluted ornamentation, which found favor towards the middle and end of the millennium. The tall jars with low shoulders from Pulur, often decorated in the upper part with a bold rendering of a human face in a schematic relief pattern, are good examples found in Early Bronze Age I contexts. Recessed necked jars with a rail (squared) rim also commonly bear plastic designs of quartered lozenges, ladder patterns, and pendant crescents. Horizontal flutes (a trait that appears to have arrived from the western regions), and vessels with slightly flattened girth (pointing to eastern developments) are later developments. Bowls of various profiles, handled pot lids that range from flat to a bevelled edge, and elaborately decorated pot stands are common shapes.

The Upper Euphrates is also the home of a distinctive painted pottery tradition restricted to sites in the Keban (Elazığ region) and Karakaya (Malatya region). Although it is associated with handmade Kura-Araxes pottery, and indeed probably derives from that tradition, it is not found further east in the Anatolian highlands and Trans-Caucasia. Clearly this handmade painted assemblage is a local tradition that developed, according to Catherine Marro, in tandem with the socioeconomic complexity of the Upper Euphrates. In a thorough study, she recognizes four groups (A–D) that can be attributed to the Early Bronze Age II (2850–2550 BC in her chronology) and another four (E–H) to the Early Bronze Age III (2555–2200 BC).[104] The general trend in this painted tradition is from one of regionalization (Early Bronze Age II) whereby small valleys are distinguished by local production and traits to one of uniformity as the centralization and complex hierarchical systems control production and exchange. The corpus of shapes is fairly limited and generally open, with globular pots and round-profiled bowls particularly common. Decorations are executed in matt red, brown or black paint on a cream to pinkish-buff background. Designs are generally geometric—zigzags, obliques and bands—are simple and often haphazardly painted with a fairly thick brush.

Eastern Anatolia

As we move eastwards from the Euphrates, into the rugged highlands that comprises the vast province of the Kura-Araxes culture, Syro-Mesopotamian influences begin to fade. Trans-Caucasian affiliations manifest themselves more prominently, but detailed insight, as for the Late Chalcolithic, is limited. Sos Höyük (Eruzurm) offers the most hope, but its restricted exposures for the Early Bronze Age preclude a full understanding of settlement layout. Nearby are the sites of Karaz, Güzelova and Pulur excavated by Hamit Koşay, but none provides a differentiated stratigraphy.[105] Further along, in the Lake Van Basin, we have Karagündüz and Dilkaya.[106]

After the formative period of the Late Chalcolithic, eastern Anatolia continued to play a pivotal role in the character of the Kura-Araxes. Within this divided landscape, this horizon is today represented by numerous mound sites that contain the accumulated debris of farming and transhumant settlements, mostly of modest proportions, averaging about 150 m in diameter. Larger sites do exist, especially in the western periphery of this culture province, along the Turkish Upper Euphrates region, and the eastern periphery, in the Ağrı province and modern Armenia, where fortified sites have been reported. The processes involved in the swift and astonishing dispersal of this horizon are still obscure, but evidence suggests the migration of people to a large extent. Whether this involved directional movement of certain groups from one region to another, or a more mosaic, "leapfrogging" model, is difficult to say, but the earlier view of a wave of people is unlikely.[107] There has been a tendency to view the Kura-Araxes assemblage as rather homogenous, whose history unfolds in a linear narrative, promoting monolithic and static notions of cultural development. The picture is far more complex. Even though, on the whole, communities tenaciously preserved fundamental elements of the Kura-Araxes culture—hearths, distinctive ceramic attributes, architectural styles, and use of space and so on—the horizon is distinguished through multiple regional adaptations, reflecting a conscious definition of group and individual identity.

We have little understanding of architecture at Sos Höyük during the Early Bronze Age I (Period VB, 3000–2800 BC), which is represented only by floor levels and a hearth. In Period VC (EB II), a freestanding, single-roomed house was founded on stone and built of mud bricks. A decorated circular clay hearth with central projections was positioned at the end of the room; bench and clay bin are standard fitments. Whereas pits define the Early Bronze Age III at Sos Höyük (Period VD), the succeeding period (Sos Höyük IV) witnesses an elaboration of Kura-

Araxes features within multiroomed houses.[108] Hearths, in particular, evolve along new lines. From the horned andirons of the Late Chalcolithic period, portable hearths develop into horse-shoe shapes with knobbed projections. Likewise the plain, round hearths fixed into the floors of Late Chalcolithic houses, develop into elaborate features with raised central horns by the early second millennium BC (Figure 5.20). At Karagündüz, juxtaposed mud brick buildings faced each other on either side of a wide street. Their rectilinear plans contrast with a circular structure partly exposed at the end of the street.

In ceramics several trends are noteworthy (Figure 5.21). During the first half of the third millennium BC, double spirals were a characteristic motif in the eastern part of the Kura-Araxes cultural province, but absent in the Upper Euphrates. In the earliest deposits at Karaz, they are

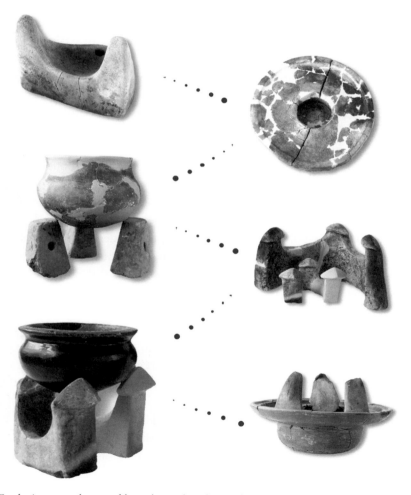

Figure 5.20 Evolutionary scheme of hearths and andirons from Sos Höyük near Erzurum, ranging from Late Chalcolithic (top) through Early Bronze to Middle Bronze (bottom)

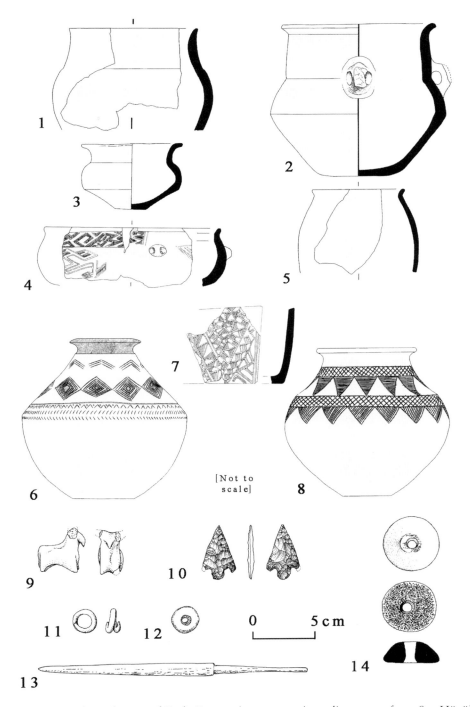

Figure 5.21 Main artefactual types of Early Bronze Age eastern Anatolia as seen from Sos Höyük (after Sagona 2000)

rather loose coils that meet at the top, whereas later, at nearby Pulur, potters preferred tighter spirals with narrower coils. Some of these spirals are in relief, whereas others are formed through a combination of grooving and relief. At Karagündüz, spiral patterns are incised on the surface and are rather crude by comparison. Impressed circles and vertical grooves, often alternating around the neck, are also a common motif. Nakhichevan handles (broad-based loops) are popular in the easternmost regions and Trans-Caucasus, but peter out as one moves west. The most common shape associated with spiral designs is the tall jar with recessed neck. Other shapes of the standard assemblage include hemispherical and straight-sided bowls, and lids with a central depression.

Around 2300 BC, or a tad earlier, the fortunes of communities living in eastern Anatolia began to change, largely because of new influences emanating from southern Caucasus. In the archaeological record of Caucasus, this is reflected in a number of large and striking elite tombs found throughout Trans-Caucasus, whose construction and contents differed markedly from the modest and simple pit inhumations of the preceding millennium. Termed *kurgan* burials and first investigated in Georgia in the Trialeti region, these new barrow inhumations and their rich assemblage, which included vessels of precious metals and, in some cases, a vehicle with four wheels of solid wood, are generally accepted as the hallmarks of a new age distinguished by fundamental social changes.

This change is also reflected in ceramics. A new array of shapes and modes of decoration, erring toward delicate and incised designs, begins to appear alongside Kura-Araxes pottery in easternmost Anatolia. These bring with them new terms derived from Trans-Caucasian burial complexes—Martkopi/early Trialeti and Bedeni.[109] How these ceramic repertoires relate typologically with the late phase of Kura-Araxes is still a matter of debate. Martkopi and early Trialeti, here lumped together, are distinguished by sharply biconical forms, a lustrous black burnished surface and incised ornamentation (Figure 5.21: 6, 8). One example from Sos Höyük also has ochre paste applied after firing. Rounded forms do occur, but incised ornamentation prevails generally in the form of pendant triangles. Bedeni pottery is lustrous. Potters used graphite and mica to produce an almost mirror-like silvery sheen, which at Sos Höyük is best seen on black vessels with a tripartite profile. These vessels are generally plain, although in Armenia they are often decorated with fine incisions and ascribed to late Kura-Araxes. The Bedeni pottery assemblage in Georgia is also characterized by straight-sided cups, spurred handles, multiple knobs and pattern burnishing, but only some of these features are present at Sos Höyük.

One of the issues that has generated considerable interest is the mode of economic subsistence practiced by the Kura-Araxes communities. Most researchers have argued in favor of a specialized strategy involving pastoral mobility. Accordingly, eastern Anatolia in the Early Bronze Age has been viewed as a landscape settled largely by nomadic stockbreeders, or at the very least by communities who practiced some form of transhumance—a subsistence strategy that involved part of a community moving with their flocks, seasonally or periodically, to different environmental zones. This picture is based mostly on three cultural attributes: The plan of certain villages—freestanding, rectilinear houses, or compounds of circular rooms—that mirror the settlement plans of modern nomadic tent sites; the apparent flimsy construction Early Bronze Age architecture, which seemed incongruous with the harsh climatic conditions of the mountains; the portability of certain artefact types such as andirons. Together these elements have fuelled the ideas of nomadism and, in turn, of rapid and extensive migrations. Recently, however, the analyses of faunal remains from Sos Höyük have provided some sobering conclusions. Two studies have argued against specialized pastoral production, suggesting instead that the inhabitants were sedentary agropastoralists whose economic management minimized risk, encouraged diversification and reflected stability—hardly the strategies of nomads.[110] Nonetheless, issues such as seasonality and transhumance need to be explored further.

In the Erzurum region, the late Kura-Araxes horizon extends into the second millennium BC, when the northern regions of Trans-Caucasus are also defined by a dark colored pottery tradition derived from the later kurgans. These dark wares are roughly contemporary to two painted pottery traditions that belong to the Middle Bronze Age. One is situated in the Malatya-Elazığ region and is similar to Khabur Ware of northern Syria. The other is concentrated on the high plateau of eastern Anatolia, southern Trans-Caucasus and northwestern Iran, encompassing the greater Aras/Araxes basin.[111] This geographical spread, crossing as it does several modern geopolitical boundaries, has generated an often confusing range of terms, including Van-Urmia, Karmir-Vank, Kizyl-Vank, Karmir-Berd, and Sevan-Uzerlik. It has also fuelled the viewed that pastoral nomads, who grazed their stock on mountain pastures, were responsible for this painted pottery tradition. Yet, despite the large quantity of intact ceramic vessels held in various museums, we know very little about these people in eastern Anatolia. The rapacious plunder of their cemeteries in recent times and research strategies that have focused on the excavation of sites in the valley floors have combined to deprive us of contextual information.

Nonetheless, systematic survey work is redressing the situation. We are now aware, for instance, that domestic pottery, as reflected from sherds collected from the surface of sites, was mostly unpainted. Conversely, painted pottery was placed in stone-lined cist tombs such as those found in the extensive and well-circumscribed cemeteries at Küçük Çatma, Suluçem, and Yuvadamı. Both conceptually and in their structure, these necropoleis are markedly different to barrow burials. Vessels are wheelmade and have a fabric that is baked to a brown or brick red color. Their exterior surface is slipped and given a perfunctory burnish. Brown or brick-red slips generally bear geometric patterns executed in black; some containers, slipped a second time with a pale color, exhibit captivating designs painted in a variety of colors.

Western Anatolia

In western Anatolia, there is no sharp break in assemblages at the onset of the Early Bronze Age to suggest an influx of new groups or significant external influences. Instead, we witness the acceleration of internal dynamics across the western peninsula that were eventually crystallized in the Early Bronze Age when the boundaries of cultural provinces became clearer. This region did, however, contribute to the population movements to the Aegean. Recent and significant genetic studies have identified intrusive clusters of Y-chromosome populations in the Aegean that connect it with western and northwestern Anatolia and Syro-Palestine.[112] The defining centuries in this process were 3300–3000 BC, a period that some regard as a phase transitional to the Early Bronze Age.[113] Conspicuous indicators of change are manifested in terms of architecture and use of space with the emergence of a settlement type often referred to as *Anatolisches Siedlungsschema*—small circular settlements of adjoining rectangular houses arranged in a radial plan centered on a large courtyard, such as Demirichöyük (Figure 5.24: 1).[114] Pottery repertoires can be baffling, but certain indicators are worth noting: The association of red slipped and burnished ceramics with black and dark-faced burnished wares; the petering out of white painted ornamentation as fluting and plastic design gained popularity; and the manufacture of jugs with rising ("beaked") spouts. Turan Efe stresses that pottery best reflects emergent sociopolitical structure in western Anatolia during the Early Bronze Age.[115]

Stronger regional characteristics became apparent during the Early Bronze Age I (3000–2700 BC), when four zones can be defined largely on the basis of ceramics (Figure 5.14):[116]

1 One, situated in the northwest, stretched from Iznik to Troy and the Dardanelles, and down past Yortan, incorporating the offshore islands. A slight variation of the *Anatolisches Siedlungsschema* is found at Troy. Overlooking the Dardanelles, the mound of Hissarlık Höyük, is one of the most celebrated sites in antiquity. Convinced it was Homeric Troy, Hienrich Schliemann led a series of excavations (1870–73, 1878–79, 1882, 1890), and in the process discovered what he thought was the "Treasure of King Priam."[117] Other campaigns followed Schliemann's—Wilhelm Dörpfeld in the 1890s, then half a century later Carl W. Blegen headed a University of Cincinnati expedition for seven campaigns (1932–38), and more recently a German–American team equipped with the latest technology and codirected by the late Manfred Korfmann, responsible for the prehistoric levels, and Brian Rose, working on the Greek and Roman levels, have extended our understanding of Troy even further.[118] These extensive investigations have produced a detailed sequence that has been divided into nine cultural periods (I–IX) and many subperiods. Our concern here is with the earliest, Levels I–V, whose internal developments have been re-interpreted in recent years. Essentially, Korfmann maintained that levels Troy I–III (ca. 3000–2100/2050 BC, or Early Bronze Age I–early III) display a cultural homogeneity, which they shared with coastal sites in western Anatolia and the islands of the eastern Aegean, enough to warrant the term "maritime Troia culture."[119] This reminds us that, when studying prehistoric Troy, we should refrain from according it primacy in the Early Bronze Age and instead assess its achievements within the context of equally significant neighboring sites.

    The earliest settlers, arriving sometime towards the end of the fourth millennium BC, had nothing to do with the Homeric period. Theirs was a small village (Troy I). Yet the need for security soon led to the construction of massive, stone fortification walls with a battered

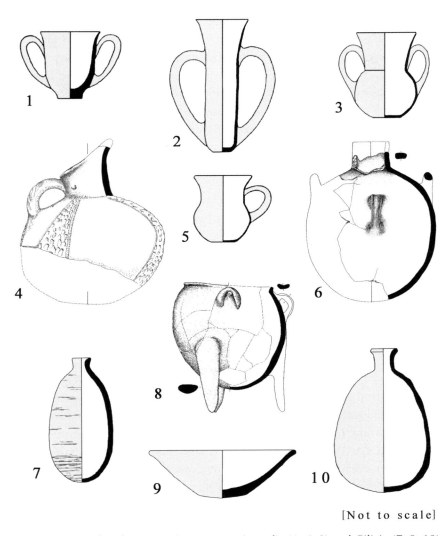

Figure 5.22 Pottery types of Early Bronze Age western Anatolia (1–6, 8) and Cilicia (7, 9, 10): **1, 2** Two-handled depas. **3, 5** Tankards. **4** Beak-spouted jar with barbotine decoration. **6** Jar with vertical lug handles. **7** and **10** Syrian bottles. **8** Tripod cooking pot. **9** Wheel-made plate

surface and multiple entrances flanked by guard towers. Along the southern section the wall still rises to height of 3 m. Within the enceinte, the community built a row of rectangular houses, not in a radial plan, usually comprising a freestanding large room, with little variation in finds between the dwellings. Among the house types is an apsidal house (103) and a distinctive type of building (House 102), the megaron, which consisted of a freestanding rectangular room with a porch at one end and a large room with a central hearth. The origin of the megaron plan has been discussed and connections with southeast Europe seem feasible.[120] Level I at Thermi, a site on the island of Lesbos, overlaps with Troy I, and its architecture vaguely conforms to a radial plan with a central courtyard. Ceramics of Troy I-Yortan cultural province are still very much dominated by black burnished vessels and dark-faced wares generally. The red slipped and burnished ceramics that found favor in the western hinterland made little headway here. Among the most characteristic forms well documented in the Troy assemblage is the conical bowl with a thickened, inverted rim (sometimes referred to as "antisplash"). They can have a flat base, or be placed on a pedestal foot, and occasionally have a horizontal lug attached just below the rim. Other simple bowls have a single handle that rises just above the rim. Incised decoration is rare and consists of rectilinear patterns filled with a white paste.

2   Another cultural province is located further inland and defined by the Early Bronze I assemblage at Beycesultan. Fine wares are distinctive for their combination of effective ornamentation, graceful forms, and high quality manufacture. Vessels are handmade, yet remarkably thin walled. They are hard fired and slipped in black and red, with exterior surfaces often brilliantly polished; interiors are usually cloth wiped. It is reasonable to suggest that some of the attributes—thin walls, fluting, and strap handles—are ceramic imitations of metalwork elements.

3   To the north of the Beycesultan zone is Demiricihöyük and the Upper Sakarya Valley, also referred to as the Phrygian–Bithynian cultural region. An excellent example of the radial plan village was discovered at Demircihöyük, in the Eskişehir Plain, where the houses shared a party wall and had a broad (back) end that abutted an enclosure wall (Figure 5.23: 1). There is little differentiation in the size of the houses, whose occupants used a communal courtyard fitted with bins and other utensils. Ahlatlıbel, outside this culture province near Ankara, is another instance of the radial plan, but as we have seen a clearer one is found a considerable distance to the east at Pulur (Sakyol) in the Upper Euphrates valley.[121] Efe has put a persuasive argument forward that the transition towards the radial plan is evidenced at Küllüoba 5–3 (ca. 3200–3000/2900 BC), where a thick layer of packed earth, up to 4 m in width, encircles a well-preserved settlement of clustered rectilinear houses, whose exterior walls form a zigzag around the circumference of the site.[122] The houses, with walls rising up to 2.5 m, face onto a central courtyard, foreshadowing the developed version exposed at Demirichöyük. The bulk of Early Bronze Age I ceramics from Demircihöyük are black topped, a style that did not really catch on elsewhere. Forms include simple hemispherical bowls with an upswung handle, occasionally decorated on the inside with a red painted cross.

4   Finally, according to Efe, enough evidence is emerging to isolate another ceramic zone in the southwest in the region of Lycia and Psidia.

The map of the Early Bronze Age II (2700–2400 BC) is a rather complicated mosaic of regional variations (Figure 5.14). The extent of the northwestern cultural region remains more or less the same. The fortress of Troy I was burnt, but the survivors constructed soon after a larger citadel, phase IIa, with two gateways (FL, FN) over its debris (Figure 5.24). This

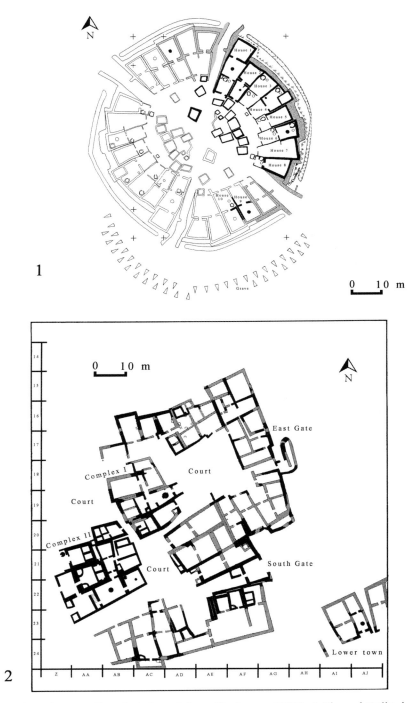

1

0 ___ 10 m

2

Figure 5.23 1 Plan of Demircihöyük (adapted from Korfmann 1983). 2 Plan of Küllüoba in the Early Bronze Age II (adapted from Efe 2007).

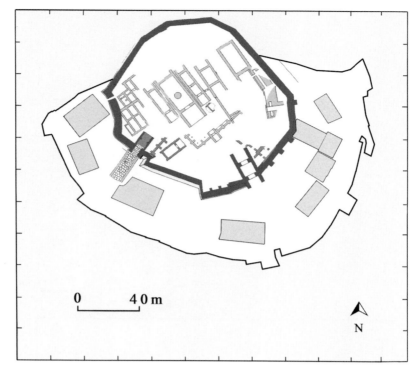

Figure 5.24 The extent of the Troy II and subsequent settlements as determined by archaeological prospection and geomorphological studies (adapted from Korfmann 2001)

settlement, Troy II, had at least 12 phases. By Troy IIc, which was also destroyed in a conflagration, we notice changes in the size of buildings in line with those of Karataş, while retaining the earlier concept of an all-encompassing fortification wall. The southwest gate (FM) is now approached by an impressive, wide, stone-paved ramp. Once inside, visitors would have been drawn to a huge megaron building (Megaron IIA), about 45 m in length and almost 300 sq m in area, which was part of a complex facing an enclosed court. Built on a large stone socle, the walls of Megaron IIA were built of mud bricks and timber. At least four other megara were constructed alongside this large building. The function of the individual buildings is uncertain, with shrine, palace, and public building all having been suggested.

By the last phase of the second settlement, Troy IIg, blocks of neat, tightly packed structures replaced the large buildings. The extraordinary "Treasures of Troy," discussed later, should be attributed to this phase.[123] Even though we have no detailed understanding of the treasure's context, it is not unreasonable to think that it was hidden or dropped in the frantic evacuation of the fortress, as fire swept through it. Judging by the settlement plan and the luxury items of gold, silver, and lapis lazuli, we can posit the view that they reflect a more hierarchical social system in which power lay in the hands of the wealthy elite. The treasures also demonstrate the contact the community of Troy IIg had with distant lands, and the high level of metallurgical skills.

Pottery begins to change both in color and shape, though on the whole the Troy II repertoire clearly evolves from Troy I. Red and tan colored vessels increased in popularity, though black polished ware was still abundant. Among the innovations is the introduction of the fast wheel in Troy IIb, which facilitated the production of new shapes such as plates and shallow dishes. The most distinctive is the *depas amphikypellon*, a two-handled tankard introduced in Troy IId (Figure 5.22: 1, 2). This and the popularity of other tankard types suggest the importance placed on feasting and drinking during Troy II. Also noteworthy is the appearance of pots and lids bearing face designs, which are essentially an evolved form of the practice of incising facial features on bowl rims in Troy I.

In the Early Bronze Age, the settlement at Beycesultan (Levels XIX–XVII) showed a marked change in plan, defined by a series of buildings that the excavators termed shrines. Beginning as a modest building in Level XVII, they developed into twin structures (Shrines A and B), with internal fittings—a pair of mud brick stelae and a horned structure—and "votive pottery" in the Early Bronze Age II. In the west Anatolian hinterland, the extensive zone of the Beycesultan Early Bronze Age I continued into the Early Bronze Age II, although subregional differences can be discerned, probably reflecting clusters of village potting traditions. The most significant development in the Beycesultan sequence is the sharp break between the ceramics of the Early Bronze Age I and II. After the destruction of Beycsultan Level XIIIa, the pottery changed markedly. Although still handmade, vessels were built with thick walls and are rather heavy. Gone are the thin fine wares. Exterior surfaces have a crackled appearance from firing, which baked vessels to a bright red or black. They are also burnished, but not to the high polish of the Early Bronze Age I. Their forms tend to be new, large and striking, in contrast to the smaller, elegant shapes of the Early Bronze Age I. Horned pedestalled bowls, large bowls on a tripod base and a high loop handle, wide-mouthed cups on three feet, and hole-mouthed jars with two twisted loop handles are among the profusion of new shapes. Grooved and ribbed ornamentation is effectively used to complement the form of vessels and is often found in combination with applied ribs, lugs and bars. All these many and striking elements suggest that while the pottery of Beycesultan Early Bronze Age II may have been manufactured locally, it is derived from traditions more akin to Troy I and Yortan.

By the middle third millennium, we start to witness some major changes in settlement plan at Karataş-Semayük. A large, independent megaron structure constructed on the highest point of the mound, overlooking the settlement, is conceptually different to the radial settlement (Figure 5.11: 2). The court along three sides of the megaron and the earthen embankment around its perimeter heighten the feeling of difference.[124] Enclosing the settlement was a palisade and beyond that pairs of ditches. These changes in architecture are likely to reflect a different level of social complexity. To this can now be added the large megaron building at Aizanoi, near Kutahya, built on a platform.[125] Even though it did not contain any fitments, its size (11 m in length), position and the attention paid to the surrounding area and slopes, which were paved with small stones, are suggestive of a special function. Meanwhile other sites of southwest—Limantepe, Bakla Tepe, and Bademğacı—have an architectural traditions redolent of Thermi.[126]

Of these, the emerging evidence from the impressive site of Limantepe is worth mentioning. The Early Bronze Age I (Level VI) and II (Level V) settlements are encircled by massive fortifications with battered lower courses and projecting bastions.[127] Today the walls rise in places to over 6 m and originally they may well have reached a height of 12 m, creating what must have been an imposing sight. Part of the site lies underwater and includes a breakwater some 30 m in length and 5m in height. This protected harbor points to the seaward orientation of the settlement, and a series of narrow storerooms may well have been used for maritime trade.[128] At Küllüoba, Efe and his team have uncovered a late Early Bronze Age II fortified settlement with a distinctively linear look (Figure 5.24: 2).[129] A complex of structures is built around an open space defined along one side by a unit that contains a megaron with stone paved porch. Other regions can be discerned, but not as clearly. Among these, the Konya Plain with its plum-red pottery and Metallic Ware shows stronger affinities with Cilicia than the western regions.

In the Early Bronze Age III, Troy changed, but not markedly. Troy III is characterized by complexes of up to three rooms built entirely of stone—mud bricks ceased to be the medium of construction.[130] Poliochni, on the island of Lemnos, affords a more extensive understanding of this compact settlement layout, especially in the later Early Bronze Age.[131] Although it does not conform to a circular plan like Troy, it too had a fortification wall, breached by a narrow entrance that is flanked by long public buildings during the earliest phase. Thermi V shows much the same plan. Main thoroughfares and side streets separate several compact units of long houses, with no indication of any large public building. Although Thermi V has an enclosure wall and the dense plan itself provides a sense of boundary, the site lacks the fortified system so conspicuous at Troy.[132] Ceramics remain largely unchanged in the Early Bronze Age III apart from the introduction of the beak-spouted jug and the increase in the amount of wheelmade, light colored vessels. A marked shift in material culture defines Troy IV–V (ca. 2100–1850 BC), which is now more aligned with the interior of Anatolia. Both levels continued to be fortified, but only traces of the walls remain. Rows of two-room houses, sharing a party wall, which face each other across a street, are now furnished with a greater number of built-in fixtures such as domed ovens, fixed hearths and benches. Pottery is now mostly wheelmade. Beak-spouted jugs with cutaway necks become popular and are associated with a new type, the red-cross bowl.

Central Anatolia

The transition between the Late Chalcolithic and Early Bronze Age I in the interior of Anatolia is quite unclear. At Çadır Höyük occupation in the Early Bronze Age began with a settlement much less substantial than its earlier counterpart.[133] It is only towards the middle stretch of the third millennium that developments become apparent, and only then in the area around Alişar, which was a fortified settlement in contact with Cilicia. This Alişar 1b ceramic horizon, found at

Kültepe too, is distinguished by red slipped surfaces and shapes, mostly cups and jugs, with distinctive outlines—narrower necks and slanting lips help define these vessels.

A well-fired and levigated pottery, known as "Intermediate Ware," replaces Alişar 1b in Level 7M (13T), and essentially marks the beginning of the Early Bronze Age III, when the central plateau began to experience a degree of cultural unity. Although many of its forms develop from the earlier assemblage, Intermediate Ware is distinguished by painted liner designs of lozenges, chevrons, and zigzags executed in purplish brown. At Kültepe this period is represented by levels 13–11 on the mound, with Level 10 belonging to the Middle Bronze Age and the establishment of Karum IV. These important historical synchronisms will be dealt with in the next chapter, but it should be noted that contact with surrounding regions—Cilicia, Syria, and west Anatolia, specifically Troy II—are already well attested in the Early Bronze Age III. The occasional "Syrian bottle," wheelmade corrugated buff cups also from Syria, and local imitations of the depas shape manufactured in Intermediate Ware and painted with red stripes are testimony to a wide-ranging network. Wheelmade depas from Kültepe Level 12, which could be accommodated comfortably in the Cilician Early Bronze Age III assemblage, are further evidence of these contacts.

Towards the end of the Early Bronze Age at both Alişar and Kültepe, Cappadocian painted ware (or Alişar III) gradually replaced Intermediate Ware. This new painted repertoire is often divided in successive stages of technical development that continue into the second millennium BC. Vessels have a reddish or buff surface that is decorated with dark brown to black geometric design composition, which increases in complexity through time. At a later stage, cream-colored panels may be painted onto red slipped vessels, and then ornamented with patterns painted in dark colors.

Cilicia

It is perhaps fitting to end these regional overviews of the Early Bronze Age with Cilicia, whose diverse affinities were very much shaped by the strong pulses from neighboring territories. Gözlü Kule, Tarsus, the main link between the Syro-Mesopotamian and Anatolian sequences, shows rapid and distinct shifts in cultural alignments best attested in ceramics.[134] Following the Amuq F horizon in the Late Chalcolithic, the inhabitants of Tarsus looked northward towards the south Anatolian plateau, making greater use of the Cilician Gates. The clearest indicator of this change is the abrupt appearance in the Early Bronze Age I of red, gritty, handmade Anatolian wares, including the beak-spouted pitcher, which displaced pale colored, wheelmade Syro-Mesopotamian ceramics of Amuq G type as the main household containers. In the Early Bronze Age II, the town of Tarsus expanded and prospered. Mud brick fortifications surrounded neatly built residential units, positioned along streets, whose household contents included tin bronzes, reflecting to the rise of metal trading communities in the Taurus. The pottery horizon continues to be varied and attests far-flung connections. From the southern plateau around Konya and

Niğde arrived buff-colored handmade pitchers with rising spouts, handled jars, and bowls painted with designs executed in a purplish paint.

Whereas buff Syrian wares, including Syrian bottles and spiral-burnished wheelmade jars, occasionally red banded, show eastern connections, red and black streak-burnish containers point to Cyprus. Pivotal for comparative chronology and testimony to long-distance contact is the occurrence of a Cilician reserved slip jug among the grave goods in mastaba G 1233 at Giza, dated to early Dynasty IV. But it was during the Early Bronze Age III that trade connections were most vigorous. During this period Cilicia's attention was sharply drawn to western Anatolia, though it never cut its ties with Syria (Amuq J), as a range of elegant goblets and bottles reflect. Connections with the west extended as far as Troy, whose presence in Cilicia is attested by two-handled *depas*, tankards, red slipped platters, and others forms we have already encountered.[135]

Metallurgy and its impact

Turkey is well endowed in metals and ores, so it is not surprising that it played a leading role in the development of pyrometallurgy. Its mountainous terrain is literally studded with metalliferous sites, including copper, iron, lead, silver, and gold, especially in the northern and eastern regions (Figure 5.25). Of these, copper, silver, and gold can occur in the native state. Throughout antiquity this beneficence positioned Anatolia well for trade, both local and long distance, but it also attracted the attention of its neighbors who coveted these resources. Combined with human ingenuity, this richness in ores also enabled the ancient Anatolian smiths, known for their technical sophistication and artistry, to play a leading role in metallurgy.

Much has been said about the Early Bronze Age Kestel Mine and the nearby mining village at Göltepe since the discovery was announced in the late 1980s.[136] Taking the later Middle Bronze Age texts of the Assyrian Trading colony period as a model, most assumed that tin was imported into Anatolia, even in the prehistoric period. Gradually, however, the majority of researchers have been persuaded by the arguments of Aslıhan Yener and her colleagues, who have provided a considerable amount of compelling evidence. But for some, nagging doubts remain. The primary concern is the relatively small amount of tin recovered from the Kestel Mine today, and the conspicuous absence of tin slag deposits at the complex. Another is the apparent paradox of prehistoric miners investing a large amount effort to extract tin from low-grade, iron-rich tin ore to supply a fledging tin-bronze industry in Anatolia. Despite these qualms, the archaeological evidence and accompanying scientific analyses provide a persuasive argument that tin ore was mined and processed on a grand scale throughout the Early Bronze Age. Radiocarbon readings indicate that Kestel was worked over various periods from about 3240 to 2200 BC, with the period of greatest activity during the second half of the third millennium, after which the mine ceased operations.

The Kestel-Göltepe complex is vast. The mine itself comprises a network of eight galleries

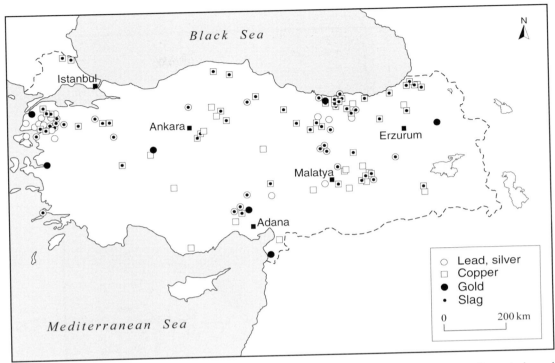

Figure 5.25 Location of the main sites in Turkey that have yielded evidence of ancient metallurgy (adapted from Wagner and Öztunalı 2000)

(Chambers I–VIII), extending in various directions (Figures 5.26 and 5.27). Some 4500 cubic meters of ore were extracted, often through precariously narrow tunnels, using fire—to create tension in the physical matrix—and large ground stone hammers to shatter the ore. The rich tin-bearing haematite ore is either gray or burgundy in color, but has a distinctive sparkle that distinguishes it from other ores. Even if the ore mined in antiquity were low grade, containing only 1% of tin like some the nodules found in the excavations, the size of the galleries point to the production of some 115 tons of tin. But it is likely that prehistoric miners at Kestel were taking out a richer grade ore, with a tin content possibly as high as 2%.[137] No less impressive is the evidence from Göltepe, the processing site established on a hilltop 2 km from the mine. Its industrial purpose is obvious. Over one ton of ceramic furnaces and crucibles covered with a tin-rich residue were recovered. Storage jars laden with ground ore, nodules waiting to be processed, hearths, and an arsenal of stone crushers reinforce the specific function of the work-shops. Göltepe was also a habitation site. The miners lived here in pit houses, measuring 4–6 m in diameter, cut into the bedrock and finished with a wattle and daub superstructure. Despite the grime the workshops no doubt produced, the inhabitants of Göltepe did not neglect their houses, repeatedly plastering their walls and decorating them with geometric relief patterns.

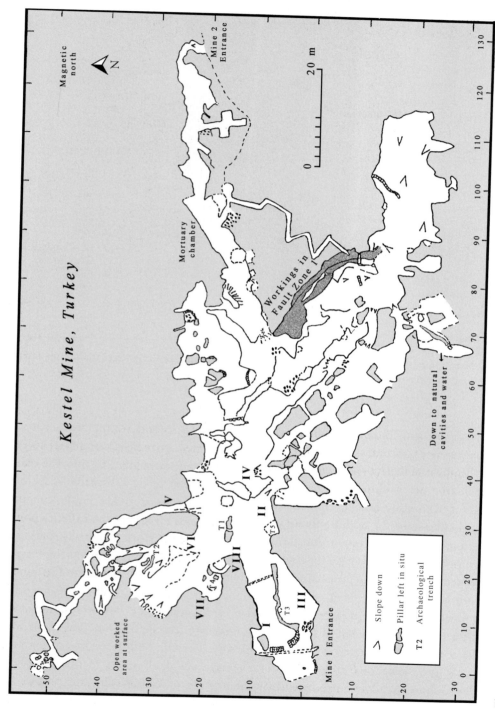

Figure 5.26 Plan of the Kestel Mine, Niğde (adapted from Yener 2000)

Figure 5.27 Kestel Mine, Early Bronze Age galleries (Photo: courtesy Aslıhan Yener)

One point should not escape us, namely the consumption of fuel that is required for mining, which must have impacted heavily on the surrounding forests.

Despite the abundance of ore-bearing sites, not all were utilized in antiquity. Over 30 prehistoric copper mining and smelting sites have been located in Anatolia.[138] Archaeological evidence associated with an ancient working, includes open pit mines (often reworked), burnt or discolored clay linked with furnaces, and metallurgical debris. The by-product of metalworking often comprises a scatter of ore fragments, charcoal, crucible debris, tuyeres, mining tools such as hammers and picks, and waste dumps in the form of slag heaps. Although Anatolia has deposits of native copper, exploited as early as the eighth millennium BC to fashion jewellery and simple tools, this form is quite rare. Instead, the bulk of copper used in antiquity was released by smelting more common ores that contain other impurities. The most conspicuous ores by virtue of their color are malachite (green) and azurite (blue).

Gold was obtained from mine (primary) and placer (secondary) deposits. Primary gold deposits occur in few areas: One is located in the Menderes Massif, in the Izmir province, while the second group is associated with quartz veins, commonly known as reef gold, also situated in western Anatolia. In both cases, the gold can be found in association with other metals such as silver, copper, and lead. Gold from placer deposits is commonly known as alluvial or native gold. Present-day alluvial deposits in western Anatolia have too low a content to be exploited, but in antiquity the sands of the Pactolus River (Sart Çay), near Sardis, famous for their gold dust were certainly worked. Native gold poses no problems to the goldsmith. A soft metal, it was shaped into jewellery from an early period without any modification.

Silver is found either as silver glance (the sulfides) and horn silver (the chlorides), or in silver-bearing ores of lead, copper, and other metals, including electrum, an alloy of gold and silver.

Native silver is rare and quite pure, and even though it occurs in the vicinity of ore deposits, it is difficult to detect because it is located well below the surface. Anatolia has many silver mines, especially in the north-central region, where the Gümüşhane area has the richest deposits in the country. These were most likely exploited by the Hittites, whereas Kaz Dağı and Ulu Dağı in the northwest supplied the Trojan silversmiths centuries earlier.

Despite the welter of publications that inform us of precocious technological achievements, the social circumstances surrounding ancient metallurgy in Anatolia have yet to be explored fully. The notion that metalworking must be considered part of the broad range of human behavior, especially magic and ritual, is a relatively new one,[139] with many archaeometallurgists preferring the view that: "The composition of the materials can give far more unambiguous information on the technology of the process which produced them than on the society that made and used them."[140] This technological view, which assumes that early metalsmiths were engaged in a rational path of discovery and experimentation, stems from Childe's influential ideas on the developmental stages of metallurgy.[141] Following his Marxist convictions, Childe stressed the importance of the industrial use of metals in cultural evolution, and adhered to the view that metallurgy was a "science," free of superstition and magic.

The process of metallurgy from mining to metalworking involves three broad stages—procurement of raw material, production of metalwork (hammering, melting, smelting, and casting), and the use of the items. In pre-industrial agrarian communities, mining was for the most part a seasonal and often short-term activity that was scheduled around the agricultural activities that always took primacy.[142] This was likely the case in Anatolia too. Beyond functional aspects, we should be aware that many cultures, from Siberia to Indonesia, saw the process of metallurgy as a confrontation with powers not of this world.[143] The positive, human response to this experience, as indeed with any confrontation with the numinous, was embodied in religious ritual—a combination of thought (myths) and action (cult)—focused on pyrotechnology. Given the difficulty of explaining the numinous, social and natural experiences are often used as metaphors as a way of communicating the mysterious processes. A mineral ore, for instance, is perceived by many cultures as a seed that gestates within the belly of an earth mother, in a constant state of metamorphosis, and eventually "procreating" into a metal.[144] Smelting too is ascribed a role, and is often viewed as the catalyst that transforms the embryonic ores into metals within the furnace (uterus). The sacredness of metalworking is also often associated with the concepts of purity and cleanliness, which are enforced through a variety of ritual behavior.[145]

Anatolian communities made significant advances in metallurgy in the Chalcolithic period, which are arguably among the most innovative anywhere in the world.[146] From the earliest appearance of copper metallurgy at Çayönü, metalworkers carried the technology forward through several stages beyond the initial hammering and annealing. Copper was now melted and cast, which meant that temperatures over 1981.4°F (1083°C) were reached. Once this barrier was overcome, smelting, the extraction of mineral ores from their matrix, was easily achieved, requiring only slightly higher temperatures. This process of experimentation soon led to another first, namely fledgling attempts to produce polymetallic substances by alloying copper with another metal.

The Chalcolithic was very much the age of copper. In the fourth millennium BC copper was smelted from oxide and sulphide ores, often containing arsenic as an impurity. Whether arsenical coppers, common in the Late Chalcolithic and earlier part of the Early Bronze Age, should be regarded as deliberate attempts to mix metals, is a point of debate. Contrariwise, the metallurgical potential of tin, as a natural alloy in the manufacture of tin bronzes, was very much understood by metalworkers of the Early Bronze Age II.

Evidence for mining and the metallurgical process itself is sparse for the Chalcolithic. While native copper could be easily collected, copper ores had to be separated from their parent rock. To do this effectively would have required the use of fire, which would have weakened the rock matrix. Relatively heavy hammers made from hard, riverine stones, usually with a meridional groove around the waist to aid hafting would then have been used to crush the matrix into coarse lumps. Other tools made of antler, bone, and wood were probably also part of the miner's toolkit, although few have survived. This process of carefully sorting out the mineral by hand picking or washing is known as *beneficiation*. The earliest attempts at smelting have left few tangible remains, owing to the simple technology that would have been used. There were no true furnaces—requisite temperatures were achieved using simple hearths and blowpipes, a process that would have left little or no slag.

Early Chalcolithic metal items are few in number. Mostly copper beads, awls, and pins from Hacılar and Mersin XXII–XXI, these objects are technologically little different from their Neolithic counterparts in being beaten from nodules of native metal. Up to this point, metallurgy was very much focused on trinkets. Major breakthroughs, however, were achieved around the beginning of the fifth millennium BC. In the Middle Chalcolithic settlement at Mersin (Levels XVII–XVI), metalworkers began to cast tools—chisels and axes mostly—by pouring molten copper into open moulds.[147] Chemical characterization of this Mersin assemblage indicates further experimentation shown by the smelting of minerals ores. While some tools are arsenical copper, others can be classed as crude tin-bronzes. Even lead, which does not exist as a native metal, was mixed with copper in one case. By the middle fifth millennium (Mersin XVI–XIV), the range and quantity of objects, now containing equal proportions of tin and arsenic, reflect the increasing confidence of the smiths.[148]

During the Late Chalcolithic period, the focus of metallurgical activity shifted to the Upper Euphrates basin, around Malatya and Elazığ, where there is very good evidence for the smelting of polymetallic oxide and sulphide ores. Analysis of residue slag, crucibles, and lumps of ore found at Tülintepe, Tepecik, and Norşuntepe (in the Altınova Plain), and at Değirmentepe (near Malatya) suggests the widespread use of arsenical copper during the first half of the fourth millennium BC. Only a few copper items have survived from these centuries—spiral rings, an awl and a hook from Norşuntepe—but they too confirm arsenic as the predominant constituent after copper. Generally, arsenic comprised about 2–2.5% of the content, with other minor additives including lead, zinc antimony, and nickel.

Metallurgy was well advanced at Arslantepe by this stage with good evidence for the smelting of polymetallic oxide and sulphide ores.[149] Nine swords (Figure 5.8: 2), the earliest swords so far documented in the world, 12 spearheads and a quadruple spiral plaque were found in a cult context in one of the Arslantepe rooms assigned to Period V. The varying amounts of arsenic in these items, the highest being found in the swords (3.25–5.8%), are a strong argument for the deliberate addition of an arsenic mineral, possibly realgar. Some of the swords bear an inlaid silver design on the hilt. A triangular pattern was excised and filled with silver, suggesting knowledge of the relatively sophisticated technique of *cupellation*, whereby silver is extracted from lead sulphide ores. Silver jewellery found in tombs at Korucutepe is a further indication that the metal was in use in the late fourth millennium BC. The Black Sea is another region with evidence for advanced metallurgy. At İkiztepe a range of arsenical copper objects bears typological and chemical similarities with those from Arslantepe.[150] Here, too, the high arsenic content appears to indicate deliberate and controlled alloying. The central and western regions of Anatolia are metallurgically less advanced than in the eastern provinces during this period, and have a limited range of items.

A unifying thread within the diversity of Early Bronze Age cultural developments is the influence of innovative metal technologies, especially in the third and final phase of this period, when even pottery imitated metallic vessels through their highly burnished surfaces and angular shapes. Anatolian smiths made full use of their land's extensive mineral and polymetallic ore resources. Bronze was not the only metal that was worked. Ceremonial artefacts and jewellery of silver, gold, and electrum were already produced by the late fourth millennium BC. By the Early Bronze Age III they dramatically increase in number and display a high level of craft skills suggestive of specialization and different metallurgical workshops. Metal inlay, casting in closed moulds (lost wax), hammering and repoussé, soldering, granulation, and filigree were among the techniques used. Concentrations of wealth such as those found at Troy, Alaca Höyük, and Horoztepe (Figure 5.28) are remarkable and also provide insights into social structures, representing as they do the worldly possessions of elite groups. Moreover, this demand for metals had economic implications, fuelling the growing commercial networks that traded both the mineral ores and the finished luxury items.

The Treasures of Troy were discovered by Heinrich Schliemann between 1872 and 1890 at Hissarlık Höyük and catalogued by Hubert Schmidt in 1902, after Schliemann's death. Schmidt identified 19 groups (Treasures A–S), comprising over 10,000 objects, if even the smallest items such as beads are counted individually.[151] According to Donald Easton, who has managed to determine the archaeological contexts of the treasures, they probably comprise 21 collections, spread across several periods.[152] The most spectacular is "Priam's Treasure" (Treasure A) discovered in Troy II. Circumstances after the Second World War saw 13 collections moved in 1945 from Berlin to the Pushkin Museum of Art in Moscow, where they remained inaccessible until 1994.

Jewellery from Troy includes diadems, earrings (basket shaped and lunate), hair rings, bracelets, torques, pins, pendants, and a range of beads. Among the most famous items are two

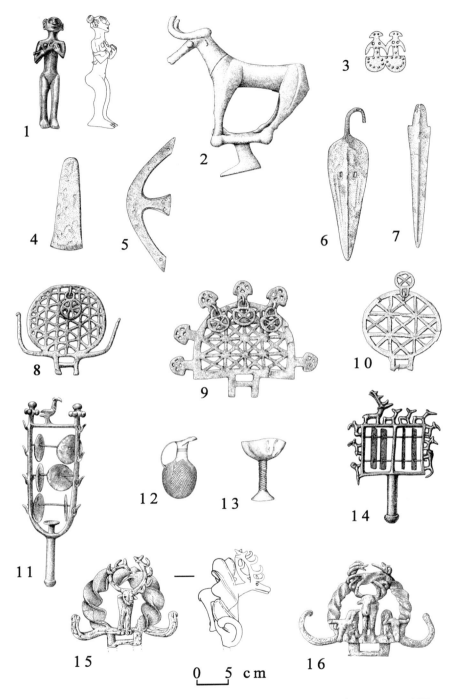

Figure 5.28 Main metal artefact types from Early Bronze Age central Anatolia: **1, 4–7, 14** Horoztepe. **2, 3, 8–13, 15, 16** Alaca Höyük (adapted from Müller-Karpe 1974)

diadems in the form of narrow bands with vertical chains, 90 on a large diadem and 64 on a small one, covered with leaf-shaped scales and ending in a pendant. Longer chains frame both sides of each diadem. The pendants, individually cut from sheet gold, are either "idol shaped," or lance-shaped. Whether the diadems were designed to decorate a cult statue, or mounted on a textile or leather headdress is unclear. In western Anatolia, similar diadems with repoussé ornamentation have been found among the grave goods at Alaca Höyük, Kücükhöyük, and Demircihüyük-Sarıket.[153] A band diadem with convex dotted decoration was also among the assemblage of the elite tomb at Arslantepe VIB, which belonged to a different (Trans-Caucasian) tradition. Basket-shaped earrings decorated with rows of granulations sometimes have pendants, and their weight has led some to suggest that they may have been attached to the hair.

The hands of different craftsmen can be seen in the method of manufacture of these earrings. Those from Treasure A, for instance, have bodies made of separate vertical wires soldered together, technically superior to the Treasures F and J earrings that are cast as solid plates and vertically incised to imitate wires. Stylistically similar earrings have been found at Poliochni and Eskiyapar, which also produced comparable examples of the Troy lobed hair rings, the most numerous category among the treasures. Beads, too, are plentiful and come in a variety of forms—flat discs, barrel shaped, and segmented to mention a few—and are made from gold, silver, bronze, carnelian, and amber. Much discussion has focused on quadruple spiral beads, represented by a large example in Treasure D, and at several other third millennium sites across Anatolia and the Near East, including the Royal Tombs at Ur.[154] These types of bead are also found in second millennium context. Their origin is disputed with both western Anatolia and northern Iran suggested as the source.[155] Among the pins, two with complex heads from Treasure O are quite extraordinary. One consists of a plate decorated with double-spiral filigree motifs and a row of six miniature vessels, which may date to late Troy II or even Troy III, and is a more elaborate version of a similar pin from Poliochni. The other comprises a flattened cylinder decorated with a central convex dot and filigree petals. Although numbering only two and seemingly insignificant, the amber beads from Treasure L assume importance as evidence of some contact with the Baltic amber network that travelled along the river valleys such as the Danube, and also as the earliest evidence of amber use in Anatolia.[156]

We have already made reference to the Alaca Höyük metalwork and its connections with Chernykh's Circumpontic "metallurgical province." The tombs and their contents will be discussed later, but reference should be made here to the quantity and range of sumptuous burial goods made from metal (gold, silver, copper alloy, and iron), bone, clay, and stone. Standards with stags, bulls, or open-worked geometric forms, are among the most striking objects (Figure 5.28).[157] In terms of jewellery, we should note the ability of the craftsmen to combine gold and silver with precious stones (carnelian, jade, and rock crystal), a technique especially favored for pins, and at the same time the conspicuous absence of filigree and granulation, obvious both at Troy and later on in Caucasus. Like the material from Troy, there is quite a repertoire of beads. Diadems are in the form of a plain gold band, ornamented with punctate design. Unique to Alaca Höyük, however, is a diadem composed of four rows of open work from Tomb H. Worth

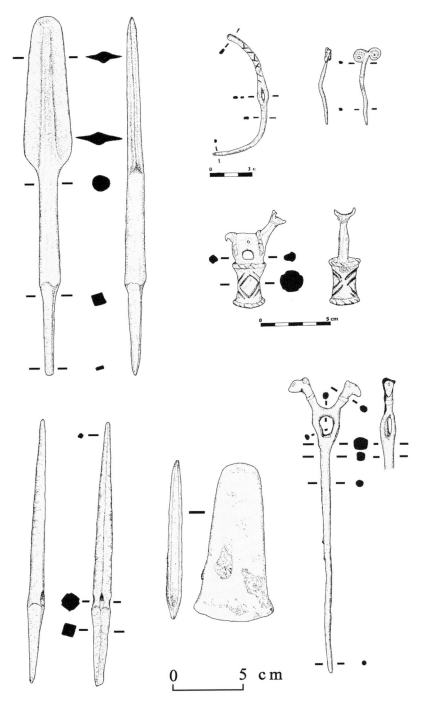

Figure 5.29 Main metal artefact types from the Early Bronze Age of southeastern Anatolia. All items are from the Birecik cemetery (adapted from Sertok and Ergeç 1999)

noting, too, are the stylistic similarities between the pendant from Horoztepe and the two Alaca Höyük brooches in the form of conjoint circles with a punctate pattern on the one hand, and various circular plaques from Caucasus. An outlier of this stylistic group is the gold medallion from the Kinneret tomb, in northern Israel, which was found in association with rock crystal beads that would be quite at home in lands further north.[158] The metalwork repertoire from tombs in the southeastern region was more standardized and consisted of a variety of pins, weapons, and tools.

WOOL, MILK, TRACTION, AND MOBILITY: SECONDARY PRODUCTS REVOLUTION

A series of innovations and economic practices based on domesticated animals that collectively have come to be known as the Secondary Products Revolution are significant, yet they have barely had an airing in Anatolia.[159] Distinguished from the initial primary stage of early farming economies when domestic animals were exploited for their meat, the secondary phase reflects a series of patterns directed towards the exploitation of a diverse range of secondary products. In Anatolia there is evidence that a significant intensification of secondary products use started about 3500 BC. Essentially, several millennia after they were domesticated, animals were put to a variety of uses other than as suppliers of meat, bone, and marrow (primary products). Cattle, for instance, provided milk, and were also bred to provide traction power (pulling a plough or vehicle). The physical makeup and role of sheep had changed too. In addition to supplying milk, years of domestication gradually reduced the length of their coarse hair and promoted the growth of the woolly layer, normally restricted to a short, winter under-coat in wild sheep. Herein lies a crucial distinction between the two types of herding practice: To obtain primary products the animals were slaughtered, whereas secondary products were extracted from living animals, ensuring a maximum yield per head of livestock. Moreover, while primary products could be harvested from both domesticated and wild animals, only domesticated animals could yield secondary products.

Detecting the use of secondary products is a difficult process that requires an evaluation of mostly indirect evidence. We have already mentioned the importance of mortality statistics of bone assemblages in determining the earliest stages of herding practices in the Neolithic, noting that young males figure prominently in a sample if meat was the main concern, because their growth slows at subadult age. A strategy aimed at milk production witnessed a different kill-off pattern. To reduce the competition for milk, most male animals were despatched as infants, providing a bone assemblage that is largely adult females. The difficulty here is the softness of infant bones that are likely to perish from the record and skew the statistics. Some argue that dairy mortality profiles are not trustworthy because lactating females fill their mammary glands with milk in response to the needs of their suckling offspring, which must be kept alive. Others have pointed out that early herders would have had various ploys, such as a surrogate offspring, to promote a mother to produce milk. A novel approach to this question is through the study of bone density. Studies currently restricted to Israel show that ancient lactating female sheep like their present-day descendants have a calcium deficiency brought about by stress and nutritional causes.[160] One thing is certain, namely that while is it possible that milk was consumed when animals were first domesticated, milk production through the maintenance of a dairy herd is a labour-intensive task that required a different management strategy. Ceramics can also provide evidence for the use of milk products. Containers that are perforated all over are not uncommon in the Late Chalcolithic period and may have been used to make cheese. Unfortunately, very little work has been done in Anatolia on the chemical analysis of lipid and protein residues on ceramic containers to identify dairy use, but the potential is significant.

The physiological transformation from wild, hairy sheep to wool-bearing domesticates appears to have been a long process, with production of wool in the Near East dated to about 3000 BC or slightly earlier. The mortality profile of a wool-bearing herd consisted mostly of adult males and females, because both sexes yield wool. But the analysis of bones is complicated by the difficulty in distinguishing male and female bones (other than through relatively rare horn cores), and differentiating between sheep and goats. Even so, a high proportion of male adults is suggestive of wool production. While no direct evidence of woolen textiles exist in Anatolia, the sharp rise in the number of bronze clothes pins points to changes in types of fastener and clothes. Pins are more suitable for open weave woolen garments rather than linen clothes spun from flax with a dense weave, or leather, which were fastened with toggles. Spindle whorls and loom weights are not such a sensitive indicator of this transition because they can be used for both flax (linen) and wool. Even so, the increase in the toolkit used for textile production is marked, especially in western Anatolia, where a site like Troy has yielded a significant number of spindle whorls and loom weights to suggest an organized, if not centralized, activity.[161]

Harnessing animal power for transport and labour was a major achievement that sparked a range of new technologies. Vehicle technology that used the wheel, initially in the form of animal-drawn carts and later as chariots of war drawn by horses or donkeys, triggered social transformations as well as economic and technological shifts. Used at first as a means of displaying power and wealth, wheeled vehicles went on to revolutionize modes of transport and warfare. The use of traction, a task suited best to males or castrates, is difficult to detect in bones, especially when only a few individuals are required. Pathologies such as osteoarthritis caused by traction stress are one indicator, but on the whole the main evidence is artefactual or derived from the landscape. In Europe, the preservation of ploughs in peat bogs, the survival of plough marks and cut ruts across fields, and pictorial representation of ploughing with cattle on rock art confirm the use of traction. In Mesopotamia, the pictographs of wheeled vehicles assign them a date around the end of the fourth millennium BC, and a little later, in Anatolia, we have models of wagons with solid wooden wheels. We have a vivid impression of the later models of these cumbersome prototype "luxury cars" of yesteryear—slow, usually four wheeled and presumably drawn by oxen—from the spectacular discoveries of vehicle remnants at Trialeti (Middle Bronze Age Georgia) and Lchashen (Late Bronze Age Armenia). Finally, we should note that pack animals, the main mode of transport other than human porterage, presumably began about 5000 years ago, when the donkey was domesticated in the eastern Mediterranean.[162] Horses appeared to have been tamed earlier, sometime after 4800 BC in the Pontic-Caspian steppes, and although they played a role in transport, later horse burials point to intrinsic value and their role as objects of status.[163]

In sum, the Secondary Products Revolution comprised another package of economic, cultural, and technological changes that were every part as significant as the primary stage of domestication. New techniques of cultivation and overland transport, no longer totally dependent on human porterage, increased both productivity and mobility. New products also expanded the range of material culture, such as woolen textiles that initiated different modes of production. Judging by later texts, this diversification of the textile industry may, in turn, have contributed to shifts in gender roles, with female labor devoted increasingly to weaving activities. Whether the demand for woolen garments would have also provided women with economic power is unclear. Finally, the use and application of secondary products manifested through new technologies and the enhancement of farms enabled elites to further control power and wealth.

BURIAL CUSTOMS

The context of deposition must form the focal point in any analysis of ancient burials.[164] Relationships between the burial structure, human remains, goods placed within the grave, and the location of the burial itself—whether beneath architecture or in a well-circumscribed cemetery—inform us of human behavior and the cognitive framework of the community. In terms of burial type, five variants can be discerned for Early Bronze Age Anatolia:[165]

1 earthen pit—a simple pit without structural walls or roof, and accessible directly from the surface
2 roofed pit—an earthen tomb with a structural roof, but no structural walls, and accessible through the roof
3 cist tomb—an architectural unit comprising an earthen tomb with structural walls and roof, and entered through the roof
4 chamber tomb—an architectural unit comprising an earthen tomb with structural walls and roof, accessible through a shaft or dromos that leads to a portal in one wall
5 ceramic container—comprising purpose-built pithoi, domestic jars, or pottery sherd envelopes that are accessed through the mouth of the container.

The bulk of burial evidence for the Early Bronze Age derives from western, north-central and southeastern provinces, and there are clear regional fluctuations in the quantity of burials. The overall number of burials excavated is relatively low across Anatolia in the Early Bronze Age I, rising dramatically in the Early Bronze Age II, especially in western Anatolia, which has some 1500 burials recorded. The quantity of burials also rises in the southeast during the Early Bronze Age II, but remains modest in the central plateau. In western Anatolia, the number of burials plunges in the Early Bronze Age III, contrasting with the spike in other regions. This variability between regions is also reflected in terms of burial types, which will now be examined.

Some 15 sites have provided the bulk of evidence of mortuary practice in western Anatolia.[166] Despite certain variations in tomb structure, on the whole, communities adhered to features so tenaciously that they must reflect a prevailing mortuary tradition. The most striking instance of this uniformity is the use of extramural cemeteries. All graves were dug in a discrete area well away from the settlement, or along its fringes, as at Karataş. Another feature is the careful and deliberate positioning of the tombs. In the great majority of cases, burials are evenly distributed with minimal overlap, and invariably oriented along an east–west axis with the head of the deceased pointing to the east. Finally, one cannot escape the sameness of the grave assemblage. The quantity and type of goods deposited with the deceased vary little from site to site. Ceramics, in particular jars and jugs, are dominant, and are followed by copper/bronze items and the occasional gift made from silver, gold, and stone.

During the Early Bronze Age II, the most common tomb type is the single ceramic container with the opening to the east. Hundreds of these pithos burials have been unearthed at Yortan and Karataş, and a good number have also been exposed at Babaköy and other sites.[167] The deceased was placed feet first in a large stump or round-based jar that was angled in the ground with the mouth at the upper end, sealed by a flat stone or large sherd. The majority of these burials (ca. 75%) were single. The remains of no more than eight individuals were found in multiple burials, with the final deposition, contracted with skull near the mouth of the jar, placed on top of the disarticulated remains of earlier depositions. A variation of this burial type is found at Demircihöyük and Küçük where two ceramic containers were placed mouth to mouth, forming the so-called *Doppelpithosgräber*, which did not contain multiple burials.[168] At Demircihöyük, Küçük, and Kusura,[169] pithos burials were part of a mixed facility that occasionally also utilized cist tombs and earthen pits. Interestingly, this mixture of funerary structures is more in keeping with central Anatolia, especially at Alişar where a similar combination was used intramurally. Furthermore, the ritual deposition of oxen, presumably part of the funerary feast, link both Demirici and the Early Bronze Age III burials at Alaca Höyük, which, as we shall see, also have north Pontic affiliations. The greatest departure from the general uniformity of the western tradition is found at Iasos, where the community buried their dead only in cist graves.[170] The excavators believe the exclusivity of cists reflects contact with the Cyclades. Despite this difference in the tomb architecture, in every other respect—distribution of grave goods and predominance of single burials—the Iasos burials conform to general west Anatolian practice.

Compared with western Anatolia the central plateau differs both in its diversity of mortuary practice and the abundance of information it has yielded for the Early Bronze Age III. Here, the Alaca Höyük royal tombs stand apart on several levels and require further elaboration.[171] Fourteen royal tombs were exposed in a discrete intramural area (27 × 30 m) in the southeast part of the mound; a further five nonroyal burials were located fringing them to the north. The stratigraphy of the royal tombs is complex. The most persuasive reconstruction is that of Gürsan-Salzman, who proposes four stratigraphically distinct groups: Burials Burials B, F, and L (EBA II/III); Burials A, A1, C, E, T, T1 (early EBA III); Burials D, D, R, and S (late EBA III); Burial H (EBA/MBA transition).[172] According to Gürsan-Salzman, all the burials lay beneath architectural complex "ABC," with only Burial H dating after its construction. The burials consisted of a rectangular pit roofed with wooden planks, occasionally supported by stones that lined the tomb, and sealed with mud brick and plaster (Figure 5.30: 1). The dimensions of the tombs varied: Widths ranged from 2 m to 4 m, lengths measured from 2 m to 8 m, and they were dug to a depth between 0.75 m and 1 m. Apart from one Burial C, which was aligned along a north–south axis, all the Alaca burials have an east–west orientation. Single burials prevailed at Alaca, except for Burial C into which three individuals were placed; in addition to a complete skeleton, Burial E had a detached skull. The deceased were laid on their right side, in a contracted position with their head pointing east. Five adult males and four females have been identified among the skeletal material, which on the basis of stratigraphy and the proximity of their tombs include three male–female pairs.

The royal tombs yielded over 700 items, with the greatest number (129) from Burial D, showing show an extraordinary wealth in metals (Figure 5.28). The grave goods can be broadly grouped into 12 typological categories:[173]

1 animal and human figurines
2 weapons
3 standards, and bull and stag statuettes
4 hooks
5 metal and ceramic containers
6 personal ornaments such as hairpins
7 utilitarian objects, comprising tools, and implements
8 diadems
9 appliqués
10 mace heads
11 seals
12 miscellaneous objects that included metal pieces and sheathing, presumably used for furniture.

Equally remarkable is the diversity of materials used—metals (copper, bronze, silver, gold, electrum, iron, lead, haematite), stones (carnelian, rock crystal, chalcedony, flint, lapis lazuli), frit, faience, pottery, bone, and textiles. But most impressive of all are the metalworking skills best evidenced by the combination of more than one metal in a single object.[174] Graves goods were deposited in the tombs according to type. Standards, figurines, and statuettes were placed in the corners of the tombs, whereas vessels were dispersed throughout the tomb, with the rest of

Figure 5.30 **1** Alaca Höyük Tomb MA (adapted from Koşay 1944). **2** Irganchai Barrow 5 (Photo: courtesy Kakha Kakhiani). **3** Treli Tomb 43 (Photo: courtesy Mikheil Abramishvili)

the items laid either on or near the deceased. Both genders were accorded grave goods. Standards and statuettes are found in most tombs, but otherwise two clusters can be discerned: One with a prevalence of maceheads and weapons, and another with tools. Gürsan-Salzman interprets this breakdown as reflecting elite and nonelite groups. But the paired male–female burials, which are supposedly related, have one individual associated with maceheads and weapons and the other with tools.

Disarticulated animal bones were found within the burials and presumably represent the remains of a ceremonial funerary feast. Between 2 and 10 animals were slaughtered, with oxen being the most common. Skulls and long bones were arranged with care on the wooden roof, interspersed with vessels and hooks, which were most likely attached to the yoke of carts originally placed in the tombs.[175] Fewer animal bones were found in the tomb and include oxen, sheep, dogs, pig, and goat. The five "nonroyal" burials are so designated on the basis of their poorer assemblages. Three of the burials were in containers and had no grave goods, the other were earthen pits with an assemblage of ceramic vessels.[176]

The extraordinary abundance of metals at Alaca Höyük, in particular gold, is staggering. Mention should also be made of the more modest metal objects found in burials at the contemporary nearby sites of Horoztepe Kalinkaya, Göller, and Oymaağaç.[177] Though looted and damaged, the pit burials at Horoztepe—Kalinkaya and Göller were pithos burials—are similar in size and form to those at Alaca. This surge of precious metals and the showiness of wealth should be seen as part of a broader phenomenon in the Cirumpontic region.[178] In the northwestern Caucasus we have the earlier Maikop culture, which first came to light in 1897 with the excavation of the Oshad barrow.[179] Now comprising some 150 burials and 30 settlements, the Maikop phenomenon has yielded a spectacular assemblage of precious items that includes no fewer than 7400 gold objects.[180] After protracted debates, involving calibrated radiocarbon analysis of secure samples, some collected from Maikop settlements, and persuasive Syro-Mesopotamian connections, the Maikop culture is generally attributed to the period around 3500–3250 BC, nearly a millennium before the Alaca "royal tombs."[181]

Southern Caucasus, too, has its share of wealthy kurgans that range from the late third to the mid-second millennium BC, to the well-known kurgans excavated by Kuftin on the Tsalka Plateau in the 1940s, which define the Trialeti horizon, and a number more. Attention should be drawn to Tomb 43 at Treli (Figure 5.30: 3), in Tbilisi, and Barrow 5 located near the village of Irganchai (Figure 5.30: 2), in southeast Georgia, which share some striking similarities with Alaca Höyük.[182] Irganchai Barrows 9 and 21 had gold artefacts, including sheathings that mirror those from Alaca.

Clearly, while these Caucasian burials and those of Alaca belong to the same general mortuary tradition, the chronological spread—from Maikop through Alaca to Trans-Caucasus—shows a long-lived tradition. That the wealth of Maikop disappears at the same time that it spikes in others regions seems to suggest that the network involving the procurement and distribution of precious metals had changed. Moreover, it seems to point to a movement of peoples who accorded prestige to their leaders through a distinctive mortuary rite.

Although part of the Circumpontic region, a totally different mortuary tradition of the Early Bronze Age III is found at İkiztepe, on the fringe of the Turkish Black Sea coast.[183] Over 600 simple earthen pit burials were exposed in an extramural cemetery that measured some 40 by 40 m. Single burial was the norm for the most part, although occasionally two or three individuals were placed in the one pit. Orientation does not seem to have been an important factor, unlike the position of the corpse, which was always placed on its back. Bronzes—weapons, tools, jewellery and emblems—formed the bulk of the grave goods, which also included objects of gold, silver, lead, stone and ceramics.[184] The distribution of goods is uneven, ranging from burials without any (about 25% of undisturbed graves) to those that had up to 14 objects. On the whole, the objects per burial were few, averaging 2.53 for males and 1.94 for females, with male burials containing mostly tools and weapons and the majority of quadruple spirals, idols, and emblems, whereas females were deposited with pottery, jewellery, some tools, and weapons. Equally significant is that age and sex were not used to determine whether a burial had no goods.

Unlike western and central Anatolia, the southeastern region had mortuary rites that changed through time in a broadly linear fashion from the Early Bronze Age Ib to the Early Bronze Age III. Two main developmental phases, centered on the use of cist and chamber tombs, can be distinguished in the Adıyaman-Urfa district, each with extramural cemeteries and burials within the settlement. At Lidar Höyük, 192 Early Bronze Age Ib–II closely packed, stone cist tombs, oriented northeast–southwest, were uncovered in a cemetery on the eastern slope. Single burials, they contained a skeleton in a contracted position and for the most part a few grave goods, mostly pottery, although occasionally the deceased was laid to rest wearing jewellery—a bronze pin or bracelet, pendant of stone or shell, or a necklace of limestone beads. Similar tombs were used for the 37 Early Bronze Age I–II burials investigated in the course of salvage operations at a large cemetery located southwest of the Birecik Dam (Figure 5.31: 1).[185] The Birecik tombs contained a range of bronze items ubiquitous throughout the southeast (Figure 5.29). Although 200 burials were recorded, the extent of destruction suggests that the original cemetery probably accommodated many more. A different combination is seen at Hassek Höyük. Its Early Bronze Age II cemetery, located at some distance (700 m) from the settlement, encompassed 94 burials in ceramic containers and three stone cist tombs.[186] Unlike the methodical linear organization of the western Anatolian burials, all these tombs were crowded together and irregularly arranged in rows. All are single burials and contained a pottery vessel or two and sometimes a bronze artefact, usually a cone-headed pin.

Titriş Höyük introduced a new concept in the Early Bronze Age II—the chamber tomb.[187] Located away from the settlement, the chamber of this one burial measured 3.5 by 5 m, and was built with blocks and capped with a stone slab. Two steps led to the side entrance, which revealed a compartment full of pottery and three skeletons—two adults and a subadult. This tomb, through its structure and multiple burials, foreshadowed developments in the subsequent period. At Titriş these chamber tombs, containing up to seven individuals, were found within its city walls, where they shared space with cist tombs. This relationship between cist and chamber is also seen at Lidar, where 13 Early Bronze Age III chamber tombs, two with a pair of chambers

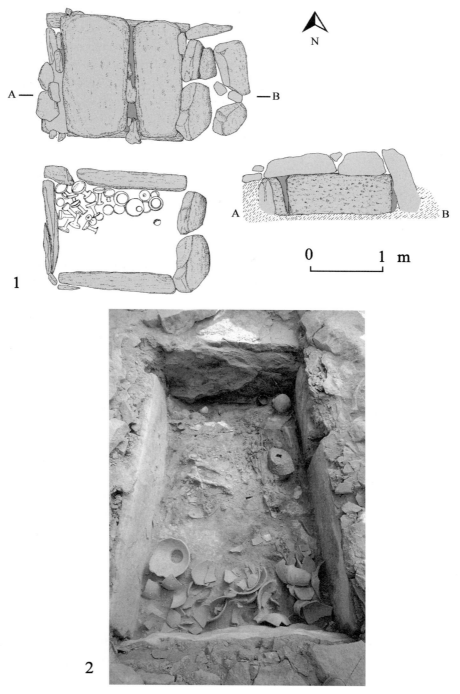

Figure 5.31 1 Cist tomb no. 163 from Birecik cemetery (adapted from Sertok and Ergeç 1999). 2 The "lordly" tomb, Arslantepe VIB (Photo: courtesy Marcella Frangipane)

joined by a dromos, were uncovered. The adjoining chamber tombs alone had 26 depositions between them.

A tomb of extraordinary significance was discovered at Arslantepe in 1996. The substantial construction of the stone cist tomb and the wealth of grave goods that include 75 metal objects, clearly point to the authority wielded by the deceased male, who has been dubbed a "lord" by the Italian excavators (Figure 5.31: 2).[188] Found in a context that enables it to be attributed to period just before the Period VIB2 settlement, this tomb is not important simply for its wares and precious metals, but for the detailed insight it can give into the events that immediately followed the destruction of the Arslantepe VIA complex. The tomb is a rectangular pit, lined with stone slabs, dug into a larger circular hollow. The tall adult male in his 30s or 40s was not buried alone. On top of the large stone slabs covering the tomb, the excavators made a rather grisly discovery. The remains of four adolescents, one male and three female, aged between 13 and 16–17 years, were found in positions that suggest they were either unceremoniously dumped into the pit, or worse still, buried alive. Each of two individuals (a male and a female) wore jewellery suggestive of some social standing: Two silver hair spirals, two copper clothes pins worn on their shoulder, and silver-copper diadem decorated with a punctate design, placed over a fine cloth, traces of which have also survived.

The older male was laid to rest on his right side, with knees bent. Around him was a considerable panoply of goods: Ceramic containers were placed at his feet, seven spearheads driven into the ground lined the walls behind his head, and a cache of metal objects were heaped in a pile behind his back. The deceased himself wore only a few items of jewellery—two silver quadruple spiral pins and necklaces with gold, silver, carnelian and rock crystal beads. The range metal objects—jewellery of precious metals, weapons, arsenical copper vessels, axes, and tools—and their ritual destruction through burial, not to mention the accompanying human sacrifice, clearly point to the wealth and power of the individual and his family. Significant, too, are the cultural connections that the grave goods reflect. The types of spearhead are indistinguishable from those found in Period VIA complex, as is the use of a silver inlay on a spearhead that recalls the geometric patterns on three of the swords from the VIA building. There is also a strong Trans-Caucasian influence. The diadems immediately bring to mind the one from Kvatskhelebi in Georgia, and spiral-headed pins generally have an eastern quality too. Finally, this mixed cultural ambience of the Malatya Plain is further shown by juxtaposition in the tomb of Mesopotamian style wheelmade jars with the handmade Kura-Araxes-style red-black vessels. This elite tomb from Arslantepe offers not only a dramatic insight into actions and decisions of people who lived about 3000 BC, but is also portrays the palpable collision of two worlds. In addition, it also demonstrates that the elite of the society, whether their affiliations lay with the urban Syro-Mesopotamian traditions or the more pastoral existence of the eastern highlands, manifested their wealth and power through metal objects. Moreover, they appear to have shared metallurgical know-how and objects themselves.

Strong Trans-Caucasian burial traditions continued to be felt in eastern Anatolia 500 years later. At Sos Höyük VD two tombs, assigned to the Early Bronze Age III, mirror two different mortuary customs that were used in southern Caucasus. One is a simple pit interment typical of the Kura-Araxes horizon. The deceased, a 19–23 year old male, was laid in a flexed position, accompanied with no more than two shell rings and a lustrous black burnished bowl. The other is a deep pit grave, sunk to a depth of 2 m, and measuring about 2.5 × 1.45 m across the top that was centred by two flat stones. At the base of the shaft lay the disarticulated and arthritic remains of an elderly man (50–60 years), who also was buried with modest remains—a black, crudely incised jar and a shell ring. Another burial from Sos Höyük is worth mentioning here, even though it is assigned to the subsequent Middle Bronze Age I (Period IVA). An even deeper shaft revealed the remains of a woman, who appears to have been bound at the hands and feet; her grave goods included an incised ceramic vessel of the Trialeti horizon and a curious Y-shaped object that had been carefully hollowed from the branch of a deer's antler. The top of the shaft was filled with stone rubble. These two burials at Sos are relatively early examples of a new burial tradition of the *kurgan* type that in the Caucasus is distinguished by a barrow of stones, which covered a variety of funerary chambers, and in some cases by a spectacular assemblage of goods, such as those at Trialeti and Martkopi (Georgia), and Kharashamb (Armenia).[189]

NOTES

1 See, for instance, Marro 2007b: 10, who places the Late Chalcolithic of eastern Anatolia within the period 4000–3500 BC.
2 For a discussion of these terms, see Yoffee 1993, 2005.
3 Rothman 2002.
4 For a discussion of seal impression terminology, see Frangipane 2007: 15–22.
5 A comprehensive listing of the most recent studies, which include no fewer than a dozen books and conference proceedings, can be found in the Algaze 2005. Equally useful is Butterlin 2003, which provides a comprehensive history of research on the Uruk world, and gathers together some of the key archaeological evidence. The key major works include Collins 2000; Lupton 1996; Moorey 1995; Postgate 2002; Rothman 2001; Stein 1999a, 1999b.
6 First published in 1993, Algaze's *The Uruk World System: The Dynamics of Early Mesopotamian Civilization*, has been published as a revised 2nd edition (2005).
7 Frangipane 1993.
8 Porada 1965.
9 Wright and Rupley 2001.
10 Helwing 2000; Frangipane 1993: table 1.
11 Mitchell 2001: table 1: 1.
12 Algaze 2005: 1290; Stein 2004: 156.
13 Algaze 2005.
14 Stein 2004: 143.
15 Behm-Blancke 1992; Behm-Blancke et al. 1981, 1984; Helwing 2002. A comparison of Helwing 2000: figures 7–8, with Algaze's model reveals disagreements in definitions, especially in what constitutes an Uruk site. Helwing prefers to discriminate between Syro-Anatolian sites (with no Uruk influence), Uruk sites (largely located from the Syrian Middle Euphrates down), Uruk sites with Syro-Anatolian elements, Syro-Anatolian sites with hybrids and so on. Perhaps most marked is her classification of Hassek Höyük.

16 Algaze 2005: 132–135.

17 Algaze 2005: 132.

18 Here one must be careful not to overstress the lack of natural resources in southern Mesopotamia. Cf. Potts 1997.

19 Helwing 2000.

20 Gülcer 2000.

21 Gülcer 2000.

22 Brown 1967: 132; Özdoğan 1977: 10 ware type 1.11; Russell 1980: 23–24, some of Group F.

23 Frangipane 1993.

24 Akkermans and Schwartz 2003: figure 7.10; Hauptman 1976: pl. 42: 3.

25 Frangipane 1993: 139.

26 Frangipane 1993: 141.

27 Frangipane 2001a: 329.

28 Trufelli 1997.

29 Braidwood and Braidwood 1960.

30 Trufelli 1994.

31 Frangipane 2000: 441.

32 Frangipane 2000: 442.

33 Palumbi 2003.

34 Stein 1999a: 145.

35 Pearce 1999; Pollock and Coursey 1995.

36 Bieglow 1999.

37 Stein 1999a: 142.

38 Frangipane and Palmieri 1983: figures 3–4; Palmieri 1981.

39 These cretulae are also termed, inappropriately according to the Arslantepe excavators, bullae, and confused with "clay sealings." For an exhaustive study see Frangipane 2007.

40 Badalyan and Avetisyan 2007; Burney and Lang 1971; Frangipane and Palumbi 2007; Kohl 2007; Kushnareva 1997; Munchaev 1975; Sagona 1984.

41 Braidwood and Braidwood 1960; Yener 2005.

42 Greenberg et al. 2006; Miroschedji 2000; Philip and Millard 2000.

43 Burney 1989.

44 For the latest reports on Sos Höyük, see Sagona 2000; Sagona and Sagona 2000.

45 Marro and Özfırat 2003, 2004, 2005; Özfırat 2007b; Sagona 1999; Sagona and Sagona 2004.

46 Sagona 2000.

47 Sagona and Sagona 2000.

48 Kobayashi 2007.

49 Chataigner 1995; Kiguradze 2000, 2001; Kiguradze and Sagona 2003.

50 Sagona and Sagona 2004.

51 Marro 2008; Marro and Özfırat 2003, 2004, 2005; Özfırat 2007.

52 I would like to thank Sepideh Maziar for sending me photographs of some the material from the 2007 excavations at Kohne Pasgah Tepesi.

53 Sagona and Sagona 2004.

54 Kiguradze and Sagona 2003.

55 Marro 2007a; Marro and Özfırat 2003: 389–390. For connections with Caucasus see Kohl 2007 and Lyonnet 2007.

56 Marro 2007a.

57 Işıklı 2007.

58 Kiguradze and Sagona 2003. See Smith (2005: 258), who questions the value of searching for the origins of the Kura-Araxes horizon.

59 Palumbi 2003: 100.
60 Rothman 2003: 95.
61 Connor and Sagona 2007.
62 Schoop 2005.
63 Duru 1994a.
64 Eslick 1988.
65 Korfmann et al. 1995; Özdoğan 1982; Sperling 1976.
66 Seeher 1992.
67 Efe 1989–90; 2003a: 92.
68 Efe 2001: 104–108.
69 Roodenberg and Alpaslan-Roodenberg 2008.
70 Alkım et al. 1988; Alkım et al. 2003; for a revision of the attributions, see Schoop 2005: 309–314. An overview is provided by Dönmez 2006.
71 Gorny et al. 2000; 2007; Steadman et al. 2007; Steadman et al. in press.
72 Schoop 2005.
73 Koşay and Akok 1957.
74 Palumbi 2007.
75 For detailed discussions, see Trigger 2003; Yoffee 2005.
76 For new view on the trajectory of urbanism in northern Mesopotamia see Oates et al. 2007.
77 Çevik 2007. See Joukowsky 1996, and Yakar 1985 and 2000 for site summaries.
78 Çevik 2005.
79 Çevik 2007.
80 Çevik 2007.
81 Şahoğlu 2005.
82 Algaze et al. 1994; Özdoğan 1977.
83 Yardımcı 2004.
84 Algaze 1999; Wilkinson 1990.
85 Rothman and Fuensanta 2003: 595.
86 Lupton 1996.
87 Rothman and Fuensanta 2003: 597.
88 Algaze 1999.
89 Abay 1997; Akkermans and Schwartz 2003; Jamieson 1993; Lebeau 2000; Lupton 1996; Rothman and Fuensanta 2003; Rova 1996.
90 For a review of the Turkish Lower Euphrates, see Gerber 2005; Rothman and Fuensanta 2003. See also Algaze 1990; Braidwood and Braidwood 1960; Fuensanta et al. 2000.
91 Jamieson 1993.
92 Algaze et al. 1995; Algaze et al. 1996; Matney and Algaze 1995; Matney et al. 1997; Matney et al. 1999.
93 Hauptmann 1987.
94 Frangipane 2001b.
95 Hauptmann 2000b: figure 1. Includes a full listing of the preliminary reports in the Keban Project Activities, published by the Middle Eastern Technical University.
96 Hauptmann 2000b: figure 2: 1–3.
97 Koşay 1976: 118.
98 Sagona 1994a: figures 68; 69: 6–9.
99 See Marro 1997, Groups A and B.
100 Hauptmann 2000b.
101 Sagona 1993.
102 Duru 1979: 69.

103 Van Loon 1978: pls 24 and 26A.

104 Marro 1997.

105 Koşay and Turfan 1959; Koşay and Vary 1964, 1967.

106 Közbe 2004.

107 Rothman 2003.

108 Sagona and Sagona 2000.

109 Sagona 2004.

110 Howell-Meurs 2001; Piro 2009.

111 Özfırat 2001, 2007b.

112 King et al. 2008: 212.

113 Efe 2003b: 89; Efe and Ay Efe 2007: 252.

114 Korfmann 1983: 222–229.

115 Efe 2003a: 92.

116 Efe 2003b: figure 1.

117 Schliemann 1880.

118 Blegen et al. 1950; Dörpfeld 1902. The latest expedition is extensively reported in the series *Studia Troica* founded in 1998; see, for instance, Korfmann 1994.

119 Korfmann 2001. See also Özdoğan 2003b.

120 Warner 1979.

121 Koşay 1976; Naumann 1971: figure 23.

122 Efe 2003b.

123 Tolstikov and Treister 1996.

124 Eslick 1988; Warner 1994: pl. 8.

125 Locher 2001.

126 Efe 2003b.

127 Erkanal 1996, 1999.

128 Şahoğlu 2005.

129 Efe 2003b: figure 5.

130 Blegen et al. 1951.

131 Bernabò-Brea 1964.

132 Aslan 2006.

133 Steadman et al. in press.

134 Goldman 1956; Mellink 1989.

135 Şahoğlu 2005.

136 See references in Yener 2000, 2008.

137 Yener 2008.

138 The basic information is to be found in the Maden Teknik Araştırmarları (MTA) inventories 1970, 1971, 1972, and Ryan 1960. Detailed and trustworthy field surveys of prehistoric copper mines and smelting sites have been carried out by Wagner and Öztunalı 2000. Also useful is De Jesus 1980.

139 Killick 2001; Knapp et al. 1998; Pigott 1996.

140 Craddock 1995.

141 Budd and Taylor 1995; Childe 1944.

142 Shennan 1998. Cf. Arnold 1985.

143 Eliade 1964.

144 Helms 1993.

145 Childs and Killick 1993; Eliade 1962; Herbert 1998; Schmidt and Mapunda 1997.

146 Chernykh 1992; Yener 2000. See also the important collection of papers on Anatolian metallurgy in Yalçın 2000, 2002, 2005.

147 Caneva 2000; Yener 2000.

148 Efe 2002.

149 Hauptmann and Palmieri 2000.

150 Özbal et al. 2002.

151 Antonova et al. 1996.

152 Easton's reasoning (2002) is more persuasive than that of David Traill (1992), who has questioned the integrity of the collections, arguing that they represent artificial groups derived from different parts of the site and from different levels.

153 Antonova et al. 1996: 199.

154 Antonova et al. 1996: 106.

155 For references see Antonova et al. 1996: 210.

156 Antonova et al. 1996, nos 227 and 228.

157 Orthmann 1967.

158 Sagona 2001.

159 Sherratt 1981, 1983.

160 Smith and Horowitz 1984.

161 Richmond 2006.

162 Rossel 2008 et al.

163 Anthony 2007.

164 Morris 1987, 1992.

165 Rankin 1997.

166 Rankin 1997.

167 Kâmil 1982; The Karataş preliminary reports were published by M. Mellink in the *American Journal of Archaeology* from 1964 onwards. Bibilographic details on the cemeteries may be found in Stech-Wheeler 1974 and Warner 1994. See also Bittel 1941.

168 Gürkan and Seeher 1991; Jansen 1991; Korfmann 1983; Seeher 1987, 2000.

169 Lamb 1936; Stewart in Lamb 1937.

170 Pecorella 1984.

171 Arık 1937; Gürsan-Salzman 1992; Koşay 1938, 1951; Koşay and Akok 1966.

172 Gürsan-Salzman 1992. For earlier reconstructions, see Orthmann 1963; Schaeffer 1948.

173 Gürsan-Salzman 1992: 114.

174 De Jesus 1980; Mellink 1956; Özyar 2000.

175 Orthmann 1967.

176 Gürsan-Salzman 1992: 91, 108–111, 150.

177 Özgüç 1964 (Horoztepe), 1980 (Göller and Oymaağaç); Özgüç and Akok 1958: 42–52; Zimmerman 2006, 2007 (Kalınkaya).

178 Chernykh 1992.

179 Munchaev 1994.

180 Avilova et al. 1999.

181 Andreeva 1977; Chernykh and Orlovskaya 2004a, 2004b; Kohl 2007; Lyonnet 2007.

182 Abramishvili 1978: pl. 12: 2; Kakhiani and Ghlighvashvili 2008.

183 Alkım et al. 2003; Backofen 1987.

184 Bilgi 1984, 1989.

185 Sertok and Ergeç 1999: figure 2.

186 Behm-Blancke et al. 1981, 1984; Behm-Blancke 1992.

187 Algaze et al. 1995.

188 Frangipane et al. 2001; Frangipane 2001b. For some excellent photographs and discussion (in Italian) by Palumbi, see also the exhibition catalogue, Frangipane 2004.

189 Sagona 2004.

6

FOREIGN MERCHANTS AND NATIVE STATES

Middle Bronze Age (2000–1650 BC)

In the early second millennium BC, more than a dozen city-states flourished in central Anatolia, their sites now marked by some of the largest höyüks in that region (Figure 6.1). It was a more urban age than the periods that preceded or followed it, seeing both the intrusion of foreign elements and the spread of sophisticated new native styles. The types of pottery and other forms of material culture introduced between 2000 and 1650 BC would prevail without a major break until the end of the Bronze Age shortly after 1200 BC. Most significantly, from this period onward one can reconstruct the past of the region on a broader basis than archaeology alone permits, since there are now substantial numbers of cuneiform tablets excavated from the soil of Turkey itself to enhance archaeology with the written word.

This documentary record is inaugurated by more than 20,000 clay tablets found at Kültepe, supplemented by a few hundred from other sites in central Turkey. They were written by Assyrian merchants who had come to trade in textiles and metals (Figure 6.2). These individuals sometimes resided in Anatolia for decades, commissioning others to do the shipping and traveling while they kept track of the commercial activities and corresponded with their homeland through the medium of cuneiform writing in their native language, the Old Assyrian dialect of Akkadian.[1] Because the merchants were only writing for the pragmatic purposes of conducting their business, the testimony of these tablets, which date between roughly 1920 and 1740 BC,[2] is in no way comparable to the literary, political, historical, and religious offerings in royal archives that the Hittites were to assemble later in the millennium. They used a professional jargon for brief notations of legal matters, shipment inventories, and loans, and their private correspondence assumes a knowledge of context that we no longer have. Nevertheless, these documents make it possible to name specific individuals and sites, say something about the linguistic makeup of Anatolia, and help us to understand the larger economic and political forces that were shaping this new urban society. The milieu in which they were written was both

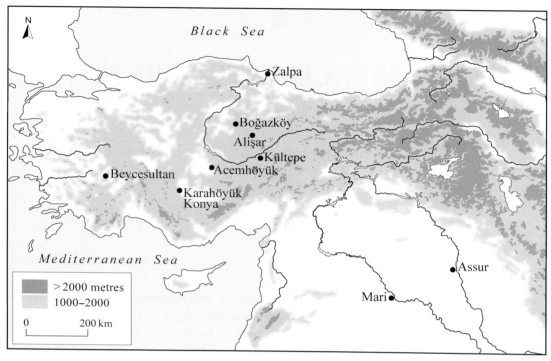

Figure 6.1 Map showing primary sites of the Middle Bronze Age

Figure 6.2 Old Assyrian merchant's tablet with Old Babylonian seal impression

cosmopolitan with recognizable foreign influences, yet dominated by a distinctively Anatolian culture which was to outlast the mercantile activity by many centuries.

THE KARUM KANESH AND THE ASSYRIAN TRADING NETWORK

The key site for this period is Kültepe (ancient Kanesh or Nesha), located 19 km northeast of Kayseri and a little southeast of where Kızılırmak (the Halys River of classical texts) begins to curve northward through the plateau on its way toward the Black Sea. It is central to the history of this period both as the archaeological site that has produced the most textual and archaeological evidence, and as the commercial nucleus of the Assyrians on the Anatolian plateau. Kanesh served as the point of contact between Assyria and the rest of central Anatolia. It was but one of a score of polities of the period that we know by name, but it appears to have played a very strong political hand as the seat of a prince who ruled from a palace whose walls enclosed an area of more than one hectare. Significantly, the Hittites later named their own language after this site, although at this time many others were also spoken there.[3] It is also appropriate to begin the discussion of this period with Kültepe since this site provides the basic stratigraphic sequence for ordering the chronology of the whole period.

The site of Kültepe is more extensive and complex than it first appears (Figure 6.3). What catches they eye is an approximately circular mound, roughly 500 m in diameter and rising 20 m above its surroundings. By itself, this is one of the largest mounds in Anatolia, but the lower lying areas that arc around its northern and eastern perimeters have produced the more spectacular finds. This lower area, off the main city mound, is known as the karum, or "quay" of Kanesh. The Akkadian word *kārum* was used to designate the harborside areas in Mesopotamian cities where trade was conducted, and although landlocked Kültepe was a port only for donkey caravans, the Assyrians applied the term to this merchant quarter and the institutions associated with it. Although we know from tablets that it contained a temple to the god Assur and an official building known as the *bīt kārim* (lit. "house of the karum") what has been found there archaeologically is a collection of private houses in which both Assyrians and native Anatolians lived.[4]

It took some time for archaeologists to establish the precise source of the Old Assyrian tablets, although it was suspected they came from Kültepe from the time they first appeared in art markets in Istanbul and Kayseri in the late 19th century AD. The main mound attracted the passing attention of a number of archaeologists, including the renowned pioneer of Anatolian archaeology, Ernest Chantre, who dug there for two seasons in 1893 and 1894. Hugo Winckler, who achieved fame for his work at the Hittite capital, also excavated for about a week in 1906.[5] These excavators were disappointed in their search for tablets, as was Bedrich Hrozny, the leader of a later Czech expedition, at least initially. The low quality of archaeological technique practiced by these early excavators did no small amount of damage to the mound. Hrozny, for example, was convinced that the palace in the center of the mound dated to the Hittite Empire,

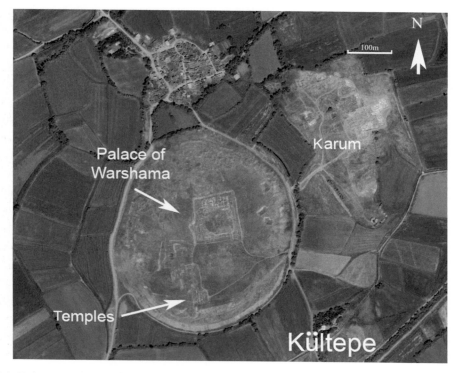

Figure 6.3 Kültepe in Google Earth photo with karum and locations on city mound marked

and reasoning that the tablets must come from below because they predated the Hittites, dug right through it.[6] We now know this palace in fact dated to the time when the Assyrians were active at the site. Despite starting in the wrong place, it was Hrozny who eventually discovered the karum. As his single field season of 1925 neared its end a local villager informed him that the clandestinely excavated tablets were not coming from the main mound at all but rather from beside it. Hrozny immediately transferred his workmen to the karum and was able to recover 1034 tablets in the time that remained.[7]

Work on a more archaeologically sophisticated level commenced at the site in 1948 with a Turkish expedition led by Tahsin Özgüç. It has continued in annual campaigns ever since, focusing primarily on the karum, but with some attention to the main mound as well. Özgüç, who directed the project into the 1990s, was able to work out the basic stratigraphy of both the citadel mound and the karum and provide the backbone of an archaeological chronology for Middle Bronze Age Central Anatolia. He discerned 18 building levels in the main mound, which are numbered from the top down. Levels 18–11 span the Early Bronze Age, and 5–1 cover the period from the Iron Age through the time of the Roman Empire. There is apparently no occupation in the Late Bronze Age, and the Middle Bronze levels, 10–6, represent the most prosperous period of the site.[8] The karum was only occupied in the Middle Bronze Age, and has its own stratigraphic sequence, normally designated by Roman numerals. The earliest two, Levels IV and III, are substantial, covering the whole area that was settled there, but have yielded no tablets. Level II is the most active period of the Old Assyrian trade and has produced the greatest number of tablets. References to Assyrian rulers and eponym officials[9] date these from ca. 1920 to 1830 BC,[10] with the great majority of the tablets probably coming from the second half of that span. This level was violently destroyed, which is no doubt how so many tablets came to be preserved. The karum was then abandoned for at least a generation. In Level Ib, dated by tablets to 1810–1740 BC,[11] the trade was resumed, but at a lower level and on a somewhat different basis. Enough time had passed that the Assyrian language had actually undergone some changes, which tablets found at other Anatolian sites also reflect.[12] Level Ia represents the much diminished and final occupation of the karum, without tablets.[13]

Publication of all the Kültepe materials, tablets and archaeological remains, has lagged, but the general picture is clear. All told, there are probably around 20,000 tablets from the karum, if one includes the ones from all excavations as well as those that turned up on the antiquities market. Alişar, Boğazköy and a few other sites in Turkey and Iraq have also produced a few hundred more Cappadocian texts. The catastrophe that ended Karum Kanesh Level II seems to have been local; all the Old Assyrian tablets from other sites belong to the Karum Kanesh Ib period, or perhaps a little later.

The tablets these Assyrian merchants left behind are valuable not just a source for the history of Anatolia in the 19th and 18th centuries BC, but also for what they have to tell us about ancient economics generally. Although they leave many things unexplained and are only part of a very large system, they provide the most detailed record of a long-distance system of trade that we have from the ancient world. They also give warning to archaeologists studying trade in other complex societies not to overestimate how much one can understand from material evidence alone. The commodities traded at Kanesh are for the most part invisible in the inventory of excavated objects, and without the tablets—which we would not have found had some more perishable material than clay been the writing material—there would be little indication that the Assyrians were here at all. In any case, let us begin with a discussion of the commercial arrangements, before broadening our horizons to the society as a whole.

What drove the trade, at least in the Karum Level II period, was the widespread demand for tin. Although bronze objects from the Early Bronze Age composed of copper and tin are not unknown and an inferior bronze was made by alloying copper and arsenic, the Middle Bronze Age is the first time that tin bronzes were produced in quantity. Turkey is rich in copper ores, but local tin supplies were apparently inadequate for the demands of the new era. We do not know precisely where the Assyrians were getting their tin since our documents only inform us about the commerce within Anatolia and between Anatolia and Assyria. It is clear, however, that the merchants of Kanesh were buying it in Assur and bringing it overland into Anatolia, where they were able to sell it for twice what they had paid. This presumably was the staple commodity that made local Anatolian princes so accommodating to these foreigners in their midst. Assyria, of course, did not have any tin of its own, and must have been importing it from elsewhere. It is clear that the Kültepe texts are showing us only one leg of a larger trading network centered in Assur. The location of the mines that produced the tin is not known absolutely, but the direction of the shipments suggest that it was coming from the east, and the richest sources known in that direction are in the vicinity of Herat, in Afghanistan (Figure 6.4).

Tin was not, however, the most profitable trade item for the Assyrian merchants in Anatolia. Along with the tin, the donkey caravans making the 1000-km trek from Assur to Kanesh brought textiles which had been manufactured in Assyria and southern Mesopotamia. While it is hard to imagine there was any wool shortage in Anatolia, the tablets show that merchants, carefully weighing shifts in fashion and demand, made a gross profit of around 200% on textiles.[14] Mesopotamian textiles may have been valued in the same way that Persian rugs are today. And what went back to Assyria? Despite all of the local goods which one would think the people living in resource-poor Assyria might want, the only thing the tablets show going back is money, that is, silver and gold.[15] The discrepancy in the weight of material going in the two directions was so great that most of the donkeys coming in from Assyria were sold in Anatolia.[16]

Kanesh was the first stop for the caravans coming to and from Assyria, but it was only one of

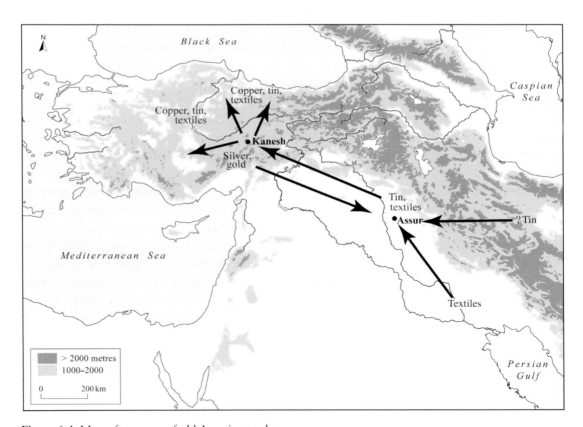

Figure 6.4 Map of patterns of old Assyrian trade

15 sites in Anatolia to have a karum. Most of the others were in major cities of independent principalities, the most famous of which were Burušhattum (Purušhanda), Duhurmit, Hattuš, Uršu, Wahšušana, and Zalpa. Of these, only the location of the karum Hattuš is confidently pinpointed archaeologically, as it was part of the site of Boğazköy, where the Hittites were later to establish their capital. Burušhattum, mentioned as a remote place in Mesopotamian texts of the third millennium, is generally felt to be one of the westernmost of theses merchant colonies, lying somewhere south of Tuz Gölü. An old Hittite story appears to locate one of the two places called Zalpa in the Old Assyria texts at the place where the Kızılırmak flows into the Black Sea.[17] There was also a secondary, smaller type of trading center known as a *wabartum*. About a dozen of these are named in Kültepe texts, and they seem to have been located in smaller villages.

Assyrian merchants moved between all of these trading posts, apparently enjoying a kind of political neutrality, trading in a wider range of commodities (including copper) than they did on the Assyria to Kanesh route. A large part of the commercial economy of Anatolia was apparently in their hands. But the local palace was involved with, and benefited from the trade the Assyrians were practicing. Incoming caravans were first unloaded in the palace at Kanesh, before their goods went on the market. The king apparently had first choice of textiles brought to the karum, taxed the merchants, and could impose embargos. There is one commodity, of no small interest in the Bronze Age, which seems to have been of specific concern to the authorities: a metal known as *ašium* or *amūtum*, which had a value eight times that of gold. Since there are not many candidates for what so valuable a material might be, it is usually thought to be meteoric iron.[18] It was rare, and its trade was restricted, if not prohibited by the authorities.[19]

The activities of these Assyrian merchants and their relationships with governmental authorities in Anatolia and Assyria are of great importance in a major debate in economic anthropology. Was the behavior of the merchants dictated by market forces that can be explained by such universal economic principles as supply and demand, or were these embedded in institutions that molded them into much more culturally specific forms that would defy such analysis? The economic historian Karl Polanyi, for example, argued that markets and abstract concepts of money—as opposed to special purpose money—were relatively recent inventions, and economic behavior in premodern societies could not be understood in terms of classical economic forces. His views had a great influence in the field of anthropology and at the time he was writing, in the mid-20th century, it was recognized that the data from Kültepe were crucial to this problem. Polanyi himself wrote an article attempting to demonstrate that the Old Assyrian merchants were engaged in treaty trade, where political agreements overrode the independence of individual merchants. More recent and detailed study of the tablets has shown this thesis to be untenable.[20] The merchants bought low, sold high, looked for bargains, avoided what taxes they could, and assumed the risks for their ventures without any support from the palace on either end of the trade route.

At Kanesh, the karum was composed of private houses in which the Assyrian merchants as well as native Anatolians resided (Figures 6.5 and 6.6). There is no visible difference between the houses of the two populations—only the tablets establish the Assyrian heritage of some of the

231

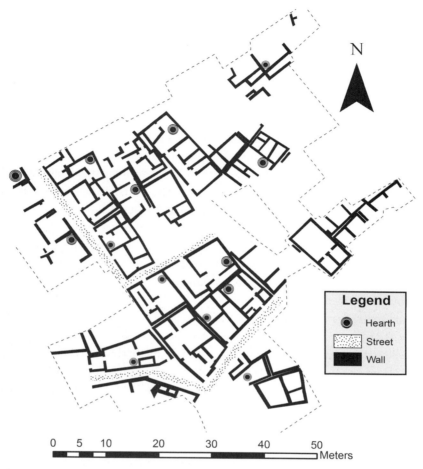

Figure 6.5 Plan of part of a neighborhood in the Karum Kanesh Level II (after T. Özgüç 1986: plan 1)

occupants. House forms were essentially built according to Anatolian traditions, more often than not in two stories. They are essentially single-family dwellings of rectilinear form, and there is not much variation in them over the various phases of the karum's occupation. A basic two-room plan was the starting point, and to this a courtyard and other rooms could be added. This is more of a western Anatolian building form than a reflection of the greater Mesopotamian tradition, where the structure looks inward and rooms are grouped around a central court. At Kültepe, the open areas around the houses were probably used a work spaces and the ground level was where most of the business was conducted. Another distinctively Anatolian construction technique was the use of large amounts of timber laid horizontally and as vertical poles to reinforce the structures. Stone foundations formed the base of the wall, and in some cases these rose quite high.

It is not surprising that few of the domestic artefacts look particularly Assyrian, apart from

Figure 6.6 Street in the Karum Kanesh, with city mound in the background (Photo courtesy Roger Matthews)

the tablets themselves and some of the seal impressions on them. The key figures in the trade, the Assyrian merchants, spent long periods of time in Anatolia—some of records suggest they stayed away from Assyria for decades—and adopted local customs. One letter, addressed to two merchants by creditors, laments: "Thirty years ago you left the city of Assur. You have never made a deposit since, and we have not recovered one shekel of your silver from you, but we have never made you feel bad about this. Our tablets have been going to you with caravan after caravan, but no report from you has ever come here."[21]

The idea that Assyria had some sort of sovereignty or empire in Anatolia at this time no longer has any credibility, but the merchants did associate with one another and enjoyed certain special privileges. They had an assembly in Kanesh which served as a court and could impose punishments in matters concerning commercial activities and there was some sort of "house" or administrative structure to coordinate activities. The physical structures associated with these, however, have not been identified. The government of Assur maintained contact with the merchants of the karum through correspondence, and emissaries were sent to coordinate negotiations with the native Anatolian political authorities.[22]

MIDDLE BRONZE AGE CITY-STATES OF THE ANATOLIAN PLATEAU

Powerful engines of social and economic development clearly transformed Anatolia in the 20th and 19th centuries BC. It is not that the sites are entirely new—most of the important Middle Bronze Age centers are built on sites that were occupied in the Early Bronze Age. Kültepe's main mound, for example, was inhabited throughout the third millennium, as was Alişar, where a pioneering American expedition in the 1920s and 1930s sought to work through a very complex series of archaeological levels in order to establish the ceramic chronology of the central plateau. What is different is the scale of these centers. The size of the central mounds expanded, and then spilled off into terraces, producing adjacent living areas like the karum.

The places that grew the most seem to have been those that lay at intersections of important avenues of communication, rather than locations on higher ground that might more easily be defended. This is not to say that their defense was neglected. These settlements were protected by massive walls which required some organized communal effort to construct. At Alişar the form of the city wall is clear. It consisted of boxes of mud brick built on stone foundations (Figure 6.7: 2). These casemates, which measured 5–6 m^2, were then filled in with packed earth, and the facade presented a kind of saw-tooth appearance when viewed in plan. Von der Osten, the wall's excavator, speculated that this unusual building principle may have been adopted to limit the damage of a breach to a confined space,[23] but it is equally possible that it was simply a the result of a system of diving up labor to produce such a large undertaking quickly. In any case, the casemate technique was to live on in the Hittite Empire, albeit in a much more refined form. At Alişar there is also an innovation that the Hittites would pick up: The postern gate (Figure 6.7: 1). This tunnel runs for 50 m, descending 9 m as it passes under the city wall 150 m from the northern gate. It is assumed that it would allow defenders of the city to engage a besieging enemy by sneak attack, outside the fortifications.[24]

Such defenses were clearly necessary, because these Anatolian principalities were politically independent of each other and no doubt frequently at war. For the most part the Assyrian documents touch only peripherally on local politics, but they do occasionally shed some light on the native authorities. In this regard, Kanesh is again the most informative site, and architectural remains are eloquent statements of power. Excavations on its citadel mound have demonstrated that it was dominated by a substantial royal establishment. While the depredations of ancient rebuilding, mining of the mound's soil by local farmers for agricultural purposes up until a century ago, and the clumsy, vain search for the source of the Cappadocian texts by early excavators uninterested in artefacts caused enormous damage to the central mound at Kültepe, Tahsin Özgüç was able to discover the basic character of several palaces here. One of these, located near the center of the mound, is roughly circular in its ground plan, although only about a third of its perimeter can be made out.[25] It was not planned as a single structure and its walls were relatively thin and composed of largely of mud brick. The pottery and small finds associated with this building date it to Level II of the karum, the time in which trade was most vigorous, giving it a construction date in the late 20th or 19th century BC. Despite the thousands of tablets found in

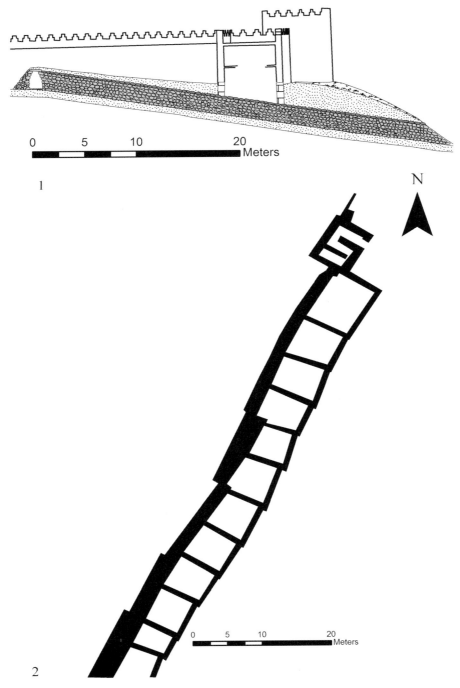

Figure 6.7 Defenses at Ališar: **1** Postern gate (after von der Osten 1937: fig. 29). **2** Casemate wall (after von der Osten 1937: fig. 24)

the karum in this period, the name of only one Anatolian king, Labarša, is mentioned.[26] We know from the tablets that merchants took their shipments "up" to the palace on arrival in Kanesh for clearance of customs and payment of duties, so it was presumably in the central area of this circle that the unloading took place.

Overlying this early palace, and exhibiting a radically different plan, is a later building known as the Palace of Waršama after one of the kings who resided there, whom we shall discuss later. It has a nearly square layout of a little more than 100 m on each side (Figure 6.8). The foundations' outer walls were made of large stones, well laid out and reinforced with timbers, in places surviving to a height of 2 m. The walls were buttressed at regular intervals and only one gateway, on the western side, has been discovered, although there is a possibility that another,

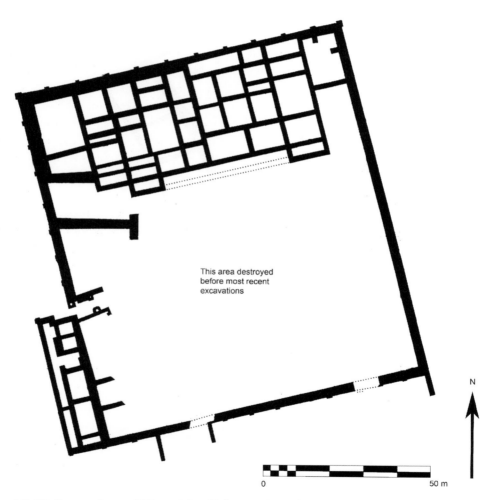

This area destroyed
before most recent
excavations

0   50 m

Figure 6.8 Waršama palace at Kültepe (after T. Özgüç 1999: plan 1)

destroyed by later building, lay on the south and offered the most direct approach from the karum. The building was constructed as a unit around a central courtyard. The rooms of the palace are best preserved on the northern and western sides. Some 50 of them have been excavated in the complex, eight in a kind of annex on the southwest side and the rest on the north and northwest sides. Some of these may be identified as storerooms and from the thickness of the walls and the presence of a staircase, it is presumed that the royal residential quarters were on a second story. Rooms on the southern and eastern sides of the courtyard have been destroyed, so it is not possible to be certain what functions were performed where in the building, or whether such things as workshops, unattested in the present state of the evidence, were truly absent. With an area of over one hectare, it does not match its famous contemporary, the Palace of Zimri-Lim at Mari (2.5 hectares), but it is the largest single building known in Anatolia up to this point and reflects the prominence of the local ruler. Seals, sealings, and pottery, while not present in overwhelming quantities, are unanimous in dating this building to Level Ib of the karum.

One other palace at Kültepe is located on the terrace area of the mound to the southeast of the citadel. This is incompletely exposed and does not seem to enclose a courtyard, as is the case with other palaces. It may have been some sort of adjunct administrative building rather than a royal residence. In any case, it was abandoned in the final phase of the site's occupation, its functions presumably transferred to the new and larger palace of Waršama.

While it is generally true that the tablets found at Kültepe shed little light on the Anatolian politics of the era, there is one conspicuous exception, which was found beside the ruins of the gateway to the later palace on the citadel. It was sent to king Waršama himself by the king of the neighboring land of Mama, and is worth quoting extensively:

> Thus says Anum-hirbi, the Mamean *rubā'um*[27] to Waršama, the Kanišean *rubā'um*, say: "You wrote me: 'The Taišamean is my slave; I shall take care of him. But do you take care of the Sibuhean, your slave?' Since the Taišamean is your dog, why does he argue with the other *šarru*s? Does the Sibuhean, my dog, argue with the other *šarru*s? Is a Taišamean *rubā'um* to become the third *rubā'um* with us? When my enemy defeated me, the Taišamean invaded my country. He destroyed twelve of my cities and carried away their cattle and sheep. He said 'The *rubā'um* is dead, so I have taken up my fowler's snare.' So instead of protecting my country and giving me heart, he not only burned up my country but created evil-smelling smoke. While your father Inar was besieging the city of Harsamna for 9 years, did my land invade your land and did it kill an ox or sheep? Today you wrote me as follows: 'Why do you not free the road for me?' I will free the road."[28]

The discovery of this document put an end to the early notion that the Assyrian merchants were operating under some sort of imperial umbrella held by Assur. The Anum-hirbi letter, on the contrary, shows a hierarchy of authority in which there are rulers of important places like Mama and Kanesh holding subordinate rulers in check—or at least that is what the king of Mama says they should be doing. There is no reference here to the Assyrians whatsoever.

It is interesting that this exercise in diplomacy had to be conducted through the medium of the Assyrian language and script. We don't know whether the scribe who took Anum-hirbi's dictation was a native Anatolian trained in Assyrian, or an Assyrian pressed into service by the palace, but the letter is a clear demonstration that literacy was Assyrian monopoly.

As noted already, the palace of Waršama is the largest palace that we have from the period of the Assyrian trading colonies, but it is not the only one. Another site of great importance is Acemhöyük, located 19 km to the west of Aksaray, adjacent to the modern village of Yeşilova. The ancient identity of this site is not entirely certain, although its excavator, Nimet Özgüç, was inclined to identify it with the famous Burušhattum,[29] which is known to lie several days' journey to the west of Kanesh. We know there was a karum at Burušhattum and indeed there is evidence for both Assyrian merchants and contact with Kanesh at the site. The mound is more oval in shape than Kültepe, measuring approximately 650 m NE–SW and 400 m NW–SE. Two palace complexes have been excavated, one known as Sarıkaya on the southeastern edge of the mound, and the other of nearly equal size, Hatipler Tepesi, in the northwest central area. The principles of building in evidence here are different from the palaces of Kanesh. Neither palace enclosed a central court, but rather all rooms seem to have adjoined one another. Hatipler may actually have been an agglutinative structure, but Sarıkaya, with its nearly square arrangement and surrounding porticos, looks planned from the outset (Figure 6.9: 1) It is possible, however, that they are separate units of the one large administrative structure.[30] In any case, both were destroyed at the same time in an extraordinarily violent fire that has turned some of the mud bricks in the walls to glass and the pottery here appears to be contemporary with the pottery at Karum Ib.

No karum as such has been excavated at Acemhöyük, although one may well lie beneath the modern village beside the site or elsewhere in the unexcavated areas around the höyük. Evidence for the Assyrian trade, however, comes from a series of bullae, or clay dockets, that were once fastened to commodities or their containers and were found in the palace storerooms. These bear seal impressions, and occasionally brief inscriptions. Interestingly, some of the latter say "to the karum Kanesh," which might have seriously misled an archaeologist in identifying Acemhöyük, had we not already been quite certain that Kültepe was Kanesh. What they do show is the latter serving in its role as a transshipment point for caravans from Assur, from which goods were moved to other sites, like Acemhöyük. One other important offering of the bullae is a reference to Shamshi-Adad, the Amorite king of northern Mesopotamia and partial contemporary of Hammurabi of Babylon, who created an empire for himself that included Assur, Mari, and Shubat-Enil (Tell Leilan). This provides an important synchronism for the Karum Kanesh Level Ib period.[31]

Evidence for the activities of Assyrian merchants has been found at several sites outside of Kültepe, but in all cases it dates to the end of the Karum Kanesh Ib period, when the trade was operating at a reduced level. At this time more of the trade seems to be within Anatolia, and, most significantly, there are few references to importing tin.[32] About 60 tablets were found at Boğazköy in private houses located below the citadel rock which was later to be the site of the

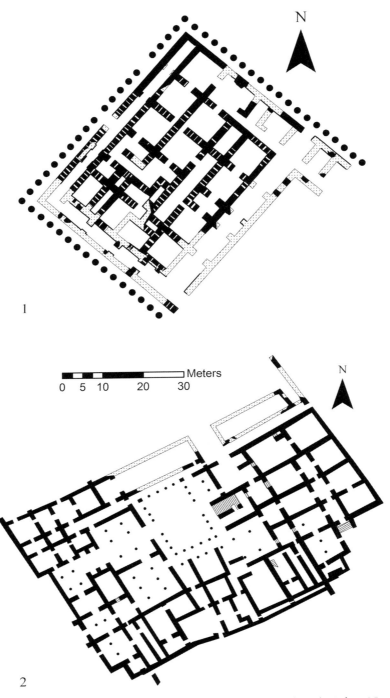

Figure 6.9 Middle Bronze Age palaces: **1** Sarıkaya palace at Acemhöyük (after N. Özgüç 1966). **2** Beycesultan palace (after Lloyd and Mellaart 1965: figs A3 and A4)

palace from which the Hittite realm was governed.[33] These were the documents of the karum Hattuš, and that city name, which is regularly written Hattuša in the following period, gives its name to the land of Hatti. Approximately 75 more tablets come from the terrace of the mound at Alişar, which was probably named Amkuwa in this period.[34]

CENTRAL ANATOLIAN MATERIAL CULTURE OF THE MIDDLE BRONZE AGE

The emergence of this prosperous and cosmopolitan society coincided with the introduction of new ceramic traditions. Some of these were relatively short lived. A rather elaborate handmade pottery, known as "Cappadocian ware" (Figure 6.10: 1), is most often seen in open bowls. First identified in Alişar Level III, it continued the trajectory of the "Intermediate Ware" of the late Early Bronze Age, but painted in multiple colors. Its geometric designs of horizontal bands, triangles, zigzags, and lozenges in red, black, and white paint make it one of the most colorful styles ever to develop in ancient Turkey. This ware does not seem to have been particularly widespread, being much rarer at sites at the north, like Boğazköy, than it is at Kültepe. It also died out in the course of the Middle Bronze Age.

Another type of decoration is more often found on larger wheelmade pitchers and open vessels (Figure 6.10: 2). They are partially or wholly covered with a red to reddish-brown slip that is burnished to a low shine. Reserved rectangular areas on the vessel shoulders and rims are decorated with dark brown geometric patterns of the same sorts that are found in Cappadocian ware, but here without the color.

Perhaps more significant is the introduction of wheelmade wares with red or brown slips that are often polished. Some of the forms of the latter are quite distinctive. They include pitchers with long beaked spouts and containers on high pedestals (Figures 6.10: 3 and 6.10: 4). Vessels with attached animal figures gracing their handles or rims are quite common. This burnished ware is informally and not entirely correctly dubbed "Hittite ware" because it continues to be used, albeit evolving gradually until the end of the Bronze Age. In the period of the merchant colonies, it became a kind of standard throughout the plateau, yet there was still some local variation. Kutlu Emre found that beak-spouted pitchers, two-handled drinking cups, and some other types tended to be squatter and thicker at Acemhöyük than at Kültepe, although the overall shapes tended to be indistinguishable.[35]

The place where the cosmopolitanism of the era comes though most clearly is in the art revealed to us by seal impressions. Most of these are associated with the trading activities of the karum, appearing on the clay envelopes of letters and sealings associated with storage, such as the dockets found at Acemhöyük. It is not surprising, therefore, that these should include a mixture of both foreign and local elements.

External influence is apparent in the very shape of many of the seals. This period is virtually the only one in which the cylinder seal, so characteristic of Mesopotamia, is in widespread use. There was a long tradition of sealing in Anatolia, but it favored the use of stamp seals rather

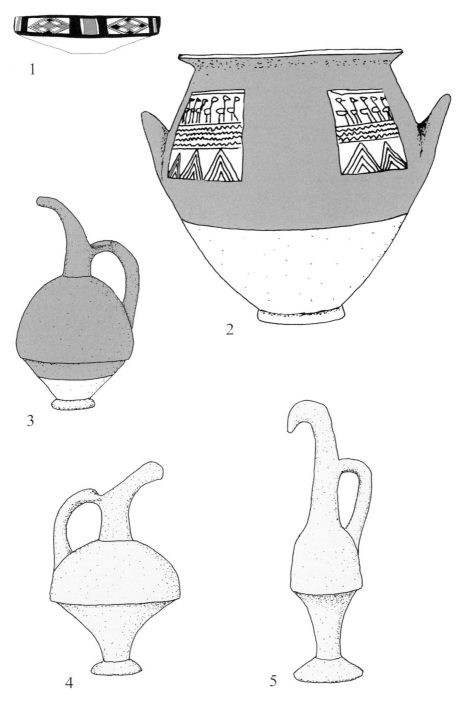

Figure 6.10 Pottery from the trading colony period: **1** Cappadocian ware (after von der Osten 1937: plate 5). **2** Panel vessel (after T. Özgüç 1986: plate 102/3). **3** Pitcher with red burnished slip on upper portion (after T. Özgüç 1986: plate 99/3). **4** Red slipped and burnished pitcher (after Bittel 1976: fig. 52). **5** Red slipped beaker jug from Alaca Höyük (after Akurgal 1962: plate 38)

than the friezes of design that come from the rolling of a cylinder. Cylinder seals were the norm in Assyria, as well as Syria, so the mere fact that they came into vogue in the trading colony period speaks for southern influence. Stamp seals, however, do not completely disappear, and one can see the waxing and waning of their importance throughout the period as a kind of index of the intensity of foreign participation in the Anatolian trade.

Nimet Özgüç, who has made several pioneering studies of the seals and seal impressions of Kültepe defines four major stylistic groups, three of which can be classed as outright imports: Old Babylonian (Figure 6.2), Old Assyrian (Figure 6.11: 1), and Old Syrian (Figure 6.11: 2). The fourth, and perhaps most interesting, is the termed the Anatolian Group (Figures 6.11: 3 and 6.11: 4). We cannot assume, however, that the style of the seal denoted the place of origin of the seal owner. Seals were valuable items, staying in use for a long time, and sometimes recut for new holders. Seals dating to southern Mesopotamia's Third Dynasty of Ur (ca. 2100–2000 BC) were used at Kültepe, although their manufacture predates the context in which they were found by centuries. It is also clear from the texts on which they appear that both natives and Assyrians made use of seals in the Anatolian Group.

Old Babylonian seals were, of course, contemporary with the trading colonies and embraced a wide number of themes. One of the most common is the "presentation scene," in which an individual is led into the presence of a seated deity by an interceding divinity. This basic motif is adopted and transformed in many of the scenes on the Anatolian Group seals. Manufacturing points for the widespread Old Babylonian seals would include not just southern Mesopotamia, but also Mari, which the Acemhöyük finds demonstrate was in contact with Anatolia. The Old Assyrian type is much more limited geographically and temporally, and is most easily distinguished by its processions of repeating figures and crude renderings of the garments of figures using parallel diagonal lines. There are at least two groups of the Syrian styles, an earlier one with groups of smaller figures and a later one with much larger, well-modeled figures.

The scenes of the Anatolian Group are most noteworthy for their clutter. Familiar Mesopotamian scenes are here, but they are transformed by the sealcutters' abhorrence of a vacuum. Spaces between larger figures are filled with animals, or parts of animals turned every which way. The gods in the presentation scenes sometimes wear the tall pointed horned crown that is much better known from Anatolia in the late Hittite Empire. In fact, many of the Anatolian deities who figure prominently in the cultic practices and mythology of later centuries, such as the Storm God and the Sun Goddess, probably find their first representation here, although we can say little of them in this period without extrapolation from the later texts.

Stamp seals never went out of use, and they appear to increase in popularity during the Karum Ib period (Figures 6.11: 5 and 6.11: 6). Generally, they have a flat stamping surface of a round or rectangular shape, and are held by a knob through which there was a hole to suspend them on a string. These tend to make smaller impressions than cylinder seals, and their themes are therefore more limited. The earliest stamp seals often have nothing more on them than hatch marks. In later periods the designs include familiar Anatolian themes, such as double-headed eagles.

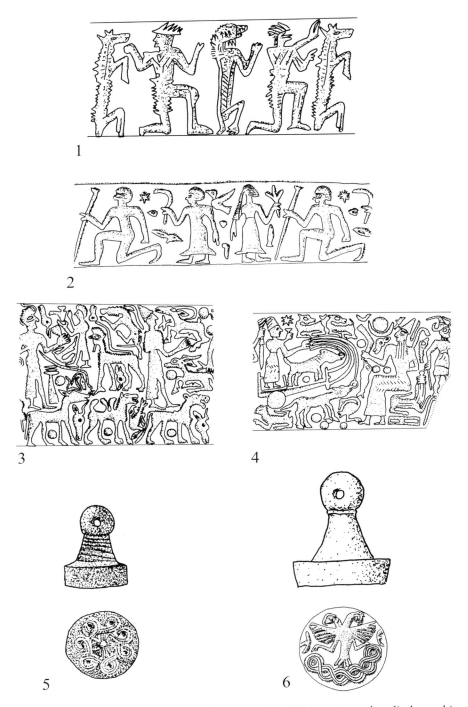

Figure 6.11 Seals and sealings of the trading colony period: **1** Old Assyrian style cylinder seal impression (after N. Özgüç 1968: plate xxvii/1). **2** Old Syrian style cylinder seal impression (after N. Özgüç 1968: plate xxix/1). **3** Partial impression of Anatolian Group cylinder seal (after N. Özgüç 1965: plate xi/31a). **4** Partial impression of Anatolian Group cylinder seal (after N. Özgüç 1965: plate viii/24b). **5** Stamp seal (after N. Özgüç 1968: plate xxxvii/4a–b). **6** Stamp seal (after Bittel 1976: fig. 78)

Kültepe and other sites of this period have also produced a large body of figurative art (Figure 6.12), much of it in the form of clay attachments to vessels, or vessels themselves formed in the shape of animals. Small, very stylized figurines were also made of lead in molds. There are a few figurines in more exotic materials, like ivory (Figure 6.12: 2), which itself indicates long-distance trade. Acemhöyük has also produced ivories, some of which show stylistic attributes such as large curls in the hair falling over the shoulders, which will reappear in Hittite art in subsequent periods (Figure 6.12: 3).

INDO-EUROPEANS IN ANATOLIA AND THE ORIGINS OF THE HITTITES

The language of the Old Assyrian texts is a dialect of Akkadian, which belongs to the larger Semitic family that dominates the Near East south of the Taurus Mountains, and most of people who are mentioned in connection with the trade have Semitic names, as one would expect. However, names of Anatolian natives are sometimes mentioned and because these provide the earliest evidence we have for reconstructing the linguistic makeup of the plateau, they are of great interest. They are a very diverse group. In a pioneering study that is admittedly somewhat dated, Paul Garelli examined the 600 non-Semitic names that were known to him and concluded that about two-thirds of these could be satisfactorily explained, although there were many ambiguities. The greatest number, not quite a majority, were Hittite, with much smaller numbers of those that could be understood as Luwian. Some belonged to the unaffiliated Hurrian language, but these individuals appear to have come from the south, and if the Hurrians had a homeland on the plateau, it was in eastern rather than central Anatolia. Another unaffiliated language is one we call Hattic or Hattian, which gave its name to the land of Hatti before the Hittites came into prominence. Garelli was puzzled that so few names of this type were represented—fewer than 40, and some of these may actually have belonged to Hittites—suggesting that perhaps the language had already died out. Other names in the tablets may be nicknames or shortened forms which cannot be affiliated with anything from the information we have.[36]

On the basis of their personal names, it would appear that the majority of the population at Kültepe spoke an Indo-European language of the Anatolian family. This is a crucial fact for both earlier and later Anatolian history, and involves a digression into one of the key battlefields of historical linguistics. When the great Indo-European language family was defined in the late 18th and 19th centuries AD, the starting point was the recognition that Greek, Latin, and Sanskrit were all descended from some common ancestor. Soon the Germanic, Slavic, Celtic, Iranian, and other families were recognized as descendants of this proto-Indo-European progenitor as the fundamental principles of historical linguistics were worked out. The search for the time and placed of origin of this ancestral language was undertaken by analyzing words common to many of its descendants. For example, many Indo-European languages share a common word for snow, but they do not have a common word for ocean. This pretty well rules out a tropical island for the homeland.

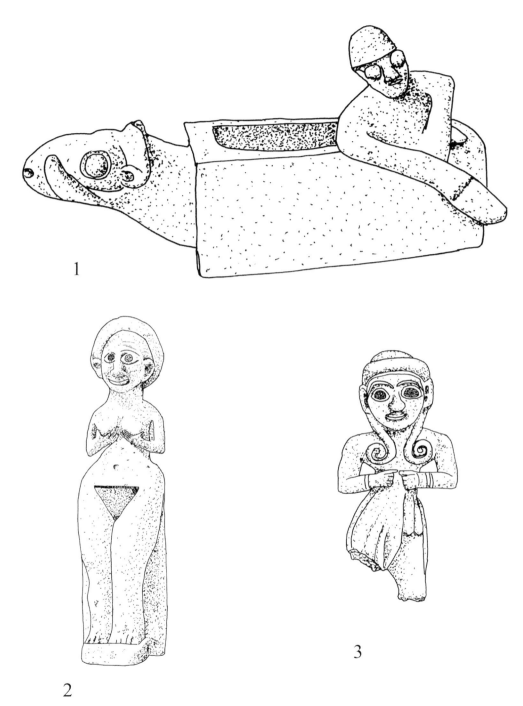

Figure 6.12 Objects of art from the trading colony period: **1** Clay vessel with figure (after Bittel 1976: fig. 71).**2** Ivory figurine from Kültepe (after Bittel 1976: fig. 33). **3** Ivory figure from Acemhöyük (after Bittel 1976: fig. 45)

When the Hittite language was deciphered in 1917 and recognized to be Indo-European, ancient Anatolia became an area of keen interest in historical linguistics. It was immediately recognized that there were two other closely related languages in the archives of the Hittites—Luwian and Palaic—and that Lydian and Lycian were members of this Anatolian family that survived into the first millennium. Hittite, Luwian, and Palaic were the oldest written Indo-European languages and the relationship of this family to the other descendants of proto-Indo-European was not particularly close. The presence of this group also posed a question for archaeologists and historians: If the proto-Indo-European homeland was somewhere in Europe or Russia, when and how did the Indo-Europeans come to Anatolia?

We still do not have an answer to this question, but archaeologists no longer look for destruction levels to identify with the Hittite invasion. Let us start from the period of the Assyrian trading colonies and work backward. We know that speakers of this Anatolian group of Indo-European languages were in the country from the appearance of their proper names. This evidence is generally not sufficient to distinguish Hittites from Luwians, but it is assumed that these languages had already begun to separate themselves from each other. By the time that we have readable texts, toward the end of the Middle Bronze Age, there is a clear geographic distribution of the Palaic language in the northwest center of the Plateau, Hittite in the center, and Luwian in southern and western Anatolia. In any case, the fact that the Anatolian speakers were only one of many different groups suggested to many that they were recent arrivals.

Not long ago, a completely different solution to this problem was proposed by Colin Renfrew, whose field of expertise is European and Aegean prehistory. He sought to tie the diffusion of Indo-Europeans to the spread of agriculture.[37] This is an attractive hypothesis for many reasons. It would, for example, explain the absence of pre-Indo-European place names in Europe. Normally names of locations are very conservative and remain in use long after the languages they come from have passed from the scene, as with the survival of many Native American place names in the eastern United States. We know that Europe was certainly inhabited before the Indo-Europeans arrived, but if this was by pre-agricultural peoples, much less numerous and not as intensively tied to specific places than the larger and sedentary populations inherent in an agricultural economy, it would explain why their languages are not reflected on the modern map.[38]

If agriculture and Indo-Europeans go together, then Indo-Europeans had been in Anatolia for a very long time before the Assyrians got there. They would no longer need to be brought in through the Caucasus Mountains or Thrace, because they were already there. For the archaeologist, this is a very attractive thesis, but for historical linguists, who date the spread of Indo-European much later, the idea is heresy. It remains a matter of controversy.

In any case, the native population of central Anatolia with whom the Assyrians conducted their business was a linguistically mixed group. Indeed, central Anatolia was to remain an area of linguistic turbulence throughout most of its history. Some languages of the period we have been discussing soon went out of use, such as the unaffiliated language known as Hattian, which gave name to the region from which the Indo-European Hittites were to exercise their later dominance. While it is inappropriate to call the native Anatolians of the trading colony period Hittites collectively, the culture that we call Hittite in the next chapter cannot be understood without reference to Kanesh and the sites with which it interacted in the Middle Bronze Age.

MIDDLE BRONZE AGE ANATOLIA BEYOND THE HORIZONS OF LITERACY

As one moves westward from Acemhöyük across the Anatolian plateau one leaves the area in which the Assyrians were directly involved in trade and thus the light of written documentation. The characteristics of the world we have been describing in central Anatolia do not otherwise vanish suddenly but rather transform gradually.

One major site, whose archaeological potential has only partially been realized is Karahöyük Konya, located 8 km south of Konya. Here too there was a massive palace, which is not dissimilar to the adminstrative structures at Acemhöyük. No karum has been located, but a large number of seal impressions has been recovered from the site. These are dominated by stamp seals, and stylistically look a little different from those found further east.[39] The pottery is roughly the same as at Karum Kanesh Ib and Acemhöyük, but again with some local variations. It has been suggested that perhaps this site was destroyed a little later than the others, and this rather than geography alone might account for some of the differences.

Further west, in the upper Meander Valley, lies Beycesultan, at site which has provided a long and important stratigraphic sequence for earlier periods in this part of Turkey. British excavators were originally attracted to it by the prospect that this might be the capital of the kingdom of Arzawa, an erstwhile rival of the Hittite in the mid-second millennium and a place known from the Amarna letters to harbor literacy. The search for Arzawa and tablets of the Late Bronze Age proved futile,[40] but an important Middle Bronze Age edifice, the "Burnt Palace" was discovered (Figure 6.9: 2). In the eyes of some, this structure, which is only partially preserved, offered parallels with the Minoan palaces of Crete, and was perhaps their inspiration, although now that we know more about Anatolian palaces of the era this view is less convincing.[41] There are no seals or seal impressions from Beycesultan, and the pottery is sufficiently different from Kültepe that it no longer makes any sense to discuss it in terms like Karum II and Karum Ib. Seton Llyod and James Mellaart have summed up the ceramic evidence as follows: "One cannot fail to notice the predominant local character of the Beycesultan pottery and that of South-west Anatolia in general. Developing on a late Early Bronze Age base with here and there an echo from the Kültepe region it remained staunchly West Anatolian."[42] Indeed, things are different enough that the dating of this palace is problematic and its excavators suggesting that perhaps the conflagration here was as late as the beginning of the Hittite Old Kingdom,[43] beyond the time frame of the Middle Bronze Age. Generally, however, one must agree with the with the excavators of Beycesultan that regional developments emerged independently in various parts of Anatolia in this period, and despite this there is a broad underlying unity in pottery of the Anatolian plateau overall.[44]

We will not discuss the picture in Turkey as a whole, beyond to say that we reach the shore of the Aegean, we are in a different world. At Miletus, on the coast, evidence for quite close contact with Middle Minoan Crete has recently been discovered in the form seals and seal impressions,[45] but there are also local indigenous styles. To the east, in the region that would much later become Urartu, the pottery is again quite different and nothing suggests this area was interacting with the Assyrian merchants or the city states of central Anatolia.

THE END OF THE TRADING COLONY PERIOD

The archives at Boğazköy contain an important historical document that provides a link, albeit obscurely, between Middle Bronze Age Kanesh/Nesha and the Hittite kingdom that was to dominate Anatolia and beyond from the late 17th century until the end of the Bronze Age. It is worth quoting some of its passages:

Anitta, son of Pithana, became king of (the city of) Kuššara. He behaved in a manner pleasing to the storm-god in heaven. And when he was in turn favored by the storm-god, the king of (the city of) Neša was [hostile(?)] to the king of Kuššara.

The king of Kuššara [came] down from the city with massed forces [and took] Neša by storm at night. He captured the king of Neša but in no way mistreated the inhabitants of Neša. He treated [them] as if they were (his) parents . . .

All the lands [arose(?)] from the direction of Zalpuwa on the Sea. Long ago, Uhna, king of Zalpuwa, had carried off our deity from Neša to Zalpuwa, but thereafter I, Great King Anitta [carried] off our deity back from Zalpuwa to Neša. I brought Huzziya, king of Zalpuwa, to Neša [alive]. (The city of Hattuša) inflicted [evil on me], and I released it. But when it later suffered from famine, their deity Halmašuitt (the throne goddess) delivered it up, and I took it by storm at night. [I] sowed cress on its grounds.

May the storm-god of Heaven smite whoever should become king after me and should resettle Hattuša.[46]

There are many ironies here. Why would the Hittites keep a record of a curse put on anyone who

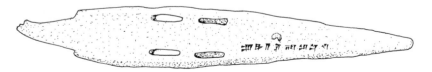

Figure 6.13 Bronze spearpoint with inscription of Anitta (after T. Özgüç 1999: plate 107)

resettled the very place they made their capital? What is the connection between the dynasty of Pithana and Anitta with the rulers who created the Hittite state a century or so later? Hittite tradition is consistent in beginning the story of their kings without reference to Anitta. There is one tie, of course, and that is that the royal line of the Hittite Old Kingdom also emerged from Kuššara, a site that has yet to be discovered archaeologically.

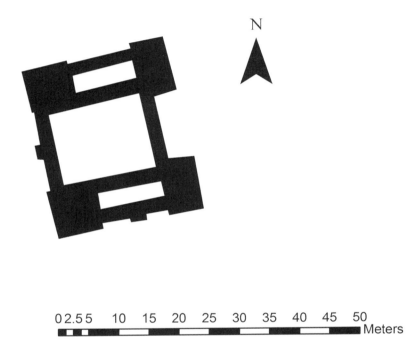

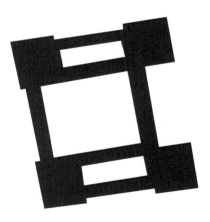

Figure 6.14 Temple plans from Kültepe (after T. Özgüç 1999: plan 7)

This Anitta is no mere figure of legend. While the text in the Boğazköy archives is written in Hittite and survives as a Late Bronze Age copy, it is written about a real figure—virtually the only one from this era remembered by the Hittites. Proof that this proclamation, however anachronistically recorded, contains a kernel of historical truth is provided by a bronze spearpoint excavated in a rather peculiar building on the terrace of Kültepe south of the Waršama palace (Figure 6.13). Inscribed on it the words "Palace of Anitta" can be easily made out. The building in which it was found deserves comment, for has a ground plan that appears to be unique to Kültepe. It takes the form of a large square room, to which rectangular wings are added, projecting in front of one side and aligned with the others. Two such buildings have now been found at Kültepe (Figure 6.14). Their monumentality, mutual similarity, and absence of features that would class them as any other type of public building strongly suggest that they are temples, as Tahsin Özgüç has assumed. The fact that the Anitta text mentions the construction of two temples, one for each of the most important gods, may not be irrelevant. If so, this spearpoint must have been a dedication there, and since the Hittite account specifies his association with the Storm God, this is one potential candidate for the deity to whom the building was dedicated. It is likely that the "Palace of Anitta" is none other than the Waršama palace, if we are to accept the claim that Anitta simply took over Kanesh and did not destroy it.

We are very much in the dark about the events that brought about the end of this period in the late 18th century BC. The later account appears to show a process of political consolidation going on, with Anitta eliminating Hattuša and Zalpa, and assuming power over Kanesh. All of the major centers that we have been considering went up in flames either during Anitta's reign or shortly afterward, and most did not recover as major centers of population or commerce.[47] Kanesh, which Anitta specifically claims not to have destroyed, suffered the same fate. When the Hittites brought Anatolia back into the full light of history after a century long dark age, they were forging a kingdom of a very different kind in a transformed world.

NOTES

1 When these tablets first attracted the attention of scholars in the 1880's, stylistic idiosyncrasies of the cuneiform writing prevented anyone from recognizing that they were written in a known language and tablets were dubbed "Cappadocian" in accordance with the name given in classical antiquity to the region of central Turkey from which they came. The name has stuck, and one still speaks of Cappadocian texts and Assyrian trading colonies in Cappadocia, even though the geographical term is an anachronism and the language is nothing other than Assyrian, a dialect of the Semitic Akkadian.
2 Veenhof 1997: 308.
3 The terminology for Hittite is confused by the fact that the language we conventionally call Hittite was called "Neshite," by its speakers. Nesha is a shortened form of the place name Kanesh (Otten 1973: 57–58).
4 T. Özgüç 1999: 117.
5 T. Özgüç 1999: 73.

6 T. Özgüç 1999: 74–75.

7 Michel 2003: 53.

8 T. Özgüç 1997: 268.

9 The Assyrians named years after officials rather than counting them. Recently, lists of these names have been discovered among the Kültepe texts (Veenhof 2000).

10 Dates are to the "Middle Chronology" of the *Cambridge Ancient History* as a convention. Many scholars, particularly in Europe, prefer a shorter chronology that would make these dates later by at least 64 years. A detailed discussion of chronology based in part on Kültepe texts, arguing that these dates should be lowered by as much as 50 years, is provided by Veenhof (2000).

11 Veenhof 1997: 308.

12 The easiest linguistic change to spot is the disappearance of final /m/ and /n/ sounds at the ends of words. In the nominative case, an Akkadian masculine word originally ended in -*um*, as in kār*um*. In the late 19th century BC this final consonant drops out, for example the kār*um* becomes the kār*u*. Writing does not always follow pronunciation immediately. The Code of Hammurabi, for example, which was written a little before 1750 BC, retains the final -m (which is called "mimation,") because it is being deliberately archaic, but less formal tablets of his time do not have it. In any case, mimation is present in the Karum II tablets, and absent in the Ib period.

13 T. Özgüç 1997: 268.

14 Veenhof 1972: 85.

15 Larsen 1967: 4.

16 Veenhof 1972: 2.

17 Otten 1973: 58.

18 Garelli 1963: 284. An indication that iron was regarded as very precious is provided by the example of an ivory box from Acemhöyük, in which small bosses of iron were elaborately set beside lapis lazuli and copper ornaments with gilded mountings.

19 Veenhof 1972: 306.

20 For a review of these issues from the perspective of an anthropologist, see Adams 1974.

21 Oppenheim 1967: 74.

22 Veenhof 1997: 308.

23 Von der Osten 1937: 4.

24 Naumann 1971: 302.

25 T. Özgüç 1999: plan 3.

26 T. Özgüç 1999: 137.

27 Usually, this term means something like magistrate, and would be inferior to someone bearing the title *šarru*, or king. In Anatolia in this period, the hierarchy seems reversed (Balkan 1957: 25–28).

28 From Balkan 1957: 8 with stylistic modification.

29 Also known as Purušhanda, and Purušhattum. It was a city of legend in Mesopotamia and its memory certainly survived into the Hittite period, all of which fits the chronology of the archaeological evidence from Acemhöyük. The identification, however, is not without controversy (cf. Steiner 1993).

30 Kuniholm reports this as a conclusion that Nimet Özgüç was leaning toward (Kuniholm 1989: 287).

31 N. Özgüç 1980: 61–63.

32 Veenhof 1997: 308.

33 Bittel 1970: 43.

34 Gelb 1935: 9.

35 Emre 1966: 140.

36 Garelli 1963: 127–169. Garelli's study of the Old Assyrian period is somewhat vitiated by his reluctance to distinguish between the Karum II and Ib periods.

37 The thesis was initially presented in Renfrew 1987.

38 Indeed, there are the non-Indo-European Basques Etruscans, Finns, and Hungarians who either occupy isolated areas or are recent, historically documented immigrants.

39 Alp 1968.

40 In fact, Hawkins (1998) has now convinced most scholars that it lies to the west, along the Aegean coast.

41 Bittel 1976: 66–67.

42 Lloyd and Mellaart 1962: 70.

43 Lloyd and Mellaart 1962: 73.

44 Lloyd and Mellaart 1962: 71.

45 Greaves 2002: 46–47.

46 Beckman et al. 2006: 21–218.

47 At a few sites, like Kaman-Kalehöyük, which lies midway between Boğazköy and Kültepe, the destruction level of the colony period is followed by a Hittite Old Kingdom level (Yildirim and Gates 2007: 295).

7

ANATOLIA'S EMPIRE

Hittite domination and the Late Bronze Age
(1650–1200 BC)

The Hittites loom over all other peoples in the early history of Anatolia in their broad exercise of political power and lasting cultural impact. Uniting the disparate principalities of central Asia Minor, they created an empire which spilled off the Anatolian plateau into Syria and vied with Egypt, Mitanni, Babylonia, and Assyria as one of the great powers of the day. The Hittites are to be respected not only for their political and military accomplishments, which are awesome enough, but also for the richness of their artistic, literary, and historical tradition. They were a force in the cultural development of Anatolia whose impact was felt long after their empire collapsed at the end of the Bronze Age.

THE REDISCOVERY OF THE HITTITES

Modern recognition of the significance of the Hittites only dawned in the last quarter of the 19th century AD. The historians and geographers of ancient Greece appear to have had no notion that a great empire had once been ruled from the Anatolian plateau. Herodotus ascribed one Hittite monument on ground he knew well, the Karabel relief (Figure 7.1), to the Egyptian king Sesostris.[1] While the Bible introduced the term "Hittite" to ancient and modern vocabularies, its testimony was composed in the aftermath of the Hittite Empire's collapse and reflects two distinct concepts that are tied to the political and social conditions of the Iron Age. On the one hand, it lists Hittites among the aboriginal inhabitants of the promised land on an equal footing with the Girgashites, Amorites, Canaanites, Perizzites, Hivites, and Jebusites.[2] "Hittites" of this kind sold land to Abraham and married their daughters to Esau. A different concept seems to apply when the term "Hittite" was generally used for kingdoms of northern Syria. According to the most frequently cited passage in this regard, Ben-Hadad's Syrian forces besieging Samaria

Figure 7.1 Karabel relief: **1** Relief from a distance in author's photo of 1975. **2** Detail with readings of hieroglyphs of Hawkins 1999 superimposed

retreated in fear of an approaching army of the kings of the Hittites and the kings of the Egyptians which they believed the Israelites had hired.[3] Such references make sense in terms of what we know of the Neo-Hittite principalities in northern Syria in the early first millennium BC.[4]

This picture began to change in the late 19th century. William Wright and A. H. Sayce began speaking of an "empire of the Hittites" in the early 1880s, basing their arguments for a major power on the distribution of monuments inscribed with a distinctive form of hieroglyphic writing. As Egyptian and Assyrian historical sources became available and intelligible to western scholars, this idea that the Hittites constituted a major power in the Late Bronze Age became irrefutable. The cuneiform documents of the 14th century BC Amarna archive, for example, showed that Egyptian kings corresponded with Hittite kings as if they were equals—a status indicating there must be something more to the Hittites than the Bible revealed. Until 1906, it was taken for granted that northern Syria was their homeland. In that year the northernmost site where "Hittite" hieroglyphs were then known, Boğazköy, began to yield a flood of documentary information that was to revolutionize our conception of who the Hittites were and the role their civilization played in the world of the second millennium BC.

The extensive ruins beside the village of Boğazköy, 154 km east of Ankara, were visited as early as 1834 by the explorer Charles Texier. The plans he later published correctly identified the surface remains of a very large building as a temple, now known as Temple I. He also published drawings of reliefs at the nearby group of rock outcrops known as Yazılıkaya, not rendering their unfamiliar style entirely successfully.[5] He suggested the site was ancient Pteria, a city of the Medes which Herodotus said lay somewhere in this general vicinity. Over the next decades, several other individuals came to map these ruins, take squeezes of the above ground sculptures, and offer other hypotheses on their ancient identity and significance. The initial excavations were undertaken in 1893–94 by Ernest Chantre, who recovered the first cuneiform tablets from the site. But it was only when an expedition under Hugo Winckler and Theodor Makridi arrived on the scene in 1906 that the spectacular royal archives of the Hittite Empire were discovered.

They actually found two major archives, which duplicate each other to a certain extent. One came from storerooms beside the ruins of the great temple that Texier had identified. The other came from atop a natural eminence known as Büyükkale ("large castle") which the Hittites had fortified as their royal residence and seat of power, in short the imperial palace (Figures 7.2, 7.3, and 7.4). From these locations came thousands of tablets and tablet fragments covered with minute writing in cuneiform script. And what tablets! These were not mundane private and commercial documents of limited scope like the Cappadocian texts discussed in the previous chapter, but the intellectual tools required for the political and ideological maintenance of the empire: Treaties, annals, prayers, rituals, descriptions of festivals, myths, literature, and royal correspondence.

At the time of the initial discoveries, Winckler, who was an expert in ancient Near Eastern languages, could only partially understand what the tablets contained. Just as the Latin alphabet is used to write many modern languages, cuneiform was employed for many ancient Near

Figure 7.2 Topography of Boğazköy, looking east

Figure 7.3 Büyükkale, looking north

Eastern ones, particularly at Boğazköy. The conventions of the writing system provided some idea of what the texts were about even without an understanding of the language itself. For example, cuneiform includes many signs that stand for words (logograms) with consistent meanings in all languages, for example, signs for "king," "palace," "sun," "god," etc. There are also signs that indicate an associated word belongs to a certain category (determinatives), like pots, garments, place names, personal names, names of gods, and objects made out of wood. Most of the signs, however, are pronounced phonetically as syllables. These generally have standard sound values in all cuneiform writing, just as letters of the Latin alphabet do whether one is writing English, French, or Danish. Thus Winckler and his contemporaries could pronounce Hittite words even if their meanings were unknown. Moreover, a fair number of the Boğazköy tablets were written in Akkadian, the *lingua franca* of the second millennium, which had been deciphered half a century earlier. With the historical information these contained, Winckler was soon able to draw up a preliminary king list and to establish that the ancient name of the city he was excavating was Hattusa,[6] capital of the Hittites.

The majority of the Boğazköy tablets, however, were written in Hittite,[7] a language virtually unknown before Winckler's discoveries. Winckler, who died in 1913, did not live to see its decipherment. The man who made the key breakthrough was Bedrich Hrozny, whom we encountered in the previous chapter as an excavator of Kültepe in search of Cappadocian texts

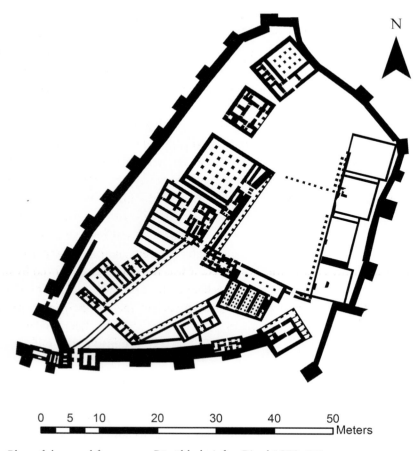

N

Figure 7.4 Plan of the royal fortress on Büyükkale (after Bittel 1970: 75)

at a somewhat later phase of his career. While the First World War brought most academic research to a halt, Hrozny was fortunate enough to travel to Istanbul in 1914 and work with the excavated Boğazköy tablets. He was inspired by parallel passages from a ritual text that we may transliterate as follows, using the modern convention of italic script to represent syllabic signs and the upper case for the Sumerian pronunciation of logograms:

nu NINDA-*an e-ez-za-at-te-ni*
wa-a-tar-ma e-ku-ut-te-ni

The first syllable, *nu*, is a kind of verbal punctuation mark that begins sentences and Hrozny also recognized that the -*ma* joined two clauses when put at the end of the first word of the second phrase, meaning "and" or "but." Verbs were regularly written at the end of sentences or phrases. These patterns become clear when one looks at hundreds of tablets. Now the logogram

NINDA is well known from Mesopotamian texts and means "bread," so the passage does something with bread, and does something else with *watar*. At this point, the Indo-European character of the language becomes obvious. One has no difficulty recognizing *ezzateni* as related to the German verb "to eat," *essen*, and the *t* in the verb endings suggests second person plural in many Indo-European languages, so the obvious translation of the passage was "you eat bread and you drink water."

Building from this insight, Hrozny was able to publish a grammar of Hittite in 1917. In the next decades philologists, for the most part German, refined our understanding of the historical and cultural content of the archives. It was soon recognized that two other Indo-European languages related to Hittite were also in evidence. One of these, Palaic, appears to have been spoken in areas to the north and west of the Hittite capital. Not many texts in it survive, and it was on the way to extinction by the time it was written down—the first recorded Indo-European language to die. The second language was Luwian,[8] spoken in southern and western Anatolia. It was to have a much longer life than Hittite itself, since although it ceased to be written in cuneiform when the Hittite empire was destroyed, it was the language conveyed by hieroglyphic inscriptions that were still being composed well into the first millennium BC. The Anatolian branch of the Indo-European family is now recognized to include two later, poorly known languages not found at Boğazköy, Lydian, and Lycian, which were dying out when they were written in alphabetic scripts related to the Greek alphabet late in the first millennium BC. No modern descendants survive.

The material culture of the Hittites has been rediscovered gradually, with no single break-through like Hrozny's recognition of the character of the language. The Hittite Empire was vast and diverse, and ultimately a political rather than a cultural entity. We learn a good deal of its history from sites in Syria like Ugarit and Emar, where Anatolian elements are far from dominant in the material assemblage. The core of Hittite civilization, of course, must be sought at the capital and from there one works outward in defining such concepts as Hittite art, Hittite architecture, and Hittite styles of pottery. Thus the German excavations at Boğazköy, which resumed in 1931 and, excepting a break during the Second World War, have continued to this day, represent a kind of anchor for Hittite archaeology. We will refer to them frequently in the discussion of various aspects of the Hittites and their empire that follows.

HISTORICAL OUTLINE

The Hittite monarchy enjoyed two phases of political prowess separated by an interval of weakness of unknown duration (Table 7.1). The first is known as the Old Kingdom (ca. 1650 to 1500 BC) and second as the Empire (ca. 1400 to 1200 BC). The historical documentation for the Hittites thus spans the break between the floating relative chronology of the Middle Bronze Age and more or less absolute chronology tied to the modern calendar of the Late Bronze Age, but does little to resolve its length. Most of the tablets excavated at Boğazköy come from

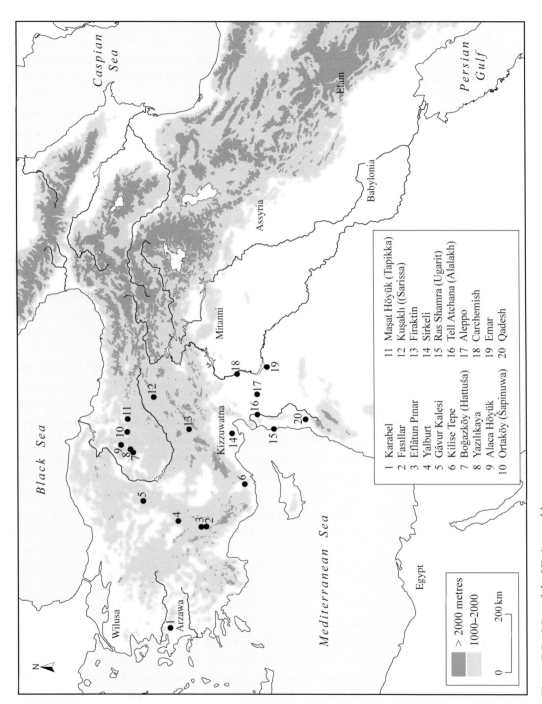

Figure 7.5 Map of the Hittite world

Caspian Sea

Black Sea

Mediterranean Sea

Persian Gulf

Wilusa

Arzawa

Kizzuwatna

Mitanni

Assyria

Babylonia

Elam

Egypt

1 Karabel
2 Fasıllar
3 Eflâtun Pınar
4 Yalburt
5 Gâvur Kalesi
6 Kilise Tepe
7 Boğazköy (Hattuša)
8 Yazılıkaya
9 Alaca Höyük
10 Ortaköy (Šapinuwa)
11 Maşat Höyük (Tapikka)
12 Kuşaklı ((Sarissa)
13 Firaktin
14 Sirkeli
15 Ras Shamra (Ugarit)
16 Tell Atchana (Alalakh)
17 Aleppo
18 Carchemish
19 Emar
20 Qadesh

> 2000 metres

1000–2000

0   200 km

N

archives which were maintained until the violent destruction of the capital a little after 1200 BC, in other words a late Empire context, but among them are earlier tablets and copies of older texts going back to the Old Kingdom. Hittite tablets, as a rule, were not dated by their authors, so although we may speak of a Hittite historical tradition and know what various kings did at certain points in their careers, the overall outline of events rests ultimately on synchronisms with Mesopotamian and Egyptian sources.

The dynasty that was to establish the Hittite power emerged from Kussara, as noted in the previous chapter. We do not know its connection with the earlier kings from that city, Pithana and Anitta. One view of the Hittite dynasty's early history appears in the Proclamation of Telipinu,[9] a text written at a time of crisis in the Old Kingdom. It begins with the following statement:

> Formerly Labarna was the Great King. Then were his sons, his brothers, his relations by marriage, his (blood) relations and his troops united. And the land was small. But on whatever campaign he went, he held the lands of the enemy in subjection by his might. He kept devastating the lands, and he deprived the lands of power; and he made them boundaries of the sea. But when he returned from the field, each of his sons went to the various lands (to govern them).[10]

The text then lists seven lands to which the sons went. This is followed by a passage that repeats the same information, verbatim except for the list of lands, for the next king, Hattusili (I), and repeats it yet again with Hattusili's successor, Mursili I.

Hardly anything is known about the earliest ruler in this proclamation, although the name Labarna resonates in the term *tabarna* which was adopted by successors to serve as a kind of royal title, much as the name of Caesar was used in the Roman Empire (see Table 7.1).[11] He may not even have been the first of the line, although the names and even existence of the kings who preceded him are poorly documented and controversial.[12]

There can be little doubt that Labarna's son, Hattusili I, the best known of the early monarchs of the Old Kingdom, was the man who brought the Hittites into the light of history and laid the foundation of the kingdom that was to dominate Anatolia for the next four centuries. His name means "the man of Hattusa" and it is pretty clearly not the one he was born with. Since it was he who moved the capital from Kussara to Hattusa he may have assumed it in honor of the occasion.

Hattusili is also the first of the Hittite kings to make use of writing, which was re-introduced to Anatolia after a century of illiteracy. His court did not revive the Old Assyrian script, but borrowed a more mainstream style of cuneiform from Syria, perhaps as a direct result of Hattusili's campaigns there. Cylinder seals, which Assyrian influence had made common in the colony period, went out of fashion. Instead, stamp seals, an Anatolian specialty going back as far as the sixth millennium, replaced them almost completely. The beginning of this trend can already be seen at the end of the trading colony age. By the same token, many of the hallmarks of

Table 7.1 Chronological listing of Hittite kings (after Bryce 2005: xvi)

Date	King	Events
1650 BC	Labarna Hattusili I (1650–1620) Mursili I (1620–1590)	Capital moved to Hattusa Campaigns in Syria
1600	Hantili (1590–1560)	Raid on Babylon First appearance of Kaska
1550	Telipinu (1525–1500)	Egyptian invasions of Syria
1500		
1450		Mitanni as dominant power in Syria
1400	Tudhaliya I/II Tudhaliya III	
1350	Suppiluliuma I (1350–1322) Mursili II (1321–1295)	Amarna Age in Egypt Campaigns in Syria Elimination of Mitanni
1300	Muwatalli II (1295–1272) Urhi-Tesub/Mursili III (1272–1267) Hattusili III (1267–1237)	Transfer of capital to Tarhuntassa Battle of Qadesh Treaty with Egypt
1250	Tudhaliya IV (1237–1209) Arnuwanda III (1209–1297) Suppiluliuma II (1207–?)	Karunta briefly holds power
1200		Destruction of Boğazköy Raids of sea peoples in Levant

the Old Kingdom and the Empire seem to have their roots in the previous era, and there was clearly a great deal of continuity between all three. This is particularly true of pottery forms, which tended to be remarkably conservative until the end of the Late Bronze Age. Red burnished pitchers with gracefully curving spouts are equally at home in the trading colony or Empire periods. Even in glyptic (seal cutting), where the transformation in the shape of the seal has just been cited as evidence of change, it should be noted that many of the motifs found on Hittite seals can be traced back to trading colony period antecedents.

The most significant change brought about by the rise of the Old Kingdom was political. The quarreling city-states of the earlier era were gone, and the greater part of the Anatolian plateau came to be dominated by a single sovereign of Hittite descent, with responsibilities for subordinate civil and military administration apportioned out to various members of his family. Hattusili had sufficiently consolidated the base of his power on the plateau that he was able to direct his attention to Syria—further afield than any Anatolian ruler had ever ventured. His campaigns there were not entirely successful. In the Amuq plain he conquered Alalakh, ending what is known there archaeologically as Level VII. But the primary polity in northern Syria, Aleppo, was able to withstand Hattusili's siege and the Hittites had to return to their heartland. Hittite records nowhere provide a rationale for invading Syria, but it was to be a recurring theme in Hittite imperialism.

Another great theme in Hittite history also resounds from the beginning of the Old Kingdom: Instability of succession. Hattusili's sons turned against him and the aging king passed over a nephew at the last moment. The grandson he named as his as his successor, Mursili I, was able to take the throne, but he was eventually assassinated and many of the kings who followed, to say nothing of their family members, fell victim to court intrigues. The Proclamation of Telipinu, cited earlier, chronicles a few generations of this turmoil and seeks to establish rules of succession. Damaged sections of the text make it all but impossible to follow the sequence or rulers, and there is little indication that much attention was to paid to the proclamation's prescriptions in practice—obscure and short-reigning monarchs succeeded one another in a diminishing realm until the kingdom's fortunes were reversed in the early 14th century.

The early part of the Old Kingdom saw its greatest military successes. Mursili I succeeded in Syria where Hattusili had failed, sacking Aleppo and bringing an end to the history of the kingdom of Yamhad. Subsequently, he led the Hittite armies on to Babylon and extinguished the dynasty of Hammurapi in 1595 BC.[13] This was not a lasting conquest, but rather a brief raid, doubtless made possible by the political weakness of Mursili's opponents in Syria and Mesopotamia. New powers, however, were on the rise, and Mursili may have encountered one of these in its formative stages on this campaign. The Telipinu Proclamation tells us that he defeated the troops of the Hurrians before noting that he brought back booty and prisoners from Babylon. Hurrians had been a population element in northern Syria and Mesopotamia for centuries by this time, and presumably eastern Anatolia as well, but in the years after Mursili's raid they were to become the dominant people in the coalescing Kingdom of Mitanni. Hurrians, as we shall see, were to have a profound influence over Hittite culture and politics—to the point where some of the later Hittite kings appear to have been Hurrians themselves, if one judges by the names they had before they came to the throne.

Historical sources for the later rulers of the Old Kingdom are meager and incoherent, but it would appear that the kingdom held its own on the Anatolian plateau while retreating from Syria. The Kingdom of Kizzuwatna, covering the Cilician Plain, achieved independence, but was bound to the kings of Hatti in the oldest treaty found in the Boğazköy archives.

Culturally the Old Kingdom established the norms which were to prevail until the end of the empire. As noted earlier, writing was re-introduced in the time of Hattusili. The pattern is one often seen in emerging states adjacent to more literate areas: First borrow a language and a script together, then use the script to write one's own language. The earliest Hittite texts are written in Akkadian, but in short order scribes started using the syllabic signs to sound out words in their own language. Some bilingual texts were written in this period, which aided modern decipherment. Although scribes were soon writing most of their tablets in Hittite, they did not neglect the Mesopotamian tradition. Not only were Hittite texts filled with Akkadian words and Sumerian logograms, but the scribes occasionally copied or wrote whole documents in these foreign languages. This came to be particularly important to them in communications dealing with lands outside of Anatolia, where Hittite was unknown.

With a specialized knowledge of Hittite writing habits it is possible to distinguish between tablets written in the Old Kingdom and those belonging to the Empire. Texts in the imperial archives sometimes exist in several copies, showing that Hittite scribes spent much of their time, as medieval monks did, copying older material to insure its survival and availability. One of the most important and frequently copied texts is the Hittite Law code, which was not only composed in the Old Kingdom, but also modified in the same period. The laws were drawn up as a list of offenses, each with a prescribed punishment. The laws themselves provide a fascinating glimpse into Hittite society, showing the interaction of merchants, slaves, freemen, soldiers, and the palace. Most cases deal with such commonplace concerns as homicide, bodily injury, matrimony, and problems with private property, but others go into more bizarre areas, such as witchcraft and sexual taboos. The copies we have often include clauses saying "formerly the penalty was X, but now it is Y." Even the Old Kingdom copies say this. Surprisingly, punishments seem to get less draconian when revised.

During the waning years of the Old Kingdom, or as some would see it the intermediate period between the Old Kingdom and the rise of Empire in the 14th century BC,[14] numerous changes took place in the political climate which reshaped the word with which the Hittites had to contend. The most immediate concern was loss of control of the mountainous areas north of the capital. In the reign of Hantili we hear, for the first time, of an unruly people known as the Kaska. Apparently too disorganized to be controlled by the usual methods through which the Hittites brought enemies into submission, the Kaska soon took over areas that were of great importance, in particular the site of Nerik, an important cult center of the Storm God. From the 15th century to the end of the Empire, the Kaska played the role of unconquerable frontier barbarians so familiar in other ancient empires like Rome and China. Unable to make treaties with them because they had no kings, unable to profit from attacking them because they had no wealth to seize, Hittite kings set up a kind of *limes* (fortified frontier) to protect their northern border, but this did not stop the Kaska from threatening the capital, even at times when the empire was one of the world's great military powers.

To the south, the Hittites remained on the sidelines for at least a century as other great powers contended for control of Syria. Egyptian pharaohs, building their empire in Asia, campaigned as far north as the Euphrates and entered into at least one treaty with the Hittites. From its center in northeastern Syria, the Kingdom of Mitanni came to dominate an arc of territory that stretched from the Zagros Mountains to the Mediterranean and for a while included the Kingdom of Kizzuwatna, thus effective blocking Hittite access to the south. These trends coincided with increasing Hurrian influence in Anatolia.

It is customary to date the commencement of the Empire to a king Tudhaliya,[15] around the beginning of the 14th century. His accession was represented as a restoration of the royal family after a usurpation by the obscure Muwatalli I, and military successes in Anatolia soon followed. In particular, Tudhaliya pushed toward the west, defeating a coalition of powers that included the kingdom of Arzawa, Hatti's most powerful rival in that region. The re-establishment and maintenance of Hittite power on the Anatolian plateau was a dynamic process over the next half century with numerous setbacks, particularly on the Kaska frontier. The most dramatic expansion of Hittite power took place under perhaps the greatest and least pronounceable of the Hittite kings, Suppiluliuma I,[16] with a return to Syria and the defeat of Mitanni. The wars that he conducted there were to lead to long-lasting domination and the creation of an administrative structure by which Hittite territory was governed. Suppiluliuma appointed two of his sons to rule as kings in Aleppo and Carchemish,[17] respectively, and the dynasty of the latter was ultimately to outlast the Empire itself.

The Hittite rulers from Suppiluliuma to the end of the empire are richly documented—so much so that we can appreciate their personalities and intimate concerns in some detail.[18] Here we can only summarize some of the major political events which have a bearing on the cultural history of the Hittites. Suppiluliuma's campaigns in Syria inevitably brought the Hittites into conflict with Egypt. Akhenaton and Tutankhamen were pharaohs at the time, and the turmoil of Egypt's religious revolution and counterrevolution undoubtedly facilitated the Hittite conqueror's work. In a celebrated incident, Tutankhamen's widow wrote to him suggesting a marriage alliance between herself and one of his sons. Suppiluliuma was incredulous, but eventually sent one of his sons. He was murdered when he reach Egypt, and the upshot was a war. Prisoners taken in Suppiluliuma's campaign of revenge were believed to have been the cause of a great plague that devastated the Hatti lands for years afterward. It is possible that this plague was so severe as to reshape the ethnic makeup of the Empire's core; from this time forward it appears that Luwian may have been the language spoken by the majority, although the chancellery still wrote in Hittite.[19] Many of the key Hittite leaders died in short order. First Suppiluliuma, then his successor, and then two Hittite princes in charge of the Hittite affairs in Syria were victims of this disease. Mursili II came to the throne as a youth, and had to more or less reconquer the kingdom. His long reign was one of constant struggle, but he ultimately extended Hatti's influence over most of western Anatolia while holding on to Syria. There were even some successes on the northern frontier against the Kaska.

Mursili's son Muwatalli, not long ago recognized as the second king of that name, succeeded to the throne and, for reasons not well understood, took the dramatic step of moving the Hittite capital from Hattusa to a city called Tarhuntassa, in the Lower Land. The precise location of this site is unknown today, but lay somewhere in the area southeast of Konya and northwest of the Cilician plain. Perhaps not coincidentally, the Kaska burned Hattusa after the court's departure. A desire to be closer to Syria may have been another motive for the move. Meanwhile Egypt gradually emerged from her period of internal chaos and sought to reassert herself in Palestine and Syria. In Muwatalli's reign an epic clash took place between the two powers at Qadesh, today Tell Nebi Mend outside of the Syrian city of Homs, in 1285 BC.[20] While the Egyptian king

Ramses II left a memorable account of the battle and claimed victory, the Hittite hold on Syria remained unshaken.

Muwatalli was succeeded by his son, who took the throne as Mursili (III), although he is better known to posterity by his Hurrian name, Urhi-Teshub. Muwatalli also had a very powerful brother, Hattusili, who was aggrieved to serve under Urhi-Teshub. Eventually he seized the throne himself, composing a detailed "apology" lambasting the iniquities of his nephew and putting forth his case for getting rid of him. It is one of the classics of Hittite royal propaganda. The capital was moved back to Hattusa, but another son of Muwatalli, Kurunta, was left to rule in Tarhuntassa with special privileges. This was to cause difficulties later. One of Hattusili's accomplishments was to enter into a peace treaty with Egypt, and there was even a marriage between one of his daughters and the by now aged Ramses II. The last two kings of the Empire, Tudhaliya IV and Suppiluliuma II were nevertheless troubled by unrest both at home and in Syria. A rectangular bronze plate once hung by chains was discovered in the upper city of Boğazköy, ceremonially buried near the Sphinx Gate.[21] On it was a treaty between Tudhaliya and his cousin Kurunta. The reason the treaty was buried has recently become clear: Kurunta rebelled against the government in Hattusa and was, for a time, able to take over the Great Kingship himself. Tudhaliya was able to recover the crown, but it is clear the kingdom had suffered yet another crisis over succession. Tudhaliya had to weather one other great setback. Assyria, now a centralized state possessed of a ruthless war machine, had began making inroads into Hittite territories. At Nihriya, on the Euphrates, the Assyrian king inflicted a major defeat on Tudhaliya's army, and thereafter the Hittite control of Syria was less secure. Tudhaliya had greater success in his conquest of Cyprus.

Suppiluliuma II, the last of the Great Kings to rule in Hattusa, also campaigned in Cyprus and was active in the Lukka lands. The circumstances under which the kingdom was lost and Hattusa destroyed are unknown, but were part of a general cataclysm that brought down civilizations all around the Mediterranean.

THE IMPERIAL CAPITAL

The archaeology of the Hittites in the Late Bronze Age is an archaeology of imperialism. It revolves around edifices devoted to defense and control; symbols of power and persuasion, and artefacts of cosmopolitan complexity. To discover its essence, one must begin at the center of command, the capital at Hattusa. This is one of the largest sites in the ancient Near East, covering an area of 167.7 ha and surrounded by a 6-km circuit of fortification wall.[22] Archaeologically is it is a palimpsest of monuments of many periods, from an Early Bronze Age occupation to Iron Age remains belonging to a time when its status as a great capital had long been forgotten. It is to the Hittite Empire, however, that the vast majority of its surviving monuments belong, and its violent destruction at the beginning of the 12th century to which we owe so much of what we know about the material world of the Hittites.

The core of the site is the limestone eminence of Büyükkale (Figure 7.3). This forms a natural fortress overlooking a gorge and dominates more level ground to the northeast, where the earliest settlement area was located. Somewhat farther to the north lies the modern village of Boğazkale, whose earlier name[23] Boğazköy, continues to be used as a designation of the whole archaeological complex. During the Old Kingdom, Büyükkale came to serve as the royal residence of the Hittite kings. Its natural defenses were enhanced by a perimeter wall with towers and buttresses, and access from the lower city was controlled through a single gateway approached by a ramp. In its final form in the 13th century, the palace consisted of a complex of monumental buildings grouped around a series of courtyards, increasingly secluded as one ascended. Only the stone foundations of these survive, leaving room for some uncertainty in how they are to be reconstructed. There were accommodations for palace personnel around the lower courtyard and the actual residence of the king was located in the highest, not far from the largest structure on the citadel, believed to be an audience hall with a grid of pillars supporting a roof over a large open space. The palace archives were discovered in three separate locations on the citadel.

The original settlement at Boğazköy stretched northwestward over lower ground from the foot of Büyükkale. Houses were built there in the Early Bronze III period, and a karum of the trading colony period has been discovered a little farther to the northwest, beyond the ground on which the largest Hittite temple was later built.[24] In the Old Kingdom this area was protected and joined to Büyükkale by a fortification wall. During the Empire the walled area of the city was vastly increased by the inclusion of the elevated ground to the south. The lower courses of these walls were built with massive, undressed stones and made more imposing by casemate construction, an older Anatolian tradition to be sure. There were towers at regular intervals and at least five major gates in the wall around the upper city. The latter were multiple chambered arched doorways flanked by towers and adjacent outer walls to control access from the outside.

Although the enemies who destroyed Hattusa put some effort into destroying the protective sculptures that guarded these gates, some of them survive at three entrances to this upper city. The best preserved relief was found[25] in the inner chamber of what is popularly known as the "King's Gate" on the eastern side (Figure 7.6). This male[26] figure, executed in such high relief that it allowed the sculptor to put the eye in natural perspective on the front of the face, rather than rendering it front view on a side view head as is customary in more shallow Hittite and Egyptian reliefs, is not, in fact, a king. He wears a horned crown, which is reserved for deities, and the Hittite Great King, unlike his Egyptian counterpart, was not god.[27] Rank in the pantheon is also reflected by the number of horns a god has on his crown, and in this case there is only one, so this gate figure is a minor protective deity. In the southwestern gateway there are two lion figures carved in protome, that is to say with their front parts emerging from the stone, but the rest of the animal not carved in the round. This tradition of having lions guarding gateways, while not original with the Hittites, is certainly one that had a long life in their artistic tradition.

The most impressive construction at the site was undertaken between these two gates, where

Figure 7.6   King's Gate: **1** Photo with replica of relief in place (courtesy Roger Matthews). **2** Plan of gateway (after Bittel 1970: 52)

Hittite architects had to modify the terrain, cutting through a ridge and building a massive higher wall in order to reduce the vulnerability of the site to attack from higher ground. Two staircases ascend the stone glacis on either side, and a subterranean tunnel runs underneath the wall at its highest point. The gateway at the summit was guarded by statues of sphinxes with elaborate headdresses, which were broken to pieces when the site was sacked at the end of the Empire.

In the lower city the most important structure is the Great Temple, or Temple I as it is sometimes designated in archaeological literature. At 62 × 45 m, it is larger than any other Hittite temple, but its general configuration is shared by many other temples in Boğazköy (Figure 7.7). It is constructed on artificial terraces, and probably dates to the 13th century, although it doubtless replaced earlier versions.[28] The temple is entered through a monumental entrance giving access to a rectangular courtyard, which appears to have been open to the elements. Rows of smaller rooms surround this courtyard, and from the absence of staircases it may be assumed that the building had only a ground floor. At the back of the courtyard is a portico and beyond this was the most sacred part of the building. The Great Temple is unusual in that it actually has two *cellae* (cult chambers), rather than the customary one. Although there is no direct testimony to prove it, size and location would indicate that it served the two most prominent deities of the Empire, the Storm God of Hatti and the Sun Goddess of Arinna. Their

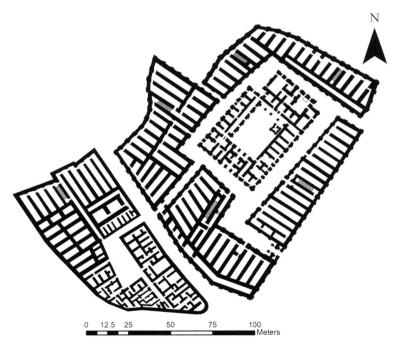

Figure 7.7 Plan of the Great Temple at Boğazköy and associated administrative buildings (after Bittel 1970: 56)

images would have stood on platforms at the back of these rooms. However, there was no direct access to the cult statues from the large courtyard where texts indicate many of the religious rituals were performed. A row of small rooms intervened and, at best, windows might have provided a limited view.

Besides the temple building itself, there are two other major components of the Great Temple complex. One is a series of magazines surrounding the temple building on all sides. These have the form of long, narrow rooms which must once have been filled with offerings and supplies essential to the cult. In some of these, on the east side of the temple, an archive comparable to, and indeed partially duplicating those found on Büyükkale was discovered. On the opposite side of the temple, some of the most massive storage jars known from the ancient world may be seen today, buried up to their shoulders and having a capacity of 2000 liters.[29] South of the temple and across a paved street from its surrounding storage complex, there was another large building, which appears to have been devoted to the administrative functions of the temple. When all of these structures are viewed as a whole, one cannot fail to be impressed by the extensive economic and administrative apparatus that supported the worship of the Empire's chief deities, irrespective of all the governmental activity taking place on the citadel of Büyükkale.

The other temples at Boğazköy are located on higher ground, in the southern or upper city (Figure 7.8). Until not long ago, only four of these were known, but in the 1980s Peter Neve began excavating in a "sacred quarter" and discovered 25 more. Some are within enclosures and other stand alone. None has associated auxiliary buildings like the Great Temple, but they do all have somewhat similar plans, including a rectangular courtyard. These Hittite temples do not appear to be related to any types found elsewhere in the Near East, nor do they descend from the temples that are seen at Kanesh in the Middle Bronze Age. If anything, they seem to be derived from traditions Anatolian courtyard house architecture.

Within the Upper City there are several other focal points of cultic interest as well as remains of administrative activities. In two separate locations there were large pools, created deliberately by retaining water produced by springs. Stone walls reinforced with a waterproofing clay formed their embankments. Not far from the largest of these, 300 m south of Büyükkale, are two arched structures that form single-room blind chambers. It has been suggested that these represent the oldest arches of stone masonry in the ancient Near East.[30] One of these, Chamber 2, had been partially dismantled in the Iron Age by people who were constructing a fortress in this area (the *Südburg*), but it has been possible for the excavators of Boğazköy to reconstruct it almost completely since many of its stone blocks were covered with a hieroglyphic inscription (Figure 7.9). These could be fitted back together like a jigsaw puzzle. The panel that forms the rear of the chamber is dominated by the figure of the Sun God in shallow relief, a large winged disc crowning his headdress. On the left entrance of the chamber, as one faces inward, is a somewhat smaller figure of Suppiluliuma II, holding a spear before him and bearing a bow on his shoulder. Curiously, he is wearing a crown with three horns on it, and thus a king is being represented here, uniquely, as a divinity. There can be no doubt about who he is, since his name is given by hieroglyphs carved in front of his face, albeit with the royal cartouche and titulary as

Figure 7.8 Temples in the upper city at Boğazköy, from Google Earth image

1

2

Figure 7.9 Funerary monument of Suppiluliuma II in the Südburg area, Boğazköy (Photos: courtesy Roger Matthews)

Great King that we would expect. He is also the author of the six-line hieroglyphic inscription that covers the length of the opposite side of the chamber.[31] While precise understanding of the text eludes us, it mentions deeds of Suppiluliuma, and includes a reference to Tarhuntassa. It can be compared to another, longer hieroglyphic text by the same king found at Yalbert, which mentions conquests in the southern part of Anatolia, although it is not clear that the Chamber 2 text is concerned with military activities.[32]

With its royal residence on Büyükkale, the Great Temple in the lower town and scores of temples in the upper town, awesome fortifications, funerary monuments, archives and debris of administration, Hattusa is an impressive seat of imperial authority. But was it a city in the sense of being a place where a substantial population actually lived? There clearly were residential dwellings in Hattusa, but more and more space within the walls was devoted to public and sacred architecture as the Empire matured. Even allowing that excavations have given priority to public buildings, it is hard to believe large numbers of people resided in the site. In its final years Hattusa was, in Peter Neve's words, a city of gods and temples.[33]

HITTITE SITES IN THE EMPIRE'S HEARTLAND

The Late Bronze Age ceramic assemblage associated with the Hittite capital is more remarkable for its standardization than its artistic qualities. It is for the most part monochrome, with so little change in basic shapes over time that it offers archaeologists only a very imprecise dating tool. Pottery of this type was termed "drab ware" by the excavators of Tarsus because it struck a contrast with the painted and otherwise more elaborately decorated wares of other periods in the sequences they uncovered. The basic repertoire was descended from forms that are in evidence at Kültepe before the Hittites came to power. The essential point, however, is that this pottery seems to have a direct association with the Hittite government, the exact nature of which remains obscure. At Gordion, which is on the northwestern edge of the area in which this pottery is distributed, it has been noted that not just the vessel shapes, but also the techniques of pottery production are the same as those at the capital, despite the use of local clay.[34] The same may be said of the Late Bronze Age pottery of Kilise Tepe in the Lower Land.[35] One index of the association, is that this pottery drops out of use when the empire disintegrates. Interestingly, the local pottery traditions that emerge after it is gone resemble the painted pottery that came before the rise of the Hittites.[36]

Hittite texts name hundreds of settlements on the Anatolian plateau, but major archaeological exposures of the Late Bronze Age are comparatively few. One reason for the discrepancy is that most of the names probably belong to rather inconsequential places. While in many cases, the majesty of the Hittite Empire may not have made much of an impact on the daily routines of villagers living outside of the capital, we know that many places had an important cultic significance to the kingdom from its beginnings. For example, there is a group of officials designated [lú]AGRIG,[37] each associated with a specific town where they played an important role in rituals.

They also controlled storehouses, not just in their towns, but also sometimes in Hattusa, where there was a storehouse assigned to that town. It appears a system of at least forty AGRIG towns was set up in the Old Kingdom, and remained basically the same until the end of the Empire.[38]

One town mentioned as having an AGRIG is Tapika, which has now been identified with Maşat Höyük thanks to the discovery of tablets there in the 1970s. This is a medium-sized site on a natural eminence, which seems to have had its heyday in the earliest years of the Empire. The site is dominated by a large public building of more than 40 rooms, built around a court-yard (Figure 7.10). The style of construction would not be out of place in the capital, and it appears to have served the needs of a local governor. The discovery of a group of imported Mycenaean vessels in one of the storerooms is particularly intriguing, given that Mycenaean pottery is virtually unknown at the otherwise cosmopolitan Boğazköy. Among the 116 tablets are a few oracle, religious, and mythological texts, but the vast majority are letters dealing with administrative matters. Many of these were part of a correspondence with the Great King in Hattusa, who is generally not mentioned by name, but can be identified as Tudhaliya III from a pair of seal impressions.[39] The tablets were written over a short period and show that the king

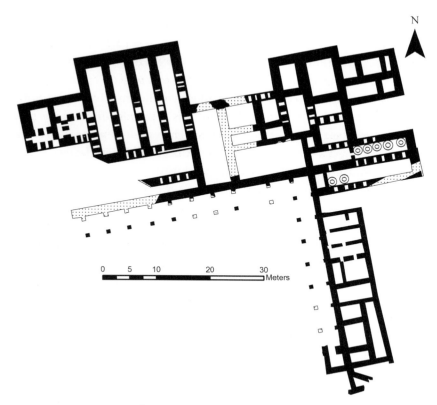

Figure 7.10　Maşat palace (after T. Özgüç 1982: plan 2)

was being kept aware of what was going on in this provincial center by a number of different officials. Maşat lay very near the Kaska frontier, and interactions with the Kaska as laborers and prisoners of war figure prominently in the letters. Not all were written to the king or the capital however; there is also correspondence with other provincial centers.

One of the places mentioned, Shapinuwa, has now yielded an archive of its own, which is many times larger than the one found at Maşat. This is the site of Otraköy, at which two public buildings have been excavated. One appears to be a sort of royal residence, if the testimony of the 3000 tablets found there is interpreted correctly. The exposed portion measures 25 × 75 m and apparently had two stories. When it burned in an intense fire, the tablets fell from the upper stories. As in the case of Maşat, these documents appear to date to the early part of the empire, and do not directly name the king. A large proportion are again letters, but these seem to have been sent to the king from various parts of the Empire. Some of the letters are between king and queen, and this has led the excavator to assume that at least one of them was in residence here. It is also of interest that almost a third of the tablets are written in Hurrian, and it would appear that the site was important in Hurrian rituals.[40]

Two other important provincial sites are currently under excavation: Kaman Kalehöyük and Kuşaklı. In both cases, there are large public buildings which served in the administration of the Empire. The general configuration of the latter is clear from survey and excavation, so we will highlight it as an example of a medium-sized Hittite provincial center. It was constructed on elevated ground and surrounded by a casemate wall enclosing 18 hectares in which there are four regularly spaced gateways (Figure 7.11).[41] On the southeast side of the acropolis, which is slightly off center in the rough circle marked out by the city wall, is a major palatial building (Building C), formed around a courtyard. Other public buildings were located nearby and one of these, Building A, yielded a small archive containing texts that relate to the king's performance a ritual in the town of Sarissa: it would appear that the local archive kept materials of local importance. Near the northeast gate there is another large temple that matches the temple plans of Boğazköy with a colonnaded central court.[42]

Thus, recent research has shown that the bureaucratic and ideological apparatus of the Hittite state was much more widely spread throughout the countryside than what the first decades of Hittitology, with their overwhelming concentration on the capital, had indicated. Archaeologists have had little incentive to excavate hamlets and farmsteads, but documents like the Hittite law code and ritual texts make it clear that the countryside was dotted with small communities. If the Old Kingdom was not the urban age that the Assyrian trading colony period had been, one can see that the activities of the Hittite imperial government gradually became more visible in the countryside with the rise of centers of provincial control like Örtaköy, Kuşaklı, Kaman Kalehöyük, and Maşat Höyük.

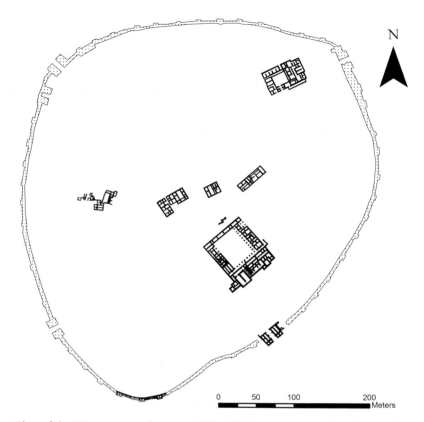

Figure 7.11   Plan of the Hittite regional center of Kuşaklı/Sarissa (after Müller-Karpe 2002: 148)

YAZILIKAYA AND HITTITE RELIGION

Yazılıkaya, "inscribed rock" in Turkish, lying outside the walls of Hattusa 1.5 km northeast of Büyükkale as the crow flies, was a site charged with religious significance for the Hittites. As its name would have it, there are indeed inscriptions there, but the chief attraction of the place today is the sculpture, which constitutes the largest collections of Hittite reliefs anywhere. The crags are arranged in such a way as to form three chambers (Figure 7.12),[43] to which access was controlled in the time of the Empire by a building that is now visible only from a few courses of stone forming its ground plan. Chamber A, the largest, is decorated with two processions of deities in which the figures increase in size and importance as they converge in a central panel. As one faces them, the procession on the left is primarily of gods, and the one on the right is primarily of goddesses, although there are exceptions to this gender rule. The much narrower Chamber B also contains sculptures of deities, but includes two representations of King Tuda-haliya IV as well. This area, or perhaps the whole site, is now thought to be a "stone house" in which the cremated remains of the king were laid to rest.[44] Both rooms were open to the

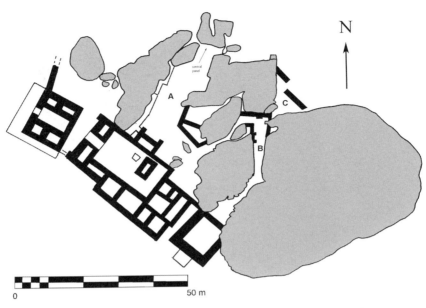

Figure 7.12 Chambers at Yazılıkaya (after Bittel 1970: 106; Bittel et al. 1975: 50)

elements, but over the years Chamber B filled with soil which protected its sculptures until they were excavated in the 20th century AD.

In the larger chamber, Room A, the reliefs remained above ground and have thus suffered considerable weathering. Travelers visited them over the centuries, long before anyone recognized their association with the Hittites, and there was much speculation as to their significance, often concocted from snippets of information about the area that classical sources gave us. Was this the depiction of a royal marriage? Greeks meeting Amazons? Now that the Boğazköy archives have come to light and more of the culture of the Hittites is understood, we can put aside such theories and recognize this as a depiction of the pantheon. The bisected oval symbol in front of many of the figures is the hieroglyphic marker of divinity, used as a determinative before the names of gods. The two largest figures, who face each other at the center of the composition, are the Hurrian storm god Tushub and the Hurrian goddess Hepatu (Figure 7.13: 1).[45] The Storm God, wearing a tall conical cap covered with horns, stands upon stylized mountain gods who bend forward as they support him. Hepatu wears a tall cylindrical headdress and a long dress, both commonly seen in representations of women in Hittite art. She is supported by a lioness.

The processions appear to be in a ranked order, with the gods and goddesses becoming smaller the farther removed they are from the central panel. The last of the gods in on the male sides, a group of twelve whom see again in Chamber B, appear to be running, as if to catch up with the rest. Most of the gods wear kilts, although a few have long coats as well. The goddesses consistently wear pleated skirts. Shoes with upturned toes are another characteristically

1

2

Figure 7.13 Yazılıkaya reliefs: **1** Central panel. **2** Gods holding up the sky (Photos: courtesy Roger Matthews)

Anatolian feature on display. We note here only a few of the identifiable personalities. Standing behind Hepatu, also on a lioness, is the god Sharruma. The only male on the female side, he is the son of the central pair. On the male side, there are two female attendants following one of the deities who appears to be male. They have been identified as Ninatta and Kulitta, the hand-maidens of the goddess Shaushga,[46] a Hurrian deity equated with the Mesopotamian Ishtar, who has both masculine (warlike) and feminine (love) qualities. She appears to be represented separately for each aspect here at Yazılıkaya, for there is another Shaushga on the feminine side. The sun and moon gods can be identified by their headdressess, and two supporting gods stand on a hieroglyph for the earth and hold up a symbol of the sky (Figure 7.14: 2).

The most unexpected aspect of this representation of the pantheon is its Hurrian character. Before the hieroglyphs could be read, it was suspected that the leading goddess would be the Sun Goddess of Arinna, not the foreign Hepatu.[47] Not just the names, but the way in which the procession is ordered appears to be Hurrian.[48] Here, at the very center of the empire at their most sacred site known to us, the Hittites seem to have been quite open minded about whom they were worshiping.

The Hittites did not claim to inhabit a "land of a thousand gods" for nothing, and Yazılıkaya is but one of many indicators of their willingness to embrace both new and old deities of all kinds. According to Bryce:

[T]he Hittites believed that the world was populated by a multitude, indeed a plenitude, of spirits and divine forces. The whole cosmos throbbed with supernatural life. Gods inhabited the realms above and below the earth. And on the earth every rock, mountain, tree, spring, and river had its resident god or spirit. These were not mere abstractions, but vital living entities.[49]

There was a core group of old Hattian deities and other local deities, but as the Hittites conquered new territory, they tended to bring in the gods of their new subjects and allies as well. One of the reasons the Boğazköy archives contain so many different languages is that rituals had to be performed for these deities in their native tongues.

Let us look at the Hurrian case in a little more detail, since the Hurrians contributed a major component to the culture of the Empire. Their history begins before the Hittites appeared, their presence in northern Syria being attested by Mesopotamian documents of the third millennium BC. By the time of the Hittite Old Kingdom, the Hurrians formed a sizable percentage of the population of northern Mesopotamia and southern Anatolia as well, but it was during the growth and expansion of the Empire that they had their greatest impact in the north. Their language is unrelated to any other tongue spoken in the ancient world, except Urartian, to which we shall return in a later chapter. Much that stemmed originally from Mesopotamia came to the Hittites through the Hurrians but their influence was not limited to transmitting the works of others; many of their own myths and rituals are found in the Boğazköy archives. The Hittite royal family itself seems to have been Hurrian because some of its rulers had Hurrian names before adopting traditional Hittite names on assuming the throne. For example, Urhi-Teshub became Mursili III.

Because the cultural borrowing is on so large a scale, it is difficult to formulate a simple statement of not just what constitutes Hittite religion, but also Hittite mythology, literature, and even art. In mythology, the most important deity was clearly the Storm God, which is not surprising in a land where the weather has such dramatic intensity. But the general concept of the storm god embraced numerous local variants who are often treated separately. Among the gods called on to witness treaties, we find the Storm God of Heaven, the Hattian Storm God, the Storm God of Halab, the Storm God of Nerik, and so forth, all in the same list. Usually the name of this god is written with a logogram, so we do not even know how the Hittites pronounced it, but the Luwain version was Tarhunt, and the Hattic, Taru. The same logogram was used for the Hurrian Teshub.[50] The supreme female deity was the normally Sun Goddess of Arinna, but we noted earlier that we find Hepatu, chief goddess of the Hurrian pantheon, in her place as the queen of heaven at Yazılıkaya. The two cannot be the same, for Hepatu had no connection with the sun. There are innumerable goddesses tied to this place or that whose name is written with the cuneiform logogram for the Mesopotamian goddess Ishtar.

In their mythological literature the Hittites showed the same flexibility. One of the most famous of their myths concerns a Hattic god who, by chance, has the same name as the Old Kingdom ruler mentioned earlier: Telipinu. For some reason, he flies into a rage, becoming so irate that he puts his right shoe on his left foot, and his left shoe on his right. He storms off in anger and his disappearance causes the reproductive powers of the world to fail. Alarmed, the rest of the gods try to find Telipinu and lure him back. A bee locates the recalcitrant god, but this just makes him angrier. Finally, through the performance of a ritual, Telipinu is returned and the land blooms again. Another, virtually identical version of this myth, has the Storm God as the central character. Another important group of myths, the Kumarbi cycle, deals with the birth of the gods and the struggle between generations.[51] The god Kumarbi emasculates his parent, but is himself impregnated with a new generation of gods when he swallows his father's genitals. Teshub, the leader of this new generation, then challenges and defeats Kumarbi. Similarities between this and Hesiod's *Theogony*, the Greek story of conflict between generations of gods, have not gone unnoticed. In another myth of the cycle, Kumarbi seeks revenge by creating a massive stone monster, Ullikumi, whom Teshub is at pains to thwart. All of the names of characters and significant locations in the Kumarbi cycle are Hurrian, but the Boğazköy tablets on which they are written are in Hittite. We do not know how extensively the Hittites modified what must originally have been a Hurrian tale.[52]

HITTITE ARCHITECTURAL SCULPTURE AND ROCK RELIEFS

Rock reliefs are one of the distinguishing art forms of the late Hittite Empire, and they are scattered over the Anatolian plateau, generally found in isolation. It is not entirely clear what their purpose was, or indeed if they had a single purpose. Some are of gods, and others are representations of the king, and, in at least one case, the queen. Stylistically, they are all close to the reliefs of Yazılıkaya and Alaca Höyük, and indeed they were probably all carved within a century. The oldest one that can be dated is a representation of Muwatalli II in very crude, almost planar relief, on the face of a cliff that overlooks the Ceyhan River in the Cilician Plain at Sirkeli (Figure 7.14: 1). Here the king wears a long coat and carries a curved staff (*lituus*), a symbol of leadership derived from the shepherd's crook, with the hooked end down, as Tudahliya IV does at Yazılıkaya. There is a small site above this cliff, but the relief cannot be seen from it. The relief is simply a marker of the king's presence, and may not be unrelated to Muwatilli's interest in the Lower Land. Another set of royal reliefs, also in a planar style, is found at Firaktin, on the other side of the Cilician Gates. Here Hattusili III and the Storm God face each other on opposite sites of an altar, while Hattusili pours a libation. To his right, his wife Puduhepa does the same before the Hurrian goddess Hepatu (Figure 7.14: 2). Here, as at Sirkeli, the identifications are made certain by Luwian hieroglyphs carved in and beside the reliefs. Once again, a political motive may be ascribed to this. Fıraktın is along an access route which connects the Hittite heartland with Kizzuwatna, from which Puduhepa came.

With other reliefs, the depictions are of gods alone. South of Ankara at the site of Gâvurkale,

Figure 7.14 Hittite rock reliefs: **1** Sirkeli. **2** Fıraktın

a fortress sits atop a conical hill. It has the typical cyclopean masonry, protecting both a fortified core and a small settlement area. On the rock face just below the summit there are two 4-m tall figures of gods, one bearded one not, striding leftward, with their hands raised before their faces. There are no glyphs visible here.

Another site with clear religious significance is Eflatun Pınar, in the Beyşehir region. It lies beside a pool fed by a spring and consists of a rectangular structure made of huge ashlar blocks (Figure 7.15: 2). Facing the water are sculptures of two large seated figures, one male and the other female. Between and beside them are mountain gods and figures who hold up winged discs over the heads of the figures. The topmost disc is incomplete, and the monument, if it were ever finished, is in disrepair. On the ground behind the platform is a broken and badly worn statue of a lion, which bears a resemblance to lions found on another unfinished piece of sculpture discovered at the nearby site of Fasıllar. This is a 7-m high stele of the Storm God in a smiting position, a replica of which now stands in the courtyard of the Archaeological Museum in Ankara (Figure 7.15: 1). It has been suggested that the Eflatun Pınar structure was the base on

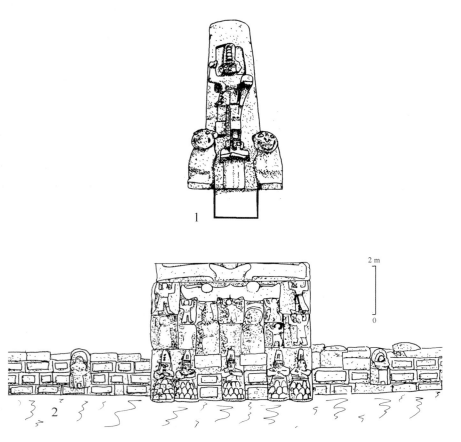

Figure 7.15 Sculptures of the Beyşehir area: **1** Fasıllar monument (after photo of replica in Bittel 1976: fig. 264). **2** Eflatun Pınar

which one, or perhaps a pair of monuments like the one at Fasıllar would have been placed. If so, it would have been an impressive, if isolated edifice. Recent excavations have revealed that the edge of the pool was also lined with sculpture. There can be little doubt of its cultic importance. Although no inscriptions are associated with the site, it is clearly imperial.

HITTITE GLYPTIC AND MINOR ARTS

The art of the Hittite rock reliefs appears in miniature on royal seals. In the period of the Empire, the basic form of the king's seal impression is circular, with a cuneiform legend running around the circumference framing the central motif. In some cases that motif consists of hieroglyphs of the royal "cartouche"—so named because it performs a function rather like that of the oblong enclosure that encircles royal names in Egyptian hieroglyphs. In the Hittite case, it is a frame formed by a sun disk over the glyphs for "great" and "king." Between these are the signs that give the personal name of the king. In one version Suppiluliuma I's name appears alongside the name of his queen.[53] There are also elaborations of the royal seal in which the king is shown in the embrace of the Storm God, or the god Sharumma. In the latter case the figures are represented just as they are at Yazılıkaya, the king wearing a skullcap and holding his staff downward while the embracing god wears a tall horned crown. A particularly well preserved sealing of the Hittite viceroy of Carchemish, Ini-Teshub, has been found at Carchemish.[54] It depicts a god and gives the name of Ini-Teshub in both hieroglyphs and cuneiform, just as a great king's seal would, but the hieroglyphs give the simple sign for king, not the imperial cartouch with the sun disc and glyphs for great king.

These royal seals of the late Empire are the most elaborate examples of a sealing tradition that can be traced back to the Middle Bronze Age (Figure 7.16). The motifs included deities riding on animals, presentations scenes, or simply hieroglyphs, which increased in number as time went on. The Hittites favored stamp seals over cylinder seals, although the latter are not unknown. There was, however, great variety in the forms that these stamps took. Most left circular impressions, but there were also prisms with multiple faces. Some had knob attachments and a few had handles that have been likened to hammers; others were biconvex discs. There were also stamp cylinders, which could be either rolled or stamped. Hieroglyphs, or signs that would later become hieroglyphs, are often part of the design elements. It is also clear that a large number of people were using seals. A remarkable discovery of over 3000 bullae from a building near Nişantepe at Boğazköy, not associated with any archive but dating to the time of the Empire, revealed 280 different personal names of princes and other officials, only a small number of whom appear in other written documents.[55]

The Hittite minor arts reflect a style that is consistent with what one sees in the monumental reliefs, although they are not particularly common finds in archaeological excavations. Some categories of artistic expression are missing, perhaps though the chance of discovery. We have, for example, no Hittite wall paintings, and almost no large-scale sculpture in the round. A

Figure 7.16 Royal seal impressions: **1** Seal of Mursili II (after Neve 1992: 58, Abb. 154). **2** Seal of Hattusili III and Puduhepa (after Neve 1992: 57, Abb. 152). **3** Impression of "Boss of Tarkondemos" (Tarhumuwa) (after Bittel 1976: 168). **4** Seal of Ini-Teshub, King of Carchemish (after Bittel 1976: 168)

number of figurines, some in precious materials like gold or rock crystal, have been found out of context, their style leaving no doubt about their Hittite associations. An 82-cm high jar found at İnandıktepe is the best preserved representative of a class of ritual vessels with ritual scenes depicted in raised relief and polychrome painted decoration.[56]

FRINGES OF EMPIRE: HITTITE ARCHAEOLOGY BEYOND THE PLATEAU

Delimiting the boundaries of the Hittite Empire is no easy matter, whether one is speaking of political control or cultural influence in some more generalized sense. This is not just because those boundaries were in constant flux, but also because the Great Kings of Hatti often exercised their dominance indirectly. A regime cobbled together by transient conquests and political deals can hardly have been expected to propagate cultural uniformity over as large an area as, for example, the Urartians were later to do. If anything, it had the opposite effect, increasing diversity and cosmopolitanism in its core area. In the sphere of language, for example, we have seen Hurrian deities in the most central of its religious shrines and the Luwian language coming to dominate the center of the kingdom where Hittite (Neshite) once held sway.

Ceramic evidence, which may be expected to be less reflective of the actions of government than monumental architecture and sculpture, defines a core Hittite area on the central plateau. The wares most intimately associated with the rise of the Hittites tend to be red polished and continue the shapes seen at Kültepe in the previous era. These "Hittite" wares are found as far west as Eskişehir and as far east as Elazığ, but they do not extend into the Pontic area.[57] Different ceramic traditions are found in the Beyşehir area, the Troad, and on the southwestern coast of Turkey.[58]

The use of imperial motifs in the westernmost part of Anatolia is demonstrated by recent revelations concerning the land of Mira, which involve two of the longest known objects of Hittite art. One of these is the relief of a king carved in a cliff face in a pass at Karabel,[59] which overlooks a land route connecting Ephesus and Sardis (see Figure 7.1). While modern scholarship has had no doubt about the Hittite character of the relief—the figure would not be the least bit out of place at Boğazköy or Yazılıkaya—it was a puzzle as to what it was doing so far from the core area of Hittite material culture.[60] The badly worn glyphs were clear enough to show that Herodotus was wrong to identify this as an Egyptian relief, but long eluded decipherment. The second is a silver object of unknown provenance, now in the Walters Gallery in Baltimore, which has the form of a royal seal: a figure accompanied by hieroglyphs indicating he is a king, framed by a circle of cuneiform. This was the first time the two types of writing had been found together, and it was dubbed the "Boss of Tarkondemos" when it was first published by Sayce in the 1880s. The cuneiform, however, was inexpertly done, and so the precise reading of both inscriptions remained unclear. In the late 1990s J. D. Hawkins recognized that the name on the Boss of Tarkondemos was the same as the one on the Karabel relief: Tarkasnawa, king of Mira. Moreover, this individual was known from recently excavated documents from Boğazköy, and the fixed geographical point for Mira provided by Karabel tied a lot of historical loose ends about western Anatolia together.[61] We now recognize that Mira was a kingdom created by Mursili II when he carved up the larger western Anatolian kingdom of Arzawa, which had been a thorn in the side of the Hittites for generations. Apasa, the capital of Azawa, can now confidently be identified with classical Ephesus, where indeed Late Bronze Age materials have been found. Mursili established a local ruler there, and ties between Mira and Hatti were renewed periodically until the end of the Empire. Tarkasnawa's father was a contemporary of Tudhaliya IV. The essential point is that Tarkasnawa may have been a Hittite ally, or even a Hittite puppet, but he was no Hittite. He came from a local line that stemmed from Arzawan nobility. Yet when it came to marking his boundary with another western Anatolian kingdom, the Seha River Land, he chose to do so with the symbolism, script, and costume of a Hittite king.

The relationship of the Hittites with the Mycenaean civilization of Greece is one of the great unresolved issues in Anatolian history. In the Late Bronze Age, Mycenaean pottery is well represented along the Aegean coast, from Troy to the shore opposite Rhodes. It is mixed with local pottery in a smaller percentage north of Miletus than it is in the area south of it, but generally speaking the assemblages of this whole area are mixed and form an area of cultural interface shared by the islands off the coast.[62] In Hittite dealings with Miletus (Millawanda), and western Anatolia generally, they came up against a great power known as Ahhiyawa, whose king was remote from them. For eight decades, scholars have debated the location of Ahhiyawa and its relationship to the Mycenaeans, wavering between a location on the Greek mainland or a location in Anatolia to which the Hittites did not enjoy direct access. As the map of western Anatolia fills in, there are few places left to put it in Asia, although the coast south of Miletus remains a possibility.[63]

In Syria, where the Hittites also exercised their political authority through treaties and descendants of Suppiluliuma residing in Carchemish served as viceroys for the area, the material imprint of Anatolian rule is quite circumscribed in the period of the Empire. We might have a different appreciation of this if the Bronze Age levels at Carchemish were excavated, but with the modern border between Syria and Turkey passing through the southern part of the site, this is unlikely to happen. While it is beyond the scope of this book to treat sites outside of Turkey in any detail, a quick glance at Ugarit and Emar, two sites in Syria which were very important to the Hittites, is instructive.

Ugarit, located only 1 km from the Mediterranean shore, was a port of trade in the broadest sense. It had been inhabited since the Early Neolithic, and in the Late Bronze Age its kings had to deal with Egyptian, Mitannian and Hittite expansion into their territory. The native population spoke a west Semitic language closely related to Canaanite, and even employed an alphabetic cuneiform script to record it, although the scribes of Ugarit made use of Hurrian, Akkadian, and Sumerian as well. The site suffered a catastrophic destruction at roughly the same time as Boğazköy, and from its ruins excavators have recovered objects of art from all over the Mediterranean, including Mycenaean, Cypriot, and Egyptian materials. One sees a very thorough cosmopolitanism here.

Where do their Hittite overlords fit into this picture? Not in architecture or monumental art, certainly, and Anatolian objects are quite rare in the record.[64] Ugaritic mythology and religion are clearly tied to local traditions. There is almost no writing in the Hittite language in the many cuneiform tablets that have been found here, but this is hardly surprising since the Hittites generally chose to write in Akkadian when dealing with peoples outside of Anatolia. It is, in fact, in tablets that Hittite authorities most clearly leave their mark, and specifically on land deeds. The tablets that perform this function have a special shape, both here at Ugarit, and in Boğazköy. Most cuneiform tablets have a flatter side, the obverse, where the text begins, and more rounded reverse, on which it may continue as the tablet is turned over, not from side to side, as the page of a book, but top to bottom. These land deeds, however, have a quite rounded obverse, in the center of which there is a large, round seal impression of the validating authority.

The archaeological evidence for Hittite control in Ugarit is thus very limited, coming mostly from texts that deal with government to government relations. There are probably more Egyptian artefacts in this port of trade than there are clear Anatolian ones. The Hittite government was content to leave a local king in charge, and local institutions functioning, while its viceroy in Carchemish, whose very Anatolian seal is certainly in evidence, oversaw things from a distance.

Things are slightly different at the frontier site of Emar, near where the Euphrates makes its great bend in the Syrian desert to flow southeastward to southern Mesopotamia and the Gulf. Emar had a long history before the Hittites, and is mentioned in texts from many sites in the Early and Middle Bronze Age. Archaeologically, however, the ruins at Mesqene with which it has been identified are Late Bronze Age and founded on virgin soil on elevated ground overlooking the Euphrates flood plain. It is apparent, therefore, that the site was moved here from some other, presumably lower lying location which has now been flooded by the Tabqa Dam, built in the 1970s. Margueron, the first excavator, argued that the new site was a construction of the Hittites, although this view has recently been challenged. What is apparent is that the Hittites were the ones to install a king here, as opposed to a city lord who had answered to the king of Mitanni. This Hittite appointee was answerable to the Hittite viceroy in Carchemish. Tablets from Emar, both legitimately excavated and looted, show a mixed population here but probably very few people who actually spoke Hittite.

The violent end of the Hittite Empire was only one event in a wider conflagration that swept the eastern Mediterranean lands at the end of the Bronze Age. The Trojan War is believed to have taken place around this time, and soon afterwards the brilliant Mycenaean civilization of Greece collapsed. The Egyptians tell of a number of warlike groups, known collectively as the Sea Peoples, who destroyed the Hittites before moving on to raid Egypt. Whether it was these people who put the Hittite capital to the torch, or older enemies taking advantage of the situation, Hattusa's age of greatness was over.

NOTES

1 *Histories* ii.106.
2 *Deut.* 7:1.
3 2 *Kings* 7:6.
4 For a summary of the various perspectives on the Hittites offered by the Old Testament, see McMahon 1992.
5 Texier's plan and drawings have been conveniently reproduced in Canpolat 2001: 100, 152–153.
6 This name also appears in English as Hattusha or Hattuša. A note on transcribing the cuneiform sibilant š is order here, for it is our transcriptions, not Hittite writing that is inconsistent. The cuneiform writing system the Hittites borrowed from Mesopotamia via Semitic-speaking Syria, had three different unvoiced sibilants, which we transcribe s, ṣ, and š. The Hittite language, on the other hand, had only one. The historical linguistic analysis of Indo-European indicates that this was pronounced like an English s, but for some reason Hittite scribes regularly chose to record it with the cuneiform signs that indicate š (pronounced as the *sh* in "shoe"). Publications vary in choosing whether to render what the Hittites wrote (for example, Hattušili), or what they probably said (Hattusili). In the previous chapter, where we were transcribing Akkadian signs, we elected to follow the writing, thus Kane*sh*. In this chapter, where we are rendering Hittite names, we will use the simple s.
7 At least this is what we have chosen to call the language. As we noted in the previous chapter, the Hittites themselves, however, called it *Nešili* or *Nešumnili*, "the speech of Nesha" or Kanesh), and by parallel with our Biblically derived term Hittite, it would be Neshite. Boğazköy was known as Hattuš in the time of the Assyrian merchants and what the Hittites called *Hattili*, "the speech of Hatti," local

to the area before the Hittites arrived, is a quite unrelated language that is called Hattic or Hattian in modern scholarship.

8   In some literature this is spelled "Luvian", but the *w* better approximates the ancient pronunciation. The *v* appears in English because translations often pass through German, which does not have the *w* phoneme that Luwian, Hittite, and English share.

9   In some English language publications, Hittite names are written with the final *s* (or *š*) of the nominative case ending, for example, Telipinus or Hattusilis. Since this doesn't always make grammatical sense in English, we prefer giving the names in their bare stem form.

10 Bryce 2005: 64.

11 Collins 2007: 37.

12 For a review of recent suggestions, see Collins 2007: 37 note 31.

13 This is the date as given by the "middle chronology" of the *Cambridge Ancient History* which is used as a convention by many scholars. The date of 1531 BC given by the "low chronology," more popular in Europe, is another alternative in a matter of uncertainty that has been investigated from a number of angles for decades without a decisive solution. For a review of the issues, and an "ultra-low" alternative, see Gasche 1998.

14 In early scholarship on Hittite history, some scholars placed a Middle Kingdom between the Hittite Old Kingdom and Empire. There was also a certain amount of inconsistency about when it began and ended. This creates the false impression that there were three phases of strong Hittite leadership, whereas in fact most of the rulers of this "Middle Kingdom" are known only by name. There is a certain validity to the linguistic distinction of "Middle Hittite" for the writing that is later than the Old Kingdom and earlier than the documents of the later Empire, from Suppiluliuma I on, but the texts that fall into this category were written in the early part of the Empire. See Archi 2003 for a review of the concepts.

15 It is probable that this is the first king of this name, but it was long believed that there was a earlier Tudhaliya in the scantily documented period between Telipinu and the rise of the Empire. So as not to upset the traditional numbering system, which would cause a great deal of confusion when it came to the quite well known figure of Tudhaliya IV, for example, the founder of the Empire is often designated Tudahliya I/II (Collins 2007: 42 note 40).

16 The name becomes a little more transparent if one translates it. *Šuppi* means "pure" or "clean" (ritually); a *luli* is a spring, and *uma* associates a word with a place. So Suppiluliuma means something like "the man from clearwater."

17 We retain the older spelling of this city employed by its English excavators. The alternative spellings, Karkamiş and Karkamiš are also in common use.

18 An excellent overview is provided by Bryce 2005.

19 Van den Hout 2006: 234–237.

20 The date is, not surprisingly, disputed, but at this point in the Late Bronze Age the range of disagreement is less than a dozen years.

21 Neve 1992: 19–21.

22 Naumann 1971: 213–214.

23 The modern village officially changed its name in 1960 (Neve 1992: 7).

24 Bittel 1970: 31.

25 A replica now stands in its place at the site; the original relief has been removed to the Museum of Ancient Civilizations in Ankara.

26 Because the bare chest of the figure is well defined, some earlier scholars sought to identify this figure as female. It was in this part of Anatolia that the legendary amazons were thought to have lived, so before people knew anything about Hittites, this was not an entirely unreasonable theory. A close observation of the sculpture, however, shows that he has hair on his chest, and the Hittites knew nothing of Amazons.

27 Hittite kings could be deified upon their death; for example, when Hattusili III says "when my father became a god" it means, "when my father died." There is also a certain divine aspect in the royal title "My Sun," used as an equivalent of "majesty," but the living Hittite king was never portrayed as a god in art, or worshiped as such.

28 Peter Neve, who completed the excavations here, suggests it may have been Hattusili III who sponsored the construction (Neve 2002: 77).

29 Seeher 2002: 21. For comparison, one of these vessels would hold more than nine standard 55-gallon (208 liter) drums.

30 Seeher 2002: 86.

31 Although the signs are very clear, this text demonstrates how imperfectly we understand Luwian hieroglyphic writing at this early phase of its development. Most of the signs here stand for words, and many are simply unknown. As the hieroglyphic script developed, particularly after the 13th century more syllabic signs with known pronunciations are used and these help to link words being written hieroglyphically with Luwian and Hittite words known from cuneiform texts.

32 Melchert 2002: 139.

33 Viz. the title of Neve 1992.

34 Henrickson 2002: 128–129.

35 Postgate 2007: 142–145.

36 Genz 2005.

37 A note on transliteration conventions is in order here. The capital letters give the Sumerian pronunciation of word sign or signs. In this case, we do not know the corresponding Hittite term, since Hittite scribes never wrote it syllabically. The superscript is used for a sign known as a determinative, which simply indicates a category to which the word belongs, here indicating that an AGRIG is a type of person. Determinatives were not pronounced.

38 Singer 1984: 127.

39 Alp 1991: 48–50.

40 Süel 2002: 163–164.

41 Müller-Karpe 2002: 148.

42 Müller-Karpe 2002: 150.

43 Our discussion focuses on the two chambers which are decorated with sculpture, A and B. The third, undecorated chamber, C, was recognized in excavations of 1966–67 and is a sort of an annex to Chamber B created by walling off a fissure in the rock behind it (Bittel et al. 1975: 49–62).

44 By the standards of other Great Kings of the Bronze Age Near East, the Hittites do not distinguish themselves in creating royal tombs. Texts inform us that Hittite kings were cremated and their remains placed in a "stone house". There were also "eternal peaks" that served as memorials to deceased kings. In the case of Tudhaliya IV, there are strong indications that the Nişantaş was the latter, and Room B at Yazılıkaya was itself the "stone house" (van den Hout 2002).

45 Bittel 1970: 96.

46 Bittel 1970: 96.

47 Bittel et al. 1975: 167.

48 Bittel 1970: 97.

49 Bryce 2002: 135.

50 Bryce 2002: 144.

51 Summarized by Bryce 2002: 222–229.

52 Bryce 2002: 227.

53 Schaeffer 1956: plate I.

54 Schaeffer 1956: plate V.

55 Herbolt 2002: 53–54.

56 Özgüç 1988: plates 36–59.

57 McQueen 1986: 102–104.

58 For a brief summary of the pottery areas, see Macqueen 1986: 102–106.

59 There were once other monuments here, probably fragments of another relief on the opposite side of the road. They disappeared when the road was widened in the late 1970s. What little can be made of them is discussed by Hawkins 1998.

60 For example, Bittel 1967.

61 Hawkins 1998.

62 For a detailed discussion of the shifting ceramic patterns over time, and a consideration of the Ahhiyawa issue, see Mountjoy 1998.

63 Mountjoy 1998: 51.

64 Schaeffer 1956: 1–163 presents the material evidence for Ugarit's relationship that was available at the time of its publication.

8

LEGACY OF THE HITTITES

Southern Anatolia in the Iron Age (1200–600 BC)

The destruction of the Hittite capital at Hattuša at the beginning of the 12th century defines a watershed in the history of Anatolia and the ancient Near East generally. From this point forward, attempts to blend the archaeology of ancient Turkey into a single thread of narrative are strained, particularly if the Anatolian plateau is the focal point. In south central Turkey and adjacent parts of Syria, Hittite artistic traditions lived on for another five centuries, albeit in a transformed socio-political environment. Eastern Anatolia, dormant in obscurity through much of the Late Bronze and Early Iron Ages, saw the emergence of a powerful empire in the form of the kingdom of Urartu, with obvious cultural ties to northern Mesopotamia as well as striking native innovations. In central and western Anatolia, where a generation ago it was assumed a dark age prevailed for several centuries, new evidence is gradually filling the picture of new peoples and polities emerging, like the kingdoms of Phrygia and Lydia.

There are some broader uniformities underlying this chaos, however. The key transformation is the nearly simultaneous collapse of the great empires that had dominated the world of the 14th and 13th centuries and the appearance of new peoples in less centralized political and economic configurations. It was not just the Hittite Empire that disintegrated; all of the other major powers of the eastern Mediterranean and Near East suffered serious reverses in the 12th century in what have been called the "crisis years." The Egyptians lost their empire in Asia and were never able to regain the glorious self-centered stability that they maintained throughout the entire Bronze Age. The Middle Assyrian Empire, which had met the Hittites along the Euphrates, receded into its core territory in northern Iraq under a series of obscure and impotent kings. The Kassite dynasty in Babylonia gave up on the building projects that had renovated many of the older cities of southern Mesopotamia as its power disintegrated. Battered by intrusions from Assyria and Elam, its last king was removed from power before the middle of the 12th century and the various native dynasties that claimed authority in Babylonia afterwards generated few documents or archaeological remains. In Iran, the Middle Elamite exuberance of power that enabled it to conquer Babylon and carry off such key monuments in the history of art as the Law Code of Hammurabi and the Stele of Naram Sin also dwindled into obscurity at the end of the 12th century. In Mycenaean Greece fortresses like Pylos, Tiryns, and Mycenae itself were violently destroyed, and the palace at Knossos on Crete likewise. In the Levant generally there was widespread devastation, most vividly illustrated in the ruins of Ugarit, where five millennia of settlement terminated in a massive—and archaeologically rich—destruction level.

A dramatic decline in literacy, material wealth, and the size of political units followed these catastrophes. Memories of this transformational era are reflected in accounts of the Trojan War and the Israelite conquest of the promised land. The 12th and 11th centuries are not a completely "Dark Age," but they were in fact a period in which more continuity was lost than in many of the dark ages that preceded it. In traditional terminology, this is the beginning of the Iron Age, although iron itself is initially almost nonexistent in the archaeological record.

What caused this upheaval? As with all great historical development, there is no shortage of speculation, and little generally accepted fact.[1] On the most superficial level, there appears to have been some sort of systems collapse, where damage to one polity released forces that damaged others. The very interrelationships that ordered the civilized world effectively transmitted disorder. Ancient historical sources finger outside invaders as the triggering factor, but modern historians find this explanation insufficient, since barbarians like the Kaska are always a potential threat and generally no match for more complex societies unless something is going wrong with them internally. Climate change, technological change, and even earthquakes have been suggested as prime movers.

THE CONCEPT OF AN IRON AGE

In this context, it is useful to revisit the somewhat antiquated concept of the Iron Age, not just to refute the once popular view that discovery of "the secret of iron" precipitated the end of the Bronze Age by giving barbarians more power, but to evaluate the importance of metallurgical technology in reshaping societies in the following centuries. As with many other broad and influential ideas that shaped the direction of archaeological research, a clear statement of the underlying theory was presented by V. Gordon Childe in the 1930s. The gist of his argument was as follows: Once the smelting technology is mastered, iron tools and weapons are cheap to make. Iron ores are common and although some locations are better than others for brining ores and the timber to smelt them together, there is never any possibility of monopolizing the production of iron or the distribution of objects made of it. Bronze, on the other hand, is always something of a luxury and a metal controlled by elites, since sources for its components, copper and tin, are restricted and must be brought together by long-distance shipment. The introduction of iron was thus a democratizing force in society, improving the tools available to non-elites for the first time since the Neolithic. The new economic and military power imparted to these lower and more populous social strata thus demanded new and more broadly embracing forms of leadership, social control, and ideological propagation. One may trace such things as the spread of the alphabet, the emergence of proselytizing religions, and eventually democracy itself back to the influence of iron.

As with all grand ideas, the devil here is in the details. Childe was inclined to see transformations in the human condition as "revolutions" and in his day the archeological record was thin enough to allow the notion of a very abrupt change from bronze to iron as the dominant blade technology. Certainly when one compares the palace-based Bronze Age societies of the 13th century with those of the 8th-century Iron Age the contrasts are striking, but one must cover a lot of time to get from one to the other, and the role of iron technology in bringing about the changes is problematic. Iron existed as a luxury metal in the Bronze Age, and it did not appear in any quantity, or in the kind of utilitarian objects that would effect Childe's "revolution," until the 10th century.

Anatolia is certainly one of the regions of the world in which the changes at the end of the Bronze Age were most dramatic. Recent archaeological research is refining our understanding of both the continuities and discontinuities of the transformation. At the site of Boğazköy, for example, there is just enough occupation in the period after the site was destroyed as an imperial center to track a pattern of change through pottery in the Early Iron Age, between the fall of the Empire and the Phrygian reoccupation of the site in the 9th century BC. In the first of three stratigraphic phases covering the 12th through the 10th centuries, there is a great increase in the amount of handmade pottery compared to the Empire, but wheelmade pottery still makes up a quarter of the sherds. Some of the forms of the vessels look very much like their imperial predecessors, but their surfaces are more polished. In the second and third phases, wheelmade pottery disappears and light colored fabrics are sometimes decorated with red painted geometric designs. There is new crude ware, poorly fired in a reducing atmosphere to create a dark gray appearance. These vessels sometimes have horseshoe or knob-shaped handles. In the Middle Iron Age, that is beginning in the 9th century, there is a substantial new settlement on Büyükaya, using a new type of pottery in which a matt-brown paint predominates.[2] These later wares are associated with the Phrygian domination of the area, which will be discussed in Chapter 10, but also appear in southern Anatolia where the Phrygians were never a major population element. In short, what appears to be happening in the area around Boğazköy is not an invasion from the west, but the evolution of local traditions.[3]

At Kilise Tepe, a site which had flourished in the "Lower Land" during the imperial period, one sees a transformation parallel to that which took place at Boğazköy. The standardized wares associated with the Hittite Empire on the plateau go out of use, and are replaced by red painted wares reminiscent of pre-imperial conditions in the area. The forms and styles of these "revivals" are not the same as the ones that appear in the north or elsewhere in Anatolia, but the replacement of broadly distributed "imperial" forms by local ones is clearly a product of the same loss of political centralization.[4]

ASSYRIA AND THE HISTORY OF THE NEO-HITTITE PRINCIPALITIES

In the world of the early Iron Age, one group of polities made direct claims to the legacy of the Hittite Empire: At various sites in the Taurus Mountains, Cilicia, and northern Syria principalities distinguished by the use of Luwian hieroglyphic writing flourished from the beginning of the 12th until at least the end of the 8th centuries BC (Figure 8.1). It was their hieroglyphic texts that led scholars of the 19th century to posit the existence of the Hittite Empire in the first place, although most of them were actually written after the Hattusa had been destroyed. The designation "Hittite" for these monuments and state must also be used with qualification. We now know that the language in question was a dialect of Luwian, not Hittite, so the increased prominence of hieroglyphic writing in the Iron Age can be argued as both continuity and discontinuity with the Empire. It is, in fact, emblematic of what was going on generally. These "Neo-Hittite", "Syro-Hittite" or "Late Hittite" principalities, as they are variously called,[5] gather

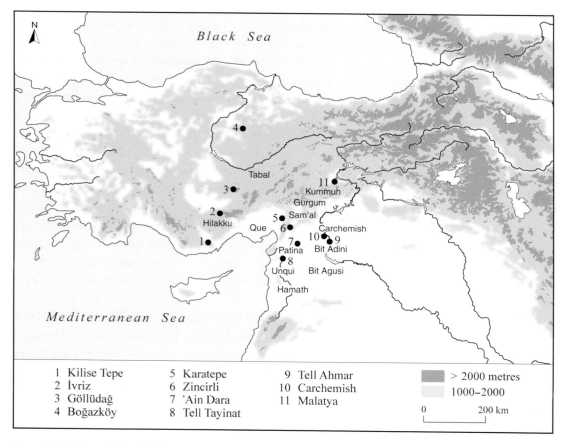

1 Kilise Tepe	5 Karatepe	9 Tell Ahmar	
2 İvriz	6 Zincirli	10 Carchemish	
3 Göllüdağ	7 'Ain Dara	11 Malatya	
4 Boğazköy	8 Tell Tayinat		

Figure 8.1 Map of Neo-Hittite sites

up some of the old elements of the defunct empire and represent them in quite new and different ways.

There are roughly a dozen political entities to be considered under these rubrics, and within and among them diversity is the watchword. To classify them collectively either as city-states or tribally controlled territories is inappropriate, and most of the known detail of their political history relates to confused and unstable dynastic succession. Starting from the north, moving down the Euphrates, then across Syria and returning to the Anatolian Plateau, the kingdoms exhibiting some degree of Hittite influence were Melid (Malatya), Kummuh, Carchemish, Bit Adini, Bit Agusi, Hamath, Patina/Unqi, Sam'al, Que, Hilakku, Tabal, and Gurgum. It is important to recognize, however, that another people, the Arameans, became prominent in the southern part of this area in the course of the Iron Age and their language ultimately came to dominate the Near East south of the Taurus Mountains. Aramean and Neo-Hittite elements are so thoroughly mixed in the societies of Syria and Anatolia in the Iron Age that drawing a firm line between Aramean and Luwian cultural entities is problematic, if not pointless. Their interactions are poorly understood and in many cases the principalities themselves appear to have been composed of different population elements.

The available textual and archaeological sources for history of these principalities do not permit us to produce a coherent chronological narrative. With archaeology, part of the problem stems from what may be the most interesting product of this cultural complex—monumental sculpture. Because they offered large and curious objects of art that could be exported to museums, Neo-Hittite sites were dug in the very early days of archaeology when little attention was given to recording contextual information. The nuts and bolts of modern archaeology such as pottery sequences, domestic remains, intrasite/intersite relationships and so forth were neglected. More recent research is making progress in this area, but there is a vast amount to time and space to cover. In this sphere, Anatolian and Syro-Palestinian archaeology blend together without sharp delineation, and the character of the Hittite survival cannot be treated without reference to the Arameans linguistically, and Syria geographically.

A second complicating factor is that the textual record of the Neo-Hittites themselves is very incomplete, and not rich in historical information. They did not make use of cuneiform, or, more to the point, clay as a writing material. Most of what survives are monumental inscriptions on stone, and these have very limited functions such as commemorating buildings and validating local dynasties. In some cases, they enable us to put together genealogies of several generations for a given principality, but otherwise they are quite provincial in their outlook. A few incised lead strips excavated at Assur and Kululu establish that Luwian hieroglyphs were indeed used for letters and purposes other than monumental display and seal legends, but the bulk of this kind of writing must have been on perishable materials and is thus unavailable to us.

The history of the Neo-Hittite states, and indeed Iron Age Anatolia generally, cannot be written without a discussion to the Neo-Assyrians, whose power came to embrace almost the whole of the Near East. While the center of gravity of their vast empire was in northern Iraq and the Neo-Hittite area was but one theater in a program of conquest which also included

Babylonia, Iran, the Levant, and Egypt, Assyrian records are our primary source of information on the broad outlines of the chronology of the Neo-Hittite states. They are also central to the study of Urartu, which is treated in the next chapter. Thus a digression on Neo-Assyrian history is in order.

Assyria's rise as a military power in the Late Bronze Age and its threat to the Hittite Empire in Syria were noted in the previous chapter. This phase is known as the Middle Assyrian period, and in the crisis years at the beginning of the 12th century, the power of Assyrian monarchs declined, rather than collapsing completely as it did with the Hittites. The succession of kings continued, although the rulers were inconsequential figures and seem to have lost control of northern Syria. At the end of the 12th century, Assyrian fortunes were briefly revived by a remarkable ruler, Tiglath-Pileser I (1114–1077), whose annals composed on clay prisms provide the first the first information on Iron Age Anatolia and the Neo-Hittite world. Crossing the Euphrates to campaign in Syria, he was also the first king to mention the Arameans. He received tribute from Ini-Teshub of Carchemish, whom he regarded as the king of Hatti.[6] He also makes intriguing references to the Kaska, who now appear in the upper Tigris area, and a kingdom called Mushki, which was later to be a major power in Anatolia, usually associated with the Phyrgians (see Chapter 10). Tiglath-Pileser's widespread conquests were a one-reign tour de force in this phase of Assyria's history, however. Two more centuries passed before another Assyrian monarch was to reach the Neo-Hittite area.

The Neo-Assyrian empire was established on a more solid basis in the reigns of Assurnasirpal II (883–859 BC) and Shalmaneser III (858–824 BC). The former again received tribute from Carchemish as he marched to the Mediterranean, and the latter struck repeatedly at a coalition of north Syrian principalities that included many Neo-Hittite states as well as places that we associate with Aramean leadership. Shalmaneser also captured the key site of Til Barsip on the east bank of the Euphrates, converting it into a stronghold which was to serve as a key Assyrian provincial center for the duration of the Empire. Effective as these conquests were, they appear to have temporarily exhausted the Assyrians. In the last quarter of the 9th century and the first half of the 8th, the powers of the Assyrian central government again went into retreat. Former Assyrian governors, such as Shamshi-ilu, whose inscriptions have been found at Til Barsip, picked up some of the slack in this period. Interestingly, if there is a candidate for the historic Assyrian queen Semiramis whose name and legends survive in classical literature and modern opera, it is Shamurramat, the mother and wife, respectively, of two of the more obscure Assyrian kings of this period.

The reign of Tiglath-Pileser III (744–727) inaugurated the final phase of expansion into the Neo-Hittite areas, and in subsequent reigns, particularly Sargon II's (722–705 BC), most of the Aramean and many of the Neo-Hittite states were absorbed into the Neo-Assyrian Empire, losing their cultural identity. Sargon himself fell on a battlefield in Anatolia, but the Assyrian hold on Syria was now firm. By the end of the 8th century, the traditions inaugurated by the Hittites in central Anatolia were dead, even in the southern areas to which they had migrated in the Iron Age.

The Assyrian Empire lasted until the last decades of the 7th century, when its great capitals were sacked by Medes and Babylonians. From that point forward, the cuneiform documentary record on ancient Turkey is very much impoverished, although by no means extinguished. As chroniclers of events in Anatolia, however, the Assyrians always had their limitations. They were never able to conquer or control very much of the highland areas, and their contact with the areas relevant to our study was uneven. It is best documented at times when the Assyrians were intruding, which can hardly be expected to coincide with the primary periods of local prosperity or dynastic coherence. Therefore, one must turn to the evidence of the Neo-Hittite societies themselves and attempt to reconcile it with the historical skeleton provided by their southern neighbors.

KEY NEO-HITTITE SITES

Two innovations of the Hittite Empire were embellished in the Neo-Hittite period, and provide us with most of what we know from native sources on the archaeology and history of the period. The first of these was the use of carved limestone and basalt slabs known as orthostats to protect and decorate the lower part of walls of public buildings. Sometimes the color alternation of these two types of stone was exploited for dramatic effect. Limestone is more subject to weathering than basalt, so there is often an unevenness in the preservation of larger compositions of this type. In any case the sculptures on orthostats, and associated architectural sculpture in the round, provide us with depictions of kings, gods, mythical scenes, funerary banquets, and so forth. In the five centuries and multiple localities in which they were produced, they exhibited changes in style, taking them ever further from the art of the Empire, although some connection can always be recognized. It is generally accepted that these sculptures inspired the development of relief sculpture in Assyria, which was underdeveloped in the Middle Assyrian period and polished to a sublime art form in the Assyrian Empire. Assyrian relief styles, in return, increasingly influenced the art of the Neo-Hittite states as the Empire extended its political influence over them.

The second Hittite imperial innovation the Neo-Hittite states brought to a new level was the use of hieroglyphic Luwian display inscriptions, which we have already noted on several occasions (Figure 8.2). Writing of this type was increasingly used in the latter period of the Empire, particularly by Suppiluliuma II, but in the Iron Age it was even more widespread and served as the only means by which the Luwian language was conveyed. Knowledge of cuneiform cannot have lapsed completely because the Assyrians continued to use it, although the Neo-Hittite princes chose not to. Orthostats inscribed with text, with or without associated sculptures, were the durable historical records of the Neo-Hittite period.

The study of the art, history, and archaeology of the Neo-Hittites principalities is an intricate endeavor, which demands specialties crossing numerous academic boundaries. We highlight here some of the better documented sites, but note that this is only a limited selection.[7]

297

1

2

0   2 cm

Figure 8.2 Luwian Hieroglyphic writing: **1** Orthostat relief of Katuwas, from Carchemish. The large figure pointing to his nose is actually the glyph for the first person singular pronoun. **2** Lead letters from Assur (after Hawkins 2000: plate 306)

Carchemish

Carchemish had a long prehistoric occupation and was already an important city when historical documents from Ebla and southern Mesopotamia began to shed light on the area in the mid-third millennium BC.[8] As we have noted already, it was the key location in the Hittite Empire's control of Syria. Despite its long and important occupation in these earlier periods, however, almost all of the archaeological exposures to date are of materials dating to the Iron Age. Yet even these, which have given us some of the major monuments of Neo-Hittite art, present a sadly incomplete picture of the site. If ever the archaeological history of a site was vexed by circumstances, it is here at Carchemish. British excavators, including C. Leonard Woolley and T. E. Lawrence, worked here in the years before the First World War, and again immediately afterward. In both instances, the work was interrupted by hostilities and the field notes and storage facilities of the expedition were destroyed.[9] After the Turkish War of Independence, the border between Syria and Turkey was drawn along the line of the Berlin to Baghdad railroad, and this has hindered further archaeological work. The citadel and most of the excavated portions of the site are in Turkey, whereas much of the outer town is in Syria.[10] Woolley, who went on to direct highly successful excavations at Ur and Alalakh, long hoped to return to Carchemish and deplored his inability to publish the small finds and pottery in the long delayed final publication on the site.[11] The excavations, which did not reach Bronze Age levels, were primarily successful for recovering Iron Age sculpture and numerous building inscriptions.

Carchemish stands on the western side of the Euphrates at an important crossing point of the river (Figure 8.3). It has a high citadel mound on which one would expect to find the palace or, if the comparably configured 'Ain Dara is a reliable model, a major temple. In any event, the top of this mound was apparently removed by Roman builders,[12] and a large modern structure and parking lot is visible there in satellite images today. Below the citadel, two fortification systems extend the site to the west and south. The nearer marks off the inner town, in which there was a group of public buildings and monumental structures which were the primary subject of archaeological investigations. The farther wall connects to this, and marks off the outer town, which is largely unexplored.

Reconstructions of the Iron Age chronology of the site find a way to order two long-running dynasties of native of rulers mentioned by inscriptions from Carchemish itself with the names kings of Carchemish noted by Assyrian inscriptions at various times. The latter provide the only fixed dates for the whole sequence. There is now a general consensus on how this is to be done—slotting the native kings into the lacunae of the Assyrian records and counting generations—although the dating is still not entirely secure.

The dynasty of kings of Carchemish established by Suppiluliumi I appears to have survived the fall of the capital at Hattusa, and it seems that Kuzi-Teshub, one of the members of this line, assumed the title of Great King of Hatti early in the 12th century—the first king of Carchemish to do so.[13] Although the Egyptian texts of Ramses III that recount the ravages of the Sea Peoples explicitly state that Carchemish was destroyed around 1190 BC, no destruction level comparable

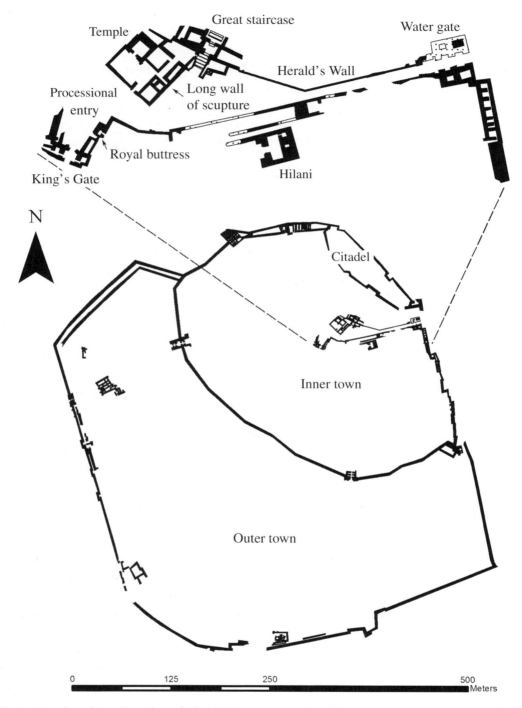

Figure 8.3 Plan of Carchemish, with detail of primary areas in which sculpture was found (after Hawkins 1976–80: 427)

to the one at Ugarit is in evidence here. The Ini-Teshub from whom Tiglath-Pileser I received tribute around 1100 BC was a descendant of Kuzi-Teshub, and the namesake of the 13th century king of Carchemish whose seal was illustrated above (Figure 7.16: 4).[14] No monuments of these kings are found at the site. There are, however, sculptures in very early Neo-Hittite styles together with inscriptions identifying otherwise unknown rulers who claim the title Great King which must belong in period between Tiglath-Pileser I and the 10th century.[15]

In the middle of the 9th century BC, the Assyrians tell us that Carchemish was ruled by a certain Sangara. Despite his importance and a certain longevity, there are again no inscriptions or other works at the site executed in his name. There is, however, an important local dynasty that must precede him. Known as the "house of Suhis," four generations of rulers are known, the last of whom was Katuwas, who is associated with a particular style sculpture (Figure 8.2: 1). This includes a distinctive type of curl in the hair of the head and beard, which can be seen in contemporary sculptures at other sites—by such means are synchronisms made in this somewhat dark age. There is no room for this dynasty in the history of Carchemish after Sangara, so it must come before him. We do not know its connection with the earlier rulers who claimed to be Great Kings, but the line should have begun in the 10th century, if not earlier. The last king of Carchemish, Pisiri, appears in Assyrian records in 738 BC. He was replaced by Assyrian governors when Sargon II brought the city into the Assyrian Empire in 717 BC. The "house of Astiruwas," several generations of local rulers who again produced hieroglyphic monuments— this time associated with an art style that was heavily influenced by Assyria—must be placed in the century between Sangara and Pisiri.[16]

There are probably more pieces of Neo-Hittite sculpture stretched over a longer period of time at Carchemish than at any other site (Figure 8.4). Most were excavated from the public buildings which had been created at different times and were probably rebuilt and modified a good deal before being abandoned. The primary architectural monuments in the inner town run from a gateway beside the river, along a major avenue, and into an area in which there was a large staircase and a temple in an enclosure. The colorful English names these were given by the excavators ("Water Gate," "Long Wall of Sculpture," "Great Staircase," "Herald's Wall," and "King's Gate") are not based on ancient texts, and the architecture itself was of secondary importance to the sculptures that adorned it. South of the road there was a palace building of the hilani type, discussed later in the context of better preserved examples from Zincirli. The Temple of the Storm God, on a platform beside the Grand Staircase is a simple, almost square one-roomed affair with thick walls and single doorway on its southwest side.

Neo-Hittite sculpture has been broadly classified into four sequential phases by Orthmann,[17] and all are represented at Carchemish. The Carchemish sculptures, which as we have seen can be put into a rough chronological framework thanks to the local inscriptions and Assyrian correlations, can then be used to order works at other sites. The earliest works are very close in style to the imperial art of the Bronze Age, and there is no question of where their inspiration came from. By the time we come to Katuwas in the late 10th- or early 9th-century proportions and styles have clearly changed. The sculptures of Yariris, who appears to have been a kind of regent

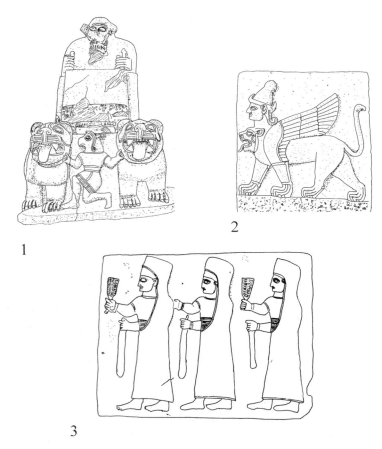

Figure 8.4 Sculptures from Carchemish: **1** God seated on lion base. The statue of the god has been destroyed (after Akurgal 1962: plate 109). **2** Spinx (after Bittel 1976: fig. 284). **3** Procession of women from Processional Entry (after Bittel 1976: fig. 287) (not to scale)

in the house of Astiruwas,[18] are executed in a very flat relief, which is reminiscent of techniques being used in Assyria at that time.

Malatya

The mound of Arslantepe, so important for our understanding of central Anatolia in the 4th millennium BC, was also an important location in the Hittite Empire. In the early Iron Age, it seems to have an intimate connection with Carchemish, since two of its kings claim descent from Kuzi-Teshub, mentioned earlier, perhaps as a kind of cadet branch of the royal line.[19] Tigalth-Pileser I noted that Malatya was part of Hatti. The pattern of subsequent interaction with Assyrian rulers is reminiscent of the situation at Carchemish, in that the authors of the local inscriptions are not named in the Assyrian records whereas other kings of Malatya are. Like Carchemish, Malatya became subject to Assyria late in the 8th century, first through local puppets and finally under Assyrian governors who may have ultimately ruled it from another city, Kummuh.[20]

Architectural remains of the Neo-Hittite period are much more limited at Malatya than they are at Carchemish, and the most interesting group of reliefs is associated with a monumental gateway which was already very much damaged before the French archaeological team excavated it.[21] These include scenes of a king whose name we render PUGNUS-mili[22] pouring libations to various gods (Figure 8.5: 1). There are probably two kings of this name, and both were descended from Kuzi-Teshub, son of Talmi-Teshub of Carchemish. Whichever these reliefs portray, their date would probably be in the late 12th or early 11th century, older than analysis of their style suggested to scholars before the connection with the Carchemish dynasty was recognized.[23] In these reliefs there appears to be a kind of narrative art being used for the first

1

2

Figure 8.5 Reliefs from the Lion Gate at Malatya: **1** PUGNUS-mili sacrificing to the Storm God (after Akurgal 1962: plate 105). **2** Gods battling monster (after Bittel 1976: fig. 279)

time in Anatolia, with the god riding up in his chariot, and then receiving the king's libations. The technique of narrative was not carried very far by the Luwians, but it probably had its influence on the Assyrians, who elaborated upon it in depictions of military campaigns. One of the reliefs shows a mythological scene of gods battling some sort of monster (Figure 8.5: 2), sometimes taken to be a depiction of the Hittite myth of the serpent Illuyanka, albeit very speculatively.

'Ain Dara

While 'Ain Dara lies just outside the borders of Turkey, it has an important contribution to make in unraveling the relationships between Anatolian and non-Anatolian elements in the Neo-Hittite tradition. It has the same configuration as Carchemish, but at a slightly smaller scale: a high mound beside a river, in this case the 'Afrin, and a large walled lower town beside it. Sherds scattered in the fields beyond the city walls hint at the existence of an outer town. Unlike Carchemish and Malatya, the ancient identity of this site is unknown, and although fragments of hieroglyphic inscriptions have been found in excavations, there are no coherent texts from the site. Neo-Assyrian texts establish that this site lay in a kingdom called both Patin(a) and Unqi, which also included the Amuq.[24] Although 'Ain Dara was clearly an important place, it was probably not the political capital, Kinalua, which is thought to be at Tell Tayinat. It was, however, the site of a temple of great importance.

The temple exhibits an interesting mix of traditions.[25] Its ground plan bears no resemblance to the Hittite temples at Boğazköy, but rather conforms to a standard arrangement that one can see developing in Syria in the Bronze Age and corresponds rather well to the Biblical description of the Temple of Solomon, which it predates. It is laid out in such a way that the approach to the holy of holies at the back of the building is a straight line from the entrance at the font, and the building has a bilateral symmetry along that axis. There is a broad porch centered on the front of building, with two gigantic column bases on either side of the entrance (Figure 8.6). From there one crosses a broad courtyard paved with large stones to a second threshold, and then another paved courtyard. At the back of this, there is a row of blocks carved in relief, on which the cult room must have been built, perhaps of wood. A raised "annex" runs along the sides and back of the temple, and there are indications that it was open to the outside at points to allow viewing of pieces of sculpture on the inner walls. Unique in the art of the Near East are meter-long human-shaped footprints carved in the entrance and the threshold between the first and second court-yards. There are a pair on the lowest step of the entrance, then a left on the next step, and across the first courtyard there is a right. It is as if a gigantic anthropomorphic god were striding into his home.

The Hittite tradition is seen in the sculptures with which the temple was decorated.[26] The row of blocks that held up the cella, now in the Aleppo Museum, are adorned with mountain gods and mixed beings with their arms elevated to support a burden. There can be no doubt about

Figure 8.6 Temple at ʿAin Dara during excavation, footprints near north arrow

their Anatolian origins, and it should be noted that this is the only place where mountain gods appear in post-imperial Hittite art. Other sculpture reinforces the Anatolian connections. The facade of the temple and the wall of the first courtyard facing the entrance were composed of gigantic lions and sphinxes placed on plinths decorated with interwoven bands (*guilloche*). The faces of these creatures were all damaged, but one complete lion and several others that were in various stages of being carved lay together not far from the temple, so one has a good idea of what they looked like (Figure 8.7). Fragments of faces found at the site have also been reassembled, and their rounded cheeks, distinctive noses, and other features bear a strong resemblance to the art of the Anatolian Plateau from the time of the Empire.

In the absence of inscriptions and with so much damage to the sculptures, the deity to whom this temple was dedicated is unknown. There is one relief of the goddess who corresponds to Ishtar/Shaushga, with both feminine and warlike characteristics.[27] This deity is represented on both the male and female sides of the procession at Yazılıkaya. But the relief is probably not the cult image that occupied the holy of holies and so cannot be confidently identified as primary subject of worship here. The dating of the ʿAin Dara temple is also problematic. Stylistically, the lions and other figures are very close to the earliest of the Carchemish sculptures, and some authorities would thus put them in the 10th century. Broken pieces of sculpture that look even earlier, some

Figure 8.7 Sphinx and lion on left of main entrance to ʿAin Dara temple

of which bear hieroglyphs, were found built into the temple ruins, and there were clearly older, if not Bronze Age versions of the temple. There was also much later rebuilding, and the temple as excavated shows many signs of rebuilding, some of which, such as a dado running around the temple base, were never completed. The temple stood open to the elements for centuries before it was filled with debris from the late first millennium BC, so its contents are of no help with the dating.

The settlement area which stretches out below the temple, however, is quite revealing about the inhabitants of the site in the Iron Age.[28] All of the pottery and small finds unearthed there are very much in the dominant tradition of Syria and the nearby Amuq plain. The sequence of ceramic changes here, such as a shift from monochrome painted pottery to red burnished and bichrome wares, are familiar to any archaeologist working in the Iron Age Levant. The only inscribed objects so far discovered are Egyptian scarabs. The Luwian elements of the temple facade do not seem to be reflected in any way in the material culture of the lower town in the Iron Age.

Zincirli

Zincirli, ancient Sam'al, offers a contrastive example of the mixing of Aramean and Neo-Hittite traditions. Excavations at the site began in 1889 as the first move in the grand tradition of German archaeological exploration of the ancient Near East,[29] which was soon to be followed by long term excavations at Babylon, Boğazköy, Assur, and Uruk. The techniques of excavation used at that time can hardly be expected to meet modern standards, but a new University of Chicago project was begun at Zincirli recently, and should reveal the kind of detail that was missing in the earlier work.

The site lies in a valley on the edge of the Amanus Mountains, very near the northern end of the Great Rift that includes the Orontes Valley, the Dead Sea, and stretches through Africa to Olduvai Gorge. The city plan is striking: A somewhat oblong citadel mound, 240 × 335 m slightly off-center in an area marked out by a nearly circular double wall 720 m in diameter.[30] The latter looks as if it were laid out by a draftsman using a compass—with regularly placed buttresses and three symmetrically located city gates (Figure 8.8: 1).

The architecture of the citadel is distinguished by palatial buildings of a form that has come to be designated *bīt hilāni*, thanks to the use of this term in Assyrian texts for a "Hittite" palatial building (Figure 8.8: 2). Its essence is a broad porch with one to three columns or pilasters in a single row at the front, behind which is a broad room with a hearth.[31] Additional rooms are grouped around this, but essentially it is a single building, not constructed around a courtyard or assembled in an agglutinative manner. The Neo-Assyrians recognized the *bīt hilāni* as a Syrian or "Hittite" palace, and came to use the term as a word for "portico" in their own land. It seems to have its antecedents in the Late Bronze Age, particularly at Alalakh,[32] and is as much associated with Aramean as with Neo-Hittite architecture, to the extent that they can be distinguished at all.

Zincirli is the most explicitly Aramean of the sites discussed in this chapter, so much so that a case could be made not to treat it as Neo-Hittite at all.[33] Only a signet ring with hieroglyphs giving the name of Bar-Rakib attests that Luwian writing was known here,[34] and even this king used Aramaic on another ring and all of his other monuments. Otherwise, the comparatively numerous inscriptions from the site are in West Semitic alphabetic scripts, including one discovered in 2008. Yet this only emphasizes the polyglot character of the cultural milieu in which Neo-Hittite principalities flourished. There are Luwian names attested at the site and Luwian inscriptions have been found not far away. Since all of the surviving documentation that we have comes from the 9th and 8th centuries, there is ample time to accommodate earlier, Luwian-speaking dynasties at the site, which have been hypothesized in the past, even if their existence is unproveable.[35] In any case, the distinction between Aramean and Luwian Dynasties may well be overdrawn. The linguistic affiliation of a ruler's personal name may say very little about what he actually spoke, and the language in which he composed his inscriptions was as likely to reflect political considerations as person ethnic ties. There is no particular reason to believe any of these elements were in conflict at Zincirli.

The styles of all of the sculptures found at Zincirli are far removed from the art of the Empire,

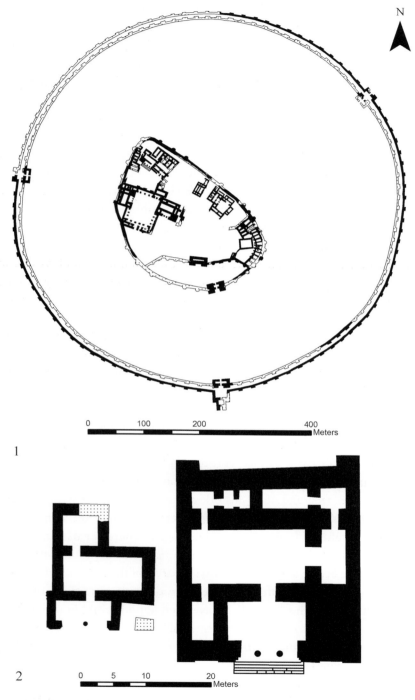

Figure 8.8 Zincirli: **1** City plan (after Wartke 2005). **2** Plans of Hilani structures on citadel (after Naumann 1971: 419)

but there are nevertheless echoes of the Hittite tradition in the subjects. One of the largest and earliest groups of orthostats was found on the southern outer city gate. The first chamber of the gate is guarded, as one might expect, by flanking lions. Along the faces of the entrance there are very crudely executed figures, only a little more than 1 m high, showing warriors, sphinxes, chariot scenes and representations of deities. These, and stylistically even earlier figures not found in situ, such as the horse rider carrying a severed head (Figure 8.9: 2),[36] are almost like cartoons. There was more monumental sculpture as well. A 3-m high statue of a ruler on a lion base found on the citadel[37] (Figure 8.9: 1) is as stiff as anything found in Near Eastern art. Later art, belonging to the 9th and 8th centuries, is much more carefully executed. The basalt portrait of a ruler who has sometimes been identified as the historically known 9th-century king Kilamuwa, although direct textual evidence for the identification is lacking, shows great detail despite its diminutive height of 50 cm (Figure 8.9: 3). A century later, Bar-Rakib's stele (Figure 8.9: 4), carved with equal care, shows strong Assyrian influence. Incidentally, the scribe who addresses him is carrying a hinged tablet, probably with wax surfaces on the inside, and a box with writing instruments: a reminder that much of the nonmonumental writing in this period was being done on perishable materials. A final phase of Zincirli's history is represented by a gigantic, and purely Assyrian, statue of the site's Assyrian conqueror, Esarhaddon.

The deities worshiped at Zincirli in the 8th century include Hadad, El, the sun god Shamash, and the moon god Ba'al Harran (Lord of the city Harran).[38] While these deities clearly have their Hittite, Luwian, and Hurrian equivalents, the terminology here gives no hint of Anatolian traditions. In sum, Zincirli is as far as anything can be from the Hittite world, and still be considered Neo-Hittite.

Karatepe

Karatepe is a fortified hilltop overlooking the Ceyhan River in northeastern Cilicia, and essentially served as a border post on an important route crossing the Taurus and connecting the Anatolian Plateau with the south. It is heavily wooded today, and the landscape around it has been transformed by the construction of a dam on the Ceyhan, but its character as a fortress is unmistakable (Figure 8.10). The site was discovered in 1946 and priority was given to excavation of two gateways in the perimeter wall, one in the north and the other in the south. These were both decorated with orthostats (Figure 8.11) and sculptures of lions and sphinxes, executed in two different styles, both quite far removed from imperial Hittite models. It has been suggested that one stylistic group of sculptures had originally adorned a 9th-century site, Domuztepe, which lay across the river.[39] The date of Karatepe itself was long disputed, but textual evidence now strongly points the late 8th–early 7th century,[40] making this one of the very last sites to produce hieroglyphic Luwian inscriptions.

Karatepe's most important contribution to modern scholarship comes from these inscriptions, for they constitute part of a substantial set of bilingual texts that was of the utmost

Figure 8.9 Sculptures from Zincirli: **1** Ruler on lion base (after Akrugal 1962: plate 126). **2** Horseman from South Gate (after Bittel 1976: fig. 297). **3** Relief of ruler of 9th century, sometimes identified as Kilamuwa (after Akurgal 1962: plate 129). **4** Bar-Rakib relief, 8th century (after Akurgal 1962: plate 131) (not to scale)

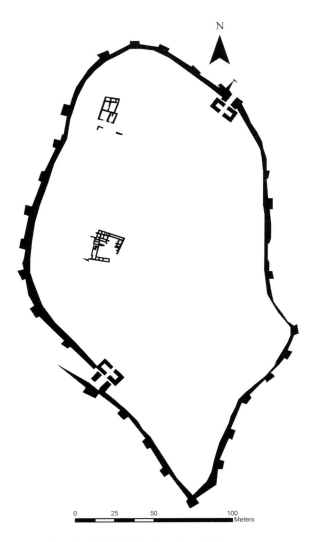

Figure 8.10 Plan of Karatepe (after Çambel 1999: plates 3 and 4)

importance in putting the decipherment of Luwian hieroglyphs on a sound footing. There are actually several inscriptions: an alphabetic Phoenician and a hieroglyphic Luwian text for each of the gates and a Phoenician text inscribed on a large statue that was found 6 m inside the south gate.[41] Before the discovery of Karatepe, the decipherment of this script had a very modest number of clues to work with. It was recognized that there were certain signs that stood for whole words, like the signs for "king" and "land," and a large number of signs that were to be read as syllables. Seals and seal impressions of the time of the Hittite empire sometimes offered short partial bilinguals by including both hieroglyphs, and well-known cuneiform signs. By trying out various values in consonant and vowel combinations, gradually and largely

Figure 8.11 Karatepe relief (after Akurgal 1962: plate 142)

independently, several scholars converged on readings that would make sense. In a stroke, the Karatepe bilinguals, which give us both by far the longest hieroglyphic inscription and a Phoenician inscription of no small importance for the study of early alphabetic writing, demonstrated the reliability of most of the readings that had been so painfully worked out.[42]

The text itself sheds some light on historical conditions in Cilicia around the time that the last filaments of the long Hittite tradition decayed into oblivion. The author of the text, whose name is now read Azatiwatas, created Karatepe and named it after himself (Azatiwataya). He had been put in power by the king of Adana, whom he calls Awariku and is generally identified with a figure known to us from Assyrian inscriptions as Urikki of Que. Azatiwatas essentially ruled as a regent of the subsequent kings of Adana.[43] He speaks of making peace with various rebels and spreading prosperity in the land, but probably did not himself rule in Adana. Karatepe does not have monuments of any subsequent rulers, and we may assume that it was abandoned not long after his rule.

Land of Tabal

The southeast central part of the Anatolian Plateau was known to the Assyrians as Tabal. It encompassed the area of Kültepe and the territory north of the Taurus, no doubt including the "Lower Land" of the former Hittite Empire. We do not know how far west it actually extended and it was not always a unified kingdom. Inscriptions from Karadağ and Kızıldağ composed by a certain Hartapus, the son of Mursili, claim the title of Great King. The dating of these is problematic, since the sculptures associated with them look stylistically late, but the writing appears to date close to the time of the Empire.[44] In any case, they are testimony to the existence

312

of a line independent of Carchemish claiming the title of Great King after the collapse of Hittite Empire. The Assyrians never penetrated this land, although they interacted with its rulers, and proximity dictated that the influence of the Phrygians, both political and cultural, would eventually be felt here. Archaeologically it has less to offer in the way of sites and monuments in the Hittite/Luwian tradition than the areas to the south and east, but it is still very much a Luwian area.

Perhaps the most celebrated Neo-Hittite relief comes from the erstwhile territory of Tabal, located on a cliff face above a stream at İvriz. It depicts a king, Warpalawas, dwarfed by the storm god Tarhunzas, to whom he pays obeisance. True to form, the god is wearing a horned helmet and kilt, but he is also holding grape vines and barley in his hands. Warpalawas is known to be a contemporary of Tiglath-Pileser III. His garments and jewellery show Phrygian traits and the rendering of his features is distinctly Assyrian—borrowings from the peoples who were to bury the Hittite tradition.

NOTES

1 For a useful review of various theories on the causes of the collapse, see Drews 1993: 33–93, who treats them in chapters headed: "Earthquakes," "Migrations," "Ironworking," "Drought," "Systems Collapse," and "Raiders" before offering his own theory of a revolution in military tactics in the remainder of the book. Dickinson 2006: 43–57 critiques the latter, adds more recent bibliography and, from the perspective of Mycenaean Greece, finds none of the traditional explanations broadly valid, but many containing aspects of the truth (p. 54)

2 Genz 2000: 38–39.

3 Genz 2000: 40–41.

4 Postgate 2007: 145.

5 When Hittite civilization first attracted the attention of European scholars, it was these monuments inscribed with hieroglyphic writing that were the focus of attention and the Hittites were regarded as an Iron Age people. The discovery of the cuneiform archives at Boğazköy made it clear that Anatolia, not Syria, and the Bronze Age, not the Iron Age, were what defined the essence of Hittite civilization. The discovery of the cuneiform archives at Boğazköy made it clear that Anatolia, not Syria, and the Bronze Age, not the Iron Age, were what defined the essence of Hittite civilization. The terminological problem has been further complicated by the recognition that the language of these hieroglyphic inscriptions is Luwian. The Assyrians and other ancient contemporaries of the Iron Age polities, however, called them Hittite, so the name is not entirely unjustified.

6 Grayson 1991: 37.

7 For a more comprehensive view of the Neo-Hittite world, two tools are essential: For inscriptions see Hawkins 2000, and for sculptures Orthmann 1971. Hawkins's corpus supersedes all previous work, and since its publication there have been few additions. While Orthmann's work is decades old, his conclusions are generally valid and no comparable overview has been produced.

8 For early references to Carchemish, and indeed an excellent overview of the history and archaeology of Carchemish generally, see Hawkins 1976–80.

9 Woolley 1952: Preface.

10 Satellite images, such as those offered by Google Earth, provide a clear view of the current status of the site at 36° 49′70″N, 38° 1′E, although the excavated areas can only be vaguely made out.

11 Woolley 1952: Preface.

12 Hawkins 1976–80: 436.

13 Hawkins 2000: 73.

14 Hawkins 2000: 73–74.

15 Hawkins 2000: 76.

16 Hawkins 2000: 76–78.

17 Designated Sph. (späthethitische) I, II, IIIa, and IIIb. See Orthmann 1971: 143–148.

18 Hawkins 1976–80: 444.

19 Hawkins 2000: 283.

20 Hawkins 2000: 283–286.

21 For a sketch plan locating the sculpture, see Orthmann 1971: 521.

22 The pronunciation of the first hieorglyph of his name is unknown, but the symbol is a clenched fist. It is customary to transcribe logograms in Hieroglyphic Luwian with their meanings in Latin as capital letters, thus "PUGNUS."

23 Hawkins 2000: 287–288. Orthmann, writing before the connection was established, tentatively dated the monuments to Sph. II, that is to say later than the earliest monuments at Carchemish (Orthmann 1971: 519–522). Bittel, in the same position, suggested a 10th- to 9th-century date (Bittel 1976: 247).

24 Assurnasirpal II marched from Hazzazu (mod. Azaz) across the river Aprê (mod. ʿAfrin) to Kunulua, the capital of Patina, which is usually thought to be Tell Tayinat, in the Amuq plain. For the text, see Grayson 1991: 217. He would have passed right beside ʿAin Dara, which is on the ʿAfrin, south of Azaz. The king he encountered was named Lubarna, clearly the same as the founder of the Hittite Old Kingdom dynasty, and testimony to the survival of Anatolian traditions here.

25 The definitive publication on the temple is Abu Assāf 1990. Since that book was published, there has been considerable restoration work at the site itself.

26 For a discussion of the "Hittite" and non-Hittite characteristics of the temple and the site of ʿAin Dara generally, see Zimansky 2002.

27 Abu Assāf 1983.

28 Stone and Zimansky 1999.

29 Wartke 2005: 7.

30 Wartke 2005: 19, 67.

31 Naumann 1971: 411.

32 Naumann 1971: 408.

33 In her extensive discussion of Luwian art and architecture, for example, Sanna Aro omits it on the ground that the monuments are written in West Semitic languages and scripts, but admits this "seems to be sort of hairsplitting" (Aro 2003: 284).

34 Hawkins 2000: 576, pl. 329.

35 Orthmann 1971: 200.

36 Orthmann 1971: 537, Taf. 55 (Zincirli A/3).

37 Orthmann 1971: 545, Taf. 62 (Zincirli E/1).

38 Wartke 2005: 86.

39 Winter 1979: 125–132. Çambel (1999: 9–12) concludes that the thesis, while stimulating, is not supported by the way the Karatepe reliefs fit together.

40 Hawkins 2000: 44.

41 The definitive publication of the Karatepe texts is Çambel 1999.

42 There was one major revision yet to come, for which the Phoenician version of the Karatepe bilingual could provide no help. Like most other early Semitic alphabets, Phoenician did not have characters for vowels, and four of the most common Luwian hieroglyphic signs were misread as vowels for many

years. In the 1970s, thanks to the discovery of some hieroglyphic inscriptions scratched on jars at Altıntepe giving well-known Urartian words for liquid capacity, the readings of these signs were corrected. The language behind the hieroglyphs was then seen to be even closer to Luwian cuneiform than previously recognized (Hawkins, Davies, and Newmann 1974).

43 Hawkins 1976–80: 410–411.
44 Hawkins 2000: 429.

9

A KINGDOM OF FORTRESSES

Urartu and eastern Anatolia in the Iron Age
(1200–600 BC)

The kingdom of Biainili, better known as Urartu, was perhaps the most powerful political entity to emerge on Anatolian soil in the pre-classical era. It did not control a territory quite as vast as the Hittite Empire, nor did it last as long, but it exhibited a stronger ability to mobilize resources and more thoroughly transformed the social, economic, and political conditions under which its subject populations lived. Ruling from Tushpa on the east shore of Lake Van, its kings controlled much of the territory that is now eastern Turkey, Armenia, and northwest Iran in the 8th and 7th centuries BC (Figure 9.1). They created an extraordinary network of fortresses and administrative centers and commanded a military establishment that rivaled Assyria. The testimony of Urartu's inscriptions, abundance of its metalwork, and scale of its architecture leave no doubt of the resplendence of this civilization.

The kingdom was also a striking anomaly in the history of the region it dominated, which is not noted for political coherence or cultural complexity. Geographic conditions would appear to militate against any kind of unity in a land where mountain chains intersect in a confused pattern of ridges and volcanic peaks. Eastern Anatolia's rivers, useless for transport, flow into a multitude of watersheds, ultimately reaching the Persian Gulf, the Black Sea, the Caspian, or the enclosed lakes Urmia and Van. Small, isolated pockets of land are found in areas where the valleys of these rivers occasionally open up, but most of the economically useful land is highland pasture. Short, dry, summers are followed by long, cold, snowy winters which limit human and animal mobility. It is not surprising that in most eras the territory that Urartu so successfully united has been characterized by low population, pastoral economies, and small settlements—if any settlements at all. In the time of the Roman Empire, and many other eras, it was a buffer zone between larger powers. For the Urartians, however, this unpromising land was the core of their polity and culture.

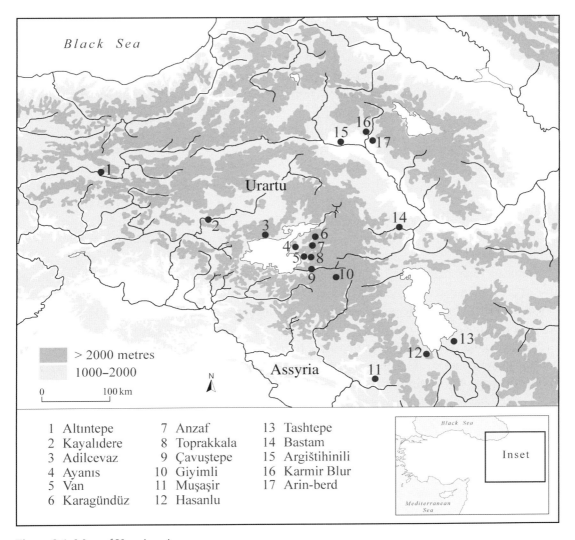

Figure 9.1 Map of Urartian sites

1 Altıntepe	7 Anzaf	13 Tashtepe
2 Kayalıdere	8 Toprakkala	14 Bastam
3 Adilcevaz	9 Çavuştepe	15 Argištihinili
4 Ayanıs	10 Giyimli	16 Karmir Blur
5 Van	11 Muşaşir	17 Arin-berd
6 Karagündüz	12 Hasanlu	

EARLY URARTU, NAIRI, AND BIAINILI

There is no simple answer to the question of where this improbable empire came from. One must distinguish between the land called Urartu, which has a long history through which it changes its geographical position somewhat, and the specific political entity that emerged around 830 BC and disappeared in the late 7th century BC. The latter was called Biainili by its own kings, but other peoples of the time, most importantly the Assyrians, called it Urartu. This is the same word modern Bibles write as Ararat; the original Hebrew did not have vowels and by the time they were put in, the original pronunciation of 'rrt had long been forgotten. "Urartian" is also routinely used today to refer both to the prevailing language and to the culture of the kingdom.

It is the geographical concept for which we first have evidence. The variants Uratri and Uruatri[1] are found in inscriptions of energetic Assyrian king Shalmaneser I (1274–1245 BC). Campaigning in the territory immediately north of Assyria, he claims to have overwhelmed a disorganized resistance:

[A]t the beginning of my vice-regency, the land Uruatri rebelled against me. I prayed to the god Aššur and the great gods, my lords. I mustered my troops (and) marched up to the mass of their mighty mountains. I conquered the lands Himme, Uatqun, Mašgun (or Bargun), Salua, Halila, Lūhu, Nilpahri (or S/Zallipahri), and Zingun–eight lands and their fighting forces; fifty-one of their cities I destroyed, burnt, (and) carried off their people and property. I subdued all of the land of Uruatri in three days at the feet of Aššur, my lord.[2]

It appears that Shalmaneser encountered a group of small, tribally organized societies, incapable of coordinated action and perhaps not entirely sedentary—a far cry from the later Iron Age kingdom. What Uruatri means geographically at this time, aside from a general location north of Assyria, is unclear.

Another geographical term of significance for this initial phase of eastern Anatolia's history is Nairi, which was invaded by another powerful Assyrian ruler, Tiglath Pileser I (1115–1077 BC). He had to cross the Euphrates and push through the mountains to reach its distant and previously unsubdued kings who lived on the shore of the Upper Sea in the west. The latter is usually assumed to be Lake Van. The upshot of the campaign sounds rather like raids into Uruatri—scores of kings are captured, cities are burned, and booty, mostly in the form of livestock, is taken back to Assyria.[3]

It is perhaps significant that the first native Urartian king to leave an inscription, writing around 830 BC in the style and language of the Assyrians, called his kingdom "Nairi." By this time, however, he was in control of a politically unified area which the Assyrians themselves were calling Urartu.

There is scant archaeological evidence for settled populations in the key area of the Lake Van basin in the 13th and 12th centuries, when the Assyrians claim to have traversed the area. Just how wild the mountains north of Assyria were before the Iron Age became clear in 1998, when 13 stelae of an unknown and unexpected type were discovered in Hakkâri (Figure 9.2). Their dating is not precisely known, but it is difficult to disagree with their discoverer's conclusion that they represent a tradition closer to the peoples of the Eurasian steppes than the Ancient Near East and probably date to some period late in the Late Bronze Age.[4]

Most of the archaeological evidence we have for the early Iron Age comes from graves, and substantial habitation sites do not appear in the Van region until the 9th century, when they arise as part of the process that culminates in the formation of the creation of Biainili's empire.[5] Cemetery sites do show a kind of cultural unity that distinguishes the Van basin from the areas

Figure 9.2 Stele from Hakkâri (after Sevin 2001: 86)

south and west of Lake Urmia. The pottery in particular shows continuity with what later came to characterize the Urartian state, in contrast to the early Iron Age gray ware traditions of northwest Iran.[6] The most extensively published of these tombs are found at Karagündüz, located in the mountains not far from Van. These consist of rectangular subterranean burial chambers containing the bones of numerous individuals—in one case as many as eighty (Figure 9.3).[7] The tombs were clearly re-entered many times, and as new interments were made, the bones of bodies previously placed here were pushed aside. Men, women, and children were all represented. The grave goods include necklaces of semi-precious stones the offerings of metal are small, but elaborate. Curiously, bronze is quite rare and the weapons, bracelets, pins, and rings that one would expect to be made of it are instead fabricated from iron.[8] There is no significant settlement of the period directly associated with this cemetery.

The Assyrians, who made numerous incursions into the highlands in the 9th century as they were re-establishing their own empire, inadvertently give us a chronology of rapidly changing social and political conditions in Nairi and Urartu. When Assurnasirpal II (883–859 BC) inaugurated his new capital at Calah (Nimrud), tribute poured in from neighboring states, among which were gifts from Gilzanu and Musasir, locations later associated with Biainili. No unified kingdom of Urartu participates in this.[9] The next Assyrian king, Shalmaneser III

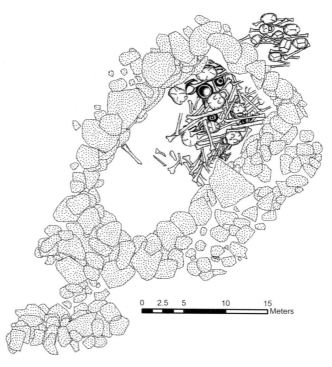

Figure 9.3 Karagunduz tomb, 9th century (after Sevin and Kavaklı 1996)

(858–824 BC) made five campaigns in the north, and in the first three of these he fought against a single opponent named Arame. He captured two of Arame's "royal cities," Arşaškun and Sagunia, neither of which has been identified archaeologically. In his 27th year, more than a decade after we last hear of Arame, Shalmaneser marched against Urartu once again, this time encountering a king whom he called Seduri. This ruler is generally felt to be Sarduri, son of Lutipri, from whom the dynasty that was to control Biainili for at least the next century was descended. He is the first Urartian king to leave any written records of his own and indeed the first ruler with whom we can associate an archaeological monument—a platform built of large stone blocks found at the northwestern foot of the 1.4-km long citadel rock at Van (Figure 9.4) The upshot of decades of Assyrian incursions into Nairi and Urartu was that power came to be concentrated in the hands dynasty ruling from a royal city at Van.[10]

Cultural innovations accompany the rise of this new state. These include new forms of art, architecture, religious expression, and language. Some of these may stem from traditional practices local to the Van basin being given more tangible expression for the first time, but others are clearly imports. The synthesis of these elements took place under the direction of the first kings of Biainili, and spread outward over eastern Anatolia and adjacent areas with in lockstep with their territorial conquests.

Figure 9.4 Van citadel from the west, with Toprakkale in the background to the left

HISTORICAL DEVELOPMENTS IN IMPERIAL BIAINILI, THE KINGDOM OF VAN

The outlines of the political history of Biainili/Urartu are provided by both native and Assyrian documents, with the latter giving the primary chronological anchors (Table 9.1). The rapid expansion of the kingdom can be traced by the spread of cuneiform inscriptions, which show where each king undertook campaigns and building projects.[11] The few inscriptions of Sarduri I are only in Van (Figure 9.5).[12] His successor, Ishpuini composed some texts in his own name, and many others jointly with his son and eventual successor, Minua. There is even one example of an Ishpuini inscription where a third generation is represented by Minua's son Inushpua, although this individual apparently died young and it is uncertain that he ever ruled as king. If it is correct to apply the principle that the inscriptions by Ishpuini are earlier than those of Ishpuini and Minua jointly, the monarchy first sought to fortify the east shore of Lake Van, and then to move into the area around Patnos, to the north. The construction of two fortresses at Anzaf, controlling the road into the Van area from the northeast was part of this effort (Figure 9.6). Sometime around 800 BC the Urartians made a thrust to the southeast, and Minua left an inscription carved into the rock of the destroyed fortress of Tashtepe, although this probably lay outside of the area that he actually sought to govern. This particular campaign, or perhaps series of

Table 9.1   Urartian king list and synchronisms with Assyrian kings

Date	Urartian kings	Assyrian kings	Events
		Assurnasirpal II (883–859)	
850 BC	Aramu ← 856 / 831 Sarduri, son of Lutipri / ca 818 Ishpuini, son of Sarduri	Shalmeneser III (858–824) / Shamshi-Adad V (833–811)	Founding of capital at Van / Assyrian decline
800 BC	Minua, son of Ishpuini / Argishti, son of Minua	Assur-nirari V (754–745)	Urartian campaigns in Iran / Expansion of Urartu in north / Founding of Erebuni
750 BC	Sarduri, son of Argishti / 743 / ? / Rusa, son of Sarduri / 714 / ? / 708 / Argishti, son of Rusa	Tiglath-Pileser III (744–727) / Sargon II (721–705)	Assyrian revival and Urartian defeat in Syria / Sargon's 8th Campaign (714) / Kimmerian invasion
700 BC	? / Rusa, son of Argishti / 673	Sennacherib (704–681) / Esarhaddon (680–669)	Massive Urartian building program
650 BC	Rusa, ? son of Erimena =? Rusa, son of? / 665 / Sarduri, son of? 639	Assurbanipal (668–627)	Last reference to an Urartian king (ca. 639) / Fall of Nineveh (612) / End of Assyrian Empire
600 BC			Medes in control of eastern Anatolia

Figure 9.5 Block in structure at foot of Van citadel with inscription of Sarduri I, in Akkadian

campaigns are historically interesting for two other reasons. First, the land known as Paršua (or Baršua) is mentioned in connection with them. This is usually taken as a very early reference to the Persians, and if so, they are either a long way from their later homeland in Fars province of Iran, or Urartians campaigned very far afield indeed. Second, this campaign may have destroyed the flourishing site of Hasanlu, where individuals executed by blows with a mace found in the ruins give testimony to the savagery of Iron Age warfare.[13]

More inscriptions of Minua survive than for any other Urartian king, and they highlight the effort he put into developing the resources of the Van area. One of his enduring feats was to bring the waters of a powerful spring to the Van basin by constructing a 50-km long canal and aqueduct which continues to operate today. Although the modern channel is now lined with concrete, the massive retaining walls that have kept it functioning for 28 centuries are still in place, as are several of the inscriptions along its course in which Minua proclaims his achievement. Minua also took his armies down the Murat Valley to the west, and went northward at least as far as the Araxes, where he constructed a city in his own name, Menuahinili.

The military achievements of the two kings who succeeded him, Argishti I and Sarduri II, respectively, are quite well documented, thanks to the survival of their annals. Those of the former are carved on the south face of the citadel rock at Van, outside an enormous

Figure 9.6 Urartian fortresses at Anzaf. Lower Anzaf in foreground, Upper Anzaf in background

multichambered rock cut tomb which was presumably the resting place of the king himself (Figure 9.7). This tomb, which is approached from above by a staircase cut in the living rock, was looted long before the modern era, but its scale made a great impression on subsequent visitors to the site. The annals themselves are not as richly descriptive as those left by Assyrian kings, but they show a very similar pattern of military activity. There was no apology or justification given for each campaign—with the support of the god Haldi, the king set out at the head of his armies at least once a year, and sometimes more often. Several lands would be conquered and at the end of each entry the quantities of prisoners and livestock taken would be listed with great precision, if not absolute honesty.[14] No defeats are acknowledged. The annual campaign was clearly an important duty of the monarch, and one assumes was important to the maintenance of the state, which would undoubtedly have had an enormous appetite for forced labor and the wherewithal to feed it, given the number of and scale of royal building projects. In one instance, for example, we are told that Argishti settled 6600 prisoners from Hatti and Supani as he founded the site Erebuni, located at Arin-berd in the modern Armenian capital of Erevan.

The founding of Erebuni and another major center at Argishtihinili (modern Armavir), which is also in the plain of Ararat, were part of a major expansion of the kingdom to the north. This proved to be the last major territorial gain for Urartu, and thereafter the area of control

Figure 9.7 Annals of Argisti I, on the face of the cliff of the Van citadel, above the stairs leading to his tomb

remained more of less stable for roughly a century. The growth of Urartu's power in the time of Minua and Argishti I was probably facilitated by Assyrian weakness in the first half of the 8th century. While undistinguished Assyrian kings campaigned "in the country" (i.e., in their own homeland) and their provincial governors usurped powers normally reserved for the king, Urartu briefly became the largest state in western Asia.

In the second half of the 8th century, the balance of power between the rival empires shifted back toward Assyria with the accession of a reformer, Tiglath-Pileser III (744–727 BC). He defeated Sarduri II in a battle on the Euphrates and ultimately marched on the Urartian capital where he claims to have set up a victory stele. These reverses do not seem to have seriously damaged Urartu, however, and from the Urartian side Sarduri II presents himself as a very successful ruler. His annals—in this case inscribed on a large stele found within a large rock niche on the north side of the Van citadel rock (Figure 9.8)—demonstrate that the pattern of annual campaigning continued. Sarduri continued to launch large construction projects, the most impressive of which was citadel of Sardurihinili (Çavuştepe) (Figure 9.9) which stretches for 1 km along a ridge in the valley of the Gürpınar, not far from Van.

Figure 9.8 Niches at Hazine Kapisi, on the north side of the Van citadel. The annals of Sarduri II were inscribed on a stele placed in the larger niche. Note the seated figure for scale

The late 8th century is perhaps the best documented period in Urartu's history, but in many ways the most confusing. A pivotal date is 714 BC. In that year Sargon II of Assyria (721–705 BC) conducted an important campaign that took him deep into Urartian territory after he defeated an Urartian king named Rusa. He left a vivid description of this campaign in a lengthy "letter" to the god Assur, which includes a description of the Urartian countryside and a detailed booty list drawn up after sacking the temple of Urartu's chief god Haldi in the buffer state of Musasir on the return journey (Figure 9.10).[15] Archaeologists have also recovered numerous intelligence reports summarizing developments in Urartu for the Assyrian court around this time, which are all the more valuable in that they were never intended for the public. These refer to dramatic events, including a catastrophic defeat for the Urartian king at the hands of the Kimmerians, a people who were to wreak destruction throughout Anatolia in succeeding decades and are mentioned here for the first time.[16]

Despite this wealth of textual evidence, most of it from Urartu's arch rival, there are problems with chronology and uncertainties about the sequence of events. Our reconstruction of the king

Figure 9.9 Walls of the western part of Çavuştepe at top of ridge, seen from the northeast

list is based on the Urartian practice of regularly giving the patronymic of a king along with his own name. For example Minua, son of Ishpuini, is succeeded by Argishti, son of Minua, who is succeeded by Sarduri, son of Argishti. Because so many Urartian sites and objects of art are associated, by inscription, with specific kings, understanding this sequence is crucial for understanding the archaeology of Urartu as well as its history. From the time of Sargon's campaign onward, we can no longer be certain of the order in which some very important Urartian kings ruled. In particular, there is currently a great deal of confusion about the sequence of three kings called Rusa (see Table 9.1). Recognition of this problem is a recent development, and the designations Rusa I (Rusa, son of Sarduri), Rusa II (Rusa son of Argishti), and Rusa III (Rusa, son of Erimena) were used confidently throughout most of the 20th century. A newly discovered inscription ties together several strands of evidence to demonstrate that Rusa III ruled before Rusa II, and perhaps even before Rusa I.[17] This uncertainty has an impact on our understanding of the final phase of Urartu's history, to which we shall return later.

Urartu clearly suffered some damage at the hands of Sargon and the Kimmerians, but this was not the end of its power by any means. In fact, its greatest days were still ahead. There does seem to be a change in Urartu's fortunes at this time. According to Sargon's annals, the king Rusa

327

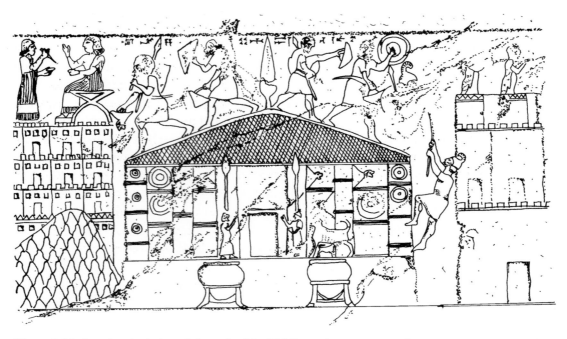

Figure 9.10 Assyrian depiction of the sack of the Haldi temple in Musasir (after drawing of lost relief from Khorsabad by Flandin, originally published by P. E. Botta, *Monument de Nineveh* (Paris: Imprimerie nationale) 1849–50)

against whom he campaigned in 714 BC was so distraught by the sack of Musasir that he committed suicide. By 708, Urartu was ruled by Argishti II, whose reign is obscure and peculiar. He does not seem have undertaken any major projects, but his few surviving inscriptions are found farther east and farther west than those of any other king: One in a tomb at Altıntepe, near Erzincan, probably on or beyond Urartu's northwestern frontier, and another halfway between Lake Urmia and the Caspian,[18] an area that reflects no Urartian cultural remains otherwise and was thus probably never integrated into the political control of the Biainili.

In contrast, Argishti's successor, traditionally called Rusa II but now understood to be the third king of that name, was probably the most powerful king Urartu ever produced. He was certainly the most energetic builder and in terms of material from controlled excavations—90% of the archaeology of Urartu is the archaeology of this Rusa.[19] The discovery of his importance has come rather gradually over the last half century, as one site after another has been excavated in Turkey, Iran, and Armenia.

One firm date for this king is provided by the Assyrian ruler Esarhaddon. He sat rather insecurely on his throne after his father, Sennacherib, had been assassinated by his elder sons, who then fled into the mountains of Shupria, another of the border states between Urartu and Assyria. In 673 BC, Esarhaddon invaded Shupria to apprehend the assassins, and presumably eliminate their claims to his throne. He clearly feared what the response of the Urartians to this campaign would be. We actually have a text in which he asks his religious advisors if Rusa, whom he says is also known as Yaya, would cause trouble about this, and his annals assure us that he returned fugitives from Urartu to Rusa in the aftermath of his campaign. There is a second Assyrian reference to a king Rusa in 655 BC, in the reign of Assurbanipal, when the latter received an embassy from Urartu. This may be a reference to Rusa son of Argishti as well.

The activities of Rusa son of Argishti would certainly suggest he had a long and prosperous reign. He built at least four major centers that we know of, and probably a great deal more. The first of these to be excavated is the ancient "City of Teisheba" at Karmir Blur (Figure 9.11). Today it lies within the city limits of the Armenian capital of Erevan, only 7 km away from Erebuni, which Argishti I had founded a century earlier. Materials in the storerooms at Karmir Blur had 8th-century artefacts with royal dedications in Erebuni, so it appears that Rusa transferred much of the material from that older site to his new center. Another major center was also created in what must have been familiar territory with the construction of Ayanis, which lies only 25 km as the crow flies from the citadel rock at Van. This site was named Rusahinili, but since another site named Rusahinili had already been built at the site of Toprakkale, near Van, the two were distinguished from each other by adding the name of a nearby mountain:

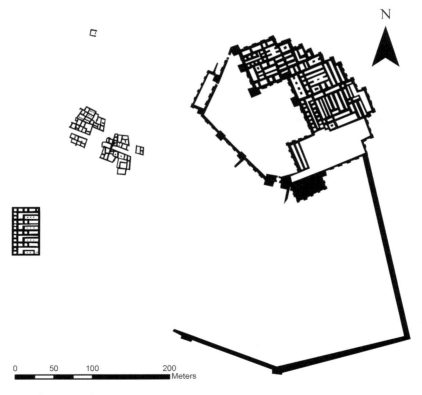

Figure 9.11 Plan of Karmir Blur

329

Rusahinili Qilbanikai ("before Mt. Qilbani") for Toprakkale and Rusahinili Eidurukai ("before Mt. Eiduru") for Ayanis. Rusa gave his name to another site located at Bastam, Iran, calling it Rusai-URU.TUR, or "Rusa's small city." Ironically, this may be the largest Urartian site ever constructed (Figure 9.12). Across Lake Van from Ayanis and Tushpa, a great citadel with an associated settlement area was also constructed at Kefkalesi, on elevated ground overlooking Adilcevaz. The only known body of monumental Urartian relief sculpture has been discovered in secondary contexts from this area, perhaps originally built into palatial and temple architecture from Kefkalesi itself, but in any case associated with inscriptions of Rusa son of Argishti. We will treat specific aspects of these sites later in more detail, but the essential historical point is that during the first half of the 7th century, Rusa the son of Argishti built the largest sites in Urartu, creating new centers in the heartland of his kingdom, and furnishing them lavishly.

Since Assyrian records of hostilities with Urartu disappear in the 7th century and Rusa himself left no annals it is sometimes assumed that this was a more peaceful era than the previous century. The discovery of a lengthy inscription on the facade of the Ayanis temple in 1997 casts doubt on this, however. While most of the text is devoted to Rusa's building activities,[20] it includes a statement that Rusa conquered the enemy lands, and deported their people. The list is impressive, beginning with the land of Assyria followed by other lands like Mushki and Hatti, which were not minor actors in the world of Iron Age Anatolia. While this list no doubt

Figure 9.12 Bastam from the east

exaggerates the extent of Biainili's power and conquests during the reign of Rusa son of Argishti, there is a clear implication that the policies of frequent campaigning and rounding up captive populations of the 8th century were still being pursued.

Archaeology makes it clear that Biainili ended violently, but the circumstances and actors in the catastrophe are unknown. Even the date is disputed over a range of approximately half a century. Rusa, son of Argishti was the last king to do any significant building or to record military conquests.[21] All of the citadels he created appear to have been violently destroyed, which is no doubt one of the reasons they have been such important archaeological sites. In their ruins have been found seal impressions of individuals who have names that sound royal: Rusa son of Rusa, Sarduri son of Rusa, etc., but these individuals bear title *asuli*, of which the significance is unknown, but does not mean king.[22] They may have been members of the royal family, but there is no evidence that they ever ruled. The last Assyrian reference to an Urartian king is provided by Assurbanipal of Assyria around 643 BC.[23] The Sarduri he mentions is a pathetic figure, begging for Assyrian favor, and no inscription or other material evidence for his existence has been discovered in Urartu.

FORTRESSES, SETTLEMENTS, AND ARCHITECTURAL PRACTICES

The material culture associated with Biainili/Urartu is almost entirely the creation of the state whose history we have just outlined.[24] Some of its features were borrowed from identifiable sources, as the Assyrian imprint on its writing and art clearly demonstrates. Other aspects are much harder to pin down, if not wholly new creations. Perhaps the most impressive accomplishments of the Urartian kings, providing the deepest insight into the civilization they governed, are seen in architecture. At all levels, from fortress building to the details of individual structures, the Urartians appear to be innovators in this sphere.

In the conditions of warfare in which the state of Biainili was formed, it is not surprising that the creation of military strongholds was the first priority of the state. Its first known site and capital was at built at Van on a spine of rock which stretches east–west for more than a mile. It is a natural fortress, presenting a vertical face on its southern side and more gradual, yet still quite precipitous slope on the north. Two deep trenches were cut through the stone of this ridge to enhance the defenses of the central part. Stone working on the citadel was not limited to fortifications, and as time went on it became crowded with cultic and mortuary structures. Little remains of the actual buildings that the Urartians erected here, but the amount of rock they hacked away to prepare foundations for them is impressive nevertheless. When possible, Urartian architects preferred to put the foundations of the walls they created directly on bedrock, and carved steps into the rock for this purpose. In addition, they prepared large horizontal surfaces at various elevations on the citadel upon which imposing buildings are presumed to have stood. Rock-cut chambers for royal tombs, in two cases approached by long staircases cut in the living rock, were made on the south side of the citadel in the course of the 8th century. The largest of these are the Argishti chambers, noted earlier, outside of which the annals of this king are carved. One area in which particularly dramatic modification of the living rock is found the north side of the citadel, were an enormous platform was carved out of the slope and two niches over 5 m tall with rounded tops were sunk into the vertical face thus created (Figure 9.8). One of these housed a stele bearing the annals of Sarduri II.[25] Running down the slope from the platform in front of these was a large grooved channel, presumably for carrying away the blood of sacrifices.

The citadel rock was the heart of ancient Tushpa (Assyrian Turušpa), the capital of of Biainili and played a role of special significance in the kingdom's history. From beginning to end, Urartian kings of claimed lordship of Tushpa as the concluding element in their titulary. Almost nothing is known of the settlement associated with this place, however. Excavations conducted on a höyük north of the citadel rock revealed some structures, but no city in the sense of a large residential area. There may be Urartian remains to the south of the citadel beneath the remains of the historic city of Van, but they are inaccessible. For an appreciation of what Urartian architects and planners created, one must look outside of the capital, to the fortresses that they erected throughout the territories they controlled.

The favored locations for construction were natural eminences that overlooked routes of communication and areas of fertile ground where irrigation could intensify agricultural productivity. These had to be high enough to be defensible, but not so high as to be isolated from the productive parts of the countryside; large enough to contain storage facilities, arsenals, and administrative buildings, but small enough to be surrounded by fortification wall. The outer walls had foundations of stone boulders rising several meters above the footings that were cut for them in bedrock. The superstructures were made of mud brick. No outer fortress wall survives to its full elevation, but depictions in art show several stories topped by crenellations and towers projecting above (Figure 9.13).[26] Wall thicknesses of 4 m and more also suggest impressive height. The walls were buttressed, sometimes with major towers at places where the angle of the wall changed. The walls of larger sites exploited the potential of the terrain, but sometimes smaller fortresses were laid out with simple rectangular plans.

The two fortresses at Anzaf were created at the end of the 9th century straddling a road approaching Van from the northeast. Lower Anzaf is the more modest of the two, but it is still very substantial, with a rectangular enclosure made of massive stones and a collection of storerooms. Upper Anzaf is a very complex site, which in its final form included buildings at several elevations, an outer town, and a massive store-room complex. On the highest point, presumably central focus of the site, was a temple with a dedicatory inscription of Minua built into one of its corners.[27]

Erebuni, in modern Erevan (to which, presumably, it gives its name), was founded by Argishti I a generation later. Here the whole citadel has been cleared and one has a good sense of its layout, despite some post-Urartian modifications. The temple lies in the heart of a compact arrangement of rows of rectangular rooms and courtyards. An inscription at its entrance records its dedication by Argishti to the otherwise unknown god Iarsha.[28] The lower parts of the walls of

1

2

Figure 9.13 Depictions of Urartian architectural elevations: **1** Bronze model of a fortress from Toprakkale now in the British Museum. **2** Stone relief from Adilcevaz bearing an inscription of Rusa, son of Argishti, now in Ankara

the temple and many of the citadel buildings are constructed of closely joined ashlar blocks, which is another characteristic of the finest Urartian buildings.

Ayanis, one of the many centers created by Rusa son of Agishti in the 7th century may serve as an example of a later Urartian site. The fortress overlooks Lake Van from a steep hill which was surrounded by a strong, regularly buttressed fortification wall. There is a monumental gateway on the southeast side, in which Rusa placed a dedicatory inscription, recording his construction of Rusahinili Eidurukai, a temple to Haldi, and agricultural works. Beside this entrance the walls are cased with carefully dressed stone. From here, one ascends through a series of court-yards whose roofs were supported by square pylons of black stone with reinforced corners. In the largest of these courtyards, near the summit of the mound is a temple of Haldi, whose facade is covered with an inscription detailing Rusa's building activities (Figure 9.14). The interior of the single room of the temple was lavishly decorated with stone inlay figures, and an alabaster podium on which the cult object once stood was incised with winged creatures and the entwined vegetation of a sacred tree design. Storerooms on the southern side of the temple area contained bronze shields, weapons, helmets, and at least one cauldron. The temple itself was adorned with bronzes, including an ornate shield with a lion head boss. Many of the objects from this area

Figure 9.14 Temple courtyard at Ayanis. Stone pylons surround main temple building (Photo: courtesy Altan A. Çilingiroğlu)

bore dedications by Rusa to Haldi. To the west of the temple complex was an area in which the excavated architecture is associated with domestic functions—clay cooking pots, bins, vats, and so forth. But luxury items such as decorative gold rosettes and carved ivory attachments fallen into these rooms indicate that elites were living upstairs. Traces of wall painting are found throughout the palace and temple area. At various places on the citadel, but particularly on its southwestern flanks, rows of long, narrow magazines stepped down the slope, each containing scores of enormous storage jars. Overall, one cannot fail to be impressed by the craftsmanship, luxury, and coordinated human effort that went into creating this citadel in the final phase of Urartu's history.[29]

Most known Urartian sites are fortresses and satellite defensive locations, not settlements. It is generally assumed that much of the population was dispersed throughout the countryside, and Sargon's letter describing his campaign against Urartu backs this up by noting scores of "settlements in the vicinity" of each fortified location he encountered. A few Urartian centers, like Karmir Blur, Bastam, and Argishtihinili (Armavir) have settlement areas outside their walls, and Ayanis is one where the variety of different types of housing are in evidence.[30] Some of the domestic structures are well planned, with stone wall bases created in exactly the same manner as they are in the fortresses. Some structures contain multiple housing units in regular blocks as if they were apartment complexes. Others, however, are ramshackle affairs in which no two walls are built in the same way. Urartu's reputation for city planning, which is based on the single dubious example of a grid-plan layout at the mysterious and probably non-Urartian site of Zernaki Tepe, is hardly reinforced by the excavations at Ayanis.

SMALLER ARTEFACTS AND DECORATIVE ARTS

The material culture and artistic traditions of Urartu must be considered in conjunction with the development of Biainili as a state. Just as we know the architecture of Urartu largely through fortresses and buildings that were built at royal command, the decorative arts and even the bulk of the mundane artefacts such as pottery, stem from the culture of government. They come into existence with the consolidation of the kingdom, and leave only shadowy vestiges after its political demise. The very media of expression in the decorative arts were bound to the upper levels of a social hierarchy, which came and went. While art from the lower levels of society tends to be ignored by students of most ancient societies, with Urartu it is particularly difficult to identify traditions that existed in the area before the state or were carried on by local populations after its demise in what might be considered a folk culture.

While some local pottery traditions of the early Iron Age, particularly a ribbed buff ware bowl, continued to be seen, a new type of red pottery appears and becomes something of a type fossil for identifying Urartian presence. Some red wares were burnished to a very high polish. This is particularly common in trefoil-shaped jugs and plates with slightly in-curving rims— essentially pottery which was used for serving food and wine. As often as not, the trefoils have hieroglyphs on their handles apparently indicating capacity. Neutron activation studies indicate that this type of pottery was generally made in the vicinity of the sites at which it is found, despite the fact that it looks the same on one side of the kingdom as the other. There are a few instances, however, at which a pot made in Bastam, for example, turns up at Ayanis.

Buried up to their shoulders in the floors of the major citadels are rows of enormous pithos jars used for storing liquids (Figure 9.15). At Karmir Blur, where virtually the whole citadel was unearthed, Piotrovsky records finding about 400 of these vessels, with a combined storage capacity of 400,000 liters.[31] At Ayanis, the largest pithoi are more than 2 m high. Many of these were marked with cuneiform, giving their capacity in the standard Urartian hierarchy of units of liquid measure: *aqarqi, terusi,* and *liš*.[32]

The sources of inspiration for Urartian figurative art lay to the south of the Taurus. When one looks at the motifs on bronzes, for example, one finds oneself in a world of sphinxes, centaurs, genii and other mixed beings who are quite familiar from the art of Assyria. The theme of winged genii fertilizing a sacred tree can be found both in the reliefs of Assurnasirpal II's Northwest Palace at Calah and on Urartian bronze helmets. It has been argued that the specific connection with Assyria has been overemphasized simply because Assyrian art is so rich and well known in comparison to the art of other parts of the Iron Age Near East. Some of the mixed beings so loved by the Urartians are also found on Babylonian objects as well. But given the clear Urartian borrowing of Assyrian writing at the time of Biainili's foundation, there is no reason to doubt a certain direct stimulation in the decorative arts.[33] Urartian art, however, never developed the narrative qualities that so distinguish Neo-Assyrian palace reliefs.

Bronzes

Urartu may have been an Iron Age society, but much of its artistic expression comes to us on bronze artefacts. There is so much bronze, in fact, that Urartu has been termed a "metalworking center," although it is the consumptive rather than the productive patterns of the kingdom that are in evidence. On the technical side, it is noteworthy that the Urartians had an ample supply of tin, which usually constitutes approximately 10% of the alloy. They also mastered the art of producing brass, which is complicated by the fact that the boiling point of zinc is lower than the melting point of copper.

The first discovered and commonly regarded as iconic pieces of statuary were part of a ceremonial throne recovered from Toprakkale.[34] They include a winged centaur with a face of stone inlay and a griffin with elaborately patterned wings. Apart from furniture fittings, bronze statues are relatively uncommon in Urartu, although the superb bronze lion head that was attached to a shield hung on the Ayanis temple deserves mention.[35]

The artistic inspiration of the Urartians is most visible in repoussé designs on belts and plaques. Bronze belts are particularly well represented. Although examples from documented excavations are relatively rare, they were apparently common in elite burials and many have

Figure 9.15 One of many magazines in the Ayanis fortress (Photo: courtesy Altan A. Çilingiroğlu)

appeared on the clandestine art market. Patterns of decoration range from simple rows of dots in several bands, to elaborate representations of mythological figures, processions, banquet scenes and city representations.[36]

A considerable number of bronze plaques were found by villagers at the site of Giyimli, south of Van, in the late 1960s and found their way into the art market. Most of these were associated with a female deity reminiscent of the Assyrian Ishtar. On some of these the official style and iconography of the Urartian court, which was highly Assyrianizing, has been hammered out by the imposition of a crude, more frontal representation of a female deity who seems to go back to an earlier local tradition, as exemplified by stone reliefs found in Hakkâri.

Not just from graves, but also from the storerooms of the major Urartian citadels come hundreds of pieces of bronze military equipment, some of it decorated with artistic motifs and much of it inscribed. Many of the bronze shields, helmets, and quivers were purely utilitarian, but they were not invariably so. Those with inscriptions frequently bear the statement "*urhiši* of RN*," where the royal names in question begin as early as Minua and end with Rusa, son of Argishti. Urishi is usually translated storehouse or magazine. There is a clear association of many of the more highly decorated pieces with temples. The celebrated Assyrian relief showing the sack of Haldi temple at Musasir shows its walls covered with bronze fittings and shields with projecting lion heads.[37] Exactly these decorations were excavated from beside the Ayanis temple.

Stone reliefs

Relief sculpture was not particularly common in Urartu, although the surviving pieces are of quite high quality. A magnificent relief of a deity standing on the back of a bull was found in a secondary context in Adilcevaz, on the north shore of Lake Van.[38] It is one of two figures that flanked a niched doorway, in all probability belonging to a temple. Its low relief and elaborately incised detail, particularly in the patterns on the garment, remind one of the art of Assyria. Large architectural blocks with reliefs of similar deities were also found at the same site, bearing inscriptions of Rusa son of Argishti. Given the quality of these reliefs, it is surprising that so few have been found, but this kind of decoration may simply be one of the many experiments in this final phase of Urartian palace building.

Seals and seal impressions

The Urartian proclivity for religious scenes is also apparent on their seals, which are known to us both as seals themselves and as seal impressions, often on tear-shaped lumps of clay that were attached to knotted cords or other objects. One particular form of seal that found general favor in Urartu was the stamp cylinder with a design cut into the sides of the cylinder that could be rolled out, and another image on the circular base of the cylinder that could be used for stamping (Figure 9.16: 1). Not all Urartian seals took this form, however, and there are numerous examples of stamp seals of various prismatic forms, including one unusual pentagonal stamp found at Bastam.[39]

Cuneiform inscriptions appear only on the seals used by kings and individuals bearing the title of *asuli* mentioned above (Figure 9.16: 2). Several royal seals of Rusa son of Argishti are known. At least three nearly identical versions show a large figure attended by a parasol bearer following in procession with a lion and a trident. Rollings of this type of royal seal have been found both at Toprakkale and Bastam.[40] Another type of royal seal of the same king has been found Ayanis: A rectangular stamp showing him under a parasol, but without attendants.[41] The inscriptions on all of these simply state "this is the seal of Rusa, son of Argishti" without giving any further titulary (Figure 9.16: 3).

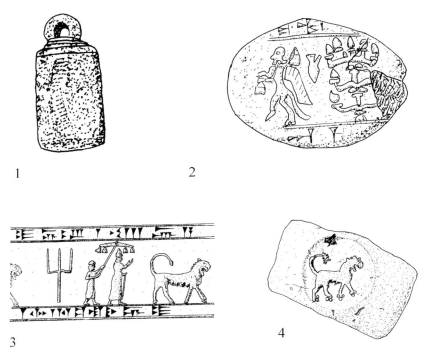

Figure 9.16 Urartian seals and seal impressions: **1** Typical stamp cylinder. **2** *Asuli* cylinder seal impression on a clay bulla. **3** Cylinder seal impression of Rusa son of Argishti, reconstructed from bullae found at Bastam. **4** Stamp impression on bulla, probably made by the end of the seal of Rusa, son of Argishti

There are two main stylistic groups of nonroyal seals: Those that are close to the royal seals in style, and those that are carved in a much cruder style. Many of the smaller stamp seals appear to have had metal mountings which leave impressions on the clay beside the main stamp. Some of these may have been used for adornment as much as sealing.

LANGUAGE AND WRITING IN URARTU

As they created their kingdom, the rulers of Biainili brought native literacy to eastern Anatolia for the first time. The source of their inspiration is clear enough: Their earliest inscriptions are in both the language and script of Assyria. It was not until the reign of Ishpuini that the Urartians began writing their own language, and they continued to use Assyrian cuneiform signs. An Urartian hieroglyphic script (Figure 9.17: 2), to all appearances not unlike Hieroglyphic Luwian, was used on pottery, seals, and bronzes, but most surviving examples of this are very short, usually single or small groups of glyphs, and provide no linguistic or historical information.[42]

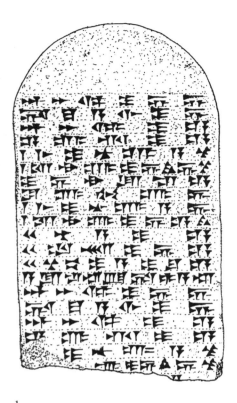

1

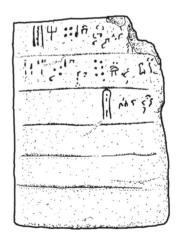

2

Figure 9.17 Urartian inscriptions: **1** Typical dedicatory stele of Minua recording the erection of a stele, now in Van Museum. **2** Hieroglyphic tablet from Toprakkale (after Wartke 1993: Taf. 86)

Because the cuneiform script used by the Urartians is essentially the same writing system employed for millennia in ancient Mesopotamia it is perfectly legible to modern scholars. Urartian scribes did not employ the full repertory of signs and tended to do most of their writing with signs pronounced as syllables rather than word signs, so their writing is not particularly complicated. Any student with training in basic cuneiform can read out an Urartian text with some confidence that he or she is approximating a correct pronunciation of the words, and thanks to the occasional sign for words like "king," "god," "city," and "palace," have a general idea of what it says.

Actually understanding the language, however, is another matter. It is not Indo-European, as Hittite and Luwian were, nor is it Semitic, like the Akkadian of the Assyrians. It has, in fact, only one close relative, Hurrian, which is not particularly well known itself. Hurrian and Urartian are perhaps to be distantly connected with modern languages of the Caucasus like Udi and Chechen, although the relationship is controversial and of no help in actually reading Urartian texts. Urartian grammar is understood in principle, but many of the details are murky.[43] Both nouns and verbs begin with a short root or stem, to which a string of suffixes are added to express grammatical details. For example, one of the numerous verbs meaning "to build" has the root *zad*, and if you want to say "he built it," you add -*u*- to indicate the verb is acting on something, and -*ni* to indicate that the actor is third person singular and the thing acted on is also singular. The language has a deeply ingrained "ergative" structure, meaning that it does not have a formal direct object in the sense that Semitic and Indo-European languages do, and that the actor or agent must me marked with a special case ending. You can get a feel for this if you regard all verbs as passive, "X is done by Y," although linguists bristle at this as an oversimplification. In any case, the actor is indicated by the ending -*še*. A particle -hi- seems to mean something like "belonging to" and is used to indicate the name of a person's father, and particle -ni- is used to separate particles in the suffix chain. So *Išpuini-še Sarduri-hi-ni-še ini* É (word sign for house, building or temple) *zad-u-ni* means "Ishpuini, son of Sarduri, built this building/temple."

Where Urartian texts repeat themselves and say simple, predictable things, we can read them; passages that are unique or complicated are only partially intelligible. One reason for our imperfect understanding is the very limited scope of the inscriptions. Almost all of the roughly 500 monumental inscriptions on stone that survive are executed in the name of the reigning king (Figure 9.17: 1). They commemorate such activities as the building of temples, digging of canals, erecting of stelae, and the ordination of sacrifices to the gods. Records of military conquests are found not only in annals, but sometimes carved into the faces of cliffs in areas where the conquests took place. In all of these royal inscriptions, there is very little creative writing—everything is in the past tense, usually in the first or third person, and the king is virtually the only actor on stage.

It is quite possible that future archaeological discoveries will alleviate some of this linguistic and historical poverty. A few dozen clay tablets and clay bullae with short handwritten cuneiform notations on them have been excavated at Urartian sites—enough to show that there were scribes actively writing letters, decrees, and economic documents. No major archive has yet been discovered, but where the tablets have been found, they are clear and well preserved. Excavation of an archive room in an Urartian citadel is a real possibility, and it would revolutionize our understanding of the Urartian language and the lives of Urartian citizens who were not kings.

URARTIAN RELIGION AND CULTIC ACTIVITIES

In all probability there was a wide variety of popular religious activity in addition to the official cult in Urartu, but it is only the latter that we know anything about. The formation of a state religion was an important step in the creation of the state of Biainili.[44] The god Haldi, whose primary cult center was at Musasir, appears in Assyrian records of the second millennium BC, but is not particularly prominent. In the reign of Ishpuini, if not earlier, he was elevated to the head of the Urartian pantheon and remained overwhelmingly the most important deity until the kingdom came to an end, after which he disappears from the historical record.[45]

The pantheon Haldi led included a few gods who are important in the Hurrian religion of the second millennium, specifically the Storm God, called Teisheba by the Urartians, and the Sun God, Shiuini (probably pronounced *Shiwini*).[46] The trio of Haldi, Teisheba, and Shiuini not only head the lists of gods in texts which ordain sacrifices, but is also invoked in the curse formulae that conclude some royal inscriptions, threatening those who damage the monument or claim it as their own. Ranking below these gods were several others who appear in multiple inscriptions and thus may be regarded as having importance in the kingdom as a whole. Scores of others, known only by name, are mentioned only once.

No Urartian Yazılıkaya has been discovered, but we get a good idea of the hierarchy from a lengthy inscription carved in an outcrop on the northern outskirts of Van. Meher Kapısı (the "Door/Gate of Mithra") as this is now known, is a false door with a frame that takes the same form as temple entrances on Urartian citadels. Within the frame is a 94-line text in which Ishpuini and Minua list quantities of animals to be sacrificed to individual gods in the month of the Sun God. The quantities and values of the animals offered to each god diminish as one moves down the list, starting with 17 bovids and 34 sheep to Haldi and finishing with individual animals for lesser gods. Below the framed text are benches and grooves carved in the rock where the animals could be sacrificed and the blood channeled off.

A unique pictorial representation of the ranking gods in anthropomorphic form appears on a fragment of a bronze shield discovered in the fortress of Upper Anzaf.[47] It shows the god Haldi impaling enemies with his *šuri*, the weapon with which he campaigns in Urartian texts (Figures 9.18 and 9.19).[48] Behind him comes a procession of gods astride animals, brandishing their own weapons. Teisheba on a lion and Shiuini on a bull are identifiable by their thunderbolts and winged sun disc, respectively, and then come other gods riding mythical animals. The identification of these is by no means certain, although the hypothesis that they follow the order of the Meher Kapısı text is not ruled out.

Meher Kapısı should not be seen as a canonical Urartian pantheon for the entire kingdom or

Figure 9.18 Bronze shield fragment from Anzaf with an inscription of Minua, showing the gods in battle (after Belli 1999; Seidl 2004: 85)

the full sweep of Urartian history, however. At other sites gods who are of minor importance or not mentioned at all on the list enjoy great prominence. For example, one of the two well-preserved temples excavated at Çavuştepe, in the heart of the citadel itself, is dedicated to the god Irmushini. He, or she, is the only named deity at this very important site[49] yet there is nothing much to distinguish him from other gods at Meher Kapısı, where he appears well down in the list. Iubsha or Iarsha, the deity of the temple at Erebuni built by Argishti I, is not mentioned on the list at all. The mountain god Eiduru is prominent at Ayanis, not unexpectedly as this mountain is used to specify the location of the site, yet he does not make the list either, even though Ayanis is not far from the cliff on which the Meher Kapısı inscription was carved. It would appear local gods were worshiped as they came to the attention of the monarchy, and that the pantheon was hardly systematized below the upper levels of its hierarchy.

The construction of temples within royal fortresses highlights the strong association of the state with religion in Urartu. One particular form of temple appears only in this context. It has a square ground plan with thick walls and reinforced corners (Figure 9.14) which suggest it took the form of a tower.[50] Near the back wall of the single room *cella* was a podium on which a cult image of some sort was presumably placed. At Ayanis there was an elaborately decorated alabaster platform in this location,[51] and in the temple Toprakkale it would appear that the first excavators in Urartu uncovered the remains of a throne.[52] Decorative schemes of the temples themselves vary, ranging from simple, unadorned ashlar masonry at Altıntepe to the elaborate

343

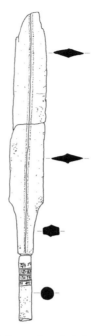

Figure 9.19 Bronze šuri (weapon) of Haldi, from Ayanis (after Seidl 2002: 92)

display at Ayanis, with an inscription covering the entire facade and inlaid animals and deities lining its interior. In any case, the embrace of church by state appears to be very close and no Urartian inscription mentions a priesthood or any other institution intervening between the king and the god.

About religious activities other than royal sacrifices, we are largely in the dark. Seals and bronzes often depict mythical creatures including protective deities, griffins, and centaurs. Fertilization of the sacred tree, a motif borrowed from Assyria, is a common theme, as is an individual standing before a seated divinity. Bronze plaques with religious themes must have something to do with a popular form of religion, albeit very obscure. Circular grooves cut into rocks on high places and elsewhere are associated with the Urartians and also speak for an aspect of religious practice that we know almost nothing about.

DEMISE

When and why did Biainili cease to exist? What enemy torched and pillaged its mighty citadels? We do not know the answer with any precision. Urartu as a geographical designation, continues to be used for some time, but there is no firm evidence that it was a political entity after 639 BC. According to the testimony of Herodotus, who had never heard of Urartu or Biainili, the Medes established their border with the kingdom of Lydia on the Halys River (Kızılırmak) in 585 BC after 5 years of war, and it seems unlikely that they would have left an Urartian state in their rear. One school of thought is that the Medes, who doubtless inherited Biainili's territory at some point, were the ones who administered the final blow to the kingdom, a few years before 590. In support of this late date, there is a reference in the book of Jeremiah, ostensibly dating to 594 BC, in which the kings of Ararat, along with the Scythians, are invoked as a force which will punish Babylon.[53] Contrariwise, we cannot be certain any Urartian document or royal building activity dates after the reign of Rusa son of Argishti, and it is hard to see how Biainili could have been an active concern for five or six decades without leaving some clear archaeological evidence of its existence.[54] If the kingdom was destroyed shortly after the middle of the 7th century, as seems likely, it would help to explain why so little memory of it survived in later historical writing. This would mean that the Scythians were the agents of destruction, and the Medes inherited nothing but ruins when they took over the territory. In the 6th century certain individuals in Mesopotamia are said to be from Urashtu, which probably just means the north. The last formal reference to it as a place is by the Achaemenid Persian king Darius I, who mentions it in the Akkadian and Elamite versions of his great trilingual inscription at Behistun, but substitutes "Armenia" in its place in the Old Persian text.

The disappearance of Urartian culture was remarkably thorough. For the most part, Urartian sites were not re-occupied—particularly those created by Rusa, son of Argishti, in the final burst of construction. When the Greek historian Xenophon passed through Urartu's erstwhile territory in 399 BC, there was little left for him to observe, and he gives no indication that he was aware that a great kingdom once existed here. A millennium or so later, the Armenian historian Moses Khorernatsi attributed the inscriptions at Van to the legendary Assyrian queen Semiramis, but he was getting his information from classical sources via Greece, not from any direct local transmission. The contrast with the Hittites, whose traditions could still be perceived five centuries after their empire collapsed, could not be stronger.

NOTES

1 The consonant renderer as *t* in these variants and the word Urartu itself was actually the equivalent of a Semitic emphatic *tet*, which is normally transcribed as at with a dot under it. Since English doesn't have this phoneme and symbols for it are absent in even the extended character sets of most word processing systems, we will follow the normal modern convention of ignoring the dot.
2 Grayson 1987: 183.
3 Grayson 1991: 21.
4 Sevin 2001: 79.
5 An overview of Early Iron Age sites in the Van area is provided by Belli and Konyar 2003.
6 Sevin 1999: 163.
7 Sevin and Kavaklı 1996: 53.
8 Sevin 1999: 162.
9 Grayson 1991: 288–293.
10 Specific sources for this are summarized in Zimansky 1985: 48–50.

11 Zimansky 1985: 48–76.

12 As this book goes to press, a new, comprehensive edition of all Urartian of texts is being published by Mirjo Salvini. The new translations, in Italian, will be conveniently organized and indexed. Therefore we have not given references to specific Urartian texts in the obsolete German and Russian collections here.

13 The end of Hasanlu IV, one of the more dramatic destruction levels in the ancient Near East, has been challenged on more than one occasion. It was originally dated to around 800 BC by its excavators, who have consistently defended that date (Dyson and Muscarella 1989) and whose arguments we find convincing. Burney and Lang 1971: 134, 145 suggest that the Urartian king might be Argishti I, which would put it a generation later. Others have opted for still later dates, and suggested that the Assyrian king Sargon II was responsible for it.

14 A table presenting the campaigns in summary, with the figures from the booty lists is given by Zimansky 1985: 58.

15 The most readily available English translation of this important document is still Luckenbill 1927: Vol 2, pp. 73–99, although more complete and up-to-date editions are in preparation.

16 Salvini 1995: 84–89 discusses the letters in question.

17 The site of Toprakkale, where the first excavations in Urartu were conducted in the 19th century AD, was long known to have been founded by a Rusa, but the Keşiş Göl stele, which records the fact, was broken and did not give his patronymic. Another fragmentary stele (Salvini 2002) from the same area, of the which the author is Rusa, son of Erimena, has now been recognized to join the Keşiş Göl stele, thanks to a duplicate which Salvini has subsequently discovered. Thus Rusa, son of Erimena, claimed to be the founder of Rusahinili (Toprakkale) and the site was a going concern in the time Rusa, son of Argishti, who therefore must come later, barring the possibility of a refounding.

18 Burney and Lang 1971: 158.

19 Zimansky 2005: 235.

20 Interestingly, it lists many places we have never heard of, but fails to mention any of the great projects like Bastam, Karmir Blur and Kefkalesi which are known from his other inscriptions. For the inscription, see Çilingiroğlu and Salvini 2001: 253–270.

21 This is assuming that Rusa, son of Erimena, ruled in the 8th century, and not in the obscure period after Rusa, son of Argishti. In addition to the evidence on the founding of Toprakkale (Rusahinili before Mt. Qilbani) noted above, the style of the art associated with Rusa son Erimena would argue for the earlier date (Seidl 2004: 124).

22 For a long time this was read [lü]A.NIN, which could be interpreted as "son of the lady" and was understood as "crown prince." The names of people bearing this title have names like Sarduri and Rusa, so this was not unreasonable. However, it is now clear that the sign for "lady" was misread, and no literal meaning comes from the new understanding of the sign. Seals of these officials regularly show winged genii fertilizing a sacred tree, and often a winged centaur on the stamping end. See Hellwag 2005 for a discussion of the reading and recognition that the holders of the title are of the royal family, but her conclusion that it means "minister of water" seems strained.

23 Salvini 1995: 111.

24 Zimansky 1995.

25 For a plan of the area, see Salvini 1995: 144.

26 For depictions on bronze belts, see Seidl 2004: 145–147. A bronze model of part of a facade shows two stories above the top of a monumental door (Wartke 1993: Taf. 28; van Loon 1966: plate 20).

27 Belli 1999: 16–28.

28 Ambiguities of the cuneiform script would also allow the reading "Iubsha" for this deity, which is the reading favored by Salvini 1995: 61.

29 A full description of the finds at Ayanis up to 1998 may be found in Çilingiroğlu and Salvini 2001. In the seasons of excavations since then, many more luxury items have been found in the storerooms of

the temple complex, including numerous bronzes, bullae and seals, but no further monumental inscriptions have been discovered.

30 Zimansky 2005.

31 Piotrovsky 1969: 140 mentions 400 pithoi but gives the capacity as only 9000 gallons, which can hardly be correct. Wartke 1993: 87 reports the capacity as 400,000 liters, which accords better with the size of the pithoi.

32 Çilingiroğlu and Salvini 2001: 308–311.

33 Seidl 2004: 207.

34 Drawings of a reconstruction, see Seidl 2004: 62–63.

35 Çilingiroğlu and Salvini 2001: 186.

36 Seidl 2004: 133–197.

37 Reproduced by Wartke 1993: 56.

38 Wartke 1993: Taf. 59.

39 Kleiss 1988: Taf. 31.

40 Kleiss 1988: Taf. 22–27.

41 Çilingiroğlu and Salvini 2001: 327.

42 A photograph of the one known tablet written in hieroglyphs, from Toprakkale, is given by Wartke 1993: Taf. 86.

43 For an up-to-date sketch of Urartian grammar, see Wilhelm 2008.

44 Salvini 1989.

45 His name appears so frequently in royal dedications and campaign inscriptions that in the early days of modern scholarship on Urartu it was erroneously believed that the Urartians called themselves the "Children of Haldi" and the Khaldaioi, a people of eastern Anatolia mentioned by Xenophon and other Greeks, were thought to retain some connection with the erstwhile state by taking the name of its chief deity. The derived terms Chaldians, Chaldian, etc., now quite obsolete, are still common enough in the literature on Urartu to cause confusion with the Chaldaeans of Babylonia, who have nothing to with Urartu.

46 Salvini 1995: 183–184.

47 Belli 1999: 34–65.

48 For many years it was believed by some scholars that a šuri was a chariot while others saw it as a sword. The dispute was settled by the discovery of a 1-m long ceremonial blade with an inscription on the handle identifying it as a šuri. See Çilingiroğlu and Salvini 2001: 172, 277.

49 The other temple at Çavuştepe has no inscription. Although it is referred to as the Haldi temple by its excavator, this is simply an assumption by default. The great majority of dedicatory inscriptions for temples in Urartu, most of which have been separated from their archaeological context, are to Haldi.

50 The ground plans of these buildings are well known thanks to the survival of their stone foundations, but how tall the buildings were and how their roofs were constructed remain controversial. The upper portions of the walls were made of mud brick, which has not survive any higher than the 3 m preserved at Ayanis. The thickness of the walls and the fact that the Urartian term used for this temple, susi, was apparently translated as "tower" in Akkadian would argue for a very tall building. It is likely that the doorways had the same proportions as the false doors of rock carvings like Meher Kapısı, which would also argue for height. On the other hand the Assyrian relief depicting the of the sack of Haldi temple at Musasir shows a building that is not particularly tall. Was the Musasir temple an Urartian susi? The bronzes found at Ayanis show that it was certainly decorated in the same manner.

51 Çilingiroğlu and Salvini 2001: 57–59.

52 There have been suggested reconstructions of this based on the finds of bronze furniture attachments that came out of various 19th-century excavations.

53 Jer 51: 27

54 Kroll 1984 makes the case for this earlier end to Urartu, which is now the prevailing scholarly view.

10

NEW CULTURES IN THE WEST

The Aegean coast, Phrygia, and Lydia (1200–550 BC)

In the course of the Iron Age, two Anatolian monarchies came to control large territories west of Urartu: The Phrygians with their capital at Gordion, succeeded by the Mermnad dynasty of Lydia, based at Sardis. The Aegean coast also saw an intensification of Greek settlement which culminated in the rise of city states like Miletus and Ephesus. These were first subjugated by the Lydians, and then, in the mid-6th century, became part of the Persian Empire, which for the first time brought the whole of Anatolia under a single sovereign, at least nominally (Figure 10.1).

In western Anatolia consideration of the transition from the Bronze to Iron Ages is colored by the rich legacy of myths, epics, and histories retroactively imposed on it by the Greek tradition. There is almost nothing in the way of contemporary written documentation, and although literacy was reintroduced with the Greek alphabet and related scripts like Phrygian, its testimony before the mid first millennium BC is quite circumscribed. The Assyrians knew little of this part of the world, which was well removed from the sphere in which they could assert their military power, and there were no native Anatolians writing in cuneiform on durable materials, as there had been in the time of the Hittite Empire or in Iron Age Urartu. Because the later historical record offered by such authorities as Homer and Herodotus is so rich, archaeologists have tended to use this to frame the questions they ask, but reconciling evidence from excavations with the historical memories of the Greeks is not always a straightforward process.

THE TROJAN WAR AS PRELUDE

Perhaps the best known episode in the history of Anatolia is the Trojan War. It configured the most remote historical horizon for the Greeks from Homer onward, who recognized it as belonging to the Bronze Age. It has provided a test case for the reconciliation of archaeology and

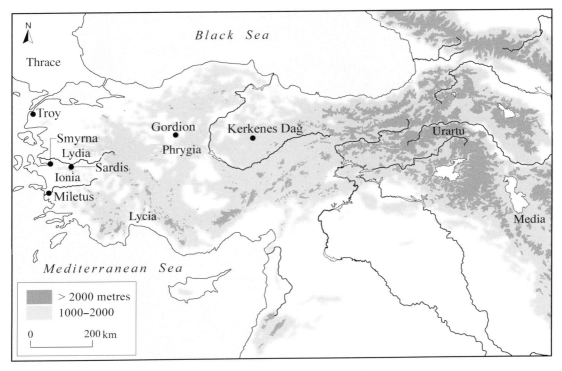

Figure 10.1 Map of western Anatolian sites of the Iron Age and Kerkenes Dağ

Greek legend from the 1870s, when Heinrich Schliemann began his excavations at Hissarlık. Despite its location on the periphery of Anatolia, Troy is the most intensively examined site in Turkey, and has been excavated over the longest period of time.

Two levels have been singled out for consideration as the remains of Homer's Troy: VI and VIIA. In some ways, the best fit for the city of the epics is Troy VI, whose prosperous citadel was occupied into the last century of Late Bronze Age. Recent exploration of the surrounding area has also identified a lower town to surrounding this citadel (Figure 10.2). This, presumably, would be the city the Hittites knew as Wilusa, which they sometimes grouped with the western Anatolian states known as Arzawa. Wilusa is a word related to an alternative Greek name for Troy, Ilion, originally written *Wilion*, of which the different endings of the Hittite and Greek variants have explanations in the grammar of the respective languages. Intriguingly, the Boğazköy archives contain a treaty drawn up with Aleksandus of Wilusa, a personal name which appears to be identical to Alexander—a name sometimes used in Greek texts as an alias for Paris, whose abduction of Helen triggered the war in the first place. The ruins of Troy VI contained significant amounts of Mycenaean pottery indicative of at least indirect exchange with the Late Bronze Age Greek world, but the archaeology of the site otherwise suggests continuity with Anatolian traditions. One can say little for certain about the ethnicity of its

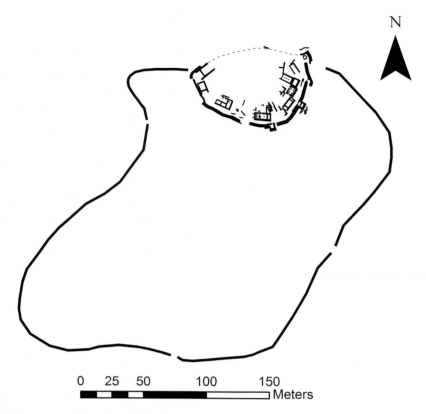

Figure 10.2 Troy VI citadel with suggested area of lower town (after Korfmann 1997–98: 370)

inhabitants in this period, for the site has failed to yield any epigraphic remains beyond a single seal with Luwian glyphs. The Hittite correspondence and treaty would suggest that literacy was not unknown there, however, and the personal names the Hittites give us could be Luwian, but are not necessarily so.[1] In any case this would be a thriving city in the right place for a confrontation with Mycenaean Greeks in the Late Bronze Age.

The case against Troy VI was argued by Carl Blegen, who led an important American expedition which worked at the site in the 1930s. He saw the destruction of Troy VI as the result of an earthquake, and thought that the level which followed without a cultural break and was thoroughly destroyed by fire, Troy VIIA, was a better candidate for the victim of a siege.[2] The dating of this level, in the early 12th century, would put it in the era of the Sea Peoples and the chaos of the collapsing Hittite Empire.

In any event, the reality of the Trojan War, if it took place at all, was imperfectly reflected in the verses of Homer, which were composed in the Iron Age centuries after the collapse of the Bronze Age world. Homer knew enough about the existence of the Bronze Age not to have his heroes armed with the weapons of his own era, but such matters as how chariots functioned on a battlefield were lost on him. The Bronze Age states of Arzawa and the existence of the Hittites had been entirely forgotten; neither did he have any conception of the literate and bureaucratic aspects of the Mycenaean polities which were their contemporaries. At the end of the second book of the Iliad, there is a list of the Trojan allies, in other words the peoples who opposed the Achaean attackers, among whom are the Thracians, Phrygians, Lycians and Carians. The principle of a coalition of west Anatolian forces may go back to a Bronze Age tradition, but the list itself, with its total ignorance of the Hittites and the powers of their day, reflects the changed world of the Iron Age.[3]

Troy VIIB, of which the first subphase is largely remains carried over from the conflagration that ended VIIA, contains pottery of the Mycenaean IIIC style, which is widely spread in sites of the Levant in levels following the destructions at the end of the Bronze Age. At Troy, but not elsewhere in Anatolia, a type of pottery known as "knobbed ware," which has its closest parallels across the Hellespont in Europe, also appears.[4] While it is difficult to be precise about exactly who is doing what, new peoples are clearly on the move in these obscure concluding centuries of the second millennium.

THE AEGEAN COAST

Greek-speaking peoples had been in contact with the Aegean coast of Turkey, if not actually residing there, in the Late Bronze Age, but the early Iron Age saw a migration to this area on a completely different order of magnitude. The geography of dialects is probably the best indicator of these population movements, which are otherwise difficult to date on the basis of the meager archaeological evidence. The first point to be made is that the people involved were new migrants and not simply local Mycenaeans left over from the previous era. Mycenaean Greek is most closely related to dialects in the Peloponnese, not the ones that spread in the Iron Age. By the time written records become available in the first millennium, speakers of the Ionic dialect occupy the islands and shoreline between Izmir and the Menderes (Meander) River, Aeolians were to the north of them, and Dorians to the south, so these groups occupied virtually the whole western coast of Turkey. This indicates several waves of westward migration from different locations on the Greek mainland, and its archaeological correlate is the appearance of Protogeometric pottery at sites along the Aegean Coast. At Miletus, in Ionia, the arrival of these new settlers is placed around 1050 BC or shortly afterward.[5]

After their arrival, these Hellenic populations on the western fringe of Anatolia maintained a self-consciously separate cultural identity from their inland neighbors, although there was obviously continual interaction between them. One follows the stylistic development of the pottery in the Ionian cities, for example, in terms that are familiar to all students of classical archaeology: geometric, orientalizing, black figure, red figure, etc. The archaeology of these coastal and island sites cannot be separated from developments on the Greek mainland. It is a vast and intensively studied subject, beyond the scope of this volume.

351

Nevertheless, the emergence of Ionia is a remarkable story. At some point in the 9th century the dozen primary Ionian city states, which included Miletus, Priene, Ephesus, and Chios among others, bound themselves together into a league.[6] Smyrna, which according to Herodotus, was not initially part of this league,[7] is the site that gives the best picture of what these cities looked like in their initial phases. Its heavily walled 8th-century settlement was densely packed with curvilinear houses, and by the late 7th century its core was still very much a fortified enclave (Figure 10.3).[8] Such are the beginnings of the great cities that were to create the world in which Homer actually lived, give rise to the birth of philosophy, nourish the field of historical writing, and helped create the artistic and literary traditions that still shape the western world. This book closes with the arrival of the Persians in the mid-6th century BC, when the era in which the whole of Anatolia and much of the Near East became Hellenized still lay in the future.

THE PHRYGIANS

Herodotus claims that Phrygians migrated into Asia from Europe, having originally been neighbors of the Macedonians.[9] There is usually assumed to be some truth to this statement, although specific confirmation of a link between Thrace and newcomers to central Anatolia in the early Iron Age cannot be demonstrated archaeologically.[10] The linguistic evidence is not incompatible with a European origin, although does not prove it either. Phrygian is an

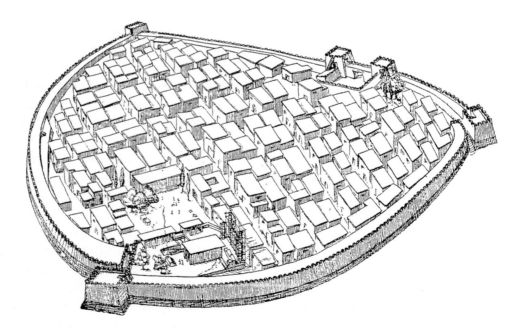

Figure 10.3 "Imaginative reconstruction" of Old Smyrna, 7th century BC (after Cook 1958–59: 15)

Indo-European language, but it is not a member of the Anatolian family to which Hittite, Luwian, and indeed Lydian belong. It is more closely related to Greek, with which it may share descent from a common sub-branch of early Indo-European.[11] There is no record of it prior to the Iron Age when the earliest inscriptions, recorded in a script that is closely related to the Greek alphabet appear in small numbers.[12] Thus the presumption that the Phrygians came into Anatolia from the west as part of the large scale migrations that took place in the Bronze Age–Iron Age transition seems reasonable, but has not been conclusively demonstrated.

There is another complication in our identification of the Phrygians archaeologically and culturally that has to do with the different perspective offered by classical and Near Eastern historical sources. We are given the term Phrygia by the Greeks, as well as two royal names which may have repeated in dynastic succession: Gordius and Midas. The Assyrians, who offer the most specific of the cuneiform sources for the period in which Phrygia was flourishing, do not mention Phrygia by name, nor do their contemporaries, the Urartians. Instead, they speak of an Anatolian kingdom called Mushki, which the Greeks, in their turn, have never heard of. Are these two names for the same place, given in the way that Europeans on all sides of the Germans have completely different terms for them, like French "Allemand" and Russian "Nemets"? Or were there really two powerful kingdoms in central Anatolia in the Iron Age, each obscuring the other from the gaze of the peoples on opposite sides?

In favor of the second theory is a very clear division in pottery types between the eastern and western parts of central Anatolia. One, first identified at Alişar is a painted pottery, with red/brown painted stags and geometric patterns on a buff surface (Figure 10.4). To the west of this, in Gordion itself, there is a quite different burnished gray ware tradition.

Against it is the fact that the most famous individual associated with each seems to have the same personal name. Mita, king of Mushki, dominated the politics of interaction with Assyria in the late 8th century, and his name sounds very much like that of the most famous ruler of Phrygia, Midas. The balance of scholarly opinion generally favors regarding Mushki and Phrygia as different terms for the same kingdom, but there are dissenters.[13] We will follow the more customary route of assuming that Phrygia and Mushki are one and the same, not least because the archaeological record is so dominated by a single site.

This key site for the archaeology of the Phrygians is Gordion, indisputably identified with Yassıhöyük, on the Sakarya River 80 km west southwest of Ankara. It is a vast archaeological complex, consisting of a citadel mound, a lower town beside it, a large and poorly defined outer town to the west, and a scattering of tumulus mounds to the north and east, the largest of which is the famous "Midas Mound." The citadel provides one of the basic chronological sequences for this region of Anatolia, its phases relevant to the Iron Age designated YHSS[14] 7 to YHSS 5, with several subphases. These were defined by Rodney Young, who directed the University of Pennsylvania's excavations here between 1950 and 1972, but refined by subsequent work of Kenneth Sams and Mary Voigt in a later phase of excavations that began in 1989. Most dramatically, in 2001, radiocarbon dates, dendrochronology, and stylistic analyses of pottery converged to push the end of YHSS 6A back to around 800 BC, more than a century earlier than Young had

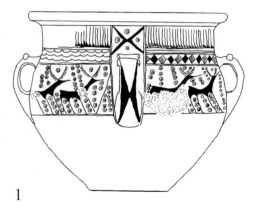

1

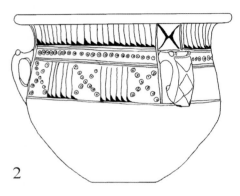

2

Figure 10.4 Alishar IV vessels from the Iron Age levels at Maşat (after T. Özgüç 1982: figs 140 (1) and 138 (2) (not to scale)

assumed, and consequently the story of Gordion and the Phrygians has been dramatically transformed (see Table 10.1).[15]

Let us review the developments at the site as we now understand them. There were both Middle and Late Bronze Age occupations on the Citadel Mound but only very small exposures have been made in them. From a limited sounding, it is possible to see that Gordion had clear cultural links to the Hittite Empire. In YHSS 8, for example, the pottery was professionally manufactured, using the wheel and favoring a few forms that were produced over and over again. Metal artefacts also appear to be of standard types for the Empire.[16] In the earliest Iron Age levels, again only exposed in a small area, there is a rather thoroughgoing change in the character of the archaeological assemblage. Undecorated, crudely formed handmade vessels predominate with a low degree of standardization. Firing temperatures appear to be lower as well. Here we are not seeing the post-imperial return to styles that prevailed before the Hittites,

Table 10.1 Key factors in the Phrygian and Gordion periods

YHSS phase	Period name	Approximate dates	Associations
5	Middle Phrygian	ca. 800–540 BC	Rebuilding and long occupation, followed by fire
6A	Early Phrygian	ca. 900–800 BC	Monumental buildings; destroyed ca. 800 BC
6B	Initial Early Phrygian	ca. 950–900 BC	Public spaces
7	Early Iron	1100–950 BC	Wattle and daub domestic architecture; hand-made unpainted pottery
9–8	Late Bronze	1400–1200 BC	Hittite imperialism

as we did at Boğazköy and Kilise Tepe, but something new, quite apart from any Anatolian traditions. The architectural remains reinforce this conclusion. Small square rooms made of wattle and daub were adjoined to create domestic structures of no great elegance or sophistication. It is hard to argue with the idea that these reflect the intrusion of a new group of people.

In the late 10th or early 9th century BC the citadel mound was dramatically restructured. In place of the simple houses, open spaces were laid out buildings of a public character were constructed. These had stone foundations and mud brick walls. No large segment of the City Mound can be seen for any of these periods, however, because they were only investigated in small areas not covered by the elaborate architecture of YHSS 6, known as the "Early Phrygian" phase.

Sometime around the middle of the 9th century BC a central authority seems to have imposed a planned series of nearly identical buildings on the whole central and eastern sector of the City Mound (Figure 10.5). The basic structural unit has a plan that has been classed as a megaron, which is to say that it consisted of a rectangular rooms in a linear arrangement with direct access from front to back through centrally placed doorways. Rows of columns helped support the roof. This basic layout was to last throughout YHSS 6, although it was subject to modification. One particular building was a little larger than the others. It had a mosaic floor and two parallel rows of columns which appear to have supported a gallery. We are without documents to inform us of what these structures were for, or even who was ruling Gordion at this time. There is some indication of an awareness of Luwian art and hieroglyphic inscriptions, but the architecture and pottery speak for a quite different culture. The particular activity that appears to be associated with these megaron buildings is weaving.[17] If these are textile factories, the industry must have organized under the auspices of the state, but we are at a loss to identify nearby trading partners who might have consumed theses products in the 9th century.

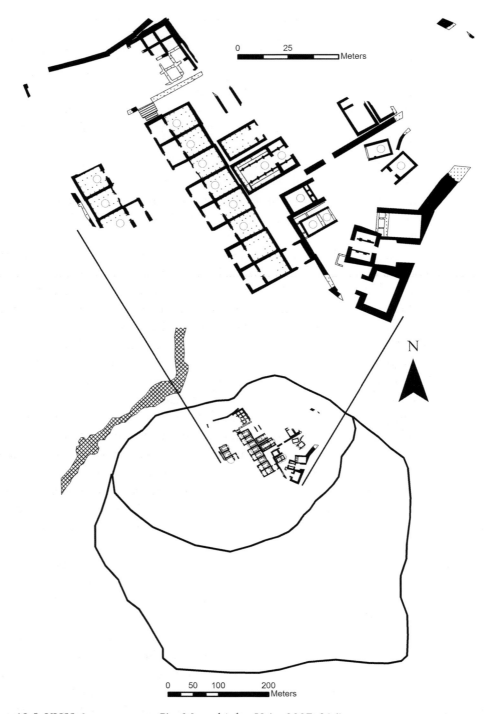

Figure 10.5 YHSS 6 megarons on City Mound (after Voigt 2007: 316)

This public architecture represents a kind of high-water mark for organization at Gordion. At the end of YHSS 6, while modest changes were being made in this area, there is a dramatic destruction level, after which much of the site was packed with a deliberate fill of debris. This seems to mark the end of a major phase of Phrygian history, but one must bear in mind that Gordion is the central and overwhelmingly dominant source of everything we know about Phrygians in this era. In order to put this destruction in context, however, we must digress to discuss some older ideas about it, which are recent enough that they are still widespread in the literature on Gordion.

Rodney Young, the excavator who did so much for the archaeology of Gordion and Phrygia generally, tied his chronological conclusions to the few known historical facts about Gordion. One of these was that the site was destroyed in the early 7th century by Kimmerians, a people we have already discussed in connection with the Urartians. There was also the prominence of Midas to contend with, in both the Greek and Assyrian traditions. Assyrian records show Mita to have been on the throne of Mushki as late as 709 BC, and, if the greatest of the tumuli around the area could not be associated with him personally, it should at least belong to the same era. Thus the destruction level of the early Phrygian city and the tumuli were all placed around the beginning of the 7th century to conform with the Kimmerian attack and the disappearance of Mushki from Assyrian records after its hours of greatness under Midas.

It should be noted that this is not an era in which radiocarbon dating could be of much help in resolving chronological issues. The span between the 8th and 4th centuries is one in which fluctuation in the amount of carbon 14 in the earth's atmosphere cancels out the rate of radioactive decay in such a way that the calibration curves are flat. An organic object that ceased to live in 750 BC contains the same amount of radiocarbon as one that died in 350 BC. Under these circumstances, dendrochronology becomes the most important tool for establishing more precise year dates, and indeed it was at Gordion that the first steps were taken toward working out a master sequence of tree rings for Anatolia—work which we have had occasion to cite on many occasions in the previous chapters. In any case, until 2001 the chronology of Early Phrgyian Gordion was discussed in late 8th-century terms, and because this was a key sequence tied, however tenuously, to historical records, much of Iron Age central and western Anatolia went with it.

Increasingly, however, there was unease about these dates. In 2000 a new set of radiocarbon samples was taken from grain in the destruction levels. Unlike wood, this would not be kept around and re-used. The upshot was that a series of reliable dates came back showing the destruction level of Early Phrygian citadel took place about a century earlier than had been thought, and is now put at ca. 800 BC.[18] This has the dramatic consequence of separating the public buildings and other clear evidence of a powerful post-Hittite state in the Early Phrygian period from the historical Midas who interacted with the Assyrians. The tumulus mounds, whose chronological position in the 8th century is secured by dendrochronological dating, no longer have anything to do with the great capital of the Dark Age. The ca. 800 BC destruction level was followed by a reorganization of the central part of the citadel mound. Many of the early structures were packed with a clay fill to create a platform upon which to build anew. While it was once believed that there was a period of abandonment of more that a century between the destruction and the rebuilding, it now appears the rebuilding started immediately.[19] The subsequent Middle Phrygian phase was a very long-lasting occupation and it, too, ended in a fire dating to around the time that the Persians came to Gordion in the mid-6th century BC. By this time Gordion had already come under the control of the other great Iron Age power of western Anatolia, Lydia.

The landscape to the east of the City Mound is dotted with burial mounds of various sizes. Altogether about eighty tumuli have been identified, most of which were constructed during the Middle Phrygian phase and a few even later. The most prominent of these tumuli have been designated with letters, and the three most prominent in terms of excavated materials are designated P, W, and MM (for Midas Mound). Each contained a single burial in a wooden tomb—in the case of P a 5-year-old child.[20]

The Midas Mound, as it is popularly known, is the site of one of the most celebrated archaeological discoveries of the 20th century. Royal tombs are almost invariably robbed, long before archaeologists can get to them. In those rare cases where they have escaped this fate, like the Royal Cemetery at Ur in Mesopotamia or the tomb of Tutankhamen in the Egypt's Valley of the Kings, it is because the very existence of the royal burials has been obscured. The Midas Mound is hardly a subtle feature in the landscape. Rising 53 m above the plain and with a base diameter of a little less than 300 m,[21] it is by far the largest of the tumuli at Gordion. Its bulk is composed of packed clay which has eroded to some extent over the centuries, so it must once have formed a taller and steeper cone, with the base having a somewhat smaller diameter than it does today. It was an obvious target for anyone who dreamed of tapping into the wealth of the king with the golden touch, and not a few people tried digging into it, only to be defeated by its mass. All this makes it remarkable that the burial chamber of this great tumulus remained undiscovered until 1957.

The burial chamber was constructed of wood in several phases (Figure 10.6). Outermost was an enclosure formed of whole logs on which the bark is still preserved, some of them more than 700 years old when they were cut. Within this chamber, a more elegant wooden chamber was made of finished planks. The body of a single individual was placed inside this room on a wooden bier. The anaerobic conditions created by packing the earth on top of this burial chamber led to excellent preservation, both of the structure and the materials that it contained. In particular the room was filled with wooden furniture carved with geometric designs of considerable delicacy (Figure 10.7). Another indicator of the stable conditions so far underground is the preservation of lumps of wax on three bronze bowls, into which alphabetic inscriptions had been incised.[22]

The lone occupant of this tomb, a man of average stature aged 61–65,[23] was clearly a person of great importance. It would appear that the funeral rites were performed elsewhere and the body was then brought here for interment along with an extraordinary inventory of grave goods. These included elaborately carved wooden screens and tables, a large number of metal vessels, the most spectacular of which were three large bronze cauldrons. The latter had attachments for

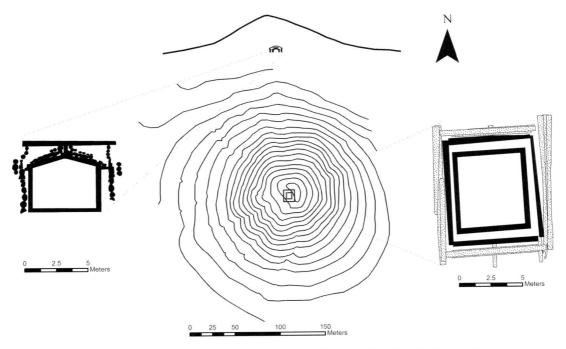

Figure 10.6 MM tumulus mound and burial chamber (after Young 1981: figs 50, 51, 61, 62)

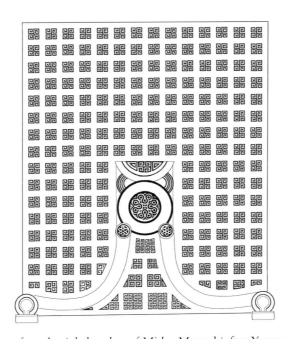

Figure 10.7 Wooden screen from burial chamber of Midas Mound (after Young 1981: fig. 104)

holding carrying rings on them in the form of bulls' heads, daemons, and sirens. The bulls' head type of cauldron was already known from an Urartian tomb excavated at Altıntepe, with which the Gordion burial is nearly contemporary. There were scores of smaller bronze vessels of various shapes: trefoil (pinched rim) pitchers, omphalos bowls,[24] rounded bowls with ring attachments, and animal-headed drinking vessels (rhyta). There were nearly 200 fibulae—elaborate safety pins for securing garments—145 of which had been wrapped together and put on a table at the foot of the bier on which the deceased lay. However, whatever textiles were included with the burial goods—and they must have been important—disintegrated before the chamber was excavated. Significantly for a royal tomb that was associated with Midas of the golden touch, there was no gold.

Who was this individual really? From the time of discovery professional opinion was that it could probably not be the Midas of Greek legend. That king was said to have died from drinking bull's blood in the wake of the Kimmerian attack (ca. 689 BC), and Rodney Young believed that a people who had just suffered a catastrophe would not have been able to build such an enormous tumulus.[25] The date of the burial chamber, which was sealed at the time of interment, has now been pushed back well into the 8th century by a combination of tree ring and radiocarbon dating. As we have noted, the latter is difficult to use in this period, but carbon samples can be taken from individual rings of 700-year sequence in the logs of the outer tomb chamber of the Midas mound. The carbon of these dates to time the living tree added the ring in its annual growth cycle. The long sequence of fluctuation can then be "wiggle-matched"—correlated with fluctuations in a master set of radiocarbon dates for the Old World generally—to match the treerings to the modern calendar. The technique is not perfect, and in 2001 researchers made the newspapers by making the Iron Age dates 22 years older than the dates they had given just a few years before.[26] The construction date is now 740 BC. This is too early for Mita of Mushki, whom we have seen was active at the end of the 8th century according to Assyrian sources. The simple fact is that we do not know who the important occupant of this tomb was, and he may not be mentioned in any historical sources.

Midas is intimately associated with another site of a quite different character. West of Gordion between the modern cities of Eskişehir and Afyon, is an area known as the Highlands of Phrygia. There are settlement mounds here which were occupied over many periods, including the periods at Gordion we have been discussing. There are also scores of tombs, shrines, and architectural facades carved into projecting rock outcrops. The grandest of these is the Midas Monument (Figure 10.8), overlooking a village with the same name as the shrine outside of Boğazköy, Yazılıkaya. The carved area is meters high and almost as wide presenting, in relief, an architectural enclosing a huge, geometric pattern of framed crosses. The design is reminiscent of some of the wooden furniture in the MM tumulus burial chamber. At the lower center is a false door and a niche. Above the roof to the left as one faces the relief, there is an inscription in large, Old Phrygian alphabetic characters. Running up the right edge of the monument is another, in somewhat smaller characters. These are not entirely intelligible, given our impoverished understanding of the Phrygian language, but it is clear that the top one mentions a dedication to

Figure 10.8 Midas Monument in the Highlands of Phrygia (Photo: courtesy Christopher Roosevelt)

Midas.[27] Since there is no evidence of scaffolding or other marks to indicate how these inscriptions might have been carved later, it is generally assumed that these inscriptions were created at the time the rest of the facade was carved, and thus it is probably a late 8th-century monument.

Graffiti in the niche appear to mention the great mother, Kybele.[28] This goddess, who was to have enormous importance as late as the time of the Roman Empire, was particularly associated with the Phrygians. Frequently represented in art flanked by lions, some have sought to see her emergence in the Neolithic figurine from Çatalhöyük (Figure 4.9: 3), and she is unquestionably Anatolian in her origins. If the Phrygians are to be considered Iron Age intruders, as Herodotus and the classical tradition would have it, they came to be remembered for their association with one of the oldest divinities of their new homeland.

THE LYDIANS

In some ways Lydia parallels Phrygia. Its archaeology is overwhelmingly known from a single site, around which are scattered tumulus mounds. In each case, its capital controlled a large territory in western Anatolia, and its kings were remembered by the Greeks as powerful monarchs. The transition between Phrygian and Lydian control at Gordion takes place in the Middle Phrygian period without a noticeable break in the archaeological record. These were, however, kingdoms of very different origins, and their similarities were probably superficial. Unlike the Phrygians, the Lydians do not appear to be new to Anatolia in the Iron Age. Although there are no well-preserved Lydian inscriptions until the fifth and fourth centuries BC, long after the kingdom had lost its independence, there is linguistic evidence enough to indicate that the language belonged to the Anatolian family within Indo-European. In other words it is a close relative of Luwian, Palaic, and Hittite, but not Phrygian. Given the very small number of texts linguists have to work with, however, is not possible to be more precise about its ancestry.[29]

The historical record on the subject of Lydia is rich, thanks largely to the *Histories* of Herodotus. Some of his best stories are found in the opening book of this masterpiece, and they are repeated with every overview of Lydia. We must restrain ourselves here, however, because Herodotus provides little useful information for the early part of the Iron Age. He claims a dynasty descended from Heracles ruled for five hundred years before the accession of Gyges, the first king for whom we have any independent evidence. One episode he reports during this span has drawn more that a little comment from later scholars, although it is probably apocryphal. In response to a prolonged famine, he tells us, the Lydians divided into two groups, one of which sailed off to Italy and came to call themselves the Tyrsenoi, that is the Etruscans.[30] Given the many mysteries surrounding the Etruscans, one of the few non-Indo-European speaking peoples in early Europe, this story has not always been rejected out of hand, although it makes no sense linguistically.

In any case, the verifiable history of the kingdom of Lydia begins in the first half of the 7th century BC, with Gyges, the founder of the Mermnad dynasty.[31] Assurbanipal records that

Gyges (Guggu), king of Lydia, sent ambassadors to the Assyrian court at Nineveh.[32] One text records that Lydia was a region on the other side of the sea and so far away that earlier Assyrian kings had not heard of it. Another says that Gyges' first messengers could not make themselves understood because their language was unknown.[33] Besides indicating that the Assyrians did not know much about Lydia, these references establish a date for the man described by Herodotus.

The line Gyges founded included four more rulers: Ardys, Sadyattes, Alyattes, and, the best known of the Lydian kings, Croesus. At the beginning of this span, Gyges had to contend with the depredations of the Kimmerians, who had by this time been ravaging Anatolia for 50 years. Herodotus's account of the rest of Lydian history focuses on the themes of the kingdom's subjugation of the Greek city-states of Ionia, and the expansion of Lydia to the east, where it confronted the Medes coming from the opposite direction. One notable event is the indecisive battle fought between the Cyaxeres, the Median king, and Alyattes. This ended with an eclipse of the sun, supposedly predicted by the first great Ionian philosopher Thales, which can be dated astronomically to 585 BC.[34] Following this, the Medes and the Lydians entered into a treaty, in which control of all of Anatolia west of the Kızılırmak went to the Lydians.

The type site for Lydian archaeology is Sardis, which was also the political capital of the kingdom. It lies 80 km inland from Izmir overlooking the valley of the Hermus River (Gediz Çayı), a major avenue of communication between the Aegean coast and the interior of Anatolia. Sherds and artefacts found out of context in the vicinity of Sardis go back as far as the Neolithic period and the earliest identified strata in the city are of the Late Bronze Age. It probably owed its existence to the commanding position of its citadel constructed on a towering crag at the edge of the Tmolus mountain range (Figure 10.9).[35] Separately fortified settlement areas surround the north and west sides of this eminence, and the Pactolus River, flowing northward to the Hermus, is a major factor in the urban topography.

American expeditions have worked at Sardis for decades, beginning with a Princeton University project before the First World War, and currently conducted by a Harvard–Cornell expedition which has been excavating almost every year since 1958. A good part of these archaeological efforts has gone into uncovering ruins, some quite spectacular, of periods that postdate the Mermnad dynasty and are thus beyond the scope of our treatment. The very scale of later building projects here, as well as a considerable amount of erosion from the slopes of the citadel, has made it difficult to get an overall view of the 7th- and 6th-century occupations that are so crucial for defining Lydia when it was a major independent civilization. Nevertheless, some key areas of Mermnad Sardis have been uncovered.

The most massive ruins of this period are a series of terraces and retaining walls on the lower slopes of the citadel. The latter are constructed of well-hewn ashlar (squared off) blocks that have inspired the suggestion that they influenced the builders of Pasargadae in the early Persian Empire.[36] There is also now a massive mud brick structure which seems to be a part of the fortification walls of the city, describing an arc well to the north of much smaller perimeter that the older city was felt to have.

Among the various places in which early Iron Age materials have been found is an excavation

Figure 10.9 Sardis citadel (Photo: courtesy Christopher Roosevelt)

area known as the "House of Bronzes." Here there is a deep stratigraphic sequence going back to the Late Bronze Age. The excavators identified three main Lydian levels, the earliest of which ends in a destruction level associated with the Kimmerians and thus Gyges, and the last with the Persian conquest.[37] A broader exposure near the Pactolus River has revealed city dwellings that seem to begin only at the very end of this sequence, suggesting that the city expanded considerably under the Mermnads.

The Lydians were renowned for their gold, the metal behind the phrase "rich as Croesus," and is is generally believed that the Lydians invented coinage. They began at some point in the 7th century with small, fixed weights or metal and eventually struck coins from units of electrum (an alloy of gold and silver). Probably before the mid-6th century they were making coins of pure elements, both silver and gold.[38] The Sardis excavations in the Pactolus North area revealed evidence for how this was refined. In an open area, roughly one hundred small hollows averaging about 20 cm in diameter were found formed in the clay ground surface. These small basins, or "cupels," were once filled with mixture of gold dust, charcoal, and lead and burned to a high temperature with a bellows. The metal would pool in the bottom of the cupel.[39]

Near this industrial area was a stone altar measuring roughly 2 × 3 m and standing 1.75 m high (Figure 10.10). It is associated with the goddess Kybele because it was adorned with sculptures of lions, the animal with which she is associated, and because a sherd with the name Kuvava (the Lydian rendering of Kybele) on it was found in its ruins. Such finds give an indication of the sorts of things that might be uncovered if the massive site of Sardis could be explored more extensively in this period.

There are several extramural cemeteries around Sardis, and as at Gordion many periods are represented. The most remarkable, however, is in the plain to the north in an area known as Bin Tepe ("1000 mounds") (Figure 10.11). Two tumuli surpass the others and have definite associations with the Mermnad Dynasty. One is associated with Gyges, and its looted burial chamber is decorated with repeated markings that might, with a stretch of the imagination, be read as symbols for GYGY. These interior walls are the earliest example of marble architecture at Sardis.[40] The other great mound, identified by Herodotus as the tomb of Ayattes, is the largest tumulus in Anatolia, surpassing even the Midas Mound in size (Figure 10.12).

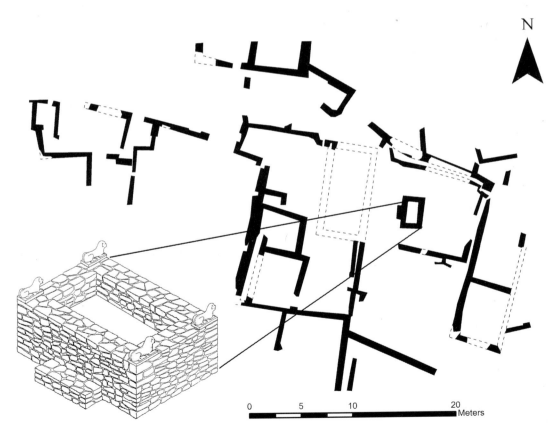

N

Figure 10.10 Kybele altar in Pactolus North area of Sardis (after Rammage and Craddock 2002: 75)

Figure 10.11 Bin Tepe (Photo: courtesy Christopher Roosevelt)

Lydian tumuli superficially resemble those at Gordion, but there are some important differences. Instead of having sealed wooden burial chambers, as the Phrygians did, the Lydian burials were essentially stone chamber tombs, with side benches and entrance ways. Again, superb workmanship on the part of stonemasons is in evidence here, and sometimes the interiors of the tombs were elaborately decorated with red, white and black painted designs. Bin Tepe is not the only place where these are found, nor were royalty the only people interred in them. Local Lydian elites constructed these tombs at various locations in the Lydian heartland.

Lydia was something of a bridging culture between the civilizations of the Near East and the Geek world. In spite of the hostilities involved in the Mermnad takeover of Ionia, one feels a distinct admiration for these kings in the writings of Herodotus. Archaeologically, East Greek and Lydian traits are so intertwined that it is often hard to tell them apart.[41] In central Anatolia the largest and best known Lydian site is Gordion, where there is no abrupt cultural break in earlier traditions to mark the arrival of the new regime.

Figure 10.12 Tomb of Alyattes (Photo: courtesy Christopher Roosevelt)

THE ACHAEMENID CONQUEST AND ITS ANTECEDENTS

On the testimony of Herodotus, the Iranian conquest of Anatolia may be conceived as having two phases: First, the expansion of the Medes into the area east of the Kızılırmak in the first half of the 6th century, and the victory of Cyrus over Croesus, which brought the Persians to the Aegean coast a generation later. Archaeology has little to contribute to this picture, for these political changes were not immediately accompanied by any dramatic transformation in material culture. The Medes, in fact, are so invisible that a case can be made that their empire was a creation of Herodotus, who assumed it must have resembled the Achaemenid Empire of his own day. The Persians were real enough, but Cyrus the Great created their vast dominions by absorbing existing empires in large blocks. His stature as a great liberator is no doubt somewhat overdrawn in Persian propaganda, but at least initially Achaemenid policy was to rule with a light hand. In Mesopotamia in 539 BC, for example, scribes simply stopped dating their tablets to the regnal year of Nabonidus, the last Babylonian king, and started dating them to Cyrus, continuing their business routines without missing a beat. It was only afterwards that new administrative structures were imposed, languages changed, and the great tradition of Meso-potamian civilization from its gods to its cylinder seals and cuneiform writing system began to wither and die. Something similar seems to have happened in Anatolia, although here the native civilizations encountered by the Iranians were less venerable and more diverse to begin with.

The political changes of the 6th century BC undoubtedly affected the site of Kerkenes Dağ, the largest pre-Hellenic site in Anatolia and in some ways the most mysterious (Figure 10.13). It lies astride a mountainous ridge 47 km southeast of Boğazköy, protected by a fortification wall whose 7-km perimeter encloses an area of 2.5 km^2 (Figure 10.14). The site has been known for roughly a century but until recently very little work was done there. It appeared to belong to a single period, and preliminary work by the University of Chicago in the 1920s established that it was post-Hittite and pre-Hellenistic. Then the site was left to itself for more than seventy years. Perhaps its very size was daunting, and there was a suspicion that its construction might never have been finished—that it might be, in essence, a hollow shell. In any case, it kept its secrets until quite recently.

For the last decade, however, Geoffrey and Françoise Summers have been conducting a technologically sophisticated project at Kerkenes Dağ which has shown this earlier neglect was

Figure 10.13 Kerkenes Dağ (Photo: courtesy Geoffrey and Françoise Summers)

Figure 10.14 City blocks of Kerkenes Dağ, as determined by remote sensing (Courtesy Scott Branting)

quite unjustified. Their team took on the whole site with a battery of remote sensing techniques, mapping its visible remains from the air and detecting its subsurface architecture. Far from being empty, the area within the walls was crowded with architectural compounds, some of them quite well appointed. Soundings revealed that it had been burned, and at least one of the major gateways in its city wall deliberately destroyed. Soon after the first trenches were opened, an ivory and gold plaque was discovered to suggest that luxury was not unknown here (Figure 10.15).

It is tempting to identify Kerkenes Dağ with ancient Pteria, a major historical site that has yet to be put on the map. Herodotus relates that Croesus, on his way to do battle with Cyrus in central Anatolia, crossed the Halys River (Kızılırmak) and entered the land of Pteria. By the treaty the Medes and Lydians had drawn up in the previous generation, this would have been Median territory. Croesus enslaved the inhabitants of Pteria's city and drove them from their homes, "though they had done him no harm."[42] If Kerkenes were Pteria it might also be something that archaeologists of eastern Anatolia and Iran have long been looking for: A full fledged Median city.

While the equation of Kerkenes and Pteria is by no means ruled out, recent excavations have shown that this cannot simply be classified as Median. No sooner had Geoffrey Summers published a paper arguing for its Iranian character[43] than he discovered the first epigraphic evidence from the site: Phrygian alphabetic inscriptions on objects of art. In a more recent publication he has argued that most of the public architecture is more reflective of western Anatolian than Median traditions.[44]

Kerkenes Dağ is a reminder of how much we still have to learn about the archaeology of ancient Turkey. Here we have an enormous creation of organized human endeavor which may well have played a significant role in key events shaping the subsequent course of civilization. We understand enough of what it contains to be able to date it, and say something about its urban layout. Discoveries at Kerkenes Dağ have followed a pattern of the archaeology of Anatolia in the Iron Age as a whole: with Herodotus as a guide, one tries to establish an historical fact, only to find complexity, contradictions, and more questions. We have learned much since Schliemann first went looking for Priam's Troy. Most of all, we have come to recognize that Turkey's archaeological riches have vastly more to tell us.

Figure 10.15 Gold and ivory attachment from Kerkenes Dağ (Photo Behiç Günel, courtesy Geoffrey and Françoise Summers)

NOTES

1 Bryce 2006: 117–122.
2 Blegen 1963: 144.
3 Bryce 2006: 127–130.
4 Belgen 1963: 169–171.
5 Greaves 2002: 77, 90.
6 Bean 1966: 22.
7 Herodotus I.143
8 Cook 1958–1959: 14–15.
9 *Histories* 7.73.
10 Tsetskhladze 2007: 304.
11 Brixhe 2008: 72.
12 The earliest Phrygian inscription, on a single sherd, appears to date to around 800 BC. The "Greco-Phrygian" forms of the letters "d" (delta) and "k" (kapa) suggest that letter shapes were borrowed from the Phoenician alphabet by the second half of the 9th century (DeVries 2007: 96–97).
13 Witke 2004.
14 Yassıhöyük Stratigraphic Sequence.
15 Table dates from Voigt 2005: 27.
16 Voigt and Henrickson 2000: 42.
17 Burke 2005.
18 There are dissenters, but one must now dismiss a great many very solid radiocarbon dates in order to hold to the traditional dating, and most of the scholars directly involved with the Gordion excavations have adopted the new chronology and re-interpreted other forms of evidence, such as ceramic chronology, to accord with it.
19 Voigt 2007: 315–324.
20 Young 1981: 9.
21 Young 1981: 79.
22 Young 1981: 273–277.
23 Young 1981: 101.
24 So named for the rounded raised projection at the center of its interior, which helped one to hold it in one's hand. This was a style of metal vessel popular in the Near East from the time of the Assyrian Empire into the Achaemenid period.
25 Young 1981: 102.
26 For the dating, see Manning et al. 2001; for press coverage, see John Noble Wilford, "So Who is Buried in Midas' Tomb?" *New York Times*, Dec. 21, 2001.
27 Berndt 2002: 9.
28 Berndt 2002: 11–14.
29 Melchert 2008: 56–57.
30 *Histories* 1.94.
31 *Histories* 1.7.
32 Luckenbill 1927: vol. 2, pp. 351–352.
33 Pedley 1968: 45.
34 Pedley 1968: 55.
35 Mellink 1987: 19.
36 Mellink 1987: 19.
37 Hanfmann 1983: 28.
38 Rammage 2000: 17–19.

39 Hanfmann 1983: 35; Rammage and Craddock 2000: 72–98.
40 Hanfmann 1983: 57.
41 Mellink 1987: 18.
42 *Histories* 1.76.
43 Summers 2000.
44 Summers 2007.

BIBLIOGRAPHY

Abay, E. (1997) *Die Keramik der Frühbronzezeit in Anatolien mit "syrischen Affinitäten"* (Altertumskunde der Vorderen Orients. Archäologische Studien zur Kultur und Geschichte des Alten Orients). Ugarit-Verlag: Münster.

Abramishvili, R. (1978) *Tbilisi: Arkheologicheskie Pamiatniki I.* Metsniereba: Tbilisi.

Abū ʿAssāf, A. (1983) Ein Relief der Kriegerischen Göttin Ischtar, *Damaszener Mitteilungen* 1: 7–8.

—— (1990) *Der Tempel von ʿAin Dārā.* (Damaszener Forschungen 3). Philipp von Zabern: Mainz am Rhein.

Adams, R. M. (1974) Anthropological perspectives on ancient trade, *Current Anthropology* 15: 239–258.

Adamthwaite, M. R. (2001) *Late Hittite Emar: The Chronology, Synchronisms, and Socio-Political Aspects of a Late Bronze Age Fortress Town* (Ancient Near Eastern Studies Supplement 8). Peeters: Louvain.

Akkermans, P. M. M. G. & Schwartz, G. M. (2003) *The Archaeology of Syria: From Complex Hunter-Gatherers to Early Urban Societies (ca. 16,000–300 BC).* Cambridge University Press: Cambridge.

Akurgal, Ekrem (1962) *The Art of the Hittites.* Thames & Hudson: London.

Albrecht, G., Albrecht, B., Berke, H., Burger, D., Moser, J., & Rähle, W., et al. (1992) Late Pleistocene and Early Holocene finds from Öküzini: A contribution to the settlement history of the Bay of Antalya, Turkey, *Paléorient* 18 (2): 123–141.

Algaze, G. (ed.) (1990) *Town and Country in Southeastern Anatolia. Vol. II: The Stratigraphic Sequence at Kurban Höyük,* 2 vols (The University of Chicago Oriental Institute Publications, Vol. 110). Oriental Institute of the University of Chicago: Chicago.

—— (1999) Trends in the archaeological development of the Upper Euphrates basin of southeastern Anatolia during the Late Chalcolithic and Early Bronze Ages, in G. del Olmo Lete and J.-L. Montero Fenollós (eds) *Archaeology of the Upper Syrian Euphrates: The Tishrin Dame Area. Proceedings of the International Symposium held at Barcelona, January 28th–30th 1998,* pp. 535–572. Editorial AUSA & Institut del Próxim Orient Antic, Universitat de Barcelona: Barcelona.

—— (2005) *The Uruk World System: The Dynamics of Expansion of Early Mesopotamian Civilization,* 2nd edn. University of Chicago Press: Chicago.

Algaze, G., Breuninger, R., & Knudstad, J. (1994) The Tigris-Euphrates archaeological reconnaissance project; final report of the Birecik and Carchemish dame survey areas, *Anatolica* 20: 1–96.

Algaze, G., Goldberg, P., Honça, D., Matney, T., Mısır, A., Rosen, A., Schlee, D. & Somers, L. (1995) Titriş Höyük: a small EBA urban center in SE Anatolia. The 1994 season, *Anatolica* 21: 13–57.

Algaze, G., Kelly, J., Matney, T., & Schlee, D. (1996) The Late EBA urban structure at Titriş Höyük, southeastern Turkey: the 1995 season, *Anatolica* 22: 129–143.

Alkım, U. B., Alkım, H., & Bilgi, Ö. (1988) *İkiztepe I. Birinci ve ikinci Dönem Kazıları. The First and Second Seasons' Excavations (1974–1975)*. Türk Tarih Kurumu Basımevi: Ankara.

—— (2003) *İkiztepe II. Üçüncü, Dördüncü, Beşinci, Altıncı, Yedinci Dönem Kazıları (1976–1980)*. Türk Tarih Kurumu Basımevi: Ankara.

Alp, S. (1968) *Zylinder- und Stempelsiegel Aus Karahöyük bei Konya* (Türk Tarih Kurumu Yayınlarından. V. dizi. sa. 26). Türk Tarih Kurumu Basımevi: Ankara.

—— (1991) *Hethitische Briefe Aus Maşat-Höyük* (Türk Tarih Kurumu Yayınları. VI. dizi. sa. 35). Türk Tarih Kurumu Basımevi: Ankara.

Alpaslan-Roodenberg, S. (2006) Death in Neolithic Ilıpınar, in I. Gatsov & H. Scwarzsenberd (eds), *Aegean–Marmara–Black Sea: Present State of Research of the Early Neolithic*. ZAKS-Monographs 5.

Ammerman, A. J. & Cavalli-Sforza, L. L. (1984) *The Neolithic Transition and the Genetics of Population in Europe*. Princeton University Press: Princeton.

Anati, E. (1968) Anatolia's earliest art, *Archaeology* 21: 22–35.

Anderson, E. W. (2000) *The Middle East: Geography and Geopolitics*. Routledge: London.

Andreeva, M. V. (1977) K voprosu o yuzhnykh svyazakh maikopskoi kul'tury, *Sovetskaya Arkheologiya* (new series) 1: 39–56.

Anthony, D. W. (2007) *The Horse, the Wheel and Language: How Bronze-Age Riders from the Eurasian Steppes Shaped the Modern World*. Princeton University Press: Princeton.

Antonova, I., Tolstikov, V., & Treister, M. (1996) *The Gold of Troy: Searching for Homer's Fabled City*. Thames & Hudson: London.

Arık, R. O. (1937) *Les Fouilles d'Alaca Höyük* (Publication de la Société d'Histoire Turque, V, Seri, No.1). Türk Tarih Kurumu Basımevi: Ankara.

Archi, A. (2003) Middle Hittite–Middle Kingdom, in G. Beckman & R. Beal McMahon (eds) *Hittite Studies in Honor of Harry A. Hoffner Jr. on the Occasion of His 65th Birthday*. Eisenbrauns: Winona Lake, IN.

Arnold, D. E. (1985) *Ceramic Theory and Cultural Process*. Cambridge University Press: Cambridge.

Aro, S. (2003) Art and architecture, in H. C. Melchert (ed.) *The Luwians* (Handbuch der Orientalistik 1/68). E. J. Brill: Leiden.

Arsebük, G., Howell, F. C., & Özbaşaran, D. N. (1992) Yarımburgaz 1990, *Kazı Sonuçları Toplantısı* 13: 1–21. T. C. Kültür Bakanlığı: Ankara.

Arututyunyan, N. V. (2001) *Korpus Urartskikh Kinoobraznykh Nadpisej*. Izdatel'stvo "gituyun" Natsional'naya Akademiya Nauk Respubliki Armeniya: Yerevan.

Aslan, C. (2006) Individual, household, and community space in Early Bronze Age Western Anatolia and the nearby islands, in E. C. Robertson, J. D. Seibert, D. C. Fernandez, & M. U. Zender (eds) *Space and Spatial Analysis in Archaeology*. University of Calgary Press: Calgary.

Asouti, E. & Fairbairn, A. (2002) Subsistence economy in Central Anatolia during the Neolithic: the archaeological evidence, in F. Gérard & L. Thissen (eds) *The Neolithic of Central Anatolia: Internal Developments during the 9th–6th Millennia Cal BC. Proceedings of the International CANeW Table Ronde, Istanbul, 23–24 November, 2001*. Ege Yayınları: Istanbul.

Atalay, S. (2005) Domesticating clay: the role of clay balls, mini balls and geometric objects in daily life at Çatalhöyük, in I. Hodder (ed.) *Changing Materialities at Çatalhöyük: Reports from the 1995–99 Seasons* (MacDonald Institute Monographs and British Institute of Archaeology at Ankara Monograph No. 39). MacDonald Institute for Archaeological Research: Cambridge.

Aurenche, O. & Kozlowski, S. K. (1999) *La naissance du Néolithique au Proche Orient ou le paradis perdu*. Editions Errance: Paris.

Avilova L. I., Antonova, E. V., & Teneishvili, T. O. (1999) Metallurgicheskoe proizvodstvo v yuzhnoi zone tsirkumpontiiskoi Metallurgicheskoi provintsii ve epokhu rannei bronzy, *Rossiiskaya Arkheologiya* 1: 51–65.

Backenofen, U. W. (1987) Palaeodemography of the Early Bronze Age cemetery of İkiztepe/Samsun, *Araştırma Sonucları Toplantısı* 2: 175–185. T. C. Kültür Bakanlığı: Ankara.

Badalyan, R. S. & Avetisyan, P. S. (2007) *Bronze and Early Iron Age Archaeological Sites in Armenia I. Mt Aragats and Its Surrounding Region* (British Archaeological Reports, International Series 1697). Archaeopress: Oxford.

Badalyan, R., Chataigner, C., & Kohl, P. L. (2004) Trans-Caucasian obsidian: the exploitation of the sources and their distribution, in A. Sagona (ed.) *A View from The Highlands: Archaeological Studies in Honour of Charles Burney* (Ancient Near Eastern Studies Supplement Series 12). Peeters: Louvain.

Badischen Landesmuseum Karlsruhe (ed.) (2007) *Vor 12.00 Jahren in Anatolien: Die ältesten Monumente der Menschheit*. Konrad Theiss Verlag: Stuttgart.

Bailey, D. W. (2000) *Balkan Prehistory: Exclusion, Incorporation and Identity*. Routledge: London.

Baird, D. (2002) Early Holocene settlement in central Anatolia: problems and prospects as seen from the Konya plain, in F. Gérard & L. Thissen, *The Neolithic of Central Anatolia: Internal Developments during the 9th–6th Millennia Cal BC. Proceedings of the International CANeW Table Ronde, Istanbul, 23–24 November, 2001*. Ege Yayınları: Istanbul.

Balkan, K. (1957) *Letter of King Anum-Hirbi of Mama to King Warshama of Kanish* (Türk Tarih Kurumu Yayınlarından VII seri, No. 31a). Türk Tarih Kurumu Basımevi: Ankara.

Balkan-Altı, N. (1994a) *Le neolithisation de l'antaolie* (Varia Anatolica 7). Institut français d'etudes anatoliennes d'Istanbul & De Boccard Edition-Diffusion: Paris.

—— (1994b) The typological characterisations of the Aşıklı Höyük chipped stone industry, in H. G. Gebel & S. Kozlowski (eds) *Neolithic Chipped Stone Industries of the Fertile Crescent. Proceedings in Early Near Eastern Production, Subsistence and Environment* 1. Ex Orient: Berlin.

Balkan-Altı, N., Binder D., & Cauvin, M.-C. (with Bıçakçı, E., Der Aprahamian, G. and Kuzucuoğlu, C.) (1999) Obsidian sources, workshops and trade in Central Anatolia, in M. Özdoğan & N. Başgelen (eds) *Neolithic in Turkey: The Cradle of Civilization. New Discoveries*. Arkeoloji ve Sanat Yayınları: Istanbul.

Bar-Yosef, O. (1994) The Lower Palaeolithic of the Near East, *Journal of World Prehistory* 8: 211–265.

Bar-Yosef, O. & Belfer-Cohen, A. (1992) From foraging to farming in the Mediterranean Levant, in A. B. Gebauer and T. D. Price (eds) *The Transition to Agriculture*. International Monographs in Prehistory: Ann Arbor.

Bar-Yosef, O. & Meadow, R. H. (1995) The origins of agriculture in the Near East, in T. D. Price and A. B. Gebauer (eds) *Last Hunters, First Farmers: New Perspectives on the Prehistoric Transition to Agriculture*. School of American Research Press: Santa Fe.

Başgelen, N. (1988) Ancient paintings see the light of day, *Image of Turkey* 16: 20–22.

Beal, R. (2003) The predecessors of Hattušili I, in G. Beckman, R. Beal, & G. McMahon (eds) *Hittite Studies in Honor of Harry A. Hoffner Jr. on the Occasion of His 65th Birthday*. Eisenbrauns: Winona Lake, IN.

Bean, G. E. (1963) *Aegean Turkey: An Archaeological Guide*. Ernest Benn: London.

Beckman, G., Goedegebuure, P., Hazenbos, J., & Cohen, Y. (2006) Hittite historical texts I, in M. W. Chavalas (ed.) *The Ancient Near East: Historical Sources in Translation*. Blackwell: Malden, MA/ Oxford.

Bednarik, R. G. (1990) On neuropsychology and shamanism in rock art, *Current Anthropology* 31: 77–80.

Behm-Blancke, M. R. (ed.) (1992) *Hassek Höyük. Naturwissenschaftliche Untersuchungen und lithische*

Industrie (Deutsches Archäologisches Institut Abteilung Istanbul, Istanbuler Forschungen 38). Ernst Wasmuth: Tübingen.

Behm-Blancke, M. R., Boesneck, J., van der Driesch, A., Roh, M. R., & Wiegand, G. (1981) Hassek Höyük: Vorläufiger Bericht über die Ausgrabungen in den Jahren 1978–1980, *Istanbuler Mitteilungen* 31: 11–94.

Behm-Blancke, M. R., Roh, M. R., Karg, N., Masch, L., Parsche, F., & Weiner, K. L., et al. (1984) Hassek Höyük: Vorläufiger Bericht über die Ausgrabungen in den Jahren 1981–1983, *Istanbuler Mitteilungen* 34: 31–150.

Belli, O. (1999a) *The Anzaf Fortresses and the Gods of Urartu.* Arkeoloji ve Sanat: Istanbul.

—— (1999b) Dams, reservoirs and irrigation channels of the Van Plain in the period of the Urartian Kingdom, in A. A. Çilingiroğlu & R. J. Matthews (eds) *Anatolian Iron Ages 4*, in *Anatolian Studies*, 49: 1–26.

—— (2001) The discovery of cave paintings in the Van region, in O. Belli (ed.) *Istanbul's University's Contributions to Archaeology in Turkey, 1932–2000.* Istanbul University Rectorate Research Fund: Istanbul.

—— (2003) Van bölgesi'ndeki yeni boyalı mağara resimleri, in M. Özbaşaran, O. Tanındı, & A. Boratav (eds) *Archaeological Essays in Honour of* Homo Amatus: *Güven Arsebük. İçin Armağan Yazılar.* Ege Yayınları: Istanbul.

—— (2006) Kars bölgesinde tarihöncesi döneme ait kayaüstü resimleri, in F. Özdem (ed.) *Kars: "Beyaz Uykusuz Uzakta".* Yapı Kredi Yayınları: Istanbul.

Belli, O. & Konyar, E. (2003) *Doğu Anadolu Bölgesi'nde Erken Demir Çağ Kale ve Nekropolleri/Early Iron Age Fortresses and Necropolises in East Anatolia.* Arkeoloji ve Sanat Yayınları: Istanbul.

Bellwood, P. S. (2005) *First Farmers: The Origins of Agricultural Societies.* Blackwell Publishing: Malden MA/Oxford.

Bellwood, P. S. & Renfrew, C. (eds) (2002) *Examining the Framing/Language Dispersal Hypothesis* (McDonald Institute Monographs). McDonald Institute for Archaeological Research, University of Cambridge: Cambridge.

Bender, B. (1978) Gather-hunter to farmer: a social perspective, *World Archaeology* 10: 204–222.

Bernabò-Brea, L. (1964) *Poliochni. Città prehistorica nell'isola di Lemnos*, Vol. I: 1, 2, (Monografie della scuola archeologica di Atene e delle missioni italiane in oriente). L'erma di Bretschneider: Rome.

Berndt, D. (2002) *Midasstadt in Phrygien: Eine Sagenumwobene Stätte im Anatolischen Hochland* (Zaberns Bildbände zur Archäologie). Philipp von Zabern: Mainz am Rhein.

Beug, H.-J. (1967) Contributions to the postglacial vegetational history of northern Turkey, in E. J. Cushing & H. E. Wright Jr. (eds) *Quaternary Paleoecology.* Yale University Press: New Haven.

Bıçakçı, E. (1995) Çayönü house models and reconstruction attempt for the Cell-plan building, in *Readings in Prehistory: Studies Presented to Halet Çambel.* Graphis: Istanbul.

—— (1998) An essay on the chronology of the Pre-Pottery Neolithic settlements of the Taurus region (Turkey) with the building remains and 14 C dates, in G. Arsebük, M. J. Mellink, & W. Schirmer (eds) *Light on Top of the Black Hill: Studies Presented to Halet Çambel.* Ege Yayınları: Istanbul.

Bieglow, L. (1999) Zooarchaeological investigations of economic organization and ethnicity at Late Chalcolithic Hacınebi: a preliminary report, *Paléoreint* 25: 83–90.

Bilgi, Ö. (1984) Metal objects from İkiztepe—Turkey, *Beiträge zur Algemeinen und Vergleichenden Archäologie* 6: 31–96.

—— (1989) Metal objects from İkiztepe—Turkey, *Beiträge zur Algemeinen und Vergleichenden Archäologie* 9–10: 119–219.

Binford, L. (1968) Post-Pleistocene adaptations, in S. R. & L. R. Binford (eds) *New Perspectives in Archaeology.* Aldine: Chicago.

Bintliff, J. L. (ed.) (1991) *The Annales School and Archaeology.* Leicester University Press: Leicester.

Bittel, K. (1941) Ein Gräberfeld er Yortan-Kultur bei Babköy, *Archiv für Orientforschung* 13: 1–28.

—— (1953) Büyükkaya, *Mitteilungen der Deutschen Orient-Gesellschaft* 86: 48–55.

—— (1955) Büyükkaya, *Mitteilungen der Deutschen Orient-Gesellschaft* 88: 24–30.

—— (1967) Karabel, *Mitteilungen der Deutsches Orientgesellschaft* 98: 1–23.

—— (1969/1970) Bemerkungen über die prähistorische Ansiedlung auf dem Fikirtepe bei Kadıköy (Istanbul), *Istanbuler Mitteilungen* 19/20: 1–19.

—— (1970) *Hattusha: Capital of the Hittites*. Oxford University Press: New York.

—— (1976) *Die Hethiter: Die Kunst Anatoliens Vom Ende Des 3. Bis Zum Anfang Des 1. Jahrtausends vor Christus*. C. H. Beck: Munich.

Bittel, K., Boessneck, J., Damm, B., Güterbock, H. G., Hauptmann, H., & Naumann, R., et al. (1975) *Das Hethitische Felsheiligtum Yazılıkaya* (Boğaköy-Hattusa Ergebnisse der Ausgrabungen IX). Gebrüder Mann Verlag: Berlin.

Blegen, C. W. (1963) *Troy and the Trojans* (Ancient Peoples and Places). Thames & Hudson: London.

Blegen, C. W., Boulter, C. G., Caskey, J. L., & Rawson, M. (1958) *Troy: Settlements VIIa, VIIb, and VIII*, Vol. IV. Princeton University Press for the University of Cincinnati: Princeton.

Blegen, C. W., Caskey, J. L., & Rawson, M. (1951) *Troy: The Third, Fourth and Fifth Settlements*, Vol. II. Princeton University Press for the University of Cincinnati: Princeton.

Blegen, C. W., Caskey, J. L., Rawson, M., & Sperling, J. (1950) *Troy: General Introduction The First and Second Settlements*, Vol. I. Princeton University Press for the University of Cincinnati: Princeton.

Bordaz, J. (1968) The Suberde excavations: an interim report, *Türk Arkeoloji Dergisi* 17.2: 43–71.

—— (1969) A preliminary report of the 1969 excavations at Erbaba, a Neolithic site near Beyşehir, Turkey, *Türk Arkeoloji Dergisi* 18.2: 59–64.

Bordaz, J. & Bordaz, L. (1982) Erbaba: the 1977 and 1978 seasons in perspective, *Türk Arkeoloji Dergisi* 26.1: 85–92.

Börker-Klähn, J. (2004) Die Leute vom Göllüldağ und im Königreich Tyana, in T. Korkut (ed.) *Anadolu'da Doğudu: 60. Yaşında Fahri Işık'a Armağan/Festschrift für Fahri Işık Zum 60. Geburtstag*. Ege Yayınları: Istanbul.

Boserup, E. (1965) *The Conditions of Agricultural Growth*. Aldine: Chicago.

Bostancı, E. Y. (1959) Researches on the Mediterranean coast of Anatolia: a new Palaeolithic site at Beldibi near Anatalya, *Anatolia* 4: 129–177.

—— (1962) A new Upper Palaeolithic and Mesolithic facies at Belbaşı rock shelter in the Mediterranean coast of Anatolia: the Belbaşı industry, *Belleten* 26 (No. 102): 252–292.

—— (1966) The Mesolithic of Beldibi and Belbaşı and the relation with the other findings in Anatolia, *Antropoloji* 3: 91–142.

Bottema, S. (1991) Dévelopment de la vegetation et du climat dans le basin méditerranéen oriental à la fin du Pleistocène et pendant l'Holocene, *L'Anthropologie* 95: 695–728.

—— (1995) Holocene vegetation of the Lake Van area: palynological and chronological evidence from Söğütlü, Turkey, *Vegetation History and Archaeobotany* 4: 187–193.

Bottema, S. & van Zeist, W. (1981) Palynological evidence for the climatic history of the Near East, 50,000–6000 BP, in J. Cauvin and P. Sanlaville (eds) *Préhistoire du Levant: chronologie et organisation de l'espace depuis les origines jusqu'au VIe millénaire: Lyon, Maison de l'Orient méditerranéen, 10–14 juin 1980*. CNRS: Paris.

Bottema, S. & Woldring, H. (1984) Late Quaternary vegetation and climate of southwestern Turkey—Part II, *Paleohistoria* 26: 123–149.

—— (1990) Anthropogenic indicators in the pollen record of the eastern Mediterranean, in S. Bottema, G. Entjes-Nieborg, & W. van Zeist (eds) *Man's Role in the Shaping of the Eastern Mediterranean Landscape: Proceedings of the INQUA/BAI Symposium on the Impact of Ancient Man on the Landscape of the Eastern Mediterranean Region and the Near East*, Groningen, Netherlands, 6–9 March 1989, pp. 231–264. A. A. Balkema: Rotterdam.

Braidwood, R. J. (1960) The agricultural revolution, *Scientific American* 203: 130–141.

Braidwood, R. J. & Braidwood, L. S. (1960) *Excavations in the Plain of Antioch*, vol. I (Oriental Institute Publications 61). Chicago University Press: Chicago.

Brain, R. (1979) *The Decorated Body*. Hutchinson: London.

Brixhe, C. (2008) Phrygian, in R. D. Woodard (ed.) *The Ancient Languages of Asia Minor*. Cambridge University Press: Cambridge.

Broodbank, C. & Strasser, T. F. (1991) Migrant farmers and the Neolithic colonisation of Crete, *Antiquity* 65: 233–245.

Brown, G. H. (1967) Prehistoric pottery from the Antitaurus, *Anatolian Studies* 17: 123–164.

Bryce, T. (2002) *Life and Society in the Hittite World*. Oxford University Press: New York.

—— (2005) *The Kingdom of the Hittites*, 2nd edn. Oxford University Press: Oxford.

—— (2006) *The Trojans and Their Neighbours*. Routledge: London.

—— (2003) History, in H. C. Melchert (ed.) *The Luwians* (Handbuch der Orientalistik 1/68). E. J. Brill: Leiden.

Budd, P. & Taylor, T. (1995) The faerie smith meets the bronze industry: magic versus science in the interpretation of prehistoric metal-making, *World Archaeology* 27(1): 133–143.

Burke, B. (2005) Textile production at Gordion and the Phrygian economy, in L. Kealhofer (ed.) *The Archaeology of Midas and the Phyrgians: Recent Work at Gordion*. The University Museum: Philadelphia.

Burney, C. A. (1989) Hurrians and Proto-Indo-Europeans: the ethnic context of the Early Trans-Caucasian Culture, in K. Emre, B. Hrouda, M. Mellink, & N. Özgüç (eds) *Anatolia and the Ancient Near East: Studies in Honor of Tahsin Özgüç*. Türk Tarih Kurumu Basımevi: Ankara.

Burney, C. A. & Lang, D. M. (1971) *The Peoples of the Hills: Ancient Ararat and Caucasus*. Weidenfeld & Nicolson: London.

Butterlin, P. (2003) *Les temps proto-urbains de Mésopotamie: Contacts et acculturation à l'époque d'Uruk au Moyen-Orient*. CNRS Éditions: Paris.

Byrd, B. F. (1994) Public and private, domestic and corporate: The emergence of the southwest Asian village, *American Antiquity* 59(4): 639–666.

Campbell, S., Carter, E., Healey, E., Anderson, S., Kennedy, A., & Whitcher, S. (1999) Emerging complexity on the Kahramanmaraş Plain, Turkey: the Domuztepe project, 1995–1997, *American Journal of Archaeology* 103: 395–418.

Çambel, H. (1999) *Corpus of Hieroglyphic Luwian Inscriptions II: Karatepe-Aslantaş*. Walter de Gruyter: Berlin/New York.

Caneva, I., Lemorini, C., & Zampetti, D. (1998) Chipped stone at aceramic Çayönü: technology, activities traditions, innovations, in G. Arsebük, M. J. Mellink, & W. Schirmer (eds) *Light on Top of the Black Hill: Studies Presented to Halet Çambel*. Ege Yayınları: Istanbul.

Caneva, I. & Sevin, V. (eds) (2004) *Mersin-Yumuktepe: A Reappraisal* (Collana del Dipartimento: Università di Lecce, Dipartimento di beni culturali1 2). Galatina: Congedo.

Canpolat, F. (ed.) (2001) *Boğazkö'den Karatepe'ye: Hititbilim ve Hitit Dünyasının Keşfi / From Boğazköy to Karatepe: Hittitology and the Discovery of the Hittite World*, 2nd edn. Yapı Kredi Yayınları: Istanbul.

Carter, E., Campbell, S., & Gauld, S. (2003) Elusive complexity: new data from late Halaf Domuztepe in south central Turkey, *Paléorient* 29.2: 117–133.

Carter, T., Conolly, J., & Spasojevic, A. (2005) The chipped stone, in I. Hodder (ed.) *Changing Materialities at Çatalhöyük: Reports from the 1995–99 Seasons* (MacDonald Institute Monographs and British Institute of Archaeology at Ankara Monograph No. 39). MacDonald Institute for Archaeological Research: Cambridge.

Cauvin, J. (1985) Le néolithique de Cafer Höyük (Turquie): bilan provisoire après quatre campagnes (1979–1983), *Cahiers de l'Euphrate* 4: 123–133.

—— (1989) La stratigraphie de Cafer Höyük-Est (Turquie) et les origines du PPNB du Taurus, *Paléorient* 15(1): 75–85.

—— (2001) *The Birth of the Gods and the Beginnings of Agriculture* (transl. T. Watkins). Cambridge University Press: Cambridge.

Cauvin, J., Aurenche, O, Cauvin, M.-C., & Balkan-Altı, N. (1999) The Pre-Pottery site of Cafer Höyük, in M. Özdoğan & N. Başgelen (eds) *Neolithic in Turkey: The Cradle of Civilization. New Discoveries.* Arkeoloji ve Sanat Yayınları: Istanbul.

Cauvin, M.-C., Gourgaud, A., Gratuze, B., Arnaud, N., Poupcau, G., & Poidevin, J.-L., et al. (1998) *L'obsidienne au Proche et Moyen Orient: du volcan a l'outil* (British Archaeological Reports, International Series 738). Archaeopress & Maison de Orient Mediterraneen: Oxford/Lyon.

Çevik, Ö. (2005) The change of settlement patterns in the lake Van basin: ecological constraints caused by highland landscape, *Altorientalische Forschungen* 32.1: 74–96.

—— (2007) The emergence of different social systems in Early Bronze Age Anatolia: urbanization versus centralisation, *Anatolian Studies* 57: 131–140.

Chataigner, C. (1995) *La Transcaucasie au Néolithique et au Chalcolithique* (British Archaeological Reports, International Series 624). Tempus Reparatum: Oxford.

—— (1998) Sources des artefacts du proche orient d'apres leur characterisation geochimique, in M.-C. Cauvin, A. Gourgaud, B. Gratuze, N. Arnaud, J. L. Poidevin, & C. Chataigner, *L'obsidienne au Proche et Moyen Orient: du volcan a l'outil* (British Archaeological Reports, International Series 738). Archaeopress & Maison de'Orient Mediterraneen: Oxford/Lyon.

Chernykh, E. N. (1992) *Ancient Metallurgy in the U.S.S.R.: The Early Metal Age.* Cambridge University Press: Cambridge.

Chernykh, E. N. & Orlovskaya, L. B. (2004a) Radiouglerodnaya khronologiya drevneyamnoi obshchnosti i istoki kurgannykh kul'tur, *Rossiiskaya Arkheologiya* 1: 84–99.

—— (2004b) Radiouglerodnaya khronologiya katakombnoi kultur'no-istoricheskoi obshchnosti (srednii bronzovyi vek.), *Rossiiskaya Arkheologiya* 2: 5–29.

Childe, V. G. (1936) *Man Makes Himself.* Watts: London.

—— (1944) Archaeological ages as technological stages, *Journal of the Royal Anthropological Society* 74: 7–24.

Childs, S. T. & Killick, D. (1993) Indigenous African metallurgy: nature and culture, *Annual Review of Anthropology* 22: 317–338.

Çilingiroğlu, A. & Abay, E. (2005) Ulucak Höyük excavations: new results, *Mediterranean Archaeology and Archaeometry* 5: 5–18.

Çilingiroğlu, A., Derin Z., Abay, E., Sağlamtımur, H., & Kayan, İ. (2004) *Ulucak Höyük: Excavations Conducted between 1995 and 2002* (Ancient Near Eastern Supplement Series 15). Peeters: Louvain.

Çilingiroğlu, A. A. & Salvini, M. (eds) (2001) *Ayanis I: Ten Years' Excavations at Rusahinili Eiduru-kai 1989–1998.* CNR Istituto per gli Studi Micenei ed Egeo-Anatolici: Rome.

Claasz Coockson, B. (2008) The house from Ilıpınar X and VI compared, in J. Roodenberg & S. Alpaslan Roodenberg (eds) *Life and Death in a Prehistoric Settlement in Northwest Anatolia: The Ilıpınar Excavations, Volume III.* Nederlands Instituut voor het Nabije Osten: Leiden.

Clottes, J. & Lewis-Williams, D. (1998) *The Shamans of Prehistory. Trance and Magic in the Painted Caves* (transl. S. Hawkes). Harry N. Abrams: New York.

Clutton-Brock, J. (ed.) (1989) *The Walking Larder: Patterns of Domestication, Pastoralism and Predation.* Unwin Hyman: London.

Colledge, S., Conolly, J. & Shennan, S. (2004) Archaeobotanical evidence for the spread of farming in the Eastern Mediterranean, *Current Anthropology* 45: 35–58.

Collins, B. J. (2007) *The Hittites and Their World* (Archaeology and Biblical Studies, No. 7). Society of Biblical Literature: Atlanta, GA.

Collins, P. (2000) *The Uruk Phenomenon: The Role of Social Ideology in the Expansion of the Uruk Culture during the Fourth Millennium B.C.* (British Archaeological Reports, International Series 900). Archaeopress: Oxford.

Connor, S. E. (2006) *A Promethean Legacy: Late Quaternary Vegetation History of Southern Georgia, Caucasus* (unpublished PhD thesis, University of Melbourne).

Connor, S. & Sagona, A. (2007) Environment and society in the late prehistory of southern Georgia, Caucasus, in B. Lyonnet (ed.) *Les cultures du Caucase (VIe-IIIe millénaires avant notre ère). Leurs relations avec le Proche-Orient*. CNRS Éditions: Paris.

Conolly, J. (1999) *The Çatal Höyük Flint and Obsidian Industry* (British Archaeological Reports, International Series 787). Archaeopress: Oxford.

Cook, J. M. (1958–1959) Old Smyrna, 1948–1951, *The Annual of the British School at Athens* 53–54: 1–34.

—— (1962) *The Greeks in Ionia and the East* (Ancient Peoples and Places). Thames & Hudson: London.

Craddock, P. T. (1995) *Early Metal Mining and Production*. Edinburgh University Press: Edinburgh.

Curtis, E. S. (1914) *In the Land of the War Canoes: Kwakiuti Indian Life on the Northwest Coast*. Documentary film restored in 1972 by B. Holm, G. Quimby, & D. Gerth.

Cutting, M. (2005) The architecture of Çatalhöyük: continuity, household and settlement, in I. Hodder (ed.) *Çatalhöyük Perspectives: Reports from the 1995–99 Seasons* (MacDonald Institute Monographs and British Institute of Archaeology at Ankara Monograph No. 39). MacDonald Institute for Archaeological Research: Cambridge.

Davis, M. K. (1982) The Çayönü ground stone, in L. Braidwood & R. J. Braidwood (eds) *Prehistoric Village Archaeology in South-Eastern Turkey* (British Archaeological Reports, International Series 138). British Archaeological Reports: Oxford.

—— (1998) Social differentiation at the early village of Çayönü, in G. Arsebük, M. J. Mellink, & W. Schirmer (eds) *Light on Top of the Black Hill: Studies Presented to Halet Çambel*. Ege Yayınları: Istanbul.

De Jesus, P. S. (1980) *The Development of Prehistoric Mining and Metallurgy in Anatolia*, 2 vols (British Archaeological Report, International Series 74). British Archaeological Reports: Oxford.

Dethier, J. (1982 [1981]) *Down to Earth. Mud Architecture: An Old Idea, A New Feature* (transl. R. Eaton). Thames & Hudson: London.

DeVries, K. (2007) The date of the destruction level at Gordion: imports and the local sequence, in A. Çilingiroğlu & A. Sagona (eds) *Anatolian Iron Ages 6: The Proceedings of the Sixth Anatolian Iron Ages Colloquium Held at Eskişehir, 16–20 August 2004* (Ancient Near Eastern Studies Supplement 20). Peeters: Louvain.

Dewdeny, J. C. (1971) *Turkey: An Introductory Geography*. Praeger: New York.

Di Nocera, G. M. (1998) *Arslantepe VIII: Der Siedlung der Mittelbronzezeit von Arslantepe*. Visceglia: Rome.

Dickinson, O. (2006) *The Aegean from Bronze Age to Iron Age: Continuity and Change Between the Twelfth and Eighth Centuries* BC. Routledge: London/New York.

Disa, J. J., Vossoughi, J., & Goldberg, N. H. (1993) A comparison of obsidian and surgical steel wound-healing in rats, *Plastic and Reconstructive Surgery* 92: 884–887.

Dixon, J. E. & Robertson, A. H. F. (eds) (1984) *The Geological Evolution of the Eastern Mediterranean*. Published for the Geological Society. Blackwell Scientific Publications: Oxford.

Dönmez, Ş. (2006) Cultural developments of the central Black Sea region before the Early Bronze Age II, in D. B. Erciyas & E. Koparal (eds) *Black Sea Studies Symposium Proceedings*. Ege Yayınları: Istanbul.

Dörpfeld, W. (1902) *Troja und Ilion: Ergebnisse der Ausgrabungen in den vorhistorischen und historischen Schichten von Ilion 1870–1894*. Beck & Barth: Athens.

Drews, R. (1993) *The End of the Bronze Age: Changes in Warfare and the Catastrophe ca. 1200 BC*. Princeton University Press: Princeton.

Düring, B. S. (2001) Social dimensions in the architecture of Neolithic Çatalhöyük, *Anatolia Studies* 51: 1–18.

—— (2002) Cultural dynamics of the central Anatolian Neolithic: the early ceramic Neolithic–late ceramic Neolithic transition, in F. Gérard & L. Thissen (eds) *The Neolithic of Central Anatolia: Internal Developments during the 9th–6th Millennia Cal BC. Proceedings of the International CANeW Table Ronde, Istanbul, 23–24 November, 2001*. Ege Yayınları: Istanbul.

—— (2006) *Constructing Communities; Clustered Neighborhood Settlements of the Central Anatolian Neolithic ca. 8500–5000 cal BC* (PIHANS 105). Nederlands Instituut voor het Nabije Osten: Leiden.

Duru, R. (1979) *Keban Project: Değirmentepe Excavations 1973* (Middle East Technical University, Keban Project Publications, Series III, No. 2). Tük Tarih Kurumu: Ankara.

—— (1989) Were the earliest culture at Hacılar really aceramic?, in K. Emre & B. Hrouda (eds) *Anatolia and the Near East: Studies in Honor of Tahsin Özgüç*. Türk Tarih Kurumu Basımevi: Ankara.

—— (1994a) *Kuruçay Höyük I. 1978–1988 Kazılarının Sonuçları. Neolitik ve Erken Kalkolitik Çağ Yerleşmeleri*. Türk Tarih Kurumu Basımevi: Ankara.

—— (1994b) Höyücek kazıları 1990, *Belleten* 58: 725–750.

—— (1996a) *Kuruçay Höyük II. 1978–1988 Kazılarının Sonuçları. Geç Kalkolitik ve Erken Tunç Çağ Yerleşmeleri*. Türk Tarih Kurumu Basımevi: Ankara.

—— (1996b) Bademağacı Höyüğü (Kızılkaya) kazıları. 1993 yılı calışma raporu, *Belleten* 60: 783–800.

—— (1997a) Bademağacı Höyüğü kazıları. 199 yılı calışma raporu, *Belleten* 61, 149–159.

—— (1997b) Bademağacı kazıları. 1995 ve 1996 yılları calışma raporu, *Belleten* 61: 709–730.

—— (1998) Bademağacı kazıları 1996, in *XIX Kazı Sonuçları Toplantısı* I. T. C. Kültür Bakanlığı: Ankara.

—— (1999) The Neolithic of the Lake District, in M. Özdoğan & N. Başgelen (eds) *Neolithic in Turkey: The Cradle of Civilization. New Discoveries*. Arkeoloji ve Sanat Yayınları: Istanbul.

—— (2000a) Bademağacı kazıları 1997 ve 1998 yılları calışma raporu, *Belleten* 64: 187–212.

—— (2000b) Bademağacı kazıları 1999 yıllı calışma raporu, *Belleten* 64: 583–598.

—— (2002a) Bademağacı kazıları 2000 ve 2001 yılları calışma raporu, *Belleten* 66: 549–594.

Duru, R. & Umurtak, G. (2005) *Höyücek: 1989–1992 Yılları Arasında Yapılan Kazıların Sonuçları*. Türk Tarih Kurumu Basımevi: Ankara.

Dyson, R. H. & Muscarella, O. W. (1989) Constructing the chronology and historical implications of Hasanlu IV, *Iran*, 27: 1–27.

Easton, D. F. (2002) *Schliemann's Excavations at Troia 1870–1873* (Studia Trocia Monographien 2). Philipp von Zabern: Mainz am Rhein.

Efe, T. (1989–1990) Three early sites in the vicinity of Eskişehir: Asmainler, Kanlıtaş, and Keskaya, *Anatolica* 16: 31–60.

—— (1990) An inland Anatolian site with pre-Vinça elements, *Germania* 68: 67–113.

—— (1993) Chalcolithic pottery from the mounds Aslanapa (Kütahya) and Kınık Bilecik), *Anatolica* 19: 19–31.

—— (1995) İç batı Anadolu'da iki neolitik yerleşme: Fındık Kayabaşi ve Akmakça, in H. Erkanal et al. (ed.) *Metin Akyurt Bahattin Devam Anı Kitabı*. ASY: Istanbul.

—— (2000) Recent investigation in inland northwestern Anatolia and its contribution to early Balkan-Anatolian connections, in S. Hiller and V. Nikolov (eds) *Karanovo III. Beiträge zum Neolithikum in Südosteuropa* (Österreichisch-Bulgarische Ausgrabungen und Forschungen in Karanovo). Phoibos: Vienna.

—— (ed.) (2001) *The Salvage Excavations at Orman Fidanlığı. A Chalcolithic Site in inland Northwestern Anatolia* (TASK Vakfı yayınları, No. 3). TASK: Istanbul.

—— (2002) The interaction between cultural/political entities and metalworking in western Anatolia during the Chalcolithic and Early Bronze Ages, in Ü. Yalçın (ed.) *Anatolian Metal II* (Der Anschnitt, Beiheft 15). Bergbau Museum: Bochum.

—— (2003a) Pottery distribution within the Early Bronze Age of western Anatolia and its implications upon cultural, political (and ethnic?) entities, in M. Özbaşaran, O. Tanındı, & A. Boratav (eds) *Archaeological Essays in Honour of* Homo Amatus: *Güven Arsebük. İçin Armağan Yazılar.* Ege Yayınları: Istanbul.

—— (2003b) Küllüoba and the initial stages of urbanism in western Anatolia, in M. Özdoğan, H. Hauptmann, & N. Başgelen (eds) *From Villages to Towns: Studies Presented to Ufuk Esin.* Arkeoloji ve Sanat Yayınları: Istanbul.

—— (2005) Neolithization in inner Western Anatolia, *Byzas* 2: 107–115.

—— (2007) The theories of the "Great Caravan Route" between Cilicia and Troy: the Early Bronze Age III period in inland western Anatolia, *Anatolian Studies* 57: 47–64.

Efe, T. & Deniz, Ş. M. Ay Efe (2007) The Küllüoba excavations and the cultural/political development of western Anatolia before the second millennium BC, in M. Alparslan, M. Doğan-Alparslan, & H. Peker (eds) *Belkıs Dinçol ve Ali Dinçol'a Armağan/Festschrift in Honor of Belkıs Dinçol and Ali Dinçol.* Ege Yayınları: Istanbul.

Efstratiou, N. (2005) Tracing the story of the first farmers in Greece—a long and winding road, in C. Lichter (ed.) *How Did Farming Reach Europe?* (Byzas 2). Ege Yayınları: Istanbul.

Ehrich, R. W. & Bankoff, H. A. (1992) Geographical and chronological patterns in east and southeastern Europe, in R. W. Ehrich (ed.) *Chronologies in Old World Archaeology*, 3rd edn, vol. I. University Chicago Press: Chicago.

Ehringhaus, H. (2005) *Götter, Herrscher, Inschriften: Die Felsreliefs der Hethitischen Grossreichszeit in der Türkei* (Zaberns Bildbände zur Archäologie). Philipp von Zabern: Mainz am Rhein.

Eliade, M. (1962) *The Forge and the Crucible: The Origins of Alchemy.* University of Chicago Press: Chicago.

—— (1964) *Myth and Reality.* Allen & Unwin: London.

Ellis, R. S. & Voigt, M. M. (1982) 1981 excavations at Gritille, Turkey, *American Journal of Archaeology* 86: 319–332.

Emre, K. (1966) The pottery of Acemhöyük, *Anadolu (Anatolia)* 10: 99–153.

Erkanal, H. (1996) Early Bronze Age urbanization in the coastal region of western Anatolia, in Y. Sey (ed.) *Housing and Settlement in Anatolia: A Historical Perspective.* Türkiye Ekonomik ve Toplumsal Tarih Vakfı: Istanbul.

—— (1999) Early Bronze Age fortification systems in Izmir region, in P. P. Betancourt, V. Karageorghis, R. Laffineur, & W.-D. Niemeier (eds) *MELETEMATA: Studies in Aegean Archaeology Presented to Malcolm H. Wiener as he enters his 65th Year.* Aegaeum 20: Liège/Austin.

Erol, O. (1978) The Quaternary history of the lake basins of central and southern Anatolia, in W. C. Brice (ed.) *The Environmental History of the Near and Middle East Since the Last Ice Age.* Academic Press: New York.

Erzen, A. (1988) *Çavuştepe I.* Türk Tarih Kurumu Basımevi: Ankara.

Esin, U. (1994) The functional evidence of seals and sealings for Değirmentepe, in P. Ferioli, E. Fiandra, G. G. Fissore, & M. Frangipane (eds) *Archives Before Writing.* Centro Internazionale di Recerche Archaeologiche, Antropologiche e Storiche: Rome.

—— (1998a) Palaeolithic era to Early Bronze Age: prehistoric Cappadocia, in M. Sözen (ed.) *Cappadocia.* Ayhan Şahenk Foundation: Istanbul.

Esin, U. & Benedict, P. (1963) Recent developments in the prehistory of Anatolia, *Current Anthropology* 4: 339–346.

Esin, U., Bıçakçı, E, Özbaşaran, M., Balkan-Altı, N. Berker, D., & Yağmur, İ, et al. (1991) Salvage excavations at the pre-pottery site of Aşıklı Höyük in central Anatolia, *Anatolica* 17: 123–174.

Esin, U. & Harmankaya, S. (1999) Aşıklı, in M. Özdoğan & N. Başgelen (eds) *Neolithic in Turkey: The Cradle of Civilization. New Discoveries.* Arkeoloji ve Sanat Yayınları: Istanbul.

Eslick, C. (1980) Middle Chacolithic pottery from southwestern Anatolia, *American Journal of Archaeology* 84: 5–14.

—— (1988) Hacılar to Karataş: social organization in south-western Anatolia, *Mediterranean Archaeology* 1: 10–40.

—— (1992) *Elmalı-Karataş I. The Neolithic and Chalcolithic Periods: Bağbası and other sites.* Bryn Mawr College: Bryn Mawr, PA.

Fairbairn, A., Near, J., & Martinoli, D. (2005) Macrobotanical investigations of the North, South and KOPAL area excavations at Çatalhöyük East, in I. Hodder (ed.) *Inhabiting Çatalhöyük: Reports from the 1995–99 Seasons* (MacDonald Institute Monographs and British Institute of Archaeology at Ankara Monograph No. 38). MacDonald Institute for Archaeological Research: Cambridge.

Fairbridge, R., Erol, O., Karaca, M., & Yılmaz, Y. (1997) Background to mid-Holocene climatic change in Anatolia and adjacent regions, in N. Dalfes, G. Kukla, & H. Weiss (eds) *Third Millennium* BC *Climate Change and Old World Collapse.* Springer: Berlin.

Fisher, W. B. (1978) *The Middle East*, 7th edn. Methuen: London.

Flannery, K. V. (1972) The origins of the village as a settlement type in Mesoamerica and the Near East: a comparative study, in P. J. Ucko, R. Tringham, & G. W. Dimbleby (eds) *Man, Settlement and Urbanism.* Duckworth: London.

—— (2002) The origins of the village revisited: from nuclear to extended households, *American Antiquity* 67: 417–433.

Frangipane, M. (1993) Local components in the development of centralized societies in Syro-Anatolian regions, in M. Frangipane, H. Hauptmann, M. Liverani, P. Matthiae, & M. Mellink (eds) *Between the Rivers and Over the Mountains: Archaeologica Anatolica et Mesopotamica Alba Palmieri Dedicata.* Dipartimento di Scienze Storiche Archeologiche e Antropologiche dell'Antichità, Universita di Roma "La Sapienza": Roma.

—— (2000) The Late Chalcolithic/EBI sequence at Arslantepe: chronological and cultural remarks from a frontier site, in C. Marro & H. Hauptmann (eds) *Chronologies des pays du Caucase et de l'Euphrate aux IVe–IIIe millenaires: actes du colloque d'Istanbul, 16–19 décembre 1998* (Acta Anatolica XI). De Boccard Edition-Diffusion: Paris.

—— (2001a) Centralization processes in Greater Mesopotamia, in M. Rothman (ed.) *Uruk Mesopotamia and Its Neighbors.* School of American Research Press: Santa Fe.

—— (2001b) The transition between two opposing forms of power at Arslantepe (Malatya) at the beginning of the 3rd millennium, *Türkiye Bilimler Akademisi Arkeoloji Dergisi (TÜBA-AR)* 4: 1–24.

—— (ed.) (2004) *Alle Origini del Potere: Arslantepe, la Collina dei Leoni.* Electa: Milan.

—— (ed.) (2007) *Arslantepe—Cretulae: An Early Centralised Administrative System Before Writing.* Università di Roma: Rome.

Frangipane, M., Di Nocera, D. M., Hauptmann, A., Morbidelli, P., Palmieri, A., Sadori, L., et al. (2001) New symbols of new power in a "Royal" tomb from 3000 BC Arslantepe, Malatya (Turkey), *Paléorient* 27: 105–139.

Frangipane, M. & Palmieri, A. (1983) Perspectives on protourbanization in eastern Anatolia: Arslantepe (Malatya). An interim report on 1975–1983 campaigns: a protourban centre of the Late Uruk period, *Origini* 12: 287–454.

Frangipane, M. & Palumbi, G. (2007) Red-black ware, pastoralism, trade, and Anatolian-Transcaucasian interactions in the 4th–3rd millennium BC, in B. Lyonnet (ed.) *Les cultures du Caucase (VIᵉ-IIIᵉ millénaires avant notre ère). Leurs relations avec le Proche-Orient.* CNRS Éditions: Paris.

French, D. H. (1963) Excavations at Can Hasan: second preliminary report, 1962, *Anatolian Studies* 13: 29–42.

—— (1998) *Canhasan Sites I: Stratigraphy and Structures*. The British Institute of Archaeology at Ankara (Monograph No. 23): London.

—— (2005) *Canhasan Sites I: The Pottery*. The British Institute of Archaeology at Ankara (Monograph No. 32): London.

French, D. H., Hillman, G., Payne, S., & Payne, R. (1972) Excavations at Can Hasan III, 1969–70, in E. Higgs (ed.) *Papers in Economic Prehistory*. Cambridge University Press: Cambridge.

Fuensanta, J. G., Rothman, M., & Bucak, E. (2000) Excavations at Tilbes Höyük, 1998', in *XXI Kazı Sonuçları Toplantısı*. T. C. Kültür Bakanlığı Müdürlüğü: Ankara.

Furst, P. T. (ed.) 1972 *Flesh of the Gods: The Ritual Use of Hallucinogens*. Allen & Unwin: London.

Gabunia, L., Vekua, A., Lordkipanidze, D., Swisher III, C., Ferring, R., Justus, A., et al. (2000) Early Plaeistocene hominid cranial remains from Dmanisi, Republic of Georgia: taxonomy, geological setting and age, *Science* 288: 1019–1025.

Garelli, P. (1963) *Les Assyriens en Cappadoce*. Bibliothèque archéologique et historique de l'institute français d'archéologie d'Istanbul XIX: Paris.

Garfinkel, Y. (2003) *Dancing at the Dawn of Agriculture*. University of Texas Press: Austin.

Garstang, J. (1953) *Prehistoric Mersin. Yümük Tepe in Southern Turkey*. Clarendon Press: Oxford.

Gasche, H., Armstrong, J. A., Cole, S. W., & Gurzadyan, V. G. (1998) *Dating the Fall of Babylon: A Reappraisal of Second Millennium Chronology* (Mesopotamian History and Environment, Series II, Memoires v. 4). University of Ghent and the Oriental Institute: Chicago.

Gelb, I. J. (1935) *Inscriptions from Alishar and Vicinity* (Oriental Institute Publications 27). Oriental Institute of the University of Chicago: Chicago.

Genz, H. (2000) Die Eisenzeit in Zentralanatolien im Lichte der keramischen Funde vom Büyükaya in Boğazköy/Hattuša, *TÜBA-AR (Türkiye Bilimler Akademisi Arkeoloji Dergesi)* 3: 35–54.

—— (2005) Thoughts on the origins of Iron Age pottery traditions in central Anatolia, in A. A. Çilinigi-roğlu & G. Darbyshire (eds) *Anatolian Iron Ages 5: Proceedings of the Fifth Anatolian Iron Ages Colloquium held at Van, 6–10 August 2001* (The British Institute at Ankara Monograph No. 31). The British Institute at Ankara: London.

—— (2007) Late Iron Age occupation of the northwest slope at Böğazköy, in A. Çilingiroğlu & A. Sagona (eds) *Anatolian Iron Ages 6: The Proceedings of the Sixth Anatolian Iron Ages Colloquium Held at Eskişehir, 16–20 August 2004* (Ancient Near Eastern Studies Supplement 20). Peeters: Louvain.

Georgacas, D. J. (1969) The name *Asia* for the continent: its history and origin, *Journal of the American Name Society* 17(1): 1–90.

Gérard, F. (1997) Un village anatolien au Néolithique: le secteur sud-ouest d'Ilıpınar, *Anatolia Antiqua* 5: 1–18.

—— (2002) Appendix II: CANeW archaeological sites database, Central Anatolia, 10,000–5000 cal. BC, in F. Gérard & L. Thissen (eds) *The Neolithic of Central Anatolia: Internal Developments during the 9th–6th Millennia Cal BC. Proceedings of the International CANeW Table Ronde, Istanbul, 23–24 November, 2001*. Ege Yayınları: Istanbul.

Gérard, F. & Thissen, L. (eds) (2002) *The Neolithic of Central Anatolia: Internal Developments during the 9th–6th Millennia Cal BC. Proceedings of the International CANeW Table Ronde, Istanbul, 23–24 November, 2001*. Ege Yayınları: Istanbul.

Gerber, J. C. (2005) *Hassek Höyük III: Die frühbronzezeitliche Keramik* (Istanbuler Forschungen 47). Ernst Wasmuth: Tübingen.

Goldman, H. (1956) *Excavations at Gözlü Kule, Tarsus*. Vol. II. *The Neolithic Through the Bronze Age*. Princeton University Press: Princeton.

Gorny, R. L. (2002) Environment, archaeology, and history in Hittite Anatolia, in D. C. Hopkins (ed.) *Across the Anatolian Plateau: Readings in the Archaeology of Ancient Turkey* (Annual of the American Schools of Oriental Research 57, 2000). American Schools of Oriental Research: Boston, MA.

Gorny, R. L., McMahon, G., Paley, S., & Steadman, S. (2000) The 1999 Alişar regional project season, *Anatolica* 26: 153–171.

Gorny, R. L., McMahon, G., Paley, S., Steadman, S., & Verhaaren, B. (2002) The 2000 and 2001 seasons at Çadır Höyük in Central Turkey: a preliminary report, *Anatolica* 28: 109–136.

Grayson, A. K. (1987) *Assyrian Rulers of the Third and Second Millennium BC (to 1115 BC)*. Royal Inscriptions of Mesopotamia: Assyrian Periods, 1. Toronto University Press: Toronto.

—— (1991) *Assyrian Rulers of the Early First Millennium BC I (1114–859 BC)*. Royal Inscriptions of Mesopotamia: Assyrian Periods, 2. Toronto University Press: Toronto.

Greaves, A. M. (2002) *Miletos: A History*. Routledge: London/New York.

—— (2007) Trans-Anatolia: Turkey as a bridge between east and west: analogies, histories and approaches, *Anatolian Studies* 57: 1–16.

Greenberg, R., Eisenberg, E., Paz, S. & Paz, Y. (2006) *Bet Yerah: The Early Bronze Age Mound*. Vol. I. *Excavation Reports, 1933–1986* (IAA Reports 30). Israel Antiquities Authority: Jerusalem.

Grinsell, L. V. (1961) The breaking of objects as a funerary right, *Folklore* 72: 475–491.

—— (1973) The breaking of objects as a funerary right: supplementary notes, *Folklore* 84: 111–114.

Gülcer, S. (2000) Norşuntepe: Dir Chalkolithische Keramik (Elazığ/Ostanatlien), in M. Frangipane, H. Hauptmann, M. Liverani, P. Matthiae, & M. Mellink (eds) *Between the Rivers and Over the Mountains: Archaeologica Anatolica et Mesopotamica Alba Palmieri Dedicata*. Dipartimento di Scienze Storiche Archeologiche e Antropologiche dell'Antichità, Universita di Roma "La Sapienza": Roma.

—— (2001) Guvercinkayasi excavation and survey of its environs, in O. Belli (ed.), *Istanbul University's Contributions to Archaeology in Turkey (1932–2000)*. Istanbul University Rectorate: Istanbul.

Güleç, E., Howell, F. C., & White, T. (1999) Dursunlu—a new lower Plesitocene atrifact-bearing locality in southern Anatolia, in H. Ullrich (ed.) *Hominid Evolution: Lifestyles and Survival Strategies*. Edition Archaeo: Berlin.

Gürkan, G. & Seeher, J. (1991) Die Frühbronzezeitliche Nekropole von Küçükhöyük bei Bozhüyük, *Istanbuller Mitteilungen* 41: 39–96.

Gürsan-Salzmann, A. (1992) *Alaca Höyük: A Ressessment of the Excavation and Sequence of the Early Bronze Age Settlement* (PhD thesis, University of Pennsylvania).

Hamilton, N. (1996) Figurines, clay balls, small finds and burials, in I. Hodder (ed.) *On the Surface: Çatalhöyük 1993–1995* (MacDonald Institute Monographs and The British Institute of Archaeology at Ankara Monograph No. 22). MacDonald Institute for Archaeological Research: Cambridge.

Hanfmann, G. M. A. (1983) *Sardis from Prehistoric to Roman Times 1958–1975: Results of the Archaeological Exploration of Sardis 1958–1975*. Harvard University Press: Cambridge, MA/London.

Hansen, S. (2006) New aspects of stone age art, *Archäologische Mitteilungen aus Iran und Turan* 38: 367–380.

Harmankaya, S. (1983) Pendik kazısı 1981, in *IV Kazı Sonuçları Toplantısı 1982*. T. C. Kültür Bakanlığı: Ankara.

Harmankaya, S. & Tanındı, O. (1996) *Türkiye Arkeolojik Yerleşmeleri I, Paleolitik/Epipaleolitik*. Ege Yayınları: Istanbul.

Hassan, F. A. (1973) On the mechanisms of population growth during the Neolithic, *Current Anthropology* 14: 535–540.

Hauptmann, A. & Palmieri, A. (2000) Metal production in the eastern Mediterranean at the transition of the 4th/3rd millennium: case studies from Arslantepe, in Ü. Yalçın (ed.) *Anatolian Metal I* (Der Anschnitt 13, Zeitschrift für Kunst und Kultur im Bergbau). Bergbau Museum: Bochum.

Hauptmann, H. (1969) Die Grabungen in der prähistorischen Siedlung auf Yarıkkaya, in K. Bittel, H. G. Güterbock, H. Hauptmann, H. Kühne, P. Neve, & W. Schirmer (eds) *Boğazköy IV. Funde aus den Grabungen 1967 und 1968* (Abhandlungen der Deutschen Orient-Gesellschaft 14). Gebrüder Mann Verlag: Berlin.

—— (1976) Die Grabungen auf dem Norşuntepe, 1972, in S. Pekman (ed.) *Keban Project 1972 Activities*, I, 5. Middle Eastern Technical University: Ankara.

—— (1987) Lidar Höyük and Nevalı Çori, 1986, *Anatolian Studies* 37: 203–206.

—— (1988) Nevalı Çori architektur, *Anatolica* 15: 99–110.

—— (1993) Ein Kultgebäude in Nevalı Çori, in M. Frangipane, H. Hauptmann, M. Liverani, P. Matthiae, & M. Mellink (eds) *Between the Rivers and Over the Mountains: Archaeologica Anatolica et Mesopotamica Alba Palmieri Dedicata*. Dipartimento di Scienze Storiche Archeologiche e Antropologiche dell'Antichità, Universita di Roma "La Sapienza": Roma.

—— (1999) The Urfa region, in M. Özdoğan & N. Başgelen (eds) *Neolithic in Turkey: The Cradle of Civilization. New Discoveries*. Arkeoloji ve Sanat Yayınları: Istanbul.

—— (2000a) Ein früheneolithisches Kultbild aus Kommagene, in J. Wagner (ed.) *Gottkönige am Euphrat; neue Ausgrabungen und Forschungen in Kommagene*. Philipp von Zabern: Mainz an Rhein.

—— (2000b) Zur Chronologie des 3. Jahrtausends v. Chr. am oberen Euphrat Aufgrund der Stratigraphie des Norşuntepe, in C. Marro & H. Hauptmann (eds) *Chronologies des pays du Caucase et de l'Euphrate aux IVe–IIIe millenaires: actes du colloque d'Istanbul, 16–19 décembre 1998* (Acta Anatolica XI). De Boccard Edition-Diffusion: Paris.

Hawkins, J. D. (1976–1980) Karkamiš, in E. Ebeling & B. Meissner (eds) *Reallexikon der Assyriologie*. Walter de Gruyter: Berlin/New York.

—— (1998) Takasnawa King of Mira: "Tarkondemos," Boğazköy sealings and karabel, *Anatolian Studies* 48: 1–31.

—— (2000) *Corpus of Hieroglyphic Luwan Inscriptions* (Studies in Indo-European Language and Culture 8), 3 vols. Walter de Gruyter: Berlin.

—— (2003) Scripts and texts, in H. C. Melchert (ed.) *The Luwians* (Handbuch der Orientalistik 1/68). E. J. Brill: Leiden.

Hawkins, J. D., Davies, A. M., & Neumann, G. (1974) Hittite hieroglyphs and Luwian: new evidence for the connection, *Nachrichten der Akademie der Wissenschaften in Göttingen, philologsich-historische Klasse* 1973/6: 145–197.

Hayadaroğlu, M. (ed.) 2006 *From Earth to Eternity: Çatalhöyük*. Yapı Kredi Yayınları: Istanbul.

Hayden, B. (1995) A new overview of domestication, in T. D. Price & A. B. Gebauer (eds) *Last Hunters, First Farmers*. School of American Research: Santa Fe.

Held, C. C. (1994) *Middle East Patterns: Places, Peoples, and Politics*, 2nd edn. Westview Press: Boulder, CO.

Hellwag, U. (2005) $^{L\dot{U}}$A.ZUM-*li* versus $^{L\dot{U}}$A.NIN-*li*: some thoughts on the owner of the so-called *Prinzensiegel* at Rusa II's court, in A. A. Çilingiroğlu & G. Darbyshire (eds) *Anatolian Iron Ages 5. Proceedings of the Fifth Anatolian Iron Ages Colloquium held at Van, 6–10 August 2001*. The British Institute at Ankara (Monograph No. 31): London.

Helms, M. W. (1993) *Craft and the Kingly Ideal: Art, Trade and Power*. University of Texas Press: Austin.

Helvenson, P. A. & Bahn, P. G. (2003) Testing the "three stages of trance" model, *Cambridge Archaeological Journal* 13(2): 213–224; with replies to reviewers 220–224.

Helwing, B. (2000) Regional variation in the composition of Late Chalcolithic pottery assemblages, in C. Marro & H. Hauptmann (eds) *Chronologies des pays du Caucase et de l'Euphrate aux IVe–IIIe millenaires: actes du colloque d'Istanbul, 16–19 décembre 1998* (Acta Anatolica XI). De Boccard Edition-Diffusion: Paris.

—— (2002) *Hassek Höyük II: Die spätchalkolithische Keramik* (Istanbuler Forschungen 45). Ernst Wasmuth: Tübingen.

Henrickson, R. C. (2002) Hittite pottery and potters: a view from Bronze Age Gordion, in D. C. Hopkins (ed.) *Across the Anatolian Plateau: Readings in the Archaeology of Ancient Turkey* (Annual of the American Schools of Oriental Research 57, 2000). American Schools of Oriental Research: Boston, MA.

Herbert, E. W. (1998) Mining as microcosm in precolonial sub-Saharan Africa, in A. B. Knapp, V. C. Piggot, & E. W. Herbert (eds) *Social Approaches to an Industrial Past: The Archaeology and Anthropology of Mining.* Routledge: London.

Herbort, S. (2002) Hittite seals and sealings from the Nişantepe Archive, Boğazköy: a prosopographical study, in K. A. Yener & H. A. Hoffner (eds) *Recent Developments in Hittite Archaeology and History: Papers in Memory of Hans G. Güterbock.* Eisenbrauns: Winona Lake, IN.

Heun, M., Schäfer-Pregl, R., Klawan, D, Castagna, R., Accerbi, M., Borghi, B., et al. (1997) Site of einkorn wheat domestication identified by DNA fingerprinting, *Science* 278: 1312–1314.

Higgs, E. & Jarman, M. R. (1969) The origins of agriculture: a reconsideration, *Antiquity* 43: 31–41.

Hodder, I. (1982) *Symbols in Action: Ethnoarchaeological Studies of Material Culture.* Cambridge University Press: Cambridge.

—— (1990) *The Domestication of Europe: Structure and Contingency in Neolithic Societies.* Blackwell: London.

—— (ed.) (1996) *On the Surface: Çatalhöyük 1993–95* (MacDonald Institute Monographs and The British Institute of Archaeology at Ankara Monograph No. 22). MacDonald Institute for Archaeological Research: Cambridge.

—— (ed.) (2000) *Towards Reflex Method in Archaeology: The Example at Çatalhöyük* (MacDonald Institute Monographs and The British Institute of Archaeology at Ankara Monograph No. 28). MacDonald Institute for Archaeological Research: Cambridge.

—— (ed.) (2005a) *Inhabiting Çatalhöyük: Reports from the 1995–99 Seasons* (MacDonald Institute Monographs and The British Institute of Archaeology at Ankara Monograph No. 38). MacDonald Institute for Archaeological Research: Cambridge.

—— (ed.) (2005b) *Çatalhöyük Perspectives: Reports from the 1995–99 Seasons* (MacDonald Institute Monographs and The British Institute of Archaeology at Ankara Monograph No. 39). MacDonald Institute for Archaeological Research: Cambridge.

—— (ed.) (2005c) *Changing Materialities at Çatalhöyük: Reports from the 1995–99 Seasons* (MacDonald Institute Monographs and The British Institute of Archaeology at Ankara Monograph No. 39). MacDonald Institute for Archaeological Research: Cambridge.

—— (2006) *The Leopard's Tale: Revealing the Mysteries of Çatalhöyük.* Thames & Hudson: London.

—— (ed.) (2007) *Excavating Çatalhöyük: South, North and KOPAL Area Reports from the 1995–99 Seasons* (MacDonald Institute Monographs and The British Institute of Archaeology at Ankara Monograph No. 37). MacDonald Institute for Archaeological Research: Cambridge.

Hovers, E., Ilani, S., Bar-Yosef, O., & Vandermeersch, B. (2003) Ochre use by modern humans in Qafzeh Cave, *Current Anthropology* 44(4): 491–522.

Howell-Meurs, S. (2001) *Early Bronze and Iron Age Animal Exploitation in Northeastern Anatolia: The Faunal Remains from Sos Höyük and Büyüktepe Höyük* (British Archaeological Reports, International Series 945), Archaeopress: Oxford.

Işıklı, M. (2007) Recent investigations at Pulur (Erzurum): observations on northeast Anatolian ceramics, in K. S. Rubinson & A. Sagona (eds) *Ceramics in Transition: Chalcolithic Through Iron Age in the Highlands of Caucasus and Anatolia.* Peeters: Louvain.

Işıklı, M. & Can, B. (2007) The Erzurum region in the Early Iron Age: new observations, in A. Çilingiroğlu & A. Sagona (eds) *Anatolian Iron Ages 6: The Proceedings of the Sixth Anatolian Iron Ages Colloquium Held at Eskişehir, 16–20 August 2004* (Ancient Near Eastern Studies Supplement 20). Peeters: Louvain.

Jackson, M. S. & McKenzie, D. P. (1984) Active tectonics of the Alpine-Himalayan belt between western Turkey and Pakistan, *Geophysical Journal of the Royal Astronomical Society* 77: 185–264.

Jamieson, A. S. (1993) The Euphrates Valley and Early Bronze Age ceramic traditions, *Abr-Nahrain* 31: 36–92.

Jansen, H. G. (1991) Vorbericht zur Geomagnetischen Prospektion der Nekropole von Demiricihüyük-Sarıket im Juli 1990, *Istanbuller Miteillungen* 41: 120–124.

Jones, A. & MacGregor, G. (eds) (2002) *Colouring the Past: The Significance of Colour in Archaeological Research*. Berg: Oxford.

Joukowsky, M. S. (1996) *Early Turkey: Anatolian Archaeology from Prehistory through the Lydian Period*. Kendall/Hunt: Dubuque, IA.

Kakhiani, K. & Ghlighvashvili, E. (2008) Bronze Age barrows in southeast Georgia, in A. Sagona & M. Abramishvili (eds) *Archaeology in Southern Caucasus: Perspectives from Georgia*. Peeters: Louvain.

Kâmil, T. (1982) *Yortan Cemetery in the Early Bronze Age of Western Anatolia* (British Archaeological Reports, International Series 145). British Archaeological Reports: Oxford.

Kansa, S. W. & Campbell, S. (2004) Feasting with the dead? A ritual bone deposit at Domuztepe, south eastern Turkey (c. 5550 BC), in S. J. O'Day, W. van Neer, & A. Ervynck (eds) *Behavior Behind Bones: The Zooarchaeology of Ritual, Religion Status and Identity. Proceedings of the 9th International Council for Archaeozoology Conference, Durham 2002*. Vol. 1. Oxbow: Oxford.

Kappelman, J., Alçiçek, M. C., Kazancı, N., Schultz, M., Özkul, M., & Şen, Ş. (2008) Brief communication: first Homo erectus from Turkey and implications for migrations into temperate Eurasia, *American Journal of Physical Anthropology* 135: 110–116.

Karabıyıkoğlu, M., Kuzcuoğlu, C. Fontugne, M. Kaiser, B., & Mouralis, D. (1999) Fecies and depositional sequences of the late Pleistocene Göçü shoreline system, Konya Basin, central Anatolia: implications for reconstructing lake-level changes, *Quaternary Science Review* 18: 593–609.

Karul, N., Ayhan, A., & Özdoğan, M. (2001) 1999 yılı Mezraa-Teleilat kazıları/1999 excavations at Mezraa-Teleilat, in N. Tuna, J. Greenhalg, & J. Velibeyoğlu (eds) *Ilısu ve Karkamış Baraj Gölleri Altında Kalacak Arkeolojik ve Kültür Varlıklarını Kurtarma Projesi 1999 Yılı Çalışmaları/Salavage project of the Archaeological Heritage of the Ilısu and Carchemish Dam Reservoirs Activities in 2001*. ÖDTÜ/METU: Ankara.

—— (2004) 2001 yılı Mezraa-Teleilat kazıları/2001 excavations at Mezraa-Teleilat, in N. Tuna, J. Greenhalg, & J. Velibeyoğlu (eds) *Ilısu ve Karkamış Baraj Gölleri Altında Kalacak Arkeolojik ve Kültür Varlıklarını Kurtarma Projesi 2001 Yılı Çalışmaları/Salavage project of the Archaeological Heritage of the Ilısu and Carchemish Dam Reservoirs Activities in 2001*. ÖDTÜ/METU: Ankara.

Karul, N., Eres, Z., Özdoğan, M., & Parzinger, H. (2003) *Aşağı Pınar I. Einführung Forschungsgeschichte, Stratigraphie und Architektur*. (Archäologie in Eurasien, 15. Studien im Thrakien-Marmara-Raum. I). Philipp von Zabern: Mainz.

Kay, P. & McDaniel, C. K. (1997) The linguistic significance of the meanings of basic color terms, in A. Byrne & D. R. Hilbert (eds) *Readings in Color, vol. 2. The Science of Color*. MIT Press: Cambridge.

Kellner, H.-J. (1991) *Gürtelbleche Aus Urartu*. (Prähistorische Bronzefunde, Abt. 12, Bd. 3). Franz Steiner Verlag: Stuttgart.

Kiguradze, T. B. (2000) The Chalcolithic–Early Bronze Age transition in the eastern Caucasus, in C. Marro & H. Hauptmann (eds) *Chronologies des pays du Caucase et de l'Euphrate aux IVe–IIIe millenaires: actes du colloque d'Istanbul, 16–19 décembre 1998* (Acta Anatolica XI). De Boccard Edition-Diffusion: Paris.

—— (2001) Caucasian Neolithic, in P. N. Peregrine & M. Ember (eds) *Encyclopedia of Prehistory, vol. 4. Europe*. Kluwer Academic/Plenum: New York.

Kiguradze, T. & Sagona, A. (2003) On the origins of the Kura-Araxes cultural complex, in A. T. Smith & K. Rubinson (eds) *Archaeology in the Borderlands: Investigations in Caucasia and Beyond*. Cotsen Institute Press: Los Angeles.

Killick, D. (2001) Science speculation and the origins of extractive metallurgy, in D. R. Brothwell & A. M. Pollard (eds) *Handbook of Archaeological Sciences*. Wiley: New York.

King, R. J., Özcan, S. S., Carter, T., Kalfoğlu, E., Atasoy, S., Triantaphyllidis, C., et al. (2008) Differential

Y-chromosome Anatolian influences on the Greek and Cretan Neolithic, *Annals of Human Genetics* 72: 205–214.

Kleiss, W. (1976) Urartäische Architektur, in H.-J. Kellner (ed.) *Urartu: Ein Wiederentdeckter Rivale Assyriens* (Ausstellungskataloge der Prähistorischen Staatssammlung, Band 2). Prähistorische Staatssammlung: Munich.

—— (ed.) (1979) *Bastam I: Ausgrabungen in den urartäischen Anlagen 1972–1975* (Teheraner Forschungen 4). Gebrüder Mann Verlag: Berlin.

—— (ed.) (1988) *Bastam II: Ausgrabungen in den urartäischen Anlangen 1997–1978* (Teheraner Forschungen). Gebrüder Mann Verlag: Berlin.

Knapp, A. B. (ed.) (1992) *Archaeology, Annales and Ethnohistory*. Cambridge University Press: Cambridge.

Knapp, A. B., Piggot, V. C., & Herbert, E. W. (eds) (1998) *Social Approaches to an Industrial Past: The Archaeology and Anthropology of Mining*. Routledge: London/New York.

Kobayashi, K. (2007) An obsidian refitting from Sos Höyük, eastern Turkey, *Ancient Near Eastern Studies* 44: 141–154.

Kobayashi, K. & Sagona, A. (2008) A survey of obsidian sources in the provinces of Erzurum, Erzincan, Rize and Bitlis, 2006, *Araştırma Sonuçları Toplantısı* 25, vol. 2. T. C. Kültür ve Turizm Bakanlığı: Ankara.

Kohl, P. L. (2007) *The Making of Bronze Age Eurasia*. Cambridge University Press: Cambridge.

Kökten, I. K. (1955) Antalya'da Karain mağarasında yapılan prehistorya araştırmalarına toplu bakış/Ein allgemeiner Überlick über die prähistorischen Forschungen in Karainhöhle bei Antalya, *Belleten* 19(75): 284–293.

Korfmann, M. (1982) *Tilkitepe: Die ersten Ansätze prähistorischer Forschung in der östlichen Turkei* (Istanbüler Mitteilungen, Beiheft 26). Ernst Wasmuth: Tübingen.

—— (1983) *Demircihüyük I. Architektur, Stratigraphie und Befunde*. Philipp von Zabern: Mainz am Rhein.

—— (1994) Troia—Ausgrabungen 1993, *Studia Troica* 4: 1–50.

—— (1997–98) Troia, an ancient Anatolian palatial and trading center: archaeological evidence for the period of Troy VI/VII, *Classical World* 91: 369–385.

—— (2001) Troia als Drehscheibe des Handels im 2. und 3. vorchristlichen Jahrtausend. Erkenntnisse zur troianischen Hochkultur und zur maritimen Troia-Kultur, in *Troia: Traum und Wirklichkeit*. Konrad Theiss Verlag: Stuttgart.

Korfmann, M., Girgin, Ç., Morcol, Ç., & Kılıç, S. (1995) Kumtepe 1993. Bericht über die Rettungsgrabung, *Studia Troica* 5: 237–289.

Koşay, H. Z. (1938) *Alaca Höyük Hafriyatı, 1936 dakı çalışmalara ve kesişere ait ilk rapor* (Türk Tarih Kurumu Yayınlarından V. Seri, No. 2). Türk Tarih Kurumu Basımevi: Ankara.

—— (1944) *Ausgrabungen von Alaca Höyük, ein Vorbericht über die im Auftrage der türkischen Geschichtskommission im Sommer 1936 durchgeführten Forschungen und Entdeckungen* (Veröffentlichungen der türkischen Geschichtskommisser, V. Serie, No. 2 a). Türk Tarih Kurumu Basımevi: Ankara.

—— (1951) *Alaca Höyük Kazısı. 1937–1939 dakı çalışmalara ve keşişere ait ilk rapor. Les fouilles d'Alaca Höyük entreprises par la societe d'histoire turque. Rapport préliminaire sur les travaux en 1937–1939* (Türk Tarih Kurumu Yayınlarından V Seri, No.5). Türk Tarih Kurumu Basımevi: Ankara.

—— (1957) *Büyük Güllücek Kazısı. 1947 ve 1949 dakı Çalışmalar Hakkında İlk Rapor. Ausgrabungen von Büyük Güllücek. Vorbericht über die Arbeiten von 1947 und 1949* (Türk Tarih Kurumu Yayınları, Seri V, No. 16). Türk Tarih Kurumu Basımevi: Ankara.

—— (1966) *Alaca Höyük Kazısı. 1940–1948 dakı Çalışmalara ve Keşişere ait İlk Rapor. Ausgrabungen von Alaca Höyük: Vorbericht über die Forschungen und Entdeckungen von 1940–1948* (Türk Tarih Kurumu Yayınları, Seri V, No. 6). Türk Tarih Kurumu Basımevi: Ankara.

—— (1976) *Keban Projesi, Pulur Kazısı 1968–70. Keban Project, Pulur Excavations 1968–70* (Middle Eastern Technical University Keban Project Publications, Series III, No. 1). Middle Eastern Technical University: Ankara.

Koşay, H. Z. & Turfan, K. (1959) Erzurum-Karaz Kazısı raporu, *Belleten* 23: 349–413.

Koşay, H. Z. & Vary, H. (1964) *Pulur Kazısı 1960. Mevsimi Calışmaları Raporu. Die Ausgrabungen von Pulur. Bericht über die Kampagne von 1960.* (Atatürk Üniversitesi Yayınları Nr. 24), Fen-Edebiyat Fakültesi-Arkeoloji Serisi Nr. 9. Atatürk Universitesi: Ankara

—— (1967) *Güzelova Kazısı. Ausgrabungen von Güzelova.* (Atatürk Üniversitesi Yayınları No. 46), Fen-Edebiyat Fakültesi Araştırmaları Seri 20. Atatürk Universitesi: Ankara.

Kozbe, G. (2004) Activity areas and social organization within Early Trans-Caucasian houses at Karagündüz Höyük, Van, in A. Sagona (ed.) *A View from The Highlands: Archaeological Studies in Honour of Charles Burney* (Ancient Near Eastern Studies Supplement Series 12). Peeters: Louvain.

Kristiansen, K. & Larsson, T. B. (2005) *The Rise of Bronze Age Society: Travels, Transmissions and Transformations.* Cambridge University Press: Cambridge.

Kroll, S. (1976) *Keramik urartäischer Festungen in Iran* (Archäologische Mitteilungen aus Iran, Ergänzungsband 2). Dietrich Reimer Verlag: Berlin.

—— (1984) Urartus Untergang in anderer Sicht, *Istanbuler Mitteilungen* 34: 151–170.

Kuhn, S. L. (2002) Paleolithic archaeology in Turkey, *Evolutionary Anthropology* 11: 198–210.

—— (2003) Flexibility and variation in the Lower Paleolithic: a view from Yarımburgaz Cave, in M. Özbaşaran, O. Tanındı, & A. Boratav (eds) *Archaeological Essays in Honour of* Homo Amatus: *Güven Arsebük. İçin Armağan Yazılar.* Ege Yayınları: Istanbul.

Kuhn, S. L., Arsebük, G., & Howell, F. C. (1996) The Middle Pleistocene lithic assemblage from Yarımburgaz Cave, Turkey, *Paleorient* 22: 31–49.

Kuhn, S. L., Stiner, M. C., & Gülec, E. (1999) Initial Upper Palaeolithic in south-central Turkey and its regional context: a preliminary report, *Antiquity* 93: 505–517.

Kuhn, S. L. Stiner, M. C., Reese, D. S., & Güleç, E. (2001) Ornaments of the earliest Upper Palaeolithic: new insights from the Levant, *Proceedings of the National Academy of Sciences of the United States of America* 98(13): 7641–7646.

Kuijt, I. (2000) Keeping the peace: ritual, skull caching, and community integration in the Levantine Neolithic, in I. Kuijt (ed.) *Life in Neolithic Farming Communities: Social Organization, Identity, and Differentiation.* Kluwer Academic: New York.

Kuniholm, P. I. & Newton, M. W. (1989) A 677 year tree-ring chronology for the Middle Bronze Age, in K. Emre, B. Hrouda, M. Mellink, & N. Özgüç (eds) *Anatolia and the Ancient Near East: Studies in Honor of Tahsin Özgüç.* Türk Tarih Kurumu Basımevi: Ankara.

Kushnareva, K. Kh. (1997) *The Southern Caucasus in Prehistory: Stages of Cultural and Socioeconomic Development from the Eighth to Second Millennium B.C.* The University Museum: Philadelphia.

Kuzcuoğlu, C., Bertaux, J. Black, S., Deneşe, M., Fontugne, M., Karabıyıkoğlu, M., et al. (1999) Reconstruction of climatic changes during the late Plesitocene based on sediment of the Konya basin (central Anatolia, Turkey), *Geological Journal* 34: 175–198.

Lamb, W. (1936) Excavations at Kusura near Afyon Karahisar, *Archaeologia*, 86: 1–64.

—— (1937) Excavations at Kusura near Afyon Karahisar, II, *Archaeologia* 87: 217–273.

Laroche, E. (1971) *Catalogue Des Textes Hittites* (Études et Commentaires 75). Éditions Klincksieck: Paris.

Larsen, M. T. (1967) *Old Assyrian Caravan Procedures* (Uitgaven van het Nederlands Historisch-Archaeologisch Instituut te Istanbul XXI). Nederlands Instituut voor het Nabije Osten: Leiden.

Last, J. (2005) Pottery from the East Mound, in I. Hodder (ed.) *Changing Materialities at Çatalhöyük: Reports from the 1995–99 Seasons* (MacDonald Institute Monographs and The British Institute of Archaeology at Ankara Monograph No. 39). MacDonald Institute for Archaeological Research: Cambridge.

Lawrence, B. (1982) Principle food animals at Çayönü, in L. Braidwood & R. J. Braidwood (eds) *Prehistoric Village Archaeology in South-Eastern Turkey* (British Archaeological Reports, International Series 138). British Archaeological Reports: Oxford.

Leach, J. & Leach, E. (1983) *The Kula: New Perspectives on Massim Exchange.* Cambridge University Press: Cambridge.

Lebeau, M. (2000) Stratified archaeological evidence and compared periodizations in the Syrian Jezirah during the third millennium B.C., in C. Marro & H. Hauptmann (eds) *Chronologies des pays du Caucase et de l'Euphrate aux IVe–IIIe millenaires: actes du colloque d'Istanbul, 16–19 décembre 1998* (Acta Anatolica XI). Institut français d'etudes anatoliennes d'Istanbul & De Boccard Edition-Diffusion: Paris.

LeBlanc, S. A. & Watson, P. J. (1973) A comparative statistical analysis of painted pottery from seven Halafian sites, *Paléorient* 1: 117–133.

Lewis, I. M. (2003) *Ecstatic Religion: A Study of Shamanism and Spirit Possession.* Routledge: London.

Lewis-Williams, D. (2002) *The Mind in the Cave: Consciousness and the Origins of Art.* Thames & Hudson: London.

Lewis-Williams, D. & Pearce, D. (2005) *Inside the Neolithic Mind: Consciousness, Cosmos and the Realm of the Gods.* Thames & Hudson: London.

Ljubin, V. P. & Bosinski, G. (1995) The earliest occupation of the Caucasus region, in W. Roebrocks & T. van Kolfschoten (eds) *The Earliest Occupation of Europe.* University of Leiden: Leiden.

Lloyd, S. & Mellaart, J. (1965) *Beycesultan Vol. II* (Occasional Publications No. 8). The British Institute of Archaeology at Ankara: London.

Locher, I. (2001) Die Frühbronzezeitlichen Siedlungsbefunde in Aizonoi, *Archäologischer Anzeiger*: 270–294.

López Bayón, I. (1988) La faune et les homes au Paléolithique moyen de Karain (quelques notes preliminaries), in M. Otte (ed.) *Anatolian Prehistory: At the Crossroads of Two Worlds*, vol. 2. ERAUL 85. Université de Liège: Liège.

Lordkipanidze, D, Nioradze, M., & Vekua, A. (2008) New discoveries from Dmanisi, in A. Sagona & M. Abramishvili (eds) *Archaeology in Southern Caucasus: Perspectives from Georgia.* Peeters: Louvain.

Luckenbill, D. D. (1927) *Ancient Records of Assyrian and Babylonia*, 2 vols. University of Chicago Press: Chicago.

Lupton, A. (1996) *Stability and Change: Socio-political Development in North Mesopotamia and South-East Anatolia* (British Archaeological Reports, International Series 627). Tempus Reparatum: Oxford.

Lyonnet, B. (2007) La culture de Maïkop, la Transcaucasie, l'Anatolie orientale et le Proche-Orient: relations et chronologie, in B. Lyonnet (ed.) *Les cultures du Caucase (VIe-IIIe millénaires avant notre ère). Leurs relations avec le Proche-Orient.* CNRS Éditions: Paris.

McCorriston, J. & Hole, F. (1991) The ecology of seasonal stress and the origins of agriculture in the Near East, *American Anthropologist* 93(1): 46–69.

McMahon, G. (1992) Hittites in the OT, in *The Anchor Bible Dictionary.* Doubleday: New York.

Macqueen, J. G. (1986) *The Hittites and Their Contemporaries in Asia Minor*, 2nd edn (Ancient Peoples and Places). Thames & Hudson: London.

Maden Teknik Araştırmarları Monograph 129 (1970) *Arsenic, Mercury, Antimony and Gold in Turkey.* Maden Teknik Araştırmarları: Ankara.

—— 133 (1972) *Lead, Silver and Zinc Deposits of Turkey.* Maden Teknik Araştırmarları: Ankara.

—— 145 (1971) *Türkiye Demir Envanteri.* Maden Teknik Araştırmarları: Ankara.

Maddin, R., Stech, T., & Muhly J. D. (1991) Çayönü Tepesi: the earliest archaeological metal artefacts, in P. Mohen (ed.) *Découverte du Métal.* Picard: Paris.

Malinowski, B. (1920) Kula: the circulating exchange of valuables in the archipelagos of eastern New Guinea, *Man* 20: 97–105.

Manning, S. W., Kromer, B., Kuniholm, P. I., & Newton, M. W. (2001) Anatolian tree rings and a new chronology of the eastern Mediterranean Bronze-Iron ages, *Science* 294: 2532–2535.

Maréchal, C. (1985) Les bracelets néolithiques en pierre de Cafer Höyük (Turquie), *Cahiers de l'Euphrate* 4: 109–115.

Marro, C. (1997) *La culture du Haut-Euphrate au Bronze Ancien: Essai d'intepretation a partir de la ceramique peinte e Keban (Turquie)* (Varia Anatolica 8). Institut français d'études anatoliennes d'Istanbul & De Boccard Edition-Diffusion: Paris.

—— (2007a) Upper-Mesopotamia and Transcaucasia in the Late Chalcolithic period (4000–3500 BC), in B. Lyonnet (ed.) *Les cultures du Caucase (VIe–IIIe millénaires avant notre ère). Leurs relations avec le Proche-Orient*. CNRS Éditions: Paris.

—— (2007b) Late Chalcolithic ceramic cultures in the Anatolian highlands, in K. S. Rubinson & A. Sagona (eds) *Ceramics in Transitions: Chalcolithic Through Iron Age in the Highlands of Southern Caucasus and Anatolia*. Peeters: Louvain.

Marro, C. & Hauptmann, H. (eds) (2000) *Chronologies des pays du Caucase et de l'euphrate aux IVe–IIIe millenaires*. Institut français d'etudes anatoliennes d'istanbul and De Boccard: Paris.

Marro, C. & Ozfırat, A. (2003) Pre-classical survey in eastern Turkey. First preliminary report: the Ağrı Dağı (Mount Ararat) region, *Anatolia Antiqua* 11: 385–422.

—— (2004) Pre-classical survey in eastern Turkey. Second preliminary report: the Erciş region, *Anatolia Antiqua* 12: 217–226.

—— (2005) Pre-classical survey in eastern Turkey, third preliminary report: Doğubeyazit and the eastern shore of Lake Van, *Anatolia Antiqua* 12: 319–356.

Martin, L., Russell, N., & Carruthers, D. (2002) Animal remains from the central Anatolian Neolithic, in F. Gérard & L. Thissen (eds) *The Neolithic of Central Anatolia: Internal Developments during the 9th–6th Millennia Cal BC. Proceedings of the International CANeW Table Ronde, Istanbul, 23–24 November, 2001*. Ege Yayınları: Istanbul.

Martirosyan, A. A. (1974) *Argishtikhinili* (Arkheologiceskie Pamyatniki Armenii 8). Akademiya Nauk Armyanskoy SSR: Yerevan.

Matney, T. & Algaze, G. (1995) Urban development at mid-late Early Bronze Age Titriş Höyük in southeastern Anatolia, *Bulletin of the American Schools of Oriental Research* 299/300: 33–52.

Matney, T., Algaze, G., & Pittman, H. (1997) Excavations at Titriş Höyük in southeastern Turkey: a preliminary report of the 1996 season, *Anatolica* 23: 61–84.

Matney, T., Algaze, G., & Rosen, S. A., with contributions by Aricanlı, S. and Hartenberger, B. (1999) The Early Bronze Age urban structure at Titriş Höyük, southeastern Turkey: the 1998 season, *Anatolica* 25: 185–202.

Matthews, R. (2002) Homogeneity versus diversity: dynamic of the central Anatolian Neolithic, in F. Gérard & L. Thissen (eds) *The Neolithic of Central Anatolia: Internal Developments during the 9th–6th Millennia Cal BC. Proceedings of the International CANeW Table Ronde, Istanbul, 23–24 November, 2001*. Ege Yayınları: Istanbul.

—— (2007) An arena for cultural contact: Paphlagonia (north-central Turkey) through prehistory, *Anatolian Studies* 57: 25–34.

Mauss, M. (1990) *The Gift: Forms and Functions of Exchange in Archaic Societies*. Routledge: London.

Melchert, H. C. (2002) Tarhuntašša in the Südburg hieroglyphic inscription, in K. A. Yener & H. A. Hoffner Jr. (eds) *Recent Developments in Hittite Archaeology and History: Papers in Memory of Hans G. Güterbock*. Eisenbrauns: Winona Lake, IN.

—— (ed.) (2003) *The Luwians* (Handbuch der Orientalistik 1/68). E. J. Brill: Leiden.

—— (2008) Lydian, in R. D. Woodard (ed.) *The Ancient Languages of Asia Minor*. Cambridge University Press: Cambridge.

Mellaart, J. (1963) Excavations at Çatal Hüyük: second preliminary report, 1962, *Anatolian Studies* 13: 43–103.

—— (1964) Excavations at Çatal Hüyük: third preliminary report, 1963, *Anatolian Studies* 14: 39–119.

—— (1967) *Çatal Höyük: A Neolithic Town in Anatolia*. Thames & Hudson: London.

—— (1970a) *Excavations at Hacılar*, vols 1 and 2. The British Institute of Archaeology at Ankara and Edinburgh University Press: Edinburgh.

—— (1970b) Anatolian before c. 4000 B.C., in I. E. S. Edwards, C. J. Gadd, & N. G. L. Hammond (eds) *The Cambridge Ancient History*, 3rd ed., vol. I, part 1. Cambridge University Press: Cambridge.

—— (1975) *The Neolithic of the Near East*. Thames & Hudson: London.

Mellink, M. J. (1956) The royal tombs at Alaca Höyük and the Aegean world, in S. S. Weinberg (ed.) *The Aegean and the Near East. Studies Presented to Hetty Goldman on the Occasion of her Seventy-Fifth Birthday*. J. J. Augustin: New York.

—— (1987) Lydia and Sardis in Anatolian context, in E. Guralnik (ed.) *Sardis: Twenty-Seven Years of Discovery*. Archaeological Institute of America: Chicago.

—— (1989) Anatolian and foreign relations of Tarsus, in K. Emre, B. Hrouda, M. Mellink, & N. Özgüç (eds) *Anatolia and the Ancient Near East. Studies in Honor of Tahsin Özgüç*. Türk Tarih Kurumu Basımevi: Ankara.

Merhav, R. (ed.) (1991) *Urartu: A Metalworking Center in the First Millennium B.C.E.* Israel Musuem: Jerusalem.

Meskell, L. & Nakamura C. (2006) Çatalhöyük figurines, in M. Haydaroğlu (ed.) *From Earth to Eternity: Çatalhöyük*. Yapı Kredi Yayınları: Istanbul.

Michel, C. (2003) *Old Assyrian Bibliography of Cuneiform Texts, Bullae, Seals and the Results of Excavations at Aššur, Kültepe/Kaniş, Acemhöyük, Ališar and Boğazköy* (Old Assyrian Archives, Studies, volume 1). Nederlands Instituut voor het Nabije Oosten: Leiden.

Minzoni-Dèroche, A. (1987) Kocapınar, site Moustérien d'Anatolie etude de l'industrie, *Bulletin de la Societe Préhistoire Française* 84: 272–277.

Moorey, P. R. S. (1995) *From the Gulf to the Delta and Beyond*. Ben Gurion University: Beersheva.

Morris, I. (1987) *Burials and Ancient Society: The Rise of the Greek City-State*. Cambridge University Press: Cambridge.

—— (1992) *Death-Ritual and Social Structure in Classical Antiquity*. Cambridge University Press: Cambridge.

Mountjoy, P. A. (1998) The east Aegean–West Anatolian interface in the Late Bronze Age: Mycenaeans and the Kingdom of Ahhiyawa, *Anatolian Studies* 48: 33–67.

Müller-Karpe, A. (2002) Kuşaklı-Sarissa: a Hittite town in the "Upper Land", in K. A. Yener & H. A. Hoffner Jr. (eds) *Recent Developments in Hittite Archaeology and History: Papers in Memory of Hans G. Güterbock*. Eisenbrauns: Winona Lake, IN.

Müller-Karpe, H. (1974) *Handbuch der Vorgeschichte*. Bd. 3, *Kupferzeit*. Beck: Munich.

Munchaev, R. M. (1975) *Kavkaz na zare bronzovogo veka*. Nauka: Moscow.

—— (1994) Maikopskaya kul'tura, in K. Kh. Kushnareva & V. I. Markovin (eds) *Epokha Bronzy Kavkaza i Srednei Azii: Rannyaya i Srednyaya Bronza Kavkaza*. Nauka: Moscow.

Naumann, R. (1971) *Architektur Kleinasiens von ihren Anfängen bis zum Ende der Hethitischen Zeit*, 2nd edn. Ernst Wasmuth: Tübingen.

Neu, E. (1974) *Der Anitta-Text* (Studien zu den Boğazköy-Texten, Heft 18). Otto Harrassowitz: Wiesbaden.

Neve, P. (1992) *Hattuša—Stadt der Götter und Tempel* (Zaberns Bildbände zur Archäologie). Philipp von Zabern: Mainz am Rhein.

—— (2002) The Great Temple in Boğazköy-Hattuša, in D. C. Hopkins (ed.) *Across the Anatolian Plateau: Readings in the Archaeology of Ancient Turkey* (Annual of the American Schools of Oriental Research vol. 57, 2000). American Schools of Oriental Research: Boston, MA.

Newton, M. W. & Kuniholm, P. I. (2004) A dendrochronological framework for the Assyrian Colony Period in Asia Minor, *TÜBA-AR (Türkiye Bilimler Akademisi Arkeoloji Dergesi)* 7: 165–175.

—— (2007) A revised dendrochronogical date for the fortress of Rusa II at Ayanis: *Rusahinili Eiduru-kai*, in A. Çilingiroğlu & A. Sagona (eds) *Anatolian Iron Ages 6: The Proceedings of the Sixt Anatolian Iron Ages Colloquium Held at Eskişehir, 16–20 August 2004* (Ancient Near Eastern Studies Supplement 20). Peeters: Louvain.

Oates, J., McMahon, A., Karsgaard, P., Al Quntar, S., & Ur, J. (2007) Early Mesopotamian urbanism: a new view from the north, *Antiquity* 81: 585–600.

Oddone M., Yeğingil Z., Özdoğan M., Meloni S., & Bigazzi G. (2003) Provenance studies of obsidian artefacts from Turkish neolithic sites: an interdisciplinary approach by INAA and fission track dating, *Revue d'Archéométrie* 27: 137–145.

Oliver, P. (ed.) (1997) *Encyclopedia of Vernacular Architecture of the World*, 2 vols. Cambridge University Press: Cambridge.

Oppenheim, A. L. (1967) *Letters from Mesopotamia*. University of Chicago Press: Chicago.

Orlin, L. L. (1970) *Assyrian Colonies in Cappadocia*. Mouton: The Hague.

Orthmann, W. (1963) *Die Keramik der Frühen Bronzezeit aus Inneranatolien* (Istanbuler Forschungen 24). Gebrüder Mann Verlag: Berlin.

—— (1967) Zu den "Standarten" aus Alaca Höyük, *Istanbuller Mitteilungen* 17: 34–54.

—— (1971) *Untersuchungen Zur Späthetitischen Kunst* (Saarbrücker Beiträge zur Altertumskunde 8). Rudolf Habelt Verlag: Bonn.

—— (2002) Kontinuität und neue Einflüsse: Die Entwicklung der späthethitischen Kunst zwischen 1200 und 700 v. Chr., in *Die Hethiter und Ihr Reich: Das Volk der 1000 Götter*. Konrad Theiss Verlag: Stuttgart.

Otte, M., Yalçınkaya, I., Kozlowski, J. K., Bar-Yosef, O., Taşkıran, H., & Noiret, P. (1995a) Technical evolution in the Lower Palaeolithic from Karain (Turkey), *Anthropologie* 99: 529–561.

Otte, M., Yalçınkaya, I., Leotard, J-M., Kartal, M., Bar-Yosef, O., Kozlowski, J., et al. (1995b) The epi-Palaeolithic of Öküzini cave (SW Anatolia) and its mobiliary art, *Antiquity* 69: 931–944.

Otte, M., Yalçınkaya, I., Taşkıran, H. Kozlowski, J. K., Bar-Yosef, O., & Noiret, P. (1995c) The Anatolian Middle Paleolithic: new research at Karain Cave, *Journal of Anthropological Research* 51: 287–299.

Otte, M., Yalçınkaya, I., Kozlowski, J. K., Bar-Yosef, O., Bayon, I., & Taşkıran, H. (1998) Long-term technical evolution and human remains in the Anatolian Palaeolithic, *Journal of Human Evolution* 34: 413–431.

Otten, H. (1973) *Eine Althethitische Erzählung um die Stadt Zalpa* (Studien ze den Boğazköy-Texten Heft 17). Otto Harrassowitz: Wiesbaden.

Özbaşaran, M. (2000) The Neolithic site of Musular—central Anatolia, *Anatolica* 26: 129–151.

Özbaşaran, M. & Buitenhuis, H. (2002) Proposal for a regional terminology for Central Anatolia, in F. Gérard & L. Thissen (eds) *The Neolithic of Central Anatolia: Internal Developments during the 9th–6th Millennia Cal BC. Proceedings of the International CANeW Table Ronde, Istanbul, 23–24 November, 2001*. Ege Yayınları: Istanbul.

Özbaşaran, M., Duru, G, Kayacan, N., Erdoğu, B., & Buitenhuis, H. (2007) Musular. 1996–2004: Genel Değerlendirme, in M. Özdoğan & N. Başgelen (eds) *Anadolu'da Uygarlığın Doğuşu ve Avrupa'ya Yayılımı: Türkiye'de Neolitik Dönem*. Arkeoloji ve Sanat: Istanbul.

Özdoğan, A. (1995) Life at Çayönü during the Pre-Pottery Neolithic period (according to the artefactual assemblage), in Section of Prehistory, Faculty of Letters, Istanbul University (ed.) *Readings in Prehistory: Studies Presented to Halet Çambel*. Graphis: Istanbul.

—— (1999) Çayönü, in M. Özdoğan & N. Başgelen (eds) *Neolithic in Turkey: The Cradle of Civilization. New Discoveries*. Arkeoloji ve Sanat Yayınları: Istanbul.

Özdoğan, M. (1977) *Lower Euphrates Basin 1977 Survey* (METU Lower Euphrates Project Publications Series 1 No. 2). METU: Istanbul.

—— (1982) Tilkiburnu: a Late Chalcolithic site in eastern Thrace, *Anatolica* 9: 1–26.

—— (1983) Pendik: a neolithic site of Fikirtepe Culture in the Marmara region, in R. M. Boehmer & H. Hauptmann (eds) *Beiträge zur Altertumskunde Kleinasiens. Festschrift für Kurt Bittel*. Philipp Von Zabern: Mainz am Rhein.

—— (1993) Vinça and Anatolia: a new look at a very old problem (or redefining Vinça culture from the perspective of Near Eastern tradition), *Anatolica* 19: 174–193.

—— (1995) Neolithic in Turkey: the status of research, in Section of Prehistory, Faculty of Letters, Istanbul University (ed.) *Readings in Prehistory: Studies Presented to Halet Çambel*. Graphis: Istanbul.

—— (1996a) Pre-Bronze Age sequence of central Anatolia: an alternative approach, in U. Magen & M. Rashad (eds) *Vom Halys zum Euphrat Thomas: Beran zu Ehren*. Ugarit Verlag: Münster.

—— (1998) Hoca Çeşme: an Early Neolithic Anatolian colony in the Balkans?, in P. Anreiter, L. Bartosiewicz, E. Jerem, & W. Meid (eds) *Man and the Animal World. Studies in Archaeozoology, Archaeology, Anthroplogy and Palaeolinguistics in Memoriam Sándor Bökönyi*. Archaeo-lingua Alapìtvány Akaprint: Budapest.

—— (1999a) Preface, in M. Özdoğan & N. Başgelen (eds) *Neolithic in Turkey: The Cradle of Civilization. New Discoveries*. Arkeoloji ve Sanat Yayınları: Istanbul.

—— (1999b) Northwestern Turkey: Neolithic cultures in between the Balkans and Anatolia, in M. Özdoğan & N. Başgelen (eds) *Neolithic in Turkey: The Cradle of Civilization. New Discoveries*. Arkeoloji ve Sanat Yayınları: Istanbul.

—— (1999c) Concluding remarks, in M. Özdoğan & N. Başgelen (eds) *Neolithic in Turkey: The Cradle of Civilization. New Discoveries*. Arkeoloji ve Sanat Yayınları: Istanbul.

—— (2002) Redefining the Neolithic of Anatolia: a critical overview, in R. T. J. Cappers & S. Bottema (eds) *The Dawn of Farming in the Near East*. Ex Oriente: Berlin.

—— (2003a) A group of Neolithic stone figurines from Mezraa-Teleilat, in M. Özdoğan, H. Hauptmann, & N. Başgelen (eds) *From Villages to Towns: Studies Presented to Ufuk Esin*. Arkeoloji ve Sanat Yayınları: Istanbul.

—— (2003b) The Black Sea, the Sea of Marmara and Bronze Age archaeology: an archaeological predicament, in G. A. Wagner, E. Pernicka, & H.-P. Uerpmann (eds) *Troia and the Troad: Scientific Approaches*. Springer: Berlin.

—— (2004) The Neolithic and the highlands of eastern Anatolia, in A. Sagona (ed.) *A View from the Highlands: Archaeological Studies in Honour of Charles Burney* (Ancient Near Eastern Studies Supplement Series 12). Peeters: Louvain.

—— (2005) The expansion of the Neolithic way of life: What we know and what we do not know, in C. Lichter (ed.) *How Did Farming Reach Europe? Anatolia-European Relations from the Second Half of the 7th Through the First Half of the 6th Millennium CAL BC. Proceedings of the International Workshop, Istanbul, 20–22 May 2004* (Byzas 2). Deutsches Archäologisches Institut: Istanbul.

—— (2006) Neolithic cultures at the contact zone between Anatolia and the Balkans: diversity and homogeneity at the Neolithic frontier, in I. Gatsov & H. Schwarzberg (eds) *Aegean–Marmara–Black Sea: The Present State of Research on the Early Neolithic: Proceedings of the Session held at the EAA 8th Annual Meeting at Thessaloniki, 28 September 2002*. Beier & Beier: Langenweissbach.

—— (2007) Mezraa-Teleilat, in M. Özdoğan & N. Başgelen (eds) *Anadolu'da Uygarlığın Doğuşu ve Avrupa'ya Yayılımı: Türkiye'de Neolitik Dönem*. Arkeoloji ve Sanat: Istanbul.

Özdoğan, M. & Başgelen, N. (eds) (1999) *Neolithic in Turkey: The Cradle of Civilization. New Discoveries*, 2 vols. Arkeoloji ve Sanat Yayınları: Istanbul.

—— (eds) (2007) *Anadolu'da Uygarlığın Doğuşu ve Avrupa'ya Yayılımı. Türkiye'de Neolitik Dönem. Yeni Kazılar, Yeni Bulgular*, 2 vols. Arkeoloji ve Sanat Yayınları: Istanbul.

Özdoğan, M. & Gatsov, I. (1998) The aceramic Neolithic period in western Turkey and in the Aegean, *Anatolica* 24: 209–232.

Özdoğan, M., Miyake, Y., & Dede, N. Ö. (1991) An interim report on excavations at Yarımburgaz and Toptepe in eastern Thrace, *Anatolica* 17: 59–121.

Özdoğan, M. & Özdoğan, A. (1998) Buildings of cult and the cult of buildings, in G. Arsebük, M. J. Mellink, & W. Schirmer (eds) *Light on Top of the Black Hill: Studies Presented to Halet Çambel.* Ege Yayınları: Istanbul.

Özdoğan, M., Yutaka M., & Dede, N. O. (1991) An interim report on excavations at Yarımburgaz and Toptepe in eastern Thrace, *Anatolica* 17: 59–121.

Özfırat, A. (2001) *Doğu Anadolu Yayla Kültürleri.* Arkeoloji ve Sanat: Istanbul.

—— (2007a) A survey of pre-classical sites in eastern Turkey. Fourth preliminary report: the eastern shore of Lake Van, *Ancient Near Eastern Studies* 44: 113–140.

—— (2007b) The highland plateau of eastern Anatolia in the second millennium BCE, in K. S. Rubinson & A. Sagona (eds) *Ceramics in Transition: Chalcolithic Through Iron Age in the Highlands of Caucasus and Anatolia.* Peeters: Louvain.

Özgüç, N. (1965) *Kültepe Mühür Baskılarında Anadolu Grubu/The Anatolian Group of Cylinder Seal Impressions from Kültepe Seals and Seal Impressions of Level Ib from Karum Kanish* (Türk Tarih Kurumu Yayınları V. Dizi—Sa. 22). Türk Tarih Kurumu Basımevi: Ankara.

—— (1966) Excavations at Acemhöyük, *Anadolu (Anatolia)* 10: 29–52.

—— (1968) *Kanis Karumu Ib Katı—Mühürleri ve Mühür Baskılar/ Seals and Seal Impressions of Level Ib from Karum Kanish* (Türk Tarih Kurumu Yayınları V. Dizi—Sa. 25). Türk Tarih Kurumu Basımevi: Ankara.

—— (1980) Seal impressions from the palaces at Acemhöyük, in E. Porada (ed.) *Ancient Art in Seals.* Princeton University Press: Princeton.

Özgüç, T. (1964) New finds from Horoztepe, *Anatolia* 8: 1–17.

—— (1969) *Altıntepe II* (Türk Tarih Kurumu Yayınlarından, Series 5, no. 27). Türk Tarih Kurumu Basımevi: Ankara.

—— (1971) *Demir Devrinde Kültepe ve Civarı/Kültepe and its Vicinity in the Iron Age* (Türk Tarih Kurumu Yayınlarından V. Dizi—Sa. 29). Türk Tarih Kurumu Basımevi: Ankara.

—— (1980) Some Early Bronze Age objects from the district of Çorum, *Belleten* 44: 467–474.

—— (1982) *Maşat Höyük II: Boğazköy'ün Kuzeydoğusunda Bir Hitit Merkezi/A Hittite Center Northeast of Boğazköy* (Türk Tarih Kurumu Yayınları V. Dizi—Sa. 38). Türk Tarih Kurumu Basımevi: Ankara.

—— (1986) *Kültepe-Kaniş II: Eski Yakıdoğu'nun Ticaret Merkezinde Yeni Araştırmalar/New Researches at the Trading Center of the Ancient Near East* (Türk Tarih Kurumu Yayınları V. Dizi—Sa. 41). Türk Tarih Kurumu Basımevi: Ankara.

—— (1988) *İnandıktepe: Eski Hitit Çağında Önemli Bir Kült Merkezi /An Important Cult Center in the Old Hittite Period* (Türk Tarih Kurumu Yayınları V. Dizi—Sa. 43). Türk Tarih Kurumu Basımevi: Anakara.

—— (1997) Kanesh, in E. M. Myers (ed.) *The Oxford Encyclopedia of Archaeology in the Near East.* Oxford University Press: New York/Oxford.

—— (1999) *Kültepe-Kaniş/Neşa Sarayları ve Mabetleri/The Palaces and Temples of Kültepe-Kaniš/Neša* (Türk Tarih Kurumu Yayınları V. Dizi—Sa. 46). Türk Tarih Kurumu Basımevi: Ankara.

Özgüç, T. & Akok, M. (1958) *Horoztepe. An Early Bronze Age Settlement and Cemetery.* Türk Tarih Kurumu Basımevi: Ankara.

Özkaya, V. & San, O. (2004) 2001 excavations at Körtik Tepe, in N. Tuna, J. Greenhalgh, & J. Velibeyoğlu (eds) *Salvage Project of the Archaeological Heritage of the Ilısu and Carchemish Dam Reservoirs Activities in 2001.* Middle East Technical University: Ankara.

Öztan, A. (2007) Köşk Höyük: Niğde—Bor Ovası'nda bir Neolitik yerleşim, in M. Özdoğan & N.

Başgelen (eds) *Anadolu'da Uygarlığın Doğuşu ve Avrupa'ya Yayılımı. Türkiye'de Neolitik Dönem. Yeni Kazılar, Yeni bulgular.* Arkeoloji ve Sanat Yayınları: Istanbul.

Öztan, A. & Özkan, S. (2003) Çizi ve nokta bezekli Köşk Höyük seramikleri, in M. Özdoğan, H. Hauptmann, & N. Başgelen (eds) *From Villages to Cities: Early Villages in the Near East.* Arkeoloji ve Sanat Yayınları: Istanbul.

Özyar, A. (2000) Noch einmal zu dem Standartenaufsätzen aus Alacahöyük, in Ü. Yalçın (ed.) *Anatolian Metal I* (Der Anschnitt 13, Zeitschrift für Kunst und Kultur im Bergbau). Bergbau Museum: Bochum.

Palmieri, A. (1981) Excavations at Arslantepe (Malatya), *Anatolian Studies* 31: 101–119.

Palumbi, G. (2003) Red-black pottery: eastern Anatolia and Transcaucasian relationships around the mid-fourth millennium BC, *Ancient Near Eastern Studies* 40: 80–134.

—— (2007) Mid-Fourth millennium red-black burnished wares from Anatolia: a cross-comparison, in K. S. Rubinson & A. Sagona (eds) *Ceramics in Transition: Chalcolithic Through Iron Age in the Highlands of Caucasus and Anatolia.* Peeters: Louvain.

Parzinger, H. (1993a) Zur Zeitstellung der Büyükkaya-Ware: Bemerkungen zur Vorbronzezeitlichen Kulturfolge Zentralanatliens, *Anatolica* 19: 211–229.

Pasinli, A., Uzunoğlu, E., Atakan, N. Girgin. C., & Soysal, M. (1994) Pendik kurtarma kazısı, in *IV Müze Kurtarma Kazıları Semineri 1993.* T. C. Kültür Bakanlığı, Anıtlar ve Müzeler Genel Müdürlüğü: Ankara.

Pearce, J. (1999) Investigating ethnicity at Hacınebi: ceramic perspectives on style and behavior in 4th millennium Mesopotamian–Anatolian interaction, *Paléorient* 25: 35–42.

Pecorella, P. E. (1984) *La Cultura Prehistorica di Iasos in Caria.* (Missione Archeologica Italiana di Iasos I. Archeologica 51). Giorgio Bretschneider Editore: Rome.

Pedley, J. G. (1968) *Sardis in the Age of Croesus.* University of Oklahoma Press: Norman, OK.

Perkins, D. (1969) Fauna of Çatal Hüyük: evidence for early cattle domestication in Anatolia, *Science* 164: 177–179.

Perkins, D. & Daly, P. (1968) A hunters' village in Neolithic Turkey, *Scientific American* 219: 97–106.

Perlès, C. (2001) *The Early Neolithic in Greece: The First Farming Communities in Europe.* Cambridge University Press: Cambridge.

Perrot, J. (2000) Réflexions sur l'etat des recherches concernant la préhistoire récente du Proche et du Moyen-Orient, *Paléorient* 26/1: 5–27.

—— (2002) On terminology in Near Eastern prehistory, in F. Gérard & L. Thissen (eds) *The Neolithic of Central Anatolia: Internal Developments during the 9th–6th Millennia Cal BC. Proceedings of the International CANeW Table Ronde, Istanbul, 23–24 November, 2001.* Ege Yayınları: Istanbul.

Peschlow-Bindokat, A. (2003) *Frühe Menschenbilder: Die prähistorischen Felsmalereinen des Latmos-Gebirges (Westtürkei).* Philipp von Zabern: Mainz am Rhein.

—— (2007) Die prähistorischen Felsbilder des Latmos, in Badischen Landesmuseum Karlsruhe (ed.) *Vor 12.00 Jahren in Anatolien: Die ältesten Mounmente der Menschheit.* Konrad Theiss Verlag: Stuttgart.

Philip, G. & Millard, A. R. (2000) Khirbet Kerak ware in the Levant: the implications of radiocarbon chronology and spatial distribution, in C. Marro & H. Hauptmann (eds) *Chronologies des pays du Caucase et de l'Euphrate aux IV-III millénaires, Institut Français d'Etudes Anatoliennes d'Istanbul, Varia Anatolica XI.* De Boccard Edition-Diffusion: Paris.

Pigott, V. C. (1996) Near Eastern archaeometallurgy: modern research and future directions, in J. S. Cooper & G. M. Schwarz (eds) *The Study of the Ancient Near East in the Twenty-First Century: The William Foxwell Albright Centennial Conference.* Eisenbrauns: Winona Lake, IN.

Pinhasi, R., Fort, J., & Ammerman, A. J. (2005) Tracing the origin and spread of agriculture in Europe, *PLoS Biology* 3: 2220–2228.

Piotrovsky, B. B. (1969) *The Ancient Civilization of Urartu* (transl. J. Hogarth). Nagel: Geneva.

Piro, J. (2009) *Pastoralism in the Early Transcaucasian Culture: The Faunal Remains from Sos Höyük* (unpublished PhD dissertation, New York University).

Poidevin, J. L. (1998) Les gisements d'obsidienne de Turquie et de Transcaucasie: geologie, geochimie et chronomterie, in M.-C. Cauvin, A. Gourgaud, B. Gratuze, N. Arnaud, G. Poupcau, J.-L. Poidevin, et al. (eds) *L'obsidienne au Proche et Moyen Orient: du volcan a l'outil* (British Archaeological Reports, International Series 738). Archaeopress & Maison de l'Orient Mediterraneen: Oxford/Lyon.

Pollock, S. & Coursey, C. (1995) Ceramics from Hacınebi Tepe: chronology and connections, *Anatolica* 21: 101–141.

Porada, E. (1965) The relative chronology of Mesopotamia. Part 1. Seals and trade (6000–1600 B.C.), in R. Ehrich (ed.) *Chronologies in Old World Archaeology*. University of Chicago Press: Chicago.

Postgate, J. N. (ed.) (2002) *Artefacts of Complexity: Tracking the Uruk in the Near East*. British School of Archaeology in Iraq: Warminster.

—— (2007) The ceramics of centralisation and dissolution: a case study from Rough Cilicia, *Anatolian Studies* 57: 151–171.

Potts, D. T. (1997) *Mesopotamian Civilization: The Material Foundations*. Athlone: London.

Pullar, J. (1977) Early cultivation in the Zagros, *Iran* 15: 15–37.

Rammage, A. (1987) Lydian Sardis, in E. Guralnik (ed.) *Sardis: Twenty-Seven Years of Discovery*. Archaeological Institute of America: Chicago.

Rammage, A. & Craddock, P. (2000) *King Croesus' Gold: Excavations at Sardis and the History of Gold Refining*. British Museum: London.

Rankin, M. (1997) *Burials and Social Structures in Early Bronze Age Anatolia* (unpublished MA thesis, University of Melbourne).

Renfrew, C. (1986) Introduction: peer polity interaction and social change, in C. Renfrew & J. Cherry (eds) *Peer Polity Interaction and Social Change*. Cambridge University Press: Cambridge.

—— (1987) *Archaeology and Language: The Puzzle of Indo-European Origins*. Jonathan Cape: London.

Renfrew, C. & Boyle, K. (eds) (2000) *Archaeogenetics: DNA and the Population Prehistory of Europe*. McDonald Institute for Archaeological Research: Cambridge.

Rice, P. M. (1987) *Pottery Analysis: A Sourcebook*. Chicago University Press: Chicago.

Richmond, J. (2006) Textile production in prehistoric Anatolia: a study of three Early Bronze Age sites, *Ancient Near Eastern Studies* 43: 203–238.

Rindos, D. (1984) *The Origins of Agriculture: An Evolutionary Perspective*. Academic Press: Orlando.

Roberts, N. (1990) Human-induced landscape change in south and southwest Turkey during the later Holocene, in S. Bottema, G. Entjes-Nieborg, & W. van Zeist (eds) *Man's Role in the Shaping of the Eastern Mediterranean Landscape*. A. A. Balkema: Rotterdam.

—— 2002 "Did prehistoric landscape management retard the post-glacial spread of woodland in southwest Asia?" *Antiquity* 76: 1002–1010.

Roberts, N., Eastwood, W. J., Lamb, H. F., & Tibby, J. C. (1997) The age and causes of mid-late Holocene environmental change in southwest Turkey, in H. N. Dalfes, G. Kukla, & H. Weiss (eds) *Third Millennium BC Climate Change and Old World Collapse*. Springer: Berlin.

Rollefson, G. O. & Köhler-Rollefson, I. (1989) The collapse of Early Neolithic settlements in the southern Levant, in I. Hershkovitz (ed.) *People and Culture in Change* (British Archaeological Reports, International Series 508). British Archaeological Reports: Oxford.

Roller, L. (2007) Toward the formation of a Phrygian iconography in the Iron Age, in A. Çilingiroğlu & A. Sagona (eds) *Anatolian Iron Ages 6: The Proceedings of the Sixth Anatolian Iron Ages Colloquium Held at Eskişehir, 16–20 August 2004* (Ancient Near Eastern Studies Supplement 20). Peeters: Louvain.

Roodenberg, J. J. (1979–80) Premiers résultats des recherches archéologiques à Hayaz Höyük, *Anatolica* 7: 3–19.

—— (ed.) (1995) *The Ilıpınar Excavations I. Five Seasons of Fieldwork in NW Anatolia, 1987–91* (PHIANS 72). Nederlands Instituut voor het Nabije Osten: Leiden.

—— (1999a) Ilıpınar. An early farming village in the İznik Lake basin, in M. Özdoğan & N. Başgelen (eds)

Neolithic in Turkey: The Cradle of Civilization. New Discoveries. Arkeoloji ve Sanat Yayınları: Istanbul.

—— (1999b) Investigations at Menteşe Höyük near Yenişehir (1996–97), *Anatolica* 25: 21–36.

Roodenberg, J. & Alpaslan Roodenberg, S. (eds) (2008) *Life and Death in a Prehistoric Settlement in Northwest Anatolia: The Ilıpınar Excavations, Volume III.* Nederlands Instituut voor het Nabije Osten: Leiden.

Roodenberg, J. J. & Gérard, F. (1996) The southwest flank of Ilıpınar: the 1994 and 1995 seasons, *Anatolica* 22: 33–48.

Roodenberg, J. J. & Thissen, C. L. (eds) (2001) *The Ilıpınar Excavations II.* (PHIANS 93). Nederlands Instituut voor het Nabije Osten: Leiden.

Roodenberg, J. J., van As, J. A., Jacobs, L., & Wijnen, M. H. (2003) Early settlement in the plain of Yenişehir (NW Anatolia). The basal occupation layers at Menteşe, *Anatolica* 29: 17–59.

Rosenberg, M. (1994) Hallan Çemi Tepesi: some further observations concerning stratigraphy and material culture, *Anatolica* 20: 121–140.

—— (1999) Hallan Çemi, in M. Özdoğan & N. Başgelen (eds) *Neolithic in Turkey: The Cradle of Civilization. New Discoveries.* Arkeoloji ve Sanat Yayınları: Istanbul.

—— (2003) The strength of numbers: from villages to towns in the aceramic Neolithic of southwestern Asia, in M. Özdoğan, H. Hauptmann, & N. Başgelen (eds) *From Villages to Towns: Early Villages in the Near East. Studies Presented to Ufuk Esin.* Arkeoloji ve Sanat Yayınları: Istanbul.

Rosenberg, M. & Davis, M. (1992) Hallan Çemi Tepesi: an early aceramic site in eastern Anatolia: some preliminary observations concerning material culture, *Anatolica* 20: 121–140.

Rosenberg, M, Nesbitt, R. M. A., Redding, R. W., & Strasser, T. F. (1995) Hallan Çemi Tepesi: some preliminary observations concerning Early Neolithic subsistence behaviors in eastern Anatolia, *Anatolica* 21: 1–12.

Rosenberg, M. & Peasnell, B. (1998) A report on soundings at Demirköy, an aceramic Neolithic site in eastern Anatolia, *Anatolica* 24: 195–207.

Rossel, S. Marshall, F., Peters, J., Pilgram, T., Adams, M. D., & O'Connor, D. (2008) Domestication of the donkey: timing, processes, and indicators, *Proceedings of the National Academy of Sciences* 105(10): 3715–3720.

Rothman, M. (ed.) (2001) *Uruk Mesopotamia & Its Neighbors: Cross Cultural Interactiions in the Era of State Formation* (School of American Research Advanced Seminar Series). School of American Research Press and James Currey: Sante Fe/Oxford.

—— (2002) *Tepe Gawra: The Evolution of a Small, Prehistoric Center in Northern Iraq.* The University Museum: Philadelphia.

—— (2003) Ripples in the stream: Transcaucasia-Anatolian interaction in the Murat/Euphrates Basin at the beginning of the third millennium BC, in A. T. Smith & K. Rubinson (eds) *Archaeology in the Borderlands: Investigations in Caucasia and Beyond.* Cotsen Institute Press: Los Angeles.

Rothman, M. S. & Fuensanta, J. G. (2003) The archaeology of the Early Bronze I and II periods in southeastern Turkey and north Syria, in M. Özdoğan, H. Hauptmann, & N. Başgelen (eds) *From Villages to Cities: Early Villages in the Near East. Studies Presented to Ufuk Esin.* Arkeoloji ve Sanat Yayınları: Istanbul.

Rova, E. (1996) Ceramic provinces along the Middle and Upper Euphrates: Late Chalcolithic–Early Bronze Age: a diachronic view, *Bagdader Mitteilungen* 27: 13–37.

Rowly-Conwy, P. (2003) Early domestic animals in Europe: imported or locally domesticated?, in J. Ammerman & P. Biagi (eds) *The Widening Harvest.* Archaeological Institute of America: Boston, MA.

Runnels, C. (2003) The Lower Palaeolithic of Greece and NW Turkey, in M. Özbaşaran, O. Tanındı, & A. Boratav (eds) *Archaeological Essays in Honour of* Homo Amatus: *Güven Arsebük. İçin Armağan Yazılar.* Ege Yayınları: Istanbul.

Runnels, S. & Özdoğan, M. (2001) The Lower Palaeolithic of the Bosphorus region, NW Turkey, *Journal of Field Archaeology* 20: 191–203.

Russell, H. F. (1980) *Pre Classical Pottery of Eastern Anatolia* (BIAA Monograph 2, British Archaeological Reports, International Series 85). British Archaeological Reports: Oxford.

Ryan, C. W. (1960) *A Guide to Known Minerals in Turkey*. Maden Teknik Araştırmarları: Ankara.

Sagona, A. G. (1984) *The Caucasian Region in the Early Bronze Age*, Vols I–III (British Archaeological Reports, International Series 214). British Archaeological Reports: Oxford.

—— (1993) Settlement and society in early prehistoric Trans-Caucasus, in M. Frangipane, H. Hauptmann, M. Liverani, P. Matthiae, & M. Mellink (eds) *Between the Rivers and Over the Mountains: Archaeologica Anatolica et Mesopotamica Alba Palmieri Dedicata*. Dipartimento di Scienze Storiche Archeologiche e Antropologiche dell'Antichitá, Universitá di Roma: Rome.

—— (1994a) *The Aşvan Sites 3. Keban Rescue Excavations, Eastern Anatolia: The Early Bronze Age* (The British Institute of Archaeology at Ankara, Monograph No. 18). The British Institute of Archaeology at Ankara: London.

—— (1994b) The quest for red gold, in A. Sagona (ed.) *Bruising the Red Earth: Ochre Mining and Ritual in Aboriginal Tasmania*. Melbourne University Press: Melbourne.

—— (2000) Sos Höyük and the Erzurum region in late prehistory: a provisional chronology for northeast Anatolia', in C. Marro & H. Hauptmann (eds) *Chronologies des pays du Caucase et de l'Euphrate aux IVe–IIIe millenaires: actes du colloque d'Istanbul, 16–19 décembre 1998* (Acta Anatolica XI). De Boccard Edition-Diffusion: Paris.

—— (2004) Social boundaries and ritual landscapes in late prehistoric Trans-Caucasus and highland Anatolia, in A. Sagona (ed.) *A View from The Highlands: Archaeological Studies in Honour of Charles Burney* (Ancient Near Eastern Studies Supplement Series 12). Peeters: Louvain.

Sagona, A. & Sagona, C. (2000) Excavations at Sos Höyük, 1998–2000: fifth preliminary report, *Ancient Near Eastern Studies* 37: 56–127.

—— (2004) *Archaeology at the North-East Anatolian Frontier, I. An Historical Geography and a Field Survey of the Bayburt Province* (Ancient Near Eastern Supplement Series 14), Peeters: Louvain.

Sagona, C. (1999) An archaeological survey of the Erzurum province, 1999: the region of Pasinler, *Ancient Near Eastern Studies* 36: 108–131.

Sagona, C. & Sagona, A. (forthcoming) The mushroom, the Magi, and the keen-sighted seer, in G. Tsetskhaladze (ed.) *The Black Sea, Greece, Anatolia and Europe in the First Millennium* BC.

Şahoğlu, V. (2005) The Anatolian trade network and the Izmir region during the Early Bronze Age, *Oxford Journal of Archaeology* 24: 339–361.

Salvini, M. (1989) Le panthéon de l'Urartu et le fondement de l'état, *Studi epigrafici e liguistici sul Vicino Oriente antico* 6: 79–89.

—— (1995) *Geschichte und Kultur der Urartäer*. Wissenschaftliche Buchgesellschaft: Darmstadt.

—— (2002) Una stele di Rusa III Erimenahi dalla zona di Van, *Studi Micenei ed Egeo-Anatolici* 44(1): 115–143.

Schachner, A. (1999) *Von der Rundhütte zum Kaufmannshaus : Kulturhistorische Untersuchungen zur Entwicklung prähistorischer Wohnhäuser in Zentral-, Ost- und Südostanatolien* (British Archaeological Reports International Series 807). Archaeopress: Oxford.

Schaeffer, C. F. A. (1948) *Stratigraphie comparée et chronologie de l'Asie Occidentale (IIIe et IIe Millénaires), Syrie, Palestine, Asie Mineure, Chypre, Perse et Caucase*. Oxford University Press: London.

—— (1956) *Ugaritica III*. Mission de Ras Shamra Tome VIII. Paul Geuthner: Paris.

Schliemann, H. (1880) *Ilios: The City and Country of the Trojans. The Results of Researches and Discoveries on the Site of Troy and throughout the Troad in the Years 1871–72–73–78–79*. John Murray: London.

Schmandt-Besserat, D. (1974) The use of clay before pottery in the Zagros, *Expedition* 16(2): 11–17.

—— (1977) The beginnings of the use of clay in Turkey, *Anatolian Studies* 27: 133–150.

Schmidt, E. F. (1932) *The Alishar Hüyük: Seasons of 1928 and 1929 Part I*. Oriental Institute Publications 19. University of Chicago Press: Chicago.

Schmidt, K. (2004) Früneolithische Zeichen vom Göbekli Tepe—İlk Neolitik Göbekli Tepe Betimlemeleri, *TÜBA-AR (Turkish Academy of Sciences Journal of Archaeology)* 7: 93–103.

—— (2006) *Sie bauten die ersten Tempel: Das rätselhafte Heiligtum der Steinzeitjäger*. C. H. Beck: Munich.

—— (2007) Göbekli Tepe, in M. Özdoğan & N. Başgelen (eds) *Anadolu'da Uygarlığın Doğuşu ve Avrupa'ya Yayılımı: Türkiye'de Neolitik Dönem*. Arkeoloji ve Sanat: Istanbul.

Schmidt, P. R. & Mapunda, B. B. (1997) Ideology and the archaeological record in Africa: interpreting symbolism in iron smelting technology, *Journal of Anthropological Archaeology* 16: 73–102.

Schoop, U.-D. (2002) Frühneolithikum im südwestanatolischen Seengebiet? Eine kritische Betrachtung, in R. Aslan, S. Blum, G. Kastl, F. Schweizer, & D. Thumm (eds) *Mauer Schau: Festchrift für Manfred Korfmann*, vol. 1. Albert Greiner: Remshalden-Grunbach.

—— (2005) *Das anatolische Chalkolithikum: Eine chronologische Untersuchung zur vorbronzezeitlichen Kultursequenz im nördlichen Zentralanatolien und den angrenzenden Gebieten* (Urgeschichtliche Studien 1). Albert Greiner: Remshalden-Grunbach.

Schrimer, W. (1988) Zu den Bauten des Çayönü Tepesi, *Anatolica* 15: 139–159.

—— (1990) Some aspects of building at the "Aceramic Neolithic" settlement of Çayönü Tepesi, *World Archaeology* 21: 363–383.

Schwarzberg, H. (2006) A new item for the Neolithic package? Early Neolithic cult vessesls in Anatolia and south-east Europe, in I. Gastov & H. Schwarzberg (eds) *Aegean-Marmara-Black Sea: The Present State of Research on the Early Neolithic: Proceedings of the Sessions held at the EAA 8th Annual Meeting at Thessaloniki, 28 September 2002*. Beier & Beran: Langenweissbach.

Seeher, J. (1987) *Demircihüyük 111, 1. Die Keramik 1*. Philipp von Zabern: Mainz am Rhein.

—— (1992) Die kleinasiatischen Marmorstatuetten vom Typ Kiliya, *Archäologischer Anzeiger*, 155–170.

—— (2000) *Die Bronzezeitliche Nekropole von Demircihüyük-Sariket. Ausgrabungen des Deutschen Archäologischen Instituts. In Zusammenarbeit mit dem Museum Bursa, 1990–1991*. Ernst Wasmuth: Tübingen.

—— (2002) *Hattusha Guide: A Day in the Hittite Capital*, 2nd edn. Ege Yayınları: Istanbul.

Seidl, U. (2004) *Bronzekunst Urartus*. Philipp von Zabern: Mainz am Rhein.

Semino, O., Passarino, G., Oefner, P., Lin, A. A., Arbuzova, S., Beckman, L. E., De Benedictis, G., et al. (2000) The genetic legacy of Palaeolithic Homo sapiens sapiens in extant Europeans: a Y-chromosome perspective, *Science* 290: 1155–1159.

Sertok, K. & Ergeç, R. (1999) A new early Bronze Age cemetery: excavations near the Birecik dam, southeastern Turkey—preliminary report (1997–1998), *Anatolica* 25: 87–107.

Sevin, V. (1999) The origins of the Urartians in the light of Van/Karagündüz excavations, in A. A. Çilingiroğlu & R. J. Matthews (eds) *Anatolian Iron Ages 4, Anatolian Studies* 49: 159–164.

—— (2001) Hakkari stelleri: Zap ırmağı kıyısında Bozkır Göçebeleri—the Hakkari stelae: a nomadic impact on the River Zap, *TÜBA-AR (Turkish Academy of Sciences Journal of Archaeology)* 4: 79–88.

—— (2003a) *Anadolu Arkeolojisi*, 2nd edn. Der Yayınları: Istanbul.

—— (2003b) The Early Iron Age in the Van region, in A. T. Smith & K. S. Rubinson (eds) *Archaeology in the Borderlands: Investigations in Caucasia and Beyond* (Cotsen Institute of Archaeology Monograph 47). Cotsen Institute of Archaeology at UCLA: Los Angeles.

Sevin, V. & Kavaklı, E. İ. (1996) *Van/Karagündüz: Bir Erken Demir Çağ Nekropolü/An Early Iron Age Cemetery* (Arkeoloji ve Sanat Yayınları Kazı Monografileri Dizisi 4). Arkeoloji ve Sanat Yayınları: Istanbul.

Sevin, V. & Özfırat, A. (2001) Van-Karagündüz excavations, in O. Belli (ed.) *Istanbul University's Contribution to Archaeology in Turkey* (transl. F. Artunkal). Istanbul University Rectorate: Istanbul.

Shackley, M. S. (2005) *Obsidian: Geology and Archaeology in the North American Southwest*. University of Arizona Press: Tucson.

Sherratt, A. (1981) Plough and pastoralism: aspects of the Secondary Products Revolution, in H. Hammond, I. Hodder, & G. Isaac (eds) *Pattern of the Past: Studies in Honour of David Clarke*. Cambridge University Press: Cambridge.

—— (1983) The secondary exploitation of animals in the Old World, *World Archaeology* 15: 90–104.

Singer, I. (1984) The AGRIG in the Hittite texts, *Anatolian Studies* 34: 97–127.

Slimak, L., Kuhn, S., Roche, H., Mouralis, D., Buitenhuis, H., Balkan-Atlı, N., et al. (2008) Kaletepe Deresi 3 (Turkey): archaeological evidence for early human settlement in Central Anatolia, *Journal of Human Evolution* 54: 99–111.

Slimak, L. Mouralis, D., Balkan-Atlı, N., Binder, D., & Kuhn, S. (2006) The Pleistocene peopling of Anatolia: evidence from Kaletepe Deresi, *Near Eastern Archaeology* 69: 51–60.

Smith, A. T. (2005) Prometheus unbound: southern Caucasia in prehistory, *Journal of World Archaeology* 19: 229–279.

Smith, B. (1995) *The Emergence of Agriculture*. Scientific American Library: New York.

Smith, P. & Horwitz, L. R. K. (1984) Radiographic evidence for changing patterns of animal exploitation in the southern Levant, *Journal of Archaeological Science* 11: 467–475.

Sperling, J. (1976) Kumtepe in the Troad: trial excavations, 1934, *Hesperia* 45: 305–364.

Steadman, S. R. (1995) Prehistoric interregional interaction in Anatolia and the Balkans: an overview, *Bulletin of the American Schools of Oriental Research* 299/300: 13–32.

Steadman, S. R., McMahon, G., & Ross, J. C. (2007) The Late Chalcolithic at Çadır Höyük in central Anatolia, *Journal of Field Archaeology* 32(4): 385–406.

Steadman, S. R., Ross, J. C., McMahon, G., & Gorny, R. L. (in press) Excavations on the north central plateau: the Chalcolithic and Early Bronze Age occupation at Çadır Höyük, *Anatolian Studies*.

Stech-Wheeler, T. (1974) Early Bronze Age burial customs in Western Anatolia, *American Journal of Archaeology* 78: 415–425.

Stein, G. (1999a) *Rethinking World Systems: Diasporas, Colonies and Interaction in Uruk Mesopotamia*. University of Arizona Press: Tuscon.

—— (ed.) (1999b) The Uruk expansion: northern perspectives from Hacınebi, Hassek Höyük and Gawra, *Paléorient* 25/1: 5–171.

—— (2004) The political economy of Mesopotamian colonial encounters, in G. J. Stein (ed.) *The Archaeology of Colonial Encounters: Comparative Perspectives*. School of American Research and James Currey: Sante Fe/Oxford.

Steiner, G. (1993) Acemhüyük Kârum Zalpa "im Meer", in M. J. Mellink, E. Porada, & T. Özgüç (eds) *Aspects of Art and Iconography: Anatolia and its Neighbors. Studies in Honor of Nimet Özgüç/Nimet Özgüç'e Armağan*. Türk Tarih Kurumu Basımevi: Ankara.

Stevanovic, M. (1997) The age of clay: social dynamics of house destruction, *Journal of Anthropological Archaeology* 16: 334–395.

Stiner, M. C., Arsebük, G., & Howell, F. C. (1996) Cave bears and Paleolithic artefacts from Yarımburgaz cave: dissecting a palimpsest, *Geoarchaeology* 11: 279–327.

Stone, E. C. & Zimansky, P. (1999) *The Iron Age Settlement at ʿAin Dara, Syria: Survey and Soundings*. (British Archaeological Reports, International Series 786). British Archaeological Reports: Oxford.

—— (2004) Urartian city planning at Ayanis, in A. Sagona (ed.) *A View from the Highlands: Archaeological Studies in Honour of Charles Burney* (Ancient Near Eastern Studies Supplement 12). Peeters: Louvain.

Süel, A. (2002) Ortaköy-Šapinuwa, in K. A. Yener & H. A. Hoffner Jr. (eds) *Recent Developments in*

Hittite Archaeology and History: Papers in Memory of Hans G. Güterbock. Eisenbrauns: Winona Lake, IN.

Summers, G. D. (2000) The Median Empire reconsidered: a view from Kerkenes Dağı, *Anatolian Studies* 50: 55–73.

—— (2007) Public spaces and large halls at Kerkenes, in A. Çilingiroğlu & A. Sagona (eds) *Anatolian Iron Ages 6: The Proceedings of the Sixth Anatolian Iron Ages Colloquium Held at Eskişehir, 16–20 August 2004* (Ancient Near Eastern Studies Supplement 20). Peeters: Louvain.

Synnott, K. (1911) *The Farmers' Handbook.* Department of Agriculture, New South Wales: Sydney.

Talalay, L. E. (2004) Heady business: skulls, heads and decapitation in Neolithic Anatolia and Greece, *Journal of Mediterranean Archaeology* 17: 139–163.

Taşkıran, H. (1998) The distribution of bifaces in Anatolia, in M. Otte (ed.) *Anatolian Prehistory: At the Crossroads of Two Worlds*, vol. 2. ERAUL 85. Université de Liège: Liège.

Thissen, L. C. (1995) A synopsis of pottery shapes from phases X to VI, in J. J. Roodenberg (ed.) *The Ilıpınar Excavations I. Five Seasons of Fieldwork in NW Anatolia, 1987–91* (PHIANS 72). Nederlands Instituut voor het Nabije Osten: Leiden.

—— (2002) Appendix I: CANeW ^{14}C databases and ^{14}C charts, Anatolia, 10,000–5000 cal BC, in F. Gérard and L. Thissen (eds) *The Neolithic of Central Anatolia: Internal Developments during the 9th–6th Millennia Cal BC. Proceedings of the International CANeW Table Ronde, Istanbul, 23–24 November, 2001.* Ege Yayınları: Istanbul.

Todd, I. (1976) *Çatal Höyük in Perspective.* Cummings Publishing: Menlo Park.

Tolstikov, V. & Treister, M. (1996) *The Gold of Troy: Searching for Homer's Fabled City.* Harry N. Abrams: New York.

Traill, D. (1992) "Priam's Treasure": further problems, in J. Herrmann (ed.), *Heinrich Schliemann: Grundlagen und Ergebnisse moderner Archäologie 100 Jahre nach Schliemanns Tod.* Akademie Verlag: Berlin.

Trigger, B. G. (2003) *Understanding Early Civilizations: A Comparative Study.* Cambridge University Press: Cambridge.

Tringham, R. (1971) *Hunters, Fishers and Farmers in Eastern Europe 6000–3000 BC.* Hutchinson: London.

—— (2000) Southeastern Europe in the transition to agriculture in Europe: bridge, buffer or mosaic, in T. D. Price (ed.) *Europe's First Farmers.* Cambridge University Press: Cambridge.

Trufelli, F. (1994) Standardisation, mass production and potter's marks in the Late Chalcolithic pottery of Arslantepe (Malatya), *Origini* 18: 245–288.

—— (1997) Ceramic correlations and cultural relations in the IVth millennium Eastern Anatolia and Syro-Mesopotamia, *Studi Micenei ed Egeo-Anatolici* 31(1): 5–33.

Tsetskhladze, G. R. (2007) Thracians versus Phrygians: about the origin of the Phrygians once again, in A. Çilingiroğlu & A. Sagona (eds) *Anatolian Iron Ages 6: The Proceedings of the Sixth Anatolian Iron Ages Colloquium Held at Eskişehir, 16–20 August 2004* (Ancient Near Eastern Studies Supplement 20). Peeters: Louvain.

Türkcan, A. U. (2005) Some remarks on the Çatalhöyük stamp seals, in I. Hodder (ed.) *Changing Materialities at Çatalhöyük: Reports from the 1995–99 Seasons* (MacDonald Institute Monographs and The British Institute of Archaeology at Ankara Monograph No. 39). MacDonald Institute for Archaeological Research: Cambridge.

Turner, V. (1966) Colour classification in Ndembu ritual: a problem in primitive classification, in M. Banton (ed.) *Anthropological Approaches to the Study of Religion.* Tavistock Publications: London.

Uyanık, M. (1974) *Petroglyphs of South-Eastern Anatolia* (Monographien und Dokumentationen die Asiatische Felsbilder). Akademische Druck- u. Verlagsanstalt: Graz.

Van den Hout, T. (2002) Tombs and memorials: the (Divine) Stone-House and Hegur reconsidered, in K. A. Yener & H. A. Hoffner Jr. (eds) *Recent Developments in Hittite Archaeology and History: Papers in Memory of Hans G. Güterbock.* Eisenbrauns: Winona Lake, IN.

—— (2006) Institutions, vernaculars, publics: the case of second-millennium Anatolia, in S. Sanders (ed.) *Margins of Writing, Origins of Cultures* (Oriental Institute Seminars Number 2). Oriental Institute: Chicago.

Van Loon, M. M. (1966) *Urartian Art: Its Distinctive Traits in the Light of New Excavations* (Uitgaven van het Nederlands Historisch-Archaeologisch Instituut 20). Nederlands Historisch-Archaeologisch Instituut: Istanbul.

—— (ed.) (1978) *Korucutepe. Final Report on the Excavations of the Universities of Chicago, California (Los Angeles) and Amsterdam in the Keban Reservoir, Eastern Anatolia, 1968–1970*, vol. 2 (Studies in Ancient Civilization). North Holland: Amsterdam.

Van Zeist, W. & Bottema, S. (1977) Palynological investigations in western Iran, *Palaeohistoria* 19: 19–85.

—— (1982) Vegetation history of the eastern Mediterranean and the Near East during the last 20,000 years, in J. L. Bintliff & W. van Zeist (eds) *Palaeoclimates, Paleoenvirnoments and Human Communities in the Eastern Mediterranean Region in Later Prehistory* (British Archaeological Reports, International Series 133). British Archaeological Reports: Oxford.

—— (1991) *Late Quaternary Vegetation of the Near East* (TübingerAtlas des Vorderen Orients A 18). L. Reichert: Wiesbaden.

Van Zeist, W. & Roller, G. J. (1994) Plant remains from aceramic Çayönü, SE Turkey, *Palaeohistoria* 33/34 (1991/1992): 65–96.

Van Zeist, W, Stapert, D., & Woldring, H. (1975) Late Quaternary vegetation and climate of southwestern Turkey, *Palaeohistoria* 17: 53–143.

Van Zeist, W. & Woldring, H. (1978) A postglacial pollen diagram from Lake Van in eastern Turkey, *Review of Palaeobotany and Palynology* 26: 249–276.

Vavilov, N. I. (1952) *The Origin, Variation, Immunity and Breeding of Cultivated Plants* (transl. K. S. Chester). Chronica Botanica Co: Waltham, MA.

Veenhof, K. R. (1972) *Aspects of Old Assyrian Trade and Its Terminology*. E. J. Brill: Leiden.

—— (1993) On the identification and implications of some bullae from Acemöyük and Kültepe, in M. J. Mellink, E. Poradam, & T. Özgüç (eds) *Aspects of Art and Iconography: Anatolia and Its Neighbors. Studies in Honor of Nimet Özgüç/Nimet Özgüç'e Armağan*. Türk Tarih Kurumu Basımevi: Ankara.

—— (1997) Kültepe texts, in E. M. Myers (ed.) *The Oxford Encyclopedia of Archaeology in the Near East*. Oxford University Press: New York/Oxford.

—— (2000) Old Assyrian chronology, *Akkadica* 119–120: 137–150.

Vekua, A., Lordkipanidze, D., Rightmire, G. P., Agusti, J., Ferring, R., Maisuradze, G., et al. (2002) A new skull of early Homo from Dmanisi, Georgia, *Science* 297: 85–89.

Verhoeven, M. (2002a) Ritual and ideology in the Pre-Pottery Neolithic B of the Levant and southeast Anatolia, *Cambridge Archaeological Journal* 12: 233–258.

—— (2002b) Transformations of society: the changing role of ritual and symbolism in the PPNB and the PN in the Levant, Syria and south-east Anatolia, *Paléorient* 28.1: 5–14.

Vermoere, M., Bottema, S., Vanhecke, L., Waelkens, M., Paulissen, E., & Smets, E. (2002) Palynological evidence for late-Holocene human occupation recorded in two wetlands in SW Turkey, *The Holocene* 12(5): 569–584.

Voigt, M. M. (2000) Çatal Höyük in context: ritual at Early Neolithic sites in central and eastern Turkey, in I. Kuijt (ed.) *Life in Neolithic Farming Communities: Social Organization, Identity and Differentiation*. Plenum: New York.

—— (2005) Old problems and new solutions: recent excavations at Gordion, in L. Kealhofer (ed.) *The Archaeology of Midas and the Phyrgians: Recent Work at Gordion*. The University Museum: Philadelphia.

—— (2007a) The splendour of women: Late Neolithic images from central Anatolia, in C. Renfrew & I.

Morley (eds) *Image and Imagination: A Global Prehistory of Figurative Representation* (MacDonald Institute Monographs). MacDonald Institute for Archaeological Research: Cambridge.

—— (2007b) The Middle Phrygian occupation at Gordion, in A. Çilingiroğlu & A. Sagona (eds) *Anatolian Iron Ages 6: The Proceedings of the Sixth Anatolian Iron Ages Colloquium Held at Eskişehir, 16–20 August 2004* (Ancient Near Eastern Studies Supplement 20). Peeters: Louvain.

Voigt, M. M. & Ellis R. S. (1981) Excavations at Gritille, Turkey: 1981, *Paléorient* 7: 87–100.

Voigt, M. M. & Henrickson, R. C. (2000) Formation of the Phrygian state: the Early Iron Age at Gordion, *Anatolian Studies* 50: 37–54.

Von der Osten, H. H. (1937) *The Alishar Hüyük Seasons of 1930–32.* Parts I & II (Oriental Institute Publication XXVIII). Chicago University Press: Chicago.

Von Wickede, A. (1984) Çavı Tarlası, in *VI. Kazı Sonuçları Toplantısı.* Directorate General of Antiquities and Museums: Ankara.

Wagner, G. A. & Öztunalı, Ö. (2000) Prehistoric copper sources in Turkey, in Ü. Yalçın (ed.) *Anatolian Metal I* (Der Anschnitt 13, Zeitschrift für Kunst und Kultur im Bergbau). Bergbau Museum: Bochum.

Warner, J. L. (1979) The megaron and apsidal house in Early Bronze Age western Anatolia: new evidence from Karataş, *American Journal of Archaeology* 83(2): 133–147.

—— (1994) *Elmalı-Karataş II: The Early Bronze Age Village of Karataş.* Bryn Mawr College: Bryn Mawr, PA.

Wartke, R.-B. (1993) *Urartu—das Reich am Ararat* (Kulturgeschichte der antiken Welt, Band 59). Philipp von Zabern: Mainz am Rhein.

—— (2005) *Sam'al: Ein Aramäischer Stadtstaat Des 10. Bis 8. Jhs. v. Chr. und die Geschichte Seiner Erforschung.* Staatliche Museen zu Berlin/Philipp von Zabern: Berlin/Mainz am Rhein.

Watkins, T. (1990) The origins of house and home, *World Archaeology* 21: 336–347.

—— (1992) The beginning of the Neolithic: searching for meaning in the material culture change, *Paléorient* 18: 63–75.

—— (1996) Excavations at Pınarbaşı: the early stages, in I. Hodder (ed.) *On the Surface: Çatalhöyük 1993–95.* MacDonald Archaeological Institute and The British Institute of Archaeology at Ankara: Cambridge/London.

Whittle, A. (1985) *Neolithic Europe: A Survey.* Cambridge University Press: Cambridge.

Wick, L., Lemcke, G., & Sturm, M. (2003) Evidence of Lateglacial and Holocene climatic change and human impact in eastern Anatolia: high-resolution pollen, charcoal, isotopic and geochemical records from the laminated sediments of Lake Van, Turkey, *The Holocene* 13(5): 665–675.

Wilhelm, G. (1986) Urartu als Region der Keilschrift-Kultur, in V. Haas (ed.) *Das Reich Urartu: Ein Altorientalischer Staat Im 1. Jahrtausend v. Chr.* (Xenia: Konstanzer Althistorische Vorträge und Forschungen, Heft 17). Universitätsverlag Konstanz: Konstanz.

—— (2008) Urartian, in R. D. Woodard (ed.) *The Ancient Languages of Asia Minor.* Cambridge University Press: Cambridge.

Wilkinson, T. (1990) *Town and Country in Southeastern Anatolia. Vol. I: Settlement and Land Use at Kurban Höyük and Other Sites in the Lower Karababa Basin* (University of Chicago Oriental Institute Publications, Vol. 109). Oriental Institute of the University of Chicago: Chicago.

Williams-Ellis, C., Eastwick-Field, J., & Eastwick-Field, A. (1947 [1999]) *Building in Cob, Pisé and Stabilized Earth*, 3rd edn. Donhead: Shaftesbury.

Winter, I. J. (1979) On the problems of Karatepe: the reliefs and their context, *Anatolian Studies* 29: 115–151.

—— (1983) Carchemish *ša kišad puratti, Anatolian Studies* 33: 177–197.

—— (2002) Defining "aesthetics" for non-western studies: the case for ancient Mesopotamia, in M. A. Holly & K. Moxey (eds) *Art History, Aesthetics, Visual Studies.* Sterling and Francine Clark Art Institute: Willamstown, MA.

Wittke, A.-M. (2004) *Muŝker und Phryger: Ein Beitrag zur Geschichte Anatoliens vom 12. bis zum 7. Jh. v. Chr. Kommentar zur TAVO-Karte B IV 8 Östlicher Mittelmeerraum und Mesopotamien Um 700 v. Chr.* (Tübinger Atlas des Vorderen Orients, Beiheft B 99). Ludwig Reichert: Wiesbaden.

—— (2007) Remarks on the early history of Phyrgia (twelfth to eighth century BC), in A. Çilingiroğlu & A. Sagona (eds) *Anatolian Iron Ages 6: The Proceedings of the Sixth Anatolian Iron Ages Colloquium Held at Eskişehir, 16–20 August 2004* (Ancient Near Eastern Studies Supplement 20). Peeters: Louvain.

Wright, H. T. & Rupley, E. S. A. (2001) Calibrated radiocarbon age determinations of Uruk-related assemblages, in M. Rothman (ed.) *Uruk Mesopotamia & its Neighbors: Cross Cultural Interactions in the Era of State Formation* (School of American Research Advanced Seminar Series). School of American Research Press and James Currey: Sante Fe/Oxford.

Yakar, J. (1985) *The Later Prehistory of Anatolia: The Chalcolithic and Early Bronze Age*, Vols I–II (British Archaeological Reports, International Series 268). British Archaeological Reports: Oxford.

—— (1994a) *Prehistoric Anatolia: The Neolithic Transformation and the Early Chalcolithic Period* (Monograph Series of the Institute of Archaeology of Tel Aviv University No. 9). Institute of Archaeology of Tel Aviv University: Tel Aviv.

—— (1994b) *Prehistoric Anatolia-Supplement No.1* (Monograph Series of the Institute of Archaeology of Tel Aviv University No. 9A). Institute of Archaeology of Tel Aviv University: Tel Aviv.

—— (2000) *Ethnoarchaeology of Anatolia. Rural Socio-Economy in the Bronze and Iron Ages* (Monograph Series of the Institute of Archaeology of Tel Aviv University No. 17). Institute of Archaeology of Tel Aviv University: Tel Aviv.

Yalçın, Ü. (ed.) (2000) *Anatolian Metal I* (Der Anschnitt 13; Veröffentlichungen aus dem Deutschen Bergbau-Museum Bochum 92). Bergbau Museum: Bochum.

—— (ed.) (2003) *Anatolian Metal II* (Der Anschnitt 15; Veröffentlichungen aus dem Deutschen Bergbau-Museum Bochum 109). Bergbau Museum: Bochum.

—— (ed.) (2005) *Anatolian Metal III* (Der Anschnitt 18; Veröffentlichungen aus dem Deutschen Bergbau-Museum Bochum 124). Bergbau Museum: Bochum.

Yalçınkaya, I. (1981) Le paléolithique inferior de Turquie, in J. Cauvin & P. Sanlaville (eds) *Préhistoire du Levant: chronologie et organisation de l'espace depuis les origines jusqu'au VIe millénaire: Lyon, Maison de l'Orient méditerranéen, 10–14 juin 1980.* CNRS: Paris.

Yardımcı, N. (2004) *Harran Ovası Yüzey Araştırması I–II/Archaeological Survey in The Harran Plain.* Eser Sahibinin Kendi Yayını: Istanbul.

Yasuda, Y. Kitagawa, H., & Nakagawa, T. (2000) The earliest record of major anthropogenic deforestation in the Ghab Valley, northwest Syria: a palynological study, *Quaternary International* 73/74: 127–136.

Yener, K. A. (2000) *The Domestication of Metals: The Rise of Complex Metal Industries in Anatolia.* Brill: Leiden.

—— (ed.) (2005) *The Amuq Valley Regional Projects, Vol. 1: Surveys in the Plain of Antioch and the Orontes Delta, Turkey, 1995–2002* (Oriental Institute Publications 131). Oriental Institute of the University of Chicago: Chicago.

—— (2008) The dynamics of local provisioning of tin during the Early Bronze Age, in Ü. Yalçın, H. Özbal, & A. G. Paşamehmetoğlu (eds) *Ancient Mining in Turkey and the Eastern Mediterranean.* Atılım University of Turkey Historical Research Applications and Research Center: Ankara.

Yener, K. A. & Hoffner, H. A. Jr. (eds) (2002) *Recent Developments in Hittite Archaeology and History: Papers in Memory of Hans G. Güterbock.* Eisenbrauns: Winona Lake, IN.

Yildirim, B. & Gates, M.-H. (2007) Archaeology in Turkey, 2004–2005, *American Journal of Archaeology* 111(2): 275–356.

Yılmaz, Y., Saroğlu, F., & Güner, Y. (1987) Initiation of the neomagmatism in eastern Turkey, *Tectophysics* 134: 177–199.

Yoffee, N. (1993) Too many chiefs? Or safe texts for the '90s, in N. Yoffee & A. Sherratt (eds) *Archaeological Theory: Who Sets the Agenda?*. Cambridge University Press: Cambridge.

—— (2005) *Myths of the Archaic State: Evolution of the Earliest Cities, States and Civilizations*. Cambridge University Press: Cambridge.

Young, R. S. (1981) *Three Great Early Tumuli*. Gordion Excavations Final Reports Volume I. The University Museum: Philadelphia.

Zimansky, P. E. (1985) *Ecology and Empire: The Structure of the Urartian State* (Studies in Ancient Oriental Civilization, No. 41). Oriental Institute Press of the University of Chicago: Chicago.

—— (1990) Urartian geography and Sargon's eighth campaign, *Journal of Near Eastern Studies* 49: 1–21.

—— (1995) Urartian material culture as state assemblage: an anomaly in the archaeology of empire, *Bulletin of the American Schools of Oriental Research* 299: 103–115.

—— (1998) *Ancient Ararat: A Handbook of Urartian Studies* (Anatolian and Caucasian Studies). Caravan Books: Delmar, NY.

—— (2002) The "Hittites" at 'Ain Dara, in K. A. Yener & H. A. Hoffner Jr. (eds) *Recent Developments in Hittite Archaeology and History: Papers in Memory of Hans G. Güterbock*, pp. 177–191. Eisenbrauns: Winona Lake, IN.

—— (2005) The cities of Rusa II and the end of Urartu, in A. Çilingiroğlu & G. Darbyshire (eds) *Anatolian Iron Ages 5. Proceedings of the Fifth Anatolian Iron Ages Colloquium held at Van, 6–10 August 2001* (The British Institute at Ankara Monograph No. 31). The British Institute at Ankara: London.

Zimmerman, T. (2006) Kalınkaya. A Chalcolithic–Early Bronze Age settlement and cemetery in northern central Anatolia. First preliminary report: the burial evidence, *Anadolu Medeniyetleri Müzesi* 2005 Yıllığı: 271–311.

—— (2007) Anatolia as a bridge from north to south? Recent research in the Hatti heartland, *Anatolian Studies* 57: 65–75.

Zohary, D. & Hopf, M. (2000) *Domestication of Plants in the Old World: The Origin and Spread of Cultivated Plants in West Asia, Europe and the Nile Valley*, 3rd edn. Oxford University Press: Oxford.

Zohary, M. (1973) *Geobotanical Foundations of the Middle East*, 2 vols. G. Fischer: Stuttgart.

Index